W9-BAI-884

Second Edition

Infant Development

Charles W. Snow

East Carolina University

Prentice Hall
Upper Saddle River, NJ 07458

Library of Congress Cataloging-in-Publication Data

Snow, Charles W.
    Infant development / Charles W. Snow. —2nd ed.
       p.   cm.
    Includes bibliographical references and index.
    ISBN 0-13-263930-0 (pbk.)
    1. Infants—Development. I. Title.
  RJ134.S66   1997
  305.232—dc21   97-28665
                                 CIP

Editor in chief: Nancy Roberts
Executive editor: Bill Webber
Acquisition editor: Jennifer Gilliland
Assistant editor: Anita Castro
Editorial/production supervision, interior design,
  and electronic page makeup: Mary Araneo
Buyer: Tricia Kenny
Cover designer: Rosemarie Votta
Cover photo: Andrew Olney/Tony Stone Images
Director, Image Resource Center: Lori Morris-Nantz
Photo research supervisor: Melinda Lee Reo
Image permission supervisor: Kay Dellosa
Photo researcher: Kim Dalton-Moss

Credits appear on p. 326, which constitutes a continuation of the copyright page.

This book was set in 10/12 Times by A & A Publishing Services, Inc.
and was printed and bound by Victor Graphics, Inc. The cover was
printed by Phoenix Color Corp.

 © 1998, 1989 by Prentice-Hall, Inc.
Simon & Schuster/A Viacom Company
Upper Saddle River, New Jersey 07458

Printed in the United States of America

10 9 8 7 6 5 4

ISBN 0-13-263930-0

PRENTICE-HALL INTERNATIONAL (UK) LIMITED, *London*
PRENTICE-HALL OF AUSTRALIA PTY. LIMITED, *Sydney*
PRENTICE-HALL CANADA INC., *Toronto*
PRENTICE-HALL HISPANOAMERICANA, S.A., *Mexico*
PRENTICE-HALL OF INDIA PRIVATE LIMITED, *New Delhi*
PRENTICE-HALL OF JAPAN, INC., *Tokyo*
SIMON & SCHUSTER ASIA PTE. LTD., *Singapore*
EDITORA PRENTICE-HALL DO BRASIL, LTDA., *Rio de Janeiro*

Dedicated

to my wife, Dora, and our daughters, Carla and Kristin

and

to infants and their parents and other caregivers everywhere

Contents

3
The Birth Process   36

4
The Newborn   53

5
Physical Growth   76

6
Health and Safety   93

7
Nutrition
and Feeding Practices   116

8
Motor Development   138

12
Social Development   222

13
Emotional Development   237

14
Infant Caregiving and Education   256

Preface

This book presents a comprehensive overview of growth and development during the first three years of life. It is designed primarily as an introductory text for courses in infant development, infant care, and early intervention. The increasing popularity of courses on infant development in institutions of higher education throughout the United States is a reflection of the interest and attention currently devoted to infant development by the academic community and the general public. The development and expansion of early-intervention programs and child-care programs throughout the United States have increased the demand for a cadre of professionals who are knowledgeable about infant development. Anyone interested in learning about infants should find the second edition of *Infant Development* informative and helpful.

This edition is a completely updated and slightly expanded version of the original text. Since the first edition was published, the research literature on almost all aspects of infant development has mushroomed. The popularity of Piaget's theory has declined somewhat with increasing interest in Vygotsky's theory, information processing models,

and dynamic systems perspectives. Consequently, every chapter has been extensively reviewed and carefully revised to include new information from theory and research on each important area of infant development.

Following the format of the first edition, the material is organized topically, with a chapter on each developmental area, except for the chapters on the prenatal and the newborn periods. The original chapter on social and emotional development has been separated and expanded into two separate chapters. Additional information has been incorporated in Chapters 4 and 9 to reflect the burgeoning research and theoretical literature on infant sensory and perceptual capacities. More attention has been devoted to cross-cultural studies and the importance of multicultural awareness and diversity. The chapter on infant caregiving and education includes expanded information about parent-child interactions and the importance of interactional synchrony. One of the unique features of this text continues to be the extended coverage of nutrition, health, and safety.

Although the text is devoted primarily to typically developing infants, the coverage on infants with special needs has been expanded. Information on developmental assessment has been added in recognition of the importance of identifying infants who are at-risk for developmental delay. A concerted effort has been made to achieve a balance between theory, research, and practical information throughout the text. Suggestions for enhancing infant growth and development are incorporated in the various chapters. I have tried to use terminology that reflects caring, sensitivity, and respect for infants and families everywhere regardless of gender, race, ethnicity, culture, and developmental abilities.

Through the years, numerous disciplines have contributed to our knowledge and understanding of infant development. This edition has been designed to retain the original interdisciplinary perspective. Information from child development and family relations, psychology, pediatrics, nursing, nutrition, biology, and other disciplines has been incorporated into the various chapters. The quotations from classical and contemporary literature, which introduce each chapter and add interest as they express a major theme, have been retained.

Several features used in the book will facilitate student understanding and learning. An introduction at the beginning of each chapter summarizes the basic topics that are covered. Important terms are highlighted and carefully defined as they occur in the text and again in the glossary for easy reference. Real-life examples are used to illustrate difficult concepts. Photographs, drawings, and tables are sprinkled throughout the book to illustrate and summarize important information. Each chapter ends with a summary of the main points.

ACKNOWLEDGMENTS

I received help from many people in the preparation of this edition. I am grateful to the following colleagues at East Carolina University (ECU) for reviewing portions of this book and making valuable suggestions: Dr. Marian Eppler, Department of Psychology (Chapters 2 and 9); Dr. Ron Dudek and Dr. John Wiley, School of Medicine (Chapter 2); Dr. Marilyn Steele, Department of Food, Nutrition, and Institutional Management (Chapter 7). I also want to express appreciation to Mara Apple, a graduate student in the Department of Child Development and Family Relations at ECU, for her invaluable assistance with literature searches and many other tasks in the various stages of manuscript preparation. The librarians in the Health Sciences and Joyner Libraries at ECU were extremely helpful in the process of identifying and obtaining essential materials. The comments of the reviewers secured by the Prentice Hall editorial staff were also valuable in planning and completing this edition. They are Patsy McCreary, Austin Community College; Lori Gregory, University of Michigan, Dearborn; Patricia Martin, Syracuse University; and Charles Bleiker, The University of New Mexico.

My wife, Dora, deserves special credit, not only for her suggestions on grammar and style but for her support and understanding during my extensive involvement with this project.

Finally, I am especially grateful to Editor in Chief, Nancy Roberts, Production Editor, Mary Araneo, Psychology Editor, Jennifer Gilliland, and other members of the Prentice Hall editorial staff for their patience and guidance in making this revised edition a reality.

CWS

1

Introduction and Theoretical Perspectives

All the world's a stage,
And all the men and women merely players.
They have their exits and entrances,
and one man in his time plays many parts,
his act being seven stages.
At first the infant, mewling and puking in the
nurse's arms.

—Shakespeare

The term **infant** is derived from a Latin word meaning "without speech." If we use the literal definition, infancy covers the period between birth and 12 to 18 months, when the baby begins to talk. However, infancy often is used to cover a broader age range, encompassing a broader age span. In this book, **infancy** includes the age span from birth to 3 years of age. Older infants who have begun to walk are often referred to as **toddlers.** The term toddler (or toddlerhood) will be used in this book when the discussion is specifically limited to infants between approximately 18 and 36 months of age. Since the first act in life's drama actually begins before birth, the prenatal period is also included as an important part of our discussion.

SOME BASIC QUESTIONS

This book is designed to acquaint you with the important concepts, characteristics, stages, and underlying processes of infant development. The basic questions we consider throughout the book are:

1. How do infants grow and develop? What are the characteristic abilities and needs of infants at various stages in their development from conception to the third year of life? How do infants differ from culture to culture?
2. Why do infants grow, develop, and behave in the ways they do? What important variables or factors influence development from conception through infancy?
3. What are the characteristics of infants who are at-risk for developmental delay, or who have a disabling condition? What are their special needs and how can those needs be met?
4. What childrearing practices facilitate the development of infants into healthy, competent individuals? How do childrearing practices differ from culture to culture?

This introductory chapter alerts you to some additional issues, recurring themes, and perspectives that are important to the study of infant development.

IMPORTANCE OF INFANCY

How far back in time can you remember? Try this exercise. Close your eyes, relax, and turn your thoughts to the earliest experiences of your life. If you are like most people, you remember very little, if anything, that happened to you during the first two or three years of your life. Can infancy be a very important period of development if we apparently have little or no recollection of what happened to us then?

The Critical Periods Debate

There is widespread agreement that infancy is a very important phase of the human life cycle. However, the extent to which infancy represents a critical period is the subject of a continuing debate. A **critical period** is the period of time when an individual is most open, or susceptible, to lasting environmental influences. We know that various organs of the body can be irreversibly damaged by exposure to environmental hazards or by deficits at delicate formation stages during the prenatal period. Whether there are comparable critical periods in psychological development is less certain.

Continuity versus Discontinuity

The theory that infancy represents a critical period of development is based upon the belief that development is continuous. Continuity of development means that humans build upon and add to previous experiences and skills throughout life. Sigmund Freud (1940) was one of the first psychologists to view experiences during the infancy years as having lifelong effects. He believed that all personality neuroses are acquired during the first five or six years of life (Rutter, 1987). Freud proposed that the first two years were the most important within that time period. For example, the child who is treated harshly and punitatively during toilet training will develop personality tendencies that are likely to last a lifetime.

A famous study by René Spitz (1945) of infants who were reared in an orphanage is also used to support the critical periods hypothesis. The infants he studied had few toys and lay in their cribs most of the time with little human contact. As a result of this deprivation of normal "mothering," the infants failed to grow and became severely depressed and withdrawn. The infants had little resistance to disease, and many of them died. Spitz believed that the severe deprivation resulted in psychological damage that was practically irreversible. However, critics point out that Spitz failed to determine whether or not the infants were normal before they were institutionalized.

On the other hand, theorists who oppose the critical-periods hypothesis believe that development is discontinuous. That is, humans respond to the world in different ways at different times as they go through life. Later stages of life are not necessarily rooted in earlier stages. Considerable evidence against the critical-periods hypothesis and in favor of discontinuity has been cited. For example, Kagan and Klein (1973) observed infants in an isolated Guatemalan village who spent the first year of life in a windowless hut with little attention from caregivers. The infants were found to be silent, apathetic, and retarded. In spite of their early retardation, however, these infants grew up to be active, happy, and intellectually competent 11-year-olds. Rutter (1985) reviewed research studies on children from severely deprived backgrounds who were subsequently placed in much better environments. He concluded that "the effects of early bad experiences can be 'neutralized' to a substantial extent by good experiences in later life . . . (p. 360). The evidence runs counter to the view that early experiences irrevocably change personality development" (p. 364).

The view of infancy as a fixed and absolute critical period of psychological development that deter-mines what happens in future stages has been, in the minds of many people, replaced with the **optimal-period** concept (Rutter, 1985). According to this position, infants are in many ways more sensitive or vulnerable to their environment than older children. As the first stage of life, infancy provides the foundation for later development. In some cases the effects may be long lasting but not necessarily irreversible. Infants are quite adaptable and malleable and have demonstrated the capacity to overcome a lot of adversity. Not all infant experiences have an impact on later development, although some experiences have long-term effects (Bornstein & Lamb, 1992).

The extent to which psychological disabilities or benefits from infancy persist depends upon a complex chain of events linking the first stage of life to the last (Rutter, 1987). The key condition under which early experiences are likely to continue or fade is environmental continuity. If the environment remains constant, the attributes (good or bad) developed in the early years are likely to be reinforced and remain stable. On the other hand, if the environment changes, children tend to change. For example, many infants who are born with prematurity, anoxia, or other birth complications, do not experience long-term problems if they are reared in an environment that is compensatory and supportive. However, if they are reared in environments that are stressful and deprived, the birth traumas are more likely to have long term negative developmental effects (Kopp & Krakow, 1983).

To the extent that critical or sensitive periods exist, Greenough, Black, and Wallace (1987) have proposed an explanation for the underlying mechanism responsible for the impact of early experience on brain development. At birth, or even before, the brain is composed of an excess number of synaptic connections among the neurons (see Chapter 5). The stimulation of the brain is important early in life because synapses need to be activated through experience within a limited time period in order to survive. The connections not activated through experience are lost through disuse. Thus instead of creating impressions on a blank slate, the lack of experience erases some of the tracings that are already there (Bertenthal & Campos, 1987).

THE NATURE-NURTURE CONTROVERSY

The discussion of critical periods and continuities of development is intertwined with the nature-nurture debate about "Which is most important, heredity or environment?" There appear to be certain physical features such as hair and eye color that are clearly controlled by heredity. When it comes to human behavior, though, philosophers and scientists for centuries have debated the relative importance of nature and nurture in human development. The nature side of the debate is represented by the **maturationists** and **nativists.** Maturationists believe that the key to growth and development is found in genetic and biological foundations. Physical growth, motor development, and other abilities proceed according to a genetic timetable. Nativists believe that infants come equipped with innate ideas, feelings, and personality traits. For example, they believe that infants are genetically endowed with the ability to understand the rules of grammar.

On the other hand, the "nurture" point of view is advocated by the **empiricists,** who believe that the course of infant development is shaped by experience. This position is based on the proposal that John Locke (1961) made in 1690 that the infant mind is a tabla rasa or "blank slate." Infants are thus viewed as passive creatures, molded by external environmental forces.

THE TRANSACTIONAL/INTERACTIONIST PERSPECTIVE

A widely accepted way of looking at heredity-environment relationships is through the **transactional perspective**. In order to understand human development we have to take into consideration the "transactions between and among individuals, their biological inner workings, and their social outer workings" (Sameroff, 1993, p 11). A major principle of this model is that heredity and environment mutually influence each other throughout the lifespan. Developmental outcomes are viewed as the result of reciprocal influences between the child and the environment. The action of the child changes the environment and then, in turn the changes in the environment affect the behavior of the child. The two factors interact and combine in ways that make infant development more than simply the sum of the two parts. For example, powerful environmental events, such as exposure to toxic chemicals or starvation can alter the genetic foundations of development. These transactions represent a powerful process that continues over time (Sameroff, 1993)

Some of the complexities of the transactional perspective are described by Scarr and McCartney's (1983) view of how hereditary and environment interact. They believe infants' genetic endowment and environmental influences operate within the context of three types of relationships: **passive, evocative,** and **active.**

The environment that parents provide for an infant is influenced by the parent's own heredity. An example of the passive gene-environment interaction is the case in which artistic parents are likely to expose the child to play materials and experiences that emphasize art. The child who has inherited a genetic predisposition to be artistic is also the recipient of an environment which pushes the child toward the fulfilment of genetic potential. In the case of evocative gene-environment interactions, infants with certain types of genetic tendencies evoke reactions from their environment. For example, parents respond differently to a child who is generally easygoing and compliant than to a child who tends to be irritable and fussy. Within the active gene-environment, children have a tendency to seek out experiences which match their genetic predispositions. This is also referred to as **niche-picking.** For example, highly intelligent children look for experiences that are cognitively challenging; thus, in some sense, they shape their own environment.

HISTORICAL PERSPECTIVES

Today infants are regarded as the most precious of all creatures. Whether or not this has always been true is a matter of debate by historians. In this section we take a brief look at two contrasting views about how infants have been treated in the past. It is important to look at the past before we can understand contemporary attitudes and practices in infant care.

Negative Views

According to many historians, before the seventeenth century infants and young children were considered to be inferior creatures and were placed at the very bottom of the social scale (e.g., de Mause, 1974; Pollock, 1983). Parents were perceived as largely indifferent to the needs of their offspring. Until the early 1800s, infants were often subjected to very cruel treatment. For example, from ancient times until the fourth century infanticide was practiced in many cultures. Newborn infants who were sickly, deformed, or otherwise viewed as a burden to their parents were killed, usually by exposure or starvation.

During the fourth century, the practice of **infanticide** was largely replaced with the practice of abandonment (de Mause, 1974). Whenever possible, problem infants were given away to be reared by substitute families or religious orders. As recently as the 1800s, many young mothers in Europe and America left their babies on the steps of a church or a mansion in the hope that they would be adopted (Langer, 1975). In addition, many wealthy parents turned their infants over to "wet nurses" for the first two years of life as a means of avoiding close contact. Love and affection generally were not considered important for infant development (Kagan, Kearsley, & Zelazo, 1978). Discipline was harsh and beating of children was common.

By the end of the 1800s, the concept of infancy as a separate and important stage in life had started to evolve. Infants were given a central role in the family, and their rights were protected by the state (Pollock, 1983). Parents gradually became more physically and emotionally involved with their infants. By the early 1900s we entered a new age of concern about the development and care of infants. Pediatrics was established as a separate field of medicine. The infant death rate declined as sanitation and medical practices improved. In the United States, public-spirited citizens worked to improve the living conditions of infants and their families.

De Mause (1974) refers to current views of infancy as reflecting a "helping mode" era.

A Contrasting View

The poor treatment of infants discussed above has been widely acknowledged, but some historians (Pollock, 1983; Hanawalt, 1977) disagree with claims that the mistreatment of infants has been widespread. Pollock (1983) believes that, apart from social changes and technological advances, childrearing practices have not changed dramatically through the centuries. According to this view, infanticide, abandonment, and other forms of cruelty to infants were practiced in the past, but not by the majority of parents. Nearly all children were wanted, and most parents were not cold and indifferent to their children's welfare. Changes have occurred in specific practices, such as feeding, and changes in parental attitudes have been observed. However, for the most part, infant care has remained remarkably consistent through different historical eras (Pollock, 1983).

STUDYING INFANTS

Although the answers to many questions about infant growth and development are tentative and incomplete, we now have more and better information than ever. During the past 20 to 30 years, our knowledge of infant development has increased dramatically. The numerous books, magazine articles, and scientific publications on infant development currently available reflect the information explosion. The rapidly growing amount of infancy research is, in part, the result of the development of some innovative methods of studying infants.

Early Techniques

The first known efforts to study and record the behavior of infants were found in several "baby diaries," the first of which was published by German philosopher Dietrich Tiedemann in 1787 (Tiedemann, 1787/1972). A **baby diary** is a day-to-day record of an infant's behavior by an adult observer, usually a parent-scientist. Diary records published by Charles Darwin (1877) and William Preyer (1888) were a little more systematic than Tiedemann's records and have received wider recognition. The information reported in baby diaries is considered to have limited value because the information may not be very objective. In addition, observations of a single subject cannot be generalized to other infants.

Jean Piaget (1951) combined the naturalistic observation method used in the baby diary with informal experiments performed on his own three infants (Miller, 1987). For example, Piaget gave an infant an object to manipulate or a problem to solve and then systematically recorded the infant's response. Piaget's conclusions about infant development based upon such observations have been widely accepted, but only because they have been verified by other researchers using more sophisticated procedures.

Current Methods

Contemporary researchers have searched for more objective and reliable methods. However, the scientific study of infants has been extremely difficult for a variety of reasons. For one thing, young infants don't talk so we can't ask them questions. They also have limited motor abilities with which to respond to stimuli. In addition, securing the baby's attention and cooperation is a problem. The baby may be too sleepy, fussy, distractable, or active to concentrate on the experimental situation. Even when an infant is cooperative, how do researchers find out what the infant is thinking or feeling before language begins? Given the challenges imposed by these limitations, researchers have had to find creative ways to assess the infant's experience of the world.

Through the years, researchers have been persistent and ingenious in designing more and better ways to measure responses they can then use to make inferences about what is going on inside the baby's body and mind (Miller, 1987). Sophisticated video cameras, computerized scanners, and other high-tech equipment are now available to monitor, record, and analyze the responses of infants. We will review a few of the ways researchers study infants at this point. You will find examples of additional infancy-research procedures throughout this book.

Habituation-Dishabituation and Novelty. Much of the research focuses on methods linked to visual preferences and habituation-dishabituation responses. You probably have had the experience of going into a store where background music is playing. You notice the music at first, but within a few minutes you are no longer listening to it. This progressive decline of response to a repeated stimulus is referred to as **habituation.** If a catchy tune comes on, you find yourself listening to the music again. If the music stops, you become aware of its absence. The recovery of interest in and response to a changing stimulus is called **dishabituation.**

To determine when an infant has habituated or dishabituated to a given stimulus, investigators measure changes in the infant's heart rate, breathing, visual activity, startle reflex, and other reactions. When an infant pays less attention to a picture, after seeing it a few times in succession, the infant is demonstrating the capacity to remember the picture. If the infant indicates renewed interest when a new picture is shown researchers infer that the infant can detect the difference between the two pictures (Trotter, 1987). Given a choice between a familiar and an unfamiliar (novel) stimulus, infants typically respond and focus on the new stimulus. Habituation-dishabituation has been used to study a variety of infant abilities, including learning, memory, visual, taste, and sound discrimination.

Visual Preference Technique. Robert Fantz (1958), a pioneer in infancy research, developed an innovative **visual preference technique** to study visual perception. In this study, an infant is placed in a special apparatus equipped with a peephole and a "looking chamber." Two pictures are hung in the looking chamber within the infant's field of vision. The pictures are separated so that the infant has to turn his or her head slightly to look from one to the other. The lighting conditions are such that an image of the stimulus is reflected in the

Figure 1-1 A System for Recording the Eye Movements of Infants
(Source: L. Hainline and E. Lemerise (1982). Infants' scanning of geometric forms varying in size. *Journal of Experimental Child Psychology, 33,* p. 241. Copyright 1982 by Academic Press. Reprinted by permission.)

infant's eye. The observer looks through the peephole and records what the infant is viewing and the amount of looking time the infant devotes to each picture or its parts. Using this procedure, researchers can determine what infants spend the most time watching and whether they can discriminate between various stimuli.

Other researchers (e.g., Hainline & Lemerise, 1982) have added high-tech electronic equipment to Fantz's original procedure (see Figure 1-1). Projectors, video cameras, monitors, and computerized data-recording equipment are now used to record the infant's smallest eye movements and detailed visual images. With this equipment, researchers can make more accurate observations and study more complex visual behaviors, such as infant scanning patterns and form perception.

Physiological Responses. Researchers have used the infant's physiological responses such as brain waves, heart rate, body temperature, and body chemistry as measures of infant responses to vari-

ous experimental conditions. Although the results of physiological tests are sometimes difficult to interpret, we are obtaining important new information about infants through these measures.

Brain Activity. Electrodes attached to the baby's head can detect changes in brain waves as viewed on an electroencephalograph (EEG) as the infant is exposed to sound, visual, or other stimuli. For example, sounds are emitted within the baby's range of hearing. If the baby's physiological hearing mechanism is functioning, the sounds produce small electrical changes in the brain that are picked up by the electrodes and shown on the EEG.

More recently scientists have developed a "window to the brain" called positron emission tomography (PET). This rapidly emerging technology employs scanners to detect glucose consumption, oxygen utilization, blood flow, and other brain activity (Chugani, 1993). A PET scan produces brightly colored images that make it possible to see what part of the brain is most active during controlled stimulation such as sounds or visual images (see also Chapter 9).

Heart Rate. Changes in heart rate can also be measured with an electrocardiogram (EKG). Changes in heart rate indicate whether an infant is paying attention to and responding to a stimulus. The heart rate slows down in response to conditions that require the infant to concentrate and speeds up under conditions that cause excitement or distress. Some scientists study an aspect of heart rhythm called **vagal tone.** This particular measure of heart rate variability is controlled by vagus nerve of the brain and is associated with breathing patterns. Vagal tone is considered to be an indicator of how well the central nervous system is functioning. Researchers have proposed that individual differences in vagal tone predict individual differences in developmental outcomes. Newborn infants with higher vagal tone may be more likely to perform better on certain tests of infant development at 8 and 12 months of age than infants with lower vagal tone (Fox & Porges, 1985; Bornstein & Lamb, 1992).

Saliva Tests. Human saliva contains a hormone called cortisol. Apparently, the amount of cortisol in the saliva varies with emotional changes related to stress. Since samples of saliva are easy to obtain from infants, researchers can analyze cortisol levels under varying conditions as an indicator of the stress an infant may be feeling. For example, researchers have found that infant cortisol levels increase in response to stressful events such as physical exams and medical treatments procedures (e.g., heel sticks), but decline during relaxing events such as short car rides (Stansbury & Gunnar, 1994).

Thermography. A marked change in facial-skin surface temperature is considered to be an indication of a change in an infant's emotional state. A drop in skin surface temperature may be an indication of stress. Such changes can be detected through the use of television cameras that are equipped with infrared sensors. The cameras are connected to computers for processing and evaluating the facial images. Japanese researchers (Mizukami et al., 1990) have used this procedure to study attachment of 10- to 16-week-old infants. The mother placed her infant in a crib and left the room after about 5 minutes. A stranger then entered the room and played with the infant for a few minutes. After the stranger left the mother returned. The facial temperature of the infant was recorded during each of the conditions. The infant typically experienced a decline in body temperature in response to a stranger, which was interpreted as an indication of stranger anxiety and awareness of the mother's absence. Thermography is a relatively new technique for assessing emotions and must undergo further use and evaluation to establish its validity and usefulness.

Facial Expressions. One of the most frequently used techniques for measuring infant emotions is the analysis of facial expressions. Theoretically, a specific facial expression is a reflection of a specific underlying emotional state. Researchers have developed detailed descriptions and coding systems for rating and analyzing facial expressions of infants as indicators of specific emotions. For example Izard (1979) has developed a detailed system for measuring specific emotional expressions called the **Maximally Discriminative Facial Movements Code (MAX).** Videotapes of infants' facial expressions are made under conditions designed to elicit emotional changes. The tapes are then played at a very slow speed so that trained observers can code the facial movements according to the criteria defined in the MAX.

Nonnutritive Sucking. A measure that is often used to evaluate the baby's responses to visual and other stimuli is provided by the sucking reflex. Researchers place a pacifier that is connected to a pressure gauge in the baby's mouth to measure the number of times the baby sucks and the strength of sucking within a given time frame. The baby is then shown pictures or provided with sounds. In some cases the baby can control the sights or sounds by varying the sucking response. The sucking rate declines as babies lose interest in a particular sight or sound and increases as the interest level increases. By varying the stimulus conditions and measuring changes in sucking responses, researchers can get a lot of information about infant preferences and capabilities.

Parent Reports. Although the accuracy and reliability of parent reports have been criticized in the past, in recent years there has been a renewed interest in the value of using parents as sources of information. Improved strategies for obtaining information from parents have made this approach more acceptable. For one thing, parent reports are currently used mainly to record infant behavior as it occurs rather than to provide retrospective information about past events. Researchers have also developed more sophisticated techniques of training parents to be observers and record information (Parke, 1989). By asking parents to observe specific behaviors and keep systematic records, researchers are able to obtain information about infants and parents that would not otherwise be available.

Observational Strategies. In order to obtain information about certain types of infant behaviors, such as social interactions, it is necessary to make direct observations of their behaviors either in laboratory or naturalistic settings. Advances in the sophistication of observational methods and procedures have made this a more reliable and useful strategy for collecting information about infant behavior. Technological advances in portable videotape and computer equipment now make it possible to collect information in homes and other nonlaboratory settings. These recordings can be analyzed in various ways at a very detailed level (Parke, 1989). For example, the observation of infant facial expressions in the study of emotions relies heavily on this technique (Parke, 1989). Systematic observations are an essential component of laboratory experiments and studies conducted in naturalistic settings, such as day-care centers.

UNDERLYING ISSUES AND RECURRENT THEMES

The study of infancy involves struggling with several basic issues and problems. Throughout this book you will be confronted with divergent views about when, how, and why infants behave in certain ways. This means that you will need to decide which points of view or which answers make the most sense to you. You will also find that several themes reappear from time to time. These recurrent themes are as basic to human development as the underlying melody or motif is to a musical composition. This section is designed to introduce some of the themes you will encounter in the study of infant development.

Norms and Individual Differences

Throughout this book we consider typical patterns of growth and development, which are referred to as **norms.** The normal age ranges for major milestones, such as the first spoken word and the social smile, are discussed. However, within these average growth and developmental trends there is plenty of room for individual differences. You should always keep in mind that no two babies are exactly alike. Human infants differ in appearance and behavior within and between racial and ethnic groups. Even identical twins differ in significant ways. Although there is an average rate and sequence of development, no infant should be thought of simply as an "average" child.

Interrelations Among Developmental Areas

In this book, infant growth and development are described in seven major domains or areas: physical, motor, cognitive, language, personality, social, and emotional. These areas are closely interrelated. When an infant makes progress in one area, there is usually a chain effect whereby development occurs in other areas as well.

Numerous illustrations of how development in one area relates to that of another area can be given. For example, the development of the ability to move around and explore the environment is accompanied by marked improvement in sensory perception. When an infant advances to a higher stage of cognitive functioning, for instance, a new milestone of language development has been reached. Changes in social and emotional development, such as smiling and stranger anxiety, are apparently related to changes in the cognitive domain.

Directions of Development

Two basic laws or principles of developmental direction are evident in the growth and development of all infants. According to the cephalocaudal principle, development proceeds from head to foot. The head and upper extremities develop and become functional earlier than the trunk and lower extremities of the body. In accordance with the proximodistal principle, development proceeds from the center of the body toward the outer extremities. For example, the arms and legs develop and become useful before the fingers and toes.

The Competent Infant

Human infants are born into the world more helpless than the young of any other species. Human infancy lasts a relatively long time. However, even at birth infants possess remarkable abilities. We used to believe that infants were blind at birth. We now know that newborns not only can see, but are capable of other sophisticated sensory functions. What you will see emerging in this study of infancy is not so much a picture of a passive infant "mewling and puking" as an active infant with an impressive amount of ability in various areas of development.

Robert White (1959) used the term **competence motivation** to describe the infant's tendency to explore and master challenges within the environment. Infants thrive on such challenges as putting a peg in a hole, finding a lost object, or saying a new word. Infants are also tough and resilient. They have a tendency to "grow toward health" (Kagan, 1979, p. 21). This means that infants are capable of overcoming a lot of adversity.

Robert Emde (1996) has identified a set of five "basic motives" that infants are equipped with at birth:

1. *Activity.* The desire to explore and confront environmental challenges.
2. *Self-regulation.* The propensity for regulating physi-

olgical and behavioral states (e.g., wake-sleep, attention, emotions).
3. *Social-fittedness.* The desire to initiate, maintain, and discontinue interactions with other people.
4. *Affective monitoring.* The inclination to monitor situations on the basis of what is pleasurable and unpleasurable, reassuring or alarming.
5. *Cognitive assimilation.* The tendency to seek out new experiences and make them familiar.

With the help of caregivers who are emotionally available and provide growth-fostering activities, these tendencies provide the impetus for an infant to achieve social, emotional, and cognitive competence.

Reciprocal Interactions

Another theme in the study of infants is the reciprocal (mutual) nature of adult-infant interactions. The socialization of infants is not a one-way process. From the beginning, infants are interactive partners in the childrearing process. Infants influence their caregivers in numerous ways, even as caregivers influence them. For example, parents respond differently to a male baby than to a female baby. A baby who is calm and easy going receives different treatment than a baby who fusses a lot and is difficult to manage. Therefore, to a significant extent, infants play an active role in creating their own environment.

THEORETICAL PERSPECTIVES

Much of the literature on infant development is written in the form of theories. Developmental theories are assumptions, hypotheses, or best guesses about how and why babies develop and behave in certain ways. Theories are important because they serve as systems or frameworks for viewing infant development and conducting research. Most theories represent a particular view of such issues as human nature, the nature-versus-nurture debate, the importance of early experiences, the ways in which individuals learn, and the stages of development. Theories vary widely in scope, complexity, scientific support, and popularity.

Some of the most important and controversial theories of development are presented in this text. Most of these theories can be divided into six general categories:

1. Behavioral theories emphasize the importance of the environment and experience in shaping the human infant. B. F. Skinner (1972) is the most well-known representative of behaviorism.
2. Nativistic or maturational theories, which stress the importance of innate characteristics, are represented by Arnold Gesell (1945) and Noam Chomsky (1975).
3. Psychoanalytic and psychosocial theories stress the importance of early experiences and the role of emotions in shaping human personality and behavior. Sigmund Freud (1917) and Erik Erikson (1963) are the major proponents of these points of view.
4. Cognitive developmental theories emphasize the interaction between genetic inheritance and environmental factors. Understanding the development of cognitive processes is the key to human behavior. Jean Piaget (1929) is a major representative of this theory. Other cognitive developmental theorists promote an information-processing approach. Rather than emphasizing stages of development, these theorists focus on the information children represent in their mind, the processes they use to transform the information, as well as their memory capacity and functions (Siegler, 1991).
5. Social contextual theorists believe that human beings are, to a large extent, products of their social and cultural worlds. In order to understand how children develop, we need to study their social and cultural background. Lev Vygotsky (1978) and Urie Bronfenbrenner (1979) are widely recognized as major contributors to this theory.

More specific information about these and other theories is provided at the points where they relate to specific features of infant development.

INFANTS AT-RISK

For the most part, this book deals with infants who conform to the developmental norms in all areas of growth and development and who are referred to as "typically developing" infants. However, many infants are born under circumstances and with challenges that may prevent them from following typical developmental patterns. These infants are referred to as infants *at-risk*. The term *at-risk* is used to refer to infants who have been exposed, or who may be exposed to conditions that are likely to result in developmental delay or atypical development. There are many diverse and complex factors that threaten development, including genetic/ biological, environmental, or a combination of factors. Two basic categories of risk have been identified: established risk and potential risk.

Established Risk

Infants placed in this category have been diagnosed with a medical condition, physical disorder, or mental condition known to result in developmental delay or atypical development. Examples of established risk are infants with a diagnosed sensory impairment (e.g., blindness or deafness), genetic disorder, congenital malformation, or failure to thrive. These infants have a 100 percent chance of experiencing developmental problems at some point in life.

Potential Risk

In many instances, infants are exposed to adverse biological and/or environmental conditions that have the potential for causing developmental problems. Prematurity, low birthweight, bleeding in the brain, or prenatal exposure to German measles or other viruses are examples of biological concerns. Severe malnutrition, neglect, and abuse are examples of environmental conditions that place infants at-risk. Poverty is a major condition that contributes to and interacts with other factors in placing infants in double jeopardy for adverse developmental outcomes. The degree of risk varies with the severity, timing, and length, and the interactions between these conditions.

Infants who are developmentally at-risk and their families have special needs for a variety of medical, educational, economic, and other intervention services that will help them reach their developmental potential. Additional information about conditions that place infants at-risk and infants with special needs will be discussed at other relevant places in the text.

DEVELOPMENTAL ASSESSMENT OF INFANTS

Developmental assessment is a process designed to obtain information about the abilities and characteristics of an infant. The information may be used for a variety of purposes, including identifying infants who may be at-risk for developmental problems (screening); verifying the presence and degree of a disability (diagnosis); planning an appropriate environment, curriculum activities, or other strategies to facilitate development (program planning); testing theories and hypotheses about various aspects of infant development (research) (Meisels, 1996).

Assessment Instruments

There are hundreds of instruments available for screening and assessing infant development. Screening instruments are designed to identify infants who show signs of developmental delay indicating the need for further assessment. These tests usually can be administered quickly so that large numbers of infants can be screened for the early detection of a developmental disability. Other assessment instruments are designed for more in-depth testing to verify and identify the existence of a specific problem. Most assessment instruments can be classified as a norm-referenced or a criterion-referenced test.

Norm-referenced tests provide specific scores or ratings that can be used to compare one infant's performance with that of other infants of the same age. One of the most widely used norm-referenced screening tests for infants and children up to 6 years of age is the **Denver II** (Frankenburg et al., 1992). The test covers four areas of development: gross motor, language, fine motor-adaptive, and personal-social. Infants who do not pass a sufficient number of age-appropriate items are referred for further testing with another instrument such as the **Bayley Scales of Infant Development–II** (see Chapter 8).

Criterion-referenced instruments assess the infant's ability to achieve specific, previously determined skills *without* comparing one infant with a group of others. **The Hawaii Early Learning Pro-file (HELP)** (Furuno et al., 1988) is an example of a widely used criterion-reference instrument. The HELP is used with infants from birth through 3 years of age to assess cognitive, language, gross-motor, fine motor, social-emotional, and adaptive (self-help) skills. This instrument is accompanied by suggested teaching/remediation activities for each of the test items.

Assessment Guidelines

The National Center for Infants, Toddlers and Families has formulated some basic guidelines for us in the assessment of infants and young children (Greenspan & Meisels, 1996).

1. Assessment should include multiple sources of information, including parent reports and direct observation. Standardized tests provide useful information, but should not be the cornerstone of assessment.
2. Assessment is a collaborative process. Participation in the process should be open to parents and other significant caregivers, as well as a variety of professionals with special expertise.
3. The assessment process should identify the child's strengths in addition to developmental delays.
4. Infants should never be separated from their parents or familiar adults and should never be challenged by assessment by strangers without a sufficient "warm-up" time.

In addition, professionals involved in the assessment process need to be aware of and sensitive to the social, linguistic, and ethnic characteristics of the families and infants they work with (Crais & Roberts, 1996). It is beyond the scope of this text to provide a comprehensive view of the assessment process and available measurements. However, in some of the chapters that follow, we will look at a few of the most widely used instruments for assessing specific developmental areas.

SOURCES OF ERROR AND CONFUSION IN STUDYING INFANTS

As you read and think about some of the information contained in this book, you may at times become confused and frustrated. Two major sources of difficulty in understanding infant development that you may encounter are the numerous contradictory theories and inconclusive research findings.

Contradictory Theories

As describe above, there are many theories about human development that present *different* views about how infants develop and why they behave in certain ways. Theories are important because they are sources of ideas for debate, study, and educational practices. However, deciding which theorist to believe or "buy into" is difficult, especially for first-time students. Keep in mind, most theories provide some "kernels" of truth and valuable insights about infant development. No one theory explains all aspects of growth and development, and each one must be evaluated on the basis of research evidence.

Contradictory Research Findings

Unfortunately, research findings on various theoretical questions about infant development are often "contradictory and inconclusive." Writers of textbooks have to sort through and interpret numerous theories and thousands of research studies. For some topics, the many available research studies reveal sufficient consistencies in their results to provide definite answers to questions about infant development. However, many other questions remain unanswered because there are not enough studies available or because several studies report contradictory findings. In addition, many studies contain methodological flaws that make their results unacceptable. Consequently, it is important to consider critically the overall weight of research evidence and avoid making firm conclusions on the basis of limited research findings.

SUMMARY

1. This book covers infant growth and development from conception to the beginning of the third year of life. Important characteristics, concepts, and underlying processes of infant development are examined and suggestions for childrearing are made.

2. As the first stage of life, infancy is considered a very important period. The extent to which infancy is a critical period in human development continues to be the subject of scientific debate. The relative influence of heredity and environment on infant development is also a topic of ongoing controversy.

3. Until the late 1800s, many unwanted infants were murdered or abandoned by their parents. Many others died of disease or abuse. During the 1900s medical care, attitudes, and childrearing practices have gradually improved. The current "helping" mode reflects an increased concern for the physical and psychological development of infants.

4. Techniques for conducting research with infants have improved dramatically since the first "baby diaries" were recorded. The use of high-tech equipment and sophisticated research procedures now make it possible to assess a variety of infant responses. Methods of obtaining information about infants are often based on the infant's tendency to habituate to stimuli after a period of exposure. Specific measures of infant responses include their visual preferences, brain waves and PET scans, heart rate, body temperature, body chemistry, facial expressions, and sucking rates. Parent reports and behavioral observations are also used to obtain information about infant functioning.

5. Some of the underlying issues and recurring themes of infant development discussed in this book are norms and individual differences, interrelationships among different areas of development, laws of developmental direction, the concept of the competent infant, and ways in which infants and adults influence each other.

6. Theories of infant development discussed include behavioral, maturational-nativistic, psychoanalytic-psychosocial, cognitive-developmental, information-processing, and social-contextual.

7. Many infants are born under circumstances and with challenges that may prevent them from following typical developmental patterns. Infants who have a genetic history, biological, or environmental background that threatens to delay or impair normal growth and development are referred to as

infants at-risk. Two basic categories of risk are established risk and potential risk.

8. There are numerous of instruments available for assessing infant development. Assessment instruments are usually classified as norm-referenced or criterion-referenced tests.

9. Basic guidelines for the assessment of infants and young children include the use of multiple sources of information, collaboration between professionals and parents, identification of children's strengths in addition to developmental delays, the presence of parents or familiar adults, and sensitivity to social, linguistic, and ethnic characteristics of families and infants.

10. Two major sources of errors and difficulty in understanding infant development are the numerous contradictory theories and inconclusive research findings.

2

Prenatal Development

Where did you come from baby dear?
Out of the everywhere into here.
                    —George MacDonald

Zygote, blastocyst, embryo, and fetus are among the terms used to label the developing human infant at various stages of prenatal development. None of these words, however, adequately conveys the profound complexity of the drama of life before birth. For centuries, scientists have attempted to understand the process of how life begins in the hidden world of the mother's womb. Although much of the mystery remains to be solved, the intricate details of prenatal development have been meticulously catalogued through the analysis of specimens of medical and spontaneous abortions at various stages of development. This chapter provides a chronological summary of the major developments during the various stages of the prenatal period. In addition, factors that affect the health and well-being of the human infant before birth, as well as after birth, are discussed.

FERTILIZATION

Prenatal development begins the moment one of the father's sperm cells (spermatozoa) unites with the mother's egg cell (ovum). Around the fourteenth day after the onset of menstrual bleeding, an egg cell is released from one of the mother's ovaries into the fallopian tube (see Figure 2-1). Occasionally two or more ova are released simultaneously and, if fertilized, result in a multiple pregnancy. An ovum is about the size of the point of a needle.

Approximately 300 to 500 million sperm are

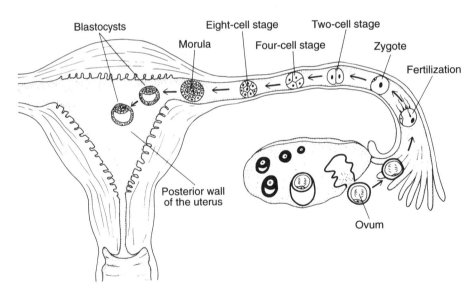

Note: The ovum is released from the ovary and passes into the uterine (fallopian) tube, where it is met and fertilized by a sperm. The zygote divides repeatedly as it passes down the uterine tube and becomes a morula. The morula enters the uterus, develops a cavity, and becomes a blastocyst. The blastocyst usually implants itself into the lining of the posterior wall of the uterus.

Figure 2–1 Ovulation, Fertilization, and Development through Implantation
Source: K.L. Moore (1983). *The Developing Human: Basic Embryology and Birth Defects* (2nd ed.). Philadelphia: W.B. Saunders Co., p. 32. Adapted by permission.

deposited in the vagina close to the mouth of the uterus (cervix) during intercourse (Pansky, 1982). Spermatozoa are much smaller than ova and cannot be seen without the aid of a microscope. Unlike ova, sperm have the capacity to move on their own by lashing their tails back and forth. Sperm swim through the cervix into the uterus and up the fallopian tubes to meet the ovum. Sperm are not capable of fertilization until they undergo a 7-hour period of conditioning, called **capacitation** (Moore & Persaud, 1993). They usually remain alive for about 24 hours, but some sperm may be capable of fertilization for up to three days.

If an ovum is not fertilized in 12 to 24 hours after ovulation, it degenerates. Only about 200 sperm reach the usual fertilization site in the widest part of the fallopian tube (Moore & Persaud, 1993). Although many of the spermatozoa may contact the ovum at the same time, only one reaches the nucleus and accomplishes fertilization. In the very rare case in which more than one sperm fertilizes an ovum, the embryo aborts, or the baby dies shortly after birth (Carr, 1971).

Artificial Insemination and In Vitro Fertilization

When a woman has fertility problems, she may elect to utilize **artificial insemination**. This is a process whereby a donor's sperm is deposited by a syringe into the vagina. The sperm are then left to find their way to the ovum. A woman may also attempt to become pregnant through **in vitro fertilization (IVF)** and "embryo" transfer. The IVF process involves the removal of several ova from the prospective mother or from a donor. The ova are then placed in a test tube or a Petri dish within a special culture fluid. Sperm are then added to the mixture. When fertilization has occurred and the cell has divided four to eight times, the embryo is transferred through the cervical canal into the uterus. Although the incidence of spontaneous abortion is higher than it is for other pregnancies, many thousands of successful IVF pregnancies have occurred since this technique was first used in 1978 (Moore & Persaud, 1993).

PREEMBRYONIC PERIOD

Fertilization marks the beginning of the **preembryonic period** of human development. This is the starting or reference point for "conceptual age" on which the timetable, or calendar, of prenatal development is usually based. The preembroyonic period lasts until the end of the second week after fertilization when the embryo begins to form. Calculated from the date of fertilization, the **prenatal period** typically lasts 266 days or 38 weeks. However, another reference point used in clinical medicine for timing the prenatal period is the first day of the last normal menstrual period (LNMP). In that case, prenatal period is extended by 14 days to a total 280 days or 40 weeks. Unless otherwise indicated, all statements in this text about age of embryonic and fetal development are based on the date fertilization occurred.

Once the ovum has been fertilized, a series of rapid changes takes place. The nuclei of the two parent cells merge, and the hereditary material from each is arranged into a blueprint for a new life. The gender of the baby is determined at that time. The mother contributes a sex chromosome that is always an X, whereas the father contributes, by random selection, either an X-bearing or a Y-bearing sex chromosome. If the chromosome is an X, the baby will be a girl (XX), if the chromosome is a Y, the baby will be a boy (XY). In rare cases the sperm may carry a mixture of sex chromosomes, which result in the development of a baby that is not genetically distinguishable as either male or female. The newly fertilized ovum is called a **zygote.** Within 36 hours, the zygote divides into two cells. As the zygote moves slowly through the fallopian tube on the way to the uterus, cell division continues. The series of rapid cell divisions results in a progressively larger number of increasingly smaller cells (Gasser, 1975).

By about the third day after fertilization, the mass of cells is composed of 12 to 16 cells and resembles a mulberry in shape. At this point, the cell mass is called a **morula** because of its knobby appearance (Singer, 1995). The morula enters the uterus about four days after fertilization. The cells, numbering about 58, cluster around a central cavity and become known as a **blastocyst**. Inside the blastocyst a small group of microscopic cells cluster to one side and begin to form the embryo and the supporting membranes.

Implantation

For two or three days, the blastocyst floats freely in the uterus. It is about the same size as the original ovum, but its content has been dramatically altered. Around the sixth day, the blastocyst attaches itself to the lining of the uterus. By this time the blastocyst has grown an outer layer of cells called **tryphoblasts**, which bury into the uterine lining by secreting enzymes that break down the cells at the implantation site. After implantation is completed, around the tenth day after fertilization, enzymatic digestion stops as abruptly as it began. The implantation is usually healed over in a scarlike cyst by the thirteenth or fourteenth day. At that time the baby is connected with the mother and circulation between the two has begun. Occasionally, implantation is accompanied by bleeding that can be mistaken for menstruation.

Not all fertilized ova become attached to the uterus. Scientists estimate that about one-third to one-half of all zygotes fail to implant and are flushed out of the uterus with the onset of menstruation (Pansky, 1982; Sadler, 1990). In addition, many of the embryos that become implanted are spontaneously aborted because of severe abnormalities (Tanner, 1990). Occasionally the zygote becomes lodged in the fallopian tube or makes its way to the abdominal cavity, the ovary, or the pelvic area.

Implantation Sites

In most cases, implantation occurs in the upper half of the uterus (see Figure 1-1). If the blastocyst becomes implanted in the extreme lower part, there is a risk of bleeding after the fourth month of pregnancy. This condition is called **placental previa** and endangers both the mother and the baby (Dryden, 1978). Implantation within the opening of the uterus (cervix) is called a **cervical pregnancy**. This situation rarely occurs but usually leads to spontaneous abortion (Moore & Persaud, 1993).

Implantation outside the uterus is called an **ectopic** pregnancy. Ordinarily ectopic pregnancies lead to the death of the embryo during the second month. In some cases the health of the mother is threatened because of excessive bleeding. In instances too rare to calculate, an ectopic pregnancy may continue long enough to result in the birth of a live baby. One such exceptional case was reported in Burlington, North Carolina, where a 32-year-old woman gave birth to a normal 6-pound, 4-ounce baby boy. The baby had developed in the mother's abdomen and was removed surgically. No one knew the woman had an ectopic pregnancy until the time of delivery (*News and Observer*, 1979).

EMBRYONIC PERIOD

The word **embryo** is based on the Greek word *embryon* meaning "a swelling." The term signifies the growth (swelling) of cells inside the fertilized ovum, as well as the beginning of all major internal and external structures of the body. The **embryonic period** covers the time from the third week after fertilization until the end of the eighth prenatal week (Moore & Persaud, 1993).

The Germ Layers

By the time the process of implantation is complete, the inner cell, a mass clustered to one side of the blastocyst, has formed a tiny disc that will develop into the embryo. At the end of the second week, the embryonic disc consists of two layers of cells. During the third week, three germ layers are formed through the process called **gastrulation**. Each of the germ layers forms the foundation for the development of various body structures (Moore & Persaud, 1993). One germ layer, the **ectoderm,** is thicker and will later form the nervous system, backbone, the skin, hair, nails, and parts of the eyes and ears. The **endoderm** will develop into the digestive tract, respiratory system, liver, and various glands. A third layer of cells, the **mesoderm,** is sandwiched between the ectoderm and endoderm. This middle layer of cells forms the circulatory, excretory, and reproductive systems, skeleton, muscles, and connecting tissues.

Supporting Membranes

Approximately three weeks after fertilization, the outer layer of cells surrounding the embryo is called the **chorion**. This membrane, which resembles a round sponge, encloses the embryo and its supporting tissues. One side of the chorion is attached to the lining of the uterus and, combined with the maternal tissues, develops into the **placenta**. A second cavity, called the **amniotic cavity** develops inside the chorion (See amnion below).

Placenta. The placenta provides the link between the mother and the embryo where exchanges of nutrients, waste products, oxygen, hormones, and antibodies take place. Unfortunately, viruses and other harmful substances can also cross over from the mother to the embryo. In addition to transporting substances between the mother and embryo, the placenta performs metabolic functions and produces hormones (Moore & Persaud, 1993). The placenta continues to develop throughout pregnancy. At three weeks it covers about 20 percent of the uterus. By five months, half of the uterus is covered. At full term, the placenta is about 6 to 8 inches in diameter, one inch thick, and weighs approximately one pound (Singer, 1995; Rugh & Shettles, 1971).

Umbilical Cord. The early embryo is attached to the placenta by a mushroom-shaped connecting stalk, the forerunner of the **umbilical cord**. The umbilical cord serves as the connecting link between placenta and embryo. The cord contains two arteries and a vein. The arteries carry blood containing waste products to the placenta, while the vein carries nutrients, oxygen, and other substances to the embryo. At full term, the cord is typically ½ to ¾ of an inch thick and approximately 20 to 24 inches long (Jirasek, 1983).

Amnion. When the embryonic disc is formed, a small space, called the amniotic cavity, is formed on one side of the inner cell mass. A larger cavity,

known as the primary yolk sac, is formed on the other side. The embryo stretches between the amniotic cavity and the primary yolk sac. As the embryo develops, the amniotic cavity enlarges within the expanding chorionic cavity. Eventually the yolk sac disappears, and the amniotic cavity totally encloses the embryo within the walls of a thin, tough transparent membrane called the amnion. The cavity is filled with a salty liquid called amniotic fluid.

The amniotic sac, often called the bag of waters, serves as a shock absorber, allows freedom of movement, and helps control the temperature of the fetus, serves as a barrier to infection, and prevents the amnion from sticking to the fetus (Callen & Filley, 1990). In the beginning, the amniotic fluid is mostly (99 percent) water that is changed every three hours through the placenta. As the fetus develops, urine and fecal matter (meconium) are secreted into the fluid. Amniotic fluid is swallowed by the fetus in increasing amounts throughout the prenatal period (Moore & Persaud, 1993). With the umbilical cord serving as a lifeline, the developing fetus floats freely within the amniotic cavity, somewhat like an astronaut in outer space.

Yolk Sac. As the amniotic sac expands, the primary yolk sac decreases in size and forms a much smaller, secondary yolk sac. The human yolk sac, unlike that of bird eggs, contains no nutrients. However, it is apparently instrumental in the transfer of nutrients to the embryo before the placental connection is made with the mother. The yolk sac also serves as a source of blood cells until the liver begins to function around the fifth week (Moore & Persaud, 1993).

Embryo at 4 Weeks

At the end of the first month of development, the embryo and its supporting membranes are about the size of a pea. During the third week after fertilization, the central nervous system begins to develop through a process called **neurulation**. The ectoderm (outer layer of the embryo) folds over to form the neural tube. The major divisions of the nervous system are produced along the length of this primitive structure (Nowakowski, 1987). The tube is open at first and contains a fluid-filled central canal. During the process of neurulation, the tube is sealed, with the top part developing into the brain as the tail end becomes the spinal cord. Three distinct bulges that will become the forebrain, midbrain, and hindbrain soon appear at the top of the neural tube (Spreen, Risser, & Edgell, 1995; Singer, 1995).

Once the neural tube is formed, cells that store and transmit information, called **neurons,** are generated with its walls. The neurons proliferate rapidly within each area of the neural tube. The cells are generally proliferated in locations that are physically separate from their intended destination within the central nervous system. Therefore, the neurons eventually migrate to their final location where they differentiate and assume their special functions (Nowakowski, 1987).

Because of the rapid growth of the primitive brain structure, the developing embryo's head makes up about one-third of the length of the body which is about one-fourth of an inch long (from crown to rump). The span of time between the third and sixteenth prenatal weeks has been identified as the "most critical period for brain development" (Moore & Persaud, 1993, p. 154).

The facial region begins to develop in the fourth week, squeezed between the forebrain and the heart. Placodes, or rounded areas of specialized thickened tissue, have developed as the locations for the eyes, ears, and nose (Moss-Salentijn & Hendricks-Klyvert, 1990).

On the opposite end, the 28-day-old embryo has a pointed tail that curls up in a C-shape toward the top of the bulbous head that bends downward. The tail will disappear by the end of the eighth week. A string of budlike structures, called somites, have formed along the outer arch of the embryo. The somites serve as the foundation of the skeleton. The arm buds develop slightly ahead of the leg buds. The limb buds are now visible as small swellings on the embryo's surface.

The U-shaped heart tube starts its first fluttering beats around the twenty-first or twenty-second day after fertilization. Like the head, the heart is large in proportion to the other organs and, at

Seven-week-old embryo.

this stage, is shaped somewhat like a light bulb. Even though it is relatively incomplete at this time, the heart is strong enough to circulate blood produced by the embryo through a primitive system of veins and arteries, the umbilical cord, and the placenta. The heart, arteries, and veins represent the first organ system to begin functioning (Moore & Persaud, 1993).

Embryo at 8 Weeks

During the second month of life the various parts of the embryo continue developing at a fantastic rate, changing almost daily. Rapid brain growth causes the head to grow to almost one-half of the total body length. The brain is developing in both size and complexity, but has not assumed control of the body at this stage. Although the embryo is still top-heavy, it is no longer C-shaped. The internal organs have continued to develop, and all the major systems are present. Some have even assumed their permanent functions. The embryo develops three successive sets of kidneys during the fourth and fifth weeks. The third set begins secreting urine by the eighth week and remains as the permanent kidneys.

The basic form of the skeleton is completed by eight weeks. However, the embryonic skeleton consists mostly of cartilage, a rubbery material found, among other places, in the end of an adult's nose. Deciduous (temporary) teeth have begun to form beneath the gums. (The primitive beginnings of some of the permanent teeth form as early as the twelfth prenatal week.)

At the end of eight weeks (fifty-six days), the appearance of the embryo is unmistakably human. It measures about 1-½ inches long from head to buttocks and weighs about ⅓ of an ounce. The embryo resembles a tiny doll with a large head, carefully formed arms and legs, and a protruding abdomen. The face is characterized by slitlike eyes and small ear lobes (Rugh & Shettles, 1971). From the beginning of the ninth week, the developing organism is called a **fetus**—a "young one." The name change signifies the completion of human form and the appearance of the first bone cells in the skeleton. A new act in the drama of life before birth has begun.

Fetus at three months.

FETAL PERIOD

Weeks 9-12

This phase of prenatal development is sometimes referred to as the "period of initial activity," because the fetus begins to move (Pansky, 1982). The fetus can kick, turn its head, curl its toes, squint, frown, move its lips, and make a fist (Rugh & Shettles, 1971). As yet, these movements are not felt by the mother. By twelve weeks, the fetus is approximately 3-½ inches (87mm) long (crown-rump) and weighs about 1-½ ounces (45gm) (Moore & Persaud, 1993). The uterus has grown to the point where the mother's pregnancy begins to "show."

The eyes have undergone further development. By the third month, the various parts of the eyeball have formed, including the cornea, lens, and retina. The optic nerves, which began to develop at four weeks, now link the eyes directly to the brain. The eyelids develop as two layers of skin that completely cover each eyeball and are sealed shut around the ninth week. They remain closed until about the twenty-sixth week.

At the beginning of the fetal stage, the head makes up at least one-half of the fetus, but the ratio gradually decreases during the remainder of the prenatal period. The immature brain has acquired its general shape. The development of the facial area is completed during the twelfth week (Spreen et al. 1995).

This time period has also been called the "period of sexual emergence" (Rugh & Shettles, 1971). The sex of an infant is determined at fertilization by the sperm that fertilizes the ovum. However, all human embryos go through a primitive stage of development when their genital systems are not distinguishable as male or female. Internally, sex differentiation begins toward the end of the second month. External sex organs begin to appear early in the fetal period but are similar in males and females until the end of the ninth week. Their mature form is clearly observable and distinguishable in the twelfth week (Pansky, 1982).

Weeks 13-16

This period is a time of rapid growth in both height and weight (Pansky, 1982). The legs grow longer as the head becomes proportionately smaller. The hands and feet are well formed. Bone cells also grow rapidly during this stage. The ears move to their normal position on the sides of the head. The fetal heart is beating at 120 to 160 beats a minute and circulating blood throughout the body (Rugh & Shettles, 1971). Heartbeats can be heard through a nonamplified stethoscope at about sixteen weeks. The fetus apparently becomes sensitive to light at this time and will turn away from bright light shown on the mother's abdomen (Bernhardt, 1987).

Weeks 17-20

The mother, on average, reaches the halfway point of her pregnancy at the nineteenth week. She begins to feel the movements of the fetus, referred to as quickening, around this time. The skin of the fetus is now covered with a waxy, cheese-like substance called **vernix caseosa**. The vernix ("varnish") forms from secretions of the sebaceous (oil) glands which then mix with flakes of dead skin. The covering protects the fetus's skin from chapping and cracking during the long immersion in the amniotic fluid. By twenty weeks the fetus is also covered with tiny, down-like hairs called **lanugo**. The eyebrows and scalp hair appear by the end of this month. The lanugo usually falls out during the seventh month, but some of it may still be present at birth.

By this age, virtually all the **neurons** have been produced (Huttenlocher, 1994). On average, over a quarter of a million neurons are generated every minute of the prenatal period (Wortan, Loftus, & Marshall, 1992). Most of these cells are generated between ten weeks and twenty weeks after fertilization. From then until maturity, the neurons grow in size, but not in numbers, as they form trillions of connections with each other. However, neuroglia (glial) cells that support the neurons continue to be added throughout the remainder of the prenatal period until sometime after birth (Tanner, 1990). The most important function of the glial cells is to produce a fatty lipid called myelin which forms around each neuron before the nervous system

reaches maturity. This process, called **myelination**, begins around twenty weeks and increases rapidly throughout the prenatal period until the brain reaches maturity. The development of the cerebral hemispheres also proceeds at a rapid pace during this period. The increasing number of cortical cells results in the shaping of the folds and convolutions that are characteristic of the mature brain (Spreen et al., 1995).

Weeks 21-25

A picture of the fetus at this time reveals a thin layer of pinkish red transparent skin. With little fat underneath, the blood vessels are clearly visible. Although still top-heavy, the proportions of the body are now more similar to those of the newborn infant. At the end of twenty-four weeks, the fetus weighs about 1-¾ pounds and measures 9 inches from the top of the head to the rump. The fetus sleeps and wakes at regular intervals (not necessarily the same as the mother's!) and has a favorite resting position. During this period, the lungs

Seven-month-old fetus.

develop and become capable of functioning with the production of surfactant, a chemical that is necessary for breathing (Needleman, 1996). The fetus may suck its thumb and engage in other reflexive activities such as swallowing and grasping. The fetus reaches the "age of viability" sometime between twenty-two and twenty-six weeks after fertilization. This means that the baby has a reasonable chance of surviving with specialized care if it is born at this time.

Weeks 26-29

The brain continues its rapid pace of growth as the outer layer of the brain (cerebral cortex) develops. The lungs have developed the capacity to breathe, even though they are not completely mature. In addition, a layer of fat is deposited beneath the skin as the weight increases to about 3 pounds. Height reaches about 16 inches from head to foot at this time. Researchers have found that fetuses blink their eyes in response to sounds, indicating that the sense of hearing is functioning at this age (Bornstein & Lamb, 1992).

Weeks 30-34

During the last few weeks before birth, the fetus rapidly puts on protective fat in preparation for life in the outside world. Its living quarters become crowded as the fetus grows to 4 or 5 pounds and measures 18 inches from head to foot.

Weeks 35-38/Birth

These weeks represent the "finishing period," the final act in the drama of intrauterine life. The baby does not change much in appearance except to add weight and height. Most importantly, the fetus acquires antibodies from the mother that provide temporary protection against some communicable diseases such as measles, mumps, whooping cough, and polio. As the placenta ages and becomes less efficient, the fetus's growth rate slows down. The end of the prenatal period and the beginning of the birth process are near.

MULTIPLE PREGNANCIES

When two separate ova are fertilized during the same ovulatory cycle, **dizygotic** (DZ) or fraternal twins are conceived. Approximately two-thirds of twins are produced in this way (Moore & Persaud, 1993). Twins may also originate from a single zygote that divides into two equal parts. When that happens **monozygotic** (MZ) or identical twins are the result. The incidence of DZ twins varies somewhat from country to country, but the number of MZ twins born each year is remarkably similar throughout the world (Benirschke, 1995).

Dizygotic twins have separate chorions, amnions, and placentas. If they implant close together chorions and placentas tend to grow together (fuse). Monozygotic twins usually develop within separate amnions, but are enclosed in one chorion and share a common placenta. In rare cases when the zygote divides within the first three days, the embryos will have separate placentas and chorions with two placentas that may be separate or fused (Dunnihoo, 1992). Other multiple births, such as triplets and quadruplets, are produced in various possible combinations of the above fertilizations.

In recent years the number of multiple births in the United States has increased dramatically. Between 1980 and 1993, the rate of multiple births rose by about 3 percent each year (Martin, 1996). Although twins account for about 98 percent of multiple births, the number of other types of multiple births has increased at a faster rate. The increase has been fueled by advances in the use of fertility drugs and in vitro fertilizations that increase the likelihood of multiple births, from twins to quintuplets (Coustan, 1996b). In addition, more older women are having babies. In typical pregnancies, the likelihood of multiple births increases with maternal age until 35 years, and then declines (Cohen, 1984).

Multiple births, especially quadruplets and quintuplets, attract a lot of attention and delight, but they can also overwhelm their families. Unfortunately, adverse birth outcomes are more common among multiple gestations. While one twin might be healthy, the other one may experience intrauterine growth delay or fail to survive. Birth defects are twice as high in twins as in singletons. Multiples are also more prone to premature birth and low birthweight (Coustan, 1995b).

INFLUENCES ON DEVELOPMENT

Each year approximately 3 to 7 percent of human newborns have a birth defect requiring medical attention (Goldman, 1984; Shepherd, 1991). It is estimated that almost one-half of the children being treated in hospitals are there because of prenatally acquired malformations. Birth defects are sometimes called congenital (meaning "present at birth") malformations. **Congenital malformations** are caused by genetic factors, environmental influences, or a combination of the two. About one-fourth of all birth defects are attributed to purely genetic factors, while environmental factors alone probably account for approximately one-tenth of such problems (Friedman & Prolifka, 1994). It is difficult to separate genetic from environmental conditions, and most malformations probably come from a complex combination of both factors. Our knowledge about the cause and prevention of these problems is, in most cases, extremely limited (Shepherd, 1991).

Genetic Factors

Genetic factors play a significant role in human development throughout the life span. At the moment of fertilization, an infant receives the genetic code that is a blueprint or set of instructions for cell division and the development of individual features. The genetic code, which is unique for each individual, is carried by genes and chromosomes. Chromosomes are spiral-shaped structures within a cell's nucleus. They contain a chemical substance called deoxyribonucleic acid, or DNA. Genes are basic units of heredity that are contained within the chromosomes. Individual chromosomes contain thousands of genes. Each parent contributes one-half of the hereditary material to the infant by means of the reproductive or germ

cells (sperm and ova) created in the testes of the father and the ovaries of the mother.

The human body contains two types of cells: somatic (body cells) and sex (reproductive cells). Each growth cell normally contains a total of 46 chromosomes. The chromosomes come in 23 matching pairs, except in cells containing an X and Y sex chromosome combination. Growth (somatic) cells for the development and replacement of body tissue are formed through the process of cell duplication called **mitosis**. During mitosis, cells divide and make exact copies of themselves. The process takes place during different stages when two daughter cells, containing the same genetic material, are created from one parent cell.

The process by which reproductive, or germ cells are formed is called **meiosis**, or reduction division. During meiosis each chromosome pair separate to form two cells. Thus, the sperm or ova produced by meiosis normally contain only a total of 23 single chromosomes. When the sperm and ovum unite at the time of fertilization, a total of 46 chromosomes is once again attained. The process of meiosis is more complicated that mitosis. Thus, there is more room for errors that result in cells containing chromosomal numerical or structural irregularities or genetic mutations.

Genes determine the infant's individual hereditary characteristics such as eye, hair, and skin color, as well as internal organ systems. Because of the complex laws of genetics, an individual may inherit a specific characteristic, such as blue eyes, even when one parent or both parents have a different characteristic, such as brown eyes. However, all genetic disorders are not inherited. Defective genes must come from one or both parents in order for a condition to be inherited. In some cases, genetic problems result from aberrations during the transmission and recombination process at the time of fertilization (Meryash, 1995).

Some human characteristics are determined by a single pair of genes, one from the father and one from the mother, whereas other traits are controlled by multiple gene pairs. Some genes are dominant, and others are recessive. When a dominant gene is paired with a recessive gene, the hereditary trait carried by the dominant gene is always present in the individual. A hereditary trait carried by a recessive gene prevails only when it is paired with a recessive gene of the same type.

The complexity of the information contained in the human genetic program is enormous. Scientists estimate that a human zygote contains 100 billion bits of information, which is equivalent to 10 million printed pages. Considering the complexity of the genetic code, it is amazing that the large majority of infants are born without defects (Goldman, 1984). Actually most fertilized cells (ovum) with chromosomal abnormalities do not survive. More than 50 percent of the fetuses that are miscarried before twelve weeks of gestational age have chromosomal abnormalities (Batshaw & Perret, 1992).

In some cases though, defects in the genes or chromosomes result in the live birth of a child with a genetic disorder. Some of the genetic problems are relatively mild and do not cause major problems, whereas others result in severe developmental disabilities. Many genetic flaws are obvious at birth, but some are "time bombs" that cause problems only later in life. Genetic disorders can be classified into four types: (1) chromosomal abnormalities, (2) single gene disorders, (3) sex-linked disorders, and (4) multifactorial inheritance.

Chromosomal Abnormalities. Disabilities may be caused by the presence of more or less than the normal 46 chromosomes, or a defect in the structure of one or more chromosomes (Widerstrom, Mowder, & Sandall, 1991). The most common disorder caused by chromosomal aberrations is **Down syndrome**. In most cases (95 percent), Down syndrome is caused by the presence of an extra chromosome (No. 21), making a total of 47 instead of the usual 46 chromosomes (Stewart, Manchester & Sujansky, 1995). Down syndrome is also caused by the presence of an extra piece of chromosome 21 which becomes attached to another chromosome (e.g., #14) during meiosis. In that case, an infant will have the usual 46 chromosomes, but the extra amount of chromosome 21 leads to Down syndrome.

Infants with Down syndrome have distinctive features. They have a relatively small head, small ears, with eyes that give an oriental appearance. The infants' hands are small with stubby fingers, a large protruding tongue, and thin straight hair. They are usually shorter than average in height. The condition results in moderate to severe mental disability. Down syndrome occurs in approximately one out of every 600 to 800 births (Meryash, 1995; Stewart et al., 1995).

Other major chromosomal abnormalities are sometimes found in the sex chromosomes (No. 23). The most frequent sex chromosome abnormality is Klinefelter syndrome, which occurs when a male child is born with two X chromosomes and one Y chromosome. **Klinefelter syndrome** may not be noticeable until after puberty. In about a third of the cases, males begin to develop feminine breasts, small testes, and very sparse beard and pubic hair. The disorder frequently results in learning disabilities and a slightly lowered level of intelligence.

A comparable sex chromosomal disorder that affects females is called **Turner syndrome**. This condition occurs when an infant is born with only one sex (X) chromosome, resulting in a total of 45 chromosomes. Turner syndrome causes delayed growth, a "webbed" neck, widely spaced nipples, and ovaries that do not function. Most females who have this disorder develop normal intelligence, but they may have visual-perceptual problems that lead to learning disabilities (Batshaw & Perret, 1992).

Problems sometimes result from defects in the structure of chromosomes involving the gain, loss, or rearrangement of chromosomal sections (Widerstrom et al., 1991). **Cri du chat** syndrome is a disorder caused by a missing section of chromosome No. 5. The cry of the infant affected by this problem resembles the meowing of a cat. Affected infants also have an unusual facial appearance, reduced head and brain size, congenital heart disease, and severe mental disabilities.

Single Gene Disorders. Many genetic disorders result from a single gene, or a pair of genes, contributed by one or both parents, following the laws of genetic transmission. These abnormalities may be classified according to a dominant, recessive, or sex-linked pattern of inheritance.

Hundreds of disorders resulting from dominant

genes have been identified, including dwarfism (achondroplasia); some forms of glaucoma; Huntington's chorea (a progressive degeneration of the nervous system); and polydactyly (extra fingers and toes). If one parent has such a disorder, each offspring has a 50 percent chance of being affected by the same problem. Dominantly inherited disorders usually cause developmental problems, but their effects are relatively mild in comparison to recessive genetic disorders.

Both parents must carry the defective recessive gene before the offspring can be affected. In such pregnancies there is a 25 percent chance that the infant will have the recessive trait. **Phenylketonuria (PKU)** is one of the major recessive genetic disorders. The infant with PKU cannot produce an enzyme necessary for the digestion of an amino acid (phenylalanine) found in milk and many other foods. The unmetabolized phenylalanine accumulates in the infant's body and, over time, causes severe brain damage. Infants born in the United States are routinely tested for PKU. The ones who are affected (approximately 260 in the United States each year) are placed on a special diet to eliminate the offending substance. When brain development is almost complete, around 10 to 12 years of age, the child can go on a regular diet.

Other recessively linked disorders that result in severe, life-threatening problems include:

Cystic fibrosis—a disease that affects the mucous, sweat, tear, and salivary glands, causing congestion in the breathing passages;

Sickle-cell anemia—a blood disease that produces malformed red blood cells and weakens resistance to infection and other symptoms. This disease primarily affects people of African ancestry;

Tay-Sachs disease—a fatal disease that causes the nervous system to degenerate. This condition primarily affects people of eastern European Jewish ancestry.

These diseases are almost always fatal, but many affected infants live for several years.

Sex-linked Disorders. A variety of hereditary disorders are caused by defective genes carried on the sex chromosomes. Most of these are recessive genes attached to the X chromosomes. Color blindness, hemophilia (deficiency in blood clotting), gargoylism (dwarfing and body deformities), and some forms of muscular dystrophy are examples of defects caused by sex-linked genes. More male than female infants are affected by such genetic abnormalities. Since males have only one X chromosome, it automatically has freedom to express any defect inherited from the mother. Females are less likely to inherit sex-linked diseases because they have two X chromosomes.

Polygenic Inheritance. Most inherited characteristics of human beings are the result of the combined effects of many genes rather than simple combinations of single pairs of recessive or dominant genes. This is referred to as **polygenic (or multifactoral) inheritance**. Characteristics that result from the combined effect of genetic and environmental factors are attributed to polygenic inheritance. Among typically developing infants, most differences such as intelligence and body size are caused by several factors. A number of common congenital disorders are also attributed to polygenic inheritance (Stewart et al., 1995). Spina bifida (exposed spinal cord), anencephaly (incomplete brain and skull), hydrocephaly (enlarged head with excessive fluid), cleft lip and palate, and congenital heart disease are examples of multifactorial disorders.

Environmental Factors

Although the human embryo is well protected in the amniotic sac, a variety of toxic substances can cross the placental barrier and cause malformations or other problems. Drugs, viruses, radiation, and other agents that cause permanent defects in infants exposed during the prenatal period are called **teratogens**. Scientists have made remarkable progress in identifying products and other environmental conditions that are associated with birth defects. However, establishing definite proof that specific substances are harmful to the unborn child is difficult because of the numerous factors involved. The effects of a drug or other compound are dependent on genetic susceptibility, stage (timing) of prenatal development, amount of exposure (dosage), length of exposure, method of exposure, interactions with other substances, maternal health, nutritional status, and other conditions affecting the prenatal environment (Hogge, 1990).

Drugs and Medications. The adverse effects of a variety of drugs and medicines have been documented in numerous research studies (Hill & Kleinberg, 1984a). Maternal use of prescription, nonprescription, and illegal drugs may affect the embryo in both dramatic and subtle ways. The most clearly observable effects are physical deformities, delayed growth, central nervous system disorders, and internal organ dysfunctions. A tragic example was seen in the use of the tranquilizer Thalidomide. In the 1960s, scientists discovered that a single dose of this drug taken between twenty-one and thirty-five days after fertilization often produced babies with severely malformed or missing limbs. More subtle effects of drugs used during pregnancy include learning disabilities and behavioral problems such as irritability or hyperactivity.

Between 40 and 90 percent of pregnant women in the United States take at least one drug, and many ingest two or more compounds. While hundreds of substances have been approved as safe for use during pregnancy, the effects of many others are not known (Levy & Koren, 1992). The drugs and chemicals that may possibly produce birth defects or other problems are numerous. The list includes illegal drugs such as marijuana, heroin, and cocaine, and many prescription and nonprescription drugs and chemical compounds given to treat epilepsy, diabetes, blood disorders, acne, and infection, as well as tranquilizers, hormones, barbiturates. A number of environmental pollutants such as lead and mercury are also listed as potential teratogens (Hill & Kleinberg, 1994a; Hogge, 1990; Levy & Koren, 1992).

There is growing concern about widely used over-the-counter medicines such as aspirin, antihistamines, diuretics, and antacids. Researchers have found an association between the mother's use of aspirin during pregnancy and the tendency of premature infants to bleed inside the brain. Studies have also found that heavy users of aspirin have an increased rate of infant mortality, low-birthweight infants, prolonged pregnancies, and hemorrhaging before and after childbirth (Turner & Collins, 1975; Collins & Turner, 1975). Acetaminophen appears to be less risky for use during pregnancy (Hill & Kleinberg, 1984b). Unfortunately, there is not enough evidence for researchers to form definite conclusions about the safety of many pain-relief compounds and many other nonprescription medicines. In view of the limited knowledge, pregnant women should check with their doctor before taking any medications or other substances.

Alcohol. During the past 20 years a large amount of research has accumulated confirming prenatal exposure to alcohol as a teratogen. Alcohol crosses the placenta and circulates in the bloodstream of the developing infant. The effects of prenatal exposure to alcohol vary on a continuum from spontaneous abortion to no observable effects (Olson, 1994). The consequences depend upon the amount of alcohol consumed, timing, and length of exposure. A host of other factors may also be involved, including the use of other drugs, dietary factors, health status, prenatal care, maternal age, and the infant's genetic susceptibility to alcohol effects (Eliason & Williams, 1990; Wekselman Spiering, Hettberg, Kenner, & Flantermeyer, 1995). Some studies indicate that consumption of alcohol combined with smoking cigarettes increases the risk of adverse developmental effects (Olsen, Pereira, & Olsen, 1991; Widerstrom et al., 1991).

Maternal consumption of large amounts of alcohol during pregnancy can lead to full blown **fetal alcohol syndrome (FAS)**. Estimates of the incidence of FAS range from 1 to 3 per 1,000 births (Olson, 1994). FAS infants suffer overall growth retardation, facial malformations, inadequate brain growth, heart defects, motor problems, skeletal defects, hyperactivity, and other difficulties. FAS has been termed the leading known cause of mental disabilities in the western world (Olson, 1994). Although many of the effects may be long lasting

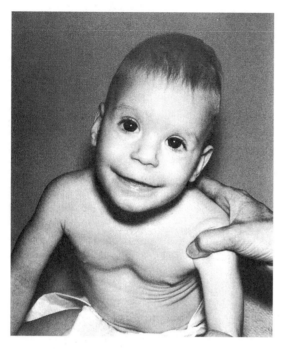

Infant with fetal alcohol syndrome. Notice the thin upper lip and wide, flat nose.

and persistent, more information is needed about the long-term effects of prenatal alcohol exposure. Researchers have not determined why some infants of alcoholic mothers suffer from FAS, while others are apparently not affected. The risk that an alcoholic will give birth to a child with FAS during her first pregnancy has been estimated to be 6 percent, but the risk goes up to 70 percent for subsequent births (Day & Richardson, 1991).

Since there is a range of alcohol-related effects, the term **possible fetal-alcohol effects (FAE)** is used in cases where the prenatal alcohol exposure has been more limited and the observable effects are not as severe as FAS. The most common effects of FAE are growth retardation and central nervous disorders. These infants tend to have decreased birthweights and suffer milder variations of some of the same problems as full-blown FAS infants, including attention deficits, impaired intellectual functioning, language deficits, sleep disorders and impaired motor functioning (Olson, 1995; Vorhees & Mollnow, 1987; Wekselman et al., 1995).

Researchers have tried to determine whether there is a safe amount of alcohol that can be consumed during pregnancy. No one has yet been able to determine exactly how much alcohol is necessary to produce fetal alcohol syndrome or other developmental problems. Research evidence indicates that the consumption of one to three drinks containing two or more ounces of alcohol each day places the fetus at risk for growth retardation (Niebyl, 1982). Scientists are not certain about whether or not smaller amounts of alcohol produce adverse effects (Eliason & Williams, 1990). Mothers are advised to avoid consuming alcohol in any amount during pregnancy since there is no known safe amount of alcohol that can be consumed at that time.

Tobacco. When the mother smokes, the baby smokes. Exposure to tobacco smoke produces an increase in the carbon monoxide in the maternal fetal bloodstreams and reduced placental blood flow. Both of these processes reduce the supply of oxygen available to the developing baby by as much as 25 percent (Levy & Koren, 1992). Smoking also tends to cause placental abnormalities that negatively affect the flow of nutrients to the fetus. The potential problems associated with smoking during pregnancy include

spontaneous abortion (Kullander & Kaellen, 1971)

reduced body weight, length, and head circumference (Miller, Hassanein, & Hensleigh, 1976; Cornelius et al., 1995)

increased perinatal mortality rates, including sudden infant death syndrome (SIDS) (Abel, 1983; Levy & Koren, 1992).

preterm birth (Niebyl, 1982)

cleft lip and cleft palate (Abel, 1983)

congenital heart disease (Himmelberger, Brown, & Cohen, 1978)

behavior disorders and learning difficulties (Abel, 1983)

Unborn babies are also adversely affected by "passive smoke" inhaled by the mother from other smokers (Roquer, Figueras, & Jimenez, 1995). The severity of effects of prenatal tobacco exposure, from active and/or passive maternal smoking apparently increase in proportion to the level of exposure (Cornelius et al., 1995).

Cocaine and Heroin. The use of cocaine and heroin by pregnant women appears to have become more widespread in recent years. Newborn babies whose mothers have been heavy users of cocaine or heroin (or a milder substitute, methadone) tend to be at increased risk for a number of problems including mortality, growth retardation, prematurity, physical malformations, irritability, poor behavioral organization, and reduced ability to interact with others (Levy & Koren, 1992). Infants may be born in an addicted state and suffer withdrawal effects characterized by irritability, shaking, sweating, and feeding difficulties. Although we can't say for sure, the long term effects of prenatal exposure to heroin appears, in most cases, to be less serious than the effects of cocaine.

Marijuana. Marijuana is one of the most frequently used illegal substances in the United States by women of childbearing age (Dahl, Scker, Williamson, Robles, & Day, 1995). In contrast to the large amount of research data on alcohol and tobacco, there is less information about the effects of marijuana on unborn infants.

Preliminary studies have not found the use of marijuana to be associated with congenital malformations and physical impairments (Cornelius et al., 1995; Linn et al., 1983; Vorhees & Mollnow, 1987). However studies have found use of marijuana during pregnancy to be associated with decreased visual responsiveness and attention, increased startles and tremors, high-pitched crying, and reduced self-quieting in newborn infants. Impaired cognitive functions at 4-years of age, as well as disturbed sleep in 3-year-olds have also been observed (Dahl et al., 1995; Fried & Makin, 1987; Lester & Dreher, 1989; Vorhees & Mollnow, 1987). Some studies have found prenatal exposure to marijuana smoke to be associated with preterm births and reduced fetal growth (Barr et al., 1984; Frank et al., 1990; Zuckerman et al., 1989) while other studies have produced contradictory results

(Cornelius et al., 1995). Overall, there appears to be sufficient evidence of adverse effects to indicate that marijuana use during pregnancy should be avoided.

Caffeine. Since most women in the United States drink coffee or other caffeinated beverages during pregnancy (Widerstrom et al., 1991), questions about the effects of caffeine on the developing baby frequently arise. There appears to be little doubt that high doses of caffeine (equivalent to 12 to 24 cups of coffee per day) produce birth defects in rats (Hill & Kleinberg, 1984a). A few human studies have associated high caffeine consumption with fetal death, birth defects, prematurity, and decreased activity and increased irritability in newborns (Hronsky & Emory, 1987; Lechat et al., 1980). However, other studies have reported no such adverse effects (Brooten & Jordan, 1983; Linn et al., 1982). Until further evidence is available, expectant mothers should eliminate caffeine from their diets or at least limit the intake of caffeine beverages to no more than 2 or 3 cups per day.

Radiation. Accidental exposure to radiation during the early prenatal period generates a lot of concern about possible birth defects, genetic abnormalities, or other problems. A study of twins conducted at the National Cancer Institute (Harvey et al., 1985) found that children who are exposed to X-rays before birth face about two-and-one-half times the usual risk of cancer. The incidence of mental retardation in Japanese children who were prenatally exposed to the World War II atomic bomb explosions is five or more times higher than in other children who were not exposed to the radiation. The most serious effects were found in the children who were exposed during the eighth to fifteenth prenatal weeks (Otake & Schull, 1984). Doctors used to X-ray women patients routinely if a multiple pregnancy was suspected, but this practice has been replaced by other diagnostic procedures.

Maternal Nutrition. Good nutrition during pregnancy is essential for a successful pregnancy and a healthy baby. Severe malnutrition may cause stillbirth, preterm birth, low birthweight, mental deficiency, and infant death during the first year of life (Annis, 1978). Apparently malnutrition is most harmful during the last three months of pregnancy. This is the period when most of the weight gain and rapid growth of the brain cells occurs (Stein et al., 1974). The nutritional status of the mother at the time of fertilization is also critical. Researchers have found that adding folic acid supplements to the mother's diet before fertilization reduces the risk of having an infant born with a neural tube defect by as much as 50 to 70 percent (Rose & Mennuti, 1995).

Maternal weight gain is considered to be one of the best overall indicators of a healthy pregnancy. Prenatal and infant mortality rates are lowest when maternal weight gains are between 24 and 27 pounds. On the average, weight gains in this range contribute to ideal infant birthweight as well as desirable maternal weight after pregnancy (Gormican, Valentine, & Satter, 1980). Women who are overweight at the start of pregnancy probably need to gain only around 16 pounds, whereas underweight women may need to gain as much as 30 pounds during pregnancy (Naeye, 1979; Satter, 1983).

When a pregnancy is planned, women frequently take prenatal vitamins in order to build up their nutritional stores before fertilization occurs. However, vitamin consumption should be carefully monitored before and during pregnancy. Studies have found that excess amounts of vitamin A (retinol) are teratogenic (Rothman et al., 1995). An excess intake of the type of Vitamin A that comes from animal products, such as dairy products or liver, and from fortified foods and vitamin supplements has been associated with birth defects in both human and animal newborns. Apparently this substance interferes with the normal brain and central nervous development during the early stages of prenatal development. It has been estimated that 1 of every 57 babies born to women who consume high levels of vitamin A is born with a birth defect (Rothman et al., 1995).

Many women report changes in food preferences and eating habits during pregnancy. In addition to pickles and ice cream, some expectant mothers develop a compulsion for eating nonfood substances. This phenomenon is called **pica**. Clay, dirt, charcoal, laundry starch, baking soda, soot, ashes, and coffee grounds are some of the items that may be consumed. Pica should be discouraged because some of the substances may be poisonous to the mother or fetus. Nonfood items replace nutritional foods in the diet and may lead to malnutrition, iron-deficiency anemia, or obesity.

Some women experience changes in their sense of smell during pregnancy that in some instances result in cravings to smell a variety of substances (Cooksey, 1995). The effect of this practice is unknown. Since the sense of smell and the sense of taste interact, the mother's food preferences may be altered, resulting in changes in nutritional status.

Maternal Age. The years between 20 and 35 appear to be the "golden age of pregnancy" (Rugh & Shettles, 1971). Teen-age mothers (especially those under 17) experience more complications during the birth process and give birth to more low birthweight babies, preterm babies, and babies with birth defects than mothers in any other age group. The death rate for babies born to teenagers is twice as high as that of older mothers (Alan Guttmacher Institute, 1981). However, it is difficult to separate the effects of age alone from the effects of poverty, since teenagers are more likely than older mothers to be poor before and during pregnancy.

At the other end of the age continuum, fetal and infant mortality rates, genetic abnormalities, and congenital malformations increase as the mother gets older (Naeye, 1983). The risk of having a child with Down syndrome increases dramatically after a woman reaches age 35. At age 35 the risk is 1 in 365, but at age 45 the chances increase to 1 in 32 (Hook & Lindsjo, 1978).

Age of the Father. For many years the age of the father was not considered to be as much of a problem as the age of the mother for the outcome of pregnancy. However, the age of the father may be an important risk factor in prenatal development. For example, Down syndrome rates double when the father is 55 years old (Stene et al., 1977; Matsungaga et al., 1978). Rare genetic disorders such as achondroplasia, Apert syndrome (facial and limb deformities), and Marfan syndrome (height, vision, and heart abnormalities) are more common among the offspring of fathers over 35 years of age (Evans & Hall, 1976). Congenital deafness and heart disorders may also be linked to the age of the father (Day, 1967).

The age of the sperm may also be important. Apparently sperm go through an aging process in which they become defective over the passage of time. Spermatozoa age in the male reproductive tract after long periods of sexual rest (Vander Vliet & Hafez, 1974). A prolonged interval between insemination and fertilization of the ovum may also cause a sperm to age beyond its optimum quality (Salisbury & Hart, 1970). Aging also occurs in sperm stored for artificial insemination. Spontaneous abortion (Guerrero & Rojas, 1975) and chromosomal abnormalities (Tesh & Glover, 1969) have been linked to aging sperm.

Maternal Emotions. Strong emotional stress, such as fear, anxiety, or anger may result in chemical and endocrine changes in the mother's blood. There is a possibility that the chemicals will enter the developing infant's bloodstream or will direct blood flow away from the placenta. High levels of stress for an extended period of time during pregnancy may increase the chances of giving birth to a baby with such problems as low birthweight, hyperactivity, cleft palate, and digestive disorders (Stechler & Halton, 1982). Maternal depression during pregnancy has been linked with excessive crying and irritability in newborn infants (Zuckerman, Bauchner, & Parker, 1990). In addition, fetuses of highly anxious mothers spend more time in a quiet sleep state and exhibit less movement during active sleep than fetuses of less anxious mothers (Groome et al., 1995).

The relationship between maternal emotions during pregnancy and the long-term effects upon development are not known. Therefore, statements about the effects of maternal emotional states on prenatal development must be made with caution. Folklore about pregnancy and childbirth tends to perpetuate the belief that a mother may "mark" her unborn child through a traumatic experience or strong emotional desires. For example, a mother may believe that her child was born with a strawberry-like birth mark because she had a strong craving for strawberries during pregnancy. There is no scientific evidence to support such beliefs, and connections between birth defects and such maternal experiences are coincidental.

Maternal Health. Physicians monitor the health of the expectant mother very carefully. Serious illnesses and infectious diseases of the mother during pregnancy may influence the well-being of the embryo or fetus. For example, if the mother is diabetic before she becomes pregnant, her pregnancy may end abruptly with a miscarriage, the baby may gain excessive weight, or may be born with a congenital defect. A few women (3 - 5 percent) develop gestational diabetes mellitus (GDM) during pregnancy. The major risk associated with GDM is overgrowth of the fetus. Extra large babies are more likely to be injured during the birth process and have a higher death rate (Lee-Parritz & Heffner, 1995). Iron-deficiency anemia and high blood pressure also are conditions that threaten the developing infant. A small percentage of expectant mothers develop toxemia (preeclampsia). This condition causes swelling and fluid retention, excessive weight gain, and high blood pressure. Severe cases can threaten the life of the mother and baby.

During the first 26 weeks of pregnancy, viral infections, such as German measles or herpes, may cause the baby to be born blind, deaf, retarded, or with other problems (Batshaw & Perret, 1992). Women who are infected with the human immunodeficiency virus (HIV) can transmit the infection to their child during the prenatal period or during the birth process. Estimates of the chances that a mother with the virus will infect her infant vary from 20 to 35 percent (Oleske, 1994; Avery, 1995). However, treatment during pregnancy with a combination of drugs has been found to lower the risk of HIV transmission (see Chapter 7). Consequently, scientists recommend that all pregnant women be tested for the HIV virus. Bacterial infections such as Group B strep are also potential causes of death and serious disabilities when they are passed on to the baby during the prenatal period or the birth process. Doctors are beginning to screen pregnant women for the infection and to administer antibiotics during labor if the woman is a carrier.

RH Factor. In some cases an incompatibility of blood types between mother and fetus is a serious threat to normal fetal development. Human blood is either Rh-positive or Rh-negative. The blood type is controlled by the genes. When the mother has Rh-negative blood and the developing baby has Rh-positive blood, an adverse reaction may occur.

The mother's blood and the baby's blood are separated by the placenta. However, during the prenatal period, and especially during the birth process, some of the baby's blood usually leaks into the mother's system. The Rh-negative mother is allergic to the biochemical substances of the Rh-positive blood and produces antibodies to fight off the foreign invaders. Normally, the antibodies do not build up in sufficient quantities to cause a problem during a woman's first pregnancy. However, if the woman has another pregnancy in which the baby is Rh-positive, serious complications may arise. The antibodies from the previous pregnancy destroy the red blood cells of the fetus.

The effects of Rh incompatibility range from mild anemia to deafness, brain damage, cerebral palsy, and death. Fortunately, an injection of gamma globulin (antibody) can be given to the Rh-negative mother soon after a Rh-positive baby is born. The injection prevents the formation of antibodies so that the next Rh-incompatible pregnancy does not have serious complications. This treatment has resulted in a decline in the death and injury rates of infants due to RH incompatibility.

Poverty. The relationship between poverty and adverse prenatal developmental outcomes is well established (Kaplan-Sanoff, Parker, & Zuckerman, 1991). Poverty affects the development of infants even before they are conceived. Economically disadvantaged mothers are more likely than wealthier mothers to have poor health and nutritional histories before becoming pregnant and are less likely to receive adequate prenatal care afterwards. They tend to experience more stress and depression, and to engage in behaviors that are potentially harmful to the developing baby, such as

substance abuse and inadequate eating patterns (Halpern, 1993). The incidence of low birthweight is two to three times higher among infants whose mothers live under poverty conditions (Kaplan-Sanoff et al., 1991).

PRENATAL TESTING

The first 38 weeks of human life spent inside the womb are potentially more dangerous than the first 38 years lived in the outside world (Bachman, 1983). Consequently, scientists are continuing to develop sophisticated techniques and equipment for monitoring the fetus and its intrauterine environment. Detection of congenital malformations or other critical problems before birth provides parents and their physicians information on which to select from the following alternatives: (1) termination of pregnancy, (2) treatment after term, (3) preterm induced delivery for early treatment, (4) delivery by Caesarean section, (5) possible surgical or medical treatment before birth (Hill & Breckle, 1983). It has been estimated that prenatal testing and diagnosis are needed in 7 to 8 percent of all pregnancies (Stewart et al., 1995).

Ultrasound

Since its introduction in the early 1950s, **ultrasound** has become the most commonly used technique for prenatal assessment (Hill & Breckle, 1983). High-frequency sound waves are bounced off the fetus to form a live video image called a sonogram. Ultrasound can be used to assess fetal growth and gestational age, locate and examine the condition of the placenta, determine the baby's sex (week 16), check for congenital abnormalities, evaluate fetal well-being, estimate the amount of amniotic fluid, and diagnose a multiple pregnancy. Ultrasound is also used to determine fetal position and as a visual guide in performing other tests and procedures. The accuracy of the procedure in detecting developmental abnormalities varies from 14 to 85 percent in low-risk populations (Garmel & D'Alton, 1994).

Ultrasound is more versatile than either X-rays

Sonogram of a five-month-old fetus.

or techniques that invade the uterus and is considered to be much safer. It has been estimated that 65 to 70 percent of women undergo at least one ultrasound procedure during pregnancy (Garmel & D'Alton, 1994). Concerns about the safety of ultrasound have persisted through the years. Researchers have reported possible associations between prenatal exposure to ultrasound and dyslexia, left-handedness, and reduced birthweight. However, other studies have not confirmed those findings (Garmel & D'Alton, 1994). As yet, there are no confirmed detrimental effects on the baby from the use of diagnostic ultrasound. The benefits of limited use of ultrasound are likely to outweigh any potential risks (Garmel & D'Alton, 1994).

Amniocentesis

In cases for which ultrasound does not provide adequate information about the condition of the fetus, an amniocentesis test may be used. Guided by a sonogram, a skilled physician inserts a hollow needle through the woman's abdominal wall into the amniotic sac. A small amount of fluid containing cells and other substances from the fetus is withdrawn for laboratory analysis. Laboratory analysis can detect more than 100 abnormalities, including genetic/chromosomal errors, biochemical disorders, and defects in the nervous system.

Amniocentesis is not typically used until around sixteen to eighteen weeks of gestation. However, medical specialists are increasingly performing early amniocentesis (EA) at ten to thirteen weeks of gestation (Stewart et al., 1995). The procedure is rather expensive and involves a waiting period to obtain the test results. Disadvantages of amniocentesis include the risk of needle-puncture injury to the fetus, spontaneous abortion, or infection. Statistics indicate that amniocentesis performed in the second quarter of pregnancy slightly (about 0.5 percent) increases the risk of spontaneous abortion (Thompson, McInnes, & Willard, 1991). The chances of fetal injury are uncertain, but estimates ranging from 0.1 to 3.0 percent of cases have been reported (D'Alton, 1994). Some studies indicate the risks apparently increase with EA, but further evidence is needed to verify those results. In either conventional or early amniotic testing, the risks are usually considered small in comparison to the benefits of the procedure.

Maternal Blood Tests

In some instances, abnormalities may be detected by testing the mother's blood for certain chemicals. The blood is analyzed to detect the presence of alpha-fetoproten (AFP), human chorionic gonadotropin (HCG), or estriol. Steadily increasing amounts of estriol are associated with a healthy pregnancy, whereas a decrease may indicate a change in the welfare of the fetus. This test is especially useful in monitoring the pregnancy of a mother who has diabetes, hypertension, or an overdue delivery. Lower levels of estriol plus an increased amount of HCG is associated with Down syndrome. An elevated level of AFP is an indication of a possible neural tube defect in the fetus. These tests are typically done at sixteen to eighteen weeks of gestation. Since maternal blood tests are not extremely reliable, they must be interpreted with care. Amniocentesis or other tests are usually used to verify the accuracy if a problem is indicated (Stewart et al.,1995).

Chorionic Villus Sampling

Physicians sometimes use a procedure called **chorionic villus sampling (CVS)** to diagnose genetic diseases early in the first trimester of pregnancy before amniocentesis can be safely performed. The ninth or tenth gestational week is considered to be the most suitable time for this procedure, although it is sometimes performed a little earlier (Brambati & Oldrini, 1986). A live sonogram is used to guide a catheter through the cervix or a needle through the abdomen to the fetal chorion. A sample of the chorionic tissue, which contains the same genetic material as the fetus, is obtained. The tissue is analyzed to determine whether suspected chromosomal, metabolic, or blood disorders are present.

The risks of CVS to mother and the fetus have been the subject of a number of investigations. Some mothers experience minor vaginal bleeding or spotting following the procedure, but further maternal complications are rarely reported (D'Alton, 1994). Studies indicate that in comparison to amniocentesis, CVS may result in a slightly greater risk of fetal loss than amniocentesis. CVS also appears to entail a slightly increased risk of limb deformities and blood vessel malformations (hemangiomas) that may lead to internal bleeding, port wine stains on the skin, or benign growths (Burton et al., 1995; D'Alton, 1994; Wynbrandt & Ludman,1991).

Fetoscopy

With the use of an instrument called a fetoscope and special lighting equipment, doctors can look at the fetus inside the womb. The fetoscope is attached to a hollow needle and inserted into the amniotic cavity as in the amniotic procedure. The fetus can then be visually inspected for physical abnormalities such as cleft palate or defective limbs. Samples of fetal skin and cells from the fetal membranes can also be obtained. The same procedure is occasionally used to conduct corrective surgery on the fetus before birth. Fetoscopy is not used until after the sixteenth week of pregnancy.

Fetal Blood Sampling (Cordocentesis)

Samples of the umbilical cord blood can also be obtained and analyzed to detect fetal blood disorders. This test is called **cordocentesis,** but you may also see it referred to as **percutaneous umbilical cord sampling (PUBS).** The procedure involves inserting a long needle through the mother's abdomen into a vein in the umbilical cord as it is viewed by means of an ultrasound scan. The blood is analyzed to detect genetic disorders, infections and other disorders. One of the advantages of this procedure is that the results can be obtained in a shorter time. This procedure is also used to give fetal blood transfusions or drugs. Some studies indicate that fetal blood sampling has a greater risk of a miscarriage than amniocentesis and should be used primarily when information cannot be obtained by safer means (D'Alton, 1994).

GENETIC COUNSELING

A genetic counselor can help prospective parents assess their chances of having a child with a genetic disorder. Prospective parents should seek genetic counseling if any of the following conditions apply: (1) either one has a blood relative with a genetic disorder; (2) they have had previous miscarriages; (3) they already have a child with a genetic disorder or with abnormal physical or behavioral development; (4) the female is over 35 years of age; (5) they are members of an ethnic group with specific genetic disorders such as Tay-Sachs disease or sickle-cell anemia; and (6) either one has a history of drug use, exposure to industrial chemicals, or other possible teratogens (Bachman, 1983).

SUMMARY

1. Fertilization of the mother's ovum by the father's sperm cell takes place in the fallopian tube. The prenatal period, which begins with fertilization, is divided into three stages: preembryonic, embryonic, and fetal. When a woman has fertility problems, she may elect to utilize artificial insemination to become pregnant through in vitro fertilization and "embryo" transfer.

2. During the preembryonic stage, the fertilized ovum, called a zygote, changes into a morula (16 cells), and a blastocyst (58 cells). The blastocyst typically begins to implant itself in the upper part of the uterus around day 6. Occasionally an ectopic pregnancy occurs when the blastocyst is implanted outside the uterus.

3. The embryonic period begins with the formation of the embryonic disc around the eighth day and continues until the eighth week of pregnancy. The growth that takes place during this period is rapid and dramatic. The size and appearance of the embryo change almost daily. During the third week, three germ layers are formed through a process called gastrulation. Each of the germ layers—ectoderm, endoderm, mesoderm—forms the foundation for the development of various body structures. The chorion, placenta, amnion, and umbilical cord develop early to function as supporting membranes for the embryo. By the end of this period the beginnings of all limbs, internal organs, and the skeleton have been established. The heart is pumping blood; the kidneys and other organs are beginning to function.

4. The fetal stage begins at the ninth week and continues until the baby is born. The name change from embryo to fetus signifies the completion of the human form and the appearance of the first bone cells in the cartilage of the skeleton. The body structures and organ systems develop further. The sex of the fetus is distinguishable. By midpregnancy, the fetus begins to move and is covered with lanugo and vernix caseosa. The complete number of neuronal cells is present in the brain. The process of myelination of the nerve cells has also begun. During the last two months of pregnancy, the fetus gains weight rapidly, increases in length, and practices many of the functions that are necessary for life in the world outside the womb.

5. The number of multiple births in the United States has increased dramatically in recent years. Twins account for about 98 percent of multiple births, but the number of other types of multiple births has increased at a faster rate.

6. Both genetic and environmental factors influence growth and development during the prenatal period. Genetic disorders are classified as chromosomal abnormalities, single gene disorders, sex-linked disorders, and polygenic inheritance. The most common disorder caused by chromosomal aberrations is Down syndrome. Huntington's chorea is a disorder resulting from a faulty dominant gene. Phenylketonuria is one of the major recessive genetic disorders. Color blindness and hemophilia are examples of defects caused by sex-linked genes. Spina bifida represents a multifactorial disorder.

7. Numerous drugs, viruses, and other environmental factors have been associated with birth defects and developmental problems. The list of substances pregnant women should avoid includes a variety of drugs and medications, alcohol, tobacco, cocaine, heroin, marijuana, large quantities of caffeine, and exposure to radiation. Inadequate nutrition during pregnancy also may cause problems such as low birthweight and mental deficiency. Maternal age, paternal age, maternal stress and health problems, maternal-fetal blood incompatibility, and poverty are additional risk factors.

8. Techniques that are used to monitor the condition of the baby and to detect developmental problems include ultrasound, amniocentesis, maternal blood tests, chorionic villus sampling, fetoscopy, and fetal blood sampling. Information obtained from tests performed before pregnancy and during the early stages of prenatal development can be used to provide genetic counseling to the parents.

3

The Birth Process

My mother groan'd, my father wept,
Into the dangerous world I leapt;
Helpless, naked, pipin loud,
Like a fiend hid in a cloud.

—Blake

Childbirth is a relatively brief period of transition between prenatal development and life in the outside world. Montagu (1964) refers to birth as a bridge between two stages of life. The birth process is marked by a series of dramatic events affecting all the participants. For the fetus, the tranquility of the mother's womb is abruptly interrupted, for better or worse, by powerful forces projecting the fetus through the birth canal. For the parents, particularly the mother, the months of waiting are coming to an end, but only after a few more exciting and stressful hours. For the physicians, nurses, or other birth attendants, decisions must be made about when and how to assist mother and baby in the process.

This chapter explores the physiology of labor, how labor begins, and what happens during each of the three stages of childbirth. The various types of delivery, the use of medication, contemporary methods of prepared childbirth, and the participation of the father in the birth process are discussed. In addition, we take a look at alternatives available for labor, delivery, and care of the baby after birth.

PHYSIOLOGY OF LABOR

The process of childbirth is commonly referred to as labor because the mother works to give birth. Normally she exerts a considerable amount of energy in pushing the baby out of the uterus. However, the process is more complex than the term labor implies. Labor is affected by the interplay of various physiological conditions, including hormonal substances, contractions of the uterus, dilation of the cervix, and the position of the fetus. In addition, psychological factors such as the mother's anxiety level and pain threshold play important roles.

The Four Ps of Childbirth

The progress of labor and delivery involve an interaction between four factors, referred to by health care specialists as the four Ps: the **passenger**, the **pelvis (passage)**, the **powers,** and the **placenta** (Benson & Pernoll, 1994). Obviously, the passenger is the fetus. The size of the fetus, the position (left or right) of the fetus in relation to the mother's pelvic structure, and the part of the fetus that first enters the birth canal are important passenger characteristics. The size and shape of the mother's pelvic structure forms the passageway through which the fetus must pass. The female pelvis has been classified into four basic types with variations, some of which provide an easier passageway than others (Wheeler, 1995). The powers of childbirth are the contractions and forces that exert pressure and force the fetus out of the uterus. The location and condition of the placenta also affect the birth process. The placenta can be an obstruction if it is implanted low in the uterus, or can cause problems if it separates from the uterus too early. Each of the factors, alone or in combination, determine whether labor and delivery are easy or difficult (Benson & Pernoll, 1994).

Onset of Labor

Calculated from the first day of the last menstrual period, the average pregnancy lasts 280 days. Approximately 95 percent of all babies are born within two weeks of this time period (or between the 266th and 294th day) (Nilsson & Hamberger, 1990). The date of birth can be estimated but not accurately predicted. Actually, scientists do not clearly understand what causes labor to begin. The answer to this mystery is obviously very important for predicting and controlling labor as well as for preventing premature births.

Researchers have tried for years to identify the factors that lead to the onset of labor. In addition to finding the mechanism controlling labor, scientists are also faced with the task of identifying whether the mother, the fetus, or both are responsible for its initiation. The process is very complicated due to the separate physiological events involved, including cervical dilation, rupture of the amniotic sac, contractions of the uterus, and placental separation.

The most recent investigations have focused on

the identification of hormones and other chemical substances that may, either singly or in combination, trigger the birth process. Oxytocin, cortisol, progesterone, and estrogen are some of the hormones that have been associated with the beginning and maintenance of labor contractions. Research studies on prostaglandin activity appear to offer the most promising clues to the mystery of human labor. Prostaglandins are members of a group of substances known as fatty acids, which are found in most body tissues and fluids. Scientists have identified at least fourteen prostaglandins that influence a variety of bodily functions, such as muscle contractions, blood pressure, reproduction, and secretion of stomach acid.

Some types of prostaglandins (PGs) have been found to be effective in inducing labor and in ripening of the cervix at any stage of pregnancy. Chemical substances that interfere with the absorption of PGs in the body inhibit labor and have been used to stop preterm labor (Gravett, 1984; Pritchard, MacDonald, & Gant, 1985; Wheeler, 1995). For example, the administration of large doses of aspirin to pregnant women act as a prostaglandin inhibitor and result in prolonged pregnancy (Biswas & Craigo, 1994). Although it is still not conclusive, evidence is accumulating to indicate that prostaglandins play a key role in the initiation of labor (Biswas & Craigo, 1994; Hirst et al., 1995). The evidence is still too fragmentary to determine whether the PGs responsible for labor originate in tissues of the fetus or the mother.

Induced Labor

In some cases, labor is started by artificial methods such as injections of prostaglandins, oxytocin, or rupture of the fetal membranes (amniotomy). The reasons for inducing labor are many and varied. Labor is usually induced as a response to a prolonged pregnancy or complications such as maternal diabetes, bleeding, excessive amniotic fluid, RH incompatibility, toxemia (infection), failure of labor to begin within 24 hours after rupture of fetal membranes, prolonged maternal infections, or intrauterine fetal death.

Induced labor may also be done because the patient lives a long distance from the hospital or simply for the convenience of the parents, the doctor, or both. Many people oppose routine induction of labor because it tends to be more unpredictable, complicated, painful, and stressful for both mother and baby (Hawkins & Higgins, 1981).

Contractions

The onset of labor is signaled by regular contractions of the uterus. A **labor contraction** is the tightening and shortening of the muscles in the uterus. The mother has no control over the contractions. When labor begins, the contractions are usually 10 to 30 minutes apart and last for 30 to 45 seconds. At the end of labor, the contractions are closer together and last from 60 to 90 seconds. Ideally, the contractions increase steadily in regularity, intensity, and duration throughout the birth process (Benson & Pernoll, 1994).

Contractions usually begin at the top of the uterus and move downward, reaching a peak and then becoming weaker. Occasionally the progress of labor is impaired by reverse contractions, which begin in the lower part of the uterus and move upward, or uncoordinated contractions in different parts of the uterus. Typically, contractions become stronger, last longer, and get closer together as labor progresses. During the process, the baby's head is pushed into the lower part of the uterus. As labor progresses, the upper part of the uterus becomes thicker and smaller, while the lower portion stretches thinner and larger. The uterus is slowly pulled upward, as if a turtleneck sweater is being pulled over the baby's head (Oxorn, 1980).

Braxton Hicks Contractions (False Labor)

The muscles of the uterus contract every 5 to 20 minutes, increasing in frequency throughout the prenatal period. These contractions are usually not strong enough to be felt by the mother until approximately the last month of pregnancy. When they are perceived by the mother, usually in late pregnancy, they are called **false labor,** or **Braxton Hicks** contractions. At that time the mother may believe that labor has begun. These contractions are irregular, short, mild in intensity, and do not cause cervical change. In contrast, true labor contractions occur at regular intervals, while gradually increasing in strength and frequency, as the cervix dilates (Troyer & Parisi, 1993).

Dilation and Effacement

The cervix is the lower part, or mouth, of the uterus that protrudes into the vagina (see Figure 3–1). During most of the pregnancy the cervix is about 1 inch (2.5 centimeters) long, with an opening about the width of the end of an unsharpened pencil (Oxorn, 1980). During pregnancy the opening is closed with a mucous plug to protect the fetus.

Throughout the prenatal period, physical and chemical changes in the uterus soften or "ripen" the cervix in preparation for the birth process. During labor, the cervix becomes shorter and thinner through the process of **effacement**. Before the baby can leave the uterus, the cervix must open to its widest capacity, which is about 4 inches (10 centimeters), or about the size of five fingers on an average hand. This process is called **dilation**. Usually effacement and dilation occur simultaneously.

STAGES OF LABOR

Preliminary Signs

Toward the end of pregnancy there are a number of signs that labor is approaching. Approximately two to four weeks before labor begins, the head of the fetus usually moves or "drops" downward into the pelvic cavity. This is called "lightening," since there is less pressure on the mother's diaphragm,

A. Prelabor. The cervix is thick and closed.

B. Early labor. Contractions, dilation, effacement, and head engagement.

C. Late labor. Cervix is completely dilated; head is in the birth canal.

D. Delivery. Baby's head begins to emerge.

Figure 3-1 Labor and Delivery.

allowing her to breathe more freely. Other warning signs include a pink vaginal discharge or a bloody "show" caused by the loss of the mucous plug from the cervical opening. Diarrhea, stomach upset, increased Braxton Hicks contractions, low back pain, and a 2-to-5-pound weight loss are other prelabor symptoms.

Rupture of Membranes

In approximately 10 percent of childbirths, the amniotic sac breaks before labor begins (Benson & Pernoll, 1994). There may be a sudden gush of water or a slow leak, depending on the size of the break in the membranes. In 9 out of 10 cases of full term pregnancies, labor begins within 24 hours after the amniotic sac breaks. The major problem the mother faces is the risk of infection. Some physicians induce labor within 3 to 12 hours, but others recommend waiting at least 24 hours for spontaneous labor to begin (Conway et al., 1984).

At one time, physicians routinely ruptured the membranes (amniotomy) if they were still intact after 2 or 3 hours of labor to speed up the birth process. This practice was criticized after researchers found that in normal labor, membranes rupture spontaneously in only 66 percent of women before the second stage. Although early rupture of the membranes may shorten length of labor, it may result in stronger, more frequent contractions that possibly reduce oxygen supply and increase fetal distress. Physicians are now more reluctant to perform an amniotomy during early labor (Spencer, 1995).

Position of the Fetus

The process of labor is dramatically affected by the position of the fetus and the body part that first enters the birth canal. Approximately 96 percent of all babies are born in the head-first (vertex or cephalic) position as shown in Figure 3-2 (Hamilton, 1984). Ideally, the smallest part of the baby's head is directed down the birth canal first, with the face turned toward the spinal column. However, the presenting part may be the face or the brow, with the head turned, in relation to the spinal column, at one of a variety of angles.

In approximately 3 to 4 percent of pregnancies, the fetus is in a **breech** position when labor begins (Hamilton, 1984). In a breech delivery, the baby is born with the buttocks, feet, or knees first, A variety of breech presentations are possible (Fig. 3–2). The **frank breech** is the most common, in which both feet are extended straight up beside the ears, and the buttocks enter the birth canal first. In a **full** or **complete breech**, the buttocks are born first, while the knees are drawn against the stomach and the feet extended downward. Breech births also occur in which the feet (**footling**) or knees (**kneeling**) are born first.

Breech births are more difficult and may take longer than normal births. The contractions are not as efficient in pushing the baby out because the largest part of the baby, the head, follows the smallest parts, the buttocks and feet. In a few deliveries (less than 1 percent) (Hamilton, 1984), the fetus is turned crosswise in the uterus in a transverse presentation (Fig. 3–2). The shoulder blade is typically positioned in the birth canal. In a transverse presentation, the baby must either be turned or be surgically removed through a Caesarean section.

Stage 1: Dilation of the Cervix

The first stage of labor, called **dilation**, begins with the first true contractions of the uterus and ends when the cervix is completely effaced and fully dilated (10cm). This stage of the birth process is the longest. In many cases, the father stays with the mother throughout labor and delivery to provide emotional support and assistance.

The dilation stage typically lasts from 6 to 18 hours for women delivering their first baby, and 2 to 6 hours for the second and subsequent deliveries. The time, however, varies widely with individuals and may be shorter or longer depending upon the 4 Ps. This first stage is divided into three phases: latent, active, and transition.

Latent phase. Contractions during the **latent** phase are usually mild in intensity to begin with, but normally become increasingly strong as labor progresses. They occur from 5 to 8 minutes apart and last about 30 seconds. A calm and relaxed attitude by the mother

Figure 3-2 Possible Positions of Fetus During Labor.
Source: H. Oxorn, Oxorn-Foote Human Labor and Birth, 4th ed., Appleton-Century-Crofts, New York, 1980. Adapted by permission.

tends to speed up dilation and decreases the amount of time needed to complete this phase. Under normal conditions, mothers are advised to walk around rather than lie down. The latent phase averages 8 to 12 hours for first-time mothers but may last up to 20 hours. This phase is usually 6 to 8 hours, but may normally last 14 hours, for women who have had other babies (Wheeler, 1995). As the cervix dilates and contractions continue, the presenting part, usually the head, moves into (engages) the pelvic outlet.

Active phase. The mother enters the **active** phase when the cervix reaches about 1-½ inches (3-4 cm) of dilation. The time between contractions decreases to about 3 to 5 minutes. The contractions last longer (45 to 60 seconds) and increase in intensity. Some women with uncomplicated labor wait until this phase to enter the hospital (Parfitt, 1977). The spontaneous rupture of the membranes most often occurs sometime during the active phases (Pritchard et al., 1985). The average time needed to complete the active phase is approximately 4 hours for the first birth and 2 hours for subsequent deliveries (Zlatnik, 1994).

Transition. The **transition** phase covers the last inch of dilation (8-10 cm.). This is the most difficult time during labor. The contractions are stronger, last longer (about 80 secs.) and are closer together. These contractions have been compared to the ocean waves on a beach during a storm, with one coming in on top of another. Feelings of irritability, discouragement, loss of control, and panic are common. Other difficulties include hot and cold flashes, disorientation, nausea, and vomiting. The mother usually feels a strong desire to push, comparable to having a bowel movement. Fortunately the transition phase is relatively short, lasting 30 to 60 minutes for first births, and about 20 to 30 minutes for subsequent births (Hassid, 1984).

Stage 2: Expulsion

The second stage of labor begins as soon as the cervix is completely open and lasts until the baby is born. The **expulsion** stage is usually a welcome relief after the difficult transition phase. The mother

may have a chance to recover her equilibrium and possibly doze between contractions. The contractions are long but less frequent (Novak & Broom, 1995). The mother can now use her abdominal muscles and diaphragm to help push the baby out of the birth canal. The baby is usually born within 30 minutes to 2 hours after this stage begins. For mothers who have given birth before, however, expulsion may last only about 20 minutes to 1-½ hours (Novak & Broom, 1995).

If the baby is in the head-first position, the head advances through the birth canal with each contraction and recedes slightly as the uterus relaxes, as if taking two steps forward and one step back. The baby's head must rotate to move through the mother's pelvic structure. The top of the head eventually becomes visible at the vaginal opening. The term **crowning** is used when the largest part of the scalp appears and does not recede between contractions.

About the time an inch (3 centimeters) of the baby's head is visible, the physician usually makes a surgical incision (episiotomy) in the perineum—the tissue between the vagina and rectum. The routine performance of episiotomies is controversial and has been questioned as unnecessary surgery (Thacker & Banta, 1983). Some physicians argue, however, that it shortens the delivery time and spares the baby's head from excessive pressure. In addition, a neat, controlled surgical incision is easier to repair and heals better than a ragged, uncontrolled natural tear (Pritchard et al., 1985; Wheeler, 1995).

Once the baby's head is out of the birth canal, the head rotates to become aligned with the baby's shoulders. The shoulders must also rotate to pass through the pelvic structure. First one shoulder emerges and then the other, followed by the buttocks and lower limbs. This part is relatively easy, since the larger head has paved the way.

When the baby emerges from the uterus, the umbilical cord is still attached. When the cord stops pulsating (or sooner if the baby is premature or in distress), clamps are applied to the umbilical cord in two places. The cord is then cut between the two clamps. Usually the physician keeps the head lowered below the vaginal opening and waits about 30 seconds before clamping the cord to allow placental blood to drain from the placenta to the newborn (Benson & Pernoll, 1994; Pritchard et al., 1985).

Stage 3: Placental Expulsion

The third stage of labor begins as soon as the baby is completely out of the birth canal and ends with the expulsion of the placenta and fetal membranes (the afterbirth). The stage of **placental expulsion** usually lasts about 5 to 20 minutes. If it extends beyond 30 minutes, the danger of excessive bleeding becomes a problem.

As soon as the baby is born, the contractions usually stop for a few minutes and then start again to expel the placenta. Oxytocin may be administered to the mother to stimulate contractions. The uterus shrinks dramatically so that the implantation site of the placenta is reduced. Since the placenta stays the same size, it typically separates or "peels off" from the lining of the uterus and is expelled during the final contractions.

Stage 4: Recovery

The recovery stage usually lasts for about an hour after the delivery of the placenta is complete. However, the length of this stage varies with hospital and cultural practices. During this period, the mother and baby are carefully observed for complications of the birth process. Although labor and delivery are complete, this stage is designated to emphasize the importance of observing the mother for excessive bleeding (Zlatnik, 1995). The episiotomy and any tears in the vaginal tissue are stitched and repaired. The stage of expulsion and the first hour after birth are considered to be the most dangerous periods in the birth process for the mother because of the risk of excessive bleeding. Currently some hospitals discharge women within 24 hours after delivery in response to demands for reduction in health-care costs. However, this policy has generated controversy because many parents and doctors feel that in some cases the mother and baby may be at risk.

CAESAREAN DELIVERY

A variety of conditions can prevent or interfere with a vaginal childbirth. When complications occur, the baby may be removed through a surgical incision in the abdomen and uterus, called a **Caesarean section (C-section)**. The transverse or breech position of the fetus, failure of the cervix to dilate, obstructions in the uterus or pelvis, excess bleeding, and signs of fetal distress are some of the conditions that might necessitate a Caesarean delivery (Hawkins & Higgins, 1981).

The number of Caesarean births in the United States more than quadrupled from 1970 to the mid-1980s, rising from 5.5 per 100 deliveries in 1970 to a peak of 24.7 per 100 deliveries in 1988. In 1993 the overall rate of Caesarean deliveries had declined slightly to 22.8 per 100 births (Paul & Miller, 1995; Clarke & Taffel, 1995). Approximately 16 to 17 percent of all 1993 Caesarean deliveries were primary, or first time births, while 7 to 8 percent were repeat Caesareans.

The increase in C-sections has been attributed to (1) improved techniques in surgery and anesthesia, (2) more concern about birth defects resulting from complications in vaginal deliveries, (3) use of more sophisticated fetal monitoring techniques to indicate fetal distress, (4) the desire to avoid breech deliveries and the use of forceps, and (5) an increased threat of lawsuits against health care providers in cases of adverse outcomes of the birth process (Hawkins & Higgins, 1981; Paul & Miller, 1995). A number of other factors have been associated with Caesarean births, for reasons that are not always understood. The rate of Caesarean births are highest in the South. The rates increase with maternal age and a pregnancy weight gain of 46 pounds or more. In addition, mothers having their first birth, who are married, and who have high educational attainment, very short gestations, low or high birthweights, and multiple delivery are more likely to have a Caesarean delivery. The overall rate is slightly lower for black than white mothers (National Center for Health Statistics, 1994).

Even under ideal conditions, the surgical procedures involved in C-sections involve greater health risks for the mother and baby than normal vaginal delivery (Brengman & Burns, 1983; Clarke & Taffel, 1995). Consequently, the high number of Caesarean births has generated a lot of concern among physicians and public health officials and has resulted in the establishment of a national health objective to reduce the overall rate of Caesarean births to 15 per 100 deliveries by the year 2000 (Clarke & Taffel, 1995). Approximately 7 to 8 percent, or about one-third, of all C-sections are performed on mothers who had a previous delivery by this method (Paul & Miller, 1995). Another national goal is to reduce the repeat C-section rate to 3 percent by the year 2000.

In the past, obstetricians took the position that once a C-section is performed, the mother must have all future deliveries in the same way, to avoid the possibility of the uterus rupturing during labor at the site of the previous incision. Research studies indicate that normal labor and delivery are possible for many carefully screened patients who had a previous Caesarean delivery (Brengman & Burns, 1983; Clarke & Taffel, 1995). During the period between 1988 to 1993 the rate of vaginal birth after previous Caesarean delivery (VBAC) doubled from 12.6 to 25.4 percent. By comparison, countries in Europe have 50 percent VBAC rate (Paul & Miller, 1995; Clarke & Taffel, 1995). Clearly some progress is being made in reducing the number of primary C-sections and increasing the VBAC rate. However, current obstetrical practices will have to change quickly in order to meet the overall 15 percent C-sections limit by the year 2000.

MULTIPLE BIRTHS

Labor and delivery of more than one fetus presents special problems. The extra crowding of the uterus frequently results in early rupture of the membranes, leading to premature labor. Although labor and delivery proceed satisfactorily in most cases, the overstretching of the uterus sometimes causes weak and inefficient contractions, delaying the progress of labor. There is also an increased risk of maternal bleeding after the birth process has been completed (Oxorn, 1980).

The birth of twins and other multiple concep-

tions may be complicated by the position of the fetuses. Usually both twins are in the ideal head-first position when labor begins, but other combinations of positions are possible. One twin or both may be in a breech position or in a transverse lie. Another rare combination is for the first twin to be in a breech position while the second twin in is in a head-first lie. In that case, the possibility exists for **interlocking** twins whereby the body of the first twin is born, but the head of the second twin descends in the pelvic structure underneath the head of the first twin. In this position the head of the first twin is trapped and cannot be born (Coustan, 1995). The second twin faces a greater risk because it occupies the less favorable position, and the uterine capacity to supply oxygen to the placenta may be reduced after the first twin is born. In most cases (80 percent) the second twin is born within 30 minutes of the first twin (Oxorn, 1980).

USE OF FORCEPS AND VACUUM EXTRACTION

Obstetrical forceps are used in some deliveries to rotate the baby's head and help the baby through the birth canal. Forceps are generally shaped like salad tongs, but they come in a variety of designs for specific applications. A physician may resort to the use of forceps when the mother cannot push the baby out because of exhaustion or the effects of medication. This instrument may also be used to speed delivery in case of an emergency such as fetal distress.

The use of forceps is controversial because of the risk of injury to the baby or mother (Hassid, 1984). The possibility of injury is greatest when forceps are applied before the baby's head is engaged in the pelvic opening. Numerous studies have consistently documented the adverse effects of using forceps before the baby's head has reached the vaginal opening. The problems identified include physical injuries and reduced long-range intelligence scores (Freedman et al., 1984; Painti, 1982). In recent years, the trend has been away from the use of forceps except under carefully defined and restricted circumstances (Dunnihoo, 1992).

A **vacuum extractor** is another instrument that is used in vaginal births. The device consists of a metal or a plastic cup that is attached to the top of the baby's head. A vacuum is generated, which causes the cup to cling to the scalp as downward pressure is applied to facilitate the movement of the head. In many countries the vacuum extractor has replaced the use of forceps, but the device is not as popular in the United States. The same precautions that limit the use of forceps are applicable to the vacuum extractor as well (Afriat & Couston, 1995; Dunnihoo, 1992).

POSITION OF THE MOTHER

Women in different cultures labor and give birth in a variety of positions, including kneeling, squatting, standing, sitting, or on hands and knees. For example, Mexican Tarahumara women often deliver outdoors. As delivery begins, the mother finds an overhead tree limb to hang on to and gives birth in a standing position. The baby falls into a soft bed of grass underneath the mother (Broude, 1995). In some places, "birth chairs" are used to support the mother as she delivers the baby in an upright sitting position.

In contrast, the mother in the United States usually labors and delivers while lying on her back (recumbent) in what is sometimes called the "stranded turtle" position. Traditionally, during delivery, the head of the delivery table is raised as the mother's knees are bent toward the abdomen with the feet flat on the surface or in stirrups (Hamilton, 1984). European women frequently lie on their sides during the delivery of the baby.

Newer adjustable beds that are currently used for both labor and delivery allow the mother to select a position (within limits) that is most comfortable (Novak & Broom, 1995). A company in Switzerland has introduced a type of chair called the ROMA Birth Wheel modeled after an ancient Egyptian "birth stone." This device consists of a seat and a head rest within a wheel-shaped tubular structure. It is powered by two remote-controlled motors that allow the mother to easily change positions from sitting to leaning backwards.

This baby was born while the mother was in a semi-reclining position on her back.

Researchers are beginning to study the effects of various maternal positions on the length of labor and on the safety and comfort of the mother and baby. Numerous studies on posture and movement by women in labor indicate that variations of upright posture, such as standing, sitting, squatting, or walking, tend to facilitate labor progress and reduce the need for pain medication. No adverse effects of these practices on the baby were reported (Troyer & Parisi, 1993).

PAIN AND LABOR

The reality of childbirth pain is universal and well documented. Melzack (1984) reviewed studies indicating that labor is one of the most intense types of pain reported by women in all cultures. There are many causes of pain during labor and delivery, including both physiological and psychological. The contractions of the uterus restrict the blood supply to the muscles, creating a painful shortage of oxygen. Pain signals are sent to the brain by the stretching of the cervix and other organs, as well as the pressure and friction on sensitive nerve endings by the baby's descent through the birth canal.

People vary widely in their anatomy as well as in their sensitivity to pain. The mother's pelvic structure and the size of the baby affect the extent to which labor is painful. In addition, the amount of pain actually experienced may be increased or diminished by the mother's emotional state. Fear, anxiety, and stress create muscle tension and may initiate chemical changes that intensify the pain of labor and delivery.

METHODS OF PAIN RELIEF

Before the discovery of ether and chloroform in the mid-1800s, people resorted to chants, rituals, body contortions, and folk medicine in attempts to find relief from the pain of childbirth. Currently, there are numerous obstetric medications as well as hypnosis and prepared childbirth training that alleviate childbirth pain. The goal in the use of pain medications is to provide a safe, more comfortable, and satisfactory delivery for the mother without adversely affecting the baby. Depending upon their functions, obstetric medications can be broadly classified as analgesics, tranquilizers, and anesthetics. Amnesic drugs that cause memory loss of varying degrees (e.g., scopalomine) are no longer used because of their unpredictable effects (Benson & Pernoll, 1994). In many cases, various types of drugs are combined to produce multiple effects.

Analgesics

Medications that reduce or eliminate pain are called **analgesics** (Novak & Broom, 1995). Narcotics, such as meperidine (Demerol), are considered to be the most effective analgesics available (Brackbill, 1979) and are widely used during labor and delivery. Unfortunately, narcotics rapidly cross the placenta and may impair respiratory functions of the newborn infant. In some cases a type of drug known as narcotic antagonist is administered to the newborn after birth to decrease these effects. Inhalant analgesics, such as nitrous oxide, are no longer widely used because of possible overdoses and undesirable effects (Coustan, 1995).

Tranquilizers

A variety of tranquilizers are given during labor to reduce the mother's anxiety and excitement. When taken in sufficient doses tranquilizers induce drowsiness or sleep. Tranquilizers are also frequently used to heighten the effects of other medications and reduce the total amount of medication needed. For example, meperidine (analgesic) and promethazine (tranquilizer) are frequently used together (Pritchard et al., 1985). Physicians vary in the specific medications they prefer to administer.

Anesthetics

Anesthetics are used to bring about partial or complete loss of sensation, either by inducing unconsciousness or by blocking the conduction of nerve impulses. Anesthetics are classified as general, regional, or local, depending upon how and where they are administered and their overall effect.

General anesthesia affects the entire body and usually induces partial or total unconsciousness. This type of medication is administered in the form of gas or an intravenous solution. General anesthesia is used occasionally for Caesarean sections or other complicated deliveries (Benson & Pernoll, 1994). Heavy general anesthesia is seldom used during normal labor because of its adverse effects on the central nervous system of both mother and baby. In addition, it can cause the mother to choke on her own gastric juices. In some cases, a woman may breathe low doses of anesthetic gases through a mask or mouthpiece to reduce discomfort or pain without losing consciousness (Novak & Broom, 1995).

Regional, or local anesthetics, sometimes referred to as nerve blocks, are substances that cause loss of feeling in a particular area of the body. A drug similar to Novocain is administered in a single injection or by continuous conduction through a small tube. The major advantage of this type of anesthesia over other obstetric medications is that it allows the mother to remain conscious and alert during the birth process. As with any medication, the main disadvantage of a regional anesthetic is the side effects. Mothers who receive regional anesthesia sometimes experience reduced blood pressure, severe headaches, and convulsions.

If given too early, or in large doses, these substances interfere with contractions, delay labor, and increase the need for the use of forceps.

EFFECTS OF OBSTETRIC MEDICATION

In addition to slowing down the birth process, most pain relief substances rapidly cross the placenta and accumulate in the bloodstream and organs of the baby. The detrimental effects on the respiratory efforts of the baby immediately after birth are clearly observable. Scientists have been concerned about possible temporary or permanent behavioral effects on the developing infant.

Numerous studies have examined the effects of obstetric medications on infant behavior. The results of the research reports have been summarized as follows (Brackbill et al., 1985): (1) Forty-seven of the studies found that obstetric medication adversely affected one or more infant behaviors, such as information-processing efficiency and attention; (2) None of the studies showed that the medication enhanced or improved infant behavior; (3) The extent of the behavioral effects was related to the potency of the drug. General anesthesia was the worst offender, whereas regional anesthesia had the least impact on the behaviors studied; (4) Few studies tested for the effects of medication beyond 6 weeks of age, and none of the studies tested beyond the first year. Therefore, long-term effects cannot be ruled out.

PREPARED CHILDBIRTH TRAINING

Many women attempt to avoid or minimize the use of medication during childbirth through childbirth-preparation classes. Prepared childbirth training has gained popularity since the 1960s as the result of concerns about the undesirable effects of medication and the desire of both mothers and fathers to participate more actively in the birth process (Gordan & Haire, 1981). There are several specific methods of prepared childbirth. The Read, Lamaze, and Bradley methods have provided the basic theoretical and methodological foundations of prepared childbirth training in the United States.

Read Method

Prepared childbirth training was introduced in the United States in the 1940s by Grantley Dick-Read, an English obstetrician (Feldman, 1978). Dick-Read believed that childbirth pain is intensified by the mother's fear and anxiety, which cause the muscles to become tense. If the muscles are tense, the contractions are more difficult and painful, and progress is slower. The increased pain leads to greater anxiety, which in turn causes more muscle tension, creating a cyclical effect. The Read method, which is sometimes called natural childbirth, interrupts the fear-tension-pain cycle through mental and physical preparation for childbirth. The training sessions include information about the physiology of labor and delivery, abdominal breathing exercises, relaxation techniques, positions for labor, and various body-conditioning exercises. The presence and encouragement of the father, who serves as a coach during labor and delivery, is considered important but not mandatory (Dick-Read, 1972).

Lamaze Method

The Lamaze method was developed by French obstetrician Fernand Lamaze (Lamaze, 1970). His approach is similar to the Read method but includes a much more structured and systematic set of instructions. Lamaze based his method on Pavlov's theory that responses can be conditioned and controlled through learning. The mother typically goes through a series of six lessons during which she learns a combination of breathing and relaxation exercises to use during the various stages of labor and delivery. As in the Read method, physical exercises and information about the physiology of labor are also included. Lamaze stressed the importance of the father (or a substitute) participating in the classes with the mother and serving as the labor leader or coach, providing emotional support and physical assistance during labor and birth.

Lamaze (1970) believed that "the pain of childbirth is neither necessary nor inevitable" (p. 41). Although contemporary Lamaze instructors do not emphasize the pain of childbirth, they recognize its reality. The goal of Lamaze training is not necessarily to eliminate pain, but to control it and make childbirth a positive experience (Ewy & Ewy, 1982). Medication for pain relief is available if needed. The Lamaze method has been the most widely used approach to preparation for childbirth (Burroughs, 1986).

Bradley Method

The Bradley method of prepared childbirth (Bradley, 1974) is much less structured or specific than either the Lamaze or Read method. Relaxation and physical and breathing exercises are demonstrated in a series of eight sessions. However, each couple is expected to find its own ways to relax and cope with the labor and delivery processes. Emphasis is placed on creating darkness and quiet and controlling other environmental variables to facilitate relaxation (Burroughs, 1986). The method is also referred to as husband-coached childbirth because the supportive role of the husband is an essential part of the process. Advocates of the Bradley method are very strongly opposed to the use of any type of medication during the birth process (Feldman, 1978).

Hypnosis

Some mothers elect to use hypnosis as an alternative to medication as a means of controlling childbirth pain. This is one of the oldest techniques of pain control during childbirth, dating back to the 19th century (Dunnihoo, 1992). There are different methods of hypnosis that vary with practitioners. The benefits of hypnosis have been favorably compared with those of prepared childbirth training (Parfitt, 1977). However, this approach is not widely used because obstetric personnel usually do not have the special training and skills needed to use hypnosis. The amount of time required to train most patients sufficiently to benefit from hypnosis is also an obstacle.

Current Approaches

Many childbirth educators are currently utilizing a broader, more diverse approach to childbirth preparation rather than a strict adherence to either the Read, Lamaze, or Bradley methods. This broader perspective is based on the need for flexibility and individualization in educating women for childbirth (Novak & Broom, 1995). The use of a more flexible teaching approach takes into consideration the wide range of women's physiological responses, coping skills, personality characteristics, and cultural backgrounds. Thus, preparation and support are provided for a wider variety of maternal behavior during labor (Novak & Broom, 1995).

EFFECTS OF CHILDBIRTH TRAINING

Research studies generally support claims that women who participate in childbirth training classes tend to (1) experience reduced pain during labor and delivery, (2) have less need for medication, (3) have lowered rates of forceps delivery, and (4) demonstrate a more positive attitude toward childbirth than women who do not receive such training (Cogan, 1980). A major factor contributing to the mother's overall favorable evaluation of childbirth is a feeling of being able to maintain control over pain perception, emotions, and behavior. Women who participate in childbirth training believe that it boosts their confidence and sense of control (Mackey, 1995). However, the results of prepared childbirth classes vary widely with instructors and individual patients. Although such classes are effective in reducing pain, most participants eventually request medication during labor or delivery (Melzack, 1984). In the past, childbirth educators have been criticized for minimizing the reality and individual variability of the childbirth experience (Lumley & Astbury, 1980), but current childbirth education classes are much more flexible and individualized (Novak & Broom, 1995).

LEBOYER METHOD

The methods of prepared childbirth discussed up to this point are procedures designed to control pain during labor and delivery. The Leboyer method is different from the others in that it involves procedures for controlling the environment in the delivery room and for handling the infant during the first few minutes after birth, French obstetrician Frederick Leboyer (1975) believes that the process of birth is traumatic for the infant and potentially leads to emotional difficulties later in life. Leboyer's method of gentle birth, sometimes called "birth without violence," is designed to help minimize the shock of the birth experience and make the transition easier from the uterus to the outside world. The delivery room is warm and quiet. The lights are dim as the baby emerges from the uterus. The newborn baby is handled gently and placed on the mother's stomach, where it is lightly massaged until the umbilical cord stops pulsating. The baby is then moved to a tub of warm bath water designed to resemble the uterine environment.

One of the first follow-up studies (Rappoport, 1976) of babies born with the Leboyer procedures indicated that they walked sooner than the average age, were easily toilet trained, and developed self-feeding skills earlier than average. Many displayed ambidextrous use of their hands. However, additional studies (Maziade et al., 1986; Nelson et al., 1980) have found no differences between Leboyer babies and babies born in traditional environments on measures of crying, motor performance, cognitive functioning, or temperament. Consequently, further evidence is needed before the effectiveness of Leboyer's approach can be assessed more completely. The complete Leboyer method is not widely practiced in the United States because of the extra time required by the medical specialists.

FATHERS' PARTICIPATION

An important outcome of the prepared childbirth movement in the United States has been increased participation by fathers in the birth process. Several years ago hospitals were very reluctant to allow fathers in the delivery room because of concerns about increasing the risk of infection and about legal issues that might arise. Hospital personnel also feared that the husband would faint or otherwise interfere with the birth process. However, most hospitals now routinely allow the father to enter

the labor and delivery room. Many fathers choose to be present for the birth of their child. The use of local anesthesia makes it possible for the father to attend even a Caesarean birth.

The presence, effective coaching, and encouragement of the father during childbirth have been associated with the mother's positive evaluation of the birth experience. Mothers sometimes perceive the father's absence or inadequate coaching as contributing to a less satisfactory childbirth experience (Mackey, 1995). From the father's perspective, being present during childbirth tends to be a positive experience. In one study, 95 percent of the fathers who were in the delivery room were enthusiastic about the experience (Entwisle & Doering, 1981). The presence of the father during childbirth may facilitate attachment (Bowen & Miller, 1980) and later involvement in child-care (Parke, 1995).

The role of the father in childbirth varies from culture to culture. The term **couvade** is sometimes used to refer to the behavior that is typical of expectant or new fathers. Such practices are usually related to magical or religious beliefs that are meant to protect the mother and baby. For example, Cubeo fathers of the Northwest Amazon are expected to stay at home during the birth process and avoid strenuous activities that might magically be harmful to the mother and baby. A widely reported, but rarely practiced, form of the couvade is associated with cases where the expectant father goes to bed and complains of abdominal pain, exhaustion, and other symptoms identified with the birth experience (Broude, 1995). Although various couvade practices are not common in industrialized societies, they illustrate the power of myth and culture over childbirth practices.

ALTERNATIVE BIRTH CARE

Rooming-In

The traditional hospital routine for postpartum (afterbirth) care has been to keep the baby in the nursery while the mother stays in a separate room, except at feeding and visitation times. This arrangement allows the mother to rest and recover from the birth process before assuming full-time care of the baby.

Hospitals have responded to parental demands for family-centered childbirth and maternity care, as well as professional concerns about the effects of early separation of mother and infant. Hospitals now allow patients to choose a "rooming-in" arrangement in which the baby stays in a private room with the mother immediately after birth or as soon as she desires. Proponents of rooming-in believe that it facilitates parent-child attachment while allowing new parents to practice child care skills under the supervision of the hospital staff. In this arrangement, the father is allowed to visit and participate in the care of the baby. Also, more and more hospitals are allowing siblings to visit the mother and baby. Such practices help other members of the family feel included in the birth process and help in the transition of accepting the new arrival.

Home Delivery

Until 1940, more than half of all babies in the United States were born at home. By 1979, however, 99 percent of all births were carried out in hospital settings (National Center for Health Statistics, 1984). In recent years there has been a resurgence of interest in homebirths, especially among middle-class parents. Women who give birth at home are usually assisted by a lay midwife, a nurse midwife (see below), or a physician.

Advocates of childbirth at home believe that women should have the choice of giving birth in the privacy of a relaxed environment where obstetric medication is not encouraged and where the support of family members makes the birth experience a more satisfying personal event (O'Connor, 1993; Sagor et al., 1983). From their perspective, under normal circumstances, a home delivery is as safe as a hospital and possibly safer because of the absence of elective invasive surgical procedures. Opponents of planned homebirth believe that the hospital is the safest place to give birth. If an unexpected emergency should occur, medical equipment and expertise are immediately available.

Comparisons of homebirths with hospital births have found no significant difference in the death rates or other risk factors, such as prolonged labor or fetal oxygen deprivation (e.g., Durand, 1992; Mehl & Peterson 1981). The risk of a serious emergency occurring in a home delivery has been estimated as less than 1 in 1,000 cases for low-risk pregnancies (Sagor et al., 1983). Women considering having a home delivery must thus weigh the small risk in relation to the anticipated benefits. In any event, a planned homebirth without the support of a competent attendant increases the risk and is not advisable. Also, women planning a homebirth should have a normal healthy pregnancy and meet general medical criteria associated with an expected normal delivery. Women who have pregnancies complicated by diabetes, hypertension, Rh incompatibility, multiple pregnancy, breech or transverse presentation, or other high risk factors should not consider homebirth (Vedam & Kolodji, 1995).

Midwives

People who call themselves midwives can be classified either as lay midwives or as nurse midwives. A lay midwife is a person who has learned by experience and apprenticeship to help mothers give birth. There is a wide variation in knowledge and skill in lay midwives and typically they have little formal training or credentials. A midwife who has completed nurses' training plus a special program in obstetrics is certified as a nurse-midwife by the American College of Nurse-Midwives. Research studies have found that skilled midwives who are backed up by medical resources have records of successful births comparable to those of physicians (Gordon & Haire, 1981; Durand, 1992).

Birthing Centers

The increased interest in homebirths and family-centered labor and delivery has led some hospitals to develop birthing rooms and maternity centers. These facilities more closely resemble the home environment and are usually less expensive than the standard hospital labor and delivery rooms. The mother labors and delivers in the same room, with the father and possibly other family members present.

Some birthing centers are located in conventional hospital settings, whereas other units are structures built separately from the main hospital. In each case, the facilities attempt to combine the best of both the home and the hospital. The safety of maternity care in both types of birthing centers is comparable to that in a conventional hospital setting (Baruffi et al., 1984). A Swedish study found that women giving birth in a birthing center used less pain medication and had overall a slightly more positive birth experience than women giving birth in a standard obstetrics hospital unit (Waldenstrom & Nilsson, 1994).

SUMMARY

1. The progress of labor and delivery involve an interaction between four factors, referred to as the four Ps: the passenger, the pelvis (passage), the powers, and the placenta.

2. Scientists do not clearly understand what causes the onset of the birth process. The most promising explanation is that the labor is triggered by chemical substances called protaglandins. When the mother has a prolonged pregnancy or other problems, the physician may induce labor.

3. The process of childbirth begins with involuntary contractions of the uterus. As labor progresses, the contractions occur closer and closer together with increasing regularity, intensity, and duration throughout the birth process. Before labor actually begins, the mother may experience "false labor," sometimes referred to as Braxton Hicks contractions.

4. The cervix has to go through the process of effacement (thinning out) and dilation (opening) in order for the mother to have a vaginal delivery

5. Some of the signs that labor is about to begin are lightening of the fetus, a bloody show, diarrhea, increased Braxton Hicks contractions, a sudden spurt of energy, and spontaneous rupture of the amniotic sac.

6. The process of labor is affected by the position of the fetus and the body part that first enters the birth canal. Almost all babies are born in the head-first position. A few babies are born in one of four different breech positions: complete, frank, footling, or kneeling. If the baby is in a transverse (crosswise) position when labor begins, the baby has to be turned or surgically removed through a Caesarean delivery.

7. Normal labor and delivery consist of three basic stages—dilation, expulsion, placental—plus a recovery period. Dilation is the longest and most difficult stage of labor. It is divided into the latent, active, and transition phases. The stage of expulsion begins when the cervix is completely dilated and ends with the birth of the baby. After the baby is born, the umbilical cord is cut and the placenta is expelled during the third stage. The recovery stage, which lasts for approximately an hour after the placenta is expelled, is a very dangerous period for the mother because of the risk of excessive bleeding.

8. A variety of conditions can prevent or interfere with a vaginal childbirth. When complications occur, the baby may be removed through a surgical incision in the abdomen and uterus, called a Caesarean section (C-section). The high number of Caesarean births in the United States has generated a lot of concern among health-care officials. The increased risk to the mother and baby associated with this method of childbirth has resulted in the establishment of a national health objective to reduce the annual rate of Caesarean births.

9. Multiple births are more difficult and complicated than single deliveries. In most multiple births, the babies are born head first, but a variety of position combinations are possible.

10. Current trends in childbirth management include the decreased use of forceps in delivery. The vacuum extractor is used instead of forceps in some instances.

11. Around the world, women give birth in a variety of positions, including kneeling, squatting, standing, sitting, or on hands and knees. By contrast, mothers in the United States often labor and deliver while lying on their back. This practice is changing due to studies indicating that variations of upright posture, such as standing, sitting, squatting, or walking, tend to facilitate labor progress and reduce the need for pain medication. Newer

adjustable beds currently used for both labor and delivery allow the mother to select a position that is most comfortable.

12. Women vary widely in the amount of pain they experience during labor and delivery, but childbirth pain is universal. A variety of analgesics, amnesiacs, tranquilizers, and anesthetics are available for the treatment of labor pains. The use of regional anesthetics is popular because the mother can be awake during the birth process. Disadvantages associated with obstetric medications include the delay of labor contractions and adverse effects on the baby's behavior, at least temporarily.

13. Traditional approaches to prepared childbirth include the Read, Lamaze, and Bradley methods. These methods differ somewhat in theory and specific procedures, but they are similar in their goal of achieving a relatively pain-free childbirth without the use of medication, while involving the father as an integral part of the birth process. Current educators are using educational methods that allow for flexibility and individuality in preparation of fathers and mothers for the birth process.

14. Prepared childbirth is generally effective in reducing the pain of labor, decreasing the amount of medication needed, and increasing the father's participation in the birth process.

15. The Leboyer method of "gentle" birth is designed to minimize the trauma of the birth experience for the infant through a carefully prepared delivery room environment. The Leboyer method differs from other prepared childbirth procedures in that it deals with what happens after the baby is born rather than events which occur during the birth process.

16. The role of the father in childbirth varies from culture to culture. In the United States, the presence, effective coaching, and encouragement of the father during childbirth have been associated with the mother's positive evaluation of the birth experience. From the father's perspective, being present during childbirth tends to be a positive experience and may facilitate attachment as well as involvement in child care

17. Current alternatives to traditional hospital procedures used in childbirth and postpartum care include rooming-in, sibling visits, home delivery, the use of midwives, and the use of homelike birthing centers.

4

The Newborn

Be careful with that new baby—it leaks.
— American Greeting Cards

In comparison to other mammals, the human infant is one of the more helpless creatures at birth. We should not assume, however, that the newborn is totally unprepared for life outside the uterus. Years ago William James, a famous psychologist, described the newborn infant's reaction to the world as "one great blooming, buzzing confusion" (James, 1890, p. 488). We now know that James greatly underestimated the sensory capacities of the newborn baby.

In this chapter we explore the ability of babies to make adjustments to life after birth. We consider the newborn's physical features, sensory and perceptual capacities, and behavior states. Part of the chapter is devoted to preterm and low-birthweight babies. Procedures for assessing the health and well-being of newborn babies are described. Finally, we review some ways to facilitate the development of full-term, preterm, and low-birthweight infants.

The neonatal (newborn) period begins with the cutting of the umbilical cord and ends when the part that remains attached to the baby falls off to form the navel. Normally this takes about two weeks. However, not everyone agrees on when the newborn period ends, so infants as old as 4 to 6 weeks of age are often classified as newborns. In this text, the neonatal period is defined as the first two weeks of life after birth. You should keep in mind, however, that when the results of research studies on neonates are discussed, the subjects may be babies of various ages.

ADJUSTMENTS TO BIRTH

The transition from the uterus to the outside environment is one of the most traumatic periods in life. At birth the baby is cut loose from the placental life support system and virtually every system of the body must adjust to a new and hostile world. Within the first 12 to 24 hours after birth the newborn must make several major adjustments, including respiration, body temperature, elimination

of body waste, and nutritional intake. However, the stress and strain of labor and delivery trigger a surge of hormones (catecholamines) that help the baby make the transition to life outside the uterus (Lagercrantz & Slotkin, 1986). The extra dose of "stress" hormones apparently helps protect the infant from asphyxia during the birth process, enhances the newborn's ability to breathe, and increases the flow of blood to the vital organs.

Respiration

Most infants begin to breathe within 20 to 30 seconds after birth (Cockburn, 1984). The first breath is largely reflexive. It is probably initiated by stimulation in the brainstem triggered by skin contact with the cold air, along with decreased oxygen and higher levels of carbon dioxide (Vulliamy, 1982). The newborn's rate of respiration is irregular, ranging from 30 to 60 breaths per minute (Novak & Broom, 1995). The newborn may have difficulty breathing because of fluid in the lungs from the amniotic sac. Normally, much of the amniotic fluid is squeezed out of the lungs as the baby passes through the birth canal. In addition, the physician removes fluid and waste products from the mouth and throat by gentle suction immediately after birth. Babies who are born through Caesarean sections tend to have more difficulty breathing at first because excessive fluid remains in their lungs. In addition, infants who are born through emergency or planned Caesarean sections, do not have the advantage of the extra "stress" hormones produced during labor that promote normal breathing (Lagercrantz & Slotkin, 1986).

Temperature Regulation

The temperature of the fetus is approximately 1°F higher than that of the mother. Fetal heat is transferred to mother through the placenta and dissipated. At the time of birth, the infant's temperature drops immediately. The decrease in temperature may be one of several mechanisms that cause the newborn to begin breathing (Ensher & Clark, 1994). Normally, the body temperature goes back up within 2 to 4 hours if the temperature-regulating

This baby is only a few hours old. Notice the grasp reflex. She is in a state of regular sleep with the eyelids tightly closed. (See Sleep States.)

mechanism located in the hypothalamus of the brain is functioning properly (Lowrey, 1978). However, even at best, temperature control in the newborn is not well established. Adults shiver or sweat to get warmer or cooler, but these mechanisms are not very efficient in the newborn. In addition, the newborn has a larger skin surface area in proportion to body size than older children and adults. There is also less fat beneath the skin for insulation. A newborn baby thus loses heat about four times as fast as an adult (Bruck, 1961).

A newborn baby must rely largely on a special kind of adipose tissue called "brown fat" for the production of body heat. This tissue is used up rapidly in babies who are exposed to cold or prolonged illness. It is deficient in preterm babies (Cockburn, 1984). Obviously, newborns should not be exposed to temperatures that are too cold or too hot. A room temperature as warm as 65 to 68 degrees is recommended as a minimum for newborns who weigh as much as 5 pounds (Spock & Rothenberg, 1992).

Eating and Digestion

Within a few hours after birth, the baby needs to begin eating or to receive nourishment through other means. Fortunately, the extra "stress" hormones produced during labor and delivery accelerate the breakdown of stored body fat that can help nourish the baby temporarily (Lagercrantz & Slotkin, 1986). Many infants show signs of hunger and are ready to utilize their sucking, rooting, and swallowing reflexes as soon as they are born. However, eating and digestion are not very efficient, so babies tend to lose a few ounces of weight during the first 2 weeks of life. Spitting up is common among newborn infants because of air that is swallowed during feeding. Occasional vomiting is also not unusual during the neonatal period.

Elimination

The kidneys are functional even before the baby is born. Two out of three infants urinate within the first 24 hours after birth (Novak & Broom, 1995). The frequency of urination gradually increases during the first few days after birth to about once an hour. The volume of urine also increases but varies with fluid intake. The newborn's kidneys do not function at full efficiency, which means that the ability to withstand dehydration or process a large amount of salty substances is very limited (Vulliamy, 1982).

The first bowel movement usually takes place within 24 to 48 hours after birth. The material eliminated is called **meconium**. This is a greenish black, semisolid substance consisting of amniotic fluid, mucus, bile, and other body secretions. If the baby is in distress during prolonged labor, elimination may occur in the amniotic fluid before birth. When that happens, there is a danger that some of the particles of meconium can be inhaled into the baby's lungs, possibly leading to pneumonia. The number of daily bowel movements varies with individual infants. The frequency may vary from one in three days to as many as ten per day (Vulliamy, 1982). The frequency tends to decrease to one or two a day as the baby gets older (Spock & Rothenberg, 1992). The bowel movements of breast-fed and bottle-fed infants vary in color, odor, texture, and frequency.

Sleeping and Waking

The newborn infant emerges from a world of darkness and relative quiet into a world of light and noise. The womb provided the fetus with a relatively consistent sensory environment. Shortly before birth the fetus sleeps and wakes at regular intervals. At birth, however, the infant is bombarded with sensory stimuli that are constantly changing. This means the newborn must adjust and regulate its sleep cycles within a new environment. We will consider the newborn infant's sleeping and waking activity further in the section on states of arousal.

PHYSICAL APPEARANCE

As seen through the eyes of the typical parent, the newborn infant is simply beautiful. Many other people, however, have images of the newborn that are not quite as flattering. Shakespeare pictured the infant as "mewling and puking in the nurse's arms." G. Stanley Hall's (1891) classic description of the newborn as "an ugly creature with its red, shriveled, parboiled skin . . . squinting, cross-eyed, pot-bellied, and bowlegged" has been widely quoted.

The beauty of the neonate is thus likely to lie in the eyes of the beholder.

At birth, the baby may be covered with a cheese-like vernix that is especially noticeable in the folds and crevices of the skin. The baby may also be splattered with spots of blood, along with bruises, scratches, and skin discolorations from the birth process. The ears may be folded or creased, but they soon reach their normal shape. The head may be elongated, lopsided, or otherwise misshapen from the passage through the birth canal. Fortunately, the skull is soft and pliable, with separate pieces of cartilage designed to overlap during the birth process. Thus, the only problem from the normal molding of the head at birth is one of temporary appearance. The genitalia of both male and female newborns are typically swollen.

The color of the Caucasian newborn's skin ranges from pale to bright pink. It may have a bluish tint if there has been a decrease in oxygen. Some babies have large red patches of skin, called strawberry nevi, which become especially noticeable during crying episodes. These and other skin discolorations tend to disappear within a few days after birth. Infants of color tend to have lighter shades of skin at birth than they do at maturity. The skin reaches its natural hereditary coloring within a few days after it is exposed to light. Infants of African, Indian, Asian, or Mediterranean descent tend to have blue-black colorations on their buttocks or lower backs called mongolian or Asian spots. These spots usually fade in early childhood and are not associated with central nervous system disorders or other developmental problems (Novak & Broom, 1995).

The individuality of the infant is obvious at birth. Some babies are born with a head full of hair, whereas others have the appearance of being bald. In addition, some of the prenatal lanugo may remain on parts of the body for a few days after birth. Permanent hair develops within a few weeks after birth. The newborn's hair may eventually change color. The newborn's eyes may also change to a darker shade or a different color. True eye color is not usually established until 3 to 6 months of age (Novak & Broom, 1995).

SENSORY AND PERCEPTUAL ABILITIES

In typically developing infants, the five basic senses—sight, hearing, touch, taste, and smell—are functioning at birth. By the second trimester of prenatal development, the eyes, the ears, the nose, the tongue, and skin are approaching functional capacity (Bornstein & Lamb, 1992). The idea that infants are passive creatures with a mind that is comparable to a blank slate (or a computer disc) is no longer widely accepted. Infants are currently viewed as partially equipped at birth to participate actively in their experiences of the world. The notion that the neonate's sensory experiences amount to only "buzzing confusion" has also been replaced with the view of the infant as capable of organizing and processing discrete impressions. However, the quantity and quality of information newborns obtain through the senses and how it is organized and interpreted continue to be the subject of scientific debate and investigation. In this section we look at a variety of sensory capacities of newborn infants. In Chapter 9 we will consider the development of sensory capacities at later stages of the infancy period.

Visual Competency

The eyes are the least well developed of all the newborn's sensory organs. It is now well established that human infants see poorly at birth (Banks & Shannon, 1993). The newborns' eyes are shorter and flatter than those of an adult. The pupils are significantly smaller, the ciliary muscles that control the lens (focus) do not function well, and the retinae are relatively immature (Banks & Bennett, 1991). The visual centers in the brain are not fully developed at birth. These immaturities affect the ability of infants to see objects clearly (acuity) and to bring objects into focus at various distances (visual accommodation). Estimates of the visual acuity of newborns vary widely, but generally indicate that newborns see about one-thirtieth as well as adults with perfect vision (Bremner, 1988; Courage & Adams, 1990). This means that their visual images, even from close up, are somewhat

blurred. However, the limited vision of newborns is not the result of deficiencies in the range or depth of focus. Evidently, newborn babies can keep objects in focus as well or better than adults. This ability doesn't help much though because they "see equally unclearly across a wide range of distances" (Banks, 1980, p. 663).

Tracking and Scanning. Even though their visual clarity is limited, newborns can locate and follow a single moving object with their eyes (tracking) for about 90 degrees. However, their eye pursuit is slow and jerky. Tracking movements become smoother and more coordinated with age. Newborn infants also engage in visual scanning of stationary objects. They apparently scan the environment, even in the dark, to find something to look at. Haith (1979) believes that neonates operate according to the following "rules" in their attempts to locate and look at interesting things:

1. When awake and the light is not too bright, open eyes.
2. If it is dark, look for a light.
3. When an object is found, look for the edges on it.
4. When the edge, or contour, is found, look up and down or back and forth across it.

Their visual exploration of faces and other objects is apparently limited to the borders and a single feature. These looking patterns indicate that newborns do not perceive whole forms and simple relationships among the elements of an object. In addition, newborn infants appear to have the innate capacity to perceive that objects remain the same size even when they are viewed from different distances—that is, objects have size constancy (Siegler, 1993). Newborns tend to prefer angles to straight lines. When given a choice between horizontal and vertical contours, they prefer the vertical (Banks & Salapatek, 1983).

Facial Recognition. Over the years researchers have tried to determine whether newborns can distinguish one face from another and discriminate between faces and other similar stimuli. We now have reasonably good evidence that newborns are capable of recognizing human faces under certain conditions. When they view moving facial images, with the features highlighted, newborns demonstrate a preference for faces to other patterns (Morton & Johnson, 1991). Shortly after birth, infants also appear to discriminate their mother's face from that of a stranger (Field et al., 1984; Bushnell & Sai, 1987). However, newborns have difficulty discriminating faces if a surrounding border (e.g., a shower cap) is placed around the face (Atkinson, 1995). Although the evidence isn't conclusive, these studies provide support for the theory that newborns are endowed with an innate preference for the human face and the ability to recognize faces.

Imitation of Facial Gestures. If you stick your tongue out at an alert newborn infant, you are likely to find that the infant will stick its tongue out at you in return. Researchers have verified the ability of newborns to imitate tongue protrusion modeled by other people (Meltzoff & Moore, 1989; 1994). Researchers have also concluded that newborn infants can imitate a variety of other facial gestures including mouth opening, lip protrusion, and head movement (Meltzoff & Moore, 1977; 1983; 1989; 1992; 1994). Crosscultural studies conducted among newborn infants in rural Nepal, Israel, Switzerland, and France (Meltzoff, Kuhl, & Moore, 1991; Reissland, 1988) have reported this behavior to be universal. Newborns apparently are biased in favor of human facial gestures since they do not imitate tongue protrusion or mouth opening modeled by inanimate objects (Abravanel & DeYong, 1991; Legerstee, 1991).

Not all scientists agree, however, that newborns can imitate a wide variety of facial gestures. After critically reviewing the studies on neonatal imitation, Anisfeld (1996) has concluded that infants only imitate the tongue protrusion gesture. Therefore, additional evidence is needed to resolve this controversy. The resolution of this question is important because if newborns only have the ability to imitate tongue protrusion, it means this early form of imitation can be explained as a type of reflex response elicited by the behavior of a model. On the other hand, if infants can imitate a variety of facial gestures, their abilities may be more advanced

and complex. This would support the view that newborn infants have the ability to engage in cross-modal transfer of information from one sensory modality to another (Anisfeld, 1996). That is, newborns actively link facial expressions they see others exhibit with internal motor sensations they feel when they engage in the same behavior.

Color Vision. We know that newborn infants are capable of responding to variations in brightness of lights. Infants as young as 2 to 4 days old prefer to look at lights of medium brightness rather than at brighter or dimmer lights (Hershenson, 1964). Do newborn infants also have the ability to see color, or is their vision limited to a black-and-white view of the world? Some researchers have concluded that infants as young as 3 days old distinguish between the basic color categories of red, yellow, green, and blue (Adams & Maurer 1983, 1984; Adams, Maurer, & Davis, 1986). Newborn babies do not do well, however, in distinguishing between similar shades within color categories (Banks & Bennett, 1991). Other researchers, however, are not as confident that newborns see any color at all. In appearing to make color distinctions, infants may simply be responding to different degrees of brightness along the color spectrum, rather than color per se. Banks and Shannon (1993) have concluded that newborn infants do not consistently demonstrate the ability to discriminate between stimuli that differ in color shade only. There is general agreement that newborns do not see colors well, if at all, either because of immaturities of color receptors in the eyes (cones), immaturities of the brain, or overall visual inefficiency. Researchers using better techniques to control for brightness may discover more definitive answers to questions about color visual capacities of newborns in the near future (Teller & Lindsey, 1993).

In any case, the ability to perceive color and to make distinctions develops fairly rapidly during early infancy. Scientists generally agree that by 2 months of age, infants can perceive the difference between two of the primary colors. The ability to discriminate among different degrees of brightness increases rapidly. This is consistent with findings that by 2 months of age, infants are able to make discriminations among degrees of brightness almost as well as adults (Peeples & Teller, 1975). Many of the fundamental aspects of color vision are reasonably adult-like by 3 months of age (Banks & Salapatek, 1983).

Scientists have speculated about whether or not color perception is culturally related. That is, do infants from different cultures classify the same wavelengths as different colors? Generally, research studies indicate that people all over the world share similar color perceptions (Bornstein, 1981). These findings support the theory that biology plays a dominant role in color perception.

Hearing

Contrary to early theories that infants are born deaf, we now know that babies hear and respond to sounds even before birth. The development of the hearing apparatus is basically complete around the fifth or sixth month of fetal life (Bredberg, 1985). Researchers have noted movements (Fleischer, 1955) and heart rate changes (Murphy & Smyth, 1962) following auditory stimulation of 7-to 9-month-old fetuses. Newborns do not hear as well as adults. They can detect sounds within the range of 40 to 50 decibels. In comparison to the typically hearing adult who detects sounds around 10 decibels, the newborn has a moderate hearing impairment (Werner & Vandenbos, 1993). However, a wide range of individual differences in hearing abilities among newborns have been identified (Siegler, 1991).

Attending to Sounds. In spite of their limitations, newborn infants are amazingly sensitive to sounds. Several studies have shown that neonates are capable of sound localization (Aslin, Pisoni, & Jusczyk, 1983). Infants as young as 2 to 4 days turn their head toward the correct location of a sound (Muir & Field, 1979). They can hear low-pitched sounds better than high-pitched sounds (Werner & Vandenbos, 1993).

Sound Discrimination. Newborn infants are able to distinguish between sounds of different pitch, loudness, and duration (Leventhal & Lipsitt,

1964). They are capable of distinguishing the difference between tones that are about one note apart on a musical scale (Weir, 1970). They also appear to be capable of distinguishing between words. In one study, newborns (1 to 2 days old) were able to recognize a word after a 24-hour delay (Swain, Zelazo, & Clifton, 1993). Neonates prefer music to noise, and vocal music to instrumental music (Butterfield & Sipperstein, 1974). Moderately low-pitched sounds and continuous or rhythmic sounds have a soothing effect on newborns. Very low-frequency and high-pitched sounds produce an opposite effect (Appleton, Clifton, & Goldberg, 1975). In addition, newborns apparently are more attentive to sounds that are of moderate duration (5 to 15 seconds) than shorter or intermittent sounds (Eisenberg, 1976).

Neonates demonstrate a preference for sounds within the range of the human voice (Eisenberg, 1976). They have been observed moving their arms and legs in rhythm to voices (Condon & Sander, 1974; Bernhardt, 1987) and tend to prefer music that is accompanied by vocal sounds (Butterfield & Siperstein, 1974). Given a choice, newborns prefer their mother's voice to other female voices (DeCasper & Fifer, 1980). They also would rather listen to the voice of a female than the voice of a male. However, they do not prefer their father's voice to those of other males, even though they can detect the differences in the voices (DeCasper & Prescott, 1984).

The preference for female voices in general and the mother's voice in particular may originate with their prenatal auditory experiences. DeCasper and Spence (1986) found that newborn infants whose mothers had read "The Cat and The Hat" to them during the prenatal period preferred that story to "The King, the Mice and the Cheese," after they were born. If infants are not born with this adult-like ability to make sound distinctions, they acquire it very quickly after birth.

Taste

Taste buds begin developing on the tongue of the human fetus at 7 to 8 weeks of gestational age with mature cells appearing at approximately 14 weeks

(Bradley, 1972). Thus, physiologically, infants enter the world prepared to experience various taste sensations. A newborn infant will smile with satisfaction when a drop of sugar water is placed on its tongue and will frown with distaste in response to a drop of lemon juice, or bitter quinine (Steiner, 1977). Thus, newborns discriminate between three basic tastes of sweet, sour, and bitter to which adults respond. Studies about newborn infants' responses to salty substances are less conclusive.

The newborn's taste for sweet is by far the dominant taste. Researchers have consistently reported that newborn infants all over the world prefer sweet substances to plain water or other substances, including milk. Their hearts beat faster (Lipsitt, 1977), and they suck faster, longer, and stronger (Crook, 1977) when they are given sweet substances as opposed to others. Apparently the sweeter the solution is, the better they like it (Desor, Maller, & Greene, 1977). There are indications that babies respond positively to sweet tasting substances even before birth (Mennella & Beauchamp, 1993). Premature infants prefer sweetened liquids to unsweetened substances (Tatzer et al., 1985). They produce more frequent and stronger sucking responses when they are given a pacifier filled with a sucrose-sweetened substance than when they are given a plain latex pacifier (Mennella & Beauchamp, 1993). The preference for sweet substances appears so early and so strong that many scientists believe the "sweet tooth" infants have at birth is an innate characteristic.

Researchers have confirmed (what every mother knows) that the taste of sucrose, given in combination with a pacifier (oral-tactile) or separately, has a calming effect on crying newborns (Blass & Ciaramitaro, 1994). It is believed that the taste sensation of sucrose or milk activates the production of opioids (substances that protect against pain).

Newborns find sour flavors distasteful. They frown and grimace when given citric acid. They even reduce their intake of a sweetened liquid when a sour substance is added (Desor, Maller, & Andrews, 1975). Newborn infants display highly negative facial reactions when given a strong bitter concentration of quinine or urea. However, they do not reject moderate concentrations of urea. In gen-

eral newborns react indifferently to salty substances. Studies measuring the facial expressions and intake amounts indicate that newborns may not detect salt (Mennella & Beauchamp, 1993). Salt was accidentally substituted for sugar in the formula of newborns fed in a hospital nursery. All of the infants drank the formula until they became quite ill (Finberg, Kiley, & Luttrell, 1963). However, some studies have shown that newborns reduce their rate of sucking in response to salty substances (Mennella & Beauchamp, 1993). In view of contradictory research findings, additional studies are needed to clarify the newborn's response to the taste of salt as well as bitter substances. The development of taste sensations and preferences will be discussed further in Chapter 7.

Smell

The olfactory system that controls the sense of smell is well developed before the baby is born (Bossey, 1980). Although the amniotic fluid contains odors, it is not known whether the sense of smell is functional before birth. There is relatively little research on the development of the sense of smell during infancy, because odor preferences are difficult to assess. Some researchers (e.g., Guillory, Self, & Paden, 1980) argue that the ability to discriminate odors does not develop until 1 month of age. However, the bulk of evidence indicates that infants have the ability to smell, at least some odors, as soon as they are born.

Within hours after birth human infants respond to a variety of odors. For example, a newborn smiles pleasurably when a piece of cotton with a banana odor is waved under its nose, but frowns in protest at the smell of rotten eggs. Like adults, newborns prefer the smell of vanilla to the odor of fish (Steiner, 1977). Newborns are especially sensitive to odors associated with their mothers and are apparently able to recognize their mothers within hours after birth through the sense of smell alone. Breast-fed newborns are able to detect the difference between the breast pad of their mothers and those of a lactating stranger. They also exhibit less movement and more sucking when they are exposed to their mothers. In addition, newborns can discriminate between underarm and neck odors from their mothers and those of a stranger (Mennella & Beauchamp, 1993). The sense of smell may play a role in the formation of attachments in humans, just as it does in animals (Lamb & Campos, 1982).

The sense of smell improves rapidly during the first few days of life. Infants are able to detect weaker odors as they get older. Lipsitt, Engen, and Kaye (1963) discovered that the amount of asafetida odor needed to elicit a response in newborns decreases with age. Breast-fed babies soon learn to detect the difference between the odor of milk from the mother's breast and milk from the breast of a stranger. MacFarlane (1975) found that such distinctions could be made by 6-day-old infants but not by 2-day-old infants. However, Russell (1976) concluded that this ability did not occur until 6 weeks of age.

Touch

Touch has been referred to as the "mother of the senses" (Montagu, 1971). Between 7½ and 14 weeks of gestational age, almost the entire surface of the embryo becomes sensitive to tactile stimulation (Hooker, 1952). It is the first sensory system to develop (Gottfried, 1984). Touch is the most complex of the senses and the most difficult to study as a separate modality. The word touch, and its synonyms contact and feel, usually refer to sensations that occur when receptors in the skin are stimulated. The sense of touch also encompasses perceptions of pain, temperature, pressure, weight, texture, firmness, and many other feelings. Touch is closely linked with sensations of the muscles and joints and with sensations of movement (Rose, 1984).

Touch plays a very important role in infant development. One of the most effective ways to soothe crying babies is to pick them up and hold them close to the body or to swaddle them tightly in a blanket. There are indications that touch, or related sensations, influences parent-infant attachment, cognitive development, sociability, ability to withstand stress, and immunological development in infants (Gottfried, 1984). Tiffany Field (1995) believes that touch or massage therapies can be used to enhance several behavioral processes and physiological functions. Massage therapy with infants involves movement of the hands over the body, stroking with pressure, and pressure without movement. She reports that infant massage has been effective in enhancing growth and development, reduction of pain, and increased attentiveness. However, touching an infant can have a positive or negative effect. The type of touching and when it occurs are important factors. A sick infant responds differently to vigorous stroking than does a well infant. The precise effects of touch are not entirely clear because of the difficulty encountered in separating touch from other sensations (Gottfried, 1984).

Perception of Pain. For many years, doctors have performed surgery on newborn infants with little or no anesthesia. This practice was based on the rationale that anesthesia is risky, and the immaturity of the infant's brain blocks out significant perceptions of pain. We now know that even premature infants experience pain. The neurological structures and pathways for the transmission and perception of painful stimuli are developed by 29 weeks of gestation (Walco, Cassidy, & Schechter, 1994).

Newborn infants respond to pain in ways that are similar to those of adults. Harrigan-Hamamoto (1983) observed crying, changes in facial expressions, fist clenching, changes in color, blood pressure, and other vital signs in newborns during a procedure used to draw a sample of blood. Lipsitt and Levy (1959) found that newborn infants are sensitive to the pain of a mild electric shock at birth. Their responsiveness gradually increased over the first four days of life. Premature infants who have surgical procedures performed with little anesthesia, display more stress responses, have higher rates of complications and mortality than infants given deeper anesthesia (Walco et al., 1994). Infants as young as 25 weeks gestational age are sensitive to heel-sticks procedures to obtain blood samples (Craig et al., 1993).

The American Academy of Pediatrics (1987) recommends using anesthesia whenever possible in operating on newborn infants. Physicians must decide whether the risk of side effects from pain medication outweighs the benefit to the infant. However, there is little reason to believe that infants are at greater risk than adults for respiratory problems from anesthesia that is carefully regulated (Walco et al., 1994).

Intersensory Perception

Most of our experiences involve simultaneous impressions from more than one sensory modality. Sights occur in combination with sounds; tastes and odors are often experienced as a blend of sensations. Newborn infants are faced with the task of integrating information they receive from different sensory systems into a unified, meaningful experience. The ability to combine information from different senses is referred to as **intersensory perception** (also referred to as **intermodal perception**). For example, when infants recognize that an object that is seen can also be touched, they are engaging intermodal or intersensory perception. As part of their perceptual experiences, infants also need to use information from one sensory system to "inform" other sensory systems. For example, infants identify an object with one of the senses (e.g., vision) through the use of information obtained only by a different sensory mechanism (e.g., touch). This process is referred to as **cross-modal transfer.**

The question of when and how intersensory perception develops has been a subject of intense debate. **Integration** theorists (Piaget, 1929; 1952) believe that the senses are independent and separated at birth. Therefore, intersensory coordination gradually emerges as the infant grows and develops. On the other hand, **differentiation** theorists (Gibson, E.,1969), believe the senses are unified at birth so that infants are, to some extent, capable of intersensory perception from the very beginning.

Research evidence tends to support the belief that infants are capable of intersensory integration at birth, at least to a limited extent. When newborns hear a sound, they attempt to find the source of the sound, apparently for visual inspection, thereby integrating sounds and sights into a single experience (Mendelson & Haith, 1976). They are also more interested in visually tracking moving objects that make a sound than objects that are silent (Rose & Ruff, 1987). In addition, newborns appear to be capable of coordinating the senses of vision and touch. Experiments show that they reach out to touch objects that move back and forth in their field of vision (Von Hofsten, 1982). Intersensory perception will be discussed further in Chapter 8.

STATES OF AROUSAL

The responses of a newborn to people and various stimuli are affected by its level of alertness, attentiveness, and activity. These conditions reflect the baby's needs and availability for contact with the outside world and are referred to as infant states. Wolff (1966) identified six states that newborn infants typically exhibit within a 24-hour period.

1. *Regular sleep.* The baby lies very still with the eyelids firmly closed. Breathing is smooth and even. Facial muscles are relaxed and the skin is pink.
2. *Irregular sleep.* The baby may jerk and startle. Facial expressions change frequently and include smiling, frowning, and pouting. The eyelids remain closed but sometimes move. Breathing is irregular and the skin may become flushed during activity.
3. *Drowsiness.* This is a transition period from waking to sleeping and from sleeping to waking. The eyelids open and close intermittently and are unfocused. Breathing is regular but rapid.
4. *Alert inactivity.* The baby is awake, with bright, shiny eyes. The face is relaxed; breathing is regular but faster than it is during sleep. The baby is happy, alert, and curious. This is the ideal state for administering newborn assessments.
5. *Waking activity.* There are frequent bursts of vigorous movements. The skin becomes flushed and breathing is very irregular. The baby may moan, grunt, or whimper.
6. *Crying.* The baby cries consistently and engages in vigorous movements. The face is twisted into a cry grimace and becomes flushed.

Newborns typically spend most of their time (67 percent) in one of the states of sleep or drowsiness (8 percent). They are alert and quiet about 10

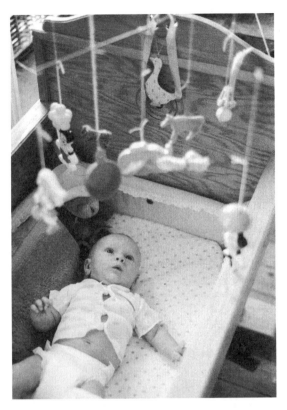

This infant is in a state of waking activity, gazing intently at the crib mobile.

percent of the time, and awake and fussy approximately 11 percent of each day (Berg, Adkinson, & Strock, 1973). Although it probably seems longer to parents, babies spend about 5 percent of their time crying. It is important, however, to keep in mind that babies vary widely in the amount of time spent in each state. While one infant may sleep and wake at regular intervals, another may be very irregular. Infant states can be altered by caregiving activities and environmental conditions. For example, infants are roused from sleep by sudden movement or temperature changes and are quieted by soothing voice tones, cuddling, and rocking.

As they get older, infants change their patterns of sleep-waking activities. When the baby is approximately 1 month of age, the amount of time it sleeps decreases markedly (Emde, Gaensbauer, & Harmon, 1976). Some infants begin sleeping through the night about this time, but infants typi-

cally do not establish such a pattern until they are about 4 months old (Parmelee, Wenner, & Schulz, 1964). Another dramatic reduction in the amount of sleep an infant needs may also be observed between 5 and 7 months of age (Emde et al., 1976). These changes may correspond with the physiological maturation of the brain.

INFANT SLEEPING ARRANGEMENTS

In the United States, most infants from middle-class families sleep in their own bed, either in their own or a sibling's bedroom. Although many parents place their newborn infant in a bassinet or crib in the parents' bedroom, this is a usually a temporary arrangement. In contrast to the United States, the cultural norm in most societies throughout the world is for infants to sleep in the same bed with the mother for the first few years of life. In some instances the infant sleeps with the father, or with both mother and father (Broude, 1995). This practice is referred to as **cosleeping** or **bed sharing.** Cultures that practice cosleeping include rural and urban, as well as technological and less technologically advanced communities (Morelli et al., 1992). Even in the United States cosleeping is widely practiced in some cultural groups. For example, infants from the eastern Kentucky Appalachian mountains sleep with their parents during the first 2 years of life (Abbott, 1992). African-American infants are more likely than Caucasian-American infants to sleep with their parents (Lozoff, Wolff, & Davis, 1984).

Through the years American pediatricians and other child rearing experts have advised parents to make separate sleeping arrangements for infants. For example, the latest edition of *Dr. Spock's Baby and Child Care* (Spock & Rothenberg, 1992) warns parents against sleeping in the same bed with their infants. Some of the concerns about cosleeping are that it may interfere with the child's independence, may become a habit that will be difficult to break, interfere with the parents' privacy, may be over-stimulating as infants get older, and may cause sleep problems (Lozoff et al., 1984).

Morelli and colleagues (1992) interviewed mothers from urban middle-class families in the United States who did not sleep with their infants. They also interviewed a group of mothers from a rural Guatemalan Mayan community whose children slept in their mothers' bed until toddlerhood. The reasons given by the American mothers for placing infants in a separate bed were based primarily on the belief that babies need to be trained to be independent, and sleeping apart facilitates that process. Other concerns of these mothers related to safety issues (smothering), establishing a difficult-to-break habit, loss of privacy and sexual intimacy, and just being "uncomfortable with the idea."

Mayan mothers regarded their sleeping arrangement as "the only reasonable way for a baby and parents to sleep" (Morelli et al., 1992, p. 608). In contrast to U.S. mothers, Mayan mothers emphasized the need to establish interdependence between parent and child. They believed that cosleeping fosters security and closeness, as well as facilitating feeding and other caregiving activities. The available space for sleeping appears to play only a minor role in sleeping arrangements.

There is little scientific evidence on the effects of cosleeping versus independent sleeping arrangements. Currently researchers are debating about whether cosleeping prevents or contributes to Sudden Infant Death syndrome (see Chapter 6). Theoretically, infant sleeping arrangements have implications for the psychological development of infants. However, isolating the effects of where the infant sleeps from the effects of other cultural practices is a difficult task. In any case, professional child-care providers who work with infants and families need to be aware of the infant's sleeping arrangement. Infants who are used to cosleeping may have difficulty in sleeping alone in a child-care facility.

BIRTHWEIGHT AND GESTATIONAL AGE

Two of the most important factors affecting the newborn's ability to survive in the outside world are birthweight and gestational age. Birthweight is easily and routinely measured, but gestational age is more difficult to ascertain. An estimate of gestational age can be made from the first day of the last menstrual period. However, this information is frequently unreliable because of reporting inaccuracies and irregular menstrual cycles. An ultrasound scan prior to 18 weeks of pregnancy can provide a fairly good estimate of gestational age. Chemical analysis of substances found in the amniotic fluid can also be used for estimating gestational age. The Dubowitz Scale (Dubowitz, Dubowitz, & Goldberg, 1970), or a simplified version (Ballard, Novak, & Driver, 1979) is frequently used to assess gestational age after the baby is born. In this test, the baby's physical flexibility, muscle tone, and physical appearance are observed to obtain a maturity rating.

Newborn infants are usually classified according to gestational age, weight, and weight for age. The following classifications are used to designate infants by their age of gestation or birthweight:

Preterm (premature)	Infants born less than 37 weeks of gestation.
Full-term	Infants born between 37 and 42 weeks of gestation.
Postterm (postmature)	Infants born after 42 weeks of gestation.
Low birthweight	Infants weighing less than 5½ lbs. (2500 grams) at birth.
Very low birthweight (VLB)	Infants weighing less than 3½ lbs. (1500 grams) at birth.
Extremely low birthweight (ELB)	Infants weighing less that 2 lbs. oz.(1000 grams) at birth.
Appropriate for gestational age (AGA)	An infant whose birth weight is between the 10th and 90th percentiles on a standard growth chart.
Small for gestational age (SGA)	An infant whose birth weight is below the 10th percentile on a standard growth chart
Large for gestational age (LGA)	An infant whose birth weight is above the 90th percentile on a standard growth chart.

Scientists (e.g., Lubchenco et al., 1963) have developed special growth charts to classify newborns on the basis of birthweight by age of gestation.

Neonatal Intensive Care. Doctors delivered Quentin 4 months premature to save his mother's life. He surprised them by exhibiting a healthy heartbeat, a pinkish color, open eyes, and a strong cry. He weighed only 14 ounces and was small enough to fit into the palm of your hand (Knight-Ridder News Service, 1991). Medical science keeps pushing back the **boundary of viability**, or how early infants can be born and still survive. Neonatal intensive care units with sophisticated equipment and health care personnel who specialize in neonatology are now available in most larger, regional hospitals. With aggressive perinatal intervention infants born as early as 23 weeks' gestation and weighing as little as one pound (454 grams) are now surviving (Wyly, 1995).

Modern medical techniques can save approximately 90 percent of newborns weighing between 2 and 3½ pounds, 66 percent of those who weigh between 1½ to 2 pounds, and approximately 33 percent of the preterm infants who weigh 1 to 1-½ pounds (Batshaw & Perret, 1992). However, the youngest survivors face extraordinary problems, some of which are caused by lifesaving medical procedures. In general, the chances of survival decline as birthweight and gestation age decrease.

PRETERM AND LOW-BIRTHWEIGHT INFANTS

Premature infants comprise approximately 7 to 9 percent of live-born infants in the U.S. Almost 4 percent of preterm babies are also LBW (Wyly, 1995). In this section we consider preterm and low-birthweight infants together because they share many of the same characteristics, risk factors, and problems. Low-birthweight infants who are products of full-term pregnancies are discussed in a separate section on SGA infants.

Physical Characteristics

Preterm and low-birthweight babies are not just smaller versions of a full-term baby, but continue to be a fetus developmentally in some respects. The youngest of these infants are covered with the downy hair (lanugo) that normally is lost before birth. The skin is paper thin and transparent. Since

A preterm infant in a neonatal intensive care isolette.

little fat has accumulated beneath the skin, the baby looks scrawny and has the wrinkled appearance of a wizened, elderly person. The ears are wrinkled and lie flat against the head, since the cartilage is not well formed. The nipples on the breast may be barely visible. The genitals are not fully developed and may be swollen in appearance. The relatively large head and abdomen are particularly striking.

In contrast to those of full-term infants, the movements of preterm infants are wild and bizarre. When lying on the stomach, the knees are stretched out to the side of the body rather than drawn underneath the abdomen. These infants do not attempt to change position very often. Unlike a full-term infant their limbs are very limp and floppy and are not likely to resist forced movement. The youngest preterm infants display few reflexes since some of the reflexes do not develop until 30 to 32 weeks of gestation (Batshaw & Perret, 1992).

Preterm Infant States

The organization of states in preterm infants depends upon the infant's level of maturity. In very young premature infants (23-27 weeks), states are diffused and not well organized. These infants display jerky movements and irregularity of breathing and heartbeats. They sleep most of the time, but their sleep is restless (active) with twitching movements. The cries of these very young preterm infants are comparatively weak, short, and infrequent. They have difficulty swallowing and sucking. Between 30 and 37 weeks of gestational age, preterm infants begin to display quiet sleep with regular respiration and less movement. However, other states are not clearly distinguishable until approximately 37 weeks (Wyly, 1995).

Problems and Complications

A number of problems make survival difficult for infants who are born too early and too small. Some of the most serious and commonly observed problems include respiratory disorders, temperature regulation, heart problems, bleeding in the brain, eye problems, blood disorders, nutrition, and infections.

Respiratory Distress Syndrome. The most frequent cause of death among preterm infants is **respiratory distress syndrome (RDS)**, sometimes referred to as hyaline membrane disease (HMD). About 8000 to 10,000 infants in the United States die each year of RDS. The death rate increases as birthweight and gestational age decrease (Henig & Fletcher, 1983). RDS occurs more frequently in males than in females, in Caucasian than in infants of color (Gleason & Durand, 1993). The problem is caused mainly by incomplete lung development and the lack of a chemical called surfactant. The underdeveloped lungs are leaky and fragile, making them susceptible to damage from ventilators. Without surfactant, the air sacs in the lungs tend to collapse between breaths. This makes breathing more difficult and inhibits the efficient exchange of oxygen and carbon dioxide. Infants do not usually have adequate levels of surfactant until about the thirty-fourth or thirty-fifth week of gestation (Ensher & Clark, 1994).

A premature infant is placed in an incubator, where the oxygen supply is carefully controlled. If the baby develops RDS, an oxygen hood may be placed over the baby's head. In extreme cases, a mechanical respirator or ventilator does the breath-

ing for the baby. Improved treatment methods have reduced the number of deaths from RDS dramatically. Ten years ago, almost three out of every four infants with RDS died. Today the large majority of infants recover from RDS within ten days to two weeks.

In some cases, steroids are injected into a mother who is about to have a preterm delivery to stimulate the baby's lungs to make surfactant. Researchers have developed a synthetic surfactant and a modified form of surfactant from calves' liver that can be given at birth to infants who have RDS, or who are at risk for developing RDS. Results so far indicate that surfactant therapy is effective in reducing infant mortality rates due to RDS (Gleason & Durand, 1993), but is not always successful. Partial liquid ventilation is a technique that is being used on an experimental basis to treat infants with severe RDS (Leach et al., 1996). The baby's immature lungs are filled with doses of an oxygen-rich liquid (perflubron) through a ventilator. The baby obtains oxygen needed for survival through the liquid. The effectiveness of this treatment has not been established

Bronchopulmonary Dysplasia. In some cases, when preterm infants who have been affected by RDS are taken off the respirator, they develop a chronic lung disease called **bronchopulmonary dysplasia (BPD)**. The walls of the lungs thicken and the mucous lining of the lungs is reduced along with the airway diameter. Therefore, the infant has to work harder to breathe. BPD can also be caused by infections, inhaling meconium into the lungs, or asphyxia. Months of oxygen therapy and treatment with various medications to keep the lungs open may be required (Batshaw & Perret, 1992).

Temperature Regulation. One problem faced by preterm and low-birthweight infants is maintaining a stable, normal body temperature. The layer of fat needed for insulation has not yet developed, and the skin surface area from which heat can be lost is relatively large. Preterm infants cannot sweat to keep cool because their sweat glands are not completely developed. In addition, the temperature-control mechanism in the brain is not sufficiently mature to regulate the body's responses to environmental temperature changes. At birth, these babies are placed in an incubator, where the temperature can be carefully maintained. For very sick newborns who require access to therapeutic devices a radiant heater is sometimes used (Gleason & Durand, 1993).

Heart Problems. Before birth the infant's heart circulates the blood through the placenta, where it receives a supply of oxygen. Most of the blood bypasses the baby's own lungs. In full-term infants, a blood vessel (ductus arteriosus) closes automatically soon after birth so that the full blood supply is channeled into the lungs. In approximately one-third of preterm infants, the duct does not close (Batshaw & Perret, 1992). If this happens, the infant will have an insufficient oxygen supply. The condition can be life threatening, and emergency surgery may be necessary. However, in recent years a new drug has been developed that frequently is successful in stimulating the duct to close on its own (Sammons & Lewis, 1985).

Bleeding in the Brain. In preterm infants, the small blood vessels in the brain are more immature and have fewer supporting cells in the surrounding tissue. Therefore, sudden changes in blood pressure or blood oxygen levels may cause blood vessels to rupture and bleed inside the skull (Sammons & Lewis, 1985). Less serious bleeding may also result from trauma to the head during the birth process. Sometimes there are no symptoms when bleeding occurs, but with severe bleeding the blood count may drop, the head may swell, and seizures may develop. Bleeding in or around the brain tissue can be confirmed through cranial ultrasound, computerized axial tomography (CAT) scans, and magnetic resonance imaging (MRI). The problem is most likely to occur in the youngest and smallest infants. Intracranial bleeding takes place in approximately 30 percent of infants who weigh less that 3½ lbs (Ensher & Clark, 1994). In some cases, the bleeding is so slight that it has little or no impact on the functions of the brain. More massive or more frequent bleeding may result in long-term motor and mental difficulties, or even death.

Retinopathy of Prematurity. A common problem found among very small and immature newborns is **retinopathy of prematurity (ROP)**. This disorder is also sometimes referred to as retrolental fibroplasia (RLF). The problem occurs when the normal progression of newly formed vessels in the retina is interrupted. If this condition continues, it causes scarring or detachment of the retina, which may lead to visual impairment or blindness (Graeber & Schwartz, 1993).

ROP has been attributed to exposure to excessive oxygen in the hospital nursery. In the mid-1950s researchers discovered that premature infants exposed to higher levels of oxygen were more likely to develop ROP than similar infants exposed to lower levels of oxygen. Since that time supplemental levels of oxygen have been carefully controlled leading to a dramatic decline in the incidence of ROP. However, in recent years, as more and more extremely ELBW and premature infants have survived, the incidence of ROP has increased (Gibson, Sheps, Schechter, & McCormick, 1990). Contrary to earlier thinking, scientists now believe excessive oxygen may not be the only cause of ROP. Even with careful control of oxygen exposure, many of the smallest and youngest infants develop ROP (Teplin, 1995). Few infants who are born later than 28 weeks of gestational age, or weighing 3½ pounds, develop this condition. Infants of multiple births are more likely to develop ROP than singletons. Fortunately, new techniques in laser and other surgeries offer promise for treatment of ROP (Ensher & Clark, 1994).

Excess Bilirubin. Preterm and low-birthweight infants frequently have a yellow-orange skin color similar to a fading tan. This condition, referred to as jaundice, is caused by an excess accumulation of bilirubin in the bloodstream and body tissues. Bilirubin is a pigment formed when red blood cells are destroyed. Preterm infants are especially susceptible to jaundice because the liver is likely to be too immature to remove the bilirubin from the blood. Normally, this problem can be corrected with phototherapy by placing the baby under a special light. White light is most commonly used in phototherapy, but blue or green lights are also used

(Ensher & Clark, 1994). In some cases a blood-exchange transfusion may be required. This can be done before birth if needed. Treatment of this problem is a high medical priority because extremely high bilirubin levels can eventually lead to brain damage.

Nutrition. Nutritional needs of preterm infants are different from those of full-term infants. The precise quantities of nutrients needed by preterm infants are still being defined (Pipes & Trahms, 1993). In addition, meeting the nutritional needs of preterm and LBW infants is a special problem because of the immaturity of sucking and swallowing abilities, as well as the digestive system. The stomach is small and the passage of its contents is very slow. The infant's capacity to metabolize fat and protein is inefficient. In addition, preterm infants are born with low nutritional stores plus the need to grow faster in order to achieve optimal "catch-up" growth (Anderson, 1993). Hypoglycemia (low blood sugar) is also a common problem in very-low-birthweight infants.

Preterm infants who are born after 32 to 34 weeks' gestation are usually able to coordinate sucking and swallowing and may feed themselves through a nipple. Infants who are born earlier or who are critically ill are usually fed through a tube inserted through the nose or mouth into the stomach and/or may be given intravenous solutions containing glucose, fat, and amino acids, and other nutrients (Committee on Nutrition, 1993). The intake of fluids and other substances has to be carefully controlled because the kidneys of the premature infant have a limited capacity to eliminate waste products. In spite of these difficulties, however, considerable progress has been made in providing nutritional care and interventions that promote the survival and growth of preterm and LBW infants. One current technique is the use of breast milk fortified with supplementary nutrients as the main diet for tube-fed preterm infants (Schanler & Hurst, 1994).

Infections and Other Problems. Preterm infants are very susceptible to infections from bacteria and viruses. Immunity to diseases, which the infant receives from the mother, is not present until 28 weeks of gestational age, and the level of immunity is rather limited at first (Vulliamy, 1982). Some of the problems, such as blood poisoning, probably result from the invasive procedures used in inserting tubes, taking blood samples, and other routines used in intensive-care nurseries. **Necrotizing enterocolitis**, a life-threatening disease that affects the bowel wall, is a special hazard of prematurity. This disorder is caused by an inadequate blood flow to the intestines or from infectious bacteria (Novak & Broom, 1995). Other problems experienced by preterm infants include apnea (a prolonged pause in breathing) and inefficient kidney function.

Risk Factors

In most cases it is not possible to determine exactly why a mother has given birth to a preterm or low-birthweight baby. Many diverse factors may increase a pregnant woman's chances of giving birth to such an infant, including the mother's age (less than 17 or more than 34 years), poor maternal nutritional status, inadequate prenatal care, low socioeconomic status, alcohol or drug abuse, smoking, infections, and diseases (Committee to Study the Prevention of Low Birthweight, 1985). Other possible risk factors include multiple pregnancy, high blood pressure during pregnancy, premature opening of the cervix, hormonal deficiency, fetal malformations, premature rupture of the amniotic sac, and unusual physical or psychological stress. Researchers have recently found that a common vaginal infection (bacterial vaginosis) may be responsible for about 6 percent of all preterm births of low birthweight infants (Hillier et al., 1995). Scientists are also studying the possibility that maternal gum disease is a major contributing factor (The Associated Press, 1997).

Many of these risk conditions for having a preterm or LBW infant are interrelated. For example, low socioeconomic status is associated with poor nutrition, stress, lack of prenatal care, and other adverse conditions. Premature deliveries are higher among African-American mothers due to a number of poverty-related reasons (Hogue & Hargraves, 1995). Not all of the factors carry the same weight. Even if one or more factors are present, the mother is still likely to give birth to a full-term AGA infant (Redshaw, Rivers, & Rosenblatt, 1985).

Prevention

Research studies have consistently shown that prenatal care can be effective, especially among women in high-risk categories, in preventing low birthweight and prematurity (Committee to Study the Prevention of Low Birthweight, 1985). Pregnant women are less likely to smoke or to use alcohol, drugs, and other harmful substances when they are aware of the adverse effects on the baby. They also are more likely to maintain better nutrition and health when they receive appropriate prenatal care. The bacterial vaginosis infection can be treated with antibiotics, thereby reducing their risk of premature delivery (Hauth et al., 1995).

The early detection of preterm labor symptoms is the most important step in preventing preterm birth. Low back pain, cramps, mild contractions, increased vaginal discharge, pelvic heaviness, and diarrhea are some signs of preterm labor (Rust & Morrison, 1993). The mother can be hospitalized and treated with labor-stopping drugs if the beginning of premature labor is detected early enough. A variety of medications are effective in postponing a preterm delivery, but there is some risk of undesirable effects on the infant. Consequently, the use of such drugs is a dilemma for patients and their physicians who must weigh the benefits versus the risks involved. Extended bed rest for mothers who are considered to be at-risk for preterm delivery is one commonly used treatment approach. However, unless the mother is actually experiencing preterm labor, bed rest has not proven to be very beneficial (Rust & Morrison, 1993). While progress is being made in preventing preterm births, some factors such as early rupture of the bag of waters are beyond the ability of medical science to control.

SMALL FOR GESTATIONAL AGE INFANTS

An infant who weighs less than 90 percent of other infants of the same gestational age is, by definition, small for gestational age (SGA). The majority of these infants are born at term, although some are classified as preterm SGA or postterm SGA (Cockburn, 1984). Full-term SGA births are usually caused by intrauterine growth retardation. Known causes of this problem include genetic conditions, congenital infections, maternal malnutrition, placental abnormalities, and maternal ingestion of adverse substances.

The majority of full-term SGA infants appear to have starved in the uterus. SGA infants tend to have even less fat and muscle tissue than preterm infants. The head appears to be larger and even more out of proportion to the rest of the body. The skin is loose and dry with very little lanugo or vernix. Typically such babies have more hair than preterm infants (Sammons & Lewis, 1985). These infants are often very active and cry vigorously (Cockburn, 1984).

SGA infants have some of the same problems as preterm infants, such as temperature regulation, but they develop some special complications of their own. They are more likely to have problems such as asphyxia (low-oxygen and high carbon-dioxide blood level) before they are born. SGA infants also frequently have trouble with hypoglycemia (low blood sugar). Since they are stressed, these infants tend to inhale meconium, which they excrete into the amniotic fluid before birth. Inhaled meconium causes breathing difficulties after birth and often leads to pneumonia. The stress placed on the heart by these breathing difficulties may result in death (Vulliamy, 1982). However, SGA babies rarely are affected by RDS (Batshaw & Perret, 1992).

SGA infants tend to remain short and underweight throughout life. They also have a higher incidence of developmental disabilities than babies whose weight is age appropriate (Batshaw & Perret, 1992). Infants who are born with VLBW and SGA have been found to be at increased risk for developmental problems in cognitive and motor functioning (Smedler et al., 1992).

EFFECTS OF PREMATURITY AND LOW BIRTHWEIGHT

The vast majority of preterm and low-birthweight infants grow up to be normal, healthy infants with little or no traces of their former condition. Advances in medical knowledge and technology since the 1960s have resulted in a decreased inci-dence of major disabilities and sensory impair-ments (Allen, 1993). Unfortunately, though, some of these infants will suffer physical impediments and other problems. The chances of having a severe disability such as cerebral palsy, mental disability, or sensory impairment increase as birthweight decreases. Approximately 5 to 15 percent of these infants will have serious or moderate degrees of such problems as visual impairment, hearing loss, epilepsy, cerebral palsy, or mental retardation (Kopp & Parmelee, 1979). Some reports indicate that the disability rate is about 18 percent for VLBW infants, and about 20 to 25 percent for ELBW infants (Hall, 1985). Follow-up studies of ELBW infants without major impairments suggest that 40 to 64 percent require special education or addi-tional services in school (Collin, Halsey, & Ander-son, 1991).

Healthy AGA premature or low-birthweight infants who have adequate nutrition usually catch up to full-term infants of the same birth date by 40 to 42 weeks of age. After that time, AGA preterm infants grow at the same rate as full-term infants (Desmond et al., 1980). SGA infants are the most likely to grow up to be smaller than their full-term peers (Hall, 1985). For example, Willie Shoemaker, the famous jockey, was an SGA baby (2½ pounds at 36 weeks' gestation). His parents kept him in a shoe box in the oven with the door open during the neonatal period (Shoemaker & Tower, 1970). Shoe-maker's adult height reached only 4 feet 11½ inches.

As a group, preterm infants demonstrate a nor-mal range of intelligence as they grow up. How-ever, their average IQ score is slightly below the average for the general population (Allen, 1993). We should keep in mind that the average may be lower because a small group of children with severe mental disability tends to pull down the group aver-age and the other preterm children may actually be unaffected.

Children who were born prematurely may not be quite ready to begin school at age 6 (Desmond et al., 1980). Some premature and low-birthweight infants therefore are more likely to have problems in academic achievement and are more likely to need special education than their full-term peers.

Poor school performance and academic difficul-ties have been reported in 23 to 48 percent of chil-dren who weighed less than 3½ pounds at birth (Allen, 1993).

In summary, during the first two or three years of life, preterm infants typically display deficiencies in behavioral organization, visual attention, infor-mation processing, motor skills, and language acqui-sition. Most of these problems tend to disappear with age, but the effects may be permanent for some children. In some instances, prematurity and low-birthweight have a "sleeper effect" whereby devel-opmental problems do not show up until these children enter school. In general, it is almost impos-sible at birth to predict how being born too soon and too small will affect any particular baby. In most cases, parents and others must "wait and see" (Ensher & Clark, 1994).

LARGE FOR GESTATIONAL AGE INFANTS

Although there is much less written about LGA babies than SGA babies, they have problems that are equally serious. LGA is most frequently caused by maternal diabetes. At birth LGA babies are likely to have too much insulin in their blood. This con-dition results in overgrowth of fatty tissue, the heart, liver, and the adrenal gland. Fortunately, brain growth is not usually affected. LGA infants are likely to have respiratory distress because excess insulin prevents the lungs from maturing. Congen-ital defects and injuries during birth are also more prevalent among LGA babies. Other problems include an extra large tongue and other body organs. The neonatal mortality rate is higher among LGA infants than AGA infants (Ensher & Clark, 1994).

POSTMATURE INFANTS

Babies born after 42 weeks of gestational age are considered to be postmature. The main risk these infants face is the aging of the placenta. After about 40 to 42 weeks' gestation, the placenta loses effi-ciency in supplying nutrition and carrying off waste products. The amount of amniotic fluid also tends to diminish in a postterm pregnancy. As a result, postmature babies are long and skinny and have dry skin that may be cracked and peeling. Asphyxia, inhalation of meconium, pneumonia, and hypoglycemia are typical problems they experience at birth (Cockburn, 1984; Vulliamy, 1982). With more accurate methods of assessing gestational age, physicians are now better equipped to prevent pregnancies from continuing too long.

INFANT MORTALITY

In recent decades there has been a steady decline in the rate of infants who die during the first year of life. However, the United States' infant mortality rate of 8.3 percent (per 100 live births in 1993) remains higher than rates for most other Western industrialized nations (Singh & Stella, 1995; National Center for Health Statistics, 1995). Approximately two-thirds of these infants die during the first 28 days of life (Novak & Broom, 1995). In the United States, black infants are twice as likely to die during the first year of life as white infants. Research studies indicate that this gap may be due primarily to the higher rate of preterm and low birthweight infants born to black mothers (Schoendorf et al., 1992; Rowland & Hargraves, 1995).

A number of factors have been associated with infant mortality. Some of the leading causes of infant mortality, in order of importance, are birth defects, sudden infant death syndrome, prematu-

rity and low birthweight, respiratory distress syndrome, complications of pregnancy, injuries, and infectious disease (Singh & Yu, 1995). In addition, poverty, poor nutrition, insufficient prenatal care, maternal health, and behavioral risk factors such as substance abuse, smoking, and sexually transmitted disease contribute, directly or indirectly, to the death of young infants.

NEWBORN SCREENING TESTS

Apgar Scale

Many physicians routinely use the Apgar Scale to evaluate the vital signs of newborn infants in the delivery room. The scale is administered within the first 60 seconds after birth to check the baby's heart rate, breathing, muscle tone, reflex irritability, and color (Table 4–1). A second assessment is usually made about 5 minutes later. Infants who are in the best condition score in the 8–10 range. A score from 5–7 warns the doctor that the baby may need help and should be carefully observed. If the score is 4 or below, the infant is in critical condition and requires emergency care. The large majority of infants score in the 7–10 range.

The Brazelton Scale

The **Brazelton Neonatal Behavior Assessment Scale (BNBAS)** was designed to assess the new-

Table 4–1   Apgar Scale

SIGN	0	1	2
A—appearance (color)	blue, pale	body pink (extremities blue)	completely pink
P—pulse (heart rate)	absent	below 100	over 100
G—grimace (reflex irritability, response to stimulation of sole of foot by a glancing slap)	no response	grimace	cry
A—activity (muscle tone)	limp	some flexion of extremities	active motion
R—respiratory (respiratory effort	absent	slow, irregular	good strong cry

Source: J. Butterfield, and M. Covey, (1962). Practical epigram of the Apgar Score. *Journal of the American Medical Association,* 181, 353. Copyright 1962, American Medical Association.

born infant's responses to the environment (Brazelton, 1973). One section of the test contains twenty items that measure the intactness of the nervous system through elicited reflexes such as rooting and sucking (see Chapter 8). The examination also contains items that score an infant on 26 kinds of behavior, including sensory responses (e.g., vision, hearing), motor maturity, alertness, self-quieting activity, and social interaction (cuddliness). The BNBAS scale is about 80 percent effective in detecting abnormalities of development in newborns; the device has been used widely in research and is also used in teaching parents about the behavior of their baby (Heidelise et al., 1979).

Assessment of Preterm Infant Behavior Scale

One of the most widely used instruments for evaluating the developmental status of preterm infants is the **Assessment of Preterm Infant Behavior (APIB)** scale (Als, 1982). The APIB is based on the BNBAS and includes some of the same items. It is designed to assess signs of stability and instability in each of the following areas: physiological functioning (e.g., heart rate, color changes), motor functioning, state organization, attention or interaction, and self-regulation. The examiner observes how well the infant responds to a series of increasingly demanding stimuli.

Hearing Screening Tests

The National Institute of Health recommends that all newborn infants be tested for hearing loss. An **otacoustic emissions** test is now available that will make it much easier to screen infants for hearing problems before they leave the hospital. In this test, which takes about 15 minutes, a probe is placed into each ear canal through which sounds are emitted. If the hearing mechanism is functioning properly, an "echo" from the baby's inner ear is transmitted through the probe and registered on a computer screen. An older procedure that can also be used is the **auditory brain stem response** test. Electrodes hooked up to computerized equipment are attached to the baby's scalp to measure brain activity while a tone is emitted through a speaker.

If the brain waves do not change, it indicates that the baby does not hear adequately. Since newborns tend to have amniotic fluid in their ears, infants are retested a few weeks later if their first test indicates there might be a hearing problem.

FACILITATING NEONATAL DEVELOPMENT

The most important thing parents and caregivers of newborns can do to facilitate the development of newborn infants is to meet their basic needs, including adequate nutrition, good health care, and affection. Burton White (1985) believes that giving an infant a "feeling of being loved and cared for" is the best thing parents can do to get their child off to a good start (p. 26). He recommends the following child-rearing practices during the first six weeks of life:

1. Handle the newborn frequently and respond promptly to its cries. A crying infant who is not hungry or in need of a diaper change can usually be calmed by swaddling (wrapping tightly in a blanket), rocking, holding and cuddling, gently bouncing, humming, providing a pacifier, or adjusting the temperature.
2. A crib mobile with contrasting colors is about the only enrichment material a newborn needs. The mobile should be designed so that it can be enjoyed from the perspective of an infant looking up rather than an adult looking down.
3. The position and location of the baby should be changed several times. A baby should be placed on its stomach (while awake) frequently during the day. This position induces head lifting and increases the visual field.
4. Develop the habit of talking to the baby when it is alert. Diaper changing and other caregiving activities are usually good times to get the baby's attention and engage in play.

Caring for Preterm and Low-Birthweight Infants

Since the early 1970s health care workers, child-development specialists, psychologists, and others have attempted to design hospital nurseries to meet the special psychological and physical needs of infants who have been born too early and too small.

For one thing, parents are encouraged to maintain regular contact with preterm and other low-birth-weight infants who must stay in the hospital for an extended period. Parents are encouraged to hold the baby and participate in feeding and other caregiving activities as medical conditions permit. In addition, researchers have introduced a variety of nonmedical interventions that have been designed to facilitate their development by sensory stimulation or stress-relieving activities.

The following special stimulation and intervention activities are often used in neonatal intensive-care units (NICU's) with preterm infants either on a regular or experimental basis:

1. Water beds and air mattresses, with or without built-in rocking mechanisms, are provided in some hospitals. When medical conditions permit, these infants are also rocked by caregivers at regular intervals.
2. Sound recordings of the mother's heartbeat and other intrauterine noises, parental voices, and even classical music are provided. However, recorded sounds are not used to substitute for human contact and live voices.
3. High-contrast pictures or mobiles in the form of black and white checkerboard or bull's eye design and other materials are placed in the infant's field of vision.
4. Infants' bodies (back of the head, neck, and back) are gently massaged, and their arms and legs are slowly moved.

Some of these interventions are based on the assumption that preterm infants are deprived of stimulation they would normally receive in the womb or postnatal experiences that are usually provided for term infants. Thoman (1993) refers to this approach as a "deficit model" in which interventions (e.g., motion and sound) are designed to resemble, as much as possible, the conditions within the intrauterine environment. On the other hand, some of the interventions are based on a "minimal stimulation" approach whereby nursery lights are dimmed, sounds are reduced, isolettes are covered with blankets to provide shade from the light, and infants are snugly surrounded with blanket rolls. Handling and routine medical checks are minimized. This approach is designed to simulate the protective features of the intrauterine environment and minimize stressful stimulation until the infant is better equipped to cope.

Numerous research studies have been conducted on the effectiveness of the various intervention techniques and models in enhancing the development of preterm infants. For example, some researchers have concluded that low-birthweight and preterm babies gain weight faster and go home from the hospital sooner if they are stimulated with gentle stroking (Field, 1995). Unfortunately, the findings have been contradictory. Some reviewers of these studies have concluded that, as a whole, the results do not justify the widespread use of such programs in NICU units (Bennet, 1987; Palmer, Capute, & Shapiro, 1988). Others have concluded that the intervention techniques have achieved positive results (Linn, Horowitz, & Fox, 1985; Mueller, 1996).

In view of the contradictory findings, Thoman (1993) has proposed an alternative "**gentlest intervention**" approach to NICU interventions. This approach is based on the theory that infants benefit most when they are allowed to respond or ignore the stimulation provided. Examples of interventions that allow infants to self-regulate the stimulation include opportunities for nonnutritive sucking that preterm infants could respond to or ignore, provision of a small beanbag so that infants can mold to it and make their own "nest," and more subdued patterns of visual stimuli (e.g., pictures of parents). Another intervention developed by Thoman (1993) is a "breathing teddy bear" that is placed in the isolette with the infant. A special air pump located outside isolette makes the bear "breathe" in adjustable rhythms to match the baby's own breathing patterns, or at a slower rate. The bear is made available to the infant to touch or move away from at will. Preliminary studies have supported the benefits of self-regulatory stimulation for preterm infants, but additional evidence is needed to be conclusive.

In any event, there is general agreement that caregivers who work with preterm infants should be aware of the infant's state and avoid intrusive or overstimulating activities. Stimulation should be provided in small increments and withdrawn if the baby appears to be stressed. Signs that a baby is overstimulated or stressed include color changes, yawning, sneezing, vomiting, eye aversion, or crying. Preterm infants need more time to warm up and respond to touch than full-term infants.

Parent-Infant Interactions in The NICU

Preterm, low-birthweight, and other infants who need to be cared for in a NICU are at increased risk for problems in early parent-child interaction patterns. These infants are more likely to be perceived by parents as less physically attractive and less responsive than babies who are born on schedule with AGA weight. The early birth of a tiny baby is likely to be accompanied by parental feelings of guilt, anxiety, and uncertainty.

NICU babies tend to avoid eye contact, smile infrequently, have difficulty in sending clear signals, and are difficult to cuddle and console. Consequently, parents of these children may respond differently than parents of healthy infants. Many parents smile less, spend less time in face-to-face contact, and make less body contact. In some cases though, parents use overstimulating touching and talking interactions in attempts to obtain responses from their baby. Infants respond to such "intrusive" behaviors by gaze aversion and turning away. Thus, parents and infants have difficulty in establishing satisfying patterns of interactional synchrony (Wyly, 1995).

In addition, parents are often overwhelmed with the tubes, respirators and other features of a high-tech NICU environment. The extensive precautions taken to prevention infections also inhibit parent-infant contact. Many parents visit infrequently because they live long distances from the hospital, have limited financial and other resources.

Recognizing the importance of early parent-infant contacts, many NICUs have established liberal visitation policies and encourage parent involvement in the nonmedical care and feeding of their infants. They also have parent education programs, support groups, and other interventions that promote parent involvement. A special type of intervention that is being used in some NICUs is **kangaroo care**. This approach originated in Bogotá, Colombia, as a means of using mothers as "human incubators" because of the lack of hospital equipment. The practice was introduced in the United States and other countries as a means of promoting tactile stimulation for the baby and facilitating parent-infant bonding through skin-to-skin contact. The mother holds the diaper clad baby between or near her breasts so that the baby has self-regulatory access to breastfeeding. The time at which kangaroo care is begun and the length of caregiving episodes varies with the condition of the baby. Fathers may also hold the baby kangaroo-style. Research studies have found that this type of care provides at least some short-term benefits for both premature infants and their families. The long-term effects have not yet been evaluated (Wyly, 1995).

SUMMARY

1. The newborn period is defined as the first 2 weeks after birth. Adjustments newborn infants have to accomplish include breathing, temperature changes, taking in nourishment, eliminating body waste, sleeping, and waking. Infants produce special "stress" hormones during labor that facilitate their survival and adjustment to life in the outside world.

2. Infants vary widely in physical appearance at birth, but the effects of the birth process are usually obvious. Skin discolorations, bruises, and a misshapen skull are some of the features displayed by many infants.

3. The five basic sensory systems—vision, hearing, touch, taste, and smell—are functioning at birth, at least to a limited extent.

4. The vision of newborns is blurred and their eye movements are jerky but these limitations do not deter their visual curiosity. Newborns scan the edges of objects and do not look much at the overall shape of objects until around 3 months. Under certain conditions, they recognize and prefer to look at human faces more than other images. Newborns imitate tongue protrusion, but their ability to mimic other facial gestures is uncertain. They appear to be capable of limited color vision. However, researchers are trying to answers ongoing questions about the color-visual capacities of newborns.

5. Newborn babies are sensitive to sounds and are capable of distinguishing between sounds of different pitch, loudness, and intensity. They prefer to listen to sounds within the range of the human voice, and the sound of their mother's voice over other voices.

6. As soon as they are born, infants apparently have the capacity to distinguish among the four basic tastes. The taste for sweet substances is predominant over other taste preferences and is probably innate.

7. Infants can detect strong odors at birth but do not respond to weaker odors until they are a few days older. Like adults, infants prefer pleasant to unpleasant odors.

8. The sense of touch is one of the earliest and most important senses to develop. It is the most complex of the senses to study and understand, but plays a very important role in development.

9. Contrary to previous opinion, newborns respond to pain in ways that are similar to how adults respond to pain.

10. Research evidence tends to support the view that infants are capable of limited intersensory perception at birth.

11. The responses of infants to sensory stimulation are affected by their particular state of awareness. Seven states exhibited by newborns have been identified: regular sleep, irregular sleep, periodic sleep, drowsiness, alert inactivity, waking activity, and crying.

12. Although there are cultural variations, most newborn infants in the United States sleep in a separate bed in a separate room. In most other cultures throughout the world infants sleep with their mother.

13. The infant's birthweight and gestational age are important factors that have a major impact on growth and development. The term "low-birthweight" is used to designate infants who weigh less than 5½ pounds at birth. Infants who are born at less than 37 weeks of gestation are called "preterm" or "premature" infants. Most preterm infants fall into the low-birthweight category.

14. Preterm and low-birthweight infants have many of the same problems and characteristics. Some of their problems include respiratory distress syndrome, chronic lung disease, temperature-regulation difficulties, heart problems, intracranial bleeding, eye problems, excess bilirubin, nutritional difficulties, and infections.

15. Small for gestational age (SGA), large for gestational age (LGA), and postterm infants also have many problems when they are born.

16. Preterm and low-birthweight infants usually catch up with the physical development of their full-term peers by the end of the infancy period. The risk of disabilities increases as gestational age and birthweight decrease. The majority of preterm, low-birthweight, SGA, LGA, and postmature infants grow up to be normal, healthy children.

17. The Apgar Scale, the Brazelton Neonatal Behavior Assessment Scale, and the Assessment of Preterm Infant Behavior Scale are assessment instruments that are widely used to determine the developmental status of newborn infants. All newborn infants should receive a hearing screening test.

18. Researchers have experimented with a variety of NICU stimulation and intervention activities for preterm and low-birthweight infants with contradictory results. There is general agreement that NICU interventions should be carefully controlled and based on the individual needs of the infant.

5

Physical Growth

*There's only one beautiful baby in
the world and every mother has it.*
—An English Proverb

As surely as life continues outside the uterus, the
baby grows. At no other time period following birth
is growth so rapid, dramatic, and clearly observable as it is during infancy. Adults are constantly
amazed at how quickly an infant changes in physical appearance. Physical growth results from two
processes—cell division and the increase in the
size of existing cells. Before birth, cell division is
the main type of growth activity. After birth, the
process shifts to the enlargement of existing cells.
This does not mean that no new cells are formed,
but the main growth function is to build on existing
structures and to replace cells that are lost through
aging, wear and tear, and physical injury.

In this chapter we consider physical changes that
occur during infancy. Clearly observable changes
in height, weight, head circumference, teeth, and
skin are discussed. We also give attention to less
obvious growth processes occurring in the internal
organs such as the brain, muscles, skeleton, and cardiovascular system. Finally, procedures for evaluating and enhancing physical growth are considered.

FACTORS INFLUENCING PHYSICAL GROWTH

Human growth is an extremely complicated process
that is affected by numerous forces including heredity, hormones, health, nutrition, socioeconomic status, sex, race, and emotional stress. Some of these
factors are considered in other chapters in connection with specific aspects of growth whereas others
are discussed at this point. Keep in mind, however,
that the precise influence of each factor is almost
impossible to determine because of the complex
ways in which heredity and environmental conditions intermix.

Socioeconomic Status

Children from higher social class groups are taller,
heavier, and grow faster than children from lower

socioeconomic groups in the same part of the country. In England, children of fathers employed in
professional jobs average about 3/4 to 1/2 an inch
taller at age 3 than those of fathers working in
unskilled occupations (Tanner, 1990). Everywhere,
infant mortality and health problems are most common among children of lower socioeconomic status. Social class differences simply reflect the
nutrition, health care, and other environmental conditions to which infants are exposed.

Illness

The effects of garden-variety childhood diseases
(measles, colds, viruses, etc.) on the growth rate
of well-nourished children are hardly noticeable.
In some cases, growth may be slowed down
slightly, but once the disease is cured, the growth
rate resumes and the infant makes up for "lost time"
(Tanner, 1990). Undernourished children do not
catch-up as easily. Children from economically
deprived environments, who have a long history of
frequent colds, ear disease, sore throats, and skin
infections tend to be smaller than other children
(Tanner, 1990). In all children, major diseases delay
growth, but the effects on body size are seldom
lasting. However, some of the illnesses to which
infants are exposed have the potential to cause
severe sensory or nervous-system impairments leading to physical disabilities.

Culture and Race

Many aspects of physical growth during infancy,
such as height and weight, vary widely around the
world, depending upon gene pools, nutrition, and
other environmental factors. At 1 year of age,
infants living in different regions of the world differ as much as 5⅕ inches in average height and 9
pounds in average weight. The shortest and light-
est infants come from South-Central and South-
east Asia (India, Vietnam, Pakistan). The tallest
and heaviest infants come from the United States
and Europe (Werner, 1979). Nail and hair growth
are more advanced in African infants in comparison
to American babies (Broude, 1995).

In the United States, black infants tend to be

slightly smaller at birth than white infants, but their skeletal development is slightly more advanced. Black infants soon surpass white infants in size and are a little taller and heavier throughout childhood as long as socioeconomic factors are equivalent (Eichorn, 1979). Birthweights of Mexican Americans are similar to those of white Americans. Japanese and Chinese infants are shorter and weigh less, on average, than infants of European ancestry (Malina & Bouchard, 1991). Japanese infants reared in America are more advanced in height, weight, and skeletal growth than Japanese infants living in Japan (Broude, 1995). The difference is assumed to be at least partially related to dietary influences. The largest physical differences in races are those of body proportion, especially of the lower extremities (Tanner, 1990; Malina & Bouchard, 1991). However, differences in shape are more observable in later years than in infancy.

Hormonal Influences

Hormones secreted directly into the bloodstream by the endocrine glands play a major role in physical growth, particularly height. Although numerous hormones affect all growth throughout the life cycle, the hormones that are particularly influential during infancy are thyroxine and human growth hormone (hGH).

Thyroxine. The thyroid gland releases **thyroxine** in response to chemical messages from the pituitary gland. Adequate quantities of this hormone are necessary for cell multiplication and subsequent growth in size. Thyroxine also is important for the stimulation of brain growth during the fetal and early infancy periods (Lowrey, 1978). To meet this need, it is secreted in greater quantities during the first 2 years of life, after which the amount is reduced until adolescence. Insufficient quantities of thyroxine (hypothyroidism) leads to brain growth failure and mental diasbility. If hypothyroidism is discovered and treated within the first 3 months of life, an infant has an 85 percent chance of developing an IQ of at least 85. The outlook is more dismal if treatment is delayed (Tanner, 1990).

Human Growth Hormone. Normal physical growth from infancy to maturity depends upon an adequate supply of **human growth hormone (hGH)**, which also comes from the thyroid gland. Human growth hormone is apparently not necessary for normal prenatal growth. However, if there is a deficiency of hGH, growth after birth is less than normal and is increasingly evident by 2 years of age (Tanner, 1990). Human growth hormone affects cell multiplication and expansion in all organs of the body except the central nervous system and some of the endocrine glands (Lowrey, 1978). Deficiency of hGH is found in approximately one out of 4,000 children (Gotlin et al., 1995). The reason for hGH insufficiency cannot be determined in most cases (Tanner, 1990).

The extent of growth retardation is related to the amount of hGH available. Children who are severely affected grow to be about one-half the size of other children (Gotlin et al., 1995). Their skeletons are normally proportioned, but they become miniature adults. However, hGH-deficient children tend to be overweight (Tanner, 1990). Fortunately, injections of hGH can be given that may stimulate normal growth. For many years after its discovery in 1956, the supply of hGH was extremely limited because it could be obtained only from the glands of human cadavers. However, the development of a synthetic form of hGH has made a sufficient supply available to treat all children who need it. Early diagnosis of hGH deficiency is important in order to obtain maximum benefit from the treatment (Gotlin et al., 1995). The ability of the body to use growth hormones is limited by the genetic potential, so hGH supplements will not stimulate a genetically small child to grow larger.

Emotional Disturbances

Disturbances in the parent-child relationship or other causes of continuing severe emotional stress result in growth failure. This condition is sometimes referred to as **psychosocial** or **deprivation dwarfism**. Apparently, young children respond to stress by reducing or completely inhibiting the secretion of growth hormone. When the stress is alleviated, the child resumes growth and usually catches up with age mates (Tanner, 1990). Short-term emotional stress connected with normal daily family living has no marked impact on growth patterns.

BODY SIZE

The three major indicators of normal body growth during infancy and childhood are weight, height, and head circumference. Measurements of these body features should be made periodically as a part of a child's routine health care. The curve of standard body growth for male and female infants can be found in Appendices 1-4.

Weight

Body weight is probably the best single indicator of growth in infancy because it represents a summary of all changes in size. Typically, a newborn baby is expected to gain about one ounce each day, averaging about 2.2 pounds each month for the first six months of life (Silver, 1984). During the last half of the first year, the weight gain slows down to about 1/2 ounce per day. Healthy infants usually double their birthweight by 4 or 5 months. Birthweight is tripled by 1 year, and quadrupled by 2 years of age.

This infant weighed 7 lbs. 7 ozs. and was 19 inches long at birth. At two months of age, when this picture was taken, she weighed 11 lbs. 7 ozs. and was 23 inches long.

Thus the average infant who weighs 7.25 pounds at birth will probably weigh about 14.5 pounds at 4 months, 22.5 pounds at 1 year, and 29 pounds at 2 years of age. During the remainder of infancy and early childhood, the average annual weight gain is about 5 pounds.

The growth of the skeleton, muscles, and body organs contribute to weight gains in infancy, but much of the body weight is due to the addition and enlargement of fatty tissue. The layer of fat beneath the skin of the fetus begins to develop during approximately the thirtieth week of the prenatal period. Body fat continues to increase until reaching a peak in growth rate from 6 to 9 months after birth. The rate of fat cell growth then gradually declines throughout infancy.

Male infants, on the average, weigh a little more than female infants. However, females have a little more total body fat than males at birth, and the difference tends to increase throughout infancy (Tanner, 1990). At birth, the average (50th percentile) male infant (7.25 lb.) weighs about ¼ pound more than the average female infant (7 lb.). The difference in weight gradually increases throughout infancy until 2 years of age, when the average male (27.75 lb.) weighs about 1.5 pounds more than the average female (26.25 lb.).

Height

The first year of postnatal life brings rapid change in height. By the first birthday, an infant has usually increased the birth length by approximately 50 percent. Thus, the average infant who measures 20 inches at birth would be about 30 inches tall at the end of the first year. During the second year, the increase is less dramatic, with a gain of about 4.5 to 5 inches, or about 24 percent of the full length. On the average, infants grow about 3 to 4 inches in the third year and measure about 3 feet tall (Silver, 1984). Typically, males remain about 1/4 to 1/2 inch taller than females throughout the infancy period. Growth in height can be restricted by chronic infections, malnutrition, and malabsorption of nutrients, severe chronic diseases, cystic fibrosis, and other developmental disorders (Illingworth, 1991). Genetic control over height is considered to be greater than genetic control over body weight (Malina & Bouchard, 1991).

Prediction of Adult Height

Tanner's (1990) relative maturity percentages are sometimes used as a rough estimate of adult height. At 2 years of age, a boy growing up in the United States will be 49.2 percent as tall as he will grow to be as an adult. A girl of the same age has reached 52.5 percent of her mature height. An average 3-year-old American female has reached 57.8 percent of her mature height, while the typical male has obtained 53.9 percent of his adult height. In general, taller than average 2-year-olds tend to become taller than average adults. However, it is not possible to accurately predict the final body size of an infant because there are too many unknown variables that can affect growth. Generally, tall parents tend to have tall children, but there are many exceptions to this trend (Malina & Bouchard, 1991).

Head Growth

The circumference of an infant's head is a major index of normal growth during infancy. At birth,

head circumference normally ranges from 12 to 15 inches, with an average of 13.75 inches. The head circumference of the typical 6-month-old infant (50th percentile) measures about 17 inches, increasing to around 18 inches at 1 year of age, and around 19 inches at 2 years. Males usually have a slightly larger head (1/4 to 3/4 inch) than females during the infancy period.

The shape of the young infant's head is noticeably different from that of an adult (Fig. 5-1). The cranium, or top of the head, is proportionately larger and more prominent in the infant. The face constitutes a much smaller part of the head. At birth, the head of an infant is approximately one-fourth of the total body length, whereas for an adult the head is only about one-eighth of total height. During infancy, the head grows slower, so there is a noticeable change in its proportion to body length.

The shape of an individual's skull is influenced by sex, race, and other factors, but the facial size is closely related to the overall growth of the head. If the brain grows as it should, the head circumference will equal the expected measurements. Head growth is considered to be a good index of brain growth. An extremely small or large head may be an indicator of atypical brain growth. However, the total body size should be considered,

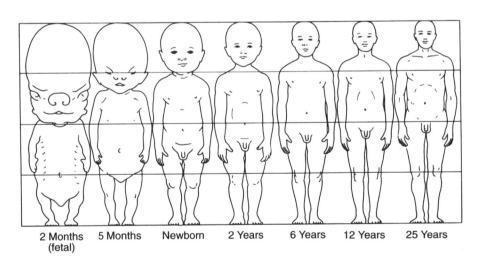

| 2 Months (fetal) | 5 Months | Newborn | 2 Years | 6 Years | 12 Years | 25 Years |

Figure 5-1   Proportionate Changes in Growth of the Head, Trunk, and Limbs.
Source: B. Anson, (Ed.) (1966). *Morris' human anatomy* (12th ed.). New York: McGraw-Hill. Used by permission.

because a large baby will typically have a large head and a small baby will usually have a small head (Illingworth, 1991). If the head circumference measures below the 3rd percentile or above the 97th percentile, the infant should be carefully evaluated for such problems as microcephaly (underdeveloped brain) or hydrocephaly (excess fluid on the brain) (Valadian & Porter, 1977).

Fontanels. The skull of an infant consists of eight pieces of bone held together by softer cartilage and connecting tissue. At birth the bones are soft and movable and may overlap so the head can more easily move through the birth canal. The narrow seams of cartilage are called sutures, while the wide sections of cartilage are called **fontanels**, or "soft spots." Four sutures and six fontanels are usually present at birth.

The two larger fontanels can easily be felt with the fingertips as soft spots in the skull. The sutures are more difficult to find and typically cannot be felt after the first few weeks. However, the sutures are not completely closed until adolescence. The largest fontanel is located in the front of the cranium. It is usuallly diamond shaped and measures about 0.4 to 2.5 inches at birth (Nelms & Mullins, 1982). The front fontanel is usually closed by 18 to 20 months of age (Valadian & Porter, 1977). The fontanel on the back of the skull is typically shaped like a triangle and measures about 0.2 inches in diameter at birth. As the skull hardens, this fontanel gradually gets smaller and is completely closed by 3 or 4 months in most infants. In some infants it may already be closed at birth (Behrman & Vaughan, 1983).

The Face. The most noticeable and complex growth of the head can be observed in the facial features. The front view of the newborn infant reveals a broad, flat appearance in comparison to the face of an adult. The flat facial appearance is a result of the baby's small, almost bridgeless nose, and cheekbones that are barely distinguishable. The profile (side view) is dominated by the cranium and forehead since the lower jaw is underdeveloped and receded (Ranly, 1980). Lorenz (1965) has noted that these facial features, in com-

bination with the infant's small size, form the "cuteness" that attracts adults to infants. This infant shape triggers nurturing behaviors, including human affection for the young of other species.

With age, the lower part of the face undergoes "catch-up growth" that changes the infant's overall appearance. The length of the face is about 40 percent complete at birth. Facial growth proceeds very rapidly during the first three years of life, after which growth is slower and steadier until maturity (Ranly, 1980). The middle of the face emerges from beneath the cranium and grows forward and downward. The bony bridge and soft tissue of the nose grow while the front sinus cavities expand so that the flat appearance of the face diminishes. In spite of the rapid growth, however, the face of an infant remains considerably less mature in appearance than an adult face.

The Eyes. One of the most striking features of an infant's face is the eyes. The eyes dominate the face of the infant until the nose becomes large enough to provide a definite separation between them. Apparently, the infant is equipped with a small nose to prevent the mother's breast from pressing against it and cutting off the air supply. In the normal full-term newborn, the eyes are approximately three-fourths of normal adult size. They grow rapidly during the first year and at a rapid but decelerating rate until the third year. Although growth of the eyes continues after infancy, it proceeds at a much slower rate (Nelson, 1996).

Various parts of the eye have different growth rates. The front part of the eye is relatively large at birth and grows less than the structures in the back of the eye. The cornea is large at birth and reaches mature size at about 2 years of age. It tends to flatten with age. The small pit near the center of the retina, known as the fovea, changes rapidly during the first year of life (Banks & Shannon, 1993). The fovea is the area of the eye that provides the sharpest vision. Overall, the shape of the eye becomes more clearly spherical with growth.

The color of the eyes tends to get darker with age in many children. In Caucasians, the eyes are typically light blue at birth but get darker and may change color as pigment is added. Infants of color

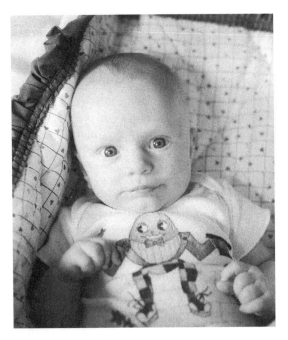

The eyes are the dominant feature of the young infant's face. Notice, also, the relatively large skull and small jaw.

typically have dark eyes at birth, so the addition of pigment is not as noticeable. Tears are often not produced when the baby cries until approximately 1 to 3 months. Beginning at birth, periodic eye examinations are recommended during infancy and childhood to detect and treat such problems as strabismus (cross-eyes), amblyopia ("lazy eye"), refractive disorders, or other problems. Visual acuity is usually measured at 2 1/2 to 3 years of age (Nelson, 1996).

The Ears. The external, middle, and internal parts of the human ear form the auditory system. The development of the ear begins with the inner ear during the fourth prenatal week (Moore & Persaud, 1993). Most of the components of the auditory system are functionally complete at birth. However, the ear canal of the newborn is shallow and straight. The supporting structure is mostly cartilage. The tympanic membrane (ear drum) is not completely closed and lies at a horizontal angle. During the first 3 years of life, the tympanic membrane closes and assumes a more mature verticle position. The ear canal gradually changes to the adult S-shape. The bends in the canal protect the ear drum from foreign bodies and sounds that are too loud. Bony formation takes the place of the cartilaginous tissue. The structure of the outer ear (pinna) has typically reached its adult form by the time of birth. Both the pinna and the ear canal continue to grow until 7 to 9 years of age when adult size is attained (Ballachanda, 1995).

Throughout the infancy period, routine physical exams of the ear should be conducted, along with hearing screening tests, to detect any structural defects, infections, or problems that might lead to hearing loss. There are 2 main types of hearing loss. **Conductive hearing loss** results from abnormalities in the ear structure, or fluid in the middle ear. **Sensorial hearing loss** results from abnormality of the inner ear, or failure of the nerves to carry sound signals from the inner ear to the brain (Shelov, 1994).

Catch-up Growth

An individual's potential body size is controlled by several genes, each of which has a small effect. Some genes do not begin to function until after birth. During the prenatal period the baby's growth is affected by the size of the mother's uterus. The uterus of a small mother thus may have a restraining effect on a baby who has the genetic potential to grow larger than average. On the other hand, an infant born to a larger mother may be larger than average even though genetically programmed to reach a relatively small adult height.

After birth, small infants who have a genetic heritage to be tall adults will usually grow faster than average for the first few months of life. Such rapid growth after the period of intrauterine growth restriction is called **catch-up growth** (Tanner, 1990). By the same genetic principle, larger-than-average infants who are destined to be small adults will grow slower than average. Thus, the baby's length at birth is not a good indicator of height at maturity. Generally, an infant will reach the genetically determined growth channel by 12 to 14 months of age. The smaller infants "catch up" earlier than larger infants who "lag down" a little later in infancy (Bax, Hart, & Jenkins, 1990). Consequently, an individual infant's height and weight percentile rankings often change considerably on a growth chart during the first 2 or 3 years of life (Malina & Bouchard, 1991).

SKELETAL GROWTH

Ossification

At birth an infant's skeleton is made up mostly of semihard, gristle-like tissue called cartilage. The skeleton is softer and more flexible in the joints. This makes it possible for babies to suck on their toes as well as their fingers! As the baby grows, the skeleton becomes harder and less flexible. The process by which minerals and other substances are added to the cartilage so that it hardens into bones is called **ossification**. Bone growth and ossification are largely dependent upon an adequate supply of nutritional and hormonal substances. Different parts of the skeleton grow and ossify at different rates. On the average, girls are more typically advanced in skeletal ossification than boys at birth. The sex difference tends to increase with age because female infants mature at a faster rate during infancy. In addition, the rate of ossification is less variable for girls than for boys (Sinclair, 1978). In general, the growth curves for skeletal weight tend to be similar to the curves for overall body weight and height (Malina & Bouchard, 1991).

The Limbs

The bone-hardening process begins in an ossification center in each piece of cartilage. At birth, primary ossification centers have begun in all of the long limb bones. Shortly before and immediately after birth, secondary ossification centers, or epiphyses, form near each end of each separate piece of cartilage. Ossification then proceeds from the end of each bone to the middle.

New ossification centers appear continuously throughout the skeleton until maturity is reached. At the same time ossification is proceeding, new lay-

ers of bony tissue are deposited on the outside of the basic structure so that the bones grow in width. The bones also grow in length and change in shape as cells are added to the epiphyses. At birth, the bones of the lower limbs and pelvic area are proportionately shorter and less advanced than the upper limbs and shoulders. However, the lower limbs grow at a faster rate and catch up with the upper part of the skeleton (Sinclair, 1978). The genetic contribution to the length and thickness of the long bones in the body has been estimated to be approximately 60 percent (Malina & Bouchard, 1991).

The Feet

The feet of the normal newborn infant are proportionately longer and thinner than those of older children. The toddler's feet are somewhat chubbier and wider than the feet of older children. The bottom typically appears flat because of external fullness of the foot pad.

Since the ankle joints are very flexible, the toes may appear to be turned too far in or out. Intoeing, a condition in which the front part of the entire foot turns in, is a common problem in young infants. This condition can result from confinement in the uterus, sleeping on the stomach, or genetic predisposition. When the baby begins to stand and walk, the problem tends to correct itself. In some cases, however, an orthopedic exam and corrective treatment treatment may be necessary (Behrman & Vaughan, 1983).

Muscles

The muscle tissue makes up about 20 to 25 percent of an infant's weight at birth. The newborn's muscle fibers are small, watery, and underdeveloped. As the baby grows, the proportion of water in the muscles decreases as protein and other substances are added. These changes result in an increase in strength and stamina. Growth of the muscle fibers is influenced by nutrition, hormones, metabolism, exercise, and health (Valadian & Porter, 1977).

Scientists generally believe that the total number of muscle fibers the human body needs are present at birth or develop shortly afterward (Tanner, 1990). Muscle fibers become longer and thicker throughout infancy and childhood. Muscles grow at about twice the rate of bones. Following the cephalocaudal principle, the muscles in the top part of the body develop a little faster than those in the lower part of the body.

Skin

A newborn infant usually comes equipped with five complete layers of skin. However, the outer layers are thinner and more delicate. The baby's outer layers of skin are also more loosely connected to the inner layers than are those of an adult. Although all of the sweat glands are present at birth, they function poorly. The glands that produce the oily secretions that form the vernix caseosa covering the baby at birth decrease production and remain relatively inactive until puberty (Lowrey, 1978). The infant's skin is thus normally dry and may flake or peel easily. Diaper rash, heat rash, allergic reactions, and skin infections are common in infants because of their delicate skin (Valadian & Porter, 1977).

In comparison to older children and adults, the skin of an infant contains less pigment (color). Infants of dark-skinned parents thus tend to have lighter skin coloring than they will have at maturity. Pigment in the skin of infants of all races increases throughout the infancy period, but the process proceeds more slowly in children with light skin (Nelms & Mullins, 1982).

Infants have a larger skin surface in proportion to their body weight than adults. Thus, an infant loses more water through the skin and has more potential for heat loss and dehydration than an adult. In proportion to adults, a baby needs more calories for maintaining basal metabolism (Eichorn, 1979).

Teeth

Ordinarily humans grow two sets of teeth in the course of a lifetime. The first set includes twenty teeth that are referred to as the **primary** or **deciduous** teeth. The word deciduous literally means to

"fall off." Primary teeth are also called milk teeth, baby teeth, or temporary teeth. Unfortunately such names may lead parents to mistakenly think that these teeth are not important (Woelfel, 1984). The primary teeth begin to develop beneath the gums as early as the twelfth week of prenatal life. The buds of some of the permanent teeth also begin to form during the fourth or fifth month of the prenatal period (Beedle, 1984).

The development of a tooth begins with a bud that forms the crown and grows downward to form the root. The enamel (outer portion) is formed slightly ahead of the dentin (inner portion). The enamel develops in microscopic layers, comparable to the rings of a tree. Severe nutritional deficits, hormonal imbalances, and prolonged or serious illnesses may disturb the formation or hardening of the teeth. For example, a 30-month-old child who has measles may develop a weakness in the enamel of the permanent teeth that are calcifying at that time.

Usually none of the infant's teeth are visible at birth. The first tooth normally begins to appear around 8 months. The central incisors (front and center teeth) are typically the first teeth to cut through the gums, followed by the lateral incisors. The sequence and approximate ages at which the primary teeth erupt are presented in Figure 5-2. The lower front teeth and second molars tend to cut through the lower jaw before their counterparts are visible in the upper jaw. The lateral incisors, canines, and first molars tend to emerge in the upper jaw earlier than in the lower jaw (Lunt & Law, 1974).

Infants vary considerably in the order, as well as the timetable, of tooth development. Variations of as much as six months from the average dates, either earlier or later, are not unusual (McDonald & Avery, 1983). The 12-month-old typically has six to eight teeth. The 18-month-old has from twelve to fourteen teeth, and the 2-year-old usually has approximately fourteen to sixteen teeth. The complete set of twenty deciduous teeth is present by 30 to 36 months in most infants.

Infants also vary in their responses to teething. Some babies are very cranky and fussy when they are cutting a tooth, whereas other babies appear to be affected very little by the process. Teething usually causes the gums to be sore, but contrary to

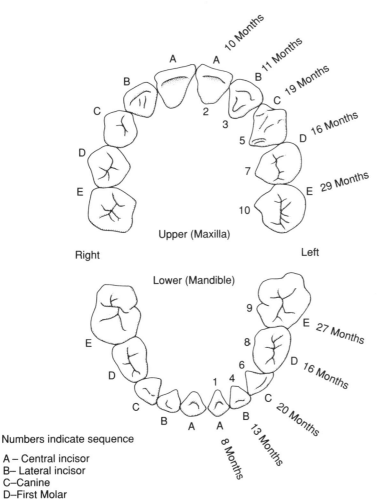

Figure 5-2 Eruption of the Primary Teeth—Age and Sequence.
Data from R. Lunt and D. Law, (1974). A review of the chronology of eruption of deciduous teeth. *Journal of the American dental Association, 89,* 872–879. Used by permission.

popular opinion, teething does not cause fever or diarrhea (Beedle, 1984). Babies try to bite on objects placed in their mouths during this stage. When teeth begin to erupt, the biting behavior may present problems for the nursing mother, who may then decide to wean the baby at that point.

Good dental care is important even for the temporary teeth. These are the only teeth a child will have until around the sixth birthday. Young children need primary teeth for chewing of food, normal appearance, and clear speech. They may reject food needed for a proper diet, such as raw fruits and vegetables, because of missing or decayed teeth. Also, decay and abscess in a primary tooth

may cause the permanent tooth developing beneath it to have a dark spot (Woelfel, 1984). More important, premature loss of primary teeth may result in problems with the timing of the eruption, spacing, and occlusion (bite) of the permanent teeth. An infant should begin regular visits to the dentist by the time all of the primary incisors have erupted, or at least by the age of 2.

BRAIN GROWTH

During the past twenty years, our knowledge of brain growth has grown by leaps and bounds with the development of increasingly sophisticated brain scanning Positron Emission Tomography (PET) technology. Although we have only begun to understand the complexity of brain development, we now know that important and dramatic changes in the structure and function of the brain occur during the infancy period.

The brain of a newborn infant is relatively large and well developed. All major lobes (sections of the brain) are clearly distinguishable. At birth, the brain typically weighs about 1 pound (DeKaban, 1970), which is roughly 15 percent of the newborn's total body weight. The brain is nearest to its adult weight than any other organ of the body, except the eye. At birth, the brain has grown to approximately 25 percent of its mature weight and by 6 months of age, nearly one-half of its adult weight has been obtained. Growth of the brain is slower during the second year, during which it reaches about three-fourths of its mature size (Tanner, 1990).

The tissue of the human brain is made up of basic nerve cells, called **neurons**, supporting cells called **neuroglia**, **myelin**, and various chemical substances. Neurons store information and carry impulses from one part of the body to another. The cell body of each neuron grows treelike branches called **dendrites**, and a longer extension called an **axon**. Dendrites are receptors of nerve impulses, and axons are the transmitters (Fig. 5-3). Dendrites and axons of separate neurons lie close together but do not touch. These connecting gaps, called synapses, are where nerve impulses are passed from one neuron to another by releasing small amounts of chemicals. Several brain chemicals, called **neurotransmitters**, which mediate transmission of impulses between neurons and synapses have been identified (Spreen et al., 1995). Three of the more familiar ones are dopamine, epinephrine, catecholamines. Concentrations of these chemicals rise and fall with brain growth activity and environmental experiences. The brain also uses glucose to perform its functions.

The human brain has more than 100 billion neurons. Recall that around the twentieth week of the prenatal period the total number of neurons the infant will ever have is complete. At this time,

unlike other body cells, they can no longer divide and multiply, or repair themselves if damaged (Dobbing, 1993). Fortunately, the human body produces an excess number of neurons. **Neuroglia (glial)** cells begin forming about the fifteenth prenatal week. Unlike the neurons, glial cells continue to increase in number until maturity of the central nervous system (Spreen et al., 1995). The glial cells, named after the Greek word for glue, make up about one-half of the brain's size and serve as support structures for the neurons. They are smaller and more numerous than neurons and do not carry messages. Once they are formed, nerve cells grow to about 200,000 times their original size. Thus, most postnatal brain growth occurs because of an increase in the size of the neurons, the addition of glial cells, and the proliferation of synaptic connections.

The brain follows an **asynchronous** pattern of growth, which means that different parts of the brain develop at different rates. The lower part of the brain develops and becomes functional before the higher structures. The parts of the brain that control the basic body functions and early reflexive activities are most fully developed at birth. The upper, or cortical, parts of the brain that control voluntary movements, speech, and other cognitive processes, are comparatively undeveloped at birth but grow at a rapid pace throughout infancy.

Synaptogenesis

The formation of synapses, or connections, between the neurons (via their dendrites and axons) is critical to normal brain growth and functioning. Synaptic development continues throughout the life span, but infancy is an important period for the establishment of neurological connections. PET scans show patterns of brain glucose utilization that are consistent with dramatic expansion of synaptic activity during the early months of life (Chugani, 1993).

Between birth and 6 months of age, synaptic development proceeds rather quickly. The sequence coincides with the appearance of various skills. During these early months, there is a tenfold increase in the number of synapses formed in the visual control center of the brain, and the connections needed for sight are essentially complete (Huttenlocher, 1994). Beginning around 2 months of age, synaptogenesis progresses rapidly in the motor cortex areas. Synaptic formation is also rapid during the first 24 months in areas of the brain that control memory functions and emotional development. From birth to 3 years, brain cirucits that are critical for language development are established. Infancy is also an important period for the generation of synaptic connections that establish the foundations for the development of math and logic functions during the childhood years (Begley, 1996; 1997).

The development of neuronal connections in the brain involves both additive and subtractive processes. During the early stages of brain development, an excess number of neurons is produced and eventually eliminated. Similarly, there is evidence of overproduction of synaptic connections among the neurons. By 2 years of age, the infant's brain contains twice as many synapses as the brain of a typical adult (Nash, 1997). After maximum synaptic density is reached in an area of the brain, fine tuning of the brain occurs through the process of synaptic elimination. This "pruning" process begins to take place as early as 6 to 12 months of age (Huttenlocher, 1994).

Scientists are not exactly sure why or how neuronal death and synaptic loss occur. Neurons may die because they do not succeed in forming connections with other neurons (Spreen et al., 1995). Synapse elimination appears to be related to expe-rience. The specific experiences of the infant determine which of the connections survive and which are "pruned." Because humans share a common genetic history of predictable experiences, the newborn's brain apparently sets up synaptic connections that are "experience expectant" (Greenough et al., 1987). That is, the human species has come to anticipate and expect certain experiences in the process of development. Therefore, the brain pathways are ready and waiting for something to happen (e.g. visual or motor activity) within a given time period.

Neurons that are stimulated by sensory and perceptual activities continue to thrive and expand, while those that are not activated do not survive. The "use it" or "lose it" principle is at work here. For example, at birth infants have a large pool of synapses that make it possible to discriminate between sounds common to all human speech (see Chapter 10). However, this ability declines during the first year of life. A possible explanation is that necessary neuronal connections are lost over time because the infant's exposure to sounds is usually limited to those of a specific language (Kolb, 1989).

Myelination

The process of **myelination** is another very important part of brain development. Myelin, a fatty substance produced by the glial cells, forms a sheath around the nerve fibers (see Fig. 5–3). The myelin sheath functions like the insulation on an electric wire to prevent short circuits. It also affects the rate

Figure 5–3 Myelination of a Neuron.
Source: I. Valadian and D. Porter, (1977). *Physical growth and development.* Boston: Little, Brown & Co. p. 134. Copyright by Little, Brown, & Co. 1977. Adapted by permission.

at which impulses travel through the nervous system. The formation of myelin thus makes the neurons more functionally capable and efficient (Spreen et al., 1995). The increase in the myelin content of the brain cells is also accompanied by the addition of connections between neurons.

Apparently, myelin begins to form on the nerve cells in the spinal cord and some areas of the brain before birth. The process continues rapidly during infancy, slowing down after the fourth or fifth year of life. Myelination is not complete in some parts of the nervous system until adulthood. Some scientists believe that myelination is related to the development of specific abilities of an infant. The appearance of specific motor abilities and muscle control thus corresponds with the formation of the myelin sheath in the area of the brain that controls those functions. However, motor abilities and sensory functions may occur without myelination, although they function less efficiently (Spreen et al., 1995).

Lateralization

The brain is divided into various parts, including the hindbrain, midbrain, and forebrain. Each area of the brain is capable of performing specialized functions in controlling body functions and mental processes. The largest part of the brain is the cerebral cortex. It surrounds the inner parts of the brain like a cap or helmet. The cortex controls thinking, memory, and language. Since the cortical areas of the brain are the last to stop growing, they are most susceptible to postnatal environmental influences (Suomi, 1982).

The cortex is divided into two hemispheres, left and right, that basically match each other in size and appearance. The cerebral hemispheres are physically connected and interact with each other, but perform different functions. For example, scientists believe the left half of the brain controls such functions as speech and language, verbal memory, mathematical reasoning, and positive emotions. The right hemisphere controls visual memory, musical functions, sense of direction, and negative emotions (Kolb & Whishaw, 1990). The process by which the different hemispheres of the brain

take on special functions is called **lateralization**. Even though certain areas of the brain appear to be highly specialized in their functions, the brain is remarkably adaptable and capable of recovery from injury. For example, very young children who suffer strokes or other brain injuries can still develop into fully functioning adults (Nash, 1997).

Critical Periods

Scientists have tried to identify critical periods of very rapid brain growth, sometimes referred to as brain growth spurts. Recall from Chapter 2 that the third through the sixteenth prenatal weeks are considered to be a critical period for brain development. During this period the brain is particularly vulnerable to teratogenic influences because the brain cells, particularly the neurons, are in a delicate stage of formation. Some scientists have identified a second critical period beginning during late fetal life and continuing through early infancy, when the brain cells increase in size and complexity (Dobbing, 1976). However, not all scientists agree about the peak, or critical periods, especially for postnatal brain growth. Epstein (1978) has proposed that postnatal brain growth occurs mainly during two periods—3 to 10 months of age and 2 to 4 years of age.

Effects of Environment and Experience

Regardless of when brain growth spurts occur, scientists generally agree that environmental hazards that are encountered at that time are likely to cause problems. Adverse environmental conditions may result in permanent reduction in brain size, total number of brain cells, quantity and complexity of cell connections, chemical composition, and functional capacity of the brain. Deprivation of oxygen, essential nutrients, or the presence of harmful chemicals, bacteria, or viruses are some of the environmental hazards that can cause brain damage. Deprivation of important environmental stimulation can also have negative impact on brain development.

The evidence for "experience dependent" critical periods in brain centers that control vision is strongest in studies using animals as subjects. For example, kittens deprived of light during the critical period of brain development beginning around one month after birth experience permanent damage to the visual system of the brain if they are kept in the dark for 2 months (Hubel & Wiesel, 1970). Although similar experiments cannot be performed with human infants, scientists believe that the development of the human visual system would be seriously damaged if deprived of appropriate experience during the first 2 years of life (Spreen et al., 1995).

The importance of environmental stimulation is seen in a series of studies of rats exposed to different levels of stimulation (Rosenzweig, Bennett & Diamond, 1972). In one group, rats were reared in an environmentally complex environment with various play objects, while another group of rats were reared in cages with nothing but food and water. The rats exposed to the enriched environment were superior to the other rats on problem-solving tasks. The environmentally enriched rats also had several regions of the cerebral cortex that were heavier and thicker, with larger neurons and more neuroglial cells. Subsequent research has also found that rats raised in an enriched environment develop a greater number of synaptic connections (Greenough et al., 1987).

Recent research investigations extend the findings of animal studies on early experience and brain development to human infants. PET images of the brains of infants reared in Romanian orphanages from birth show the devastating effects of extreme deprivation in infancy (Begley, 1997). The temporal lobes, which receive sensory information and regulate emotions, were extremely underdeveloped in comparison to the brains of children who were reared in family environments. The orphanage-reared children suffered cognitive disabilities and emotional problems stemming from neglect and impoverished living conditions.

Evidence is thus rapidly accumulating to show that appropriate environmental stimulation is essential for the growth and maintenance of synapses that affect the complexity of the nervous system. However, the amount, type, and quality of the stimulation is crucial. "If the normal pattern of experience occurs, a normal pattern of neural organization

results. If an abnormal pattern of experience occurs, an abnormal neural organization pattern results" (Greenough et al., 1987, p. 544). Consistent and repetitive activities rather than infrequent experiences build the brain's circuitry. Certain types of experiences are more beneficial than others. For example, the stimulation infants receive from listening to TV is apparently less effective in producing language development than parent talk (Begley, 1997). Overstimulation may be as detrimental to brain development as understimulation. Most infants receive adequate experience for normal brain development through "average" experience and do not need "super" enrichment.

CARDIOVASCULAR SYSTEM

Heart

Growth of the heart during the first four to six weeks after birth is very slow. Following this period, the heart grows steadily and rapidly throughout infancy. At the end of the first year, the weight of the heart has doubled; by the second year it has tripled (Moore, 1978). The shape of the heart also matures rapidly. At birth, both sides of the heart are about the same size. After birth, the left side of the heart typically grows more rapidly than the right side (Malina & Bouchard, 1991). By the second or third year of life, the outline of the infant's heart is very similar to that of an adult (Lowrey, 1978).

The heart rate of the newborn infant is rapid and subject to wide fluctuations. The 120 to 140 beats per minute is about twice the normal rate of an adult. The heart rate decreases to about 110 beats per minute between 1 and 2 years, and to 105 beats per minute between 2 years and 4 years of age (Stangler, Huber, & Routh, 1980). Heart rates are more variable in infants than in adults, and heart murmurs are common. In most cases, such murmurs do not indicate a serious problem and usually disappear by age 1 (Lowrey, 1978). There are no sex differences in heart rate averages during infancy, although slight differences appear at around 10 years of age (Malina & Bouchard, 1991).

Blood Pressure

Normally blood pressure increases throughout infancy. The blood pressure of the full-term newborn is 75/50 as compared with the typical 100/60 of an infant 2 to 4 years of age (Stangler et al., 1980). Premature infants typically have lower blood pressure readings than full-term infants. Blood pressure is more variable in infants than in adults. However, some of the variability reported in blood pressure is probably a result of the difficulty of obtaining accurate and consistent measurements. Some of the fluctuations may be attributed to rapid shifts in infant states, such as sleeping or crying, which tend to cause the blood pressure to change.

EVALUATING PHYSICAL GROWTH

Records of an infant's height, weight, head circumference, and height:weight ratio should be maintained and compared periodically with normative growth standards. Various tables and growth charts are available for this purpose, but the tables and growth curves produced by the National Center for Health Statistics—or NCHS (1976) are the best ones currently available. The charts are based on a large number of healthy, well-nourished infants and children in the United States. Although the NCHS charts do not represent much of the world's population, the World Health Organization has adopted them as the international standard of growth for the first 5 years of life. The growth status of any infant can be compared with that of other children of the same sex and age. There are other specialized charts available for assessing the growth status of infants and children affected by Down, Turner, and Klinefelter syndromes and achondroplasia, a form of short-limbed dwarfism (Needham, 1996).

The child's status is interpreted according to percentile rankings. Various measurements can be plotted on a growth-curve chart (see Appendices 1-4, pages 322–325), which gives a graphic illustration of the child's relative standing in comparison to that of other infants of the same age. To use one of the charts, find and point with one index finger to the child's weight in the vertical column. With the other index finger, point to the child's age in the horizontal row. Move the two fingers along the two lines until they meet. The intersection represents the child's percentile ranking. Measurements should be plotted at three- to six-month intervals throughout infancy to obtain the growth curve.

The middle line, or 50th percentile, in each chart represents the median or standard value and is a commonly used point of reference. Infants with measurements between the 25th and 75th percentiles are considered to be growing normally. Rankings between the 10th and 25th percentiles or between the 75th and 90th percentiles may or may not represent typical growth. Infants who fall above the 95th percentile or below the 5th percentile, or whose growth drops down more than 2 percentiles, should be evaluated for nutritional, health, or other problems that might be affecting their growth trajectory (Needham, 1996; Stangler et al., 1980). Typically, infants and children stay within one or two growth channels or percentile lines on the growth chart. However, during the first 2 years of life many infants dramatically shift percentile rankings upward or downward as their growth trajectory "catches up" or "lags down" to their genetic potential. Thus, many infants who are growing as they should fall outside the 5th and 95th percentiles (Needham, 1996).

FACILITATING PHYSICAL GROWTH

The infant's basic physical needs include food, elimination, warmth, sleep, rest, exercise, cleanliness, health, and safety. As long as caregivers consistently meet these basic needs, infants usually grow to fulfill their full genetic body-size potential. Facilitating physical development thus means routinely providing adequate nutrition, bathing, diapering, dressing, and sleep and rest periods for an infant (Gonzalez-Mena & Eyer, 1980). In addition, regular health-maintenance checkups (including appropriate dental care) and prompt medical treatment for illnesses are extremely important.

The infant's social, emotional, and other psychological needs are closely linked to the physical needs. Therefore, the manner and attitude with which caregivers meet the infant's physical needs are important. Infant caregivers should not be aloof or indifferent as they provide routine physical care. Rather, parents and other caregivers should touch, cuddle, and talk to the infant in tender, loving ways as they meet basic physical needs.

SUMMARY

1. Physical growth is influenced by a variety of environmental factors. The factors discussed in this chapter are socioeconomic class, illness, culture, race, emotional disturbances, and hormonal influences.

2. The three major indicators of body growth are height, weight, and head circumference. Male infants usually weigh a little more and are slightly taller than female infants at birth and throughout the infancy period. Infants normally double their birthweight during the first four or five months, triple it by the end of the first year, and quadruple it during the second year of life. Infants usually increase their birth length by 50 percent during the first year and an additional 24 percent during the second year of life. Taller than average 2-year-olds generally grow to be taller than average children and adults, but there are many exceptions.

3. The average head circumference increases from 13.75 inches at birth to approximately 19 inches by the end of two years. Two soft spots, called fontanels, may be felt on the newborn infant's head. The fontanel on the back of the head is usually closed by 3 or 4 months of age. The larger fontanel in front is closed by approximately 20 months of age.

4. The infant's facial features are broader and flatter in appearance than an adult's. The lower jaw is underdeveloped and receded. The eyes are the most noticeable feature of an infant's face because of the relatively small nose. The infant's eye color tends to darken during the early months of life.

5. The ear canal of the newborn is shallow and straight. The tympanic membrane (ear drum) is not completely closed and lies at a horizontal angle. During the first three years of life, the tympanic membrane closes and assumes a more mature verticle position as the ear canal gradually changes to the adult S-shape.

6. The infant's feet are proportionately thinner and longer than those of older children, but the feet of toddlers are somewhat chubbier and wider.

7. Muscle tissue makes up about one-fourth of the newborn baby's weight. As the baby grows, the muscle fibers become longer and thicker.

8. A newborn infant comes equipped with five complete layers of skin but the outer layers are thin and delicate. The infant's skin is dry and may flake or peel easily. In comparison to older children and adults, the skin of an infant contains less pigment (color).

9. The infant's deciduous teeth begin to develop as early as the twelfth prenatal week. The first tooth, however, is not visible until approximately eight months after birth. The complete set of twenty temporary teeth is usually present by 30 to 36 months.

10. The brain of the newborn infant is relatively large and well developed, but continues to grow rapidly during infancy, reaching 75 percent of its mature size by the end of two years. The infant brain may be especially vulnerable to environmental disturbances. Brain growth after birth consists primarily of increases in the size of the neurons, the growth and formation of neuroglial cells, the formation of synaptic connections, and the myelination of the nerve cells.

11. The formation of synapses, or connections, between the neurons is critical to brain functioning. Infancy is an important period for the establishment of synaptic connections. The development of the neuronal connections in the brain involves both additive and subtractive processes. As the baby grows, the different parts of the brain become more specialized through the process of lateralization.

12. Some scientists believe that the embryonic and early fetal period, and the period from late fetal life through early infancy are critical periods for brain development. Scientists generally agree that environmental conditions, including sensorimotor experiences, play a major role in the formation of synaptic connections in the brain.

13. The heart of the infant grows rapidly during infancy and triples in size by the second year. The

heart rate gradually decreases, while the blood pressure increases during infancy.

14. Standardized growth charts can be used to monitor an infant's height, weight, and head circumference. Infants who are ranked above the 95th percentile or below the 5th percentile on one or more aspects of growth should receive further evaluation. If the basic physical needs of infants are adequately met, they are likely to fulfill their genetic potential for body growth.

15. Caregivers can facilitate an infant's physical development by consistently providing adequate nutrition, routine physical care, sleep and rest periods, regular health-maintenance checkups, prompt medical treatment for illnesses, and emotional nurture.

6

Health and Safety

Eat no green apples or you'll droop
  Be careful not to get the croup
  Avoid the chickenpox and such
  And don't fall out the window much.
    —Edward Anthony

From the beginning of life, infants are confronted with countless hazards that threaten their health and well being. Numerous viruses, bacteria, and other microorganisms can invade an infant's body resulting in reactions ranging from the common cold to life-threatening infections such as acquired immune deficiency syndrome. Infants are also confronted with a plethora of safety hazards, such as poisons and unsafe toys, as they explore their world. Unfortunately, we have to add abusive treatment and neglect to the list of obstacles that potentially threaten the survival of many infants.

In the first part of this chapter we consider the immunizations and other precautionary measures that can be taken to protect infants and prevent the spread of deadly communicable diseases. We will look at the major symptoms of illness in infants along with some of the "garden-variety" and life-threatening illnesses for which no permanent immunizations are available. We also consider the horrors of child abuse and neglect, including treatment and preventive measures. The second part of this chapter is devoted to a discussion of the leading causes of death due to unintentional injuries among infants and how such injuries can be controlled.

IMMUNITY DURING INFANCY

Infants are more susceptible to infectious diseases because of the relative immaturity of the immune system. Newborn infants have some resistance to a number of infectious diseases because of the antibodies they receive from the mother during the prenatal period. The mother may be immune to communicable diseases such as diphtheria, German measles, mumps, and polio because she has had either the disease or a vaccine (Reinisch & Minear, 1978). Even so, newborns are especially vulnerable to infection. If the mother does not have

immunity against the disease, no protection can be passed on to the baby. In addition, the newborn's immune system is relatively immature and does not provide the same level of protection against most diseases as adults.

Infants are especially vulnerable to infections between 6 months and 2 years of age. Most immunities received from the mother are gone by 6 to 12 months of age. Infants may then become more vulnerable because their immune systems are still not sufficiently mature to fight off many organisms. Also, they have not had sufficient exposure to accumulate a repertoire of antibodies in combating many common infections. Fortunately, infants do not have to fight the battle alone. There are hundreds of antibiotic and therapeutic drugs to help fight off most infectious microorganisms and other diseases, in addition to vaccines available to protect infants against some of the serious contagious illnesses. By 3 years of age the immune system is much more mature (Anderson et al., 1994).

IMMUNIZATIONS AGAINST COMMUNICABLE DISEASES

Through the years, a number of vaccines have been developed to provide immunity against many of the life-threatening communicable diseases infants and young children face in growing up. Routine immunization of infants and young children has dramatically decreased the rates of serious illness and death from infectious diseases. Immunization is begun early in life so that the baby will have time to build up the level of protection necessary to avoid getting the diseases. Currently, vaccines are available to protect infants against ten infectious diseases.

Immunization against specific communicable diseases is required in all 50 states before a child can enter school or a child care program. Unfortunately, many infants do not get their vaccinations early enough to prevent the outbreak and spread of the diseases. On a worldwide basis, 2 million children die each year because of measles; 600,000 die because of whooping cough. Nearly 1 million newborn infants die each year from tetanus contracted through the umbilical cord incision, and

30,000 to 50,000 are crippled because of polio (Colburn, 1986). Current estimates indicate that only 37 to 56 percent of 2-year-olds in the United States have received the recommended vaccines (Centers for Disease Control, 1995). A top priority of the U.S. Department of Health and Human Services is to immunize 90 percent of the nations' 2-year-olds by the year 2000 (National Center for Health Statistics, 1995).

Immunization Schedule

Recommendations and guidelines for the immunization of infants and young children are based on medical knowledge, judgments of public health officials and doctors, and the availability of safe and effective vaccines. The list of vaccines infants should have, and when they should be obtained is revised as new scientific information becomes available. The schedule currently recommended for the routine immunization of healthy infants is given in Table 6-1. Delays and deviations from the schedule

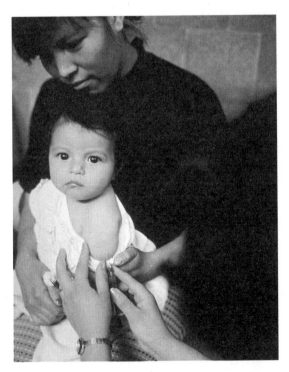

This baby is being prepared for an immunization.

may be recommended by an infant's doctor because of health concerns, reactions to previous immunizations, or other individual needs. It is extremely important for parents to obtain the complete series of immunizations for an infant as recommended by a health-care professional to establish the maximum level of immunity.

In addition to the regularly scheduled immunizations, a tuberculin skin test (PPD) is usually administered at 1 year of age, or earlier, if an infant has been exposed to tuberculosis (TB). If the test is positive, a chest X-ray will be made to determine whether or not the baby actually has an active case of the disease. If TB is evident, the baby will be treated with medications (Shelov, 1994). A vaccine to prevent TB is used in some countries with high rates of the disease and limited health-care facilities. This vaccine is not currently used in the United States because of the low incidence of TB and questions about the effectiveness of the vaccine (Anderson et al., 1994).

The immunization schedule no longer includes routine vaccination for smallpox. Fortunately, smallpox has disappeared to the extent that it is no longer considered a threat throughout the world. Actually, health officials consider the risk of complications from the smallpox vaccine to outweigh the risk of catching the disease. If 95 percent or more of infants and children worldwide can be immunized, it may be possible to virtually eliminate many other communicable diseases as well (Gold, 1996).

Some of the vaccines such as diphtheria, tetanus, pertussis (DTP), and haemophilus type b (HIB) are combined and given in a single injection. One advantage of this practice is that the baby has to be stuck with a needle only once instead of four times. The practice also saves time and is therefore less expensive. The use of combined vaccines and the administration of a series of vaccines during the same visit has been found to be as safe and effective as dispensing vaccines in individual doses (CDC, 1995).

Adverse Reactions

Although modern vaccines are extremely safe and effective, there is a slight risk of side effects with all

Table 6-1 Recommended Immunization Schedule (Birth-6 Years) — United States*

VACCINE	BIRTH	1 MO	2 MO	4 MOS	6 MOS	12 MOS	15 MOS	18 MOS	4-6 YRS
Hepatitis B (Hp-B)	Hep-B	Hep-B	Hep-B		Hep-B				
Diphtheria (D); Tetanus (T); Pertussis (aP or P)[1]			DTaP	DTaP	DTaP		DTaP or DTP		DtaP or DTP
Haemophilus influenzae type b (Hib)[2]			Hib	Hib	Hib	Hib			
Polio[3]			IPV	IPV		OPV	OPV		OPV
Measles-Mumps-Rubella (MMR)						MMR			MMR
Varicella (Var)							Var		

*Recommended vaccines are listed under the routinely recommended ages. Shaded bars indicate range of acceptable ages for vaccination. The schedule was approved by the Advisory Committee on Immunization Practices, the American Academy of Pediatrics, and the American Academy of Family Physicians. It is effective for 1997 but is subject to change. Check with a physician or a local Department of Health for updates.

[1]Two types of pertussis vaccine are currently available (aP and P). The newer type of acellular (killed) pertussis vaccine (aP) is the type currently preferred for all doses.

[2]Three Hib vaccines are available for use. If type PRP-OMP (MERCK) is administered at 2 and 4 months of age, a dose at 6 months is not required.

[3]Two polio vaccines are currently available for use: inactivated poliovirus vaccine (IPV) and oral polio vaccine (OPV). The IPV type is currently recommended for the first two doses while the OPV is recommended for subsequent doses. However, parents and physicians may choose OPV or IPV for all doses.

Source: Centers for Disease Control (1997). Recommended childhood immunization schedule - United States, January - December, 1997. *Morbidity and Mortality Weekly Report, 46,* 35-37.

of these substances. Minor reactions, such as a fever, swelling around the site of the injection, and general discomfort for a few hours are common. However, the possibility of more severe complications has been associated with some of the vaccines. The greatest concern centers around the potential risk of the polio and the pertussis (whooping cough) vaccines.

Polio. There are two types of vaccine available for immunization against polio: oral polio vaccine (OPV) and inactivated polio vaccine (IPV). Both vaccines increase immunity to polio, but only the OPV prevents a person from carrying and possibly spreading the virus. OPV is more potent because it induces immunity in the intestines where the virus multiplies (CDC, 1995). However, use of the OPV is controversial because it causes an average of 8 cases of paralytic polio each year out of 4 million doses given in the United States. IPV is made from a killed virus and carries no risk of polio.

In order to reduce the risk that infants will acquire polio from the OPV vaccine, health officials currently recommend replacing the first two doses of OPV with the safer inactivated vaccine (CDC, 1997). The first two doses IPV are used to boost immunity to the virus before the more potent oral vaccine is given (see Table 6–1). Infants are more likely to get polio from the first dose of OPV than subsequent doses. Two OPV doses are still recommended between 1 and 6 years of age.

Pertussis. The pertussis vaccine has also generated negative publicity because adverse effects on the central nervous system are occasionally reported after a child has received this vaccine. In response to concerns about the safety of the pertussis vaccinations, a newer type of this vaccine has been developed and approved for use in the DTP vaccination schedule (see Table 6-1). This type of vaccine (referred to as aP for "acellular pertussis") is safer because it is made with only part of the pertussis germ instead of the entire bug.

The new acelluar pertussis vaccine is the preferred vaccine for all 4 doses in the series (see Table 6–1). However, the older whole-cell vaccine continues to be an acceptable alternative. Regardless of which vaccine is used, the benefits of the protection far outweigh any risks associated with immunization.

Newer Vaccines

Varicella (Chickenpox). Varicella, commonly called chickenpox, is a relatively mild, highly contagious disease caused by the varicella zoster virus. Nearly everyone in the United States who is not immunized will develop chickenpox. Most cases of chickenpox occur among children between 2 and 10 years of age (Gershon & LaRussa, 1992). Chickenpox causes itchy blisters that may spread over most of the body and in some of the mucous membranes, depending on the severity of the infection. Other symptoms include fever and headaches. Complications from chickenpox in otherwise healthy infants are uncommon, but can be serious. The greatest risk is for infants under 1 year of age and older adults. The most common complications include bacterial skin infections, pneumonia, encephalitis, meningitis dehydration, and hepatitis. Complications from chickenpox currently result in 50 to 100 deaths each year, but the number of deaths has declined in recent years due to the availability of better medical treatment (Holmes et al., 1996).

Treatment of chickenpox depends upon the age and general health of the infected child. In most cases, medication to control itching and fever is all that is required. Aspirin should be avoided because of the risk of Reye syndrome. An antiviral drug called acyclovir is sometimes used to treat severe cases of chickenpox, especially when a child has other health problems. After many years of scientific research, a safe and effective vaccine has been approved for use in the prevention of varicella. In 1996, the Varicella Zoster Virus Vaccine was added to the list of recommended immunizations for children ages 12 to 18 months or older who have not had the disease (Holmes et al., 1996). This vaccine is not currently required and is offered on an optional basis.

Haemophilus Influenzae Type B. Although **haemophilus type b (HIB)** is not as well known, it is more dangerous than most other childhood diseases. HIB has been compared with paralytic polio in the seriousness of its effects (Clements, 1992). HIB occurs most frequently, and is most serious, among infants between six months and one year of age. In 1985 a vaccine was introduced to protect two-year-old infants against this disease. Currently, there are three types of Hib vaccines licensed for use with infants (CDC, 1997). Infants typically receive 4 doses of a Hib vaccine by 12 months of age (see Table 6–1).

Before the availability of an effective vaccine, HIB was the most common cause of meningitis in infants and children, and a major cause of pneumonia, severe infections of the skin, throat, ears, joints, and blood stream (Anderson et al., 1994). Approximately 3 percent of infants and children who are infected with HIB in the United States die, while many others suffer permanent brain damage, hearing loss, mental disability, or learning problems (Clements, 1992). The use of the HIB vaccines is expected to result in a dramatic decline in the incidence of this devastating disease.

Hepatitis

The term **hepatitis** refers to an inflammation of the liver caused by viruses, toxic substances, or drugs (Anderson et al., 1994). Most cases of hepatitis are caused by one of five different viruses that enter through the mouth and make their way into the bloodstream (Krugman et al., 1992). The most common forms of hepatitis that infect infants are type A and type B (Anderson et al., 1994). Hepatitis A is typically a mild illness in infants. Only about 25 percent of infected infants display any symptoms (Townsend, 1993). Hepatitis B is less contagious and therefore less common among infants and young children. However, Hepatitis B is more serious because the virus can continue in the body and eventually cause chronic infections, cancer, or cirrhosis of the liver. Symptoms of both Hepatitis A and B infections are similar and include fever, diarrhea, a general sick feeing, dark urine, light colored stools, and jaundice (Anderson et al., 1994; Townsend, 1993).

Hepatitis A is extremely contagious in group child-care situations, especially in large day-care centers with infants under 2 years of age. This infection spreads primarily from contact with feces during the diaper changing process. Lack of sanitation, particularly hand washing, is one of the major factors contributing to its spread. Hepatitis B is mainly transmitted through infected blood products and through saliva to a lesser extent. Since 1991, a series of 3 vaccinations for Hepatitis B has been recommended for all infants (CDC, 1997). The first dose is usually given during the newborn period (see Table 6–1). Currently, scientists are working to develop a vaccine for Hepatitis A (Townsend, 1993). With proper treatment, serious complications from these forms of hepatitis are rare.

SYMPTOMS OF ILLNESS IN INFANTS

Numerous symptoms accompany illness in infants. Some of the more common symptoms parents and other caregivers should attend to include general discomfort (malaise), loss of appetite, vomiting, congestion, runny nose, fever, cough, diarrhea, skin rash, listlessness, crying, and irritability. An infant may exhibit one or more of the symptoms, and the symptoms could be caused by one problem or a combination of problems. Generally, parents tend to be most concerned about fever, vomiting, and diarrhea.

Fever

A temperature higher than 100°F (37.5 C) by mouth, or 101°F (38 C) by rectum is usually considered to be a **fever** (Schmitt & Roxann, 1994). The degree of fever is not always a good indication of the extent of an illness, especially for infants younger than 2 or 3 months of age. Infants tend to have a higher temperature in response to illness than older children (Shelov, 1994). Although fever in an infant should always be considered important, it is often dramatic without being serious. Even high fevers in the range of 104° to 105°F (oral) may not be harmful.

The most frequent causes of fever in infants

under 2 years of age are upper respiratory infections, viruses, gastroenteritis, and ear infections. Examples of more serious, but less common, illnesses that cause fever are septicemia (infection in the blood) and pneumonia (McCarthy, 1979). A major concern associated with fever in young children is the danger of convulsions resulting in brain damage. The risk of convulsions is the greatest between 6 months and 5 years of age (Shelov, 1994). However, only around 4 percent of children with fever develop convulsions (Schmitt & Roxann, 1994).

Parents should call a doctor if an infant is (1) younger than 3 months and has a rectal temperature of 100.2°F or higher; (2) between 3 and 6 months of age and has a rectal temperature of 101°F or higher; (3) older than 6 months and has a fever of 103°F or higher (Shelov, 1994). However, parents are advised to avoid "fever phobia"—the tendency of over anxious parents to treat low-grade fevers with unnecessary medications (Schmitt & Roxann, 1994). Parents should avoid giving aspirin to a baby with a fever because aspirin is linked with a very serious illness called Reye syndrome that can result in damage to the brain or liver, or death.

Vomiting

Some infants vomit easily and frequently; others vomit only in response to extreme stomach distress. Vomiting may result from one or more of a long list of causes, ranging from food reactions to motion to viral infections. The decision about when to seek medical attention is not always clear. Generally parents are advised to contact a doctor if any of the following apply:

1. The baby vomits repeatedly.
2. Vomiting is accompanied by diarrhea, a fever, or convulsions.
3. The baby has ingested something unusual that may be poisonous.
4. Vomiting is preceded by a fall or blow to the head.
5. There are indications of stomach pain or other discomfort.
6. Vomiting episodes extend beyond 24 hours.
7. Blood or bile (greenish material) appears in the vomit (Shelov, 1994).

One of the main dangers associated with vomiting is dehydration. To prevent this from happening, the child should be given water and other fluids as recommended by the doctor. Parents should obtain advice from their health-care provider during the first well-child checkup about guidelines and procedures to follow when the child vomits.

Diarrhea

Diarrhea is defined as an increase in the frequency, fluidity, and volume of bowel movements. One or two watery bowel movements a day is not unusual for an infant, but three to five is considered mild diarrhea. Diarrhea is one of the most frequent problems encountered by infants and young children. During the first three years of life, an infant is likely to experience at least one to three severe episodes of significant diarrhea (Gellis & Kagan, 1986).

Viruses are the most frequent cause of diarrhea in infants under 2, especially during the winter months. Other causes of diarrhea are bacteria, side effects from oral medications, or parasitic infections (Shelov, 1994). Food is usually not the source of the problem in most severe cases of infant diarrhea in the United States. However, dietary changes sometimes result in mild diarrhea. The symptoms usually subside in 72 hours. Diarrhea is often preceded or accompanied by other symptoms, such as respiratory congestion or a cough (Gellis & Kagan, 1986). An infant is in danger of dehydration if severe diarrhea continues. The risk of dehydration is increased if diarrhea is accompanied by vomiting.

Diarrhea is the leading cause of death among children in undeveloped countries, accounting for 23 percent of the deaths of children under 5 years of age (United Nations Children's Fund, 1996). **Oral rehydration therapy** is a simple but highly effective means of treating diarrhea. Infants who show signs of dehydration are given a special solution to drink containing water, salt, glucose, and other ingredients to replace fluid losses. The World Health Organization (1985) operates oral rehydration therapy programs in undeveloped countries for preventing infant mortality due to diarrhea.

COMMON ILLNESSES OF INFANTS

While many of the life-threatening infectious diseases of infants can be controlled through immunizations, there are numerous other illnesses and health problems which cannot be. It is not possible in this chapter to consider all the diseases to which infants are susceptible, but some of the disorders that occur most frequently are briefly discussed. Parents should obtain a medical guide such as The American Academy of Pediatrics' *Caring for Your Baby and Young Child* (Shelov, 1994) or *Dr. Spock's Baby and Child Care* (Spock & Rothenberg, 1992). The American Academy of Pediatrics recommends that parents take an infant to a doctor at least 8 times before age 2 for checkups, immunizations, and screening for disabilities. Annual checkups are recommended after 2 years of age (Shelov, 1994).

Colds and Respiratory Infections

Infections of the respiratory tract include a wide variety of problems ranging from the common cold to severe pneumonia. This class of diseases represents by far the most frequent illnesses of childhood in the United States. Most infants have 8 to 10 colds in the first two years of life (Shelov, 1994). Infants who attend a group child-care facility have more colds and other infectious illnesses than other infants (see Chapter 14). More than 150 different viruses have been identified as possible causes of colds and coldlike illnesses. Infants are more likely than adults to have a fever with a cold (Marks, 1985). They have special difficulty with the nasal congestion caused by a cold because of the inability to blow their nose and clear the nasal passage. Furthermore, very young infants are often instinctive nose breathers and have a great deal of difficulty breathing through the mouth when the nasal passage is obstructed. The main concern about colds is not so much the cold itself, but the potential side effects, such as ear and throat infections, bronchitis, and pneumonia. Although there is no prevention or cure for the common cold, secondary infections can be treated with antibiotics.

Ear Infections

Inflammation of the middle ear, **otitis media**, is the most common infectious illness of childhood in the United States. Approximately 85 percent of all U.S. infants have at least one middle-ear infection before they are 3 years old (Arnold, 1996). The highest incidence is in children 6 to 24 months of age (Shelov, 1994). Otitis media is found more frequently among male infants, lower socioeconomic groups, Native Americans, infants with cleft palate or other craniofacial anomalies, and those with allergic rhinitis (Arnold, 1996).

Otitis media is a secondary infection caused by bacteria that are usually not associated with the primary illness. Streptococcus, pneumonia, and haemophilus influenzae are the most common infecting bacteria. The infection produces a sticky fluid that may gradually accumulate because the tubal passage tends to be swollen and blocked. The symptoms include earache, fever, drainage, and hearing impairment in those who have recurrent infections. However, infants cannot be relied on to give direct signs that they have otitis media. They tend to give only general signs of distress, such as irritability, crying, and loss of appetite. Some infants and toddlers may rub their ears or stop babbling or talking as much. The condition may persist for weeks without any signs of ear pain or other symptoms. Otitis media usually clears up within a week or two of treatment with antibiotics. In some cases fluid build-up in the middle ear may persist after ear aches and other signs or symptoms are gone. This condition is referred to as **otitis media with effusion**. In persistent cases, tubes, resembling small buttons, may be inserted into the ear to promote drainage of fluid (Klein, 1992). Chronic ear infections may cause hearing loss, which can interfere with language acquisition and/or cognitive and social development.

Pneumonia

The term **pneumonia** is used to refer to a variety of reactions of the lungs to infectious and noninfectious agents (Walter & Shurin, 1992). There are several types of pneumonia which vary with the location and extent of the affected lung. Approximately 80 percent of all pneumonia cases occur among children under 7 years of age, with the peak incidence in 2- to 4-year-olds. Boys are more susceptible to pneumonia than girls (Marks, 1985).

Pneumonia is usually caused by bacteria and viral infections, but it may also result from ingesting fungi, food, powder, or other foreign substances into the lungs. Infants who have pneumonia develop a cough and have difficulty breathing. Fever is usually present. With modern medical treatment, death and long-term complications are rare. However, pneumonia can be life threatening to infants and toddlers who have nervous system disorders or other health problems that tend to affect the breathing mechanism or immune system.

Croup

Respiratory viruses often produce an infection of the air passages leading to the lungs. This condition is commonly referred to as **croup**. The swelling and irritation result in hoarseness, labored breathing, and the characteristic cough, which has been compared to the bark of a seal (Marks, 1985). Croup is usually accompanied by symptoms common to all infectious diseases, such as general discomfort, loss of appetite, and fever. Croup occurs mostly in infants between 6 months and 3 years of age and is seen mainly between October and March (Shelov, 1994).

Croup can be very frightening to children and to parents because of severe coughing and breathing difficulties. The disease is rarely life threatening unless it goes untreated. Doctors typically treat mild croup by adding moisture to the air to aid breathing. More serious and complicated cases may be treated with medications as indicated by the originating infection. The most severe cases may require hospitalization (Marks, 1985).

Roseola Infantum

Roseola infantum is a mild disease that affects mainly infants from 6 months to 3 years of age. The disease begins with a high fever which drops after three to five days. A rash of small, discrete

pink spots usually appears on the upper part of the body as the fever subsides. Roseola is believed to be the most common cause of fever and rash in infants under 2 years of age. Approximately 30 percent of all infants develop this disease. Apparently, the only risk it poses to infants is convulsions from the high fever. Roseola is caused by a herpes type virus (Krugman et al., 1992).

Thrush

A common infection that attacks young infants is **thrush**. White patches, resembling milk curds, develop inside the baby's cheeks and on the tongue. The mouth becomes sore, which causes difficulty in sucking and eating. Thrush is caused by yeast (candida), which is a normal and usually harmless inhabitant of the mouth. Infants are particularly susceptible to thrush because of their low immunity and tender skin. Malnutrition, antibiotics, and other drugs can lower the infant's resistance to thrush infections. Newborn infants may develop thrush from the yeast acquired from the birth canal during delivery. Thrush is not serious, but like other yeast infections, it may be difficult to cure. Persistent thrush can be a sign of abnormalities in the immune system (Anderson et al., 1994).

OTHER HEALTH CONCERNS

Diaper Rash

Sooner or later, most infants have diaper rash. The skin covered by the diaper becomes red and irritated. Most cases of diaper rash are mild with no serious risks. However, if untreated, a skin infection can develop. Diaper rash is usually produced by prolonged contact with urine or feces. Soap and detergents left on the skin or in the diapers also contribute to the problem. If the rash lasts more than 72 hours, a type of fungus called candida is likely to invade the skin and make the condition worse (Weston, Lane, & Weston, 1980).

The treatment of diaper rash includes frequent changes of diaper, careful washing, and exposing the affected area to air as much as possible. Protective ointments, antibacterial creams, or anti-yeast preparations are often prescribed. If cloth diapers are used, boiling or soaking them in an antiseptic solution and rinsing them in vinegar may help. The use of boric acid or any ointment containing mercury is not recommended (Weston et al., 1980).

Allergies

An allergic reaction is the body's response to substances that an individual has difficulty tolerating. Substances (allergens) that commonly cause allergic reactions include food, things that are inhaled (pollen, dust, mold, mildew, etc.), things that touch the skin (chemicals, soaps, plants, fabrics, etc.), insect bites, and nonspecific factors such as health and emotions (Crook, 1975). Almost any substance is a potential allergen to someone. Allergic reactions include a runny nose, sneezing, congestion, watering and itching eyes, skin rashes, headaches, and wheezing (asthma). Infections from other diseases interact with allergies so that an allergy may make an infection worse, or an infection may make an allergy worse.

Allergies have been ranked as the sixth-leading cause of doctors' visits for infants under 1 year of age and the fifth-leading cause between 1 and 14 years of age (Allergy Foundation of America, 1971). About one in five infants develops allergies (Leach, 1984). Development of an allergy requires time, so infants usually do not exhibit adverse reactions to substances the first time they are exposed. For example, an infant who becomes allergic to penicillin may receive one course of treatment with the drug without any ill effects. The second or third treatment may make the infant very ill because the body has manufactured antigens to fight off the offending substance. An allergic illness that occurs during the infancy period depends largely upon the environmental factors to which an infant is exposed. (Food allergies are discussed in Chapter 7.)

In infants, allergies most often take the form of eczema. Three-quarters of all childhood eczema cases develop in the first year of life (Price, 1984). The first signs of eczema are bright red, itchy patches of inflamed skin on the cheeks. The rubbing and scratching lead to runny sores on the face

and scalp. In some babies the eczema spreads to other parts of the body. Babies with severe eczema are subject to serious secondary infections (Price, 1984). Allergies also may result in coldlike symptoms including sneezing, runny nose, coughing, headache, and a sore throat.

Colic

Infantile **colic** is one of the most common complaints for which parents seek medical assistance. Approximately 10 to 30 percent of all American babies develop colic (Overby, 1996). The colicky infant is one who cries inconsolably for long periods of time, day in and day out, as if in pain. The cry sounds associated with colic have been described as different from the infant's usual, noncolicky cry. The cry has been described as a loud, high-pitched, intense, piercing, angry scream that may be accompanied by breath holding (Lester et al., 1992). Crying is often accompanied by arching of the back, extending or pulling up the legs, or other agitated motor movements. Other symptoms of colic include an enlarged stomach, increased bowel sounds, spitting up, and difficulty sleeping. Episodes of colic occur most frequently between 6:00 P.M. and midnight. The condition usually begins around 2 weeks of age and may persist for 4 months or longer (Treem, 1994). Health care professionals have found colic difficult to define, explain, and treat.

Reports on possible sources of colic tend to be contradictory and confusing. In general, there is no one condition that causes colic in all babies. Different babies cry excessively for different reasons. In some cases, colic may be caused by an allergic reaction to protein in formula milk or allergens in breast milk. In other cases, the problem may stem from various gastrointestinal problems such as irritable bowel syndrome, esophageal reflux (flowing back of digestive juices into the esophagus), or the production of excessive stomach gas due to the inability to absorb carbohydrates (Treem, 1994). Colic is often attributed to unusual sensitivity of an infant to stimulation (Shelov, 1994). Although there is no conclusive evidence that colic originates from parental stress or anxiety, parents may compound the problem in frustrated efforts to stop the crying.

Attempts to find a cure for colic have been as frustrating to scientists as attempts to find a cause. Recommendations for treating colic vary as widely as explanations of why colic occurs. Apparently breast-feeding does not protect infants from colic since a similar number of breast-fed and formula-fed infants have this problem. Changing the bottle-fed baby's formula, or eliminating cow's milk and other potentially irritating foods from the nursing mother's diet is often recommended. Other methods of eliminating stomach distress include the use of antacids, antiflatulents, or fiber supplements (Treem, 1994). Other treatments that are recommended include swaddling, rocking, walking with the baby in a body carrier, running an appliance (e.g., a vacuum cleaner) that has a rhythmic sound, giving the baby a pacifier, and placing the baby stomach down across your arm or legs (Shelov, 1994). Some pediatricians have found that counseling parents on how to respond to excessive crying can be helpful (Taubman, 1984). Parents should avoid attempts to treat colic that might endanger the child. For example, in one tragic case, a 1-month-old baby died after being exposed to the heat of a hair dryer. The parents had heard that placing a colicky baby near a clothes dryer would have a soothing effect. They apparently thought the hair dryer would work just as well. Babies should not be left unattended in a rocking device or wrapped in heavy blankets that might cause overheating. Parents usually try a number of different things before finding something that helps. In most cases a baby will outgrow colic by 6 months of age.

ACQUIRED IMMUNE DEFICIENCY SYNDROME (AIDS)

Anyone who has watched television or read a newspaper since the early 1980s is familiar with the term **acquired immune deficiency syndrome,** commonly referred to as **AIDS.** This relatively new and terrifying disease results from infection with the human immunodeficiency virus (HIV). Infants acquire HIV from their infected mothers during the prenatal period, the birth process, or during breast-feeding. Infants can also become infected with the HIV virus through blood transfusions. However, this route of transmission has been virtually eliminated in the United States since careful testing and treatment of donated blood began in 1985. The chance of an infant of an infected mother being born with HIV is approximately 20 to 25 percent (Boland & Oleske, 1995). Scientists have found that the risk of prenatal transmission of HIV can be reduced by approximately 30 percent if the mother is treated with antiviral medication (AZT) during pregnancy (Parks, 1996; Fiscus et al., 1996). However, concerns have been expressed about the possibility that infants who are exposed to AZT during the prenatal period may face an increased risk of developing cancer in childhood (Health Watch, 1997).

The HIV virus attacks the immune system and eventually results in acquired immune deficiency syndrome (AIDS). Infants with AIDS are at extremely high risk for infection with many different viruses, bacterial infections, and other disorders. By contrast, such infectious agents pose little or no risk to infants with normal immune systems (Bale, 1990). The onset of AIDS is usually marked by a variety of medical problems. The symptoms include intermittent fevers, recurrent diarrhea, weight loss, and failure to thrive. The liver, spleen, and lymph nodes are often enlarged. As time passes, almost all infants are affected by opportunistic and recurrent infections such as middle ear infections, eye infections, cold sores and thrush in the mouth, pneumonia, herpes, bronchitis, bacterial infections, salmonella, bone and joint infections, and internal organ abscesses (Batshaw & Perret, 1992).

Infants with AIDS do not produce antibodies in response to vaccines for common childhood diseases. Consequently, they are at increased risk for life-threatening complications from episodes of diseases such as measles and mumps. HIV infected infants may also experience a variety of neurologic complications, including central nervous system infections, lymphomas of the brain, strokes, and abnormalities of the peripheral nerves. The neurologic features of AIDS lead to a progressive decline in motor, cognitive, social, and language functions, as well as the development of weakness, spasticity, loss of balance, paralysis, or seizures (Bale, 1990).

In most cases, HIV is dormant for a period of time before AIDS symptoms appear. Approximately 20 percent of infants who are infected with HIV at birth quickly develop full-blown AIDS. In the majority of cases though, the disease progresses more slowly. There is some evidence that the AIDS symptoms appear earlier in infants whose mothers are seriously affected by the disease at the time of delivery (Blancheet al., 1994). Until recently, most HIV infected infants displayed AIDS symptoms by 2 years of age and died by age 6. Currently, the median age at which AIDS is likely to be diagnosed has been estimated to occur at 4.1 years, somewhat later than previous occurrences (Mawhinny & Pagano, 1994).

With recent advances in medical treatments many HIV positive infants survive into their teens (Oleske, 1994). A key discovery has been the effectiveness of combining AIDS medicines. No one of the drugs is effective alone, but used together these drugs apparently deter the HIV virus from reproducing. There is new hope that AIDS will become a chronic manageable disease, or even curable, and that HIV will not necessarily be a death sentence to infants who are infected. Scientists are also more optimistic about eventually finding a vaccine that will effectively prevent the spread of the HIV virus.

SUDDEN INFANT DEATH SYNDROME

On a warm, sunny afternoon Sharyn and Joe sat on their deck while their infant daughter, Lynn, slept in a baby carriage between them. When Joe picked up Lynn a few minutes later, inexplicably she was dead (Hermes, 1981). Similar incidents are repeated all too often throughout the United States. In most cases of this type, the cause of death is attributed to sudden infant death syndrome since no medical reason can be found.

Sudden infant death syndrome, usually referred to as **SIDS,** is defined as the sudden death of any infant under 1 year of age which cannot be

explained by medical history, a complete autoposy, and examination of the death scene (Willinger, James, & Catz, 1991). The terms **cot death** and **crib death** are also used to describe this phenomenon. Although unexplained sudden death has affected infants throughout human history, SIDS was not identified as a medical syndrome until the early 1960s.

During 1993, the most recent year for which data is available, SIDS accounted for 14 percent of the deaths of infants under 1 year of age (U.S. Bureau of the Census, 1996). SIDS is the leading cause of death among infants between 1 month and 1 year of age (Willinger, 1995). The number of SIDS deaths reaches a peak between 2 and 4 months of age with the incidence decreasing as infants get older (Dwyer & Ponsonby, 1995). SIDS rarely occurs before 1 month of age. Death rates vary from country to country and from state to state. Although the incidence has declined in recent years (Freed et al., 1994), SIDS continues to be a threat to the well-being of infants everywhere.

Factors Associated with SIDS

During the past twenty-five years a massive amount of information has been accumulated in the search for an answer to the SIDS mystery. Scientists have identified a number of factors that are statistically associated with an increased risk of SIDS. The following trends have been reported:

1. Exposure of a baby to tobacco smoke before or after birth increases the risk of SIDS (Blair, et al., 1996; Dwyer & Ponsonby, 1995).
2. Infants who sleep in a prone (stomach) position or put to bed in a side position are at increased risk for SIDS (Fleming, et al., 1996; Guntheroth, 1995)
3. SIDS occurs more frequently among economically disadvantaged families (Guntheroth, 1995).
4. The risk of SIDS is highest for first-born infants (Guntheroth, 1995).
5. Preterm, low-birthweight infants, and infants of multiple births tend to have an increased risk of SIDS (Dwyer & Ponsonby, 1995).
6. The incidence of SIDS is higher among infants whose mothers are characterized by one or more of the following conditions: are less than 20 years of age, do not receive adequate prenatal care, engage in sub-

stance abuse, have a short interval between pregnancies, suffer from anemia or an infectious disease during pregnancy (Dwyer & Ponsonby, 1995; Willinger, 1995).

7. SIDS occurs at increased rates during the winter months (Dwyer & Ponsonby, 1995).

8. The incidence of SIDS is substantially higher among male infants than it is among female infants (CDC, 1996).

Possible Causes

The factors described above provide information that can be used in reducing the chance of an infant being affected by SIDS. However, the exact medical explanation for SIDS remains the subject of ongoing scientific investigations. Through the years researchers have pursued several theories in their attempts to solve the SIDS mystery. Leading theories that researchers have investigated include the search for a faulty gene; prolonged apnea (breathing stops for 20 seconds or longer) produced by an obstruction of the air passages or a defective breathing reflex mechanism; suffocation while rebreathing carbon-dioxide due to poor air circulation while sleeping on soft bedding, or sleeping with the parent(s); cardiovascular disorders such as irregular heartbeat; central nervous system defects; hypothermia (chilling); hyperthermia (overheating); or a combination of some of these conditions (James, 1985; Kelly & Shannon, 1982).

In spite of the proliferation of theories and research studies, scientists have not yet been able to determine the reason why SIDS occurs. Currently, investigators are trying to find the physiological mechanisms associated with the prone sleeping position since SIDS rates are higher for infants who sleep in that position (Dwyer & Ponsonby, 1995). It appears unlikely that there is one single physical defect or illness that causes SIDS (Freed et al., 1994).

SIDS Prevention

Until the cause (or causes) of sudden infant death is determined, no completely effective means of prevention can be developed. However, the most successful approach to reducing the incidence of SIDS has been public awareness programs, such as the "Back to Sleep" campaign that promote placing infants in the back position for sleeping. The number of SIDS deaths has dropped 50 percent or more in countries that have conducted effective campaigns to reduce the number of infants sleeping on their stomach. Although some parents place an infant in side position for sleeping, researchers have found that practice may be as risky as the stomach position. Babies placed on their side tend to roll to their stomach (Fleming et al., 1996).

In addition to placing an infant on its back for sleeping, the "Back to Sleep" campaign recommends keeping the infant in a smoke-free environment before and after birth. British researchers have concluded that the number of SIDS deaths can be reduced by almost two-thirds if parents follow both recommendations (Blair et al., 1996). Parents are also advised to keep the sleeping room temperature at a comfortable (moderate) level, to participate in prenatal and postnatal health care, obtain immunizations for the infant on schedule, and when possible, breast-feed the baby. Caregivers should not place soft bedding such as pillows, comforters, cushions, or stuffed toys under the baby, and ensure that the baby's face does not become covered (Willinger, 1995).

Another approach to the prevention of SIDS is the use of a monitoring device that sounds an alarm if the baby stops breathing or the heart stops beating. Unfortunately, there are no reliable ways to identify infants who should be equipped with such devices. Physicians frequently recommend monitoring infants who have had a life-threatening episode of apnea or who have other risk factors for SIDS. For example, infant siblings of SIDS victims are sometimes equipped with a monitor.

The use of monitoring devices has been controversial. The monitors are not totally reliable because they sometimes give false alarms or fail to alarm if there is a problem. A number of studies have found home monitoring programs to be associated with a decrease in the incidence of SIDS (Freed et al., 1994). However, monitors cannot guarantee that SIDS will not occur (American Academy of Pediatrics, 1985). Experts generally agree that the use of a monitoring device is useful for infants at risk for SIDS, if only to give reassurance to parents (Milner, 1985).

Currently researchers are trying to decide whether infant-parent cosleeping (see Chapter 4) may be a means of preventing SIDS, or actually a risk factor for SIDS occurrence. McKenna and colleagues (1994) have found that cosleeping alters sleep patterns so that infants are aroused more frequently during the night. The researchers believe that these partner-induced sleep interruptions and transitions may provide the infant with practice in self-arousal, or the use of other physiological mechanisms that may prevent SIDS. They point out that the lowest rates of SIDS in the world occur in Asia where infants typically sleep with their parents. Oher scientists believe cosleeping may actually be a risk factor for SIDS (Byard, 1994). In New Zealand and Australia, bed sharing has been associated with a higher incidence of SIDS (Kilkenny & Lumley, 1994; McKenna & Mosko, 1993). Additional research is needed before this question will be resolved.

CHILD MALTREATMENT

Every year more than 1 million children in the United States are victims of various forms of abuse and neglect (Wiese & Daro, 1995). Since statistics were first collected in 1960s, the number of reports of suspected cases of child maltreatment has increased each year (Leventhal, 1996). Approximately 13 percent of the victims of child maltreatment are under 1 year of age, while approximately 26 percent are from 2 to 5 years of age (U.S. Bureau of the Census, 1996). Maltreatment is the most frequent single cause of death in infants between 6 and 12 months of age. Almost all murders of children younger than 3 years of age are the result of child abuse by a parent or caretaker (Heins, 1984). Adult's abuse and neglect affect infants in many ways. The various forms of maltreatment are typically classified as physical abuse, neglect, emotional abuse, and sexual abuse. Some victims, particularly infants under age 3, are subjected to multiple forms of abuse (Mrazek, 1993). Infants also increasingly witness violent acts among their families, in the media, and community.

Physical Abuse

Physical maltreatment is difficult to define precisely because of disagreements about the difference between discipline and abuse, as well as how to distinguish between intentional and unintentional injury. One widely accepted definition of a physically abused child is "any child who receives nonaccidental physical injury as a result of acts or omissions on the part of his parents or guardians" (Kempe and Helfer, 1972, p. xi).

According to the latest national survey, conducted in 1994, physical abuse represents approximately 21 percent of all confirmed cases of child maltreatment (Wiese & Daro, 1995). Abused children are beaten severely, burned, poisoned, and punished in many other ways. A variety of "weapons" may be used to inflict injury on a child, such as a belt, a pan, a fist, or a lighted cigarette. The extent of injuries varies from minor bruises and abrasions to broken bones, permanent nervous-system damage, and death. Reports of child abuse similar to the following appear frequently in the news:

> He was only three years old . . . and by the time police arrived with a document declaring Michael M. to be a neglected child, it was too late. He was already dead. . . . The mother's live-in boyfriend allegedly beat the child for wetting his pants. The beatings were allegedly administered with a large belt buckle and lasted through the morning into early afternoon. . . . The mother led police to a muddy ditch where the dead child had been buried. (Slater, 1983, p. 26)

Bruises are the most common manifestations of physical abuse. The shape of the injury may resemble the object used (Johnson, 1996). Head injuries are the most common cause of death from physical abuse (Leventhal, 1996).

Shaken Impact Syndrome. The form of abuse most frequently reported for victims under 1 year of age has been called the **shaken infant syndrome** (Eagan, Whelan-Williams, & Brooks, 1985; Leventhal, 1995). Adults often grab an infant by the arms or shoulders and shake vigorously. This action may cause stretching and tearing of the tender blood vessels in the brain. The brain can also be damaged from bumping against the inside of the skull. Violent shaking can lead to bleeding in the brain and eyes as well as whiplash injury to the neck bones and muscles. The following is an excerpt from a case report:

> An 11-month old female was taken to the emergency room after she was found lying on the floor unconscious. The stepfather reported that the child fell from the couch but later admitted that he had 'shaken' the child to wake her from her nap in an attempt to adjust her sleep schedule and 'slapped' her to gain her attention. (Eagan et al., 1985)

Recent studies have indicated that shaking alone may not be responsible for the more severe brain injuries observed. Many of the shaken babies also display signs of injuries that are likely to have been caused by the impact of the head striking the crib, bed, floor, or other hard surface as the baby was being shaken. Because physicians often have trouble determining whether bleeding in the brain results from the shaking and/or an impact, the term shaken infant syndrome has been replaced with **shaken impact syndrome** in the medical literature (Leventhal, 1996).

Neglect

Child neglect refers to the willful failure of parents or other designated caregivers to meet the child's basic needs for food, clothing, shelter, medical treatment, and affection. This type of maltreatment occurs a little more than twice as often as physical abuse. Child neglect does not typically receive as much public attention as physical abuse. However, the following is a case that made the news:

> Four children, ages one through four, were found crying from hunger and thirst in an apartment where they had been left alone for 45 hours. Police reported the children were filthy and the stench from human waste was almost unbearable. (Family Life Council of Greater Greensboro, 1973, p. 1)

Children under the age of 2 are especially vulnerable to **nonorganic failure to thrive (NOFTT)**. Most cases of NOFTT can be attributed to inadequate feeding. These infants do not gain weight and grow on schedule. In most instances emotional neglect is also involved. Approximately 5 to 15 percent of these infants also suffer physical abuse. A few of these infants actually die of starvation (Johnson, 1996). NOFTT occurs less often after age 2 because older infants are better able to obtain food for themselves (Mrazek, 1993).

Emotional Abuse

Emotional abuse involves verbal assaults, unreasonable demands, scapegoating, isolation, and other treatment that undermine the child's self-esteem. It also includes ignoring the child and withdrawing love and nurturance needed for normal growth and development. Emotional abuse is the most difficult kind of abuse to legally define, detect, and prosecute. Emotional abuse accounts for approximately 3 to 4 percent of all substantiated cases of child maltreatment.

Emotional abuse is often accompanied by physical or other forms of abuse. **Factitious Disorder by proxy** (formerly "Munchausen syndrome by proxy") is a disorder involving emotional abuse and other forms of maltreatment. In this relatively rare disorder, the parent, usually the mother, fakes or creates symptoms of illness in an infant or child. The parent persistently takes the child to various health-care professionals for treatment (Oates, 1996). The parent may fabricate symptoms of illness, or actually cause symptoms by exposing the child to poisons, infectious agents, or physical trauma. The caretaker's motivation is apparently to gain attention from family members and health-care providers as a result of the problems created (Johnson, 1996).

Sexual Abuse

Sexual abuse includes any activity with a child before the age of legal consent for the sexual gratification of an older person (Johnson, 1996). Approximately one-third of the victims of sexual abuse are under 6 years of age (Schmitt & Krugman, 1992). Sexual abuse of infants usually involves genital fondling and oral-genital contact. Such cases are difficult to detect because infants cannot evaluate this behavior or let other people know what has happened (Mrazek, 1993). Sexual abuse is most often committed by family members and nonrelatives who are responsible for taking care of the child (Johnson, 1996).

Characteristics of Child Abusers

Why does child abuse occur? How could any sane parent or adult abuse a helpless child? Attempts to find answers to such questions have focused largely on the characteristics of abusive parents. Many abusive parents have little knowledge of normal child growth and development, and their ignorance results in unrealistic expectations of a child. They also tend to be afraid of spoiling their children, or they strongly believe in the value of physical punishment as a means of discipline (Mayhall & Norgard, 1983).

Child abusers cannot usually be distinguished from their neighbors and are generally classified as "normal" people. Only about 10 percent of abusive adults are likely to be insane or have criminal tendencies (Baxter, 1985). No two abusive parents are exactly alike, but they are often characterized as being immature, lacking in self-esteem, impulsive, self-centered, and rigid (Mrazek, 1993).

Child maltreatment occurs among families of all economic and educational levels. However, child maltreatment tends to be reported more frequently among parents and adults who are poor and less educated. The link between economic stress and child abuse is clearly seen in the rise in child maltreatment cases during periods of high unemployment. Parents involved in child abuse are often isolated, without friends and support from relatives (Krugman, 1984; Leventhal, 1996). Mothers who neglect their children tend to have had a negative attitude toward the pregnancy (Mrazek, 1993).

The belief that child abusers were themselves abused as children by their own parents is widespread. However, after reviewing research studies on this issue, Kaufman and Zigler (1987) concluded that unqualified acceptance of the theory that child abuse is usually transmitted from generation to generation is unfounded. Although being maltreated as a child puts a person at risk for becoming abusive, the majority of mistreated children do not grow up to be abusive parents. Approximately one out of three people who were abused or neglected as children will mistreat their own children (Kaufman & Zigler, 1987).

Infants are most often abused by their biological parents. However, foster parents, adoptive parents, stepparents, grandparents, siblings, other relatives, friends, baby sitters, and other child-care providers, inside and outside the home, are frequently involved (American Medical Association, 1985). Even older siblings and other children are perpetrators. Most incidents of abuse occur at home, and the abusive parent is more likely to be the father or another male than the mother or another female (Leventhal, 1996). Parents and other adults are not the only people who maltreat infants. On August 8, 1996, NBC News reported that an 11-year-old female had been convicted of murdering a 2-year-old infant at an unlicensed day-care center where she worked.

Characteristics of Abused Children

In searching for answers about why child abuse occurs, researchers have attempted to identify physical and behavioral characteristics of victims that may contribute to their own mistreatment. Young infants are unable to escape and are totally dependent on their caretakers. They often trigger an adult's violent response through inconsolable colicky crying. Older infants evoke abusive behavior by their inability to obtain or maintain control over elimination or impulsive behavior. Difficulties in eating and sleeping are other typical behaviors that abusive parents report as evoking their anger (Krugman, 1984). Although having a difficult temperament is frequently identified as a major risk factor for child maltreatment, research evidence does not support this conclusion.

Prematurity and low-birthweight have frequently been associated with child maltreatment. Theoretically, parents have more difficulty in becoming emotionally attached to these infants because they are isolated during the important early days after birth. Although some studies have found evidence that prematurity and low-birthweight are risk factors for child abuse, other studies have not supported such claims. Studies that have controlled for social class and other important variables have found that premature and low-birthweight babies are no more frequently involved in child-abuse cases than other infants (Leventhal, Edgerter, & Murphy, 1984). Also, researchers have not been able to verify the popular belief that failure to bond with an infant soon after delivery is a risk factor for child maltreatment (Mrazek, 1993).

Usually only one infant in each family is mistreated. It appears that the child becomes the focal point and thus a scapegoat for all the parental anger and frustration (Solomons, 1984). Statistically, females are slightly more likely to be maltreated than males (U. S. Bureau of the Census, 1996).

Effects of Child Maltreatment

The effects of child maltreatment are devastating and long-lasting in most cases. Children less than 3 years of age are biologically more vulnerable than older children. Consequently, the effects of abusive treatment are more devastating. Most fatalities due to maltreatment occur within this age group (Mrazek, 1993). If they survive, abused infants suffer long-lasting physical and mental disabilities. Damage to the brain leaves them with mental retardation, seizures, learning disabilities, and hearing or other sensory impairments. Even when severe physical impairments are not obvious, mistreated children may have lower-than-average intellectual, language, and motor abilities, leading to lower academic achievement and developmental delays (Mayhall & Norgard, 1983). Abused children also suffer emotional scars, which may make them extremely shy, withdrawn, depressed, or angry (Mrazek, 1993). Many abused children have difficulty trusting other people and forming close relationships. They may become excessively aggressive, growing up to commit violent or criminal acts against society (Baxter, 1985). In one study abused toddlers reacted more aggres-

sively to other children's distress (Main & George, 1985). For example, a 22-month-old boy began to cry loudly after his mother left him at the child-care center. A 28-month-old boy, who had been beaten with a belt buckle and witnessed his mother being stabbed, ran over to the boy and hit him in the head, screaming, "No! No!" (Zeanah, 1994).

Effects of Exposure to Violence

Infants who live in violent environments often witness adults and older children arguing, fighting, and murder. While newborns and very young infants may appear to be too cognitively immature to interpret the meaning of what they see and hear, the psychological effects are surprisingly traumatic for most infants under 3 years of age. Infants are indirectly affected when parents fight because the caregiving activities may be altered in negative ways. Depressed parents tend to talk less, display sad facial expressions, and interact less frequently with an infant (Osofsky & Jackson, 1994). We know far too little about the experience of violence in infancy, but information is emerging about some of the consequences. Some of the symptoms displayed by these infants and children include acting out an event in play, nightmares, social withdrawal, exaggerated startle responses, and aggression (Zeanah, 1994).

Treatment and Prevention

The complexities of child abuse require a wide range of treatment and prevention strategies. Efforts to treat abusive parents and their victims include individual therapy, family counseling, placing children in foster care or crisis nurseries, and short-term residential treatment for the entire family (Starr, 1979). Parents Anonymous is a volunteer organization that has been very effective in working with abusive families. The large majority of abusive parents can be helped with appropriate treatment and support. Approaches to the prevention of child abuse include parent-education programs, and hospital maternity-ward practices to facilitate parent-child bonding. The most effective method of preventing physical abuse and neglect has been extended home visitation (MacMillan, MacMillan, & Oxford, 1993). Home visitor programs usually focus on providing training in parenting along with emotional support for low-income single mothers and other parents who may be at risk for becoming child abusers.

INFANT SAFETY

Nearly all children are involved in one or more accidents while growing up. Actually, medical and safety experts are attempting to get people to use **unintentional injury** and **injury control** instead of **accidents** and **accident prevention**. The term "accident" implies a chance event, or even an "act of God" that cannot be controlled. This often leads to a fatalistic attitude that becomes a barrier to decreasing the number and the severity of injuries among infants and children. Use of the terms unintentional injury and injury control are more personal and focus on the possibility of injury reduction (Rivara & Brownstein, 1996). Although deaths due to unintentional injuries have declined during the past 10 years, they remain the leading cause of death for infants and children 1 to 4 years of age. For infants under 1 year of age, unintentional injuries are the fourth leading cause of death (National Safety Council, 1996).

Injuries happen in strange and unexpected ways before caregivers realize what is happening. A letter that appeared in "Dear Abby" (1981) described how a toddler fell into an ice chest and drowned. The same letter-writer reported another incident, in which her 14-month-old grandson wiggled down and hanged himself from the strap of his highchair when the baby sitter left the room for a few minutes.

Risk factors that are related to the frequency of injuries include age, sex, and socioeconomic status. The first year of life is the most dangerous. Injuries take the lives of more babies during this period than any other age under 16 years (National Safety Council, 1996). About one-half of all fatalities among infants occur before 5 months of age, and more than two-thirds occur by 7 months. During later infancy, the number of such deaths levels off (Metropolitan Life Insurance Co., 1985). Tod-

dlers are especially susceptible to burns, drowning, falls, and poisoning. They are increasingly mobile and curious but lack judgment to know what safety hazards to avoid.

At every age of life, the injury rate is larger for males than for females. Death rates from unintentional injuries tend to be about 25 percent higher for male infants than for female infants (Metropolitan Life Insurance Co., 1985). Either by nature, nurture, or both, boys are typically more active and aggressive in exploring their environment. Thus, they are more likely to be exposed to hazards. Parents also tend to be more protective of female infants.

Causes of Unintentional Injury Deaths

Motor Vehicles. By far the leading cause of deaths attributed to unintentional injuries during infancy is motor vehicles (Table 6–2). Approximately 900 infants and young children (Birth-4 yrs.) died in 1995 (the most recent year for which information is available) as the result of motor-vehicle collisions. The death rate attributed to motor vehicles is highest for infants under 12 months of age (National Safety Council, 1996). Very young infants are more likely to be riding in the front seat held in someone's arms. They are especially vulnerable to head injury because of the soft spots in the skull and a top-heavy body. Fortunately, the number of deaths due to motor vehicles is declining.

Most motor-vehicle deaths and serious injuries

Table 6–2 Leading Causes of Unintentional Injury Deaths Among Infants (0-4 years)—1995

RANK	CAUSE	NUMBER
1	Motor vehicle	900
2	Fires and burns	650
3	Drowning	500
4	Suffocation (ingested objects)	240
5	Falls	90
6	Poisoning (solids and liquids)	70
7	Firearms	30

Source: National Safety Council (1996). *Accident Facts.* Chicago: Author. Used by Permission.

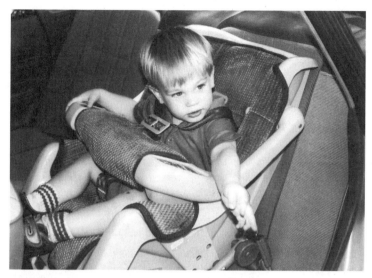

An infant in a car safety seat.

could be prevented through the proper use of infant safety seats. A ten-year research study conducted in the state of Washington found safety seats to be 80 to 90 percent effective in preventing deaths and major injuries to infants and children under 5 years of age (Scherz, 1981). Every state has a law requiring the use of automobile safety restraints for infants and children. The laws have succeeded in increasing the use of infant safety seats, thereby decreasing the death rate. Unfortunately, though, not all infants are provided this protection. While approximately 80 percent of adults now wear automobile seat belts, the usage rate for child safety seats is only 65 percent (Consumer Reports, 1995).

For maximum protection, parents should obtain a safety seat that is designed for the infant's age and weight. The seat should also be certified as meeting government safety standards, including protection in a head-on crash. The seat must be buckled tightly and securely, preferably in the center rear seat. An infant safety seat should not be installed in the front passenger seat within range of an air bag that can strike a severe blow to the baby's head.

Fires. Burns resulting from fires is the second-leading cause of death during the first three years of life due to unintentional injuries (see Table 6–2). Most fire victims die of asphyxiation and inhalation of poisonous substances rather than from burns,

but infants are more sensitive to heat from flames than older children or adults because of their thin, tender skin. Infants also suffer burns from hot water, grease, steam, heating and cooking appliances, and electrical shocks. Injuries often occur when unattended toddlers turn on the hot water faucet or bite into an electrical cord. Although such burns do not usually cause death, the injuries can be serious. Most injuries involving fires and burns occur in the home (Kane, 1985).

Drowning. Water is another safety hazard for infants. Drowning is the third-leading cause of fatal injuries during infancy. Drownings are most likely to happen when infants are left in bathtubs or near swimming pools. Infants drown even in ice chests and toilets. Dr. Jay Arena (1985), a pediatrician, wrote to newspaper columnist Ann Landers asking her to warn parents about the danger of 1- and 2-year-olds drowning when the toilet seat is left up. He reported three cases in which toddlers stumbled and drowned in the toilet bowl.

Suffocation. During the first four years of life, suffocation is the fourth-leading cause of deaths from unintentional injuries. However, for infants who are under 1 year of age, suffocation due to choking is the leading cause of fatal injuries. Suffocation accounts for one-fourth of all deaths due to unintentional injuries during the first year of life.

The first two months are especially hazardous (Metropolitan Life Insurance Company, 1985).

Young infants choke primarily on food or vomit because of their immaturity in swallowing and the tendency to cough up substances that obstruct the respiratory passages. Next to food, balloons are most often involved in choking deaths of infants, followed by tiny balls and marbles (Rimell et al., 1995). Crawling infants take special delight in finding small objects such as safety pins, buttons, or small parts of toys. Everything small enough to fit is automatically placed in the mouth, where it may be swallowed. Some infants are able to pull off and swallow pieces of the plastic coverings on their disposable diapers, which can result in choking.

Infants also suffocate by getting their heads trapped in plastic bags and between the rails of baby cribs, cradles, stair rails, and playpens. A ten-year study conducted by the U.S. Consumer Product Safety Commission found that 45 percent of all the victims of head-entrapment were under 12 months of age (Miles, Rutherford, & Coonley, 1983). Babies are also found strangled by drapery cords or cords from toys or other objects. The period when this type of strangulation is most likely to occur is between 9 and 12 months of age (Rutherford & Kelly, 1981).

Falls. Deaths due to falls have been declining in recent years, but continue to be ranked as the fifth cause of unintentional injury deaths (National Safety Council, 1987, 1996). Countless other infants receive nonfatal cuts, bruises, fractures, and other types of injuries from falls each year. Falls from highchairs, cribs, and walkers, are frequent causes of injuries to infants under 2 years of age. Babies also fall from tables, cabinets, and other high places when parents leave them momentarily. Crawling infants and toddlers are more likely to fall down stairs, out of windows or grocery carts, off playground equipment, and from numerous other places. Toddlers who live in high-rise apartments are especially at risk. Falls occur mainly when caregivers leave them unattended in hazardous places.

Poisoning. Each year about 2 million children under 5 years of age swallow or breathe potentially

This toddler is in a very dangerous situation which could have been avoided if these toxic substances had been properly stored in a "child-proof" location.

dangerous substances (Kane, 1985). The number of deaths from poisoning due to the ingestion of toxic substances among children between birth and 4 years of age declined from 150 in 1986 to 70 in 1995. Poisoning ranks as the sixth-leading cause of unintentional injury deaths among infants (National Safety Council, 1996). The number of poisonings peaks at 2 years of age (Dart & Rumack, 1994). Fortunately, most cases of poisoning do not result in death. Poisoning cases usually occur as the result of insecure storage of toxic substances. The list of poisonous substances found in homes and yards is almost limitless. Medicines are the toxic agents most frequently swallowed by children. Other substances frequently ingested include cleaning products, bleaches, drain cleaners, pesticides, and petroleum products (Dart & Rumack, 1994). Lead paint chips, which flake off the walls of old buildings, are especially dangerous. The toxic effects of poisons are more damaging to infants than to adults because of the immaturity of infants' organs (Kane, 1985).

Infants and toddlers between 1 and 3 years of age are especially vulnerable because they are curious, active, and capable of getting into cabinets, drawers, and other places where toxic substances are likely to be kept. Adults find it difficult to anticipate and control the children's growing ability to get into things. Since 1970, the federal government has required child-resistant packaging for medicines and numerous other potentially harmful substances commonly used in the home. The number of children poisoned by aspirin and other medicines has declined substantially because of the use of safety containers. However, safety experts warn parents not to be lulled into a false sense of security. Containers are frequently left open, and young children can be very resourceful in finding ways to open "child-proof" containers.

Nonfatal Injuries

So far our discussion has focused mainly on the incidence and causes of death due to unintentional injuries. However, these statistics represent only a part of the injury picture. Each year, countless numbers of infants are treated in physicians' offices and hospitals for a variety of injuries. The leading causes of nonfatal unintentional injuries to infants and children ranked in order of frequency are falls, motor vehicles, drowning, fire/burns, and poisoning (Rivara & Brownstein, 1996). These injuries are sometimes severe and result in long-term or permanent physical disabilities, neurological impairments, or other problems.

Injury Control

Even though, ironically, the infant mortality rate due to intentional injuries (child maltreatment) is increasing, the number of unintentional injury deaths has declined in recent years. Scientists estimate that 90 percent of childhood injuries can be avoided. Efforts to control injuries include public safety awareness and educational campaigns, the development of new safety devices (e.g., car safety seats), stricter government-mandated product-safety standards, and environmental control (Rivara & Brownstein, 1996).

One of the most important steps an infant caregiver can take in injury control is to "baby proof the environment" by making regular safety checks of the home and other places where infants live and play. For example, medicines, cleaning supplies, and other substances with toxic-warning labels should be kept in a locked cabinet or a place that is not accessible to an active toddler. Food, cleaning products, and medicines should never be stored in the same area. Plants should be kept out of reach. Razor blades, knives, and other sharp objects should be removed from drawers within the reach of infants and toddlers. Electrical outlets not in use should be covered with safety plugs. Cords on appliances should not be accessible to infants. Floors should be checked regularly for small objects such as coins, tacks, pins, paper clips, and marbles. Smoke detectors should be installed on each floor of the house and in all bedrooms.

Equipment or furnishings may need to be moved, added, removed, or modified. For example, stair railings, baby cribs, or playpens which might trap a baby's head should be modified. Stairs should be blocked at the top and bottom. Play yards should be fenced in. Severe burns can be avoided from tap water by lowering the thermostat setting to below 120 degrees. Infants should not be placed in mobile walkers. The American Academy of Pediatrics has recommended a ban on the manufacture and sale of infant walkers because of the risk of injury associated with their use (Committee on Injury and Poison Prevention, 1995). Numerous other things can be done to provide a hazard-free, "baby-proof" environment. However, there is no substitute for constant vigilance on the part of caregivers.

Toy Safety

All toys and play materials for infants should be selected with safety precautions in mind. Toys that have small parts which can come off and become lodged in the windpipe, ears, or nostrils are among the most hazardous. Materials such as balloons, buttons, marbles, and chalk should not be available to young infants.

Toys for infants and toddlers should not have sharp edges or points, should not be made of glass or brittle plastic, should not have cords or strings more than 12 inches long, and should not be put together with easily exposed straight pins, wires, or nails. Balls or other spherical objects less than 1 3/4 inches in diameter have been banned in toys designed for infants (Rimell et al., 1995). Even after carefully selecting toys, adults should supervise their use and examine them from time to time to be sure that wear and tear have not made the toys unsafe.

In Case of an Injury

Infant caregivers should be prepared to act quickly in case an injury occurs. Emergency telephone numbers, including the number of a poison-control center, should be posted on or near the telephone. A first-aid kit and an emergency-action chart should be readily available. In case poisoning occurs: (1) remove any remaining substance from the skin or mouth; (2) call the doctor or a poison control center immediately; and (3) follow their instructions. A bottle of ipecac syrup should be kept on hand to induce vomiting. However, it should be used only if recommended by a medical specialist.

SUMMARY

1. The human immune system consists of special cells produced by the body to destroy disease producing organisms. In addition, the defense system produces antibodies following exposure to harmful substances to build up resistance to future invasions.

2. Newborn infants usually have some temporary resistance to a number of communicable diseases as the result of antibodies obtained from the mother during the prenatal period. Infants are especially vulnerable to infections between 6 and 12 months of age.

3. Infants should receive a complete series of immunizations against hepatitis B, diphtheria, tetanus, pertussis, polio, haemophilus influenzae type b, measles, mumps rubella, and chickenpox. Vaccines should be given at ages recommended by medical authorities.

4 The polio and pertussis vaccines have been controversial because of concerns about the risk of severe adverse reactions. However, the benefits of all immunizations far outweigh any risks involved.

5. The most common symptoms of illness in infants are general discomfort, loss of appetite, vomiting, congestion, runny nose, fever, coughing, diarrhea, skin rash, listlessness, crying, and irritability. Parents are usually most concerned about fever, diarrhea, and vomiting.

6. Common illnesses and health problems of infancy include colds and respiratory infections, otitis media, pneumonia, croup, roseola, thrush, diaper rash, allergic reactions, and colic.

7. AIDS is a relatively new and deadly disease that results from the human immunodeficiency virus (HIV). The chances that an infant will acquire the virus from an infected mother during the prenatal period or during birth are approximately 20 to 25 percent. The length of time between the acquisition of the HIV infection by an infant and the appearance of AIDS symptoms has increased in recent years. New medications for the treatment of AIDS are proving to be effective in reducing the chances of an infant being born with HIV, and extending the life expectancy of infants who become infected.

8. The leading cause of death of infants between 1 month and 1 year of age is sudden infant death syndrome. A number of factors, such as prematurity and low-socioeconomic class, statistically increase an infant's chances of being affected by SIDS. The reason infants die suddenly and unexpectedly remains a scientific mystery. Recommendations for preventing SIDS include placing infants on their back for sleeping and avoiding exposure to tobacco smoke. These and other preventive measures have been found to be effective in dramatically reducing the number of SIDS deaths.

9. Each year thousands of infants are victims of physical abuse, neglect, emotional abuse, and

sexual abuse. Infants are mistreated by their parents and other people in many and varied ways. Factors associated with child maltreatment include unrealistic expectations of infants, low-socioeconomic class, alcoholism, teenage- or single-parent status, and such personal characteristics as immaturity. Many child abusers were abused by their own parents. Usually only one infant in each family is abused. Infants who survive child abuse may suffer long-lasting physical, mental, and emotional problems. The most effective approach to preventing child maltreatment has been extended parent training through home visitation.

10. Each year many infants are seriously injured or killed by a variety of unintentional injuries. The first year of life is the most dangerous, but at every age more boys than girls are involved in accidents. The leading causes of unintentional injury deaths during infancy are motor vehicle collisions, fires and burns, drowning, suffocation, falls, and poisoning.

11. Parents and infant caregivers should take careful steps to prevent injuries by baby-proofing the environment and selecting toys that are free of safety hazards.

7

Nutrition and Feeding Practices

A baby is fed with milk and praise.
—Mary Lamb

Nutrition is fundamental to growth and development. The maintenance of nutritive balance during the early months of life is especially important because it lays the foundation for physical health and mental functioning throughout life. Prenatal and infant nutrition affects the quality and quantity of body cells and fluids, skeletal and dental development, and the body's susceptibility to disease. It is difficult to think of any aspect of infant growth and development that is not directly or indirectly influenced by nutrition.

In this chapter we consider the nutritional needs of infants and how these needs can best be met during various stages of the infancy period. Nutritional concerns and feeding problems such as anemia, food allergies, and obesity are discussed. We also take a look at the consequences of malnutrition and signs of nutritional adequacy. Suggestions for feeding infants are provided.

NUTRITIONAL NEEDS

Nutrition is the process by which the body uses food and other substances in the digestive system (McLaren & Burman, 1982). Infants need nutrients for the maintenance and growth of the skeletal system and body tissues, as well as energy to support activity and life-sustaining processes. Nutritionists have had difficulty determining the exact quantities of nutrients needed by infants or humans in general, so opinions vary as to ideal diets for individuals at all ages. Factors that affect an individual's nutrient needs include body size, rate of growth, activity level, basal metabolism, and nutritional reserves stored in the body. Nutrient needs in proportion to body size are greatest during infancy and decline with age (Pipes & Trahms, 1993).

RECOMMENDED DIETARY ALLOWANCES

Current scientific knowledge about healthy human nutritional needs has been summarized in terms of **recommended dietary allowances (RDA)** and published by the Food and Nutrition Board of the National Research Council (1989). The RDAs are defined as "the levels of intake of essential nutrients that, on the basis of scientific information, are judged by the Food and Nutrition Board to be adequate to meet the known nutrient needs of practically all healthy persons (National Research Council, 1989, p. 1)." Basic categories into which nutrients are categorized include energy, carbohydrates, fat, protein and amino acid, vitamins, minerals, and water.

Energy

An infant must have sufficient energy in the diet to maintain physical activity, growth, and physiological processes such as breathing, digestion, and blood circulation. Energy needs are met by foods containing fats, carbohydrates, and protein. Fat is the most calorically concentrated nutrient. Approximately 40 to 50 percent of the energy needed by infants is supplied by fat (Pipes & Trahms, 1993). Carbohydrates are also major sources of dietary energy for infants. Lactose, an ingredient found in milk, is the primary carbohydrate in the young infant's diet.

Infants need to be provided with calories throughout the day because of their limited intake capacity. If energy needs are not met, infants grow at slower-than-normal rates and may lose weight, but an excessive caloric intake may result in an overweight baby. Energy requirements per unit of body size are highest during the first few months of life and gradually decline as the rate of growth decreases (Pipes & Trahms, 1993).

Protein

In addition to energy needs, infants require protein for the development of new body tissue as well as the synthesis of enzymes, hormones, and other compounds (Worthington-Roberts & Williams, 1996). Protein needs vary according to age, growth rate, body size, and caloric intake from fats and carbohydrates. The protein requirements decrease in proportion to body weight as the infant gets older and the growth rate decreases. Infants who do not receive enough protein in their diet to meet their individual needs grow more slowly than normal. An extended time period of severe protein deficiency usually results in the cessation of growth. On the other hand, too much protein may also inhibit growth or, for young infants, overload the kidney capacity (Cox & Gallagher-Allred, 1980; Woodruff, 1978).

Vitamins

A **vitamin** is an organic substance in food which is essential for growth and maintenance of life. Vitamins perform a variety of functions in the human infant. Many of the vitamins participate in the metabolism of energy and protein, whereas others interact with various nutrients to produce growth of bones and mucous membranes, and the synthesis of vital compounds (Pipes & Trahms, 1993). Care should be exercised in controlling the infant's intake of vitamins. Excessive amounts of some vitamins (e.g., A and D) are stored in the body and can be harmful. On the other hand, vitamin deficiencies can lead to a variety of nutritional disorders, depending upon the specific vitamin. For example, a deficiency of vitamin C may result in scurvy. The small blood vessels become so fragile that they break and bleed at the slightest pressure. Vitamin D deficiency causes rickets, a softening of the bones possibly resulting in bowlegs or other malformations. Vitamin K is especially important for normal blood coagulation.

Minerals and Water

Minerals are inorganic nutrients, such as calcium, phosphorus, iron, and zinc, that are important in the regulation of body fluids and metabolic processes. They are also structural components of the skeletal system, teeth, and body tissues (Pipes & Trahms, 1993). An excessive intake should be avoided because some of the minerals can be stored in the body and reach toxic levels.

Water is also an essential component of the body. The body of the newborn infant is approximately 75 percent water. The total body water as a percentage of body weight decreases throughout the first year of infancy to 60 percent, which is comparable to the adult proportion (Pipes & Trahms, 1993). Infants need water to replace liquid lost from skin, lungs, and the eliminative organs, and to provide a small amount for growth needs (Foman, 1993). Infants need more water in proportion to their body weight than adults. Under normal conditions the amount of water in breast milk or properly diluted formula is adequate to meet the nursing infant's needs. Care should be taken to replace water lost during periods of very hot weather or illness that leads to vomiting and diarrhea. Infants who can communicate their needs should be given water on demand.

STAGES OF INFANT FEEDING

The Committee on Nutrition (1980; 1993) of the American Academy of Pediatrics recommends that infant feeding be considered in three stages: (1) the nursing period, (2) the transitional period, and (3) the modified adult period. The nursing period is the time, usually the first six months of life, during which breast milk or formula is the source of all nutrients. The transitional period begins around 4 to 6 months with the addition of specially prepared semisolid food to the diet. The modified adult period corresponds to the toddler age (1 to 2 years), during which the majority of the nutrients come from the family table. The stages overlap so that an infant typically begins one stage before finishing another. Ideally, the rate at which an infant progresses through the stages is determined by the growth rate and developmental changes in the nervous system, by digestive capacity, and by kidney function. In most cases, however, prevailing sociocultural attitudes tend to be more powerful sources of influence than scientific information in determining the rate at which infants are encouraged to move from one stage to another.

Stage 1: The Nursing Period (Birth to 6 Months)

During the nursing period the baby is given a liquid diet of breast or formula milk. Newborn babies are equipped with rooting, sucking, and swallowing reflexes which facilitate the intake of liquids. In addition, an extrusion reflex causes the infant to push solid food out of the mouth when it is placed on the back of the tongue. The feeding reflexes gradually diminish during the first three or four months of life and are replaced by voluntary control over sucking and swallowing, as well as tongue and lip movements. The nursing period is also characterized by immature kidney and digestive capacity and by the absence of teeth with which to chew.

Choice of Feeding Method. The most important question to be answered during the nursing period is whether the baby will be fed with maternal milk or a processed formula. At the turn of the century, almost all infants in the United States were breast-fed (Martin & Beal, 1978). Over the years, cow's milk and other types of commercial formula gradually replaced breast milk as the most frequently used alternative for meeting nutritional needs during the early months of life (Committee on Nutrition, 1976a).

A resurgence of interest in breast-feeding in the United States occurred during the 1970s as more mothers from all socioeconomic classes breast-fed their babies (Martinez & Dodd, 1983). The incidence of breast-feeding (initiated during the mother's hospital stay after childbirth) peaked in 1984 at 59.7 percent and gradually declined to 52.2 percent in 1989 (Ross Mothers Survey, 1996). However, after 1989 the rate of breast-feeding began to rise again. In 1995, the incidence of breast-feeding was back up to 59.7 percent. The level of breast-feeding is highest among college educated, high income, mothers above 30 years of age (Ross Mothers Survey, 1996). Rates of breast-feeding are lowest among mothers who are young, less educated, black, Hispanic, economically disadvantaged, unmarried, and less than 20 years of age (Gielen et al., 1992; Ross Mothers Survey, 1996; National Center for Health Statistics, 1995).

On a worldwide basis, the incidence and length of breast-feeding are declining in some places while in others, breast-feeding has increased (Wray, 1991). The resurgence in the number of mothers who are choosing to breast-feed in the United States can be attributed to efforts to promote breast-feeding by nutritionists, medical specialists, and information published in scientific publications, popular magazines, and books. The LaLeche (pronounced LaLaychay) League promotes breast-feeding through the development of local support groups and the publication of "how-to" information. The goal of the United States Department of Heath and Human Services is to have 75 percent of infants breast-fed at birth (National Center for Health Statistics, 1995).

The choice of feeding method is usually made by the sixth month of pregnancy. A variety of social, cultural, educational, and psychological factors are involved in the decision relative to breast-feeding. The mother's decision about breast-feeding may be based more on the advice of family members, friends, and cultural norms than on scientific argu-

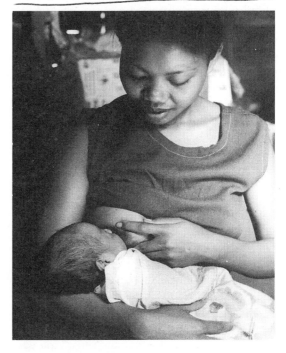

The importance of breast-feeding is emphasized by nutritionists and health-care specialists.

ments (Alexy & Martin, 1994). Maternal employment can adversely affect the length of breast-feeding, but does not appear to be a major factor involved in the initial decision. Strong approval of breast-feeding by the father has been associated with a high incidence of breast-feeding among middle-class families (Littman, Medendorp, & Goldfarb, 1994).

Advantages of Breast-feeding. A variety of arguments have been used to convince mothers that "breast is best." The reasons include both physiological and psychological advantages for the infant and the mother as well. The major reasons for breastfeeding are summarized below.

1. *Nutritional superiority*. Through the years, manufacturers of infant formula have been able to develop substitutes for maternal milk that meet basic infant energy and nutritional requirements (Committee on Nutrition, 1993). However, the protein and other ingredients in human milk differ qualitatively from the protein in cows' milk and other formula substitutes (Jelliffe & Jelliffe, 1977). Breast milk proteins and fat are easier for the infant's body to digest and absorb. In addition, the waste products are more easily processed by the immature kidneys of the infant. Human milk is used by scientists as a standard for determining the nutritional needs of infants during the first six months of life (Foman, 1993).

2. *Formula contamination and dilution*. Breast milk is sterile and is not subject to contamination. In mixing formula for bottle feeding, there is a possibility of using contaminated water or the wrong amount of water. Problems resulting from improper formula mix may not happen very often among well-informed mothers with adequate resources. However, the proper use of bottle milk is a problem of major concern in underdeveloped countries where bacterial contamination, under dilution, or over dilution of formula mixture is more likely to occur (WHO/UNICEF, 1981).

3. *Infection protection*. In contrast to formula substitutes, human milk contains substances that provide infants with protection against viral and bacterial infections. Newborn infants acquire antibodies from breast milk. These antibodies increase

the infant's resistance to a variety of intestinal microorganisms while the immune system matures. There is increasing evidence that respiratory infections, ear infections, and diarrhea occur less frequently among breast-fed babies (American Academy of Pediatrics, 1978; Dewey, Heinig, & Nommsen-Rivers, 1995; Wood & Walker-Smith, 1981). Breast milk may also help protect an infant against other conditions such as early-onset diabetes and sudden infant death syndrome, but additional research is needed to substantiate such conclusions. The protective effect of breast milk is greatest during the first six months for infants born in substandard economic conditions (Wray, 1991).

4. *Allergy protection*. Breast-fed infants are apparently less susceptible to allergic reactions, such as eczema and asthma than bottle-fed infants, during the early months of life (Gerrard et al., 1973; Eastham & Walker, 1977). Pipes and Trahms (1993) believe that breast-feeding is the best way to prevent food allergies from occurring during early infancy. However, not all scientists are convinced that breast-feeding contributes significantly to allergy prevention. There is general agreement that cows' milk protein is a common allergenic substance in infancy and that allergic reactions to breast milk are uncommon (Worthington-Roberts & Williams, 1996). However, it is possible that allergens from the mother's diet may enter her breast milk and result in an allergic reaction by a sensitive infant (Perkin, 1990).

5. *Health of the mother*. There is general agreement among physicians that breast-feeding causes the uterus to contract after pregnancy, facilitating return to its normal size and reducing the danger of hemorrhage (Martin & Beal, 1978). Indirectly, breast-feeding may be beneficial to mothers in some places by lengthening the interval between pregnancies through cultural norms that promote postnatal sexual abstinence (Nicoll et al., 1994). It has also been suggested that the incidence of breast cancer is lower in countries where breast-feeding is widely practiced (McLaren & Burman, 1982). Some researchers have found indications that prolonged lactation reduces the risk of breast cancer (Byers et al., 1985). However, the evidence is not

sufficiently strong at this point to advise women to breast-feed specifically to decrease the risk of cancer (Byers et al., 1985).

6. *Psychological benefits*. Some people believe that breast-feeding offers a superior psychological intimacy that results in emotional and cognitive advantages over other feeding situations. Since the mother has to hold the infant close to her body, there appears to be a certain amount of warmth, nurturing, and skin contact inherent in breast-feeding situations. Klaus and Kennell (1982) believe that breast-feeding is one of the procedures that facilitate the development of mother-infant bonding. However, claims that there is a relationship between breast-feeding and bonding have been disputed. Analyses of mother-infant interactions have shown that breast-feeding does not necessarily provide a comfortable or nurturing relationship with the mother (Kulka, Walter, & Fry, 1966).

Through the years, researchers have tried to find a relationship between infant-feeding methods and later psychological functioning, including socioemotional and cognitive development. The results of an eight-year longitudinal study found no relationship between breast-feeding and measures of social adjustment (Fergusson, Horwood, & Shannon, 1987). A New Zealand study failed to find differences in motor coordination, verbal ability, intelligence, and behavior problems among 3-year-old children who had been breast-fed and other 3-year-olds who had been bottle-fed (Silva, Buckfield, & Spears, 1978). However, several other investigators have found breast-feeding to be associated with higher scores on measures of cognitive performance (e.g. Taylor, 1977; Morley et al., 1988; Rogan & Gladen, 1993). A study conducted in England (Lucas et al.,1992) found that preterm infants who were fed breast milk through a tube obtained higher scores at 18 months and at 7-8 years on measures of intelligence. Critics point out that advantages associated with breast-feeding might be attributed to subtle differences in attitudes, motivation, and practices associated with the choice to breast-feed that are difficult to control (Dobbing, 1993). Consequently, additional research evidence is needed to support claims to that breast-feeding contributes to cognitive gains.

Formula Feeding as an Alternative. The evidence favoring breast milk as the best food for young babies is conclusive and compelling. Consequently, the superiority of breast-feeding over formula feeding is rarely questioned. However, many mothers do not breast-feed for a variety of reasons. In some instances, mothers prefer not to breast feed because of feelings of revulsion, embarrassment, fear, uncertainty, or concerns about having an adequate milk supply. In other cases, mothers cannot breast-feed because of illness (e.g., tuberculosis, cancer), alcoholism, use of certain medications, or insufficient milk production. In addition, the following problems and disadvantages have been associated with breast-feeding:

1. *Difficulties for working mothers*. There are usually restrictions placed upon working mothers which make it difficult or impossible for them to breast-feed satisfactorily. While some mothers are willing to fight for the right to unrestricted breast-feeding during working hours, others are less assertive. Statistics show that the incidence and duration of breast-feeding are lower for working mothers than for nonworking mothers throughout the world (Martinez & Dodd, 1983; King & Ashworth, 1991). This trend probably reflects the difficulties perceived and encountered by mothers who work. Some mothers pump the milk out of their breasts and store it for bottle feeding when they are not available for nursing. Other mothers provide formula to substitute for breast-feeding at such times.

2. *Fathers are left out of the feeding process*. When the mother nurses the baby, the father has little role, if any, in feeding the baby. In some instances, feelings of jealousy and other psychological difficulties experienced by a husband may result in a negative and nonsupportive attitude toward breast-feeding (Waletzky, 1979). However, at least one father found a way to play a role in the breast-feeding process. A medical journal article (Wollman, 1981) reported a case in which a father successfully breast-fed his daughter after receiving hormone injections. In addition, a bra-like device that holds a bottle is available for fathers who want to simulate the breast-feeding experience. Most fathers, though,

would not consider such approaches to be viable alternatives.

3. *Drugs, toxins, allergens, and infectious agents in breast milk.* Breast milk can contain viral and other infections if the mother is ill (Committee on Nutrition, 1976a). Recent evidence indicates that the AIDS virus (HIV-1) can be transmitted through breast milk. In industrialized countries, women with HIV-1 are advised not to breast-feed (Nicoll et al., 1994). However, scientists differ as to whether HIV-infected women in developing countries should breast-feed. The problem is to determine if the risk of transmitting AIDS through breast milk outweighs the risk of a child's early death from diarrhea or other illness resulting from contaminated formula milk (Worthington-Roberts & Williams, 1996).

Lactating mothers are advised to take medication only under the supervision of a physician since many drugs move from the bloodstream into the milk. Examples of drugs that should not be taken are anticoagulants, most laxatives, radioactive drugs, tetracycline, some drugs used to treat cancer, migraine headaches, arthritis, manic depressive illness, and drugs of abuse (Williams, 1996). Environmental contaminants such as PCB may also get into the mother's milk supply.

Breast-feeding and Formula Feeding in Perspective. The American Academy of Pediatrics (1982) has concluded that the benefits of breast-feeding are so numerous that pediatricians and other professionals should strongly promote the practice. The effects of breast-feeding vary somewhat with the environment into which the infant is born, including socioeconomic status, sanitation conditions, and the nutritional status of the mother (Wray, 1991). Breast-feeding is especially important in underdeveloped countries where poor sanitation, poor nutrition, and a high incidence of infectious diseases exist. Apparently some breast-feeding is better than no breast-feeding.

However, it must be recognized that the choice of breast- or formula-feeding involves multiple and complex physiological, cultural, and psychological factors. In any case, mothers who cannot or do not wish to breast-feed should not be reprimanded

or criticized. They should be given assurance that normal growth and development are possible with the proper use of substitute formulas (Foman et al., 1979). Maternal milk-fed infants and infants that are fed with appropriate formula and supplements of vitamins and minerals apparently grow equally well within similar environmental conditions (Barness, 1990).

Choice of Formula. The mother who bottle-feeds her baby has several options in the selection of formula. Premodified milk formulas are available in powdered, concentrated, and ready-to-feed containers. Formulas are available under different brands, with or without iron fortification and with slight variations in nutrient content. Milk-based formulas are generally satisfactory for full-term infants. Milk substitute formulas, usually made from soy milk or protein hydrolysate, are available for infants who are allergic to cows' milk protein. However, about 15 percent of infants who are allergic to cows' milk are also allergic to soy-based formula (Committee on Nutrition, 1976a; 1993).

The two most popular formulas are the concentrated liquid and ready-to-feed formulas (Johnson, Purvis, & Wallace, 1981). Condensed milk, skim milk, low-fat milk, goat milk, and nondairy creamers are not nutritionally acceptable for infant feeding during the first 2 years. Regular whole cows' milk should not be given to infants under 6 months of age because it may cause a small amount of intestinal bleeding resulting in iron deficiency anemia (Committee on Nutrition, 1985; 1993). Errors in preparing infant formula, such as the addition of too much or too little water, can lead to problems.

Dietary Supplements. Nutritionists generally agree that some dietary supplementation is necessary during the nursing period. Opinions vary, however, as to the specific feeding schedule and the amounts and type of supplements needed. Infants are typically given supplements of vitamins C and D, iron, and fluoride, depending upon age, whether the infant is breast- or bottle-fed, formula choice, and fluoride content of the water. Infant caregivers should very carefully follow the physician's instructions to avoid excessive or inadequate amounts of vitamins, fluoride, and iron. There is some evidence that infants from economically disadvantaged families who most need nutritional supplements are least likely to receive them, while infants from more economically advantaged families who least need dietary supplements are more likely to be given supplements they don't need (Curtis, 1990).

Schedule versus Demand Feeding. Another decision that must be made in feeding infants is whether to schedule feedings every three or four hours, or to follow a baby-led, self-demand approach. In many cultures, such as Chimalteco infants of Guatemala, a baby is nursed throughout the day and night when it cries. However, in other cultures babies are fed on a more limited schedule. For example, Jamaican mothers tend to nurse their babies an average of four times a day (Broude, 1995). Over the years, recommendations in the child-rearing literature have variously emphasized feeding babies on a schedule, or feeding them any time they get hungry. For example, all of the articles published in 1920 recommended tight feeding schedules, but in 1948, 100 percent of the articles advised self-demand schedules (McCandless, 1967). In recent years the emphasis has continued to favor demand feeding and self-regulation by the infant (Foman, 1993). Some research evidence supports the practice of providing food to babies in small, frequent feedings rather than in larger amounts at more widely spaced intervals (Fabry & Tepperman, 1970).

On a cautionary note, parents must be careful to distinguish hunger cues from other distress signals in order to avoid overfeeding or underfeeding. Satter (1990) believes that feeding goes best when parents look for cues from the child to guide the feeding process. The parent who is most successful in feeding attends to the signals from the infant about hunger and satiation and responds positively to the child's unique emotional make-up and feeding skills.

Stage 2: Transitional Period (4 to 12 Months)

The second stage of infant feeding is called the transitional period because the baby is changing from a completely liquid diet to a diet consisting mainly of soft or semisolid baby food. The baby is "in transition" between a milk diet and adult table food. The major issues to be considered during this period are (1) developmental characteristics of the infant, (2) the process of weaning, (3) when to introduce semisolid food, and (4) what foods and supplements to include in the diet.

Developmental Characteristics. The 4- to 6-month-old infant who is ready to enter the transitional period has matured physically enough to eat and digest soft, semisolid foods comfortably. By 4 or 5 months of age, the feeding reflexes have been replaced by voluntary muscle control. Sucking and rooting are voluntary, and the extrusion reflex has diminished or disappeared. The mouth is larger in proportion to the tongue and more easily accommodates a spoon. The normal infant is able to maintain a sitting position and hold the head erect without support. By 6 months the digestive system is more mature and can process a wider range of protein, fats, and carbohydrates. The kidneys have a greater capacity to handle increased eliminative loads with less water.

Weaning. The World Health Organization (WHO/UNICEF, 1981) defines weaning as the process by which milk-fed infants gradually become accustomed to the range of foods characteristic of the society into which they are born. Parents are likely to interpret weaning as the process of taking away the breast or bottle. Weaning is difficult to define with precision because there are a variety of transitions that may be made. The process of weaning may include a partial transition from breast to bottle, from a bottle to cup, from liquids to solids, and from caretaker-administered feeding to self-feeding (Gesell & Ilg, 1937). In most cases, weaning tends to be based on cultural traditions and personal preferences rather than scientific recommendations.

Weaning practices vary widely from culture to culture. In the United States, infants are typically weaned by 1 year of age, if not sooner. However, in 83 percent of 159 societies across the world, mothers wait until infants are at least 2 years of age before weaning. In some cultures children may still be nursing at three years or older (Broude, 1995). In many places, such as the Taira Okniawa of Mexico, women generally breast-feed until they are five- or six-months pregnant with another baby. Among the Gusii people of Kenya, mothers like to wait until infants can walk before they are weaned. Consequently, extended breast-feeding is an incentive to prevent a new pregnancy before the current infant begins to walk (Broude, 1995). However, late weaning does not mean that infants are exclusively breast- or bottle-fed. King and Ashworth (1991) report that small food supplements, such as gruel and fruit, are commonly given to infants in several African countries, Malaysia, and the Caribbean.

Some babies wean themselves easily, while others are more reluctant to give up the breast or bottle. Whether weaning is easy or difficult depends upon the readiness of the infant and the pressure exerted by the parent. In some cultures, such as Mixtecans of Mexico, infants are weaned abruptly. Once the mother decides to wean her baby, she never offers the breast again. If the baby protests, a woman may attempt to make nursing distasteful by rubbing bitter herbs or dirt on her nipple. In some cases the baby may be sent to stay with relatives for a day or two (Broude, 1995).

Professionals in the field of childcare tend to favor gradual weaning rather than an abrupt "cold turkey" approach (Wood & Walker-Smith, 1981). Some people advocate "baby-led" weaning, which allows infants to nurse until they are ready to give up the breast or bottle, as long as appropriate supplementary foods are given. Babies who are allowed unrestricted nursing typically wean themselves between 18 months and 3 1/2 years (Waletzky, 1979). Some babies lose interest in breast-feeding as early as 6 months of age. However, other children may act as if they will never wean on their own, as the following anecdote illustrates.

A mother was sitting in the reception room of her pediatrician's office. As she was waiting her turn, she was breast-feeding her baby. Another lady waiting beside her was observing the process with great interest. Finally, when she could restrain herself no longer, she said to the nursing mother, "Isn't that baby a little too old to still be breast-feeding?" Before the mother could respond, the baby paused momentarily, then raised itself up and said, "Mind your own business, lady!" (Wood & Walker-Smith, 1981, p. 170).

Mothers who breast-feed are encouraged to continue the process for at least 6 months, especially in undeveloped countries. Some pediatricians believe there is no reason for discontinuing breast-feeding before 18 to 20 months of age as long as other foods are introduced into the diet by 5 or 6 months to achieve an adequate nutritional balance (Foman et al., 1979). On the other hand, it is possible that prolonged breast- or bottle-feeding can promote undesirable nutritional habits whereby milk replaces other important nutrients in the diet. Infants who are breast-fed exclusively for longer than 6 months may become malnourished. Infants who are bottle-fed over an extended time may expose their teeth to sweetened liquids for longer periods of time, leading to tooth decay (Satter, 1983).

Freudian theorists have hypothesized that weaning practices may influence the development of habit patterns and personality traits such as non-nutritive sucking, aggressiveness, and impatience. Various researchers have attempted to test this hypothesis. However, a variety of studies have failed to demonstrate any consistent relationship between the time of weaning from breast or bottle and the development of child or adult personality patterns (Caldwell, 1964).

Age to Begin Semisolid Food. The German word **beikost** (pronounced bei'kost) is sometimes used to refer to baby foods other than milk or formula. The terms semisolid, nonliquid, strained, and supplementary food are also commonly used to mean the same thing as beikost. The appropriate age to begin beikost has been the subject of debate and controversy through the years. Between 1920 and the early 1970s the age for introduction of semisolid food in the United States declined from the customary age of 1-year-old to as young as the first weeks of life (Worthington-Roberts & Williams, 1996). Currently, there is wide agreement among health-care professionals and nutritionists that the best time to introduce semisolid food is from 4 to 6 months of age.

Various medical groups (Committee on Nutrition, 1980; Canadian Paediatric Society Nutrition Committee, 1979) have expressed concern about possible harmful effects of introducing significant amounts of semisolid food at 1 or 2 months of age. The practice of feeding infants any food other than breast or formula milk before 4 to 6 months of age is strongly discouraged. The reasons for delaying the introduction of semisolids until that time are

1. The extrusion reflex (tendency to push food out of the mouth) does not disappear until 3 or 4 months of age.
2. The neuromuscular coordination necessary for the swallowing of semisolids is not fully developed until 16 to 18 weeks of age.
3. The nutritional values of solid foods are inferior to milk or formula in meeting specific needs of infants for the first 5 to 6 months of life.
4. Semisolid foods impose a higher eliminative load upon immature kidneys.
5. The addition of solids may diminish the immune protection conferred by breast milk.
6. The addition of solids increases possible sources of allergic reactions.
7. Introduction of solids before the infant is able to indicate a desire for food and before the extrusion reflex disappears probably represents a type of forced feeding.
8. There is no evidence of obvious nutritional benefits.
9. The early introduction of semisolid food may interfere with establishing sound eating habits and may contribute to overfeeding.
10. There is no evidence that the addition of semisolid food helps babies sleep through the night.

There are no absolute guidelines for timing the introduction of semisolid foods, except that the decision should be individual in relation to the developmental level and needs of each infant. According to the American Academy of Pediatrics (Committee on Nutrition, 1980), supplemental foods should be introduced when the infant can sit with support and has good neuromuscular control of the neck and head at about 4 to 6 months of age.

Order of Introduction of Different Foods. Caregivers are advised to introduce one new single food ingredient at no less than weekly intervals. The purpose of the procedure is to identify specific food allergies as they occur (Committee on Nutrition, 1993). The typical sequence for the introduction of various types of food is given in Table 7-1. Infant cereals, which provide additional energy and iron, are usually introduced as the first semisolid food. The use of single-grain, rice-based cereals should be given first because they are the least likely to cause an allergic reaction. Iron-fortified cereal is frequently given to satisfy iron requirements. Vegetables may be better accepted if they are introduced before fruits (Canadian Paediatric Society Nutrition Committee 1979), but this is not a widespread opinion among infant nutritionists (Foman et al., 1979).

Juices should be given to the baby when the ability to drink from a cup has developed (Committee on Nutrition, 1993). However, fruit juice should be limited to less than 12 ounces per day. Excessive fruit juice consumption has been associated with growth problems, including short stature, obesity, and nonorganic failure to thrive (Dennison, Rockwell, & Baker, 1997; Smith & Lifshitz, 1994). In addition, many infants have allergic reactions to fruit juices (Foman, 1993). Meats and other high-protein foods, such as eggs, are usually introduced last because they place more strain on the digestive and eliminative processes. Home-prepared strained foods are just as nutritious as commercially prepared baby food. Precautions must be taken to avoid spoilage of any type of food provided (Committee on Nutrition, 1985).

Stage 3: Modified Adult Period (1 to 2 years)

Children begin to imitate adults very early in life—even in eating patterns. Although there is considerable individual variation, many babies move away from infantile eating schedules and baby food by the time they are 1 year of age. The modified adult period is characterized by (1) the development of

Table 7–1 Suggested Ages for the Introduction of Semisolid Foods and Table Foods

FOOD	AGE (Months)		
	4 TO 6	6 TO 8	9 TO 12
Iron-fortified cereals for infants	Add		
Vegetables		Add strained	Gradually delete strained foods, introduce table foods
Fruits		Add strained	Gradually delete strained foods, introduce chopped well-cooked or canned foods
Meats		Add strained or finely chopped table meats	Decrease the use of strained meats, increase the varieties of table meats
Finger foods such as arrowroot biscuits, oven-dried toast		Add those that can be secured with a palmar grasp	Increase the use of small-sized finger foods as the pincer grasp develops
Well-cooked mashed or chopped table foods, prepared without added salt or sugar			Add
Juice by cup			Add

Source: Trahms, Christine M. & Pipes, Peggy L. (1997). *Nutrition for infancy and childhood* (6th ed). WCB/McGraw Hill. Used by permission.

self-feeding skills; (2) the change from chopped (junior) baby food to food from the family table; and (3) the increasing significance of the psychosocial value of food. This period overlaps with the transition period (second stage) because infants may be eating baby food and adult food at the same time. Some infants may even continue to nurse (stage 1) from breast or bottle during this stage.

Development of Self-feeding Skills. Beginning around 1 year of age, many of the skills that are essential for self-feeding are being developed and refined. The average baby has changed the pattern of eating from sucking to rotary chewing movements. Some of the teeth have developed to the point of being useful in biting and chewing solid food. Control of the lips and tongue, which is essential in drinking from a cup, has developed. Infants usually manage to hold a cup and drink with only minor spilling early in the second year.

Voluntary hand-to-mouth movements, a finger-thumb grasp, and the ability to hold and let go of

eating utensils have developed around 7 or 8 months of age. Wrist control, essential in using a spoon efficiently, develops between 12 and 18 months. According to Gesell and Ilg (1937), the 2-year-old is relatively efficient at spoon feeding. The willingness of the parent to allow the baby to practice self-feeding is a very important factor in determining when the skill is accomplished.

During the modified adult period, the baby moves from the caretaker's lap, or an infant seat, to the highchair for meals. The rapidly developing language skills and cognitive capacities play an expanded role in the feeding process. The baby learns to recognize different foods by such features as taste, texture, aroma, and name. Specific foods are given verbal labels, which facilitate requests for food and the statement of food preferences. The feeding process thus takes on an added social and psychological significance during this period.

The age at which children are expected to feed themselves varies widely among cultures. For example, in Tarong families of the Phillipines,

This 11-month-old infant has begun to feed himself with a spoon, but at this age he often gets more food on his face than in his mouth.

infants are encouraged to eat by themselves by one or two years of age. In Indonesia, Javanese mothers may feed their children until they are five or six years old (Broude, 1995). In many cultures, the task of self-feeding involves the ability to use a spoon, chop sticks, and other eating utensils. However, in others the process of self-feeding is simplified because few, if any, eating utensils are available.

Taste and Food Preferences. Research investigations on the extent to which taste sensitivity and preferences change during infancy are rather limited. Beauchamp and Cowart (1986) found that infants younger than 4 months old did not detect the difference between plain and salty water. However, between 4 and 24 months of age, they actually enjoy sipping salty water. Like adults, by 2 or 3 years of age they prefer water plain and food with salt. Other studies also indicate that 2-year-olds prefer salted to unsalted foods, and this preference continues throughout childhood (Weiffenbach et al., 1979).

The newborn infant's preference for sweet sub-stances continues throughout infancy and can be intensified through experience. At 6 months of age, infants who have been given sugar water as a pacifier exhibit a stronger preference for sweet substances than infants who were not given the sugary solution (Capaldi & Vanderbos, 1991). Two-year-old infants who had been regularly fed sugar water by their mothers consumed more sucrose solutions, but not more plain water than infants who were not fed sugar water (Beauchamp & Moran, 1984). However, when the researchers added sucrose to Kool-Aid, no differences were found between infants based upon their past exposure to sweet-tasting water. Thus, the effects of experience with sweet-taste preferences may be modified by interactions with other taste sensations.

Other studies support the idea that the infant's early taste experiences affect later preferences. Freitas (1984) found that infants who tasted a wide variety of foods early in life were more accepting of new foods and preferred a wider range of foods than infants who had tasted only a few foods early in life. Until about 2 years of age, infants willingly ingest almost anything, although their taste preferences affect the amount they ingest (Capaldi & VandenBos, 1991). For example, breast-fed infants will spend more time at a nipple that is producing garlic flavored milk than one that is not (Mennella & Beauchamp, 1991). Even early indirect exposure to what adults eat through breast-milk flavors may be a powerful source of influence on later food preferences. After 2 years of age, infants need more exposures to develop a food preference. Between 2 and 3 years of age, sweetness and familiarity are the major factors that account for food preferences (Capaldi & VandenBos, 1991).

Nutritional Requirements and Food for the Older Infant. When the infant changes from baby food to table food, it is important to take another look at nutritional requirements. During the 1- to 2-year period, the infant's caloric needs are relatively low, but protein needs for the growth of muscles and body tissues remain high (Anderson, Chin, & Fisher, 1982). Protein, caloric, and other basic nutritional requirements can be met with menus prepared from the four basic food groups—milk, meat,

Table 7–2 Basic Four Food Plan for Infants

FOOD GROUP	DAILY SERVINGS BY AGE	
	6 TO 12 MONTHS	18 TO 36 MONTHS
Milk (and dairy products)	16–24 oz.	2–3 cups
Meats, fish, eggs	2 (½ oz.)	2 (½ oz.)
Fruits-vegetables	4 (1–2 tbsp.)	4 (2–3 tbsp.)
Bread-cereal	4 (¼ adult size)	4 (⅓ adult size)

Source: E. Satter (1983). *Child of Mine: Feeding with love and common sense.* Palo Alto, CA: Bull Publishing Co. Adapted by permission.

fruits and vegetables, and bread and cereals (Table 7–2).

An adequate supply of iron (15 mg./day) should be included in the diet during this period. Meats and iron-enriched cereal products are major sources of iron. Some nutritionists advise that the use of iron-fortified infant cereals be continued through the second year of life as the best source of easily digestible iron (Committee on Nutrition, 1976b). Consumption of more than 16 to 24 ounces of milk per day and sugary snacks may result in an inadequate intake of iron-containing foods (Satter, 1983).

Unless adequate fluoride is available in the water supply, the continuation of fluoride supplements is recommended until age 16. However, the fluoride intake should be carefully monitored to avoid tooth pitting and discoloration. For maximum absorption by the body, fluoride should be given between meals (Committee on Nutrition, 1985). Additional mineral or vitamin supplements are not needed during this feeding period if a balanced diet is provided.

Social and Psychological Aspects of Infant Feeding. Although research studies have failed to find a definite relationship between infant-feeding practices and personality adjustment, the psychosocial implications of food and the process of eating during infancy are still considered to be very important. Bruno Bettleheim (1970) believes that "the ability to control oneself, to wait, to work now for future rewards," as well as one's "entire attitude to the world" is conditioned by the eating experience (p. 16). According to Erikson (1963), the regularity and procedure with which an infant

is fed are very important ingredients in the establishment of basic trust. "The first demonstration of social trust in the baby is the ease of his feeding. . . ." (p. 247).

From the beginning, feeding a baby is not simply a one-way process, something that a caretaker does to a child. Rather, it is a process which occurs as a concert between caretaker and baby. Even the newborn is an active participant in the feeding situation. Individuality is expressed early in the infant's own unique approaches to nursing and feeding styles (Barnes et al., 1953). Caretakers also bring their own personality characteristics, expectations, and attitudes to the feeding situation. The underlying parental attitudes are likely to be more potent than actual parental practices in feeding infants (Caldwell, 1964). In any event, success in feeding and the psychosocial consequences of the feeding process ultimately depend upon the interactions between infants and their caretakers. The process of meeting the infant's need for nourishment cannot be separated from the infant's need for nurturance.

As the infant grows older and moves to the highchair, new opportunities for social interchange with the family at mealtimes are provided. The process of eating takes on increasing meaning in the establishment of autonomy and self-control. At this stage, as in earlier stages, the supportive parent will let the child take the lead and support the child's initiative. According to Satter (1990), the role of the parent is to choose feeding methods based on the child's level of development, select appropriate food, remain present in the feeding situation but restrained enough to accept the child's lead.

The role of the infant is to expand feeding skills, explore new food preferences, and determine how much to eat. The toddler's refusal of new food and the insistence on particular food preferences is one way of expressing the need for autonomy and individuality. Infants who reject new foods initially accept the same food later after repeated neutral exposure (Birch & Marlin, 1982).

There is a danger that food will become a battleground between parent and child and take on a negative dimension. Approximately 25 to 35 percent of feeding interactions tend to be negative and problematic. Common problems reported by parents include poor food acceptance, eating too much or too little, immature feeding skills, and bizarre food habits (Satter, 1990). Infants learn early that food may be used as a means of controlling behavior and attracting attention. Usually, relaxed parents who are willing to give their child choices and freedom to establish food preferences (within limits) avoid unnecessary power struggles and get through the period with minimum frustration.

SPECIAL NUTRITIONAL CONCERNS AND FEEDING PROBLEMS

A number of problems are related to infant nutrition and feeding practices. Special concerns that are the focal point of current discussion and research activity include iron-deficiency anemia, food allergies, dental caries, infantile obesity and its relationship to adult obesity, and the effects of sodium intake in early life on the development of hypertension in adulthood.

Iron-Deficiency Anemia

Iron deficiency is the most common specific nutritional deficiency usually encountered in infants and young children in the United States (Woodruff, 1978). An inadequate supply of iron in the diet can lead to **iron-deficiency anemia.** This condition involves an insufficiency in the number or size of blood cells which limits the ability of the blood to carry oxygen (Shelov, 1994). Iron deficiency is most prevalent between 6 months and 3 years of age (Committee on Nutrition, 1993). Small, premature infants become more susceptible to iron deficiency when their low prenatal iron stores are depleted after about 2 months of age. The risk period for full-term infants begins around 4 to 6 months of age. The highest incidence of the condition is found among lower-socioeconomic populations and low-birthweight infants (Committee on Nutrition, 1976b). Iron deficiency results in poor growth and lowered resistance to infection. Evidence of the association of iron-deficiency anemia with problems in psychomotor and mental development is also accumulating. Studies from various cultures have found lower mental and psychomotor test scores among anemic infants, as compared with infants who were not iron deficient (Filer, 1990; 1995). Symptoms of iron-deficiency anemia include poor appetite, irritability, poor skin color, and listlessness.

The importance of preventing and treating iron-deficiency anemia throughout the world is increasingly evident. Iron-fortified milk should be used for formula-fed infants. Full-term infants who are breast-fed should usually begin receiving iron supplements between 4 and 6 months. Iron supplementation is recommended for breast-fed preterm infants at 2 months of age (Committee on Nutrition, 1993). Sources of iron supplements include fortified, commercially prepared infant formula and cereal. Iron-containing drops are available for preterm infants who are breast-fed.

Adverse Reactions

Infants display a variety of adverse reactions to food including allergies (immunologic reactions), carbohydrate intolerance, especially milk and fruit juice, and toxic reactions resulting from food contamination, including breast milk (Bock & Sampson, 1994). Reliable estimates of the incidence of adverse reactions to food are difficult to find because symptoms are often erroneously attributed to food. For example, Bock (1987) studied a group of 480 children from birth to their third birthdays. Although 43 percent had an adverse reaction that was attributed to food, only 8 percent of the symptoms were considered to be truly food related. The incidence of true food allergies during the first 3 years of life is estimated to be approximately 1 to 2 percent of children, with the prevalence declining as children get older (Bock & Sampson, 1994).

A wide range of symptoms have been associated with allergic reactions to food. The most common symptoms include gastrointestinal episodes of abdominal pain, vomiting, and diarrhea. Skin rash is a commonly reported symptom, but may involve other conditions that are enhanced by food reactions. Respiratory tract symptoms that can be attributed solely to adverse food reactions are uncommon among infants. Contrary to popular opinion, there is little evidence to indicate that food products, such as sugar, lead to hyperactivity (Bock & Sampson, 1994). Because the symptoms are varied and may also result from other sources, the specific foods that are the culprits are hard to identify. To further complicate the problem, children may outgrow certain food allergies but become susceptible to new food intolerances with changing age.

Milk, wheat, eggs, corn, and citrus fruits are foods most frequently identified in allergic reactions in babies (Speer, 1973), but any food is a potential offender. Milk allergy is a problem for an estimated 3 to 7 percent of formula-fed infants (Goldstein & Heiner, 1970). Some children also react adversely to breast milk. In some cases the elimination of cows' milk from the mother's diet has solved the problem for breast-fed babies (Jakobsson & Lindberg, 1978). The usual procedure for identifying the cause of an allergic reaction is to remove a suspicious food from the diet and introduce it again a week or so later to determine if the symptoms recur. Blood tests are widely used for assessing food allergies. Skin tests are sometimes used in extreme cases, but they present special problems for infants.

Dental Caries

Dental caries represents one of the most common problems resulting from nutritional and feeding inadequacies. Although the rate of dental caries in the United States has decreased considerably in recent years (Brunelle & Carlos, 1990), dental health continues to be a major concern during the infancy period. Nutrition plays a critical role in the development of healthy teeth from the sixth week of the prenatal period through the adolescent period. The state of dental health is, to a large extent, a reflection of dietary adequacy. The major nutrients required for normal tooth development are protein, calcium, phosphorus, Vitamin A, Vitamin D, and ascorbic acid. The value of fluoride, in combination with an adequate diet, in the prevention of dental caries has been well documented (Committee on Nutrition, 1979; Pipes & Trahms, 1993).

A characteristic pattern of dental caries which is frequently observed in infants and young children is **bottle-mouth syndrome** (also called nursing-bottle syndrome, and baby-bottle tooth decay). The problem is characterized by extreme damage to the upper and sometimes the lower front teeth. The teeth decay and may break off at the gum line. The pattern of decay results from the pooling of milk around the teeth. Children who are habitually given a bottle while going to sleep are particularly susceptible to bottle caries. The use of pacifiers coated with sugary substances, or bottles containing sweetened beverages or fruit juice also increase the risk of bottle-mouth syndrome.

Obesity

Obesity is a problem of special concern during infancy because of the widespread belief that a fat infant tends to become a fat child, who, in turn, becomes a fat adult. An obese infant is one whose body mass index (BMI) falls at the 95th percentile or above. The BMI is defined as weight/stature squared $[(kg/cm)^2]$(Barness & Curran, 1996). Obesity can result from an increase in fat cell numbers (hyperplasia) or an increase in fat cell size (hypertrophy). Theoretically, there are two critical periods for the development of fat cell numbers—infancy and adolescence. Excessive weight gain during a critical period may result in excessive numbers of fat cells, which may be permanent. Thus, later weight loss may be difficult because it can be accomplished only through reduction in cell size (Knittle, 1972). Some scientists believe that obese infants have a moderately increased risk of becoming obese adults (e.g., Barness & Curran,

1996). However, existing studies on the relationship between obesity in infancy and obesity in adulthood are contradictory and inconclusive.

Whether an infant grows up to be fat or skinny depends to some extent upon genetic factors. Research studies of adopted infants and twins suggest that human fatness and obesity are more closely related to heredity than to early eating habits. Stunkard and his associates (1986) studied 540 adults in Denmark who had been adopted as infants. The adoptees tended to develop a body weight that more closely resembled that of their biological parents than of the parents who reared them. In another study, Stunkard, Foch, and Krubec (1986) found the incidence of obesity to be twice as high in identical twins as in nonidentical twins. The results of both studies are consistent with earlier findings (Mayer, 1965) that only 14 percent of the offspring of two normal-weight parents become obese. In comparison, 40 percent of infants with one overweight parent and 80 percent of those with two overweight parents become obese.

None of these studies should be interpreted to mean that infants of overweight parents inevitably become obese. Neither do the studies mean that parents do not have to pay attention to what infants are fed. The research does suggest, however, that parents who are overweight need to make special efforts to keep their infants from overeating. In addition to dietary control, parents need to develop other strategies to prevent obesity, such as providing increased opportunities for age-appropriate exercise activities. Obesity is not inevitable and can be prevented.

The association between the high intake of fat and raised cholesterol levels, leading to heart problems in adults, have led to questions about whether or not infants should be placed on a low-fat diet. Scientific information about the optimal content of fat in the diet of infants is very limited. No relationship between blood cholesterol levels and cholesterol levels in adulthood has been established. Therefore, at the present time, scientists do not recommend placing infants on modified-fat or low-cholesterol diets. Also, cholesterol screening tests are not considered useful (Finberg, 1990; Tarim, Newman, & Lifshitz, 1995).

In any case, parents are advised to avoid overfeeding infants foods of any type. Moderation should be followed to avoid dietary extremes resulting in nutritional deficits or obesity (Tarim et al., 1995). The growth of infants should be carefully monitored by a physician's growth chart to avoid obesity (see Appendixes). In the event that obesity has developed, the infant is usually not placed on a weight-loss diet. Rather, the emphasis is placed on restricting further excessive weight gain until normal body proportions with normal increments in height are obtained (Canadian Paediatric Society Nutrition Committee, 1979). Satter (1990) advises parents of obese children to teach children to eat in a way that reflects the child's internal cues of hunger, appetite, and satisfaction, rather than imposing weight reduction diets.

Sodium and Hypertension

An increasing amount of concern has been expressed in recent years that the amount of sodium usually included in the diets of infants may be excessive. Cross-cultural studies have found that population groups with high sodium diets have a higher incidence of hypertension than groups with a low sodium intake. Studies on rats show certain genetic strains developing hypertension in adulthood when subjected to high sodium diets in infancy (Dahl, 1972; Committee on Nutrition, 1993).

Subsequent research studies (e.g., Whitten & Stewart, 1980) using human subjects have failed to establish that sodium intake in infancy is a contributing factor in adult hypertension. Yet there remains a reasonable possibility that controlling sodium intake during infancy and childhood may be a preventive measure for the people who are susceptible.

Baby food manufacturers have responded to the concern about controlling sodium intake and no longer add salt to commercially prepared infant foods. Infant dietary surveys have found that the average sodium intake has declined in recent years (Committee on Nutrition, 1993). Parents are advised to avoid adding salt to baby food they buy or prepare at home (Committee on Nutrition, 1980).

CONSEQUENCES OF MALNUTRITION

Worldwide, malnutrition is one of the leading causes of illness and death in infancy (Barness & Curran, 1996). Malnutrition is a condition in which there is either a deficit or an excess of one or more essential nutrients needed by the body tissues (Santos, Arrendo, & Vitale, 1983). This condition can result from either insufficient or excessive nutrient intake, or inadequate absorption of food into the infant's system. There are various degrees of malnutrition, ranging from mild to severe.

Malnutrition is considered to be the most widespread and serious problem affecting infants and young children in the world (Santos et al., 1983). Nearly a third of the children under age 5 in undeveloped nations are severely malnourished (United Nations Children's Fund, 1996). The effects are numerous and varied. Specific symptoms or conditions resulting from varying nutritional problems include growth delay or failure, rickets, anemia, dental caries, obesity, and lowered resistance to disease. Malnutrition also has serious behavioral consequences such as listlessness, withdrawal, and mental retardation. The ultimate outcome of malnutrition depends upon its timing, severity, and duration.

Protein Energy Malnutrition

On a worldwide scale, **protein energy malnutrition (PEM)** is a major health problem in many developing countries (Avery & First, 1994). This condition results in growth retardation or failure and possibly mental disabilities (McLaren & Burman, 1982). Cases of PEM become evident between 4 months and 2 years of age, when infants from poverty backgrounds have been weaned from breast milk. The main features of mild to moderate PEM are growth retardation, lowered resistance to infectious diseases, and a diminished activity level. The first effects on growth are characterized by

1. a slower rate of linear growth and weight gain
2. delayed bone maturation, resulting from low protein and calcium intake

3. a decrease in midarm circumference, due to muscle wasting
4. normal or diminished weight:height ratio
5. normal or diminished skin-fold thickness, which reflects loss of fat stores (McLaren & Burman, 1982, p. 114).

Growth retardation may be compounded by the higher incidence of infectious diseases that occurs in an infant subjected to PEM. The lack of sufficient calories (energy) in the diet causes the baby to be listless and apathetic. There is a danger that caretakers will interpret this quiet behavior as a sign of a "good" baby and fail to see it as a problem.

The most severe forms of malnutrition include the conditions known as **kwashiorkor** and **marasmus.** Marasmus is more frequent in children under 1 year of age and kwashiorkor is found more fre-

These children are suffering from kwashiorkor. Notice the swollen stomach, skinny arms, and loss of hair.

quently among children 1 to 6 years of age (Monckberg, 1991). Kwashiorkor is caused primarily by insufficient protein in the diet and usually occurs in the second, third, or fourth year of life (Wood & Walker-Smith, 1981). The child who suffers from kwashiorkor has a swollen appearance (edema) but has little muscular tissue under the skin. Skin ulcers, loss of hair, irritability or lethargy, weakness, and growth failure are other characteristics of the condition.

Marasmus is caused by insufficient food intake (starvation) in general, but a deficiency of calories in particular. It typically appears in the early months of life. The marasmic child has lost most of the subcutaneous fat and appears to be mostly skin and bones. The condition may include chronic diarrhea, vomiting, irritability, or apathy (McLaren & Burman, 1982). Either marasmus or kwashiorkor leads to death if left untreated. These diseases are usually not found in the United States, although rare cases are found from time to time.

Catch-up Growth

Obviously, the effects of malnutrition can be devastating to the human body. To what extent do children have the capacity to recover from severe PEM that has resulted in stunted growth? There is reasonably strong evidence that human beings have an amazing capacity for **catch-up growth**. A group of Johns Hopkins University doctors (Graham & Adrianzen, 1972) studied children who had been hospitalized for malnutrition between 3 and 15 months of age in Lima, Peru. The children eventually achieved normal physical growth after they were removed from their impoverished environments and placed in homes where they were given adequate nutrition and medical care. Other studies (e.g., Galler & Ross, 1993; Winick, Meyer, & Harris, 1975) have found similar results.

The evidence is not conclusive, however, and not all researchers are equally optimistic about the possibility of reversing the effects of nutritional growth failure. It is possible that stunted growth that begins with even a moderate degree of PEM in infancy might have adverse consequences in old

age or even in the next generation (Gurney, 1979). A critical factor is the age at which intervention is begun. Recovery has been found to be more complete when treatment is begun before 6 months of age than when intervention is begun later (Monckeberg, 1991).

Malnutrition and Brain Growth

The effects of malnutrition on brain growth and mental functioning have been the subject of speculation and intensive investigation. Evidence is accumulating to show that severe early malnutrition is likely to alter the structure and function of the brain. Both animal and human studies have found that early malnutrition of the marasmus type reduces the number of brain cells, brain size, and head circumference. In addition, myelination, structural organization, and biochemical composition of the brain may be adversely affected (Winick, 1979). However, the timing of the nutritional deficit is critical and the starvation must be severe. The periods of growth when the brain is most vulnerable to damage coincide with times "when the brain is increasing its weight particularly rapidly" (Dobbing & Smart, 1974, p. 164). The first growth spurt when the brain is most vulnerable to starvation probably begins with the last trimester of fetal growth (about 30 weeks' gestation) and continues through the first 18 months after birth (Martin, 1973). There are no known effects of malnutrition on the brain until that time, with the exception of folic acid deficiency which can result in hydrocephaly, neural tube defects, and spina bifida (Dobbing, 1993). Another vulnerable period coincides with the rapid myelination of the brain during the second postnatal year through the third and fourth years (Spreen et al., 1995).

Severe nutritional deficits that occur during the periods of rapid brain growth tend to cause permanent damage (Winick, 1976). Studies on the effects of undernutrition of rats during early life have found deficits in both body and brain growth that were permanent even after a lengthy period of nutritional rehabilitation (Bedi, 1987). Whether or not the effects are permanent is likely to be determined by the timing, duration, and severity of the malnutrition. The effects of mild short-term malnutrition on brain growth at any time are thought to be inconsequential.

Malnutrition, Learning, and Behavior

To what extent does malnutrition in infancy adversely influence learning and intellectual performance over the course of a lifetime? Various researchers have tried to assess the impact of nutritional deficits on psychological development. One of the first studies was conducted in the early 1960s in Mexico City by Cravioto and Robles (1965), who tested twenty infants hospitalized for kwashiorkor. All of the infants were found to be below the age norms for physical and mental development. The study revealed that infants with the earliest (ages 3 to 6 months) and most severe degree of malnutrition showed fewer signs of recovery from developmental deficits than infants with later (15 to 42 months) and less severe nutritional deficits.

Galler & Ross (1993) studied the effects of severe malnutrition during the first year of life on 160 children in Barbados over a 23-year period, comparing their development with an equal number of children who had no history of malnutrition. In contrast to some other studies, social-class factors were controlled. The malnourished infants who were placed in an adequate nutritional environment generally achieved "catch-up" physical growth by the time they reached puberty. However, the researchers found that 60 percent of the previously malnourished children, as opposed to 15 percent of the well-nourished children suffered from attention deficit disorder that persisted into adulthood.

The results of the Barbados study tend to show that malnutrition that occurs during the first year of life plays a major role in impaired intellectual development (Galler & Ross, 1993). Adequate nutritional intervention alone is apparently not sufficient to reverse the long-term effects of malnutrition on mental development. However, other researchers (Grantham-McGregor, Schofield, & Powell, 1987) have found that children, malnourished as infants, who were given cognitive stimulation in addition to improved nutrition performed

at normal or near-normal levels on tests of mental performance.

Researchers have had difficulty separating the effects of nutritional deficits from other environmental factors. Malnutrition may exert its major influence on learning indirectly by causing changes in attention, motivation, and responsiveness (Beal, 1980). The undernourished baby is listless, easily tired, irritable, withdrawn, and less inclined to seek or be responsive to mental stimulation (Barrett, 1987). The infant's inactivity and lack of responsiveness may result in decreased social interchanges with parents, other caregivers, and peers. The malnourished child's greater susceptibility to illness also increases the social isolation.

SIGNS OF NUTRITIONAL ADEQUACY

Generally, the signs of nutritional adequacy are related to growth rate, appetite, muscle tone, activity pattern, and appearance of the oral cavity (Lewis, 1979). One of the best indicators of good nutrition is a consistent, steady growth rate, which generally parallels the normal curve on a standard growth chart. Usually the appetite will correlate positively with the growth rate, allowing for temporary variations for illness and changes in routines. The muscles should be firm to the touch and should have good motor reactions. Behaviorally, the baby should be alert, inquisitive, happy, and responsive. Malnourished children are listless, withdrawn, and often irritable. The mucous membranes inside the mouth as well as the lips, tongue, and gums should be reddish pink. The tongue normally has a slightly rough appearance. Any teeth that are present should remain bright and free of cavities or pitting (Lewis, 1979).

FEEDING INFANTS WHO HAVE SPECIAL NEEDS

Infants who are born with disabling conditions such as Down syndrome, cystic fibrosis, cerebral palsy, seizure disorders, inborn errors of metabolism, and numerous other conditions require adjustments in dietary and feeding procedures. Nutritional needs of these infants vary widely and need to be considered on an individual basis. For example, many infants with development disabilities (e.g., Down syndrome) have slower growth rates and diminished motor activities. Unless dietary modifications are made to reflect their lowered energy needs, these infants soon become overweight.

In other cases, infants have problems with poor sucking ability and motor coordination (e.g., cerebral palsy) that affect their ability to feed themselves. These infants have higher energy needs and may be underweight (Cloud, 1993). Infants with metabolic disorders (e.g., phenylketonuria) will experience brain damage unless their intake of food products containing phenylalanine or other aversive substances is carefully controlled. Preterm and low-birthweight babies also have special nutritional needs that are discussed in Chapter 4.

Parents and other caregivers need help in determining what and how to feed infants who have development disorders because of their unique need. Cloud (1993) recommends that nutritionists, doctors, nurses, occupational and/or physical therapists, and other specialists work together in assessing nutritional needs and counseling caregivers.

Public Assistance Programs

Various programs have been developed to help improve the nutritional status of infants who are at risk for malnutrition. Internationally, the World Health Organization has been active in developing educational and food-distribution programs to help meet the needs of undernourished infants, especially in undeveloped countries. In the United States, a number of nutritional programs are operated by federal and state agencies. The Food Distribution and Food Stamp programs funded by the U.S. Department of Agriculture help low-income families obtain the foods they need for good health. The Child Care Food Program is another federally funded program that helps meet the needs of infants and young children enrolled in child-care centers. The Special Supplemental Food Program for Women, Infants, and Children (WIC) provides nutrition education and food supplements to preg-

nant women and mothers, as well as food supplements for women, infants, and children from low-income families. The WIC program is a federally funded program that is operated by local health departments or other authorized community agencies (Kendrick, Kaufman, & Messenger, 1988).

SUGGESTIONS FOR FEEDING INFANTS

Unfortunately, feeding infants is not an exact science and the advice given to parents is often contradictory and controversial. Parents should make decisions about feeding practices only after obtaining current information from their pediatrician and other professional sources. The following are some examples of generally recommended feeding practices for each feeding stage (Hinton & Kerwin, 1981; Lewis, 1979; Satter, 1983, 1990).

Nursing Infants

1. Breast-feed the baby for the first 6 months of life if possible.
2. Engage in eye contact and cuddle the infant during feeding sessions. Talk and smile but not constantly. Look for and respond to infant cues.
3. Hold the baby securely but allow freedom to move. Avoid using bottle props to replace a caretaker's lap.
4. Allow infants to decide how much to eat as well as the feeding tempo. Allow the baby to pause and return to eating as desired. Discontinue feeding when the infant loses interest in feeding. Avoid giving infants breast or bottle to stop their crying that is resulting from needs other than hunger.
5. To avoid bottle-mouth syndrome, do not allow an infant to go to sleep with a bottle containing anything but water after teeth begin to appear. Sweetened liquids should not be given in a bottle.
6. Avoid giving an infant honey in any form because of the risk of botulism.

Transition Infants

1. Let the child take the lead. Allow the child to touch the food and finger feed.
2. Do not mix cereal or other foods with milk and give it from a bottle.
3. Make the first solid food thin and smooth. Use a small

spoon to place the food on the middle of the tongue, but do not exert pressure. Give very small amounts of any new food at the beginning.

4. Introduce new foods one at a time at one- or two-week intervals and observe for allergic reactions. Do not mix foods until each has been introduced separately.

5. Allow all infants to have food preferences. Offer infants a variety of foods over time.

6. Do not add salt or sugar to an infant's food. Foods containing refined sugar should be limited.

Toddlers

1. Serve food at lukewarm temperature in bite-size pieces and small portions. Provide child-size utensils and comfortable seating. Provide soft finger foods, with no choking hazards, for self-feeding.

2. Encourage self-feeding as soon as the infant can hold a spoon, manage a cup, or other culturally approriate utensils. Be tolerant of spills and messiness.

3. Establish mealtimes and feeding routines.

4. Provide meals in a pleasant, relaxed atmosphere. Keep mealtime conversation happy and pleasant. Allow for a premeal rest period when possible.

5. Avoid rigid rules about the amount of food to be eaten. Do not force toddlers to eat by coaxing or by offering treats or bribes.

6. Give toddlers between-meal snacks; toddlers need more frequent feedings than adults. Snacks should consist of small amounts of nutritious, low-sugar foods. They should be carefully spaced, usually midway between meals.

7. Children over 2 years of age may begin following adult guidelines which limit dietary fat to more than 30 percent of total calories.

SUMMARY

1. For healthy growth and development, infants need a diet that provides a daily balance of calories, protein, vitamins, minerals, and water.

2. The three stages of infant feeding are the nursing period (birth to 6 months), the transitional period (4 to 12 months), and the modified adult period (1 to 2 years).

3. Through the years, rates of breast-feeding have fluctuated. Following a period of decline between 1984 and 1989, the percentage of mothers who breast-feed their babies is currently on the rise.

4. An increasing amount of scientific evidence is being used to support recommendations that mothers should breast feed their newborn infants for six months if possible.

5. Generally, professionals recommend feeding infants on demand rather than on a predetermined schedule. Parents should observe an infant carefully for cues to guide the feeding process.

6. Recommendations on the age for weaning infants vary widely. In the United States, most infants are likely to be weaned by the end of the first year of life. However, weaning practices vary widely from culture to culture.

7. The recommended age for the introduction of semisolid food into the diet of an infant is from 4 to 6 months.

8. Infants develop the motor-coordination skills for efficient self-feeding by 2 years of age. The demands placed on infants for the development of self-feeding skills vary across cultures.

9. The infant's basic nutritional needs during the modified adult period can be met with menus planned from the basic four food groups: milk and dairy products, meat, fruits and vegetables, bread and cereal.

10. Food and mealtime become increasingly significant for socioemotional development, as the infant gets old enough to sit independently with adults at mealtime.

11. The most common nutritional problem of infants in the United States is iron-deficiency anemia. Adverse food reactions, dental caries, obesity, and excessive sodium intake are other nutritional problems and concerns during infancy.

12. Protein energy malnutrition (PEM) is a common nutritional problem among infants throughout the world. The physical effects of PEM include retardation of physical growth, lowered resistance to infectious diseases, kwashiorkor, and marasmus. Infants have an amazing ability to overcome the effects of malnutrition if intervention is begun soon enough.

13. Severe malnutrition occurring during the prenatal period and early months of life is likely to result in permanent damage to the developing

brain. Malnutrition may also cause learning deficits as the result of a diminished level of responsiveness and exploratory behavior.

14. Some of the signs that infants are receiving adequate nutrition are a normal growth rate, good appetite, firm muscle tone, curiosity, and alertness.

15. Nutrition needs and self-feeding abilities of infants with special needs vary widely and must be considered on an individual basis.

16. A variety of public-assistance programs is available in the United States and throughout the world to help parents meet the nutritional needs of their infants.

8

Motor Development

The loving mother teaches her child to walk alone. She is far enough from him so that she cannot actually support him, but she holds out her arms to him. She imitates his movements, and if he totters, she swiftly bends as if to seize, so that the child might believe that he is not walking alone. . . . And yet, she does more. Her face beckons like a reward, an encouragement. Thus, the child walks alone with his eyes fixed on his mother's face, not on the difficulties in his way. He supports himself by the arms that do not hold him and constantly strives towards the refuge in his mother's embrace, little suspecting that in the very same moment that he is emphasizing his need of her, he is proving that he can do without her, because he is walking alone.

—Søren Kierkegaard

As soon as an infant is born, or perhaps even before, the struggle to establish control over the body begins. The changes that occur in the infant's ability to control the movement of the muscles of the body are referred to as motor development. During the first 3 years of life, the child progresses from a relatively helpless infant state of motor activity to a state of independence and mobility. The development of basic motor skills during infancy forms the foundation for the more elaborate and refined motor acts of later childhood.

The numerous motor behaviors that emerge during the infancy period can be classified under the following general headings: (1) reflex movements, (2) eye-hand coordination, (3) achievement of an upright position and locomotion, (4) self-care activities. This chapter focuses on the characteristic patterns and processes of motor development in each of these categories. Initially, let us consider how motor development is interrelated with other areas of infant development and the factors that influence the acquisition of motor skills.

INTERRELATIONSHIPS OF DEVELOPMENTAL AREAS

The development of motor skills is a complicated process involving coordination between the nervous system, the skeleton, muscles, and sensory mechanisms. Consequently, motor development influences and is influenced by other components of the growing infant. During infancy an important indicator of mental functioning is the ability to carry out motor acts. At the same time, the acquisition of motor skills allows the infant to move and explore the environment in order to satisfy curiosity and obtain knowledge. In Piaget's (1952) view, the sensorimotor activities of infancy provide the foundations of intelligence (see Chapter 9).

Held and Hein's (1963) classic study of kittens showed that self-produced movement (e.g., creeping, walking, reaching) is important for perceptual development. More recent evidence from a variety of studies with human infants shows that dramatic changes in perceptual-cognitive, social, and emotional changes occur when infants begin to move around on their own (Bertenthal, Campos, & Barrett, 1984). Self-produced locomotion promotes the development of perceptual abilities, spatial orientation, fear of heights, and the ability to remember where hidden objects are located (see Chapter 9). It also facilitates concept formation and the differentiation of emotions (Bertenthal & Campos, 1987; 1990).

The development of an infant's body awareness and self-image are also derived to some extent from information obtained through sensorimotor activities. As infants use their bodies and experience success or failure in motor acts, they form self-opinions that are closely interrelated with overall personality development. The establishment of physical independence through motor control leads to feelings of self-confidence, psychological security, and independence. On the other hand, feelings of dependency and inadequacy tend to inhibit the acquisition of motor control.

FACTORS INFLUENCING MOTOR DEVELOPMENT

Maturation versus Learning

As in other areas of development, scientists debate the relative contributions of maturation and learning to motor development. Several classic research studies have been used to support the view that motor development is largely controlled by the process of maturation. For example, Gesell and Thompson (1934) gave one identical twin six weeks of practice in a variety of motor tasks, while they gave the other twin no opportunity for practice. Within a three-week period after the training ended, the twin who had not been given special instruction made more progress than the twin who had been trained. These researchers concluded that practice does not make any difference until a child is biologically ready to acquire a particular motor skill.

Further support for the importance of maturational influences on motor development is cited by Casaer (1992). Infants who remained in a cast between 5 and 12 months of age began to walk soon after the cast was removed. After a few days there was no difference in their walking ability as

In some cultures, infants are carried on the mother's back for several months.

compared to children who started earlier. Another classic study, by Dennis (1941), reached a similar conclusion. Hopi Indian infants who were tied to a cradleboard on their mother's backs for much of the first nine months of life were compared to a group of infants from Western culture who were allowed relatively unrestricted movement. Since both groups of infants began to walk at about the same age, Dennis concluded that walking must be maturationally determined.

On the other side of the question, Bower (1977), a Scottish psychologist, believes that opportunities for learning "have a great deal to do with the rate and direction of motor development" (p. 91). In one of Bower's experiments, babies were given practice in reaching for a dangling object. These babies obtained a more mature pattern of reaching and grasping several weeks earlier than a control group of infants who had no comparable experience. Learning experiences were thus considered to have been influential in the acquisition of these particular skills. Currently, scientific opinion supports the view that both maturation and experience are important. Results of cross-cultural research discussed below indicate that variations in child-rearing practices can influence the acquisition of motor skills.

Dynamic-Systems Approach

Thelen and Fogel (1989) explain the development of motor skills in terms of a dynamic-systems approach. This perspective represents a compromise between extreme maturation and learning points of view. Multiple factors and processes contribute to the acquisition of motor skills. The human body is composed of biological systems. The sensory, skeletal, muscular, and motor systems are examples of some major components. In order for the infant to accomplish the tasks involved in walking and other motor skills the body systems must work together. These body systems develop within a cultural context and are influenced by social systems such as mother-infant dyads. Emphasis is placed upon ways in which these biological and social systems cooperate and interact in the process of the acquisition of motor skills. The term "dynamic" is used to reflect the concept that changes involving growth and skill acquisition in one area or system will have an impact on performance in another.

An increasing number of researchers are using dynamic systems as a theoretical framework for conducting studies on motor development (Fogel, 1997). For example, researchers have used a "moving room" situation to study how the development of postural control of infants is affected by information obtained from the visual and vestibular (balance) sensory systems (Bertenthal & Campos, 1990). Infants sit or stand on a platform inside a room constructed with hanging walls that swing back and forth while the floor remains stationary. When the room moves forwards, observers determine if the infants are tricked into the false perception that they have swayed backward and react by swaying forward to maintain balance rather than falling down.

The results of moving-room studies show that 3 day old infants integrate visual information with postural responses by moving their heads in the opposite direction of the moving wall (Woollacott, 1992). By 7 to 9 months of age infants make appropriate adjustments in posture to compensate for the perceptions of the wall movements. According to Berthenthal and Campos (1990), this is a significant development because it means that infants are capable of monitoring their motor movements through both visual and vestibular information at about the time they start creeping.

Researchers have found that there are plateaus and regressions throughout infancy in the ability to use visual and vestibular information in maintaining balance. For example, after the onset of creeping there is a decline in the infant's ability to effectively use visual information from the "moving" wall to maintain balance. However, this ability returns again about the time the infant learns to stand (Woollacott, 1992). The changes in sensitivity to visual information in maintaining posture control and balance are not easy to explain. They may be the result of changes in the nervous system that occur during transition periods after infants accomplish one task and get ready for another (Haywood, 1993; Woollacott, 1992).

Body Size

The sizes of the various parts of the body affect its resistance to movement (Newell, 1984). Body size and proportions are apparently related to the age at which some of the motor milestones are achieved. The relationships are not simple, however, and are most clearly observed in infants who represent extreme differences in body measurements (Malina, 1973b). For example, slender infants with relatively long legs walk earlier than shorter infants with shorter legs (Bayley, 1935; Shirley, 1931). Garn (1966) found that leaner infants attained better scores on a variety of early motor tasks than heavier infants.

Muscle Strength and Tone

The development of the ability to control body movements and postures is affected by muscle strength and muscle tone. **Muscle strength** involves the amount of force that the muscles in a particular body part can exert while pushing or pulling against resistance. Muscle strength is affected by a number of factors including exercise, body chemistry, nervous system activity, skeletal size, and the amount and properties of muscle tissue (Fetters, 1996). In general, muscle strength improves as fibers increase in size and overall mass throughout the infancy period (Malina & Bouchard, 1991). Muscle strength also improves as infants increase activity and mobility.

Muscle tone refers to the amount of tension in the muscles when the body is in a state of rest (Smith, 1989). Muscle tone provides the foundation for the control of body posture, balance, stability, and voluntary movements. Muscle tone is controlled by the central nervous system. Underlying muscle tone is usually viewed in terms of a continuum ranging from **hypotonia** (decreased tone) at one end and **hypertonia** (increased tone) at the other end (Fetters, 1996). Normal muscle tone is dynamic and fluctuates according to movement requirements. Muscle tone that is too limp (hypotonic) or too rigid (hypertonic) interferes with the control of motor activity. Muscle tone quality generally improves with the maturation of the nervous system during the infancy period. Infants with neurological impairments may have motor problems due to atypical muscle tone or strength.

Cultural and Ethnic Influences

Cross-cultural studies consistently show that traditionally reared infants from underdeveloped countries are more accelerated in motor performance than infants from Western culture (Werner, 1979). Their advanced motor development has been attributed to such childrearing practices as frequent sensorimotor stimulation, participation in adult activities, exposure to multiple caregivers from extended families, and freedom from restrictive clothing and playpens. For example, West Indian mothers use a series of stretching exercises and massage routines from about the second or third months to stimulate active movements (Hopkins & Westra, 1988). At the end of bathing, usually when the baby is wet, the baby is suspended by both arms and gently shaken up and down. Next the mother holds the baby up by one arm and then the other, and then holds the baby upside down by the ankles. The mother also grasps the baby's head on both sides while pulling upwards to stretch the baby's neck. Infants are also propped with cushions that are gradually removed for independent sitting. Later in the year, the baby is held and stimulated to walk up the mother's body, and eventually encouraged to take steps on the floor while being held by the arms in a standing position. Researchers found these infants to be superior in head control, sitting alone, and standing up when held, in comparison to infants who do not receive this type of stimulation (Hopkins & Westra, 1988). On the other hand, infants reared in cultures where they are restricted by heavy clothing and where interactions with caretakers are quiet and passive tend to lag behind in motor activities. Differences in motor development that result primarily from cultural influences, however, tend to disappear by the end of the infancy period.

Research studies comparing infants from different racial and ethnic groups in the United States on motor performance are rather limited. There is some evidence that African-American infants demonstrate precocity in motor development (King & Seegmiller, 1973). Studies tend to show that, on average, African-American infants reach the motor milestones identified in the Bayley Motor Scales at a younger age than Caucasian-American infants (Bayley, 1965; Capute et al., 1985; Haywood, 1993). However, socioeconomic differences and other environmental conditions may account for the differences since those factors have not been well controlled in existing studies. Comparisons of motor development among preschool-age African-American and Caucasian-American children have found no conclusive differences (Haywood, 1993).

Nutrition

Nutrition may affect motor development in two ways. First, inadequate nutritional intake may cause damage to the nervous system, resulting in impairment of intersensory functioning. The child may thus have problems in processing and efficiently utilizing sensations, perceptions, memory, and attention in acquiring motor skills. Second, nutrition affects strength and energy level. Undernourished infants are apathetic and lack sufficient physical vigor and endurance to pursue motor activities (Smoll, 1982).

The relationship of nutrition to motor development is dramatically illustrated by cross-cultural studies of infants from poverty-stricken environments where breast feeding is heavily utilized. During the first six months of life, infants from these cultures compare very favorably with infants from more economically advantaged environments. However, during the second half of the first year, when breast milk alone becomes insufficient to meet nutritional needs, there is a steady decline in the psychomotor performance of these infants. Motor development begins to decline even earlier if the period of breast feeding is shorter (Werner, 1979).

DEVELOPMENTAL TRENDS

Motor Biases

Infants demonstrate preferences or **biases** in motor activities. They generally prefer to work on developing new motor skills. Levin (1983) points out that babies tend to give themselves homework assignments such as "work on crawling," or "practice standing now." For example, once infants discover that the hand can be used to touch an object, they practice over and over until they have achieved and refined their ability to reach, touch, and pick up an object. Fourteen-month-old Kristin tried to make a lid fit on a small plastic bottle. She had formed the idea that caps go on bottles if you twist them. However, she could not quite get the threads on the cap to fit the threads on the bottle. She would twist and turn until she became frustrated. Then she would throw the pieces away in anger. She returned to the same task over and over until she had mastered the skill.

Infants can be observed engaging in repetitive movements such as rocking on hands and knees, head banging, kicking, and scratching. These patterns of movements are sometimes referred to as **rhythmical stereotypies** (Thelan, 1981). Infants tend to use stereotypies as a means of preparing for later, more coordinated movements. Thelan (1981) believes that infants are programmed at birth to engage in rhythmic movements. These activities are viewed as normal responses that facilitate motor development.

Mass to Specific

General movements develop before specific movements. In the newborn, the legs and arms usually move at the same time. As the baby grows, the capacity to make specific movements with individual body parts increases. An infant can eventually move the arms without moving the legs, then one arm without the other, and finally one finger at a time. For example, if a newborn's foot is touched with an ice cube, the whole body moves in a generalized response. An older infant responds

to the ice cube by withdrawing the specific foot that has been touched.

Hierarchical Integration

The simplest and most elementary skills develop first and become more complex as they are combined to form more elaborate movements. An infant who grasps a raisin between the thumb and index finger and places it in a bottle is integrating four basic skills—reaching, grasping, placing, and releasing—to complete a more difficult pattern of activity.

Developmental Direction

Motor development generally follows the laws of developmental direction. According to the **cephalocaudal** principle, the infant obtains control of the arms before the legs. Reaching develops before walking. Following the **proximodistal** trend, control of the arms is established before control over the wrist and fingers is obtained. In the hand, control over the index finger develops first, followed by control over the third, fourth, and fifth fingers in that order (Tanner, 1990). While the laws of developmental direction are generally true, there are exceptions according to Cratty (1979), particularly in the proximodistal trend. In his estimation, the laws of developmental direction need further refinement.

REFLEXES

The first movements newborn infants exhibit consist mostly of reflex activities. A reflex is an automatic or involuntary response to a specific stimulus. The reflexes are controlled by the lower brainstem and spinal cord. As the upper part of the brain matures, the reflexes are mostly replaced with voluntary movements. The newborn infant is equipped with a variety of primitive reflexes (Illingworth, 1991).

Some of the reflexes, such as sucking, have obvious survival value. However, the importance of many of the reflexes is not clear. In general, the reflexes are considered to be indicators of the maturity and intactness of the nervous system. Several reflexes can be easily observed in young infants. If a reflex fails to appear or disappear at the appropriate age, some type of neurological problem may exist. A few of the key reflexes are described below.

Rooting and Sucking

Newborn infants are equipped with rooting and sucking responses that allow them to obtain nourishment. Touching a newborn infant in the corner of the mouth will trigger a rooting response in which the head is turned in the direction of the stimulus in search of something to suck, preferably a breast or a bottle containing milk. In concert with the rooting reflex, the newborn begins sucking reflexively as soon as a finger or a nipple touches the mouth. The rooting reflex begins to disappear by 3 months of age. The sucking reflex is gradually replaced by voluntary sucking.

Grasp

The palmar grasp reflex is easily elicited by placing a finger or small object in the palm of the baby's hand. The grasp may be so tight and strong that the baby's weight can be supported for an instant. The palmar grasp becomes weaker after the first month and is replaced by voluntary grasping by 3 or 4 months of age.

Moro

The Moro reflex is a response to a loud noise or sudden loss of support. It may be elicited by holding an infant with one hand supporting the head and the other behind the back. The hand supporting the head is lowered abruptly, allowing the infant's head to fall an inch or two. The baby responds by quickly stretching the arms outward and bringing them together in a hugging motion. The back is arched and the hands curl slightly, while the knees are drawn toward the stomach. The Moro, sometimes called the embracing reflex, is typically present at birth and begins to disappear around 3

months of age. It cannot be observed in most infants after 4 or 5 months of age. The Moro is one of the most widely used reflexes in the neurological examination of infants (Bench et al., 1972).

Babinski

If a finger or a pencil is rubbed along the inner side of the young infant's foot from heel to toe, the big toe will move upward while the other toes fan inward toward the bottom of the foot. This is the Babinski reflex, which develops just before birth in full term infants and typically disappears between 12 and 16 months of age.

Tonic Neck

There are two types of tonic neck reflexes: the asymmetrical, in which one side of the body is dominant, and the symmetrical, in which both sides of the body are balanced. Of the two, the asymmetrical tonic neck reflex (ATNR) is the more widely known. It can be elicited by placing an infant on its back and turning the baby's head to one side. One arm and leg are extended in the direction in which the head is facing. The other arm is bent at the elbow with the hand placed near the head. This is similar to a "fencing" position. The ATNR is most commonly observed during the first two or three months of life. It usually fades out by 4 to 6 months.

The symmetrical tonic neck reflex (STNR) may be observed by holding the infant under the stomach and bending the head up and down. When the head goes up, the arms go down while the legs are raised. Raising the head has the opposite effect. The reflex must disappear before an infant can learn to crawl, since the arms and legs must move independently of the head. The STNR typically disappears by 7 months.

Stepping

Infants typically exhibit a stepping or walking reflex at birth or soon afterward. When held upright with bare feet touching a flat surface, an infant will take rhythmic steps forward. The stepping reflex usu-

The tonic neck reflex position.

ally disappears by the fifth month of age. However, Thelen and her colleagues (1984) believe that the stepping reflex cannot be elicited after five months because the infant's legs have grown too heavy to lift. She found that infants who gained weight most rapidly between 2 and 6 weeks of age made the fewest reflex stepping movements during that time period (Thelen et al., 1989). Additional experiments were conducted in which 4-week-old infants were partially submerged in water to reduce the effects of leg weight (Thelen, Ulrich, & Jensen, 1989). The results revealed that stepping movements increased in rate and speed.

Influence of Reflexes on Voluntary Movement

The extent to which reflexes facilitate or interfere with voluntary movement is a major question in infant motor development. From one point of view, reflexes form the basis for later voluntary motor activities (Newell, 1984). Reflexes are considered to be responses that an infant may incorporate efficiently into the process of establishing voluntary motor skills. In support of this position, researchers have found that exercise of the stepping reflex during the first nine weeks of life can lead to an earlier beginning of voluntary walking (Zelazo, Zelazo, & Kolb, 1972). Similar effects of reflex exercise have been found for crawling (Lagerspetz, Nygard, & Strandwick, 1971) and grasping (Bower, 1977).

On the other hand, reflexes are sometimes viewed as behaviors that inhibit the onset of vol-

untary movements (Newell, 1984). According to this position, a reflex response must disappear before a related voluntary motor movement can be established. For example, the plantar reflex must disappear in the feet before an infant can stand and walk. Otherwise the bottoms of the feet tend to curl up and fail to provide a firm foundation for walking.

The relationship between the establishment of voluntary motor skills and reflex activities is obviously a complex issue. Both points of view have some validity. Apparently some of the reflexes evolve into voluntary motor responses, and with practice, facilitate their early onset. At the same time, other reflexes stand in the way of emergence and development of some motor skills. From a dynamic systems perspective, reflexive activities are viewed as interacting with other body systems in the emergence of motor skills.

DEVELOPMENT OF HAND CONTROL

Eye-Hand Coordination

The development of the ability to locate, grasp, and manipulate objects is a major task in motor development. This very complex task requires the voluntary coordination of eye, arm, hand, and finger movements. There are two major stages in the development of eye-hand coordination, which include a variety of changes during the infancy period.

Stage 1: Prereaching. Some scientists (Cratty, 1979; Trevarthen, 1978; Williams, 1983) believe that infants are equipped at birth with an underlying "motor prewiring" through which vision and kinesthetic sensations work together to produce reaching and grasping movements. Newborn infants apparently reach for or swat at objects in their visual field (Bower, Broughton, & Moore, 1970; Von Hofsten, 1982). Moving objects are more likely to elicit arm movements than stationary objects. Such movements, however, are referred to as prereaching, in contrast to later reaching (Bushnell, 1985; Von Hofsten, 1984).

Researchers have identified several characteristic features of prereaching activities. During this stage, infants are rarely successful in touching, not to mention grasping, the target object. They do not shape the hand to correspond with the object properties. They move their arms very rapidly, withdrawing the hand immediately without making corrective adjustments in the trajectory or path of the hand (Bower, 1982; Bushnell, 1985). Prereaching infants do not appear to look at both the reaching hand and the target object in their reaching attempts. Rather, the eye-hand coordination of newborn and very young infants seems to be based on a primitive combination of kinesthetic (sensations of movement from the muscles and joints) and visual responses.

Prereaching movements are visually elicited rather than visually guided (Bushnell, 1985). That is, an infant sees an object and reaches out for it automatically as part of the same response pattern. The reaching response is apparently triggered by the sense of vision rather than the thought of obtaining and manipulating the object. The main function of prereaching behavior is thus considered to be attentional rather than intentional (Von Hofsten, 1982).

The quantity and quality of prereaching activities change with age. Major changes become evident by 7 weeks of age (Von Hofsten, 1984). The amount of reaching activity declines while the intensity of staring increases. A baby seems to grasp an object with the eyes, mentally dropping it and picking it up again (Williams, 1983). Around this age, infants have a tendency to spend a lot of time looking at their hands. Apparently the increased visual attention inhibits and alters reaching behavior. Burton White (1975) believes that the visual discovery of the hands around 6 or 7 weeks is a major milestone in infant development.

When the 7-week-old infant occasionally reaches for an object, the form is different from neonatal reaching. The hand is held with the fist closed during reaching rather than remaining open as it was earlier. As the infant gets older, the amount of reaching activity goes up again, and the hand opens as it reaches an object. The changes that occur in reaching activities have been attributed to reorganization of the systems of the brain as the baby matures and moves from reflexive to voluntary responses (Von Hofsten, 1984).

Stage 2: Visually Directed Reaching. The infant begins to acquire the ability to engage in visually directed reaching some time between 3 and 5 months (Bushnell, 1985). Williams (1983) describes this stage as "the regulation of grasping/manipulative responses through intensified visual activity." Vision is involved in determining both the position of the target and the position of the hand (Von Hofsten, 1992). The infant first locates an object with the eyes and attempts to pick it up. Frequently, the baby loses sight of the object and fails as in earlier eye-hand coordination efforts. However, when this happens, the baby intensifies visual fixation, adjusts the reaching movements, keeping the hand and object in view until the goal is obtained.

As the infant builds on previous experiences, visually directed reaching becomes smoother and more successful with age. Toward the end of the first year, infants are very accurate in reaching so that targeted objects are obtained with few, if any, corrections in hand trajectories. In order to pick up and manipulate large objects, infants need to use both hands in coordinated movements. At around 7 months of age infants reach for an object with one hand or both hands simultaneously, depending on the size, weight, and shape of the object (Fagard, 1990). They begin to coordinate the movements of both arms independently and use both hands cooperatively in reaching for and grasping objects around 8 months of age (Haywood, 1993).

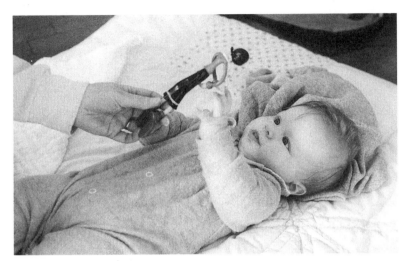

This baby is engaged in visually directed reaching.

Prehension

After the grasp reflex disappears at approximately 4 months of age, the infant begins to work on **prehension**—grasping an object between fingers and thumb. Halverson (1931) identified ten stages that occur between 26 and 52 weeks of age in the acquisition of adultlike grasping skills (see Table 8-1 and Figure 8-1). In the early stages, the infant uses only the fingers and the palm in picking up an object, such as a small cube. Initially an infant rakes at a tiny object, such as a pellet, without picking it

Table 8–1 Milestones of Fine Motor Development

MOTOR ACTIVITY	AVERAGE AGE (MONTHS)	MOTOR ACTIVITY	AVERAGE AGE (MONTHS)
Prehension of cubes		Prehension of pellets	
Reaches—no contact	4	Rakes with whole hand	5.5
Reaches—makes contact	5	Inferior scissors grasp	7.4
Primitive squeeze	5	Scissors grasp	8.2
Squeese grasp	6	Inferior pincer grasp	9.2
Hand grasp	7	Neat pincer grasp	11
Palm grasp	7	Inserts pellet in bottle	12
Superior palm grasp	8	Other	
Inferior forefinger grasp	9	Turns pages, two or three	
Forefinger grasp	12	at one time	18
Superior forefinger grasp	12	Inserts shoelace through	
Voluntary release of cube	11	safety pin	24
Builds tower of four cubes	18	Turns single page	30
Builds tower of seven		Tries to cut with scissors	36
cubes	24		
Aligns train of four cubes	24		
Builds tower of ten cubes	36		

Sources: H. Halverson. (1931). *Genetic Psychology Monographs, 10,* 107–286. Reprinted with permission of the Helen Dwight Reid Foundation. Published by Heldref Publications, 4000 Albermarle St., NW, Washington, DC 20016. Copyright 1931.; Knoblock, H., Stevens, F., & Malone, A. (1980). *Manual of Developmental Diagnosis.* New York: Harper & Row. Used by permission.

up. As soon as the ability to use the thumb (finger-thumb opposition) is acquired at approximately 9 months, grasping skills develop faster. By approximately 1 year of age, an infant can pick up cubes and pellets in an adultlike fashion, with a thumb and forefinger pincer grasp.

Object Manipulation

Once infants develop the ability to grasp and pick up objects, they spend a large amount of time engaging in manipulative activities. The way in which an infant interacts with an object varies according to age. Uzgiris (1967) observed how infants between the ages of 2 and 24 months manipulate a variety of objects including a rattle, a small doll, and a piece of aluminum foil. The earliest infant interactions with objects were characterized by holding, mouthing, and visual inspection. As they grew older (4 to 10 months), infants acquired

the ability to manipulate objects by banging, shaking, examining (turning, poking, probing, etc.), dropping, and throwing. Between 1 and 2 years of age, their object manipulations became more socially oriented through showing, extending, or naming activities (Uzgiris, 1967).

Bushnell and Boudreau (1993) condensed patterns of object manipulation by infants into the following stages:

1. **Clutching** (birth through 3 months). During this stage, object manipulation is largely controlled by the palmar grasp reflex. Typically, objects are clutched in one hand and brought to the mouth. The fingers may move in a "kneading" pattern.

2. **Rhythmical Stereotypies** (4–10 months). At the beginning of this stage infants establish elementary eye-hand control and exhibit more differentiated finger movements. They engage in repetitive finger and hand movements (rhythmical stereotypies) that peak in frequency at 6 or 7 months. These stereotypies

Figure 8–1 Types of Grasping Behavior.
Sources: H. Halverson. (1931). *Genetic Psychology Monographs, 10,* 107–286. Reprinted with permission of the Helen Dwight Reid Foundation. Published by Heldref Publications, 4000 Albermarle St., NW, Washington, DC 20016. Copyright 1931.; Knoblock, H., Stevens, F., & Malone, A. (1980). *Manual of Developmental Diagnosis.* New York: Harper & Row. Used by permission.

include scratching, rubbing, banging, squeezing, poking, waving, and passing objects from one hand to the other.

3. **Complementary Bimanual Activities** (10 months plus). At this point the infant uses both hands in object manipulation. One hand may be used to hold an object in place, while the other hand is used to manipulate or explore its parts. The hand and finger movements are more focused on exploring object properties rather than repetitive movements. At about 1 year of age infants are able to make the complex hand movements essential for advanced haptic perception, or the recognition of object properties through handling (see Chapter 9).

Hand Preference

Many organisms display a preference for one side of the body in performing certain movements. Rats tend to exhibit a paw preference, and even grasshoppers have a favorite scratching leg (Hecaen & Ajuriagurra, 1964). Human beings may begin to demonstrate a preference for one hand or the other in reaching and grasping as early as the infancy period.

Infants begin to demonstrate a hand preference when they reach for objects as early as 5 months of age (McCormick & Maurer, 1988; Butterworth & Hopkins, 1993). At that age, most infants reach predominantly with their right hand, although the incidence of left handedness is higher than it is in the adult population. However, many infants display an irregular pattern of handedness, shifting from one side to the other or using both hands about same amount of time (Butterworth & Hopkins, 1993). By 18 months to 2 years of age, most infants have established a hand preference that does not change as they get older. In some cases, though, permanent hand preference is not established until 3 or 4 years of age

Questions about whether hand preference is controlled by heredity or environmental influences have been debated for a long time. Some scientists believe that, although genetic factors may be involved, handedness is largely controlled by environmental factors related to imitation and instruction (Illingworth, 1991). Support for this position is found in a study which showed that young infants imitated the hand preference of their mothers during episodes of manual object play (Harkins & Uzgiris, 1991).

Overall, scientific evidence tends to support the position that hand preference is mainly determined by biological (including genetic) factors (Butterworth & Hopkins, 1993). Boklage (1980) believes that hand preference is linked to the organization of the brain, which is established early in the prenatal period. Evidence from his study of 800 twins reveals that if either one or both parents were left-handed, they were 50 percent more likely to have a left-handed child. Left-handedness occurs almost twice as often in twins as in singletons. These findings are consistent with the theory that hand dominance is a reflection of brain lateralization. That is, a left-handed person has a dominant right hemisphere and vice versa.

Other researchers have found that the incidence of left-handedness is higher among infants who are born prematurely, and/or who experienced respiratory distress during the birth process (Fox, 1985). Still other scientists suggest that left-handedness is a result of increased testosterone levels during fetal development (Bryden & Steenhuis, 1991). We need more research to better understand the biological mechanisms related to handedness and how environmental factors are involved.

Throwing and Catching

Infants do not develop much proficiency in throwing. However, the ability to throw objects begins to emerge as early as 6 months, when babies accidentally release and hurl objects they are waving about or shaking (Espenschade & Eckert, 1967). As voluntary release is established, infants soon learn that dropping objects has an interesting effect. They delight in dropping or throwing spoons and other objects from the high chair to hear the noise as well as to watch someone pick them up. The first attempts at throwing are usually a stiff underhand motion (Cratty, 1979). Seventy-five percent of infants develop the ability to throw a small ball overhanded by 24 months of age (Frankenburg et al., 1992).

The ability to catch an object requires much more

eye-hand coordination and perceptual ability than does throwing an object. Consequently, infants make little progress in this area. The baby's first efforts at catching are typically trying to stop a rolling ball (Hottinger, 1977). The first successful attempts to catch an object thrown into the air usually occur around 3 years of age (Williams, 1983).

POSTURE AND LOCOMOTION

Posture represents the adjustments of the body in relation to the forces of gravity. Postural abilities an infant must develop include achieving head control, sitting, and standing. Posture provides the base of support for body movements. **Locomotion** is the ability to move from place to place.

Prerequisites for Locomotor Skills

The development of locomotion involves the strength and coordination of the muscles and joints in organized response patterns. The ability to maintain a sense of balance and postural control under changing conditions, such as the location of objects and surface slopes, are related processes. These abilities gradually emerge after 6 months of age. By the time an infant is ready to crawl, the senses of vision and balance are sufficiently integrated for the infant to coordinate arm and leg movements with environmental cues. The ability to creep and crawl sets off a chain of experiences that lead to new and increasing levels of perceptual abilities and motor achievements (Bertenthal & Campos, 1990; Bushnell & Boudreau, 1993).

Emerging Locomotor Skills

The achievement of mobility increases the infant's opportunities for exploration and is necessary for learning and the development of independence. Although learning to walk is the most dramatic and important locomotor task of infancy, it is preceded and followed by an orderly progression of several other significant milestones (see Table 8–2).

Head Control. Establishing control of the head is the first step toward achieving an upright position

TABLE 8-2 Milestones of Gross Motor Development

MOTOR ACTIVITY	AVERAGE AGE (MONTHS)
Sits with support—head steady	2.3
Rolls over—back to stomach and stomach to back	3.2
Sits alone—steadily	6.6
Crawls	7.0
Stands—holding on	7.2
Creeps	9.0
Walks—holding on	9.2
Walks alone—steadily	12.3
Walks up steps alone (can hold to rail)	16.6
Throws ball overhand	20.3
Jumps up—both feet off floor	23.8

Sources: Frankenburg, W., Dodds, J., Archer, P., Bresnick, B., Maschka, P., Edelman, N., & Shapiro, H. *Denver II Training Manual* (2nd ed.). (1992). Denver, CO: Denver Developmental Materials, Inc.; Knoblock, H., Stevens, F., & Malone, A. (1980). *Manual of Developmental Diagnosis.* New York: Harper & Row. Used by permission.

and independent locomotion (Gesell, 1954). Head control is defined as the ability to keep the head steady in an upright position and move the head at will. The neck muscles of the newborn are not strong enough to support the weight of the disproportionately large head for more than a few seconds. In addition, the relative immaturity of the nervous system makes voluntary control of head movements difficult for the newborn.

The beginning of head control may be observed when the baby raises the head far enough to clear the chin from the surface for a few seconds. Most infants accomplish this task during the first 2 months of life. When lying on the stomach, an infant can routinely hold the head so that the face makes a 45-degree angle with the surface at approximately 2 months of age (Frankenburg et al., 1992). On average, infants acquire the ability to hold their head steady when held in an upright position at around three months (White, 1975).

Rolling. The infant's first attempt at locomotion is rolling from one side to the other. An infant rolls by turning the head, twisting the trunk, and using a leg to push the body over. Cratty (1979) believes that the body-righting and visual-tracking reflexes are responsible for the infant's first attempts to roll over. The baby catches sight of a moving object and turns the head to follow it. The turned head triggers the righting reflex, which causes the body to flip over. Another possible explanation for some of the early rolling activity is that an infant accidentally turns from the stomach to a side position due to poor control of a shift in weight. From the side position the infant can turn to the stomach or back. As an infant gains more muscle strength and control, rolling movements become smoother, more coordinated, and deliberate.

Ordinarily an infant accomplishes the ability to roll from stomach to back before working on the more difficult task of rolling from back to stomach. Infants typically develop the ability to roll over completely from stomach to back and from back stomach between 2 and 6 months of age (Frankenburg et al., 1992).

Sitting. As the infant gradually gains control over the muscles in the trunk of the body, sitting alone becomes possible. Most babies are able to sit alone momentarily without support between 5 and 6 months of age (Frankenburg et al., 1992). During their first attempts at sitting alone, infants lean forward to gain added balance and support

(Gallahue, 1982). On average, an infant can maneuver into a sitting position from lying down, standing, or other postures by 8 to 9 months of age (Frankenburg et al., 1992).

Crawling. About the time an infant can sit alone and roll onto the stomach, crawling movements are likely to follow. In **crawling**, the head and chest are raised while the stomach maintains contact with the surface. The weight of the head and shoulders rests on the elbows and hands, which are used to slide the body forward or backward. The legs usually drag, although they may sometimes be used to push forward or pull backward. Most infants begin crawling around 7 months (range = 4.5 to 9.5 months) (Burnett & Johnson, 1971).

Creeping. As the baby becomes a proficient crawler, and muscle strength increases in the legs, efforts are made to advance to the creeping stage. Infants begin to creep around 8.5 months (range = 5 to 14.5 months) (Burnett & Johnson, 1971). **Creeping** is defined as locomotion on the hands and knees or hands and feet. The technical definitions of crawling and creeping may be confusing because the meanings are usually reversed in common usage. Keep in mind also that different sources may use these terms interchangeably or in different ways. Thinking of the terms alphabetically—crawling before creeping as it occurs developmentally—

This baby is beginning to make crawling movements on his hands and stomach.

may help you remember their sequence and therefore the technical definitions.

When infants first attempt to creep, they slowly and deliberately move one limb an inch or two at a time. With practice, the movements become smoother, more efficient, and faster. Most babies exhibit a pattern in which the arm movement is followed by movement of the opposite leg. However, about 20 percent of all infants follow the arm movement by moving the knee on the same side of the body (Cratty, 1979). Infants are individuals, though, and tend to use a variety of positions and movements in creeping and other forms of locomotion.

The importance of self-produced locomotion for perceptual, emotional, and social development in infancy was emphasized in the beginning of this chapter. Bertenthal, Campos, and Barrett (1984) have linked the acquisition of the ability to move around on four limbs to the emergence of many of the developmental changes (e.g., wariness of strangers and heights) taking place between 7 and 9 months. Once infants begin to creep, their view and experience of the environment changes in important ways. Creeping contributes to the emergence of other abilities by enhancing the infant's ability to extract information from the environment and make more precise calculations of distances through the coordination of visual-motor cues (Berthenthal et al., 1984).

Hitching. A few infants learn to move around by an unusual method referred to as hitching, or scooting. **Hitching** is defined as locomotion in a sitting position. The baby uses the legs, heels, and sometimes the hands to slide the buttocks along the floor. Some infants can scoot along quite rapidly and may use hitching as a substitute for creeping or walking. For example, at 20 months of age, Sue was attending a nursery-toddler class in which she was the only child who had not learned to walk. However, she could participate in the activities and keep up with the others by skillful hitching movements. Although her parents and teachers were concerned, physical and neurological examinations revealed no problems. She was walking by 2 years of age.

Standing. Infants typically begin to stand by pulling themselves up and holding onto furniture. One of the infant's motivations for standing is to extend the range of grasping and reaching for attractive objects above eye level. Most infants begin to pull themselves to a standing position by using chairs or other furniture between 8 and 10 months of age (Frankenburg et al., 1992).

Standing up to furniture is followed by cruising. This activity consists of moving around, usually sideways, holding onto furniture or other objects. As infants gradually gain stability in pulling up and cruising, they develop enough confidence to let go of their support for a few seconds. Infants typically accomplish the task of standing alone with stability between 10 and 13 months (Frankenburg et al., 1992). Once they achieve this milestone, they soon proceed to the more interesting task of walking alone.

Walking. From the parents' point of view, the baby's first independent steps may represent the most significant accomplishment of infancy. From the baby's perspective, walking opens up a new world. The average age for walking alone is approximately 12 months. However, 25 to 90 percent of infants walk alone steadily between 11 to 15 months (Frankenburg et al, 1992). Infants are often referred to as toddlers from the time they begin to walk until they achieve a stable pattern of walking around 24 to 36 months of age. In comparison to other species, human infants walk relatively late. Thelen and her colleagues (1984) believe this happens because infants are top-heavy, with large heads and short legs, and, therefore, have trouble balancing their bodies in an upright position.

In the initial stage of walking, the legs are spread apart for a wide base of support (Cratty, 1979). The toes are pointed outward with the knees slightly bent. The arms are held out for balance as the legs move in rigid, high-stepping, halting movements. The baby has difficulty maintaining balance and falls easily (Gallahue, 1982). Some infants may walk sideways as a carry-over from early cruising movements.

One of the tasks in learning to walk is to move

over surfaces with different slopes without falling. Apparently infants acquire experience with slanted surfaces during the creeping stage that prepares them for this activity. Researchers have found that creeping infants differentiate between shallow and steep slopes, but do not use that information to avoid hazardous inclines. By 14 months of age, toddlers make adjustments in their movement patterns to compensate for different surface levels (Eppler, Adolph, & Weiner, 1996).

Toddlers progress to a more advanced stage of walking rather quickly, although for several weeks they may resemble a "duck out for a jog" (Fogel, 1997, p. 270). With practice, the walking pattern becomes more balanced and smoother, the toes point straight ahead, and heel-to-toe contact replaces flatfooted slipping (Gallahue, 1982). The length of the steps tends to increase with age. Walking improves throughout the infancy period, but a mature, adultlike pattern does not emerge until around 4 to 7 years (Scrutton, 1969).

Running. Young children begin to run soon after they begin to walk. Toddlers may take a few rapid steps to maintain balance even before they master walking. Toddlers who are just beginning to walk sometimes move their feet as rapidly as possible in order to reach the next base of support (Williams, 1983). Running is defined as "a series of smoothly coordinated jumps during which the body weight is borne on one foot, becomes airborne, is then carried on the opposite foot and again becomes airborne" (Slocum & James, 1968). The feature that distinguishes running from fast walking is the phase in which the body briefly leaves the supporting surface (Wickstrom, 1983).

Running begins its developmental course around 18 months of age. In the initial stage of running, the leg swing is short and limited. The stride is stiff and uneven. There is no observable time when the feet are not in contact with the surface. By 2 years of age, most infants can run well enough to meet the minimum standards of true running (Gesell, 1940). They can move a little faster and the length of the stride has increased. There is a limited but clearly observable flight phase. The arm and leg

movements are more balanced and coordinated (Gallahue, 1982). Although a mature running pattern is not established during the first three years of life, infants make a remarkable amount of progress.

Climbing. An infant may attempt to go up stair steps on all fours before developing the ability to stand alone or walk. These initial climbing efforts are an extension of creeping and generally coincide with early attempts to stand. After they begin to walk, infants will attempt to climb stairs in an upright position with the assistance of an adult. These early efforts consist of a "mark time" pattern in which the child leads with the same foot on each step. Wellman (1937) found that children, using this same pattern, can climb a long flight of stairs and a ladder by 24 months of age. Climbing with an alternating foot pattern begins to occur around 3 years of age (Cratty, 1979).

Jumping. The first attempts to jump (off low steps) may be observed in infants at about 18 months of age (McClenaghan & Gallahue, 1978). Infants like to jump off the last step as they are descending stairs with assistance. This seems to be a preliminary phase in development before they obtain the ability to jump up and down from a standing position (Williams, 1983). The average age for jumping off the floor with both feet is approximately 24 months (Frankenburg et al., 1992).

SELF-CARE ACTIVITIES

Self-care skills such as dressing, toileting, and self-feeding (see Chapter 7) vary widely among toddlers. The development of these abilities is largely dependent upon biological maturation but is also related to internal motivation and parental influences. Some infants insist on doing things for themselves very early, whereas others are more passive and dependent. Self-care activities are sometimes called **adaptive** behaviors and are closely associated with social development as well as motor development. The infant cannot develop into an independent and autonomous individual until self-care activities are mastered.

Dressing

Gesell (1940) observed that infants learn many things in reverse order. This observation is especially applicable to dressing skills. Infants begin to remove articles of clothing long before they can put them on. During the first 12 to 18 months of infancy they are more concerned about taking clothes off than putting them on. They take special delight in pulling off their shoes, tied or untied, as well as their socks. By 20 months, most infants (75 percent) can purposefully remove at least one article of clothing (Frankenburg et al., 1992).

Infants begin to push their arms through sleeves and hold out their feet for shoes shortly before they are 1 year old. However, most of their dressing skills develop between 18 months and 3 years. During this period, most infants begin to put on their

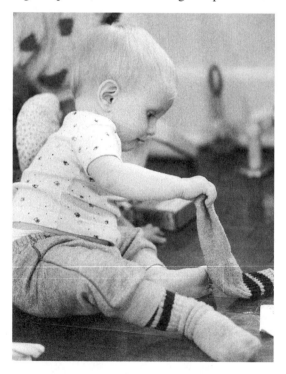

This infant can take the sock off but is not successful in putting it back on.

shoes, shirts, sweaters, and most other articles of clothing. Most children accomplish the task of self-dressing without help by 3 years of age except for tying shoes and buttoning or zipping difficult garments.

Elimination Control

A major developmental task that begins during infancy is the establishment of control over the sphincter muscles, which control bowel and bladder movements. At birth, elimination is a reflexive act that is subject to conditioning. Infants can be conditioned to empty the bladder or bowels as early as a month or two. However, infants are not usually ready to begin to establish voluntary control over these functions until they are 15 to 18 months old (Illingworth, 1991).

Many child-development experts advise parents to wait until an infant is at least 2 years old before beginning toilet training. White (1975) believes that toilet training should not be attempted between 14 and 24 months of age, because the infant is entering a period of negativism. Two-year-olds are more cooperative and usually train themselves in a short period of time. Infants who begin the process of toilet training before 18 months of age tend to take longer to be completely trained than infants who start around 24 months (Shelov, 1994).

Across cultures, toilet training practices vary widely. For example among the Gussi people of Africa, toilet training begins after the child is weaned and can walk well. The mother takes the child to a spot outdoors and tells the child what to do, or tells the child to do what the other children do. Factors that influence cultural traditions and practices include the availability of indoor plumbing, climate, modesty standards, the amount of clothing children wear, and sanitation standards. In most societies, serious toilet training begins between 1 and 3 years of age (Broude, 1995).

Elimination control is usually established in the following sequence: bowel control, daytime bladder control, nighttime bladder control. Children are usually ready to begin toilet training when they can use a word to label the process (such as "pee-pee"); remain dry for 2 hour intervals or naps;

express discomfort with wet diapers; and display signs that a bowel movement or urination is about to occur (American Academy of Pediatrics, 1993). Some children are cooperative and accomplish training easily with minimum guidance and assistance. In some instances, parents have to initiate the process with more structure and guidance. The process works best when parents are relaxed, use lots of praise, provide clear, consistent instructions, and avoid conflicts of will.

IMPEDIMENTS TO MOTOR DEVELOPMENT

Some atypical variations in motor development are common among infants and disappear with age. However, persistent delays and variations in motor performance may be signs of a neuromotor disorder. Conditions that interfere with the motor development of infants are numerous and varied. Vision problems, mental disabilities, and cerebral palsy represent developmental challenges to an infant's motor functioning.

Visual Impairment

Vision is obviously a very significant factor in motor development. Surprisingly, though, blind infants tend to achieve some of the tasks of motor development at about the same time and in the same sequence as infants who can see. Blind infants look at their hands with their unseeing eyes (Illingsworth, 1983), begin to sit alone, roll from back to stomach, take stepping movements when their hands are held, rise to their hands and knees, and stand alone within the normal age range (Adelson & Fraiberg, 1974). However, blind infants experience considerable delay in achieving self-initiated mobility and in reaching for objects.

Fraiberg and her colleagues (Fraiberg, 1971; Fraiberg, Smith, & Adelson, 1969) developed a guidance program to help blind infants with the achievement of reaching and mobility. Their program focused on the coordination of the ear and hand in reaching for objects, parent-child games, and the use of sound lures as incentives to mobility. Bower (1977) equipped a 16-week-old blind infant with a device that produced echoes from objects. The baby was able to reach accurately and grasp silent objects, even distinguishing two different objects. Scott, Jan, and Freeman (1977) have produced a guidebook for parents of visually impaired infants and toddlers that contains suggestions for helping these children with motor-skill development.

Mental Disabilities

Research findings generally indicate that infants with lower-than-average intelligence experience delay in achieving the normal milestones of motor development (Wickstrom, 1983). The extent of the delay depends on the level of mental disability and physical or nervous-system disorder. Studies of infants affected by Down syndrome (see Chapter 2) have found timing problems in the activation of muscle responses needed for posture control (Woollacott, 1992). Infants with Down syndrome tested at 22 months of age displayed muscle response behaviors comparable to patterns found at 8 to 10 months of age in typically developing infants. Hypotonia, muscle weakness, and joint instability are other problems shared by infants with Down syndrome that contribute to delays in motor development (Fetters, 1996).

In some areas of motor functioning, however, children with mental disabilities may be more alike than different from other children. For example, Kaminer and Jedrysek (1983) recorded the age of walking in 200 infants representing all levels of mental disability. The majority of children walked by the normal age of 17 months. Only when the babies were extremely disabled was walking delayed beyond 17 months. Also, early walkers were found even among this group.

Cerebral Palsy

One of the most common and serious disorders associated with motor impairment in infants and toddlers is **cerebral palsy**. Infants with cerebral palsy have difficulty with movement, posture, and muscle tone. This condition is caused by brain damage that occurs during the prenatal period, the birth process, or after birth. The incidence of cerebral palsy is higher among preterm and low-birthweight infants than in full-term infants (Batshaw & Perret, 1992). There are different types of cerebral palsy depending on the severity of the problem. The type of cerebral palsy is usually classified in terms of the quality of muscle tone and the areas of the body affected (Fetters, 1996). The effects of cerebral palsy vary from mild motor problems involving one side of the body to severe impairment involving the trunk and all four extremities. Some of the signs of cerebral palsy in infants include the persistence of primitive reflexes, weak, prolonged head lag, muscle tone that is unusually floppy or stiff, and lopsided or unusual creeping movements (Batshaw & Perret, 1992; Shevlov, 1994).

ASSESSING MOTOR PERFORMANCE

Numerous multi-domain scales include components for the assessment of gross and fine motor development during infancy. For example, the motor scale from the **Bayley Scales of Infant Development - II** (described in Chapter 9) is one of the most reliable and widely used norm-referenced instruments for assessing motor development of infants. The two instruments described below were exclusively designed to evaluate the motor performance of infants.

The **Alberta Infant Motor Scale (AIMS)** (Piper & Darrah, 1993) is one of the newest tools designed to evaluate motor performance of infants from birth to 18 months of age. Infants are observed in a variety of postures by a trained professional. One strength of the AIMS is that it includes evaluation of the quality of motor movements and is not based merely on major milestones or reflexes. The AIMS can be administered in 20 to 30 minutes.

The **Movement Assessment of Infants (MAI)** (Chandler, Andrews, & Swanson 1980) is one of the most widely used tools designed to identify infants with cerebral palsy and other motor problems (McLean et al., 1996). This test covers muscle tone, primitive, automatic reactions, and

voluntary movement in infants from birth to 12 months of age. An overall score of normal, abnormal, or questionable is calculated. Norms are not available at the present time for comparison. The MAI is administered by a physical or an occupational therapist trained in its use.

FACILITATING MOTOR DEVELOPMENT

A variety of infant-stimulation programs have been developed to assist parents and other caregivers in helping infants enhance their motor skill development. Some of these programs have been designed specifically for infants with motor delays (e.g., Connor, Williamson, & Siepp, 1978), and others are intended for use with typically developing infants (e.g., Gerber, 1981; Prudden, 1964; Levy, 1973). Ridenour (1978) advises parents to avoid motor-stimulation programs that claim to greatly enhance an infant's future motor or intellectual performance.

Many parents use an infant walker (mainly between 5 and 15 months of age) to encourage mobility, and exercise. This device, consisting of a frame on wheels with leg holes, is designed to support a prewalking baby with feet on the floor while the infant is learning to walk. However, there is no evidence that walkers have any positive effects on the motor development of infants. Any possible benefits of infant walkers are far outweighed by the risk of injury and even death from their use. Injuries resulting from infant walkers have increased steadily since 1994. Walker-related injuries have been reported in 12 to 40 percent of infants who use this device. Most injuries and deaths are caused by falls from the walker turning over or by the walker falling down stairways (Committee on Injury and Poison Prevention, 1995). The frequency of walker-related injuries has prompted the American Academy of Pediatrics (Committee on Injury and Poison Prevention, 1995) to recommend that the manufacture and sale of mobile infant walkers be banned, and that efforts be made to educate parents about the hazards and lack of benefits of infant walkers.

The following principles are recommended for use by parents and caregivers in promoting infant motor development:

1. Activities and materials should be developmentally appropriate within the various stages of motor development (Weiser, 1982).
2. Caregivers should not try to hurry development. Babies get ready for the next stage by mastering what they are doing in the present stage (Gonzalez-Mena & Eyer, 1980).
3. Stimulation activities, such as games and exercises, should be provided in each area and stage of motor development (Weiser, 1982). The Uzgiris-Hunt (1975) Scales of Psychological Development suggest many age-appropriate motor activities.
4. Movement activities should be staged so that infants can solve problems without relying on adult help or encountering adult interference (Weiser, 1982).
5. A variety of toys and materials designed to facilitate motor development should be made available to an infant. However, such objects should usually be placed within the infant's reach rather than directly in the hands (Pikler, 1968).
6. Infants should be placed in situations where they are most free and least helpless during the waking hours (Gonzalez-Mena & Eyer, 1980). Playpens, infant seats, highchairs, swings, and jump chairs should not be used for extended periods of time (Gerber, 1981; Prudden & Sussman, 1972). Parents should carefully supervise infants who are using such equipment because of the risk of injury (Ridenour, 1978).
7. Infants should frequently wear as little clothing as temperature and social settings allow in order to facilitate maximum freedom of movement (Pikler, 1968; Prudden, 1964).
8. Model and demonstrate some activities for infants to imitate such as banging two blocks together, stacking blocks, and putting objects in containers (Machado & Meyer-Botnarescue, 1997).

SUMMARY

1. Motor development plays an important role in the development of intelligence, perceptual skills, emotional development, self-awareness, and other aspects of infant development.
2. Factors influencing motor development include heredity, maturation and learning, body size, muscle strength, muscle tone, cultural practices, and nutrition.
3. According to the dynamic-systems approach, the human body is composed of various biological systems (e.g., sensory, muscular) that must work together for the acquisition of motor skills. Through the use of a "moving room," researchers have found that development of postural control of young infants is affected by the use of information from the visual and vestibular (balance) sensory systems
4. Infants display a tendency to practice a new motor activity until it becomes a skill. Motor development proceeds from general to specific responses and from simple to complex skills. Motor development follows the cephalocaudal law of developmental direction, and with some exceptions, the proximodistal law as well.
5. Newborn infants are equipped with numerous reflexes. Key reflexes observed during infancy are rooting, sucking, grasping, Moro, Babinski, tonic neck, stepping, and stretch responses. These reflexes are considered to be indicators of the maturity and integrity of the nervous system. Some of the reflexes apparently facilitate the development of motor skills with practice, whereas others may inhibit the emergence of voluntary control.
6. Eye-hand coordination is established in two stages between birth and 3 to 5 months of age. Prehension, the ability to grasp an object between fingers and thumb, develops in several stages between 4 months and 12 months of age. The infant who has developed prehensory skills spends a lot of time mouthing, visually inspecting, examining, and manipulating objects in numerous ways.
7. Permanent hand preference is established in most infants by 2 years of age. Although evidence is not conclusive, research tends to support the position that hand preference is mainly determined by biological factors.
8. To achieve an upright position, the infant establishes head control (3 months), sitting alone (5–6 months), and standing alone (6–10 months). The development of locomotion begins with rolling (16–22 weeks) and progresses through the stages of crawling, creeping, and sometimes hitching. Infants

usually begin to walk alone by around 12 months of age. Climbing, running, and jumping develop toward the end of the infancy period.

9. Infants typically accomplish most of the skills needed in undressing and dressing themselves between 8 months and 3 years of age. Parents are advised to wait until the infant is 2 years old before beginning toilet training.

10. Some of the conditions that delay and impede motor development include visual impairment, mental disabilities, and cerebral palsy.

11. Numerous scales are available for the assessment of motor development during infancy, including the motor scale from the **Bayley Scales of Infant Development – II,** the **Alberta Infant Motor Scale,** and the **Movement Assessment of Infants.**

12. A variety of programs have been developed to facilitate motor development during infancy. However, parents should use developmentally appropriate activities and not try to hurry motor development.

9

Intellectual Development

What is the little one thinking about?
Very wonderful things no doubt! . . .
Who can tell what a baby thinks.
                                    —J. G. Holland

When do infants begin to think? How do they think? How soon do learning and memory begin? What does an infant know? These and other questions about the development of intelligence in infants have been the target of numerous inquiring minds. One of the characteristics of human intelligence is to try to find out how that intellectual capacity evolved. During a child's infancy, we have opportunities to observe the development of intelligence almost from the very beginning. Although we have only scratched the surface, our knowledge of cognitive development has increased dramatically during the past 30 years.

This chapter focuses on some of the factors that influence intelligence, some important theories of cognitive development, perceptual development, some of the ways infants learn, and the development of infant memory. We also look at some of the instruments that are used to assess infant intelligence. Finally, suggestions for facilitating cognitive development during the infancy period will be considered.

DEFINITIONS

Definitions of intelligence are numerous and varied. Wechsler (1944) defined intelligence as "the capacity of the individual to act purposefully, think rationally and deal effectively with the environment" (p. 3). Piaget (1954) defined intelligence in terms of an individual's capacity to adapt to the environment. There is widespread agreement among experts from various fields that intelligence consists of at least three elements—the ability to think abstractly or reason; the capacity to accumulate knowledge (memory); and the ability to solve problems (McCormick, 1996).

Cognition is a term that is closely associated with intelligence. The two terms are frequently used to mean the same thing. Technically, though, cognition refers to all the mental processes, such

as thinking, remembering, use of language, problem solving, and concept formation. The cognitive processes thus make up the functional component of intelligence. In this chapter the terms intelligence and cognition are used interchangeably.

INFLUENCES ON INTELLIGENCE

The extent to which intelligence is controlled by heredity or by environment has been intensely debated for centuries. Today the most widely accepted point of view is that heredity and environment interact in complex ways to shape intelligence. However, researchers have attempted to determine the relative contribution of each factor.

Heredity

The position that heredity is the dominant force in intellectual development has been represented most vigorously by Arthur Jensen (1969). Jensen claims that approximately 80 percent of the differences in IQ scores is the result of genetic factors. Thus if one child obtains an IQ score of 120 and another obtains a score of 100, 16 points of the 20-point difference (.80 x 20) are the result of heredity. Jensen's claims have been controversial and not widely accepted.

Still, there is no doubt that intelligence is influenced by heredity. Plomin and colleagues (Plomin & Defries, 1980; Plomin, DeFries, & McClearn, 1990) have concluded that the difference in IQ scores which can be attributed to genetic factors is no more than 50 percent. Most researchers have been reluctant to accept a specific percentage as valid because of the difficulties involved in separating genetic from environmental factors. Scientists such as Scarr and Weinberg (1978) believe that it is impossible to assign a specific percentage to the contribution of heredity to intelligence.

Environment

In combination with heredity, numerous environmental influences potentially affect intellectual development. Most of these factors, including health, nutrition, and prenatal and perinatal influences, are covered in other chapters. At this point we need to consider three additional potential sources of influence during infancy: the family environment, cultural factors, and socioeconomic factors.

Family Environment. Research studies have tended to confirm the assertion that family influences play a very important role in the development of intelligence. In the Harvard Preschool Project, White and his associates (1973) conducted extensive observations of the home environment of 31 infants through the first 3 years of life. They concluded that the infants who were assessed to be the most intellectually competent experienced parent-child interactions superior to those of the infants who were less competent. A four-year longitudinal study of 193 mothers and their infants (Bee et al., 1982) found that measures of home-environmental quality and parent-infant interaction taken in the first year of life are good predictors of later IQ and language development.

Socioeconomic Status. Children from low-socioeconomic backgrounds consistently score lower on measures of intelligence than do their middle-class peers. However, these differences do not begin to appear until after the first 18 months of life (Golden & Birns, 1976). By 3 years of age, the child's IQ score has been affected by such socioeconomic indicators as parental education, occupation, and income (Bayley & Schaefer, 1964). For infants living in poverty a variety of factors can lead to cognitive delays. Adverse conditions commonly faced are inadequate nutrition, insufficient health care, exposure to toxic substances, and inappropriate stimulation (Kaplan-Sanoff, Parker, & Zuckerman, 1991). Fortunately, infant-intervention programs can prevent the decline of IQ scores attributed to the effects of poverty (see Chapter 14).

Cultural Factors. Cross-cultural studies have generally found more similarities than differences in cognitive development of infants throughout the world. The sequence and timing of sensorimotor milestones, smiling, separation anxiety, the order of stages of language development (Rogoff & Morelli, 1989), the ability to interpret the meaning of facial expressions and perceive whole-part relationships (Berk & Winsler, 1995) are similar for infants from all cultures. After reviewing numerous investigations, Super (1981) concluded that infants from one particular culture or race generally do not show more rapid cognitive development than infants from other cultures or races, except under conditions of minimal stimulation or malnutrition. Kagan and Klein (1973) found that infants living in an isolated village of Guatemala were delayed two to three months in achieving a variety of cognitive milestones such as object permanence and symbolic aspects of play. The delays were attributed to the inadequate stimulation they experienced during their first year.

Even though infants from all cultural backgrounds are alike in many ways, cultural influences are a primary factor in infant development. There is increasing evidence that social and cultural factors are a powerful source of influence in shaping and transforming children's thinking (Berk & Winsler, 1995). According to Vygotsky (1978), learning is inseparable from social and cultural activities. In order to understand children, therefore, we must understand the social and cultural contexts in which they develop (Berk & Winsler, 1995). Vygotsky's ideas will be considered in more detail after we look at Piaget's cognitive developmental theory.

PIAGET'S THEORY

The theory of Jean Piaget has most widely influenced contemporary understanding of the development of infant intelligence. Piaget did not agree with the nativist view that infants are born with basic concepts and knowledge structures. He also disagreed with the environmentalist position that the newborn infant's mind is a tabula rasa (blank slate) and all knowledge is acquired through experience. Instead, Piaget's theory is based on the belief that intelligence develops through an interaction between internal (genetic) and external (environmental) influences.

Key Concepts

For Piaget (1952), making progress in cognitive development is based on scheme building. A **scheme** is a basic pattern of action, thought, or knowledge that is used to interact with the environment. Schemes can be classified as either motor or mental. Motor schemes are organized patterns of action such as sucking a bottle, picking up a toy, or walking. Mental schemes are concepts, ideas, or images that make up the thought processes. Mental and motor schemes are used together and are difficult to separate, as when an infant produces a sound (motor) to form a word (mental). Schemes are the building blocks of intelligence. They make up the structure of the mind and serve as basic units of behavior. At any given age, a person's intelligence is based upon the number, complexity, and flexibility of the available schemes.

Schemes are built and modified through the process of adaptation. Piaget believed that adaptation is the key to intellectual functioning. In order to survive and get along in the world, an individual must make changes and adjustments in thought and action to fit new situations. Adaptation takes place through two related processes—**assimilation** and **accommodation**. Assimilation is making the environment fit you. In assimilation, the individual makes use of substances or information through existing schemes. A young infant who spots a new object will probably pick it up and try to eat it or bang it on something. If the toy is small enough, the baby can exploit it without making any modifications in existing behaviors. In some cases an infant assimilates information (perceptions) from the environment by forcing it to conform or fit in with existing ideas or understandings (schemes). For example, an infant may learn the word *cat* and associate it with a four-legged, furry animal. The infant may then use that particular scheme (cat) to apply to a dog or other animals. Thus, in assimilation, the infant uses and tries to preserve existing structures.

Accommodation is making yourself fit the environment. It is the process whereby an individual's schemes are altered to fit new information or experiences. When a breast-fed baby is given a bottle

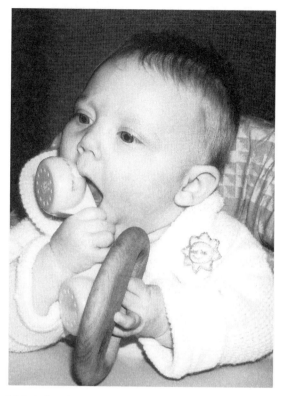

This infant is practicing assimilation by exploring the object with the mouthing scheme.

for the first time, the sucking scheme has to be modified to fit the shape, size, and milk flow of the new nipple before it is effective. The infant who calls all four-legged animals "cat" will eventually learn that the "cat" scheme only applies to certain animals. In some cases a new scheme has to be created because there is no existing scheme available into which new information can be accommodated. Accommodation is the mechanism through which variability, growth, and change occurs.

Assimilation and accommodation are complementary processes that usually operate in concert. The two processes may be observed when an infant adjusts the mouth (sucking) to accommodate the shape of a new nipple while at the same time taking in or assimilating nourishment and pleasurable sensations. In this instance, assimilation and accommodation have reached a state of equilibrium or balance. The infant has reached a state of adaptation to the environment. However, the equilibrium or state of balance between assimilation and accommodation does not last, and one process or the other dominates temporarily. When assimilation and accommodation are out of balance, the result is usually cognitive conflict. The infant is then motivated to restore equilibrium by searching for a solution. Cognitive development advances as the baby produces more sophisticated schemes in order to adapt and change.

Piaget's Stages

According to Piaget, cognitive development proceeds through a series of orderly stages. Although the approximate age at which each stage occurs has been identified, not everyone goes through the stages at the same rate or chronological age. In some instances, a person may "straddle," or be in two stages, at the same time. However, the order in which individuals progress through the stages does not vary. The basic stages Piaget identified are the sensorimotor period (birth to 2 years), the period of preoperational thought (2 to 7 years), the period of concrete operations (7 to 11 years), and the period of formal operations (11 to 15 years). The sensorimotor period, which corresponds with infancy, is considered further.

Sensorimotor Period

The first two years of life are called the sensorimotor period because the baby relates to the world by coordinating information from the senses with motor activities of the body. Piaget (1952) introduced the idea that thought arises from action. In the beginning of life, knowledge is not separated from activities. The young infant looks at an object and reflexively reaches for it without thinking about the process. As the baby gets older, the repetition of motor activities provides the basis for development of mental schemes, or ideas of the mind. During most of the sensorimotor period infants do not have concepts or ideas and thus are not capable of true thinking (Mandler, 1990).

The period of sensorimotor intelligence is divided into six stages. The infant is working on several tasks during the various substages. These tasks include imitating the behavior of others, developing intentional behavior, and understanding object permanence, cause-effect relationships, and time and space concepts. A summary of the cognitive changes that occur during each of the stages of the sensorimotor period follows.

Stage 1: Exercising Reflex Schemes (Birth–1 Month). A newborn infant is equipped with some basic reflex schemes such as sucking, looking, and crying. The baby's actions during this stage consist primarily of exercising these innate reflexes. The main accomplishment during this substage is the increased efficiency and complexity of reflexive behaviors. For example, the baby uses the sucking scheme on different objects and assimilates taste and other pleasurable sensations in the process. With experience and practice, the sucking reflex becomes more efficient and adapted to satisfying both nutritive and nonnutritive sucking needs. The other reflexes are also modified and become more efficient and discriminating if the infant has opportunities for practice.

Stage 2: Primary Circular Reactions (1–4 Months). The reflex schemes have become more complex through repeated use and now serve as the basis for new patterns of behavior. Piaget labeled these new schemes "primary circular reactions." Responses in this stage are called primary because they are centered in the baby's own body, and because they are the first of a series of circular reactions. A circular reaction is a response that stimulates its own repetition.

At the beginning of this stage, the baby may be observed repeating over and over interesting and pleasurable behavior patterns that have been accidentally discovered. One of the first primary circular responses an infant demonstrates is thumb-sucking. A major accomplishment in this stage is the infant's growing ability to coordinate and combine various schemes. Piaget (1952) observed his daughter Jacqueline turning her head to locate the sound of his voice at age 2 months and 12 days. Her action represents the intercoordination of the looking and hearing schemes. At this stage, the infant also begins to anticipate the occurrence of events on the basis of past experience. An infant may begin sucking movements the minute it is picked up and placed in the position to nurse. In so doing, the infant demonstrates an elementary understanding that there is a sequence to certain events. This forms the basis for the infant's understanding of time.

Stage 3: Secondary Circular Reactions (4–8 Months). The circular reactions are now labeled as secondary for two reasons. For one thing, this stage represents the second in the series of circular reactions. The main reason, though, is that the infant's repetitive behaviors now focus on events or objects outside the body. The stage 3 infant is concerned with a result produced in the external environment. Unlike primary circular reactions, these are not reflexive behaviors, but schemes that have been acquired through learning.

Secondary circular reactions are the result of accidental or random behaviors which produce something that attracts the infant's attention. The following is an example:

> One day when Dimitri was 4 months old, he was lying on his back in his crib looking at his multicolored animal mobile . . . when he suddenly kicked one of his feet and banged the side of the crib. The movement of his leg against the crib bars caused the mobile to sway . . . Dimitri watched the mobile's movement until it stopped. As soon as the mobile was still, he looked away and then looked back at it again. No movement. Now he again looked away, but this time catching sight of his foot. Then he kicked his foot again but not hard enough to make the crib, and hence the mobile, move. He became slightly agitated and kicked both feet, this time with success. Dimitri lay perfectly still, his eyes fixed on the dancing animals. When they stopped moving, he kicked both feet and waved his arms until he moved the crib enough to activate the mobile (Sherrod, Vietze, & Friedman, 1978, p. 104).

When Dimitri made the connection between the moving mobile and his own movements, he repeated the action and established a secondary circular response.

The stage 3 infant begins to develop an awareness of the object concept. Infants have to learn that objects are external or separate from themselves and continue to exist even though they are not visible (object permanence). At this point the infant will search for an object if it is partially visible. If an infant drops an object and loses sight of it, the infant will attempt to visually anticipate its new location. This usually happens only if the baby has caused an object to disappear. The concept of **object permanence** thus is only partially developed in stage 3.

Stage 4: Coordination of Secondary Circular Reactions (8–12 Months). For the first time, the infant exhibits behaviors that Piaget called truly intelligent. Schemes are now mobile and flexible enough to be generalized to new situations. Babies can use existing schemes to overcome obstacles or solve simple problems. The infant can also combine and coordinate several different schemes to reach a goal. This stage is thus called coordination of secondary circular reactions (schemes).

Stage 4 infants demonstrate intentional, goal-directed activity, which is one of the first signs of intelligent behavior. Piaget described how he placed his hand in front of a matchbox his son Laurent was trying to obtain. Laurent hit his father's hand to move it aside in order to get the box. When Piaget replaced the hand with a cushion as an obstacle, Laurent also hit the pillow so that he could grasp the box. In this example, we see how an existing scheme is adapted to apply to a new situation. The "hitting" scheme that Laurent used to make a mobile move in stage 3 was applied to obtain the desired object.

We can also see in Laurent's means-to-an-end behavior a major step in the understanding of cause-effect relationships. Up to this point, an infant acts and waits for something to happen, but with no real understanding of how effects occur. It was as if things happened by "magic" or that objects obeyed the baby's wishes. At this stage, however, infants begin to be aware that their own actions create results: If you hit a mobile, it moves.

The development of the object concept takes another step forward in this stage. The infant's increased understanding of the permanence of objects is evident when the infant searches for an object that has disappeared. If a ball rolls under a chair, the infant will try to find it there. An infant will also remove a cover from an object that is completely hidden. At this stage, infants love to play "peek-a-boo" and "hide-and-seek" games based on the disappearance and reappearance of people and objects.

The concept of object permanence is not completely established, though. The infant cannot think of an object as having an independent existence apart from the actions performed on it. If an object is placed under one cover (A) and then under another (B), the infant will look only under the first cover (A). The infant will find a ball that is hidden under a handkerchief but will continue to look under the handkerchief if the ball is hidden the second time under a pillow even while the infant watches. At this stage, the object is still connected with the infant's previous success in locating it at point A, so the search ends at that location. Piaget believed that the infant thinks there is more than one object involved in the game. In other words, there is an object at A and another just like it at B.

According to Piaget, the beginning of true imitation occurs in this stage. Imitation involves the capacity to copy the actions, sounds, or other characteristics exhibited by a model. Before stage 4, infants engage in what Piaget called reflexive or pseudoimitation. This is an early form of imitation that is based on a response the child has already demonstrated or finds easy to mimic. For example, an infant will readily imitate cooing and other sounds the infant has already made. Infants can be taught to imitate adults waving "bye-bye" and performing other actions, but Piaget did not call these behaviors true imitation because they require constant practice and encouragement.

Now, at stage 4, infants can imitate actions that involve movements they cannot see themselves perform, such as wrinkling the nose. They also begin to imitate new sounds. For example, one mother was surprised after she angrily hung up the phone to hear her 1-year old mimic her perfectly with the word "*Damn!*" (Pulaski, 1978).

Stage 5: Tertiary Circular Reactions (12–18 Months). Tertiary means third-order, or third in a series. Piaget used this term to describe how the baby's intellectual activities reach a more complex and advanced level of proficiency. The infant still engages in repetitive activity, but deliberately makes variations to see what happens. The stage 4 infant was satisfied with producing the same result over and over. The stage 5 infant wants to use a familiar combination of schemes to produce something new and different. This marks the beginning of curiosity and creative activity.

Piaget (1952) described how Laurent dropped pieces of bread and other objects from various body positions and locations. In the previous stage he would have been interested simply in the act of letting go, to observe the same result over and over. At stage 5 he was more interested in observing where the object landed, particularly in relation to the position from which he let it fall. Piaget referred to this type of activity as directed groping.

Through the use of tertiary circular reactions, the infant solves simple problems by trial and error. Like a budding scientist, the infant experiments to find new ways to accomplish a goal or solve a problem. New combinations and variations of schemes are attempted until the infant finds one that works. For example, babies discover they can obtain an object that is out of reach by pulling on the tablecloth on which the object is resting. Such behavior indicates that the stage 5 baby displays a certain amount of practical intelligence.

The infant continues to make progress in understanding the various features and functions of objects. The stage 5 infant is able to walk, which brings increased opportunities for contact with more objects and opportunities to see their relationship to one another in space. The baby learns more about physical properties such as size, weight, and texture. During the previous stage, the infant was interested in taking objects apart, putting them into containers, and dumping them out. Now the infant is interested in putting the pieces of an object together and exploring the relationship between different objects and their containers.

The understanding of cause-effect relations reaches a new level during this stage. Infants now begin to recognize that actions result from the behavior of other people as well as their own. They are thus becoming slightly less egocentric. When an object moves, they may look for the source of the movement outside of their own activities. For example, Piaget (1954) slowly moved Laurent's stroller with his foot. Laurent leaned over to the edge of the carriage to find what was making it move. As soon as he saw his father's foot on the wheel, he gave a smile of understanding.

The concept of object permanence also improves. The infant can now follow and locate an object that has been hidden in three successive locations. However, the infant must see the movements. If not allowed to watch where the object disappears at any point, the baby becomes confused and will look for it only at the first location. Apparently it is not yet possible for the infant to imagine what might be happening to an object while it is out of sight.

Like the object concept, the development of imitation parallels cognitive development. Stage 5 infants are capable of more accurate and extensive imitations. They can imitate behaviors that are not in their repertoire, but they require some "groping," or trial and error. In keeping with the tendency to experiment, they vary the actions or sounds of the model to observe the result.

Stage 6: Invention of New Means Through Mental Combinations (18-24 Months) At last the infant begins to think before acting. The ability to represent objects and events by mental images (symbols) develops during this stage. The infant no longer has to "discover" solutions to problems through trial and error, but is capable of inventing solutions by combining mental schemes.

Piaget (1952) gave his daughter, Lucienne, a matchbox containing his watch chain. He left a small opening so that she could see the chain inside. Her first efforts to get it out with her index finger were unsuccessful. Next, she looked at the opening and began to open and close her mouth, wider and wider. She then put her finger into the opening of the box and slid the cover back far enough to reach the chain. Lucienne gave an indication of what she was thinking when she opened and closed her mouth. Piaget concluded: "This new type of behavior pattern characterizes systematic intelligence" (Piaget, 1952, p. 331).

The ability to represent actions through mental pictures makes it possible for an infant to imitate a model faster and more accurately. The infant can, for the first time, imitate a model that is no longer present. Jacqueline observed a little boy stamping his feet while engaging in a temper tantrum. The next day she screamed and stamped her feet in a similar fashion (Piaget, 1962). This is called deferred imitation.

The concept of the object permanence is fully developed at this stage. The baby now has a mental image of the object which is independent of an immediate sensory impression of the object itself. The object has an independent, enduring existence even though it cannot always be seen. Infants are not as easily fooled when an object disappears, even though part of the process may be invisible. They search in various places where they have found objects hidden before.

Evaluation of Piaget's Theory

Presently, there is sufficient evidence to support some of the basic sequences of development outlined in Piaget's sensorimotor stages. On the other hand, researchers have found evidence to challenge many of Piaget's assumptions. There is an increasing amount of research indicating that infants accomplish some of the cognitive tasks earlier than Piaget's timetable suggests. The studies of Mandler (1990) and Baillargeon (1993) indicate that infants are far more sophisticated in their cognitive abilities than Piaget believed. As noted in Chapter 4, newborns appear to be capable of imitating facial and other expressions. Also, the results of several studies on object permanence are viewed as incompatible with Piaget's ideas. Piaget based his belief about the timetable for the development of the object concept on the willingness or ability of an infant to manually or physically search for a hidden object. It is possible, however that infants do not manually search for an object because of motor limitations, memory limitations, motivational factors, or the understanding of how to search. Bower (1982), Baillargeon (1993) and others conducted studies that relied on looking rather than the manual tasks used by Piaget and others. The results of these investigations indicate that infants as young as 3½ to 5½ months of age understand, to some extent, that objects exist and retain their physical properties even when they are not visible.

In spite of findings that apparently contradict Piaget's theory, many scholars have rushed to defend Piagetian theory (e.g., Glassman, 1994; Lourenco & Machado, 1996). Decarie and Ricard (1996) contend that upon closer examination, research findings on object permanence and imitation do not necessarily constitute evidence of cognitive skills that violate Piaget's basic theory. These and other supporters of Piaget are convinced that his theory continues to provide a valuable framework for understanding infant development. Even if Piaget underestimated the timetable for the emergence of some of the infant's cognitive abilities, his portrayal of the sequence in which cognitive functions emerge remains less controversial. As Piaget's theory undergoes reappraisal, other theories are gaining popularity. Two such theories that we will consider are Vygotsky's sociocultural theory and information-processing theories.

VYGOTSKY'S THEORY

For Piaget, sensorimotor activities are the most important activities during infancy that promote cognitive development. For Vygotsky (1978), the interchanges between the infant and other people represent the key to cognitive change. He agreed with Piaget that infants learn through the manipulation of objects. However, Vygotsky believed that the significance of object play cannot be separated from the cultural context. "The path from object to child and from the child to object passes through another person" (Vygotsky, 1978, p. 30). All higher mental activities, such as attention, memory, and problem solving are rooted in social behavior that becomes internalized by the child. The following is a brief overview of some of Vygotsky's main ideas.

Key Concepts

Vygotsky believed that language plays a central role in shaping mental functioning. Language is considered to be a "tool of the mind" that enables the infant to transfer socially generated knowledge to internal, self-regulated thought. The language environment in which the child is reared is crucial to intellectual growth. Vygotsky's ideas about language development will be considered further in the next chapter.

Vygotsky described the key to learning in terms of the **zone of proximal development (ZPD)**. At any given time in a child's life the continuum of learning includes tasks that a child can do without assistance, tasks that a child can do with help or guidance, and tasks that are completely beyond the child's capacity. The ZPD represents the middle region which consists of the motor activities or concepts a child is capable of mastering with the help of an adult or a more advanced peer. For example, 2-year-old Pia could only put together a 4-piece puzzle, but with some coaching from her mother she quickly learned to "work" a more difficult puzzle of six pieces.

Barbara Rogoff (1990) introduced the term **guided participation** to describe the process by which children develop through involvement in the practices of their community. Children learn as they actively participate in culturally structured activities with the guidance, support, and challenge of companions who impart a wide variety of skills and knowledge. Children are not just passive recipients of cultural experiences, but are viewed as "apprentices" who collaborate and participate in real-life activities and problem solving with more skilled, knowledgeable, but supportive, others.

Rogoff and her collaborators (1993) examined how toddlers (12 to 24-month-old) and their caregivers in four cultural communities shared activities through guided participation. They observed families in two middle-class communities from Turkey and the United States. These families were compared with Guatemalan Mayan and Indian tribal families from two non-middle class communities. In the two middle-class communities the goals and methods of guided participation involved an emphasis on verbal instruction, adult play with young children, and provision of "lessons" within single events and dyadic participation. Within the non-middle-class communities, the toddlers were more likely to be exposed to guided participation that involved nonverbal instruction. They were also expected to learn through observation and participation in multiple events in a larger group context. Similarites in guided participation as well as differences were found. The results were not viewed as establishing the superiority of one cultural practice over another, but as support for Vygotsky's views on the importance of cultural influences on cognitive development.

Evaluation of Vygotsky's Theory

Vygotsky's theory has been given high marks for how well it reflects the real world of children (Thomas, 1996) and its sensitivity to the diversity of children (Miller, 1993). It has been criticized for the vagueness of some of the concepts related to the zone of proximal development, and for insufficient attention to how children develop within the zone (Miller, 1993). In comparison to Piagetian theory, there is much less research on Vygotsky's theory due to the complexities of studying children in a cultural context. Vygotsky's ideas have been mostly applied to older age groups due to his emphasis on the importance of language (Berk, 1996). In recent years, however, Rogoff (1990) and others (Berk & Winsler, 1995) have extended his ideas downward to the infancy period.

INFORMATION-PROCESSING APPROACHES

Although information-processing theories are quite different from Piagetian theory, Piaget's ideas have had a formative influence on their development (Siegler, 1991). Some theorists have used an information-processing approach (e.g., Rutkowska, 1993; Siegler, 1991) to revise, refine, and rethink Piaget's theory. Actually information-processing theories are numerous and varied. Consequently, they are often referred to as a framework rather than a theory (Siegler, 1991). For our purposes we will look at a few basic ideas that characterize this approach.

According to the information-processing framework, the functions of the brain are compared to the operation of a computer (Thomas, 1996). Information is entered into the computer (input), processed within the machine (throughput), resulting in a response (output). The input and output features of information processing can be observed, but what happens during the internal processing phase remains unseen and is, therefore, the key to understanding human cognition. Thinking basically is information processing (Siegler, 1991). Therefore, information-processing theorists attempt to explain the infant's internal mechanisms for manipulating information and how the components interact to produce behavior (Thomas, 1996).

A key element in our understanding of cognitive functioning is the process by which information is entered (encoded) into the brain through the sense organs and how it is perceived (processed) by the infant. Other key components of information-processing approaches are the structure and function of attention, perception, and memory. The quality of a child's thinking at any age depends on the capacity to receive and store information, how much information a child can access and keep in mind at one time, and the ability to operate on the information to solve problems and achieve goals (Siegler, 1991).

A basic goal of information processing theorists is to identify the inner mechanisms that are responsible for developmental changes and how they work to produce cognitive growth (Siegler, 1991). The acquisition of cognitive skills that improve the way information is processed is one mechanism of development. As children get older their knowledge about various aspects of the physical world (e.g., objects) and social world (e.g., people), knowledge about memory, and strategies for remembering information improve. Another proposed mechanism of development is the changes that take place in the rate of acquiring and processing information. Theoretically, these abilities improve with age and experience.

Evaluation of the Information-Processing Approach

The information-processing approach has been a useful model for analyzing the complexities of the thought processes. This approach has been rated highly for the emphasis that is placed on the use of research findings in analyzing and forming conclusions about cognitive processes. Much of the research on infant perception and memory is currently conducted from an information-processing perspective (Miller, 1993). This approach has contributed greatly to new research findings and to our understanding of the cognitive, "computational" competencies of infants described in the next sections on perception and memory.

On the other hand, information processing has been criticized for failing to come up with a comprehensive, integrated theory of human development. This approach focuses primarily on how infants think and does not adequately consider how they develop physically, emotionally, and socially within a cultural context (Thomas, 1996). In addition, some people object to depicting infants and children as "little computers." However, proponents of information-processing views are quick to point out that the computer model is just an analogy and that children are viewed as more than simply "machines."

PERCEPTUAL DEVELOPMENT

Cognition is dependent upon sensation and perception. These processes supply data for mental activity, including thinking, learning, remembering, and problem solving. Although sensation and perception have traditionally been defined as separate processes, contemporary psychologists tend to view the two processes as lying along the same continuum (Steuer, 1994; Wortman, Loftus, & Marshall, 1992). Practically speaking, it is difficult to determine where sensations leave off and perceptions begin. Thus, **perception** is often defined as the process whereby information gathered by the senses is interpreted by the brain.

Recall from Chapter 4 that the senses are remarkably well developed in newborn infants and that newborns possess perceptual abilities that are truly amazing. We now need to consider how perceptions change during the infancy period. Information-processing researchers and others have focused mainly on visual and auditory perceptions, and to a much lesser extent on tactual (touch) perceptions. In addition, researchers have been concerned with the ability of infants to coordinate perceptions from different sensory modalities (see intersensory perception later in this chapter; also see chapter 4).

Our understanding of perceptual development has been heavily influenced by Eleanor Gibson's view of infants as active, self-motivated learners (1969; 1992). According to Gibson, perception is a process that develops over time as the baby becomes capable of increasingly finer, more complex, discriminating, and accurate perceptions. In the process, infants search for information from the environment in the form of **invariant features** of objects and events. Infants are viewed as "preattuned" to pick up the features that are consistent and unchanging and are able to filter out irrelevant information (Miller, 1993). For example, they detect overall patterns in the shape of objects, such as squares and forms.

Infants also tend to look for **distinctive features** that distinguish one object from another. This tendency enables the infant to distinguish between faces on the basis of differences in noses, ears, hair line, and other individual features. In adddition, infants' perceptions are guided by the principle of **affordances.** That is, infants look for things in the environment that are useful to them, or **afford** them opportunities for action, such as surfaces that will support standing. For Gibson (1992, p. 234), "perceiving is itself a mechanism of learning" and "the key to knowledge." Many of Gibson's ideas have been supported by existing research, although her theory is not universally accepted.

Operating from various theoretical perspectives, researchers are accumulating an increasingly large body of literature on the perceptual and cognitive abilities of infants. The research literature is far too vast and complex to cover completely in this text. Therefore, we will look at some highlights and major conclusions about infant visual, auditory, and touch/ haptic perceptual abilities. Current views of perception emphasize that we are biologically equipped at birth to perceive the world in certain ways, that newborns have amazing (although limited) perceptual abilities, and that many aspects of perception reach adultlike capacity during the second 6 months of life (Siegler, 1991).

Vision

Researchers have made remarkable progress in understanding infant visual perception since the 1960s. We have learned a lot about what objects and events they attend to, their ability to discriminate the properties of objects relative to their color, motion, depth, and other properties, as well as their ability to locate still and moving objects.

Visual Acuity

Even though newborn infants have a limited visual capacity, their ability to see objects improves rapidly. In the first 6 months after birth the infant's visual acuity improves dramatically. By 1 year of age, visual acuity is estimated to be approximately 20/50. Normal adult 20/20 vision is typically achieved about 4 years of age (Teplin, 1995). Visual acuity is affected by the amount of contrast between an object and its background, and by spatial frequency of an object's patterns, such as squares on a checkerboard. Young infants see best at low spatial frequencies (e.g., a checkerboard with a few, large squares) for maximum contrast. As they get older, infants prefer to look at progressively higher spatial frequencies and do not need as much contrast (e.g., a checkerboard with a larger number of smaller squares). This indicates they are able to see more details (Siegler, 1991).

Object Perception

Infants spend much of their time looking at objects. Recall that newborn infants scan the edges of faces and still objects. By 2 months of age, infants tend to focus on and scan the internal features of objects (Haith, Bergman, & Moore, 1977). Objects are perceived as distinct, single units that are separate from other objects and surfaces (Spelke & Hermer, 1996). At this age they prefer to look at more stimuli with more complex patterns (Brennan, Ames, & Moore, 1966), and stimuli that have high-contrast contours and curves (McCall & Melson, 1970). By 3-to-4 months of age the infant's object-perception abilities have blossomed. For example, 4-month-old infants were exposed to a rod that was moving back and forth behind a block so they could see only the rod's top and bottom. The infants' responses indicated that they perceived the rod as a unified object rather than two separate pieces (Kellman & Spelke, 1983).

Facial Perception. You read in Chapter 4 that newborns prefer to look at moving human faces over other similar stimuli. In spite of this impressive beginning, studies indicate that this preferential tracking of faces disappears between 4 and 6 weeks of age (Johnson et al., 1991). The disappearance is probably due to the inhibition of a reflex-like behavior by the development of higher forms of brain activity. By 2 to 3 months of age, infants again clearly demonstrate a preference for the natural arrangement of human facial features over various scrambled facial images (Maurer & Barrera, 1981). At this stage, infants do not need motion to detect facial features. By 6 months of age, infants have developed the ability to discriminate young from old faces and male from female faces. They also remember and discriminate between the faces of strangers (Carey, 1996). Six- to eight-month-old infants display a relatively sophisticated ability to discriminate facial features on the basis of attractiveness. Like adults, they tend to demonstrate a preference for attractive faces (Langlois et al., 1987).

Object Number. Researchers have tried to determine whether or not infants can discriminate between small numbers of items. Groups of 8-, 10-, and 12-month-old infants were habituated to two objects (rabbits) as they disappeared and reappeared in a gap between two curtains—an expected event (Arterberry et al., 1993). The situation was changed whereby only one rabbit appeared in the opening—an unexpected event. Out of the three age groups, only the 12-month-olds looked longer at the unexpected than at the expected event. These findings suggest that by 12 months of age, infants are capable of a crude form of counting.

Other studies, however, indicate that by 4 or 5 months of age, infants can discriminate one object from two and two objects from three. For example, Wynn (1992) presented 5-month-old infants with a series of displays in which two objects were manipulated in various numerical combinations. She concluded that these infants could clearly perceive the arithmetic operation being performed and calculate the results. There is no suggestion, though, that infants actually "count" the objects. Rather, infants identify numbers through **subitization**, a quick and effortless perceptual process that people can apply in looking at three or four objects and knowing how many there are without going through the process of enumeration (Siegler, 1991). If young infants can do this, there is support for the belief that human infants are innately endowed with the ability to perform simple mathematical operations.

Depth Perception

Much of the research on visual capabilities of infants has been directed toward finding out when depth perception develops. Depth perception involves such things as seeing objects in three dimensions, judging the size and distance of objects, and perceiving heights of drop-offs. Infants need to be capable of depth perception in order to avoid falling down stairs, bumping into furniture, and grasping objects.

Monocular and Binocular Cues. Through the years, researchers have explored questions about the ability of infants to use monocular and binocular cues in depth perception. **Monocular cues** are cues that can be perceived through one eye working alone. By placing a blindfold over one eye of an infant, researchers are able to observe the infant's reactions to pictorial cues, such as shading and textures used by artists to create depth. Infants are capable of accurate depth perception through the use of pictorial and other types of nonmoving monocular cues by approximately 7 months of age (Granrud & Yonas, 1984; Granrud, Yonas, & Opland, 1985). However, infants perceive depth on the basis of monocular cues around

3 to 5 months of age if the stimuli are moving (Siegler, 1991).

Binocular cues are cues that are only available when both eyes focus on an object. Since the two eyes are separated, each eye picks up information from a slightly different angle. Try closing one eye and then the other to view a scene. You can easily perceive that it is not necessary to use both eyes to perceive depth. However, depth perception is more accurate and efficient with the use of binocular cues. For example, infants are more accurate in judging the distance of objects when using binocular vision than monocular vision (Granrud et al., 1984).

How soon do infants view the world from a binocular perspective? While infants can focus both eyes on the same target (convergence) as early as 1 month of age, they evidently do not have the capacity to use binocular cues efficiently until about 3½ months of age (Held, 1993). Binocular perception, as well as other aspects of perceptual development, are heavily dependent upon maturation of the nervous system, but visual experience plays a significant role.

There may be a critical period for the development of binocular perception. Researchers (Banks, Aslin, & Letson, 1975) have studied binocular functioning in children who were born with strabismus. Children who have this condition cannot focus both eyes on the same target and do not perceive binocular cues. Fortunately, this problem can be corrected by surgery. If normal focus is restored before 3 years of age, complete binocular depth perception is achieved. However, if the condition is corrected later than 3 years of age, binocular vision appears to be permanently impaired.

The Visual Cliff. The most well known studies of depth perception are based on the visual cliff technique developed by Gibson and Walk (1960; Walk & Gibson, 1961). These innovative researchers created the illusion of a visual cliff by using a special table with a checkerboard-patterned surface covered by a sheet of clear plexiglas. One side of the table has a drop-off of several feet. Infants who can crawl typically avoid the side with the drop-off even though it is covered by plexiglas

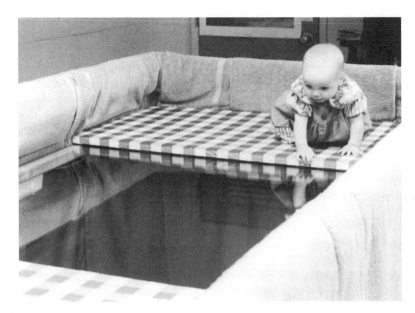

This infant is facing the challenge of the "visual cliff."

(Gibson & Walk, 1960). However, infants as young as 1½ to 3 months of age respond differently to the deep drop-off than they do to the shallow side of the visual cliff (Bertenthal & Campos, 1990). These responses can be interpreted to mean that babies perceive depth before they become mobile. An alternative explanation is that the infants are simply responding to two different visual patterns without any appreciation for the differences in depth.

In any case, though, infants do not display fear or wariness of the "visual cliff," regardless of age, until they gain experience in moving around by themselves (Campos, Bertenthal, & Kermoian, 1992). Thus, motor activities play an important role in the type of depth perception that causes an infant to avoid heights. Experience obtained through independent locomotion apparently allows the infant to judge height more accurately and develop the impression that heights are dangerous and should be avoided.

Motion Cues

One of the most important factors in an infant's ability to perceive depth and discriminate object properties is motion. Although it might seem more difficult for infants to extract information about a moving object than a stationary object, it is evidently easier for an infant to "visually" explore or manipulate an object in motion (Bornstein & Lamb, 1992). The ability to perceive depth through monocular and binocular cues involving motion develops well ahead of depth perception limited to cues from motionless stimuli (Arterberry et al., 1993).

Infants are attracted to moving objects from the beginning of life. Their eye movements are jerky at first as they track moving objects and do not reach adult efficiency until 6 months of age (Aslin, 1993). However, their sensitivity to rapidly moving objects is high during the first month of life. Apparently the ability to perceive rapidly moving objects develops ahead of the ability to respond to very slowly moving objects (Kaufmann-Hayoz, 1991). By 3 months of age infants have an uncanny ability to use motion-carried information in their perceptions. For example, infants are able to extract information from visual motion patterns to distinguish objects from their background surfaces (figure-ground relationships), as well as the perception of object shapes, spatial relations, and other properties (Arterberry, et al., 1993; Kaufmann-Hayoz, 1991). Motion studies also show that young infants perceive that (1) objects move cohesively and maintain their external boundaries; (2) objects move continuously, tracing a path as they move; and (3) objects move independently and influence each other's motion only on contact (Spelke & Hermer, 1996).

Auditory Perception

Changes in sensitivity to sounds are to be expected throughout the infancy period for several reasons. Structurally, the size and shape of the external ear, the ear canal, the middle ear cavity, and the sound conductive mechanism continue to change into middle childhood. In addition, the part of the brain in which sound is interpreted is quite immature at birth and improves with age (Muir, 1985). Finally, as the nervous system matures, the ability of the infant to concentrate, select, and attend to sounds improves. Until about 3 months of age, infants hear lower-pitched sounds better than higher-pitched sounds. As they get older, this pattern reverses so that by 6 months of age, infants are more sensitive to sounds at higher frequencies (pitch). By 24 months of age, an infant's ability to detect sounds of the highest frequencies is much like that of an adult (Werner & VandenBos, 1993).

Sound Localization. Recall that newborn infants are capable of locating the direction from which a sound originates. However, for reasons not altogether understood, the ability to orient toward sounds apparently declines during the second and third months. It reappears by 4 months of age (Aslin et al., 1983). This is called a *U-shaped curve* of development since the ability is present at first, then declines, and then reappears. By 6 to 7 months of age infants use sounds to locate objects in space when no visual cues are available. For example, infants can reach accurately for a noise-making object coming from a variety of locations in total darkness (Perris & Clifton, 1988; Clifton, Perris, & Bullinger, 1991). One of the sound features they apparently use at 6 months of age for auditory depth perception is changes in sound pressure level (intensity of decibels) (Litovsky & Clifton, 1992). The ability to identify the location of sounds continues to improve throughout the infancy period.

Sound Discrimination. Numerous studies have demonstrated that very young infants can make distinctions between very similar sounds. One group of researchers (Eimas et al., 1971) taught two groups of 4-week-old babies how to turn a tape player on by sucking on a pacifier connected to a control device. While one group of babies was allowed to listen to "pa pa pa" sounds, the other group heard "ba ba ba" sounds. The babies in both groups soon habituated to the sounds and stopped sucking, which turned off the speakers. When the taped sounds were reversed between the two groups, renewed sucking was generated to keep the new sound going. The researchers concluded that the infants could discriminate between the very similar sounds of *p* and *b*. They also hear the difference between a variety of vowel sounds, such as *a* and *e* (Kuhl, 1981). At 4 months of age infants can match vowel sounds to the face of the person making the sound (Kuhl & Meltzoff, 1982).

Studies have also confirmed that babies not only discriminate between very similar speech sounds (Moffitt, 1971; Eilers & Minifie, 1975), but are also aware of differences in voice inflection (Morse, 1972) and pitch (Moffitt, 1971). They prefer to listen to recorded speech or vocal music over instrumental music or rhythmic sounds (Butterfield & Siperstein, 1974). In addition, babies prefer female voices at the time they are born. Within a few weeks they can discriminate between their mother's voice and other voices (Eimas, 1975). The ability to make some fairly sophisticated distinctions between similar speech sounds develops rapidly. If infants are not born with this adultlike ability to make sound distinctions, they acquire it very quickly after birth. Additional information about the perception of sounds used in speech will be presented in Chapter 10.

Haptic Perception

In recent years, researchers have been increasingly interested in the ability of infants to acquire information about the properties of objects through touch and handling sensations (Bushnell & Boudreau, 1993). This process is referred to as **haptic perception**. Infants rub their hands and fingers back and forth across the surfaces of objects, enclose their hands around an object, squeeze objects, push, pull, and move objects up and down. Researchers are finding that infants learn about the size, shape, temperature, texture, and weight of objects through these haptic exploratory procedures.

An example of how researchers have studied haptic perception is found in the experiments of Streri and Spelke (1988, 1989). They conducted experiments to determine whether infants can perceive the unity and boundaries of objects they touch and manipulate but cannot see. Four-month-old infants were given two separate rings, one in each hand, under a cloth that blocked their view. In a separate condition, the rings were also connected to each other with a rod so that they moved only together. Under a third condition the rings were connected with elastic so they could be moved independently. The infants were found to perceive the two rings as separate objects when they could be moved independently, and a single object when they were held rigidly together.

Bushnell and Boudreau (1991; 1993) used findings from the existing research studies to project a general timetable for the development of haptic perception. Infants can probably distinguish the size and distinct object shapes (e.g. a solid disc from a ring) with their hands beginning at approximately 3 months of age. Haptic perception of temperature, hardness, and texture begin to emerge at approximately 6 months of age. Weight perception becomes evident at about 9 months of age. Haptic perception of shapes that are similar in features but differ in spatial arrangement (configurational shape) emerges last at 12 to 15 months.

The development of haptic perceptual abilities appears to be enhanced by the infant's experiences acquired through motor activities (Bushnell & Boudreau, 1993). Infants who just sit and look at objects, or who swat at objects and miss them, have more limited perceptual experiences than infants who can grasp objects and explore their properties.

Intersensory Perception

During the past 20 years we have learned that young infants are capable of surprisingly large and diverse multimodal perceptual abilities that improve with age. Remember that infants have at least some capacity to coordinate and integrate information from different sensory modalities soon after they are born. These abilities improve with age (Bahrick & Pickens, 1994; Rose & Ruff, 1987). However, there is some evidence that infants who are at-risk because of prematurity and/or social factors (poverty) have problems in cross-modal transfer (Rose, 1994).

In a rather ingenious experiment, Meltzoff and Borton (1979) provided 1-month-old infants with a smooth object attached to a pacifier and a rough, nubby one attached to another pacifier. The infants were allowed to suck, but not view, each of the two objects. They were then given the pacifiers to look at, along with new objects larger than those used for sucking. The infants showed a definite preference for looking at the objects with which they had become familiar through sucking. This experiment indicates that very young infants have the ability to engage in cross-modal transfer from the oral-tactile to the visual-perceptual systems.

At the age of 3 or 4 months, infants can match pictures with recorded sounds. This ability is determined by showing infants separate films of two events at the same time. As the moving pictures are projected side by side, a sound track that matches only one of the films is played. When infants look longer and more often at the pictures that are synchronized with the sounds, it is assumed that they have made a correct match (Spelke, 1979). By 5 months of age infants are able to coordinate visual-distance perceptions with auditory-distance cues. At this age, infants correctly match increases or decreases in sounds with the images of approaching or retreating toy trains and automobiles (Pickens, 1994; Schiff, Benasich, & Bornstein. 1989). Additional studies, reviewed by Bahrick & Pickens (1994), indicate that by 5 or 6 months infants are capable of a wide variety of rather complex intersensory functions. For example, 4- and 7-month-old infants were shown films of the faces of an unfamiliar child and an adult of the same gender positioned side by side. The child and the adult recited a nursery rhyme in synchrony with one another. The synchronized voice of only one of them was also played. While the 7-month-old infants were able to match the appropriate faces and voices, the 4-month-olds could not (Soutulo, Hernandez, & Bahrick, 1992). Seven-month-olds also coordinate facial motion and/or vocal sounds with facial expressions to discriminate happy and angry facial expressions (Soken & Pick, 1992; Walker, 1982; Walker-Andrews, 1986). In addition they can match the corresponding pitch of an impact sound with the color and shape of the object that strikes the surface (Walker-Andrews, 1994).

MEMORY

Do infants remember what they perceive and learn? How soon does memory begin? How long do infants remember? Questions such as these are significant because memory is one of the most important components of intelligence. Information-processing theorists focus on the infant's capacity to encode (take in) information, store it, and selectively bring it to mind as needed. Various terms are used in discussing memory development, including sensory, short-term, long-term, recognition, and recall memory.

Sensory memory consists of the immediate sensory impressions that persist for less than a second after a stimulus is gone. The information is stored for just an instant and is sometimes referred to as the **sensory register**. It is replaced by other sensory stimulation unless it receives further attention so that the information is transferred to the short-term memory. We know that sensory memory is functional at birth since newborn infants attend to sights and sounds and tend to prefer some stimuli to others. Sensory memory is one type of memory that apparently changes little with age (Hoving et al., 1978).

Short-term memory consists of information that is stored only temporarily. It is sometimes referred to as the conscious part or **working memory** that is receiving attention at the moment (Siegler, 1991). The amount of time involved is generally considered to be about a minute (Helms & Turner, 1976). For example, studies on object permanence suggest that 8-month-old infants can

remember the location of a hidden object for approximately 70 seconds (Arterberry et al., 1993). The longer an item is kept active in short-term memory, the more likely it is to be transferred to long-term memory (Siegler, 1991).

Long-term memory involves the ability to recall information after days, weeks, and even years have passed. Some information and experiences are stored permanently. Short-term memory develops ahead of long-term memory. Both improve with age during the infancy period. Memory length will be discussed further, in connection with two basic types of memory—recognition and recall.

Recognition Memory

The ability to recall whether a stimulus has been previously experienced is referred to as recognition memory. An infant who, upon request, selects a picture of a cat from an animal book is demonstrating this type of memory. There is little doubt that newborn infants display recognition memory. The ability to recognize a stimulus that triggered a response is not possible without a minimum working memory. The conditioned responses that have been demonstrated in numerous experiments with newborns constitute evidence of their capacity to remember (Olson & Strauss, 1984). The ability to store information in short-term memory increases dramatically in infants from all racial and ethnic groups around the world between 8 and 12 months of age (Kagan, 1981b).

There is also evidence that newborns have the capacity for long-term memory. Babies less than 55-hours old remembered a specific reinforcement schedule for as long as 10 hours after a single learning session (Panneton & DeCasper, 1982). Newborn infants (over 24-hours old) also appear to remember specific sounds for at least a 24-hour period (Swain, Zelazo, & Clifton, 1993). However, due to the immaturity of the nervous system, the newborn's capacity to remember is probably limited to a primitive form of recognition memory.

Within the first month or two, infants show signs of an emerging capacity for long-term retention of information. Researchers have found that 1-month-old infants can remember a conditioned response for about two days in some experiments (Ungerer, Brody, & Zelazo, 1978) and for as long as ten days in others (Little, Lipsitt, & Rovee-Collier, 1984). By 2 months of age, infants have demonstrated that they remember for almost three weeks how to move a crib mobile (Davis & Rovee-Collier, 1983). However, the infants remember the response only if they receive some prompting (called reactivation). As you would expect, 2-month-olds forget more rapidly than 3-month-olds, who remember the procedure for a month or more with prompting (Greco et al., 1986).

The period between 3 and 7 months of age is a time in which memory shows a dramatic improvement (Olson & Strauss, 1984). The information-processing skills have improved remarkably as the result of physiological maturation, increased attention span, improved motor skills, and the acquisition of a substantial amount of knowledge. The infant can learn more complex information faster and remember it for longer periods of time (Rovee-Collier & Shyi, 1992). Fagan (1971) found that 6-month-old infants recognize a variety of stimuli for as long as fourteen days without prompting. Long-term recognition memory is routinely displayed by infants between 3 and 6 months of age (Daehler & Greco, 1985). One significant change that apparently occurs at around 3 months of age is that the physical setting (context) in which learning takes place becomes important. From 3 to 6 months of age contextual cues play an increasingly important role in memory retrieval. Six-month-old infants who learned to move a mobile by kicking or pressing a lever to view a moving toy train had difficulty remembering how to do the same task when they were placed in a different environment (Borovsky & Rovee-Collier, 1990; Hartshorn & Rovee-Collier, 1997).

The speed of memory retrieval increases between 3 to 6 months indicating that information is processed more rapidly with age (Rovee-Collier & Shyi, 1992). As infants get older, they also demonstrate accurate recall of specific events over increasingly longer periods of time. Children as young as 11 months have accurate recall for specific events after a short delay. Infants as young as 13 months can recall events for as long as eight months. Over

short delays of a week or less, infants do not need to be reminded. If the delay is one month or longer, memory is enhanced with repeated experience or reminding or both (Bauer, 1996).

Recall Memory

Recall memory is the ability to remember something that is currently not available to direct sensory perception (Mandler, 1984). A baby who can tell you the name of the family dog is demonstrating recall memory. The ability to think begins with recall memory. Piaget linked recall memory with deferred imitation and symbolic thinking (mental images), and the use of language. Piaget thus argued that this type of memory does not emerge until 18 to 24 months of age. However, there is an increasing amount of evidence that infants are capable of elementary recall memory much earlier.

Results of studies on infant attachment and separation anxiety are sometimes used to argue that infants possess at least a rudimentary form of recall memory by around 6 months of age (Schaffer, 1979). Since attachment and separation anxiety (typically established at around 6 months of age), involve the ability to remember that the parent exists even when out of sight, this capacity implies that recall memory has been established.

One method researchers have used to study recall memory has been to ask parents to keep diaries of their child's memory behavior over a period of time. Using this approach, Ashmead and Perlmutter (1980) found examples of recall memory in infants between 7 and 9 months of age. In one case, a 9-month-old girl kept some ribbons that she played with in the bottom drawer of a chest. One day she opened the drawer but could find no ribbons. She opened all the drawers until she found her ribbons in the top drawer. The next day she looked for her ribbons in the top drawer. Anecdotal records such as this seem to provide evidence of long-term recall memory. However, other researchers believe that this type of research lacks scientific objectivity (Daehler & Greco, 1985).

Researchers have also used **elicited imitation** to test nonverbal infants' recall memory (Bauer & Wewerka, 1995). In elicited imitation, props such as nesting cups are used to model an action or a sequence of actions. The props are then given to an infant who is encouraged to imitate the actions observed. After a period of hours or days, controlled by the researchers, the props are made available again to the infant to determine if the original actions will be repeated without the benefit of a model to observe. By 9 to 11 months of age infants reproduce actions involving a single object after a 24-hour delay (Meltzoff, 1988a). At 13 to 14 months of age, infants can reproduce limited actions after a one-week delay (Bauer & Hertsgaard, 1993; Meltzoff, 1988b). Toward the end of the second year of life, infants remember multistep sequences for two to six weeks, and for as long as eight months if they are given verbal reminders (Bauer & Wewerka, 1995).

HOW INFANTS LEARN

Learning is the acquisition of knowledge or skills through experience. Infants begin to learn even before they are born. However, for a number of reasons, learning is generally more limited during infancy than at other stages. For one thing, the brain and nervous system are very immature. The interconnections between the various cells have not yet been completely established. The sensory organs that affect the infant's perceptual capacity have not reached their peak functional capacity. The infant's limited attention span, motor skills, and language ability are additional factors affecting the capacity to learn. All of these limitations affect the infant's ability to collect, process, store, and retrieve information. In spite of these immaturities, however, much learning takes place during infancy. The ways in which infants learn are numerous and varied.

Conditioned Responses

Behavioral psychologists believe that all learning is the result of conditioned responses. This theory is based on the principle that infants learn through actions that are reinforced, punished, or ignored. There are two types of conditioned responses—classical and operant.

Classical Conditioning (Respondent). Infants frequently exhibit the same response to a particular stimulus each time it is encountered, such as turning the head when the cheek is stroked (rooting reflex). In classical conditioning, an infant learns to transfer the response to a different stimulus that initially elicits the response. This type of conditioning is based on the principle that when two different stimuli appear close together, the response to one of them will be transferred to the other (Baldwin, 1967). For example a buzzer can be set off each time the cheek is stroked to elicit the rooting reflex. A baby will eventually turn its head in response to the buzzer alone. An infant thus learns to associate a new stimulus (buzzer) with an old response (rooting reflex). This is referred to as a new stimulus-response connection.

Researchers have observed classical conditioning in unborn infants during the last three months of the prenatal period. Spelt (1948) found that a loud sound would cause a fetus to move each time the noise was made. The loud sound was paired with a vibration of the mother's abdomen. After a number of simultaneous repetitions, the vibratory stimulus alone was effective in causing the infant to move. A later study using ultrasound images confirmed Spelt's conclusion (Birnholz & Benacerraf, 1983).

Researchers have also demonstrated classical conditioning in infants soon after birth. Connolly and Stratton (1969) paired the Babkin reflex, in which the mouth opens when pressure is applied to the palms, in 2- to 4-day-old infants, with a neutral buzzing noise. When the noise was presented by itself, the infants exhibited mouth-opening movements characteristic of the Babkin reflex. Researchers (Blass, Ganchrow, & Steiner, 1984) also gently stroked the foreheads of newborns (2 to 48 hours of age) while feeding them a sucrose solution. The infants were thus conditioned to exhibit the facial expressions related to sucking through stroking alone. The use of classical conditioning is limited to the responses that infants already exhibit.

Younger infants are harder to condition than older infants. The emotional responses of older infants are particularly susceptible to classical conditioning. Numerous environmental encounters become sources of infant fears. Carla, a toddler, was stung by a bee while she was playing on her swing set. After that experience she was afraid of all flying insects. Babies frequently begin crying as soon as they see a doctor or anyone else dressed in a white coat. They have learned to associate the coat, initially a neutral stimulus, with painful examining or treatment procedures such as injections.

Operant Conditioning (Instrumental). If a response to a stimulus is followed by reinforcement, the chances are increased that the response will be repeated when the stimulus is repeated. By the same token, responses that are punished or receive no reinforcement are less likely to be repeated. In operant conditioning, the reinforcement follows the response that, in the beginning, occurs spontaneously. In classical conditioning, the infant has no control over the events through which stimuli occur. However, in operant conditioning the infant's response, or lack of response, determines whether a reinforcer will follow (Sameroff & Cavanagh, 1979).

Researchers have not found a method by which operant conditioning can be studied in the unborn infant. However, there is ample evidence that newborn infants can be conditioned. In fact, operant conditioning is easier to obtain in newborns than classical conditioning (Columbo, 1993). Examples of this type of learning are found in experiments that have successfully conditioned newborns to alter their head-turning (Siqueland, 1968) and sucking (Sameroff, 1968) responses to receive a reinforcer.

Operant conditioning, like classical conditioning, depends upon the ability of an infant to emit a specific response. Consequently, the variety of behaviors that can be conditioned in infancy is limited. As with classical procedures, the operant-conditioned responses are obtained easier and faster as the infant gets older, especially after 6 months of age (Lamb & Bornstein, 1987). Sameroff and Cavanagh (1979) believe that there is a 7- to 9-month shift in the behavioral organization of an infant. During this time, changes occur in the emotional, cognitive, and physiological domains which greatly facilitate

conditioned responses as well as other types of learning. The acquisition of the ability to move around on all four limbs (creep) is a major factor in the developmental advances taking place between 7 and 9 months of age (Bertenthal, Campos, & Barrett, 1984).

In older infants, operant-conditioning procedures are often used to shape behavior. This involves reinforcing gradual changes, or successive approximations, in the infant's behavior until the desired behavior is obtained. Parents often use this procedure with their infants. An example is found in the infant's use of the word "Da-da." When the baby first says "Da-da," it is reinforced by praise, hugs, and other positive responses no matter when the sound is made. Later, parents respond positively only if "Da-da" is repeated in the presence of the father. Finally, the term is reinforced only when the infant uses it to designate the father.

Imitation

One of the most easily observed ways that infants learn is through imitation. At around 6 weeks of age, imitation begins to play an increasingly important role in learning (Rosenblith & Sims-Knight, 1985). Older infants imitate actions from a variety of models, including adults, children, and television characters. Parents are primary models, as the following example indicates: At 15 months, Candy is very imitative—"Often when she picks something up from the floor, she wipes it on her dress. That's what her mother does with anything Candy will put in her mouth again" (Peterson, 1974, p. 37).

Imitation is frequently combined with operant conditioning in the learning process. An initial response is produced by an infant because it has been copied from a model. If the behavior is considered desirable, the infant receives responses that are rewarding so the behavior will continue. At 2 years of age, Kristin was encouraged to observe her mother use the bathroom as a way to begin toilet training. As soon as Kristin began to imitate her mother's behavior she was reinforced with verbal praise, "Good, Kristin! That's good!" The verbal reinforcement that was used in facilitating toilet training was so effective that Kristin began to imi-

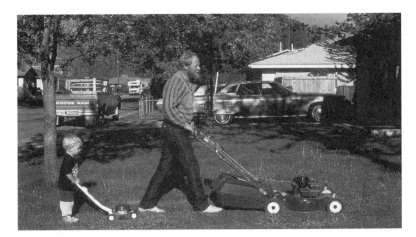

An example of imitation.

tate her mother in the use of praise. One day, while observing her mother use the bathroom, Kristin said, "Good, Mommy! That's good!"

Learning Through Play

Play is one of the basic ways infants learn. To an infant, "play is learning and learning is play" (Sroufe, 1977, p. 93). No one needs to teach infants to play. Their play is voluntary, intrinsically motivated, and freely chosen (Johnson & Ershler, 1982). Piaget (1962; 1971) viewed play as opportunities for infants to test reality through acts of assimilation. Sounds, objects, and other stimuli are freely manipulated to serve the infant's own particular needs. Piaget divided cognitive play during infancy into two basic stages: sensorimotor play and sym-

bolic play. Within each stage, the complexity of play changes with the baby's cognitive maturity and competence.

Sensorimotor Play. During the first three or four months of life, infant play is focused on body movements that provide sensory pleasure. Repetitious kicking movements and sucking the fist are typical activities. Infants also begin to play with cooing and other sounds as soon as they are capable. At approximately 6 months of age, an infant typically plays with one object at a time (Fenson et al., 1976). This earliest object play involves mouthing, shaking, banging, inspecting visually, and shifting from one hand to the other.

After about 9 months of age, the simple, undifferentiated type of play declines and is gradually

Infants are sensory creatures who use simple, everyday experiences, such as bathing, for play and stimulation.

replaced by function-relational play with two or more objects (Belsky and Most, 1981). The infant begins to figure out how some objects "work" (e.g., a toy telephone dial). At first, two objects may be used together indiscriminately, without regard to their appropriate relationships (e.g., placing a hairbrush in a cup). Later the infant learns to combine objects in ways that exploit their appropriate relationships, such as placing a lid on a pot. During this stage, infants usually prefer new toys to old ones (Ross, 1974), and complex toys to simple ones (McCall, 1974).

Pretend (Symbolic) Play. The earliest form of symbolic play begins around 12 months of age when the infant begins to perform simple "pretend" activities. In the beginning, pretend play involves activities directed toward the self, such as making drinking sounds using an empty cup, or using a doll brush on the infant's own hair (Belsky & Most, 1981). As infants get older, their pretend play is directed toward others (dolls are fed "pretend" bottles of milk), and they begin to substitute "pretend" objects for the real thing (a stick becomes a bottle of milk). The most sophisticated level of pretend play is called double substitution (Belsky & Most, 1981). This happens when a toddler uses two "pretend" materials in a single play sequence. Thus, a stick becomes a "doll" and a bottle cap is used as a cup to feed the "doll."

Learning Through Scaffolding

Theorists and educators who share Vygotsky's views (Berk & Winsler, 1995) use the concept of **scaffolding** to describe how infants benefit from their experiences. The term scaffolding (as in building construction and repair) is used to describe how adults use special structures of social encouragement to promote children's learning. Basically, scaffolding takes the form of tutoring that offers assistance when necessary for mastery, but prompts children to assume responsibility for their own learning as much as possible (Berk & Winsler, 1995). The following is an example of how a mother helps her 2½-year-old child put a puzzle together:

Child: *Oh, now where's this one go?* (Picks up a blue piece and looks at the form board.)
Mother: *Which piece might go here?* (Points to the bottom of the puzzle.)
Child: *His hat?* (Picks up another piece, but tries the wrong one).
Mother: *See if you can find a piece that looks like this shape.* (Points to the bottom of the puzzle again).
Child: *The red one!* (Tries it, but can't quite get it to fit.)
Mother: *Try turning it just a little more this way.* (Gestures to show her.)
Child: *There it fits!* (Picks up another piece and says:) *"Now this green one should fit here. Oh, I need to turn it just a little! Look mom, this one fits too!"*) (Adapted from Berk & Winsler, 1995, p. 27).

Adults should be careful, though, not to interfere unnecessarily with the child's attempts to solve a problem. The key to scaffolding is to wait until the child is about to give up and provide just enough assistance to keep the child working on the task (Gonzalez-Mena & Eyer, 1997).

ASSESSING INFANT INTELLIGENCE

"Intelligence is what the tests test" (Boring, 1923, p. 35). Although this widely quoted statement is not an adequate definition of intelligence, it is an indication of the importance that has been attributed to testing intelligence. The assessment of intelligence in infancy is viewed as especially important in the early detection of mental disabilities, as well as in determining the extent to which intelligence changes from infancy to adulthood.

The accurate measurement of infant intelligence has proved to be very difficult, from the standpoint of both test construction and test administration. Eliciting an infant's attention and cooperation can be a major obstacle to testing, especially when the infant is being tested by a strange person in a strange place. Intelligence tests for children and adults typically have a large verbal-skills component, whereas intelligence tests for infants are comprised primarily of sensorimotor functions. Scarr-Salapatek (1983) believes that the type of intelligence displayed by infants during the first two years is not comparable to the cognitive skills that evolve later in life. Thus, infant test scores are not reliable predictors of intellectual functioning in later years.

In spite of these problems, though, infant intelligence scales (sometimes referred to as developmental schedules) are useful for specific purposes when interpreted appropriately. They are widely used in screening programs to identify infants with potential mental disabilities. Researchers have also used these measures for a variety of purposes, such as assessing the influence of intervention programs on the development of intelligence during the infant years. The following examples represent some of the older and newer instruments that are available for assessing infant intelligence.

Gesell Developmental Schedules

Arnold Gesell (1925) was one of the pioneers in the assessment of infant development. Gesell and his co-workers at Yale University made extensive observations on the normal developmental patterns of infants and young children. Gesell's schedules were designed primarily for the purpose of determining the integrity and functional maturity of the nervous system between 1 month and 6 years of age. The scales are divided into five major areas: adaptive (e.g., problem solving), fine motor, gross motor, language, and personal-social. A separate score is obtained for each of the five areas, plus an overall score that is labeled the Developmental Quotient (DQ). Gesell intended for this instrument to be used as an indicator of total development rather than of intelligence per se. A short version of the test is available for use as a developmental screening inventory. Cattell (1940) used Gesell's schedules as a basis for the development of a test (**Cattell Infant Intelligence Scale**) specifically designed to measure intelligence over the age span of 2 months to 30 months.

Bayley Scales of Infant Development–II

The Bayley Scales of Infant Development–II (Bayley, 1993) is the most widely used norm-referenced instrument for assessment of the cognitive performance of infants and toddlers (Meisels, 1996). It is used in early intervention programs and research settings. The **Bayley–II** is administered to infants from 1 month to 42 months of age. This test is divided into three separate scales that can be used independently or in combination for assessment purposes. The Mental Scale is designed to assess such functions as sensory/perceptual abilities, memory, learning, language development, and problem-solving ability. This scale results in a standard score which is labeled the Mental Development Index (MDI). The Motor Scale measures skills such as body control, large- and fine-motor skills, and manipulative ability. The results of this scale are expressed as the Psychomotor Development Index (PDI) score. The third scale, the Behavior Rating Scale, allows the examiner to rate the infant's attention, orientation, motor quality, and emotional regulation. It provides four subscale scores in addition to an overall score.

Uzgiris-Hunt Scales

The Uzgiris-Hunt Ordinal Scales of Psychological Development (Uzgiris & Hunt, 1975) are based on Piaget's description of cognitive development during infancy. The term "ordinal" indicates that the test items are arranged, or ordered, according to the level of difficulty. The first items on the scale should be passed at an earlier age than subsequent items. The scales reflect Piaget's belief that all infants go through the tasks involved in sensorimotor development in the same specific order, although not necessarily at the same age.

The Uzgiris-Hunt Scales consist of six subscales: (1) the development of visual pursuit and the permanence of objects; (2) the development of means of obtaining environmental events; (3) the development of vocal and gestural imitation; (4) the development of operational causality; (5) the construction of object relations in space; and (6) the development of schemes relating to objects. Each scale includes seven to fourteen steps in the developmental progression from birth to 2 years of age. The highest step achieved on each of the six subscales forms an infant's developmental profile. No single, overall score is provided.

The Uzgiris-Hunt Scales provide the most in-depth assessment of infant cognitive development of any instrument available (Horowitz, 1982). The scales may be especially useful in early-intervention programs because they measure very small steps in sensorimotor development. However, this instrument has not been used as widely as other infant assessment scales because of the complexity and the amount of time required for administration. Dunst (1980) has developed a simplified version of the scales that requires less time to administer.

FACILITATING INTELLECTUAL DEVELOPMENT

Some of the research and theoretical information currently available on the development of intelligence in infants has been translated into suggestions for caregiving activities. Piaget and Vygotsky did not develop practical applications of their theories, but others have. For example, Lehane (1976) has produced a guidebook of 100 Piagetian-based activities for helping infants learn. Numerous other resources offer suggestions for facilitating cognitive development during infancy (e.g., Fowler, 1980; Gonzalez-Mena & Eyer, 1997; Leach, 1976; Machado & Meyer-Botnarescue, 1997; Marzollo, 1977; Painter, 1971; Sparling & Lewis, 1979).

Greenfield and Tronick (1980) have developed a list of techniques for use in teaching babies how to use play materials, solve problems, and "scaffold" learning. Some of these techniques, listed in order from the simplest to most complex, are as follows:

1. Simplify the activity. For example, in introducing nesting cups, give the infant only the smallest and largest ones in the set. This is a useful teaching technique for infants under 6 months of age.

2. Point to and touch the important parts of a new activity, such as the space on a puzzle board that matches the piece of puzzle the baby is holding.
3. Show the infant how to do an activity or solve a problem (after about 6 months). For example, let the infant watch you place one block on top of another.
4. Tell the baby what to do next in an activity. This technique, obviously, is only appropriate when words are used that an infant can understand. Use short, simple phrases, such as "Turn it over" and "Put it here." The other techniques may be used in combination with telling.
5. Allow infants to use self-teaching as much as possible. Avoid interfering in activities when help is not needed or wanted.

Parents and other caregivers are advised to avoid the pressure-cooker approach to early learning in an attempt to create a "super-intelligent" baby. Doman (1982, 1984) believes that parents can teach an infant math or almost any subject. However, too much emphasis on early intellectual achievement can result in the "hurried-infant syndrome" (Elkind, 1981). When infants are expected to achieve too much, too soon, a level of stress is created that may result in behavior problems at the time or at a later stage of development. White (1985) believes that superiority in the intellectual domain is frequently obtained at the expense of progress in other areas of equal or greater importance. Infants learn more efficiently with better results when they are developmentally ready to master a task. Infants with developmental disabilities obviously need more specialized assistance and learning materials than typically developing infants.

SUMMARY

1. Intelligence consists of the ability to think, to solve problems, to learn, to remember, and to adapt to the environment. Cognition refers to all the mental processes, such as thinking and remembering, that make up the functional component of intelligence. In this chapter the terms intelligence and cognition are used interchangeably.

2. Intelligence is influenced by heredity and

environmental influences. The family environment, socioeconomic background, and cultural experiences are important environmental factors.

3. The theory of Jean Piaget has been widely influential in the contemporary understanding of intellectual development during the infancy period. Piaget's theory is based on the development of schemes through the process of adaptation and two related processes: assimilation and accommodation.

4. Piaget identified four basic stages in the development of intelligence. The stage that corresponds with the first two years of life is the sensorimotor period. This period is divided into six substages: (1) exercising reflex schema; (2) primary circular reactions; (3) secondary circular reactions; (4) coordination of secondary circular reactions; (5) tertiary circular reactions; and (6) invention of new means through mental combinations.

5. By the end of the sensorimotor period, infants have typically developed the ability to understand cause-effect relationships, object permanence, simple problem solution through insight, and deferred imitation. However, evidence is accumulating to indicate that infants accomplish some of these tasks earlier than Piaget's estimated ages.

6. According to Vygotsky's theory, cultural influences play a central role in shaping cognitive development. Language development provides the foundation for intellectual advancement. Learning takes place within the zone of proximal development and is facilitated through guided participation.

7. The key elements of cognitive development, according to information processing, include the individual's capacity to perceive, store, recall, and utilize information.

8. The infant's ability to see objects clearly improves dramatically during the first year of life. As they get older, infants prefer to look at more complex and detailed patterns. They can discriminate between a variety of human facial features. By 12 months of age infants are capable of subitization, whereby they "count" up to three objects. Their ability to discriminate various features of objects reaches adultlike levels by the time they are 1 year of age.

9. Infants use both monocular and binocular cues in depth perception. Depth perception is more accurate with the use of binocular vision that emerges at approximately 3½ months of age. Infants indicate a sophisticated ability to perceive when they avoid the "visual cliff." This form of depth perception is affected by the infant's experiences obtained through self-produced locomotion.

10. The ability of infants to perceive depth and discriminate object properties is heavily influenced by motion cues. The ability to discriminate the properties of moving objects develops ahead of the ability to detect the features of nonmoving objects.

11. Infants hear better as their auditory system matures. By 6 to 7 months of age infants can use sounds to locate objects in the dark. Very young infants discriminate between similar sounds and exhibit definite sound preferences.

12. Between 3 and 12 months of age, infants develop the capacity to discriminate between the size, temperature, hardness, texture, weight, and shape of objects through the use of haptic perception.

13. Young infants display the ability to coordinate and use information from different sensory modalities. By 5 or 6 months infants are capable of a wide variety of rather complex intersensory functions.

14. Infants are capable of learning through both classical and operant conditioning processes from birth. Imitation is another mechanism through which infants learn, beginning at approximately 6 weeks of age. Infants also learn through play, which progresses through two basic stages: sensorimotor and pretend, or symbolic, play. The infant's sensory organs are pathways through which learning takes place.

15. Newborn infants are capable of both short- and long-term recognition memory at a very elementary level. Memory capacity improves with age, especially between 3 and 7 months. Recall memory develops later than recognition memory. Infants are capable of the recall memory based on situational cues at approximately 7 to 9 months of age. During the second year of life, infants display

an increasing ability to recall more complex events for longer periods of time.

16. Infant intelligence test scores are not reliable predictors of intellectual functioning in other stages of life. However, infant intelligence scales, or developmental schedules, are used for screening programs and research purposes. The **Bayley Scales of Infant Development–II** is the most widely used instrument for assessment of the cognitive performance of infants and toddlers.

17. A variety of materials and recommended activities are available for stimulating the development of infant intelligence. However, parents and other caregivers are advised to avoid early learning activities that attempt to create "super-intelligent" infants.

10

Language Development

Out of the mouths of babes and sucklings
Thou hast brought perfect praise.
                    —Psalm 8:2; Matthew 21:16

One of the most fascinating and exciting things to observe about babies is the process of language development. Parents and scientists alike are captivated by how children learn languages. For parents, language represents a communicative link with their child and the key that opens the door to the child's inner world. Communication is at the center of the relationship between the parent and child.

Language is a complex system of mutually agreed-upon symbols used to express and understand ideas and feelings. In its broadest meaning, language refers to an act or acts that produce some kind of interchange or communication between two or more people (Bangs, 1982). The symbols used in language include vocal utterances, written expressions, and body movements such as hand gestures and facial expressions. **Speech** is the vocal or oral component of language and refers to the production of spoken words or other meaningful sounds. The terms speech and language are frequently used interchangeably, but technically they are not synonymous.

Scientists have been astonished at the predictability of language development and at how easily babies learn to talk. Normally, all children pass a series of "milestones" at approximately the same age, regardless of the language they acquire (McNeil, 1970). For a long time, observers of language development were content to plot these major milestones and record children's utterances. More recently, however, they have been concerned with why and how language is acquired. This chapter summarizes the processes involved in language acquisition, the progress infants make in developing language competence, and some of the biological, psychological, and social influences.

THEORIES OF LANGUAGE DEVELOPMENT

There are several theories about how human language is acquired. Theorists differ on the relative influence of innate, biological mechanisms, and environmental experiences in language acqusition. Theorists also differ in their views about the relationship between thought and language. Some of the major theories representing extreme and moderate views are described below.

Behavioristic Theory

Skinner (1957) proposed that language, like any other behavior, can be explained as conditioned responses. When infants make sounds that resemble adult speech, such as "mama," adults reinforce them with smiles, hugs, or other positive responses. Other behaviorists (e.g., Bandura, 1977) add imitation as a factor that plays a key role in language acquisition. These behaviorists stress the importance the language environment, especially the availability of speech models to copy. Behaviorism has been criticized, among other things, for failing to adequately explain the creative use of language, the production and comprehension of novel utterances (Bryen, 1982), and the rapid rate of language development during infancy.

Nativistic Theory

There is little doubt that human infants are uniquely equipped to acquire language. However, the extent to which language development is controlled by biology has been the subject of extensive debate. Nativists argue that progress in language development is closely linked to the maturation of the brain. Language acquisition is remarkably predictable and similar among humans. Children normally pass a sequence of milestones at about the same age, regardless of the language or cultural conditions. In addition, progress in language development during the early years appears to be synchronized with progress in motor development. The two functions thus appear to be commonly controlled by the maturation of the central nervous system.

Nativistic theory is based on neurological studies that have shown that verbal function in humans is controlled by specific speech centers in the brain. For most people, perhaps as many as 95 percent, language is located in the left cerebral hemisphere.

Lenneberg (1967) asserts that there is a critical period for language acquisition beginning around the age of two and ending at puberty. He maintains that speech functions have not been localized in a particular region of the brain as early as infancy. His theory is based on studies showing that if injury occurs to the left side of the brain in infancy or childhood, the right side of the brain apparently takes over the language functions so that normal speech is possible. As the child grows older, the speech functions become increasingly lateralized, with less flexibility to compensate for damage. Other theorists (Krashen, 1973; Kinsbourne, 1978) assert that lateralization of the brain occurs much earlier than Lenneberg proposed.

Chomsky (1968), another leading proponent of nativism, has proposed that human infants are equipped at birth with a Language Acquisition Device (LAD). This device is analogous to a computer that is prewired or programmed to acquire language. Babies are programmed to sort out the underlying rules and principles of their native language. The many similarities in the timetable of language acquisition for children all over the world tend to support Chomsky's theory. However, infants do not acquire language as quickly or as easily as his theory proposes. Chomsky's theory does not provide a complete explanation for the hows and whys of language development.

Cognitive Developmental Theory

According to Piaget, language development is rooted in the cognitive development that occurs during the sensorimotor period (see Chapter 9). The infant has to develop the concept of self as a distinct person separate from other objects and understand the concept of object permanence before speech can begin. In Piaget's view, development of language also depends upon the acquisition of knowledge through touching, tasting, manipulation, and other experiences with objects and people. As the child's cognitive capacities and thoughts become more elaborate and complex through the years, language acquisition becomes more sophisticated and complete.

Not all cognitive developmental theorists agree with Piaget's view that thought shapes language development. Whorf (1956) took the opposite view when he hypothesized that the language we learn determines the way we think. For example, we view an orange as a round piece of fruit because we have attached those verbal labels to it. If oranges had originally been labeled as square, purple smalzes, we would perceive oranges in those terms. Thinking is thus dependent upon language.

Vygotsky's Theory

Vygotsky's (1962) theory represents a middle ground on questions about the relationship between thought and language. He proposed that language and thought develop at the same time and eventually become interdependent. In early infancy, language and thought develop separately along parallel lines because they are both related to the same underlying cognitive ability. However, at about 2 years of age, language and the thought processes merge as the infant acquires the capacity to understand the symbolic meanings of words. Language then begins to facilitate thought, and the two processes become interdependent. Siegler (1991) has concluded that, overall, the research evidence tends to support Vygotsky's position.

Vygotsky also viewed language as socially generated rather than biologically given. The social origins of language are found in the cultural group as infants, children, and adults interact and communicate. Language starts out as a means for social communication and interpersonal influence. Eventually, language that starts out as a social tool for mediating relationships between people becomes internalized. When that happens (during the second year of life), language becomes "a tool of the mind" to direct thinking, organize perceptions, and to communicate with one's self (Miller, 1993). Advances in thinking are made possible as the child's language "tools" become increasingly more sophisticated. However, language development always occurs within the sociocultural context. Children are not just passive recipients of cultural influences, but are active participants in the process. They use their own mental processes to make sense of the information and experiences they encounter (Berk & Winsler, 1995).

Vygotsky believed that language is initially transferred from the social world to the child's cognitive world through **private speech**. This type of speech appears around 30 months of age and is defined as inner speech or "self-talk." Private speech is not addressed to other people but is used for self-communication in solving problems and regulating one's own behavior. Through the use of private speech older infants begin to transfer the regulation of behavior from others to the self (Berk & Winsler, 1995). For example, Tyrone's mother told him not to touch the buttons on the television. One day Tyrone's mother observed him looking at the TV, shaking his head, and saying "No! No!" to himself.

Interactionist Theory

The interactionist perspective emphasizes the interplay between biological abilities and environmental influences in language acquisition (Bohannon, 1993). This approach to language development combines elements of other theories including nativist, behavioral, and sociocultural theories. The innate capacities of the infant provide the structural foundations, determine the sequence, and set the timetable for language acquisition. The specific elements and characteristics of the language the child acquires are determined by environmental influences. Thus, both biology and environment are indispensable and work together in language development. However, the two are not simply added together, but interact in complex ways to produce language. Bruner (1982) explains the role of environmental experiences in language acquisition as " . . . a subtle process by which adults artificially arrange the world so that the child can succeed culturally by doing what comes naturally, and with others similarly inclined" (p. 15). An example of the infant's early sensitivity and responsiveness to the language environment can be found in studies by Condon and Sanders (1974). They found that newborn infants sometimes move their limbs in synchronous rhythms that match the tempo and sounds of adult speech. Interactionist theorists also emphasize the important contribution of the infant as an influence upon the people who provide the language environment.

STRUCTURAL COMPONENTS OF LANGUAGE

To understand the process of language acquisition, we must first know something about the nature and structure of language. All spoken languages consist of five basic components:

1. Phonology: the distinctive sound features of speech and the rules for their combinations.
2. Morphology: the way sounds are combined to form words and other units of meaning.
3. Syntax: the way words are combined to form sentences.
4. Semantics: the definitions of words and the meanings of sentences.
5. Pragmatics: the practical functions of language and the ways it is used to communicate.

These components overlap and are interrelated in usage. Each language has a set of rules governing the components and their relationships. Developing language proficiency involves mastering these rules.

Considering the complexities involved, human infants typically make remarkable progress toward mastering their native language. Infants are mostly occupied with developing phonological proficiency. However, they also work on the other features of language, sometimes separately and sometimes simultaneously, until the five components are combined in an elementary fashion by the end of the first 3 years of life. A summary of the major milestones in language development, shown in Table 10–1, illustrates the progress made in the various components during the first two years of life.

Phonological Development

Each spoken language is made up of a set of basic, distinctive sounds, sometimes referred to as **phonemes**, which are used to form words. There are two major classes of phonemes—segmented and suprasegmented. The segmented phonemes consist of the vowels and consonants. The suprasegmented phonemes include the sounds of pitch, into-

Table 10–1   Milestones of Language Development

AGE	PHONOLOGY	MORPHOLOGY AND SEMANTICS	SYNTAX	PRAGMATICS
Birth	Crying			
1 Month	Attends and responds to speaking voice			
2 Months	Cooing, distinguishes phoneme features			
3 Months	Vocalizes to social stimulus			
4 Months	Chuckles			Pointing and gestures
6 Months	Babbling			
9 Months	Echolalia	Understands a few words		Understands gestures: responds to "bye-bye"
12 Months	Repeated syllables, jabbers expressively	First word		Waves "bye-bye"
18 Months		Comprehends simple questions, points to nose, eyes, and hair, vocabulary of 22 words	Two-word utterances, telegraphic speech	Uses words to make wants known
24 Months		Vocabulary of 272 words	Uses pronouns and prepositions: uses simple sentences and phrases	Conversational turn-taking

Sources: Taken from the Bayley Scales of Infant Development, Copyright © 1969 by the Psychological Corporation. Reproduced by permission. All rights reserved. Biological Foundations of Language. Lenneberg, E. Copyright © 1967. John Wiley and Sons, Inc. Reprinted by permission of John Wiley and Sons, Inc. McCarthy, D. "Language Development in children." In *Manual of Child Psychology.* L. Carmichael (ed.). Copyright © 1954 by John Wiley and Sons, Inc. Reprinted by permission of John Wiley and Sons, Inc.

nation, juncture, and stress, which constitute the "melody" of a language (Bryen, 1982). To master the sound system of a language, infants must learn to discriminate and combine the phonemes into meaningful words. Apparently infants master the phonemes of their language by discovering the contrasting or distinctive features. Each phoneme is learned in context with another sound rather than one at a time. The first distinction infants make is between vowels and consonants.

Early Sound Perception. You will recall that most babies are born with the sensory capacity to hear distinction between sounds. Within a few days after birth, infants are responsive to speech and other sounds resembling the human voice. Very young infants are capable of discriminating practically every phonetic contrast on which they have been tested (Aslin et al., 1983). Not only do infants hear subtle differences between sounds, but can evidently organize many of them into distinct categories (e.g., p's and b's). Young infants are able to distinguish between sounds even when the rate at which they are spoken varies (Miller & Eimas, 1983).

Studies also show that very young infants perceive sound contrasts even in languages other than their own (Juscyck, 1995). Thus infants are equipped with the capacity to make sound discriminations necessary for learning any of the world's languages to which they are exposed. During the second half of the first year the general capacities for sound perception begin to evolve so that infants are more specifically equipped to deal effectively with native sound patterns (Juscyck, 1995). Weir (1966) found that the babbling sounds produced by Polish infants can be distinguished from the babbling sounds of English infants at 5 months of age. Other cross-linguistic studies confirm that by the end of the first year infants select and prefer sounds and arrangements of sounds from their own linguistic background (Boyson-Bardies, 1994).

Development of the Speech Mechanism. The production of meaningful utterances involves the complex coordination of the respiratory system and vocal tract by the nervous system. To produce a desired sound, we transmit a set of instructions, usually unconsciously, from the brain to our respiratory system and vocal tract. When we are ready to speak, an airstream is released from the lungs into the vocal tract, which includes the throat, mouth, tongue, nasal cavity, and other organs. The type of sound produced depends upon the tautness of the vocal cords, the position of the tongue, the shape of the lips, whether the air passes through the mouth, nasal cavity, or both, and the speed and

continuity of the airstream (Lindfors, 1980). Obviously defects in the speech mechanism, such as a cleft palate or brain dysfunction, will affect sound production.

The speech mechanism of an infant is in an almost constant state of anatomical change. According to Kent (1980):

> The infant's vocal tract differs from that of an adult in four major respects: The infant's tract is shorter; the pharynx is shorter and wider in relation to its length . . . ; the mouth is flatter than in the adult because of the absence of teeth, and the tongue more evenly fills the mouth (p. 39).

The vocal tract lengthens and changes its relative anatomical relationship as the baby grows. These changes affect the patterns of sound produced, which means that the motor control of speech has to be continuously modified during the course of development.

Crying and Reflexive Vocalizations. The first sound a baby makes is likely to be a cry. In the beginning, crying and "vegetative noises" such as burps, hiccups, coughs, grunts, and sneezing are involuntary behaviors that are biologically rooted (Menn & Stoel-Gammon, 1993). The crying of the newborn thus serves no intentional communicative purpose. However, as the baby grows older, crying becomes associated with specific stimuli, such as hunger pains, and is a signal to the caretaker that the baby has a need to be met.

Wolff (1969) studied the cries of infants during the first six months of life to identify the emotional quality conveyed by sounds. Of the four main types of cries that were identified, the "basic," hunger cry was the type which occurred most frequently. Other types of cries were a "mad" or angry cry, a cry caused by pain, and a "fake" cry. Fake crying is a more purposeful type of crying behavior that begins around the third week and is described as "of a low pitch and intensity; it consists of long drawn out moans which occasionally rise to more explicit cries, and then revert to poorly articulated moans" (Wolff, 1969, p. 98).

Both adults and children can distinguish between various types of cry sounds. In one study, adults

Crying usually means that the baby is trying to get the attention of the caregiver.

were able to distinguish between tape-recorded cries of pain and cries indicating hunger (Zeskind et al., 1984). Even children as young as 7 years of age are capable of distinguishing different types of cries (Berry, 1975). There is some indication that mothers are more skillful than nonmothers in identifying infant cries (Sagi, 1981), but not all studies support this conclusion (Rosenblith & Sims-Knight, 1985). However, parents are more accurate in identifying the different types of cries of their own babies than those of a strange baby (Wiesenfeld, Malatesta, & DeLoache, 1981). In reality, parents and other adults interpret the cries of infants not only on the basis of sound quality, but within the context of situational cues (e.g., nap time, feeding time) as well (Adamson, 1995).

Researchers have also studied the cries of babies with developmental abnormalities. In one such study (Wasz-Hocket et al., 1968), the cries of infants with brain injuries were compared with the cries of babies without such injuries. The researchers concluded that the sounds produced by the babies with brain damage were quite different from the cries of infants with no signs of brain injury. Such differences are apparently obvious to parents. Zeskind (1983) found that the cries of high-risk infants could be distinguished from low-risk

infants' cries by Anglo-American, Cuban-American, and African-American mothers, regardless of their previous experience with infants.

Cooing.   Sometime between 1 and 3 months of age, the types of prespeech sounds commonly referred to as **cooing** begin to emerge. In contrast to crying sounds, which are signals of distress, cooing sounds are usually sounds of contentment and happiness. Babies everywhere cry and coo alike. The appearance of cooing is related to physical and sensory changes that take place around 6 or 8 weeks of age, including increased visual attention, and greater control of the tongue (Mussen et al., 1974).

Cooing sounds are open, vowel-like, gurgling noises, such as "aaah" and "oooh." Unlike crying, cooing involves the use of the tongue and lips in sound production. The earliest cooing sounds consist of vowels that come from the front of the mouth and use the tongue, such as /e/ as in bee and /u/ as in blue (Irwin, 1948). The term cooing most likely arises from the predominance of the /u/ sound (Dale, 1976). A few consonants formed in the back of the mouth appear in cooing, such as /k/ as in kite and /g/ as in goat (Cruttenden, 1970). Vowel sounds are frequently preceded by a consonant to form sounds like coo and moo.

Babbling. Between 6 and 10 months of age, the infant's vocalizations take on an increasingly speech-like quality. At this point, the baby enters the babbling period. **Babbling** is the repetition of consonants and vowels in alternating sequences ("ba ba ba," "ga ga ga," "da da da"). The emergence of repetitive syllables in the infant's vocal repertoire is one of the most important milestones of speech development. The sounds are sometimes referred to as reduplicated babbling (Stark, 1979). Babbling is distinguished from cooing by a closer resemblance of sounds to the syllables of words. The transition from cooing to babbling is due to increasing control over the vocal mechanisms (Menyuk, 1982). However, babies continue to coo and tend to shift back and forth between cooing and babbling in their vocalizations for several weeks.

During the babbling period the repetition of syllables (e.g., "na na na") is accompanied by distinctive intonational patterns as babies begin to explore the suprasegmental aspects of phonology. The sounds take on a definite rhythmic and melodic quality. The sound play of this period has been compared to practicing scales on a piano (Hopper & Naremore, 1978).

Between 6 and 12 months, the infant's sound repertoire expands. While vowel sounds predominate during the cooing stage, with the onset of babbling there is a shift toward the dominant use of consonants (Menn & Stoel-Gammon, 1993). Sounds and sound combinations never heard from parents have been identified in the babblings of infants. As strange as it may seem, sounds that babies find difficult to produce later in words are produced frequently in babbling (Ervin-Tripp, 1966). Toward the end of the babbling period, the sounds that are not included in the native language begin to drop out of the infant's repertory. Many infants go through a period, immediately before the onset of speech, when they babble less frequently.

The babbling sounds of infants from all language backgrounds are remarkably similar. The babbling of an American infant cannot be distinguished from that of Chinese or Mexican infants (Olney & Scholnick, 1976; Oller & Eilers, 1982).

Although we cannot say for sure that no differences in babbling occur, studies suggest that differences are hard to find in the light of overwhelming similarities and rare occurrence of nonuniversal sounds. Even deaf infants babble (Lenneberg et al., 1965). Babbling begins at about the same age in deaf children as in hearing children and is similar, though perhaps a little more monotonous. Deaf children tend to stop babbling earlier than hearing children because of the lack of auditory feedback (Whetnall & Fry, 1964).

Jargon. Around 10 months of age, infants begin to utter long strings of sound combinations that are sometimes referred to as **jargon** or **conversational babble**. These sophisticated babbling sounds are rich in intonation and are frequently made with gestures and eye contact. Although these vocalizations may be a complex form of sound play, in many instances they appear to reflect an infant's effort to engage in conversation. To caregivers, it may seem as if these infants are using their own language to form complete sentences. In combination with contextual cues, jargon can sometimes be interpreted to convey requests for objects or to have other meanings (Menn & Stoel-Gammon, 1993). At this point, the baby begins to make the transition from the prespeech to the speech stage.

Significance of Prespeech Sounds. The relationship of crying, cooing, and babbling to each other and to later stages in the acquisition of speech has been the subject of debate and controversy. Some theorists believe that crying sounds have no relationship to cooing and babbling, and that none of the prespeech sounds are important in the development of speech. According to this discontinuity view, cooing and babbling sounds are simply vocal play and have little, if any, effect on later speech.

Research evidence now favors a continuity view of the relationship between early sounds and speech development. According to this perspective, prespeech sound stages and later stages of speech are connected (Hopper & Naremore, 1978). Stark (1978) found indications that early crying and later cooing vocal behaviors are integrally related. Sound features present in crying and reflexive vocal tract activity are apparently incorporated in vocal expressions of pleasurable cooing. The voice and breath control developed during crying and fussing are important factors in the emergence of cooing.

Other researchers (Oller et al., 1976) also offer support for the significance of babbling in the development of speech. For example, the phonetic content of babbling indicates that infants exhibit preferences for certain consonant-vowel clusters that are later found in meaningful words. Longitudinal studies indicate that children's phonological patterns in early meaningful speech consist of many of the sound patterns they used in babbling (Menn & Stoel-Gammon, 1993). Although the role of babbling and other prespeech utterances in language development is still not clear, this experience appears to be an important preliminary step in gaining articulatory control of the vocal apparatus. Infants use this sound play to explore the potentials of their vocal tract as neuromotor and other biological foundations of speech mature (Papousek & Papousek, 1991). In addition, these sounds provide practice in the production of certain sound sequences, intonations, and pragmatic aspects of speech.

Morphological Development

When an infant has learned to pronounce phonemes, the next task is to combine them into units of meaning, referred to as **morphemes**. At this stage the child begins to work on the morphological component of language—the formation of words with the proper endings to express grammatical elements such as tense, gender, number, person, and case. Morphemes are the smallest meaningful units of language (Gleason, 1993). Some words consist of a single morpheme, while others are composed of multiple morphemes. For example, the word *boy* is a single morpheme, trustworthy consists of two morphemes, *trust* and *worthy*, and the word *opened* consists of the morphemes *open* and *ed*. A sentence is a collection of morphemes, but there may be more morphemes than words.

First Words. The baby's first word is generally considered one of the most significant milestones in speech development. Researchers have difficulty in determining precisely when an infant utters a first word because of the difficulty in separating babbling sounds from meaningful utterances (Adamson, 1995). Near the end of the first year of life, babbling consists largely of reduplicated monosyllables, (e.g., "na na" or "ma ma"). The first word is thus likely to be a babbled utterance such as "ma-ma" or "da-da," which becomes associated with a specific person as parents reinforce increasing accuracy in their usage. The mother doesn't appreciate the baby referring to a strange man as "da da," so she says, "No! That man is not your daddy!" Infants' first words are similar in all languages because they tend to begin with consonants and end with vowels that are repetitive. It is therefore no accident that all over the world the names for parents, *mama, papa,* and *dada* are often the first words babies begin to use (see Table 10–2) (Siegler, 1991). However, not all first words are babbled consonant and vowel combinations. Some children produce words without a vowel, such as "mmm" or "shhh", as a first word (Menn & Stoel-Gammon, 1993).

Different ages for the appearance of the first word have been reported by researchers. This is partly due to the difficulties involved in interpreting the meaning of specific sound combinations as well an individual differences in speech development. Generally,

Table 10–2   Early Words for Mother and Father in 10 Languages

	MOTHER	FATHER
English	mama	dada
German	mama	papa
Hebrew	eema	aba
Hungarian	anya	apa
Navajo	ama	ataa
Northern Chinese	mama	baba
Russian	mama	papa
Spanish	mama	papa
Southern Chinese	umma	baba
Taiwanese	amma	aba

Source: Reproduced by permission from: Robert S. Siegler (1991). *Children's Thinking* (2nd. ed.). Englewood Cliffs, NJ: Prentice-Hall, Inc.

the average age cited in these reports is about 11 to 12 months. The range of 8 to 18 months includes most observations recorded for typically developing children (Darley & Winitz, 1961; McCarthy, 1954). If the first word does not appear by 18 months, there may be reason to suspect problems in the physiological, cognitive, or environmental foundations of language (Whitehurst, 1982).

Characteristics of First Words. The first words produced by infants are mostly nouns and references to things that move, things that can be acted upon, or objects of particular interest or familiarity (e.g., ball, car, cat). Verbs, adjectives, adverbs, and prepositions are acquired later, usually in that order. While vowels dominate the cooings and babblings of the infant, consonants occur more frequently than vowels during this phase (Bryen, 1982). The first words tend to

1. be single syllable words such as "go" or "no";
2. be reduplicated (repeated) monosyllables such as "ma-ma" or "bye-bye," or
3. end with ie or y (birdie, doggie, sissy);
4. begin with consonants such as /s/, /b/, /d/, /t/, /m/, or /n/ followed by a variety of vowel sounds that are made at the front of the mouth (Beck, 1979);
5. appear one at a time;
6. refer to objects or events familiar to the child.

The repetitive quality of the babbling period carries over into many of the child's early words. Babbling continues during this period but diminishes in frequency as the repertory of meaningful words expands.

Many of the infant's early words are learned through the process of association between objects, people, and actions (Bloom, 1993). The infant hears a word and enters it into memory along with information about the context in which it is used. For example the word "shoe" takes on meaning as the parent uses the word in dressing the child. After sufficient encounters with the word, the infant vocalizes the word "shoe" during the dressing sequence. Later the parent may show the child a shoe, or a picture of a shoe, and ask "What is this?" The word is thus reinforced in a more general context. The first 50 distinct words they produce

include words for people (mommy, baby), household objects (clock), utensils (cup), animals (dog), activities and states (up, on), and routines (night-night) (Clark, 1995).

Development of Meaning (Semantics)

Mastery of the semantic features of a language includes vocabulary development and understanding word meanings and relations of words within sentences. Infants concentrate mainly on the first task of developing a mental dictionary of individual word definitions. As the baby grows, new words are added and definitions of old words are revised and expanded. Toward the end of the second year of life, infants demonstrate a developing cognitive sophistication that provides the basis for the development of meaning (Bangs, 1982).

Vocabulary Development. Building up a repertoire of words is a critical task in language acquisition. From the time the infant utters the first word, vocabulary development proceeds at an increasingly rapid rate. The vocabulary grows rather quickly during the last half of the second year with the infant's increasing mobility and expanding knowledge and experience with people, objects, and events. The rate of spoken vocabulary acquisition is depicted in Table 10–3 . By the time a child

Table 10–3   How the Infant's Vocabulary Grows

AGE (MONTHS)	NUMBER OF WORDS	GAIN
8	0	
10	1	1
12	3	2
15	19	16
18	22	3
21	118	96
24	272	154
30	446	174
36	896	450

Adapted from M. E. Smith (1926). An investigation of the development of the sentence and the extent of vocabulary in young children. *University of Iowa Studies in Child Welfare, 3,* (5), p. 54. Used by permission.

is 30 months of age the vocabulary should be too large for a parent to easily count. If it is less than 150 to 200 words, it is probably too small (Coplan, 1995). Although some research suggests that in the English language infants learn nouns before verbs, the proportions probably depend upon the words they hear (Clark, 1995).

Vocabulary development involves expansion and elaboration of the various meanings of words already acquired. Many words used by infants are overextended or overgeneralized to apply to situations, objects, or persons not included in the conventional adult meaning. For example, Eva first said the word "moon" while actually looking at the moon. She then used the word moon while looking at half of a grapefruit, a lemon slice, a crescent shaped piece of yellow paper, and other similarly shaped objects (Bowerman, 1978).

Infants also underextend words by using them

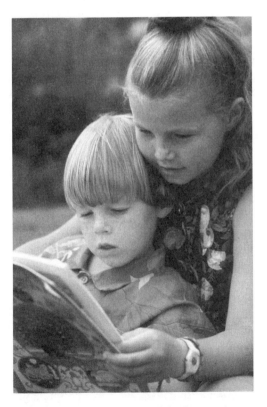

Reading to a toddler and naming pictures is an excellent way to enhance language development.

too narrowly and specifically. A child may think that the word car applies only to the family car rather than to cars on the street or to cars in picture books. A word such as "bye" may be used only when someone is leaving the child's own house. According to Clark's semantic features hypothesis (Clark, 1973), underextensions represent the first stage in the process of learning new words. The child begins by identifying one or two meanings of a new word and adding more features until the word, over a period of time, corresponds to the adult definition. Thus, in the process of adding new meanings to words, children often use words too broadly. Overextensions and underextensions are often reported in children's speech throughout the single-word period (Bloom, 1993).

One of the most interesting aspects of vocabulary development is the way infants create their own versions of adult words. A child's version of "Santa Claus" may be "Slaus Slaus," or a bottle may be a "baber." Obviously, such words are the product of mispronunciations or simplifications of adult usage. However, other words are the result of the child's own creation for which there is no adult version. The infant who called a pacifier a "bye" and money "bee" was not approximating adult word sounds. English-speaking infants make up their own version of nouns, verbs, and adverbs beginning around 2 years of age (Clark, 1995).

Why babies simplify adult words is not clearly understood, but it probably results from their limited articulatory skills (Clark & Clark, 1977). Children have been observed simplifying words by omitting final consonants ("out" = "ou"), reducing consonant clusters ("step" = "dep"), or reduplicating syllables ("water" = "wa wa") (Bryen, 1982; Smith, 1973). In other instances, infants create their own words from sounds or features associated with an object. A bell is called a "ding-ding," or a cow a "moo-moo." Clark (1995) suggests that infants construct new words from elements they already know (word roots and endings), and rely on simplicity to make the least adjustment possible. She gives the example of a child describing a wet newspaper as "soaky" (instead of soak+ed).

Many infants experience a rapid increase in the number of words they add to their vocabulary between 18 and 24 months. This is sometimes referred to as a **vocabulary spurt**. After this period, vocabulary growth remains fairly constant throughout childhood. This explosion in vocabulary is probably due to a combination of factors (Bloom, 1993). For one thing, major improvements in the thought processes take place toward the end of the second year of life. Advances in the understanding of object concepts and in the ability to sort objects into categories leads to increased ability and motivation to learn words. At this time infants also discover that everything has a name. Bloom (1993) also suggests that the vocabulary spurt is related to the infant's increased understanding of the relation between words and the ability to use one word to recall another. Finally, increases in social interactions and verbal exchanges with caregivers connected with the infant's growing awareness of the value of words may be a major impetus in learning words at this time.

Receptive Speech. The meaning the infant attaches to what other people say is called **receptive speech**. Babies usually understand more words than they can say at all stages of language development. The first signs of word comprehension appear at approximately 9 to 10 months of age when infants respond to verbal commands such as "No!" or "Clap your hands!" (Adamson, 1995). Infants typically understand a few words such as mommy, daddy, and bye-bye, well before they say their first word (Ervin-Tripp, 1966). They may understand words for three or four months before they try to say them. By 13 months of age, an infant typically has a receptive vocabulary of about 50 words (Adamson, 1995). Toward the end of the second year, 2-year-olds usually can understand and carry out two or three related requests combined in a single utterance (Bzoch & League, 1991). By 3 years of age, a child's receptive vocabulary includes approximately 800 words (Coplan, 1995).

Mastery of Syntax

Children learn the **syntax** of a language when they (1) can join words into sentences and (2) understand multiple-word sentences said by others (Wood, 1976). Infants begin to put two words together around 18 months. This stage represents an important milestone in language acquisition. The infant's utterances become more representative of formal grammar as many of the rules of syntax are applied without explicit guidance.

Holophrastic Speech. Holophrases are single-word utterances that are roughly equivalent to whole phrases or complete sentences (McNeil, 1970). For example, when baby Maria says "ball," she may mean "There is a ball" or "Bring me the ball." Children normally use variations in voice inflections or gestures to help the listener distinguish between ambiguous meanings. In some instances, however, such words are hard to interpret without gestures or situational cues.

The extent of children's knowledge about sentence structure in using holophrastic utterances has been the subject of debate and controversy for several years. From one point of view, the one-word sentence implies a certain grammatical structure that cannot be represented in a single-word utterance. By definition, a single word cannot be a sentence. On the other hand, other investigators maintain that holophrases are the product of the child's increasing cognitive awareness and limited verbal skill for self-expression (de Villiers & de Villiers, 1978).

Two-Word Utterances. Some infants remain in the one-word stage for several weeks or months, but others begin to combine words soon after they produce their first single word utterance (Clark, 1995). The typically developing infant begins in a halting and uncertain manner to put two words together at approximately 18 months of age. The transition from one-word to two-word utterances has begun. In keeping with this developmental progression, deaf infants who are learning sign language begin to use two signing combinations at around 18 months of age (Bates, O'Connell, & Shore, 1987). Many infants go through a brief phase in which strings of single words are produced in succession with pauses and separate intonations for each word. When the child reaches that point, the appearance of two-word utterances is imminent, and "Baby. Chair." becomes "Baby chair." (Bloom, 1973). The appearance of two-word combinations typically coincides with the time when the child has acquired a vocabulary of about 50 words (Lenneberg, 1967).

Roger Brown (1973) identified five stages of language acquisition based on the average length of the child's utterances. An infant enters the first stage when the average sentence length (ML) is more than one word. The infant enters a new stage each time the ML increases by 0.5. Infants work carefully on the correct grammatical structure of their sentences as they increase the average length of their utterances. Brown (1973) studied the speech of infants from such diverse languages as Spanish, Finnish, and Russian. He found that children from each of the different language environments used words with similar meanings and combined them in the same way.

Two-word utterances are more definite indicators than holophrases that the child is learning the rules for putting words together in proper order. Such utterances are almost always constructed according to basic grammatical rules, with the subject first and the verb second. Even at this early stage, infants combine words with meanings that fit together in a sensible statement. For example, you may hear a toddler say "Daddy eat!" but not "Eat Daddy!" Some children build up word combinations through the use of a small number of words they combine with a variety of other words in fixed patterns, such as *more* milk and *more* juice. (Clark, 1973).

Telegraphic Speech. Brown (1973) referred to the two-word expressions of infants as telegraphic speech because they are similar to a telegram, which omits all but the key words. The concept of telegraphic speech focuses on the efficiency and simplicity of the child's speech, as in "See truck?" instead of "Do you see the truck?" Such sentences consist mainly of nouns and verbs occurring in the order that corresponds to adult usage (Brown & Fraser, 1963).

Elaborated Sentences and Clauses. At approximately 2 years of age, infants begin pro-

ducing three-word sentences. Between 2 and 2½ years of age infants produce many two- and three-word sentences, and a few utterances with as many as six words (Crais & Roberts, 1996). With increasing age and a more extensive vocabulary, infants form longer, more complex sentences. They add other parts of speech to noun and verb combinations. Between 2 and 3 years they begin to use conjunctions such as *and, then, after,* and *if* to link sequences of words. (Clark, 1995). By 3 years of age typically developing children often speak in grammatically correct sentences using the present tense (Coplan, 1995).

Pragmatic Aspects of Language

At the same time infants are working on phonology, semantics, and other components of language, they are becoming increasingly proficient in the **pragmatic** aspects of language. **Pragmatics** refer to affective language behavior or social competency in language (Bangs, 1982). The essence of pragmatics is that language is used functionally—to do things (Hopper & Naremore, 1978). Pragmatics include the following features: (1) rules governing conversations; (2) selection of appropriate verbal as well as nonverbal language to convey intended meaning; and (3) proxemics—the proximity of physical distance people maintain in their interpersonal interactions (Wood, 1976).

Early Language Functions. Very young infants learn to use crying, cooing, and other prespeech sounds as well as body language to communicate their needs and influence the behavior of others. Halliday (1975) identified seven basic functions of language that may be practiced by infants:

1. Instrumental—getting needs met *(I want)*.
2. Regulatory—controlling the behavior of others *(Do as I tell you)*.
3. Interactional—relating to others *(Me and you)*.
4. Personal—expressing self-awareness *(Here I come)*.
5. Heuristic—exploring the environment *(Tell me why)*.
6. Imaginative—creating an environment *(Let's pretend)*.
7. Informative—communicating information *(I've got something to tell you)*.

Halliday concluded that infants are capable of using the first four functions by 10½ months, and that functions five and six are added by 18 months of age. The seventh function appears around 22 months.

Children learn how to use different forms of language when addressing different people to achieve different goals. From a young age they realize that not everyone should receive the same type speech (Clark, 1995). For example, 2-year-olds have been observed using a small, high-pitched voice and very short sentences in talking to dolls, talking for dolls, and in talking to babies (Sachs & Devlin, 1976).

Nonverbal Communication. Nonverbal communication includes various body movements, postures, facial expressions, and gestures such as pointing, reaching, approach-avoidance behavior, smiling, and eye contact. The acquisition of nonverbal communication apparently parallels verbal expression. As verbal abilities become more complex, the child acquires greater varieties and fluency in the use of gestures and facial expression (Hopper & Naremore, 1978).

Out of 63 gestures identified in a study of 1,803 infants, the one most frequently reported at 8 months of age was "extends arms upward" in the unmistakable universal signal that says "Hold me" or "Pick me up" (Fenson et al., 1994). The pointing gesture that appears around 9 to 12 months of age is another major communication device used by babies everywhere to attract the attention of another person (Bates et al., 1987; Desrochers, Morissette, & Ricard, 1995). It is also a means of saying "Look at that!" or "I want that!" (Bower, 1977). At approximately 1 year of age, babies begin to look at objects other people point to (Lempers et al., 1977). Infants begin to point to themselves at approximately 18 months of age (Bates et al., 1987). They continue to use gestures after they begin to talk. The toddler who can say "milk" may still point to the refrigerator instead of speaking, or point at the same time a request is made.

Eye contact plays a major role in the communication rituals between caretaker and child very early in an infant's life. Smiling also is a very important early facial expression that facilitates adult-infant interactions. Eye contact and smiling are complementary behaviors that serve to instigate and maintain interaction sequences with infants. The absence of eye language and smiling presents extraordinary problems for a parent in communicating and establishing emotional intimacy. Mothers of blind infants sometimes find their babies perplexing and unresponsive and have difficulty knowing what their babies want (Fraiberg, 1974).

Conversational Turn-taking. Infants apparently learn some of the basic rules of polite conversation such as taking turns, recognizing one's turn to speak, and not dominating the conversation even before they say their first words. Parents apparently encourage turn-taking in interactions with infants as early as 1 month of age by phrasing questions and responses in such a way that burps, yawns, and blinks may be considered as a conversational turn (Snow, 1977). Infants reciprocate by making sounds such as a coo and waiting for responses. Turn-taking is also found in games such as peek-a-boo and build-and-bash (the parent builds and the child bashes) (de Villiers & de Villiers, 1979). These playful "dialogues" prepare the infant for more sophisticated conversations during the linguistic stage.

Proxemics. Hall (1969) identified four zones of space people maintain in communicating under various circumstances: (1) the intimate zone (0–6 inches); (2) the personal zone (1½–2½ feet); (3) the social zone (4–7 feet); and (4) the public zone (12–25 feet). Children learn to use space in their communications in developmental stages. Infants typically prefer to communicate in the intimate zone. They engage in touching, hugging, and vocal interchanges in the intimate and personal zones. After 3 years of age, children gradually establish preferences for the less intimate zones, which involve less body contact and greater physical distance (Wood, 1976).

Crib Talk. Not all infant speech involves interactions with other people. Between 2 and 3 years of age, some toddlers talk to themselves just before going to sleep. These monologues are referred to as **crib speech**. Katherine Nelson (1989) analyzed tape recordings of the speech of an infant named Emily made over a 15-month period between 21 and 36 months of age. Some examples of Emily's earlier and later crib talk are (Nelson, 1989):

(22 months) . . . when Daddy comes in . . . then Daddy get Emmy . . . (p. 221)

(28 months) . . . we are going at the ocean . . . ocean is a little far away . . . (p. 163)

(33 months) . . . actually it's Stephen's koala bear . . . when Stephen wakes up, I'll have to throw his koala bear in his room . . . (p. 160).

These crib monologues are used by infants (1) as a pleasurable form of advanced vocal play; (2) to practice and expand their emerging language skills; and (3) to represent, sort out experiences, and make sense of their world (Nelson, 1989).

FACTORS INFLUENCING LANGUAGE DEVELOPMENT

Parent-Child Interactions

Researchers and language specialists emphasize the importance of the interactions between infants and their caretakers, particularly the mother, in the acquisition of language (Leavitt, 1980). During the early months of life, parent-infant interactions provide the natural environmental context and foundations for language acquisition. Bruner and his colleagues (1983) believe parents create a language acquisition support device (LASD) which equals Chomsky's LAD in importance. Opportunities for learning experiences that foster language occur daily in conjunction with routine caregiving activities. During diaper changing, feeding, and other daily dyadic interactions, parents tend to encourage eye contact, vocal production, vocal imitation, turn taking, and the use of gestures. Many of the interactions involve contingent responses in which the baby's behavior depends upon a response from the parent and vice versa (Papousek & Papousek, 1991).

The mere presence of a newborn infant elicits vocal overtures from adults. By 2 months of age infants begin to reciprocate with sounds that sometimes match the pitch of the parent's voice. Vocal play interactions between infants and adults increase in number with the infant's age. In one study, of vocal interactions between 2-, 3-, and 4-month-old German infants and their parents, 82 percent of the episodes were initiated by the infant (Papousek, Papousek, & Harris, 1987). Parents answered the infant's sounds with matching turns almost two-thirds of the time. In contrast, the infant answered only 17 percent of parent initiated sounds. Regardless of parent-infant differences in initiation and response patterns, this type of interactional vocal play is considered a powerful influence on language acquisition as well as socialization.

Variations in vocabulary size have been attributed to the amount of language exposure provided infants by their parents. Talkative parents tend to have children with larger vocabularies (Huttenlocher et al., 1991). Hart and Risley (1995) conducted a two-year long study on 42 infants, ages 1 to 2 years, and their families in which they observed the amount of speech parents used with their infants and other parenting characteristics. By 3 years of age, 86 to 98 percent of the words recorded in each child's vocabulary consisted of words also recorded in their parents' vocabularies. The characteristics of parental language and interactions that fostered speech competency included large amounts of diverse speech, responsiveness to child utterance, encouragement of autonomy, and talk about relations between things and events.

Baby Talk. The special language mothers use in talking to their infants is sometimes referred to as **motherese** (Newport, Gleitman & Gleitman, 1977) or **baby talk** (Brown, 1977). Mothers from all linguistic communities tend to talk to their babies in much the same way. The mere presence of an awake infant elicits motherese (Trehub, Trainor, & Unyk 1993). Kaye (1980) has summarized the following characteristics of "motherese":

1. A higher pitch, greater range of sound features, more varied tones.
2. Simplified words and special forms, such as potty and mama.

3. Shorter and simplified utterances, slower pace, and occasional whispering.
4. Immediate repetition and more repetition of the same words or phrases over a period of time.
5. Restriction of topics to the child's world.

The rise in pitch that generates a falsetto quality is perhaps the most notable aspect of baby talk.

Mothers, fathers, other adults, and even children in cultures all over the world adjust their speech when addressing infant listeners (Trehub et al., 1993). Fernald and her associates (1989) compared sound modification in mothers' and fathers' speech to preverbal infants in French, Italian, German, Japanese, British English, and American English. In all languages, mothers and fathers spoke with higher pitched sounds, shorter utterances, and longer pauses in infant-directed speech than in speech directed to adults. Fernald (1989) found that objective adult listeners could identify the communicative intent (e.g., comfort, attention-bid) of the speaker in infant-directed speech more accurately than in adult-directed speech. However, cultural variations in baby talk have been noted. For example, Japanese mothers tend to use repetitive nonsense syllables and imitations of their infants' sounds more than American mothers. Japanese mothers also seem to spend more time soothing their infants with vocalizations as compared with American mothers (Trehub et al., 1993). Higher pitch and exaggerated baby-talk sounds do not appear to be as prevalent among southern rural African-American parents, Kaluhi families in New Guinea, and Quiche-Mayan parents in Guatemala (Sachs, 1993).

There are indications that a type of "motherese" extends into the songs mothers sing to their infants. The practice of singing to infants is observed throughout the world. Apparently, mothers and other caregivers almost everywhere sing lullabies to soothe their babies and put them to sleep. This practice has been observed in cultures as diverse as the Cuna Indians of Panama, the Hazara tribe of Afghanistan, and traditional Vietnamese families. Trehub and her colleagues (1993) identified the following characteristics of lullabies similar to infant-directed speech: word reduplication, sequence repetition, a low and narrow pitch range, elongated vowels, and common words incorporated into rhythmic patterns.

The importance of motherese is more than the provision of sounds or words for the baby to imitate. What caregivers are mainly attempting to accomplish when they use baby talk is to communicate, to understand, to be understood, to engage and maintain infant attention, to communicate affect to the infant, and facilitate speech and language comprehension (Brown, 1973; Fernald, 1984). Evidently the mother's efforts are not wasted. Studies of vocal interactions between young infants and their mothers have found that infants as young as 3 months of age vocalize in response to their mother's speech (Bates et al., 1977; Lewis & Freedle, 1973). Infants match the pitch of the parent's voice, sometimes engaging in vocal "duets." They prefer infant-directed speech over adult-directed speech, and approving over disapproving infant-directed tones (Trehub et al., 1993).

Motherese and other forms of vocal play between caregiver and infants eventually include a variety of playful interactions and ritualized games. German mothers have been observed engaging in playful "headbutting" games with their infants as they make playful flow of rythmnic sounds (Papousek, Papousek, & Harris, 1987). Blowing on the baby's stomach, tickling, playing "I'm gonna getcha" are other examples of the types of games parents everywhere play with their infants. Some theorists believe that other forms of children's play originate in these early dyadic interactions combining vocal and social games (Papousek et al., 1987).

Turn-Taking. The baby appears to be trying just as hard as the mother to communicate. The process of verbal interchanges between infant and caretaker encourages turn-taking, which prepares the child for later linguistic communication (Bruner, 1978). Apparently, the baby is almost instinctively following the rules of polite conversation. As mother and child take turns vocalizing to each other, the process evolves into what has been referred to as the "fine-tuning" of the baby's language by the parent. Maternal vocalizations are thus adjusted to match the child's changing linguistic abilities according to cues from the child (Bruner, 1978).

Fine-Tuning. The process of fine-tuning the baby's speech may involve the techniques of prompting, echoing, and expansion (Dale, 1976). For the preverbal child, a parent may talk and make sounds while feeding or bathing the child, such as "You are a sweet baby—Yes—Ooh—Ooh—," which prompts the child to reciprocate with sounds. For the older infant, the parent may prompt by asking, "What do you want?" as the child points to the refrigerator. In echoing, the parent imitates or repeats the child's utterances, which stimulate the child to continue to vocalize. Expansion is similar to echoing, but with something added to the child's utterance by the adult, as in: "Mommy's dress." "Yes, this is Mommy's blue dress." In the following interchange all three processes are used:

Mother: (Pointing to a ball); *What's that?* (Prompting)
Child: *Ball.*
Mother: *Ball.* (Echoing)
Child: *Blue ball.*
Mother: *Yes! It's a round, blue ball.* (Expansion).

These techniques represent a form of scaffolding (discussed in Chapter 9) and are consistent with Vygotsky's theory of facilitating language acquisition within the Zone of Proximal Development.

Joint Attention. Parents and infants often communicate through the process known as **joint attention.** This happens when infant and caregiver focus on the same object, sounds, or events. Most of what we know about joint attention involves episodes of joint visual attention (shared looking). For example, an adult might notice a bright red ball that has captured the baby's attention. The adult looks back and forth from the infant to the ball to indicate mutual interest and attention. The adult then comments "Ball! Red Ball!" Adults also initiate joint looking episodes by moving objects into the baby's

field of vision, by pointing at objects, and by making eye contact with the baby and then shifting their gaze to something they want the baby to see. Infants call attention to objects they want to share with adults by shifting gaze, pointing, making sounds, and by physical contact (e.g., tugging). Such interactions usually elicit adult naming or other comments that help infants label objects and other features of the environment. Babies typically engage in sustained shared looking with adults at approximately 12 months of age (Corkum & Moore, 1995).

There is a growing amount of evidence to support the significance of joint attention as a powerful means of communication and language acquisition. For example, infants are more likely to acquire a correct word for a novel object (*dodo*) if they are looking at the object while it is being named than if their attention is focused on something else (Dunham, Dunham, & Curwin, 1993). Toddlers make faster progress in vocabulary acquisition when mothers label features of the environment during joint attention episodes (Dunham & Dunham, 1992). On the basis of existing studies it is not possible to determine whether the adult contributes more to the language acquisition in joint attentional episodes, or whether the child controls the process. An alternative explanation favored by Dunham and Dunham (1992) is that the process is a mutual one in which both adult and child make important contributions to language acquisition during joint attention episodes.

Father-Infant Speech

Does father-infant speech display the same modification and characteristics as mother-infant interchanges? Unfortunately, information on father-child verbal interactions is more limited. The available information indicates that fathers' speech to their babies is similar to that of mothers, but with some notable differences. Fathers adjust their speech to baby talk, or "parentese," when talking to young infants. Like mothers, they use shorter phrases and repeat sounds more frequently when talking to an infant than when talking to an adult (Belsky &

Volling, 1987). However, fathers, in contrast to mothers, tend to omit the falsetto rise in pitch (Trehub et al., 1993). Also, fathers are less likely than mothers to sing lullabies to infants. Instead, they tend to sing popular songs or folk tunes, improvising words or melodies and often embedding the infants' names into the words (Trehub et al., 1993).

In contrast to mothers, fathers tend to use fewer repetitions and expansions of child utterances (Giattino & Hogan, 1975), but use more imperatives and directives. An example of an imperative is "Come and get your toy truck!" Fathers appear to misunderstand children's utterances more often and to be less attentive and less attuned to their children's speech (Gleason, 1975). Rebelsky and Hanks (1971) found that fathers in the United States spend little time interacting with their very young infants (up to 3 months old). However, a study of German parent vocal interactions with their 2-, 3-, and 4-month-old infants did not find any difference between mothers and fathers in the number of parent initiated vocal play episodes, the length of the interactions, or the number of parent vocalizations (Papousek, Papousek, & Harris, 1987). Infants were less responsive to their fathers, though, in repetitive sounds per episode. Although some studies (Rebelsky & Hanks, 1971) report that fathers spend more time talking with male offspring than with female children, others have found no such differences (Hart & Risley, 1995).

Gender Differences

Through the years researchers and scholars have had difficulty deciding whether or not gender is an important factor in language acquisition. In 1982, Shepherd-Look concluded that research has not found gender differences in the age of beginning to talk, age of first sentences, mean length of utterances, picture vocabulary ability, word comprehension, or word production. More recently, studies of infants and toddlers have found a female advantage in certain aspects of verbal ability, such as vocabulary and length of utterances. (Morisset et al., 1995). For example, a study of gender differences among toddlers from economically disadvantaged families found differences favoring girls

on spontaneous utterances at 20 to 30 months of age. However, no gender differences were found at 24 and 36 months on standardized tests of language development (Morisset et al., 1995). A large scale study to develop norms for a parent-report inventory of infant communicative development found female scores on several aspects of language ability to be slightly higher than males (Fenson et al., 1994).

What can we conclude from such contradictory information? Overall, the evidence from existing studies tends to show that female infants and toddlers, on average, display superior performance on some measures of language development. However, gender differences are much smaller than previously believed and probably account for no more than 1 to 2 percent of individual differences in language ability during the early years (Fenson et al., 1994).

Twins

Researchers have found that twins and other children of multiple births have more problems in language development than children from single births. In comparison to singletons, twins tend to lag behind in language ability (McCarthy, 1954; Drillien, 1964). This difference has been attributed the fact that they develop a "twin language" or private communication system of their own that includes gestures and jargon. However, there are indications that such an "autonomous" language may not be used exclusively by twins, but may be communication patterns used by other children to communicate with their peers (Bakker, 1987). In any case research on language development in twins is complicated by factors such as prematurity, low birthweight, and other developmental problems that are more prevalent among twins than singletons. A study on language development among twins conducted in Sweden did not find any significant delays in language development among twins at 4 years of age when birthweight was controlled (Akerman & Thomassen, 1991). Thus, factors other than "twinness" per se may account for much of the language delay found among many twins.

Multilingualism

Under certain circumstances, being born into a family in which more than one language is spoken may be an obstacle in the early stages of language acquisition. Infants from bilingual families have trouble separating phonological components of the languages until about 3 years of age, unless there is a marked separation of a situation or speakers (Ervin-Tripp, 1966). However, many children who are exposed to two languages during infancy tend to show few differences in language development when compared to monolingual children (Padilla & Lindholm, 1976). Even when early difficulties are present, children eventually speak each language without one interfering with the other (Obler, 1985). The optimal way for infants and young children to learn two languages at the same time is keeping the contexts in which they are used separate. For example one parent can use one language consistently, while the other parent uses the second language. Another approach is for one language to be used in the home, while the second language is used in the child-care facility or preschool environment (Taber-Flusberg, 1994).

Social Class Differences

Infants from upper and middle social-class environments are generally considered to have a linguistic advantage over infants from lower social classes. Socioeconomic status (SES) is generally found to be associated with the quality of the language environment, including the amount of talk and complexity of expression. Hart and Risley (1995) found that middle-SES parents of 11- to 18-month-old infants average 535 utterances per hour of which 321 were addressed to the baby. By comparison, lower-SES parents average 521 utterances per hour, of which 283 were addressed to the baby. However, the effects of social class on language acquisition do not, in most cases, become evident until the second and third years of life (Golden & Birns, 1976). Morisset and her colleagues (1995) studied language development among toddlers from age 13 months through 36 months of age who were from poverty backgrounds. Language delays did not become observable until after 24 months of age. This is consistent with other studies demonstrating the emergence of social class differences in language during the third year of life (Fenson et al., 1994).

Individual Differences

The study of language development involves, to a large extent, the identification of typical patterns displayed by infants all over the world. Researchers, however, are also interested in individual differences in language acquisition. Some infants are producing two- or three-word sentences while others of the same age are still struggling with the first words. One study (Snyder et al., 1981) found variations in the one-word vocabularies expressed by 13-month-old infants ranging from 0 to 45 words. An interesting (but not verified) anecdote about the famous Scottish philosopher, Thomas Carlyle, is sometimes used to illustrate precocious language development. At 10 months of age Carlyle had not said any words, but when he heard a baby crying was reported to have said, *"What ails thee, Jock?"* From then on he spoke in complete sentences (Illingworth, 1991).

Nelson (1973) identified individual stylistic differences in how children acquire and use early words. Some toddlers use a **referential** style whereby they acquire a large number of words that refer mainly to objects. Their speech is used mainly for sharing information about objects ("ball"), one word at a time. Other toddlers use an **expressive style**. Their speech is more socially oriented and consists mainly of pronouns and action words. Expressive toddlers tend to have smaller vocabularies, but compress them into phrases ("getit") to communicate feelings and wants.

Individual difference in language styles and other aspects of language acquisition have been attributed to variations in caregiver styles and interaction patterns. Researchers have found that parents use verbal styles of interaction that tend to match and support the style (referential or expressive) used by the child (Goldfield, 1987). Other possible sources of individual variations include maturational status at birth, disabilities, intelligence, underlying brain mechanisms, and personality factors.

PROBLEMS IN LANGUAGE ACQUISITION

Due to the individual differences in the developmental patterns, communication disorders are often not detected during the early months of life unless an infant has an obvious developmental disability such as cerebral palsy, Down syndrome, or a cleft lip. Communication disorders are usually identified much later in infants who are typically developing in other areas. Parents should have an infant screened for potential problems if the infant has not spoken any words by 2 years of age, or is not responsive to words and sounds of others. The number one cause of speech and language delays during infancy is hearing loss (Billeaud, 1993). Consequently, hearing loss should be identified as early as possible.

Hearing screening tests should be administered periodically, especially to infants who are at-risk for developmental delay, who have persistent incidents of otitis media, or who display any indications of hearing loss. Some possible signs of hearing loss that parents, caregivers, and teachers should look for are

1. lack of responsiveness to loud noises;
2. cessation of babbling after a few months;
3. failure to produce words soon after the first year of age;
4. failure to form two-word phrases by 2 years of age;
5. failure to produce simple sentences by 3 years of age;
6. cessation of vocabulary growth after it begins (Tweedie, 1987).

LANGUAGE ASSESSMENT INSTRUMENTS

Most general infant-assessment scales, such as the Bayley–II (Bayley, 1993), have sections for measuring language performance. In addition, there are several instruments specifically designed for screening and assessing infant-toddler communication skills. Two frequently used standardized scales are:

The Receptive-Emergent Language Test-2 (REEL-2) (Bzoch & League, 1991). The REEL-2 is a checklist that is used to screen infants from 1 to 36 months of age for potential delays in receptive and expressive language skills. The examiner obtains information about the child by means of a parent interview. The scale provides a receptive and expressive communication quotients and age-equivalent scores, and an overall language score.

Sequenced Inventory of Communicative Development-Revised (SICD-R) (Hedrick, Prather, & Tobin, 1984). The SICD-R is classified as a diagnostic instrument for measuring the communication skills of infants and children between the ages of 4 months and 4 years. It is designed to assess sound awareness and discrimination, comprehension, motor, vocal, and verbal expressions. Information is obtained from parents, but some of the test items are administered to the child. The test results produce a receptive communication age score and an expressive communication age score.

FACILITATING LANGUAGE DEVELOPMENT

Although theorists differ about the extent to which language development can be facilitated through environmental stimulation, the importance of exposure to a supportive and enriched environment is being increasingly recognized. The following are examples of activities that can be used by parents and other caretakers to enhance communication and language development during the various stages of infancy. Keep in mind, however, that these activities should be natural, spontaneous, informal, and free from pressure on the infant to "perform."

Birth to 6 Months

1. Imitate the baby's facial expressions, gestures, and sounds. Maintain eye contact and talk to the baby during diapering, feeding, and other routines (Senter, 1983).
2. Engage in turn-taking with the infant. Initiate the cycle when the baby is quiet and alert by making a series of sounds ("ooh-ooh," "ah-ah") (Senter, 1983).
3. Play records with soothing sounds for the baby. Sing lullabies while rocking the baby.
4. When talking to an infant at this age, frequently keep your face about 12 to 18 inches from the baby's, so

that the baby can watch your face and lips (Meier & Malone, 1979).

5. Gently bounce the baby on your knee and sing songs like "trot-a-little-horsey" (Sparling & Lewis, 1979).

6. Say the baby's name frequently (Cataldo, 1983).

6 to 12 Months

1. Continue activities suggested above (except number 4).

2. Play peek-a-boo. Vary the game by attaching a cloth to the top of a mirror. Ask "Where is (baby's name)?" and raise the cloth to let the baby see the reflected image (Sparling & Lewis, 1979).

3. Say "Hi" when you come close to the baby. Wave and say "bye-bye" when you are leaving the room (Sparling & Lewis, 1979).

4. Play pat-a-cake.

5. Toward the end of this age period, read simple short stories when baby is quiet and alert. Avoid forcing the child to be quiet or sit still (White, 1975).

6. Carry the child around the house or other places on "word walks," and point to objects of interest (Meier & Malone, 1979).

7. Use a tape recorder to record the infant's sounds and play them back (Meier & Malone, 1979).

12 to 18 Months

1. Continue activities suggested for 6 to 12 months.

2. Talk to the baby during bath time about soap, water, washcloth, and toys. Discuss how they feel and what they do (Sparling & Lewis, 1979).

3. Use learning exercises such as the following: Find a book with stiff pages with only one brightly colored object on each page. Place the book where the baby can see, point to the picture of an object, and say, "See the _____." Point to the "_____." "Where is the _____?" If the baby makes any sounds, repeat the sounds or words vocalized (Meier & Malone, 1979).

18 to 24 Months

1. Continue reading and naming objects from books at least once a day.

2. Listen carefully to what the child is trying to say, and respond positively. If the words are not clear, venture a guess (e.g., "You want some water?")

3. Repeat and expand the child's one- or two-word utterances into complete sentences. For example, if the

baby says, "Go bye-bye," respond by saying, "You want to go outside?"

4. Continue to structure games and activities to stimulate language (e.g., This little piggy).

5. Be very specific when giving instructions and directions to your child. Instead of saying, "Bring me your things," say, "Bring me your shoes and socks." Then expand further by saying, "I see you brought your blue socks." (Sparling & Lewis, 1979).

6. Raise or lower your voice from time to time to make sounds more interesting. Sing your words at times.

SUMMARY

1. Language is a complex system of mutually agreed-upon symbols used to express and understand ideas and feelings. Speech is the vocal component of language, which includes expressive and receptive functions.

2. Behaviorists maintain that language is acquired through systematic reinforcement, whereas nativists claim that infants are innately equipped to master language. Cognitive developmental theorists stress the importance of cognitive processes. Vygotsky emphasized the cultural origins and functions of language. Interactionist theorists stress the interplay between biological and environmental influences in language acquisition.

3. Language consists of five components: phonology (sounds), morphology (words), syntax (structure), semantics (meaning), and pragmatics (social usage). Developing proficiency in a language involves mastering the rules governing the various components.

4. The ability to produce speech sounds is affected by the development of the vocal mechanism, which changes rapidly during infancy.

5. The prespeech sounds include crying, cooing, babbling, and echolalia. The significance of these sounds for language development has been the subject of debate and controversy. Research studies indicate that each type of prespeech sound is an important link in the chain of language acquisition.

6. The first word represents a major milestone in morphological development and usually appears

around the child's first birthday. Its appearance marks the transition from the prespeech stage to the speech stage. The first words produced by infants are mostly nouns and references to things that move and capture their interest.

7. Semantic development is based upon the infant's growing cognitive capacity to acquire new words, add new meaning to old words, and understand relationships among words.

8. Vocabulary development is an important task in language acquisition that proceeds rapidly after 18-months of age.

9. Word comprehension (receptive speech) progresses ahead of word production (expressive speech) during all stages of language development.

10. Infants begin to acquire the grammar (syntax) of their language when they can understand and produce multiple-word utterances. The first two-word combinations, sometimes called telegraphic speech, are usually produced around 18 months. However, some linguists believe that sentence-like words, called holophrases, may be the first indicators of syntactic awareness. Between 2 and 3 years of age, infants produce longer and more complex sentences.

11. Infants demonstrate their growing competency in the pragmatic aspects of language early in life by using crying, cooing, and other prespeech sounds to interact with adults and get their needs met. They use "crib talk" as a form of vocal play, to practice language usage, and make sense of their experiences.

12. Parent-child interactions are an important influence on language acquisition during infancy. Mothers use their own special language, called "motherese," in talking to their babies. Language acquisition is facilitated by parent-infant interactions that are characterized by episodes of turn-taking, fine-tuning, and joint attention.

13. The speech of fathers to infants is similar to "motherese," but there are some notable differences, such as fewer repetitions and expansions of the baby's utterances.

14. Gender differences probably account for only 1 to 2 percent of individual differences in language acquisition during infancy.

15. Twins may be at a disadvantage in language acquisition, but other correlated factors may be responsible for their language delay.

16. Infants from bilingual families are faced with challenges in language acquisition, but usually demonstrate few problems in language ability. The best way for infants and young children to learn two languages at the same time is for adults to keep the contexts in which they are used separate.

17. Infants from economically impoverished environments are generally considered to have a disadvantage in language development. However, the effects of social class on language acquisition do not usually become evident until the second and third years of life.

18 Individual differences in language development have been attributed to stylistic differences in how children acquire and use early words, variations in caregiver styles and interaction patterns, maturational status at birth, disabilities, intelligence, underlying brain mechanisms, and personality factors.

19. The number one cause of speech and language delays during infancy is hearing loss. Parents should have infants screened periodically for potential problems.

20. Examples of standardized scales that are used to assess the language competency of infants are the REEL-2 and the SICD-R.

21. Parents and other caretakers are advised to use a variety of informal games and stimulating activities to enhance language development during infancy.

11

Personality

I am the only ME I AM
who qualifies as me;
no ME I AM has been before
and none will ever be.
      —Jack Prelutsky

An infant is a person, even from the beginning of life. Although parents are frequently preoccupied with routine caregiving activities, they quickly recognize the uniqueness and individuality of their newborn infant. Even identical twins display their own unique behavior patterns. Jan is quiet and placid, while her sister Jean is active and exuberant. One of the most important features distinguishing one baby from another is personality.

The term personality has many general meanings as well as specific definitions. The following definition has been widely used: "**Personality** refers to more or less stable internal factors that make one person's behavior consistent from one time to another, and different from the behavior other people would manifest in comparable situations" (Child, 1968, p. 83). Personality is thus viewed as the sum total of the internal qualities and enduring patterns of behavior that establish a person's individuality.

In this chapter we examine a number of concepts and theories associated with the development of infant personality. Two important components of personality that emerge during the infancy period—temperament and the concept of self—are discussed. Finally, the practical implications of the theoretical and research literature for facilitating personality development during infancy are considered.

THEORIES OF PERSONALITY DEVELOPMENT

There are numerous theories about what makes up human personality and how it develops. For our purposes, however, we consider the four most influential and prominent theories: the classical psychoanalytic theory of Sigmund Freud; Erik Erikson's contemporary psychosocial theory; the behavioristic theory of B. F. Skinner; and Maslow and Rogers' theory of self-actualization.

Freud's Psychoanalytic Theory

Freud was probably the first theorist to emphasize the importance of infancy and the first few years of life in personality development. He believed that the "child is father of the man," and that the basic personality structure is formed by the fifth year of life (Hall & Lindzey, 1978). Consequently, the experiences a person has during infancy have a profound influence on the adult personality.

Freud identified three major components of personality: the id, the ego, and the superego. The id is the biological part of personality that is present at birth. It includes the basic instincts and physiological urges such as hunger and libido (sexual energy). The id provides the energy that motivates the personality. According to Freud, the newborn infant has a very simple personality consisting solely of the primitive urges of the id. The infant seeks immediate gratification and has little ability to tolerate tension created in the id when needs are not met.

The irrational, pleasure-seeking, uninhibited id remains part of the personality throughout life. However, people cannot realistically always have what they want as soon as they want it. Consequently, a second part of the personality, the ego, develops during infancy to exercise control over the id's instinctual urges. The ego is the rational, planning, and organizing part of the personality. Its primary function is to help the id find ways to achieve gratification that are, in the long run, most satisfactory.

The gradual emergence of the ego during the infancy period lays the foundation for the formation of the superego during preschool years (ages 3 to 5). The superego consists of the conscience and the ego-ideal (the person you would like to be). It functions primarily to inhibit the impulses of the id that are socially unacceptable and works to perfect moral behavior (Hall & Lindzey, 1978). The superego is often in conflict with the id, while the ego works to reconcile the differences. If the ego is not successful in resolving the conflict, personality problems may develop.

According to Freud, personality develops through a series of stages: oral, anal, phallic, latency, and genital. The personality is shaped by the quality of the experiences related to the area of the body that is dominant in each stage. Only the two stages that occur during the infancy period will be discussed in more detail.

The Oral Stage (Birth to 18 Months). During the first part of infancy the oral region—the mouth, tongue, and lips—is dominant. Feeding experiences, nonnutritive sucking, and other sensations incorporated through the mouth provide the infant's first experiences of pleasure and frustration. If the baby receives too much or too little gratification through the mouth, oral fixation is likely to occur. Oral fixation through deprivation results in such personality traits as pessimism, self-depreciation, and passivity. Opposite personality characteristics develop from overindulgence in the oral stage.

The Anal Stage (18 Months to 3 Years). Toward the end of the infancy period, the anal region of the body gradually becomes the focal point of the baby's experiences. During this stage, bowel movements become a source of pleasure and potential conflict. The toilet training that typically begins during this period is likely to have long-term consequences. If the infant is treated too harshly, a personality dominated by excessive orderliness, stinginess, stubbornness, and compulsivity is likely to develop. On the other hand, overpermissiveness in toilet training can result in the opposite personality traits.

Erikson's Psychosocial Theory

Erik Erikson was a follower of Freud, but he disagreed with some of Freud's ideas. Erikson (1963) reinterpreted Freudian theory, with more optimism about human nature and an emphasis on cultural influences. He translated Freudian theory into completely different, more contemporary terms.

Erikson's theory is usually discussed in relation to eight psychosocial stages of development, from birth through old age. The personality forms as the individual passes through this series of interrelated

stages. Each stage involves a conflict, or crisis of emotional opposites. The quality of the individual's experience in each stage determines how the conflict is resolved. The emotional crisis that occurs in each stage must be resolved before personality development can proceed smoothly in succeeding stages. The first two stages occur during the infancy period.

Trust versus Mistrust (Birth to 18 Months). Erikson's first stage, trust versus mistrust, roughly parallels Freud's oral stage. The trust versus mistrust stage is considered to be the most critical because it provides the foundation for resolving crises and developing a healthy sense of identity in other stages of life. The basic psychosocial attitude the infant must develop in this stage is that the world and the people in it can be trusted. According to Erikson (1963), consistency and continuity of experience provide the foundation for the sense of trust to develop.

Infants are inclined to be uncertain and mistrusting because their knowledge about the world is very limited. Some feelings of mistrust are normal and healthy. However, if the baby is treated harshly and the basic needs are not consistently met, feelings of mistrust are reinforced and become dominant. Distrustful infants have difficulty separating from their mothers and may exhibit other emotional problems later in life.

Autonomy versus Shame and Doubt (18 Months to 3 Years). The second period coincides with Freud's anal stage. Developing a sense of autonomy begins with the feeling of being in control of one's body during infancy. With increasing mobility, infants begin to explore their environment. They want to see new places and things, undertake new activities, and generally do things for themselves. During this period they also become capable of establishing bowel and bladder control. They frequently have difficulty staying within designated boundaries and complying with adult wishes. The negativism that is characteristic of toddlerhood results from the need for autonomy.

The crisis of this period occurs when the infant's natural inclination to be self-assertive collides with

As he explores the environment, this toddler is developing a sense of autonomy.

adult demands and restrictions. A major area of potential conflict is toilet training. The successful resolution of the crisis involves the parents' willingness to allow reasonable freedom without being overly permissive. Problems occur when parents are too restrictive or overprotective and impose unrealistic expectations. The child may develop a dominant sense of shame and doubt. Such a child suffers from feelings of incompetence, insecurity, and unworthiness.

Skinner's Behaviorism

According to B. F. Skinner (1961), personality is nothing more than a collection of behavior patterns. The personality is acquired over time, response by response. In contrast to Freud, Skinner rejects the idea that there are internal personality mechanisms such as an ego, or unconscious motivational forces. He identified no personality components or devel-

opmental stages. To Skinner, we are products of our environment (Hall & Lindzey, 1978).

The main concern of Skinner and other behaviorists is how behaviors are acquired and extinguished. Skinner's system consists mainly of laws or principles that control the formation of stimulus-response relationships. To understand personality, you need only to understand an individual's conditioning history. An infant becomes passive and compliant if the responses of parents and other caregivers reinforce that particular type of behavior. The infant's personality is not as complex and fully developed as an adult's because the infant has had fewer experiences. Each infant develops a unique personality because of a history of unique experiences (Hjelle & Ziegler, 1976).

Self-Actualization Theory of Maslow and Rogers

In contrast to behavioral theorists, Maslow (1970) and Rogers (1961) believe that individuals are free to choose what they want to be. Implicit in this theory is the idea that infants are born with the urge to grow. Under favorable conditions, individuals are always striving to develop all their capacities and inner potential. This process is referred to as **self-actualization,** which is the main motivational force of personality.

The core personality component is the self-concept, which begins to develop during infancy. It provides the basic mechanism through which a person interprets experiences and ultimately behaves (Lazarus & Monat, 1979). The self-concept is defined and discussed more fully in the next section.

The self-actualizing tendency is a strong force for growth that is evident even during infancy. For example, infants persist in learning to walk and performing other tasks in spite of great effort and the pain of falling down. This persistence results not simply because the infant is genetically programmed to walk, but also because of a strong tendency for growth (Lazarus & Monat, 1979). Since personality is in a constant process of change, Maslow and Rogers did not emphasize one period of life, such as infancy, as more important than any other period.

Evaluating Personality Theories

Personality has proven to be as difficult to study as it has been to define. Consequently, there is no overwhelming research evidence in favor of any single theory. Each theory has been praised as well as criticized. As a student of infant development, you will have to decide which theory you prefer. Many people prefer an eclectic approach, combining the best and most promising ideas from several different theories. In the remainder of this chapter, some of the attributes of infant personality that have become the focal points of current research are considered.

THE DEVELOPMENT OF SELF

Two-year-old Ginny grabs her doll from Michael and says, "Mine." Another toddler, Tanya, notices her picture on the nursery school bulletin board and tells her teacher, "That's me." As these incidents clearly indicate, 2-year-old children have developed an awareness of themselves as individuals distinct and separate from others. In all probability, a primitive form of self-awareness exists much earlier than this (Lewis & Brooks, 1978; Brownell & Kopp. 1991).

Many psychologists believe that the self-concept is the core of the personality and a primary determinant of behavior. In many ways the cognitive, social, and emotional competencies of infants and toddlers are tied to the development of a sense of self. The self serves as a frame of reference for organizing and integrating the experiences of infants in relation to where they are, what they do, and what they want, or intend (Kopp & Brownell, 1991). Generally, self-concept refers to the images, attitudes, and feelings one uses to describe or think about oneself as an individual. Other terms that are sometimes used to describe the self-concept and its development include "self-image" and "sense of self."

Subjective and Objective Self

The development of self involves subjective and objective dimensions. Subjective self-awareness includes experiences connected with one's own motor movements, body functions, and internal states such as hunger, pain, and temperature (Lewis, 1991). The subjective self also includes the awareness of oneself as distinguished from other people and objects in the world. The more advanced subjective features emerge from an early "intuitive" or primitive level of self-awareness (Brownell & Kopp, 1991). Objective self-awareness involves the capacity of infants to "know that they know" and to "remember that they remember" (Lewis, 1991). The objective self includes the ability to observe and talk about the experiences of the subjective self. According to Lewis (1991), objective self-awareness is necessary to experience certain emotions, such as shame, guilt, and embarrassment.

Several theorists (e.g., Lewis, 1991; Kagan, 1991; Stern, 1985) believe that the self consists of multiple components or levels. They use different labels, such as the ecological self, the interpersonal self (Neisser, 1991), the physical self, the social self, the active self, the interpersonal self (Damon & Hart, 1982), the core self, or the verbal self (Stern, 1985) to identify various "selves." The extent to which "multiple selves" function as separate entities or represent parts of a single, unified self is a matter of debate.

Levels of Self-Understanding

Psychologists do not agree on exactly how the self-concept develops and functions. However there is general agreement that three important accomplishments in self-concept development take place during the first three years of life—self-awareness, self-recognition, and self-definition. Like other concepts, the self-concept is subject to change throughout the life cycle. Infants gradually progress through these various stages, or levels of self-understanding. Early in life, primitive, subjective forms of self-awareness emerge out of perceptions associated with body functions and sensorimotor experiences. These initial subjective glimmerings of self-awareness gradually evolve into more sophisticated, objective self-awareness that involves the ability to think about oneself "thinking about oneself" and "knowing that one knows" (Lewis, 1991).

Self-Awareness. In the beginning, an infant has to develop **self-awareness**, i.e., an awareness of being distinct and separate from other people and objects. Margaret Mahler, a Freudian theorist, believes that infants must go through a second birth, one that is psychological in nature (Mahler, Pine, & Bergman, 1975). She refers to this process as **separation-individuation**. Separation involves the child's emerging self-consciousness, or "hatching" from a symbiotic (interdependent) union with the mother. Individuation consists of the achievements that contribute to the child's identity as an autonomous person.

The separation-individuation process takes place mainly between the fourth month and the third year of life. Prior to this time, the infant has gone through two preliminary stages—autistic and symbiotic—and developed a dim awareness of having needs met by an outside source. Mahler conceptualized the development of the self as a struggle between separateness and relatedness, reflected in the baby's ability to handle separation from the mother. The infant's resolution of the oneness-separateness conflict between the ages of 5 and 18 months ultimately shapes the adult personality. Thus, in theory, successful acquisition of a favorable self-concept depends largely upon the quality of the mother-child interactions.

Much of the research on the development of self-awareness in infants has been conducted by Lewis and Brooks-Gunn (1979). They have identified three periods in the infant's self-other differentiation (Lewis, 1986, 1987):

Period 1:0 to 3 Months. This period is characterized initially by the predominance of reflexive interactions with caregivers and objects. These interactions serve as a basis for the beginnings of self-other differentiation, which starts to emerge at the end of this period.

Period 2:3 to 8 Months. During this period, the infant makes additional progress in the distinction between self and others through active learning. However, self-awareness is not totally achieved yet because an infant cannot make self-other distinctions in all situations.

Period 3:8 to 12 Months. At this time, complete self-other differentiation is accomplished. Awareness of the self as unique and permanent in time and space is evident.

Thus, self-awareness is well developed by 1 year of age.

Self-Recognition. The ability of infants to correctly identify images as their own is called **self-recognition**. The development of visual self-recognition has been explored in experiments designed to determine when infants can understand the significance of their own reflection in a mirror. Lewis and Brooks (1978) observed infants from 6 to 24 months of age with a mark of rouge on their faces. None of the 9- to 12-month-old babies responded to the mark when they looked in the mirror. One-quarter of the babies in the 15- to 18-month age range, and three-quarters of the 21- to 24-month-olds touched the mark on their own face as if to say, "That's me!"

Infants recognize their own pictures at about the same age as they identify their reflections in a mirror. By 2 years of age most infants can recognize a picture as their own and distinguish between it and a picture of another baby (Lewis & Brooks, 1974). Infants can also identify themselves in a videotape at this age (Brooks & Lewis, 1976).

Bertenthal and Fischer (1978) believe that the development of self-recognition is related to the acquisition of the object concept (Chapter 8). These researchers presented a series of tasks designed to assess the development of the concept of object permanency in a group of infants between the ages of 6 and 24 months of age. The same infants were also given a test to determine their ability to recognize their own mirror image. The ages at which the infants achieved each of the stages of self-concept development closely coincided with the ages at which they progressed through a series of steps leading to the acquisition of the object concept. The concept of self apparently develops in much the same way as other concepts (Maccoby, 1980).

In summary, research studies indicate that infants begin to recognize their own visual images by the end of the first year, but this ability is not very well developed at that age. By approximately 18 months of age, a more sophisticated level of visual self-recognition can be clearly observed in some infants. Almost all infants demonstrate the ability by the time they are 2 years old (Lewis & Brooks, 1978).

This toddler is beginning to recognize the reflection in the mirror as her own image.

Toddlers from nomadic tribes in the Middle East who have never seen a mirror demonstrate self-recognition when they see themselves in the mirror for the first time (Pipp-Siegel & Pressman, 1996). The emergence of self-awareness thus closely parallels the development of intelligence.

Self-Definition. With advances in cognition and expressive language ability, infants progress beyond self-recognition to **self-definition**. When infants have a concept of themselves as physical beings, they begin noticing differences and making comparisons between themselves and others on various dimensions such as age, size, and gender (Stipek, Gralinski, Kopp, 1990). Self-definition occurs when the self-concept is further defined and elaborated through the use of verbal labels. Stern (1985) referred to this level of self-concept formation as the "verbal self." At this stage, they can define themselves categorically in terms of personal pronouns (*I, me, you*), gender identity, personal attributes (*little, curly hair*), and possessions (*mine, yours*).

The appropriate use of the pronouns *I, me,* and *you* represents the acquisition of verbal labels for the self. It is also an indication that an infant has developed a self-concept that includes the perspective of others. Some infants begin to use their own name as early as 15 months (Brooks-Gunn & Lewis, 1982). Personal pronoun usage follows a few months later. Most toddlers use *I* (along with *me, my,* or *mine*) as their first personal pronoun around 20 to 22 months of age (Charney, 1980; Maccoby, 1980). This pronoun is frequently used interchangeably with the child's own name or the word *baby* (Maccoby, 1980). The second pronoun most toddlers use is *you,* which appears at about 2 years of age (Charney, 1980).

Young children have difficulty using pronouns correctly because they can be used to refer to different people. For example, *I* and *my* sometimes refer to the child's mother, the father, or other people, depending on who is speaking. The pronoun *you* is even more confusing because it is frequently used to refer to the baby as well as other people. Consequently, an infant may say such things as "you go" for "I go." Surprisingly, though, most infants have little difficulty using pronouns correctly (Maccoby, 1980). The proper use of pronouns is an indication that the infant's self-concept is becoming more objective, more socialized, and slightly less egocentric.

Self-descriptive statements such as "I play" or "I can do this" increase in frequency around 2 years of age (Kagan, 1981a; Stipek et al., 1990). In addition to knowledge about the self's physical features (e.g., "I have red hair"), the 2-year-old is aware of the self's capabilities and actions ("I play"). Awareness of capabilities ("I can't!") is cognitively more advanced than the awareness of physical features (Damon & Hart, 1982). An infant who demonstrates such awareness has taken a further step in the development of self-knowledge.

Sperry and Sperry (1995) studied the self-references of rural African-American toddlers recorded from their conversations about past and fantasy events with parents and other adults. Their statements reflected objective understanding of self in relation to physical, social, active, and psychological dimensions. Some of their comments were: "I have a stomach" (physical); "I gonna bite you" (active); "nobody let me" (social); "I'm not crying" (psychological) (Sperry & Sperry, 1995, p. 53). Boys tended to describe themselves in the context of fantasy events, whereas girls talked more about past events.

Age (or size) and gender are also features that infants use very early in the development of a self-concept. Infants are able to distinguish adults from babies between 6 and 12 months of age (Lewis & Brooks-Gunn, 1979). By the time they are one year old, infants exhibit more social responses to strange babies than to strange adults (Brooks-Gunn & Lewis, 1979). Presumably, infants perceive other infants as more similar to themselves than adults. Infants discriminate between male and female adults on the basis of voice and facial differences by the end of the first year of life (Fagot & Leinbach, 1993). The ability to tell the difference between boys and girls emerges in the second year of life. Gesell (1940) found that one-third of the 2-year-olds and three-quarters of the 3-year-olds he questioned knew whether they were boys or girls. Most children can correctly label photographs of themselves and others as a "boy" or "girl" by 2½ to 3 years of age (Etaugh, Grinnel, & Etaugh, 1989). However, they do not yet understand that gender is constant, as the following quotation indicates: *Teacher: "Lisa, are you a girl or a boy?" Lisa (age 3): "I'm a girl, but when I'm 4, I'll be a boy"* (Edwards, 1995, p. 54).

Self-Esteem

An infant's self-concept and self-esteem develop together. **Self-esteem** is one's self-evaluation based on the self-concept. The self-concept is the descriptive part of the self, whereas self-esteem is the evaluative and emotional component of the self. Other terms that are sometimes used as synonyms for self-esteem are self-love, self-respect, self-acceptance, and self-worth. A child who has a positive self-concept will have a high level of self-esteem, whereas a negative self-concept will result in a sense of low self-esteem.

The amount of respect, acceptance, and concerned treatment infants receive from their caregivers is especially important in developing a healthy sense of self-esteem (Coopersmith, 1967). Infants learn very powerful lessons from the countless small interchanges that occur with the caregiver each day. According to Stern (1985), the response of the parent must match or be harmonious with the baby's response. For example, the infant squeals with delight and the mother, in turn, gives the baby a gentle bounce. This is a response that matches and acknowledges the baby's level of excitement. If the parent consistently overresponds or underresponds, the baby's sense of self will be negatively affected. The development of self-esteem is affected by the extent to which infants perceive themselves as good or bad, pleasing or displeasing to their caregivers. The parent who usually scolds and frowns when changing a diaper may be communicating that the infant is a "bad" person. On the other hand, the parent who talks pleasantly to the infant during diaper changing is, in effect, saying, "You are a good person."

The development of self-esteem is also influenced by the child's ability to cause things to happen and control the behavior of others (Coopersmith, 1967). This ability is referred to as the infant's **perceived personal effectance** (Lamb, 1981a). Infants learn very early in life the extent to which they can or cannot control their world. At approximately 12 months, they are typically capable of determining when their behavior has had an effect and when it has not (Piaget, 1952). Black and other minority infants face problems develop-

A child's self-esteem is influenced by the ability to solve problems and "make things work."

ing feelings of control as they grow up because of overt and subtle forms of racial discrimination.

Infants experience a sense of power or helplessness depending upon whether or not they can accomplish what they set out to do. Gunnar (1978, 1980) found that 12-month-olds were considerably less afraid of a scary toy when they could control it than when they could not. Before that age, infants could not determine that they were completely in control of the circumstances activating the toy. Realistically, infants experience feelings of power at certain times and a sense of weakness at other times. For healthy self-esteem to develop, an infant needs to learn how to manage both types of feelings. When one feeling or the other—power or weakness—predominates, self-esteem suffers. "Healthy personality growth is always between the extremes" (Weiner & Elkind, 1972, p. 32).

The importance of caregiver-child interactions and other relationships are critical in the establishment of a healthy self-image. However, it is also important to recognize multiple influences and sources of information in the development of self-knowledge and self-esteem, including biological changes and experiences affecting central nervous system functions, cognitive and perceptual development, temperament, and emotional differentiation.

Self-development of Infants with Developmental Disorders

Infants with developmental disorders, such as Down syndrome, are vulnerable to problems in the development of the sense of self. Many of these infants are confronted with a variety of neurologically and other biologically based limitations that inhibit their perceptual processes and delay progress in self-understanding. Self-recognition of visual images by infants with Down Syndrome (DS) does not occur until around 3 years of age (Mans, Cicchetti, & Sroufe, 1978). Infants with DS are also delayed in using personal pronouns, and other language to describe their internal states, and actions. However, even though they lag behind, infants with DS go through the same stages in the development of self-understanding as typically developing infants. Their responses to visual images indicate that their feelings about themselves are basically positive (Cicchetti, 1991).

THEORY OF MIND

The infant's self-concept is developed in relation to other people. At some point in time the child recognizes that other people are separate individuals who have internal mental states including thoughts, feelings, intentions, and beliefs that are different from the child's own states of awareness. The ability to consider the psychological states of other people is referred to as **theory of mind**. In order to have a fully developed theory of mind a person must (1) understand that others have thoughts and beliefs that may differ from their own, and (2) understand that others sometimes have beliefs that may be false (Thomasello, 1995). For example, when children have developed an operational theory of mind they can hide from other people and reason as follows: "Mommy is looking for me in the closet, because she thinks I am hiding there; she doesn't know I am under the bed!" (Baron-Cohen, 1994). Theory of mind is viewed as a central mechanism that underlies communication, social development, and self-reflection. Children use their theory of mind to make sense of the behaviors of other people and events in the world. Researchers have found evidence that children who suffer from autism have an impaired theory of mind (Baron-Cohen, 1994).

The age at which children typically develop a theory of mind is a matter of debate. According to Piaget, children are ignorant about the theory of mind until 6 or 7 years because of egocentric thinking. Researchers and scholars generally believe that by 4 years of age, and possibly by 3 years of age, children have a rather sophisticated level of reasoning about their own mental states and those of other people (Wellman, 1994). For example, 3-year-olds use mental terms such as "think" and "know," and have begun to understand that people have, at times, beliefs that are false. They also understand that adults can be deceived, and they will tell lies to adults under certain conditions (Lewis, Stanger, & Sullivan, 1989).

Some scholars (e.g., Thomasello, 1995) believe infants exhibit the first glimmerings of a theory of mind between 1 and 2 years of age. For one thing, infants begin to demonstrate a sensitivity to the desires of other people when they point to and hand objects to adults in joint attention episodes (see Chapter 10). Joint attention episodes also imply that infants understand that their own visual field is shared by others. In addition, young infants look at the facial expressions of adults as social reference cues to guide their own behavior. Thomasello (1995) views such episodes as evidence that infants understand other people as having intentions or feelings that may be different from the infant's own experiences. At the very least these behaviors appear to be forerunners to a fully formed theory of mind and play a vital role in its development.

TEMPERAMENT

Much of the theoretical debate, as well as research, on infant personality has focused on the development of temperament. There are numerous theories of temperament. Definitions of temperament vary somewhat among theorists. One of the earliest definitions was developed by Chess, Thomas, and Birch (1965): **Temperament** is "the basic style which characterizes a person's behavior" (p. 32). Temperament has also been defined as individual differences in the behavioral expressions of emotionality and arousal (Campos et al., 1983). The following definition of temperament combines most of the common features of various theories: Temperament "refers to the stable behavioral and emotional reactions that appear early and are influenced in part by genetic constitution" (Kagan, 1994, p. 40).

Some theorists believe that temperament is the developmental forerunner, or the basic early raw material from which adult personality is formed (Buss, 1989). The terms temperament and personality are thus often used as synonyms. Other theorists, however, view temperament as one of the components of personality (Strelau, 1994). Personality is thus perceived as containing other characteristics, such as the self-concept, values, and motivation, that are broader than those encompassed by temperament. Currently researchers are trying to determine the extent to which infant temperament characteristics can be accounted for by five major adult personality factors (Angleitner & Ostendorf, 1994; Hagekull, 1994). However, the debate about the relationship between temperament and personality is likely to continue for some time.

Measurement of Temperament

The most frequently used method of assessing infant temperament is parent and caregiver reports (Bates, Wachs, & Emde, 1994). The **Infant Temperament Questionnaire** (Carey & McDevitt, 1978) is an example of a commonly used scale. However, temperament researchers question the accuracy and validity of parental and other caregiver questionnaires. Parent ratings of the same child may vary from time to time and from parent to parent. Parental perceptions of an infant's temperament are influenced by the parents' sex, race, socioeconomic status, mental health status, marital status, and satisfaction. Parents who report higher levels of anxiety and make more negative statements about themselves rate their infant's temperament more negatively (Wolk et al., 1992) Thus, temperament may be in the minds of parents as much as in the behavior of the infant.

Consequently, laboratory observational ratings of temperament (e.g., **Laboratory Temperament Assessment Battery**; Goldsmith & Rothbart, 1991), and naturalistic observation rating scales (e.g., Bates & Bayles, 1984) have been developed as alternatives to parental ratings. In addition, psycho-physiological measures such as heart rate, cortisol secretion, and electrical activity in the brain are currently used as measures of emotional changes that are considered to be indicators of temperament. A combination of measures is considered to be the best approach to the assessment of temperament for research purposes. Parent and teacher questionnaires can be useful in clinical and educational settings as long as the potential inaccuracies are kept in mind (Bates et al., 1994).

Dimensions of Temperament

A variety of dimensions or components of temperament have been identified (e.g., Buss & Plomin, 1975; Rothbart, 1981; Thomas & Chess, 1977). The nine components developed by Thomas and Chess (1977) in a long-term research study have been widely used:

1. *Activity level.* Inactive versus active motor behavior (reaching, crawling, sleep-wake cycle).
2. *Rhythmicity.* Regularity of schedule; predictability versus unpredictability of behavior (eating, sleeping, etc.).
3. *Approach or withdrawal.* Typical initial response to a new stimulus (people, food, toys, etc.).
4. *Adaptability.* Response to change in routine (bedtime, feeding, travel, etc.).
5. *Sensory threshold.* Level of stimulation needed to evoke a response (noise, pain, light, etc.).
6. *Intensity of response.* Energy level of response (crying, body movements, etc.).
7. *Quality of mood.* The degree of pleasant, happy, and friendly behavior versus unpleasant, unhappy, and unfriendly behavior.
8. *Distractibility.* The extent to which extraneous stimuli (noise, objects, etc.) interfere with or change ongoing behavior.
9. *Persistence and attention span.* Length of time an activity is pursued and the continuation of an activity in the face of interruptions or obstacles.

Thomas and Chess (1985) found that three basic temperamental patterns of behavior could be identified soon after birth. About 65 percent of the infants in their study were classified in one of the following groups:

1. *The Easy Child.* Babies in this group display regularity, respond positively to new situations, adapt quickly to change, and exhibit a relatively mild and generally positive mood. These babies quickly develop regular schedules of sleeping and eating. They smile a lot, accept most frustrations with little protest, and are easily comforted. They are a joy and a delight to their caregivers. About 40 percent of the babies in the Thomas and Chess study displayed this temperament pattern.
2. *The Difficult Child.* At the opposite end of temperamental extremes, these babies are irregular in body functions and are slow to develop good eating and sleeping routines. They cry longer and louder than other babies. The difficult child does not adjust easily to new foods, strangers, or changes in routine. This group comprised about 10 percent of the sample. Such an infant requires a lot of patience, stamina, and resourcefulness on the part of parents and other caregivers.
3. *The Slow-to-Warm-Up Child.* These babies are characterized by mild intensity of reactions (positive or negative). Although they are very active, infants in this group do not respond well initially to new situations. A mildly negative response can be observed in such a baby's first bath or encounter with a new person. However, over time and without pressure, the slow-to-warm-up infant will make appropriate adjustments and display quiet interest and enjoyment. About 15 percent of the infants studied were in this category.

Not all infants can be placed into one of these three groups on the basis of temperamental characteristics. Also, the percentage of infants identified by Thomas and Chess in each group does not necessarily represent the general population. Most children display a wide range of behavioral styles between the extremes and do not fit neatly into a particular category. "Easy" children are not always easy, and "difficult" children are not difficult in all situations (Thomas & Chess, 1985).

The concept of the "difficult child" has been especially controversial. Doubts about the usefulness of this classification have been expressed (Rothbart, 1982). If an infant is labeled "difficult," parents and other caregivers may focus on the negative characteristics of the child. By expecting the child to be difficult, problem behaviors may develop as a kind of self-fulfilling prophecy in which the child behaves as expected. On the other hand, the difficult child classification has been defended as a useful way of explaining to parents how infants vary in behavioral style and for planning childrearing strategies.

Other temperament researchers believe the nine "dimensions" or categories of temperament identified by Thomas and Chess should be reduced to a smaller list. For example, Bates and colleagues (1994; Bates, 1994) have proposed the following three general dimensions, or dispositions, that characterize temperament: (a) *negative emotionality,* including anxiety, inhibition, irritability, and fearfulness; (b) *positive emotionality*, which includes enthusiasm, excitement, happiness, and sociability; and (c) *constraint,* consisting of responsiveness to social control and self-restraint versus impulsivity. Kagan (1994) has summarized temperament characteristic into two basic contrasting types: *inhibited* and *uninhibited.* Inhibited infants display a shy, timid, and fearful profile of behaviors. Uninhibited infants present a behavioral profile that is bold, sociable, and outgoing. Currently, researchers are trying to reach an agreement on the basic dimensions of temperament.

Origins of Temperament

There appears to be widespread agreement that temperament is based on inborn biological foundations that interact with environmental influences to produce individual behavior characteristics (Bates, 1994). Researchers and clinicians are continuing their efforts to sort out the relative contributions of genetic, biological, and environmental influences. Twins and adopted children have been used as subjects in attempts to isolate genetic influences. If temperament is inherited, identical twins should be more alike temperamentally than fraternal twins. Adopted children would be expected to

display temperamental characteristics that more closely resemble those of their biological parents than of their adoptive parents. Evidence from these studies indicates that genetic factors are at least in part responsible for an individual's temperament (Plomin, Chipuer, & Loehlin, 1990).

For example, the results of extensive studies comparing siblings, twins and adopted children have produced estimates of the contribution of heredity to temperament ranging from 10 (Plomin & DeFries, 1985) to 57 percent (Braungart et al., 1992; Plomin & Saudino, 1994). Traits that appear to be inherited include shyness (Daniels & Plomin, 1985), emotionality, activity level, and attention span (Campos et al., 1983; Goldsmith, 1983; Saudino & Eaton, 1991; Braungart et al., 1992). There are indications that genetic influences on temperament become more evident as the infant grows older (Goldsmith & Campos, 1982; Plomin & DeFries, 1985).

Researchers have begun to use laboratory analysis to identify specific genes, or a combination of genes, that affect temperament in humans as well as animals (Bates, 1994). For example, Plomin and Saudino (1994) compared nine children who were rated by their mothers as being low in activity with nine children who were rated as highly active. They found that highly active children more frequently had a genetic marker that might be associated with their elevated activity. However, this is only a preliminary finding that must be confirmed in future studies, and scientists are a long way from establishing a definite link between temperament and specific genes.

Other scientists are attempting to locate biological roots of temperament within the brain (Steinmetz, 1994) and body chemicals (Gunnar, 1994), although studies have yet to produce conclusive findings. For example, the level of progesterone has been linked with the temperamental traits of intensity and approach-withdrawal. Infants who are classified as "easy babies" tend to have higher amounts of progesterone (Weissbluth & Green, 1984). Synthetic progestins administered to mothers to prevent threatened abortions may increase aggressive behavior in their infants after birth

(Reimish, 1981). Our knowledge about hormones and infant temperament is limited, but the list of body chemicals that are potential sources of influence is growing.

Cultural and ethnic factors play an important role in the development of temperament. Friedman (1981) compared the temperament of newborn Chinese, Japanese, and Caucasian-American infants. Chinese and Japanese infants were calmer, more passive, less excitable, and more adaptable than Caucasian infants. Chisholm (1981) found that Australian aboriginal infants were less irritable and more easily soothed than Caucasian-American infants. The extent to which such differences in temperament are attributable to variations in genetic backgrounds, childrearing practices, or other cultural influences has not been determined.

Continuity of Temperament

There is an increasing amount of agreement among researchers that at least some characteristics of temperament are relatively enduring. The identification of temperamental characteristics that are consistent and stable throughout the life span continues to be the subject of numerous investigations. For example, does a baby who is highly active continue to display similar temperamental characteristics as an older child and an adult? Hagekull (1994) found that intense and active infants tended to be active 4-year-olds. Negativity, shyness, and impulsivity were also temperamental characteristics that persisted from infancy into childhood. Kagan (1994) found that the response styles of inhibited and uninhibited 2- to 3-year-olds continued to be evident when they reached adolescence. Extreme temperamental characteristics appear to be somewhat more persistent over the years than more moderate temperamental characteristics.

Temperament does not, however, always follow a consistent, predictable course over time. Thomas and Chess (1985) traced the development of temperamental traits from infancy through adolescence. Some of their subjects displayed clear-cut consistency in one or several characteristics. On the other hand, some subjects were consistent in certain aspects of temperament during one period and in other aspects during other times. They found that some of the subjects changed completely on a number of temperament traits.

Temperament and Parent-Infant Interactions

An infant's temperamental characteristics obviously have an impact upon interactions with caregivers and other people. Fussy babies who cry a lot are likely to evoke more negative social responses than infants who are calmer and more easygoing. The baby who is friendly and approachable is likely to obtain more positive responses than the infant who is shy and withdrawn. Of course, the temperament and expectations of parents and other primary caregivers have to be taken into consideration.

The way the temperament of an infant matches the caregiving style of the parents greatly influences the socialization process. This is referred to as the **goodness-of-fit** between infant and caregiver (Thomas & Chess, 1977). Different styles of parenting are needed for the shy, inhibited infant than for the infant who is bold and uninhibited. Researchers have found that mismatches between infant temperament and parenting reactions increase the risk of behavior problems in childhood. Irritable infants who had angry, punitive parents, displayed more angry, noncompliant, and less confident behavior as 2-year-olds than less irritable infants who experienced similar parental responses (Crockenberg, 1987). Other researchers have found that the combination of difficult temperament and poor parent-infant relationships increases the risk of hostile behavior problems at 7 to 8 years of age (Sanson et al., 1991).

ENHANCING PERSONALITY DEVELOPMENT

Parents and other caregivers can make a positive contribution to the personality development of infants in numerous ways. The following are examples of some recommended activities and practices.

Promoting a Positive Sense of Self

1. Parents should select a baby's name with great care. Names should not be sexually ambiguous, difficult to spell or pronounce, or the basis for undesirable nicknames, initials, or rhymes, nor should they be otherwise exceptionally odd within the context of the child's cultural heritage.
2. Hold the young baby in front of a mirror and play games such as touching and naming body parts or making faces; say "See _____ in the mirror?" (Sparling & Lewis, 1979). Give the baby an unbreakable mirror to play with at about 2 months of age.
3. Take the baby's picture at various ages and look at them together with the baby, pointing out such characteristics as hair and eyes (McDonald, 1980).
4. Minority infants should be given dolls and toys that match their color and ethnic heritage, along with other dolls, toys, and materials. Parents should talk positively about characteristics of the body in ways that include skin color. In naming colors, point to the child's arm to indicate "brown," "black," "red," or "yellow" (Comer & Poussaint, 1976).
5. Play games using various various body parts (e.g, "This little piggy"). Sing songs about feet, hand, noses. Make up you own songs (Machado & Meyer-Botnarescue, 1997).

Establishing Basic Trust

1. Respond to the infant's cries and other signals promptly and consistently. Smile, talk, and relate to the infant cheerfully during caregiving routines.
2. Don't try to sneak away unnoticed when leaving the baby with a substitute caregiver. Never leave without saying goodbye.
3. "Peek-a-boo" and "hide-and-seek" are excellent games for teaching the baby that people disappear and return (Sparling & Lewis, 1979).

Promoting Autonomy

1. Encourage infants to do things for themselves as much as possible (e.g., pull a sock part of the way off or on and let the infant finish the task). Suggest solutions to problems without taking over.
2. Give the infant choices when possible and reasonable (e.g., what to eat or wear, things to do, materials to use, and ways to spend time).
3. Handle the infant's negativism with positive responses, firmness, and understanding. Avoid using shame as a response to undesirable behavior.
4. Allow the child to explore the environment, particularly new places, as freely as possible within the limits of safety, available supervision, and situational restraints.
5. Play games with infants that facilitate motor control (see Chapter 5).

Matching the Baby's Temperament

1. Accept and enjoy each baby's individuality.
2. Try to find caregiving strategies that match the baby's behavioral style. For example, infants who are more active and difficult to manage need more structure, more environmental control, and less stimulation. Very young infants who are sensitive to being touched sometimes respond favorably to being held on a pillow. Avoid trying to force "noncuddlers" to be held closely (see Chess, Thomas, & Birch, 1965; Brazelton, 1992).

SUMMARY

1. Personality is the total of the internal qualities and enduring, observable patterns of behavior that make up a person's individuality.

2. Freud emphasized the importance of childrearing experiences during infancy in shaping personality development. He identified three components of personality: id, ego, and superego. Personality development progresses through the oral and anal stages during infancy. If infants and children are treated too harshly or too permissively in each stage, personality problems are likely to arise.

3. The two stages of personality growth identified by Erikson that occur during infancy are trust versus mistrust, and autonomy versus shame and doubt. The emotional crisis that occurs during each stage must be resolved before healthy personality development can proceed.

4. According to Skinner, personality is simply a collection of behavior patterns that are acquired over time through the process of conditioning.

5. The main motivational force shaping personality is self-actualization according to Maslow

and Rogers. The basic component of personality is the self-concept. Maslow also identified a hierarchy of needs that must be met in the process of personality development.

6. One major component of personality that emerges during the infancy period is the self-concept, or the "sense of self." The development of self involves both subjective and objective dimensions. Three important accomplishments in the development of the self-concept occur during infancy: self-awareness, self-recognition, and self-definition.

7. Self-recognition, the ability of infants to correctly identify mirror or other images as their own, is demonstrated by most infants around 2 years of age.

8. Infants indicate that they have progressed beyond self-recognition to self-definition when they begin noticing differences and making comparisons between themselves and others on various dimensions such as age, size, and gender.

9. Self-esteem is one's self-evaluation based on the self-concept. Infants need respect, acceptance, and positive treatment from caregivers for the development of a healthy sense of self-esteem.

10. Infants with Down syndrome experience delays in self-concept development, but go through the same stages in the development of self-understanding as typically developing infants.

11. Theory of mind, or the ability to consider the psychological states of other people, is viewed as a central mechanism that underlies self-reflection. Infants may be exhibiting the appearance of a primitive theory of mind between 1 and 2 years of age when they point to and hand objects to adults in joint attention episodes, and use social-reference cues to guide their own behavior.

12. Temperament refers to the relatively stable behavioral and emotional reactions that appear early and are influenced, at least in part, by heredity. Many infants can be classified as temperamentally "easy," "difficult," or "slow-to-warm-up." Currently, researchers are trying to reach an agreement on the basic dimensions of temperament.

13. At least some characteristics of temperament, such as negativity, shyness, and impulsivity, appear to be relatively enduring from infancy through childhood. Temperament does not, however, always follow a consistent, predictable course over time. Researchers and clinicians are continuing their efforts to sort out the relative contributions of genetic, biological, and environmental influences.

14. Parents and other caregivers are advised to use childrearing strategies that promote a positive sense of self, establish basic trust and autonomy, and "fit" the baby's temperament.

12

Social Development

*When the first baby laughed for the
first time, the laugh broke into a
thousand pieces, and they all went
skipping about, and that was
the beginning of fairies.*
                                    —J. M. Barrie

Babies are social beings from birth. The newborn's
slightest expressions elicit responses from parents,
siblings, and strangers. As they get just a little older,
infants become partners in the give-and-take of
human relationships. Their interactions with other
people, including adults and peers provide the cornerstone for developing awareness and social competency. In this chapter we explore social
development during infancy. As you read this material, keep in mind that social development is largely
inseparable from emotional and personality
domains.

SOCIALIZATION PROCESSES

Socialization is the "process by which the newborn child is molded into the culture . . . and hence
becomes an acceptable person in that society"
(Smelser & Smelser, 1963, pp.102–103). Socialization involves establishing satisfactory relationships with other people and conforming to the
cultural standards. Infants become socialized
through interactions with parents and other people. The process of socialization involves learning
that other people are necessary and becoming
dependent on them. Almost as soon as this awareness develops, however, infants must begin to move
in the direction of establishing independence. The
crying, clinging behavior of the baby must be eventually replaced by more mature forms of social
behavior, such as verbal requests and independent
locomotion.

THE SOCIALLY COMPETENT INFANT

Social competence refers to an infant's ability "to
make use of environmental and personal resources
to achieve a good developmental outcome" (Waters

& Sroufe, 1983, p. 81). Socially competent infants
possess the skills necessary to get their needs met
and to accomplish their desired social goals.

Burton White (1985) has identified some of the
abilities an infant must eventually develop to
become socially competent:

1. Getting and holding the attention of adults in socially
   acceptable ways.
2. Expressing affection and annoyance when appropriate.
3. Using adults as resources if a task is too difficult to
   accomplish alone.
4. Showing pride in personal accomplishments.
5. Engaging in role-play and make-believe activities.
6. Leading and following peers.
7. Competing with peers.

These social abilities gradually emerge and develop
during the first two years of life. The socially competent infant makes behavior changes as needed to
conform with age-appropriate expectations. For
example, very young infants get the attention of
adults by crying, but older infants are expected to
use other means to get their needs met.

Parents of socially competent infants are accessible (but not overwhelming) and spend time interacting with their babies (White & Watts, 1973).
They organize a stimulating, safe, and nonrestric-
tive environment in which the infants can develop
a sense of autonomy. The type of discipline that is
positive, affectionate, and encouraging of autonomy is also a very important ingredient in the development of social competence. Infants who are
exposed to discipline that is negative, rigid, and
overprotective demonstrate less social competence
(Clarke-Stewart & Fein, 1983).

EARLY SOCIAL BEHAVIORS

The social behaviors of the infant are numerous
and varied. A timetable for the development of
some of the major milestones of social development is given in Table 12–1. Keep in mind that
social and emotional development are closely interrelated and most of the topics discussed under the
heading of social development are applicable to

Table 12–1 Milestones of Social Development

BEHAVIOR	USUAL AGE (MONTHS)
Knows mother by sight	1–2
Social smile	2–3
Social laughter	3–4
Notices and begins to interact with peers	3–6
Holds out arms to be held	5–6
Plays peek-a-boo	5–8
Shy with strangers	8–10
Plays pat-a-cake	9–10
Waves bye-bye	9–10
Gives a toy when asked	11–12
Negativism begins	11–12
Plays interactive games (e.g., tag)	24–30
Dresses self with supervision	30–36

Sources: Taken from the Bayley Scales of Infant Development, Copyright © 1969 by the Psychological Corporation. Reproduced by permission. All rights reserved. Frankenburg, Dodds, & Fandal, 1973; Knobloch, Stevens, & Malone, 1980. Used by permission.

the discussion of emotional development in the next chapter. Social relationships have a strong emotional component. The infant's social behaviors are based on emotional states of the infant as well as the emotional responses of others. Some of the early emotional indicators of the infant's growing social awareness and responsiveness include smiling, laughing, and crying.

Smiling

One of the earliest social behaviors is the social smile. Smiling usually reflects positive affect (joy, pleasure, delight) and is the "most significant aspect of social development to occur in the first half-year of life" (Bower, 1977, p. 49). The onset of a true social smile is a major milestone in social development. However, distinguishing social smiling from other types of smiling behavior is not an easy task. Infants' smiles have been classified in two categories—endogenous and exogenous (Spitz, Emde, & Metcalf, 1970).

Newborn infants can sometimes be observed smiling while they are asleep. These smiles are called **endogenous**, or spontaneous, smiles because they are passive and internally controlled. They appear to be triggered by changes in the level of arousal affecting central nervous system activity (Wolff, 1963). Contrary to what parents are sometimes led to believe, the newborn is not smiling because of "gas" or hunger sensations. Endogenous smiles cannot be thought of as indicating any conscious awareness of happiness or other emotions (Sroufe, 1977).

Within a week or two after birth, another type of smile can sometimes be elicited by gentle stimulation such as high-pitched baby talk or blowing on the baby's stomach. Such stimulation apparently increases the level of nervous-system excitation or arousal. A tiny smile follows within 6 to 8 seconds as the baby relaxes (Sroufe, 1977). These smiles are labeled **exogenous** because they are triggered by stimuli that are outside the infant (Wolff, 1963). The first elicited smiles, like the spontaneous smiles, are only partial smiles limited to the corners of the mouth.

During the second week of life, infants begin to smile when their eyes are open. Such smiles usually occur only when an infant is sated with food, drowsy, and "glassy-eyed" (Wolff, 1963). The smiles may occur spontaneously or can be elicited by the caregiver's voice. By the third week of life, babies begin to smile when they are fully awake and attentive. These smiles are fuller and more expressive. A nodding head accompanied by a high-pitched voice is a more potent stimulus for eliciting smiling at this age than a voice alone (Sroufe & Waters, 1976).

As they get older (4 to 5 weeks), infants smile in response to silent moving faces, sudden appearance of objects, and pat-a-cake games. At this point, sights are more effective than sounds in evoking smiles. As Bower (1977) points out, "the first complete smile appears to be elicited by the human voice; later the controlling stimulus shifts to the human face" (p. 38).

The age at which a **true social smile** appears is a matter of debate. Wolff (1963) considers the infant's first smile in response to a human voice, which occurs around 3 or 4 weeks of age, to be the

The social smile displayed by this infant is a major milestone of development.

beginning of true social smiling. The prevailing opinion, though, is that the social smile appears at approximately 6 to 8 weeks. At this point, the stimulus is clearly social, because the infant smiles in response to human faces (Emde, Gaensbauer, & Harmon, 1976).

Between 3 and 6 months of age, infants become more discriminating in their smiling behavior. Adults have to work harder to elicit smiles from them. They are less likely to smile at familiar stimuli unless a new feature is introduced. At the same time, however, infants smile at a wider range of stimuli and smile more often over the first two years of life. The frequency of smiling increases during the third and fourth months at about the same rate in infants from many cultures around the world (Super & Harkness, 1982). Mothers from all cultures and races appear to be equally capable of eliciting smiles from their infants, although their techniques vary from culture to culture (Super, 1981). Apparently the development of smiling is related to the infant's growing cognitive awareness and sophistication (Lewis & Michalson, 1983).

Laughing

There is a considerable amount of individual variation in the age at which infants begin to laugh. Infants typically begin to laugh between 2 and 4 months of age (Walden & Garber, 1994). At first, infants laugh only in response to physical stimulation such as tickling or to intense sounds such as "boom boom boom." Beginning at six months of age, infants laugh more at visual and social stimuli. Interactions such as peek-a-boo games or the mother shaking her hair or crawling on the floor elicit laughter (Sroufe & Wunsch, 1972).

During the second year of life, infants begin to laugh at things they can participate in, such as reaching for a protruding tongue (Sroufe & Waters, 1976). Babies thus progress developmentally from laughter produced from physical stimulation to laughter based on cognitive interpretations (Sroufe, 1977). The developmental progression of laughter may be seen when the same stimuli that make younger babies cry (e.g., mother wearing a mask), make older babies laugh.

Crying

Crying has been defined as the highest "state of arousal produced by nervous system excitation triggered by some form of a biological threat . . . such as hunger, pain, sickness or insult, or individual differences in threshold for stimulation" (Lester, 1985, p. 12). Crying begins as a reflex response that has survival value. It is designed to elicit nurturing and protective responses from the baby's caregivers.

The amount of crying typically increases until about 6 weeks of age, followed by a gradual decline as the infant gets older (Milgrom, Westley, & McCloud, 1995). Although the evidence is not conclusive, it appears that babies cry less often when their caregivers respond promptly and consistently (Bell & Ainsworth, 1972). Decreased crying and fussiness at night have been associated with increased holding and carrying throughout the day

(Hunziker & Barr, 1986). Cross-cultural studies have found less prolonged crying in societies in which infants remain close to the caretaker and in which extended carrying and rocking are practiced (Hunziker & Barr, 1986). However, infant caregivers should not get the impression that they need to extinguish all crying. A certain amount of crying is necessary for the infant's behavioral organization and normal physiological functioning. Crying allows the infant to reduce tension and serves an as important regulatory mechanism for adjusting internal states.

The social functions of crying change with age. For the first six months of life, infants cry to attract attention so that their physical and psychological needs will be met. Crying is also one way an infant tells a caregiver that it wants to be let alone. In other cases, crying may be used as a means of releasing energy or tension. However, there are periods when infants cry for no apparent reason. Some of the young infant's unexplained crying may be due to maturational changes in the brain that occur between 3 and 12 weeks of age (Emde et al., 1976).

Crying, like smiling, progresses from internal to external sources of stimulation and control (Hodapp & Mueller, 1982). During the newborn period, infants cry primarily because they are hungry, too hot or cold, or otherwise physically uncomfortable. Crying is also used by infants as a self-calming mechanism and a means of emotional regulation. As they get older, infant cries can be traced to external stimuli such as loud noises, "looming objects," frustration with play objects, fear of strangers, and the disappearance of the mother. After three months, crying changes its function to take on more intentional social, cognitive, and emotional communicative expressions (Lester, 1985; Milgrom et al., 1995).

Infant cries reflect an increasingly negative emotional tone from 12 to 18 months of age. Excessive crying and temper tantrums tend to reach a peak from 15 to 18 months of age. Around 24 months of age there are fewer crying episodes and a shift toward more positive emotional expression (Kopp, 1992). During the toddler years, crying

behaviors are frequently connected with caregiving episodes, such as diaper changing, getting hurt from falls or other injuries, and separation from parents (Kopp, 1992).

INFANT-ADULT PLAY

Although the importance of play has been emphasized in previous chapters, play also is an important process in social development. Play is the vehicle by which infants and toddlers practice the social skills needed for successful interactions with others. During the first year, infants' play partners are usually adults. The characteristics of infant-adult social play change as the infant matures. Whaley (1990) proposes the following stages, or levels, of infant-adult social play:

1. *Complementary/Reciprocal Social Play* (birth to 4 months). During this phase, play consists mainly of face-to-face interactions such as smiles, sounds, and gazes, with the adult as the "object."
2. *Complementary/Reciprocal Play with Mutual Awareness* (4 to 8 months). The focus of play shifts to objects provided by the adult, who observes and provides support as needed.
3. *Simple Social/Simple Object Play* (7 to 13 months). The role of the adult shifts to that of a "consultant" and base of support as infants locate their own objects and playthings. They begin "parallel" play with peers.
4. *Object Play with Mutual Regard* (13 to 18 months). The infant attends to objects and adults at the same time through games and conversations.
5. *Simple Parallel Play* (18 to 24 months). The toddler now plays independently, but with adults or peers nearby.

Beginning with the first phase, play progresses from mutual engagement to independent play by the child during the last phase.

Uzgiris and Raeff (1995) have identified three types of parent-child play that evolve during the infancy period: interpersonal play, object play, and symbolic play. **Interpersonal play** involves face to face interactions, social games, or routines. These playful interactions provide opportunities for infants to enjoy and practice socially appropriate ways of interaction and communication. In many cultures, parents play interactive games such as "peek-a-boo," "I'm gonna getcha," and the "this little pig went to the market" as soon as babies are responsive. Imitation is another type of interpersonal game. For example, the infant coughs reflexively and the mother playfully imitates the cough. The infant coughs again intentionally, the mother coughs, and the game has begun (Whaley, 1990). Physical play, particularly among fathers and infants, is another form of interpersonal play that occurs as infants get older.

Object play involves toys and play materials and is characterized by less mutual engagement than interpersonal play (Uzgiris & Raeff, 1995). During object play, parents serve as the infants' audience and function as a facilitator through comments and other responses. Parents structure and guide play through the provision of objects. Object play reflects the infants' culture and parental values in the socialization of infants and toddlers. For example, some American parents and childcare providers attempt to promote multicultural awareness through the provision of dolls or other figures representing people of different races. Among !Kung families of Africa, objects are valued as things to be shared, rather than personal possessions. Natural objects, such as grass, stones, and nutshells are used as objects of play. Grandmothers train infants to share objects by guiding them in handing objects to other people (Draper & Cashdan, 1988).

Symbolic play is the use of pretend games and/or objects to represent something else (e.g., a block becomes a gun). Between 1 and 2 years of age, infants and parents engage in joint episodes of symbolic play (Dunn, 1986). Both parents and infants initiate symbolic play at various times. As infants get older, symbolic play involves less parent participation and more independent play by the children (Uzgiris & Raeff, 1995). Symbolic play provides important socialization experiences by enabling toddlers to act out social roles (e.g., "mothers" and "fathers") that are not available to them in real life. Since symbolic play frequently involves the use of objects, it is difficult to distinguish from object play (Uzgiris & Raeff, 1995).

SOCIAL BEHAVIOR WITH PEERS

The socialization process involves interactions with the child's age mates, or peers. Infants in most societies begin to interact with each other very early in life. Whaley (1990) believes that early adult-infant play provides the foundation and social skills needed for infant peer interactions. However, Hanna and Meltzoff (1993) point out that competence with peers and adults may develop simultaneously. That is, at the same time they are developing competence in their interactions with adults, infants are developing competence in relating to their peers. In any event, research evidence is accumulating to show that meaningful social encounters occur among infant peers in everyday encounters.

Early Peer Interactions

Information about peer interactions during the first year of life is limited because the significance of these early interactions for socialization has been questioned (Whaley & Rubenstein, 1994). However, the existence of social exchanges between infants during the first year of life is well documented (Eckerman & Whatley, 1977). Early infant behavior directed toward a peer is relatively infrequent, brief, and simple. One study (Finkelstein et al., 1978), conducted in a day-care center, found that infants made contact with adults about seven times more often than they did with other babies.

The earliest infant interactions take the form of exploratory behaviors. At about 2 months of age, infants begin to look at other infants. Around 3 or 4 months of age, an infant will reach out and touch another infant. Most interactions of infants consist of a single overture and a response. In many instances (38 to 50 percent), social overtures of one infant to another do not elicit a response (Hartup, 1983). Even at this age, though, infants direct more sociable reactions (smiling, vocalizations, reaching) toward an actual infant than a mirror image (Field, 1990).

Smiles and vocalizations may be observed between infants by 6 months of age. When infants master a particular skill, such as babbling, they begin to use it to relate to a peer (Mueller & Vandell, 1979). Infants exhibit turn-taking behaviors in peer play at the end of the first year of life (Ross & Lollis, 1987). As soon as they become mobile, infants follow and attempt to make physical contact with one another, exploring each other's eyes, mouths, and ears (Vandell & Mueller, 1980). Their interactions become increasingly social and more complex as their skills in other areas (e.g., language) become more fully developed (Campos et al., 1983).

Toddler-Peer Interactions

The frequency and complexity of peer interactions increase rapidly with age. By two years of age, toddler-peer interactions are characterized by more repetitive, reciprocal, and cooperative patterns (Asher, Erdley, & Gabriel, 1994). They play run-and-chase and a variety of active games. Observations of peer interactions in group day care and informal play groups have shown that toddlers use imitation as a principal mechanism for relating to each other as well as extending their knowledge and skills (Meltzoff & Moore, 1993). Negative and aggressive behaviors, such as biting and hair pulling, increase during the second year (Mueller & Vandell, 1979) along with positive social behaviors. However, as infants get older, the proportion of negative interchanges relative to positive ones decreases.

Observations of toddlers, ages 18 to 25 months, in a French child-care center revealed various patterns of peer interactions (Sinclair, 1994). One pattern of play involved collaboration between two, and occasionally three, partners. In these episodes, the toddlers exchange objects. One child gives a small toy to the other child, who hands it back to the first one. This pattern may be repeated over and over. The children are more interested in the interactions of giving and taking than the objects that are passed back and forth. Another pattern of peer interaction involved shared activities and division of labor. One child performs part of a task, while other children carry out other parts. For example, one child puts a cylindrical container on a table, a second child adds another beside it, followed by several other children who put all the similar containers they can find on the table. These observations are consistent with those of Verba (1994) who

An infant will reach out and touch another child at an early age.

found that peers as young as 13 to 17 months put together their ideas and actions to solve problems and achieve shared goals.

Toddlers are capable of forming genuine friendships with each other. An infant-peer friendship has been defined as a relationship characterized by "proximity seeking, sharing, positive affect, and play, . . . with the two friends specifically preferring each other as interaction partners" (Vandell & Mueller, 1980, p. 190). Howes (1987) found that 51 percent of children between 16 and 33 months of age engaged in reciprocal friendships that were maintained for at least a year. Toddler friendships are characterized by loyalty, helping, sharing, togetherness, mutual interests and preferences (Whaley & Rubenstein, 1994).

Press and Greenspan (1985a) followed the development of a friendship between two children in a toddler play group over a year's time. During that year their friendship progressed through several stages, from attraction and exploration to including other children in their friendship circle. They shared such activities as looking at books, working puzzles, and loading and unloading trucks and containers together. The following incident illustrates how their friendship included the discovery and sharing of humor:

> Dan and Ned's first shared joke happened like this: One day at snack time, when the children were 21 and 23 months old, respectively, Dan slapped his hand on a small blob of applesauce that had fallen from his spoon onto the table. He then looked across the table at Ned and wriggled with pleasure. Ned stared, caught his breath in surprise, and then laughed the most infectious belly laugh ever heard in that room. Dan was delighted and responded by repeating his act, after which Ned again dissolved in laughter (Press & Greenspan, 1985a, p. 28).

Like older children and adults, toddlers are distressed when their friendships are terminated. Whaley and Rubenstein (1994) reported a case in which Orly left a child-care group, leaving her friend Carly behind. Carly "regressed to using a bottle more frequently and went back to wearing diapers" (p. 396).

Toddler-Peer Cultures

Corsaro and Eder (1990) believe that children form a "peer culture" that includes a set of shared routines, productive activities, values, and concerns that are separate from the world of adults. In some ways peers are as important as adults in children's acquisition of social skills and knowledge. Experiments with 14- to 18-month-old infants show that they observe and readily imitate behavior modeled by their peers in laboratory, home, and day-care settings even after a 48-hour delay (Hanna & Meltzoff, 1993). The extent to which infants form their own peer culture has not been determined. However, an increasing number of infants participate daily in some type of group child day care. Once they enter child-care settings, toddlers begin to develop a strong group identity.

Researchers are studying the nature and characteristics of infant peer interactions in groups and other contexts along with questions about the influence of peers on individual development. A major feature of peer culture from the earliest years consists of challenges to adult authority and attempts by children to gain autonomy and control over their own activities (Corsaro & Eder, 1990). Between 14 and 24 months of age, toddlers begin to find amusement in forbidden behaviors and share in the laughter of their older siblings as a challenge to adult authority (Dunn, 1988). Nursery school children find ways to circumvent rules imposed by teachers. For example, they "smuggle" forbidden toys or other objects from home to covertly share with their peers (Corsaro & Eder, 1990).

Influences on Peer Interactions

Peer interactions are affected by a variety of factors. Prior experience with peers, siblings, and older children tends to contribute to the ability of an infant to engage in peer interactions (Campos et al., 1983; Shirley, 1931). These interactions are more frequent and complex among infants who are acquainted with each other and who play in dyads (twos) rather than in larger groups (Campos et al.,

1983). Infants from disadvantaged backgrounds tend to be less willing to interact with peers than infants from middle-class families (Press & Greenspan, 1985b).

Infants interact more with peers when they are in a familiar setting than in an unfamiliar place. Infants typically reach out to peers more frequently in their own home than in someone else's home (Field, 1990). The availability of toys, the types of toys, and the play space available also affect peer interactions. Infants interact more with peers in floor play with several toys than in play pens with a more limited number of toys (Field, 1990). Large, nonportable toys facilitate more frequent and positive interactions, whereas small toys generate more exploration, conflict and negative interactions (Brownell & Brown, 1992). Infants tend to interact more with each other under "toy absent" conditions than they do under "toy present" conditions (Vandell, Wilson, & Buchanan, 1980). Several studies indicate that infants and toddlers are more sociable and display more complex interactions with each other in the absence of toys (Brownell & Brown, 1992).

Familiarity with playmates also affects peer interactions. Studies of infants in group settings indicate that infants engage in more body contact, touching, imitative behaviors, and smiling with acquaintances than with strangers. Peer interactions were observed in a nursery school at the beginning and the end of a semester in a group of infants younger than 15 months of age and in another group of older toddlers (Roopnarine & Field, 1983). The number of interactions increased in both age groups during the semester.

The influence of parents appears to be critical in determining the quantity and quality of peer interactions. Toddlers who are not securely attached to their mothers have been observed initiating the greatest number of social overtures to unfamiliar peers. However, toddlers who are securely attached to their mothers are more effective in peer interactions (Jacobson et al., 1986). Socially competent infants typically have socially competent parents. Researchers (Vandell & Wilson, 1987) found that 6- and 9-month-old infants who had extensive turn-taking experiences with their mothers engaged in extensive turn-taking interactions with a peers.

MORAL DEVELOPMENT

The process of moral development involves learning and internalizing the rules and principles that govern human behavior. Moral values include such universal standards as honesty, truth, justice, respect for life, and concern about the welfare of others. Morality also includes social conventions concerned with manners and other rules that vary from culture to culture. Moral development includes cognitive functions involved in making moral judgments and the development of a set of emotions (e.g., feelings of guilt) related to the development of a conscience and other internal mechanisms for regulating actions. Infants function at a premoral level and are not expected to understand moral principles. Neither are they considered as being "morally" accountable for their actions. However, moral development has its roots in infancy. The socialization of moral behaviors begins as soon as infants understand their first words and become mobile. Very early infants hear words such as "No!" and "Don't touch!" that are designed to set limits on their activities. In addition, the emergence of feelings of empathy and guilt are viewed as motivating factors in early moral behavior (see Chapter 13).

Emde and his colleagues (1991) have identified some of the processes through which morality is shaped during infancy. They believe that early moral development is based on information and feelings acquired as "procedural knowledge." This type of knowledge is obtained through experiences outside of awareness and memory. For example, infants demonstrate procedural or functional knowledge of one of the rules governing reciprocity of human behavior when they engage in turn-taking interactions with caregivers. The infant's turn-taking capacity may be the earliest expression of the "golden rule"(do unto others as you would have them do unto you). Although infants demonstrate the capacity to behave in accordance with a variety of moral rules, they do not need to remember or conceptualize these rules before they are acquired.

Infants internalize "do's" and "don'ts" through social referencing and negotiation with caregivers (Emde et al., 1991). During the second year of life, toddlers increasingly turn to caregivers for behavioral cues about how to deal with uncertain situations. Such repeated interactions with caregivers lead to the internalization of some rules for the self-regulation behavior. Emde, Johnson, and Easterbrooks (1987) found that 2-year-olds behave in accordance with social rules and expectations as long as a caregiver is present for social referencing. They also found that toddlers often "tested" the limits of mild parental prohibitions. For example, if an infant was moving toward a tape recorder and the parent expressed a slight "No, No" head shake, the infant might continue toward the tape recorder until the parent responded with a sterner prohibition. At this stage, toddlers often negotiate with caregivers about the rules by persistence, charm, or acts of "cuteness." Through such interactions with their caregivers, infants internalize strategies of negotiation. These negotiation strategies are useful in helping one resist temptation or gain approval for behaviors that might otherwise by questioned.

The toddler years lay the foundation for moral development, including respect for authority, and compliance with reasonable rules and requests. By three years of age, children typically have internalized rules that govern the "do's" and "don'ts" of behavior in a variety of situations. They have also formed a set of moral emotional "signals" that guide their behaviors (Emde et al., 1991). Their language ability and cognitive capacity now make it possible to discuss moral rules and principles. The results of studies using "moral dilemmas" indicate that, at this age, children show evidence of having internalized rules and feelings of empathy involved in acts of compassion. For example, Buchsbaum and Emde (1990) presented a play situation to 3-year-olds that involved the need to get a bandage for a hurt child. The children were told that there was a rule prohibiting them from going to the bathroom shelf where the bandages were

located. The children understood and struggled with the dilemma and many found a way to achieve a positive outcome.

Most children tend to value kindness over cruelty and "good" over "bad" behavior (Kagan, 1994). However, during the second and third years of life children also display evidence of immoral behavior. In spite of their capacity for empathetic feelings, they take pleasure in breaking rules and exhibit behaviors that are intended to upset or hurt others (Dunn, 1987). Thus, the process of socialization for moral development not only involves encouraging prosocial acts, but helping children control antisocial behavior as well.

Prosocial Behavior

In general, parents and other caregivers encourage infants to display prosocial responses in their interactions with others. Prosocial behaviors include a variety of positive, socially desirable activities, including sharing resources, nurturance, helping, and cooperation. Such prosocial behaviors are considered to be important for the development of **character**—an individual's "general approach to the dilemmas and responsibilities of social life" (Hay et al., 1995, p. 24). Character is an important component of moral development.

Sharing. One of the earliest prosocial behaviors exhibited by humans is sharing. Shortly before their first birthday, infants begin to share resources with other people, including their own age mates (Hay et al., 1995). At around this time, infants begin to offer their food, toys, and other possessions, including their pets, to their companions. They point to objects they wish others to see. They share new toys as often as old ones, scarce resources as well as ones that are plentiful (Hay et al., 1991). For example, Joshua, a toddler who came to his neighbor's door for Halloween "trick or treat" attempted to dump his bag of candy into the bowl of candy that was held out for him to select a treat. At first a toddler may extend an object, but show ambivalence about giving it up. However, by 18 months of age, virtually all toddlers everywhere show, offer, and give objects to others (Hay et al., 1995).

Because sharing is so strong and common among toddlers, this behavior is considered to be innate. At this age, sharing behaviors do not appear to be affected by social reinforcement or modeling. Simply requesting an object from a toddler, or engaging in games of give-and-take, have been found to be the most effective ways of increasing rates of sharing (Hay, 1994). Children who do not share at all between the ages of 18 and 36 months are more likely to display behavior problems (Hay et al., 1995). Since young autistic children do not show or offer objects to their companions, the absence of sharing behavior may be an early sign of autism (Hay et al., 1994).

As infants grow older, the tendency to share with others evidently becomes weaker and more individualized. Twenty-four-month-olds are less likely to share in response to a peer's interest in an object than are twelve-month-olds (Hay, 1994). In a laboratory setting, 3-year-olds are less likely to share objects with their mothers than are 2-year-olds (Hay et al., 1995). Researchers have found that sharing occurs at relatively low rates in preschool classrooms (Hay, 1994). As children grow older they become aware that it is not always in their own best interest to share indiscriminately. This may be the reason why preschool children are more likely to share with their friends than with casual acquaintances (Hay, Castle, & Jewett, 1994).

Compliance. The child's willingness to modify behavior in accordance with the expectations of caregivers is generally considered to be a prominent indicator of prosocial tendencies. Even though toddlers are notorious for their negativism, they tend to comply with requests more often than they refuse (Hay et al., 1994). Children generally tend to become increasingly obedient during the second and third years of life (Howes & Olenick, 1986). However, compliant behavior is likely to vary according to the situation (what is being demanded) and a child's relationship with the person making the request (Schneider-Rosen & Wenz-Goss, 1990). When commands are unambiguous and are made

with sensitivity, toddlers tend to take delight in pleasing their caregivers (Edwards, 1995).

Antisocial Behaviors

Negativism and Aggression. About the time they start becoming mobile, infants begin to hear commands from caregivers intended to protect them from dangers and disapproval, such as "Get that button out of your mouth!" or "Don't pull on the cat's tail!" In many instances, older infants and toddlers refuse to comply with caregiver requests. In other instances, children do not comply because they do not understand the request or have forgotten a previously stated limit. Kopp (1992) has identified a variety of behaviors that are characteristic of resistance including negativism (No!), physical resistance (kicking, throwing), crying, ignoring, arguing (why?), and negotiation (excuses, bargaining). They may refuse to eat, take a bath, or go to bed. Ignoring, or other passive behaviors, and direct defiance are strategies used by younger toddlers. Bargaining and direct refusal are more typical of older toddlers (Kopp, 1992).

Noncompliance. Noncompliant and negativistic behavior reaches a peak at about two years of age and gradually declines during the preschool years (Edwards, 1995). This is why the stereotype of "the terrible two's" has been applied to this age period. However, this pattern of behavior does not apply to all two-year-olds and may be more prevalent among American-Caucasian toddlers reared in highly stimulating and demanding middle-class families than in other cultures (Kopp, 1992).

Adults can encourage compliance by telling the child in advance when a change of activity is necessary. "As soon as the cartoon is over, we will be going home." Adults should not insist on instant obedience. Parents and other adults should also avoid nagging and repeating demands over and over. The adult should be sure that the child hears and understands the instructions (Laishley, 1983). The toddler's "no" should not be interpreted literally (Weiser, 1982), because it may be an experimental response to see what will happen. Children usually comply willingly if the adult is firm and positive, as in the following example:

> Two-year-old Karen was busily engaged in caring for her baby doll right before lunch time. The teacher approached, saying "Let's go to the sink, Karen, and I'll help you wash your face and hands." "No!" Replied Karen. The teacher smiled, took Karen by the hand, and said "Come on, Karen, it will only take a minute, and then it's time to eat. Let's go." Karen smiled and teasingly pretended a reluctant walk over to the sink (Weiser, 1982, p. 197).

If adults are reasonable, firm, and kind in their demands, children tend to respond favorably.

Temper Tantrums. Negativism and noncompliance often take the form of kicking, screaming, throwing objects, and other violent behavior. Temper tantrums are the toddler's way of responding to behavioral restrictions, denial of wishes, and other frustrations that conflict with the desire for control and independence. Tantrums are common around the world, although parental responses vary among and within cultures (Broude, 1995). If adults respond appropriately, most toddlers grow out of this behavior. Brazelton (1992) believes that temper tantrums at this stage result from the toddler's inner turmoil and a struggle between dependence and independence. He advises parents to stand back and allow the child to gain inner control. In some cases it may be necessary to prevent the child from attacking someone or destroying property. In a group situation the child needs to be removed until the tantrum subsides. However, the child should not receive special attention in the process. Above all, this behavior should not be reinforced. A child should not be allowed to use a tantrum to obtain a desired goal. Adults need to remain as calm as possible and avoid angry, violent responses.

Hitting. Toddlers hit each other to protect or regain possessions or out of a sense of frustration and loss of control. Hitting is also a means of playful aggression without hostile intent. When one child hits or pushes another, the caregiver quickly assesses the situation to see what happened. For older toddlers it may not be necessary to intervene because they often work things out on their own. For younger toddlers and in cases of a child being a bully, the caregiver needs to respond. The caregiver should eye contact with the aggressor and state firmly: "Hitting is not allowed because it hurts!" At the same time, an alternative response is suggested: "I know that Seth made you angry when he took your hat, but you need to ask him to give it back, or come to me for help" (Leavitt & Eheart, 1985). The child who continues to be aggressive can be removed from the situation briefly but should be given praise and reinforcement for solving conflicts at other times in nonaggressive ways.

Biting. Day-care providers who work with toddlers typically report biting to be one of the most common and difficult behavior problems. Caregivers need to understand that infants bite other people for different reasons. Some bite out of a sense of curiosity, playfulness, or the need to satisfy oral urges. For other infants, biting may result from attempts to protect their space, their possessions, or to obtain scarce resources. Biting can be handled in much the same way as other aggressive acts, with firmness and suggestions for alternative ways (e.g., "Use your words!") to respond to frustration. Most of the attention should be focused on the child who has been bitten. It is not advisable to bite the child in return or to tell the victim to bite back. This response is generally not effective and may only reinforce biting behavior. In group situations, biting behavior can be prevented or minimized by providing plenty of toys, interesting activities, and close supervision, while avoiding too many adult restrictions.

GENDER-ROLE SOCIALIZATION

Gender-role acquisition is a critical component of the socialization process. To some extent, gender differences in behavior can be attributed to genetic factors and hormonal influences. The degree to which actual behavioral differences between males and females are determined by biological endowment or childrearing practices has not been determined. Similarities as well as differences in male and female behaviors have been found in different cultures. Scientists generally believe that from the beginning of life, a wide variety of social and cultural influences combine with biological influences in shaping gender-related behaviors. Cross-cultural studies show that parents in different societies throughout the world socialize their sons and daughters in different ways (Garcia Coll & Meyer, 1993). The infancy period is often considered unimportant in sex-role development. However, upon close examination we find that powerful environmental influences are in operation during this period and an impressive set of gender-related concepts and behaviors have been acquired by 3 years of age (O'Brien, 1992).

In the United States, babies typically receive the "pink" and "blue" treatment with color-coded blankets, presents, and clothes as soon as their gender is known (Fagot, 1995). Adult perceptions, expectations, and treatment of an infant depend to some degree upon the infant's gender. Researchers have found that adult descriptions of infants vary depending upon sex-stereotyped dress. An infant dressed as a girl is more likely to be described as "frail" and "sweet," whereas a baby dressed as a boy is more likely to be described in terms such as "tough" and "sturdy." Babies' facial expressions are also interpreted differently depending upon their perceived gender identity (Condry & Condry, 1976).

The extent to which parents provide different socialization experiences for male and female infants varies among families. In most American families, boys and girls have different sets of toys. Generally, girls are given more latitude than boys to display cross-gender behaviors, especially by fathers. For example when a 2-year-old boy pushed his sister's doll carriage down the sidewalk, the father commented, "Look at the little sissy!" However, studies indicate that differences in parental sex-role socialization practices for male and female infants may not be as consistent and widespread as commonly believed (Fagot, 1995; Fagot &

Hagan, 1991). Parents often use the child's behaviors as cues to guide their responses. There are some indications that parents begin to display more traditional gender-stereotyped responses to infants about the same time infants display gender-related knowledge and behaviors (Fagot, 1995). This indicates that infants are not passive creatures but active participants in the sex-role socialization process. Even though parents may try to avoid gender stereotyping in their childrearing practices, the effects of other caregivers, peers, television, and other cultural influences often counteract parental efforts.

Researchers have looked at the emergence of gender-based behaviors during the infancy period. Few reliable behavioral differences in newborn male and female infants have been observed (O'Brien, 1992). However, some gender differences such as aggression and assertiveness in play emerge very early (Jacklin & Maccoby, 1983). The appearance of other infant sex-typed behaviors evidently coincide with the ability of infants to label their own gender between 2 and 3 years of age (Fagot, 1995). Toddlers who understand labels for boys and girls tend to play more with same-sex playmates, avoid female-typed toys and play longer with male-typed toys than the toddlers who cannot label their gender (Fagot & Leinbach, 1989; Weinraub et al., 1984).

Gender awareness affects children in other ways. In one study, when asked to approach another child, children as young as age 3 stopped farther away when the other child was of the opposite gender (Wasserman & Stern, 1978). Previously unacquainted 33-month-old children of the same sex were observed to engage in higher levels of social behavior when playing with a same-sex peer than an opposite-sex peer (Maccoby, 1990) As they approach 3 years of age, children begin to increasingly demonstrate a preference for same-sex peers as play partners. Although many of their gender-based perceptions and behaviors are somewhat fragile and unstable, by 3 years of age children have adopted much of their culture's sex-typed division of activities and attributes (O'Brien, 1992).

ASSESSING SOCIAL DEVELOPMENT

There are relatively few standardized instruments specifically designed to assess social skills of infants. The **Vineland Adaptive Behavior Scales** (Sparrow, Balla, & Cicchetti, 1984) are available in three forms to assess the ability of individuals to take care of themselves and get along with others from birth to adulthood. Since these scales cover a wide age range, their usefulness in screening young infants for social competence is somewhat limited. Several standardized instruments, such as the **Battelle Developmental Inventory** (Newborg et al., 1988) contain subscales for assessing social skills.

Assessments of infant social skills are best observed in natural contexts such as play (Odom & Munson, 1996). The observation of infants as they play in structured and unstructured settings is a relatively new procedure for assessing social development as well as other abilities. Although various scales are available for use in play-based observations, **Transdisciplinary Play-Based Assessment (TPBA)** is one of the most widely used approaches (Linder, 1993). TPBA is conducted by a team of professionals and a parent who observe the child in a play session. The session consists of various phases of structured and unstructured activities in which the child interacts with a facilitator, plays alone, with a parent, and with a peer. Team members record their observations on forms provided and determine the child's level of functioning. The information is used to make recommendations for facilitating development.

FACILITATING SOCIAL DEVELOPMENT

There are numerous practices and activities that parents as well as other caregivers can use to promote healthy social development. In general, the most important thing is to give the infant a feeling of being cared for and loved. The following are some recommended principles and practices.

1. Allow babies to have moments of peace. It is important to respect an infant's desire not to interact with people or other outside stimuli from time to time (Provence, 1967). However, the infant's cries for help should never be ignored.
2. Read toddlers stories that have very simple "moral" lessons (Lickona, 1986).
3. Make up rhymes for rules to help toddlers remember (Lickona, 1986).
4. Encourage independency and self-sufficiency. In general, avoid doing things for infants that they can do for themselves.
5. There should be opportunities for the baby to be part of the adult world. An infant should have opportunities to interact with adults of both sexes, and various ages, racial, and ethnic backgrounds.
6. Provide a variety of culturally and developmentally appropriate toys and materials for infants (see Chapter 14), but do not allow toys to substitute for personal interactions.
7. Play interactive games with infants such as "peek-a-boo" and "pat-a-cake" as soon as they can reciprocate such interactions. Increase the complexity of games (e.g., pretend "tea parties") as infants get older.
8. Provide opportunities for toddlers to play with other toddlers in carefully supervised situations.

Additional suggestions may be found in sources such as Bromwich (1980); Cryer, Harms, & Bourland, 1987; Grasselli and Hegner, 1980; Karnes, 1982; Silberg, 1993; Sparling and Lewis, 1979; Weiser, 1982; and White, 1985.

SUMMARY

1. Socialization is the process by which infants learn to behave in accordance with cultural expectations through interactions with parents and other people.

2. Socially competent infants possess the ability to relate to other people effectively and to get their needs met. Mothers of socially competent babies are accessible, create a safe, stimulating environment, and provide appropriate discipline.

3. Social smiling, laughing, and crying are the first indicators of the infant's social awareness. The

age at which the first true social smiles typically appear is debatable and depends on the criteria that are used to define smiling. The earliest age at which social smiling is considered to appear is 3 or 4 weeks. Babies begin to laugh at 3 or 4 months of age. Crying is a reflexive activity that is present at birth but becomes more socially responsive with age.

4. Play is an important vehicle by which infants and toddlers practice the social skills needed for successful interactions with others. Infant-adult social play goes through 5 phases, progressing from mutual engagement to independent play. Three types of parent-child play evolve during the infancy period: interpersonal play, object play, and symbolic play.

5   The earliest infant-peer social interactions begin at approximately 2 months of age, when infants look at each other. Their interactions become more complex and frequent with age as they begin to combine smiling and laughter with playing games.

6. By 2 years of age, toddler-peer interactions are characterized by more repetitive, reciprocal, and cooperative patterns. Toddlers form genuine friendships that include loyalty, helping, sharing, togetherness, mutual interests and preferences.

7. Peer relationships are important in children's acquisition of social skills and knowledge. Toddlers form a "peer culture" that includes a set of shared routines, productive activities, values, and concerns that are separate from the world of adults. Peer culture encourages challenges to adult authority and attempts by children to gain autonomy and control over their own activities.

8. Peer interactions during infancy are influenced by social class, the social setting, availability of toys, and parent-infant attachment.

9. The process of moral development involves learning and internalizing the rules and principles that govern human behavior. Moral development has its roots in infancy as infants learn "do's" and "don'ts" through social referencing and negotiation with caregivers. By 3 years of age, children typically have internalized rules and formed morally based emotional signals that govern behavior in a variety of situations.

10. Prosocial behaviors exhibited by infants include sharing and compliance with adult requests.

11. Antisocial behaviors include noncompliant and negativistic behaviors that reach a peak at 2 years of age. Negativism and noncompliance often take the form of temper tantrums. Infants and toddlers express their aggressive tendencies through hitting and biting their peers.

12. Gender-role acquisition is a critical component of the socialization process that begins during infancy. Although many of their gender-based perceptions and behaviors are somewhat fragile and unstable, by 3 years of age children have adopted much of their culture's sex-typed division of activities and attributes.

13. Instruments and procedures that are used to assess infant social development include the **Vineland Adaptive Behavior Scales**, **Battelle Developmental Inventory**, and **Transdisciplinary Play-Based Assessment**.

14. Parents and other caregivers can use a variety of games and activities to promote healthy social development, independency, and self-sufficiency.

13

Emotional Development

Moving between the legs of tables and chairs,
Rising or falling, grasping at kisses and toys,
Advancing boldly, sudden to take alarm,
retreating to the corner of arm and knee,
Eager to be reassured, taking pleasure
In the fragrant brilliance of the Christmas tree. . .
                                    —T. S. Eliot

The above quotation illustrates the richness of the emotional life of infants as they explore their world. Virtually all the infant's interactions with people and things in the environment are punctuated with various nuances of emotional moods and expressions. Emotional development encompasses the origin and differentiation of specific emotions. It also includes developmental changes in emotional expression and the infant's understanding of emotions in themselves and others. In this chapter we will take a look at the general course of emotional development during the first three years of life. We will consider some of the theoretical issues involved in scientific discussions of emotional development along with potential influences on emotional expression. The formation of attachment between infants and their caregivers and the importance of infant-caregiver interactions will be discussed. The infant's self-regulation of emotions and the understanding of emotions expressed by others will also be considered. Finally we will look at infant mental health along with some ways to facilitate emotional development.

DEFINITIONS

The first question we must consider is "What is an emotion?" The term **emotion** comes from a Latin word meaning to "excite," "stir up," or "agitate." In common usage, emotions are often described simply as "feelings." Scientifically, however, emotions are defined more broadly than mere feelings. Greenspan and Greenspan (1985) define emotions as "complex, subjective experiences that have many components, including physical, expressive, cognitive, and organizing, as well as highly personalized, subjective meanings" (p. 7). **Affect** is a term that is often used interchangeably with emotion.

Technically, affect is used to refer to the subjective feeling component and the expressive component of emotion (Sroufe, 1996). The experience and expression of emotion involve complex changes in facial expressions, body movements, respiration, heart rate, blood pressure, hormonal, and other bodily changes. Current views emphasize the functional aspects of emotions in establishing, maintaining, or disrupting relationships between the infant and other people (Campos, Campos, & Barrett, 1989).

THEORIES OF EMOTIONAL DEVELOPMENT

The varying definitions of emotions are the result of many divergent theories about their nature, function, and development. Theories of emotional development can be summarized in terms of biological, socialization (learning), interactionist positions, and systems perspectives. The biological model emphasizes that an infant is innately equipped, or prewired, with emotions. The young infant's emotions are viewed as comparable to sneezes and knee jerks. They are "unlearned, biologically controlled and subject to relatively little socialization influence" (Lewis & Saarni, 1985, p. 2).

According to socialization, or learning, theories, emotional development is shaped chiefly by social influences. This approach does not deny the existence of biological foundations but places more emphasis on environmental experiences. In recent years, theorists have tended to adopt an interactionist perspective whereby emotions are seen as a synthesis of biological and socialization processes. The innate potential for emotional expression is realized in different ways, depending on the infant's experiences with caregivers and other socialization circumstances (Murphy, 1983).

A widely accepted variation of the interactionist perspective is dynamic systems theory (see also Chapter 8). According to this theory, emotional development involves the complex interplay between multiple response systems within the infant and external sociocultural influences. Response systems within the infant include cognitive, motor, and neurophysiological processes. Examples of influential social systems are parent-child dyads and other caregiver-infant combinations.

INFLUENCES ON EMOTIONAL DEVELOPMENT

Physiological Factors

Most definitions of emotion acknowledge the involvement of numerous body processes. Researchers are still trying to determine the extent to which physiological processes influence emotion on the one hand, and are influenced by emotions on other hand. According to Sroufe (1996), developmental changes in the brain parallel emotional development during the infancy period. We know that certain regions or networks of the brain and nervous system are connected with emotional activity. For example, the area of the brain referred to as the amygdala appears to be a key structure in mediating fear and anger responses (LeDoux, 1993). In addition, numerous neurochemicals (e.g., catecholamines) and hormones (e.g., cortisol) have been identified as possible influences on emotionality (Panskepp, 1993; Walden & Gerber, 1994).

Emotional experiences are affected by a complex interplay between various structures of the brain body chemistry that mutually influence each other in ongoing processes. For example, researchers have found that stress elevates the level of cortisol in the brain. Over time, high cortisol levels contribute to the death of brain cells, reduce the synaptic connections, and alter the emotional circuitry of the brain (Gunnar et al., 1996). Affected infants have more difficulty in developing feelings of empathy, forming attachments, and in establishing emotional control (see Chapter 5). In contrast, infants who develop positive attachments to their caregivers not only maintain lower levels of cortisol, but recover from stressful situations more quickly (Newberger, 1997).

Temperament and Emotion

Recall from the previous chapter on personality development that various theories of temperament include emotional reactions and sensitivity as major components. The infant's temperamental characteristics probably exercise a major influence on emotional expression. Researchers have found temperamental characteristics, such as activity level and soothability, to be related to the expression of both positive and negative emotions (Derryberry & Rothbart, 1984). Temperament may also affect the type of environmental stimuli that elicit emotional responses in infants (Yarrow, 1979).

Socialization of Emotions

Emotions develop within the context of social and cultural environments. The term **socialization of emotions** means that the infants' emotions are influenced, over time, by the responses of parents and other caregivers. Processes that contribute to the socialization of emotions include classical and operant conditioning, punishment, direct instruction, imitation, and identification (Walden & Garber, 1994). Parents influence their babies' emotions through selective reinforcement with facial expressions and other behaviors. A study by Malatesta and Haviland (1982) illustrates how parents condition the emotional expressions through the use of facial responses. They videotaped mothers interacting with their infants during a period of a few months. The mothers tended to respond with more facial expressions that reinforced the display of positive behaviors in their infants. Over time, the infants' number of positive behaviors increased while the negative behaviors declined.

The sex of an infant is likely to influence the socialization of emotional behavior. In face-to-face play, mothers tend to respond differently to the same emotional expressions of male and female infants. Mothers tend to smile more at boys than at girls (Malatesta & Haviland, 1985). When female infants display anger, mothers tend to display angry facial expressions in return. However, mothers are more like to display facial expressions of sympathy when male infants display anger (Malatesta & Haviland, 1982). Mothers also give a greater variety of emotional responses to a female's emotional expressions than to a male infant's. Malatesta and Haviland (1985) believe that male infants are more excitable, so mothers soon learn to limit their range of emotional response to avoid overstimulation. The exposure to more diverse emotional stimuli may partially explain why girls are better than boys at understanding emotional expression. However, few sex differences in the expression of emotions emerge during the infancy period (Zahn-Waxler et al., 1984). Researchers have not found any evidence of gender differences in security of attachment formed between infants and parents (Carlson et al., 1989).

Since parent-infant interactions are partially controlled by the infant, it is necessary to look at differences in the behaviors of male and female infants that are likely to have an impact on parent-infant relationships. According to Benenson (1996) males prefer physically assertive behavior while females prefer a more gentle style of interaction. Male infants tend to engage in more gross motor activity than females. In the first year of life, males tend to be more irritable than females. Newborn females, more than males, engage in eye contact, are more sensitive to the sound of another infant's crying, and are more responsive to caregivers' efforts to relieve the infant's emotional distress.

Culture and Emotions

Cultural influences play an important role in establishing the emotional climate and the extent to which infants are exposed to various emotions. Each culture has patterns of emotional expression that are somewhat distinctive. For example, Utku Eskimo people do not traditionally express anger overtly, nor use anger in childrearing (Briggs, 1970). They disapprove of anger and seek to express it through the socialization of their children. In a cross-cultural study (Caudill & Schooler, 1973), American infants made more happy vocalizations than Japanese infants. At 30 months of age, American infants were more emotionally expressive and independent. Japanese parents are indulgent with their infants and tend to shield them from exposure to strong emotional reactions such as anger and sadness. Thus, when anger is expressed, Japanese children display more upset than children who have been more often exposed to

such outbursts (Miyake et al., 1986). In contrast, Banoi infants in Tailand are encouraged to vent their anger very early in life (Broude, 1995). Expression of hostility is accepted throughout the childhood years.

Social-class differences in maternal interpretations of infant emotions have also been found. Lower-class mothers who were separated from their infants labeled their infant's reactions as anger more frequently than middle-class mothers (Lewis & Michalson, 1983). Thus, adults from various cultural and subcultural backgrounds are likely to socialize the emotional displays of their infants in different ways (Zahn-Waxler, Cummings, & Cooperman, 1984).

Cognitive Factors

Emotional development and cognitive development in infancy are generally viewed as interdependent processes. Most emotional responses are based on the interpretation of stimuli and events as pleasant or unpleasant, threatening or nonthreatening, or neutral. The emergence of advanced emotions is dependent upon the infant's cognitive ability to interpret specific eliciting conditions. For example, stranger fear does not emerge until an infant can make cognitive comparisons between faces and perceive a strange face as unfamiliar and threatening (Lewis, 1993). Guilt, shame, and embarrassment are emotions that depend on cognitive functions associated with the emergence of self-awareness (Walden & Garber, 1993). Sroufe (1996) contends that emotional development during infancy parallels cognitive changes outlined by Piaget during the sensorimotor period.

THE EMERGENCE OF EMOTIONS

Scientists who study emotional development have been interested in determining when various emotions first appear. There is general agreement that most of the emotions emerge and develop during the first three years of life. However, due to differences in theories, terminology, and research methods, researchers disagree on the exact timetable for the development of specific emotions. Scientists also debate whether or not emotions can be classified within 2 or 3 overall categories (e.g., anger/frustration; wariness/fear; pleasure/joy) or as seven or more separate and distinct emotions (fear, anger, sadness, etc.). Research tends to support the existence of a number of discrete emotions (Izard, 1993). In this text, an effort has been made to combine information from variety of viewpoints and research findings. Table 13-1 encompasses the approximate ages, ranging from youngest to oldest in months, identified by various researchers for the appearance of various emotions.

Newborn infants display general emotional states of distress, discomfort, or pain. They also display signs of excitement and interest in the environment, and they seem to be relaxed and content at times (Lewis, 1993). However, the emotional life of the newborn is rather limited. Yet, within the first three years of life emotions develop rapidly in concert with developing self-awareness and cognitive understanding. Between the first few days of life and 3 months of age, infants begin to display signs of sadness and disgust. By the time an infant is 6 to

Table 13–1 Infant Emotions: Age Range of Development

EMOTION	AGE (MONTHS)
Distress/discomfort/pain	Birth
Interest/excitement	Birth
Disgust	Birth–3
Sadness	Birth–3
Pleasure/delight/joy	2–7
Surprise	3–6
Anger	4–7
Wariness/fear	4–9
Rage	7–18
Affection/love	18–36
Empathy/sympathy	18–36
Embarrassment	24–36
Guilt	24–36
Pride	24–36
Shame	24–36

Sources: Izard & Malatesta, 1987; Lewis, 1993; Sroufe, 1996.

9 months old, surprise, joy, fear, and anger/rage have emerged. The more complex emotions, including affection/love, sympathy/empathy, guilt, embarrassment, pride, and shame are not expressed until sometime between 18 and 36 months (see Table 13–1). We will consider the development of pleasure/joy, anger, anxiety/fear, and sympathy/empathy in more detail as they emerge during the infancy period. Information on the development of other emotions during the infancy period is more limited.

Pleasure-Joy

The development of pleasure and joy in young infants is revealed mainly through their smiles and laughter (see Chapter 12). The exact age at which the infant's smiles and laughter actually reflect an underlying state of pleasure and happiness is not known. The argument has been made (Emde et al., 1976) that the neonatal smile represents a positive or pleasurable emotional tone, since smiling has not been observed when infants are distressed. However, the signs of pleasure and joy are more definite by 3 months of age when infants smile at familiar events and faces they recognize (Lewis, 1993). Sroufe (1996) believes smiling and laughter responses mostly result from the buildup and release of tension as infants encounter various exciting and uncertain events.

Anger

Mothers and scientists alike have reported expressions of anger in the cries and facial expressions of infants as early as the neonatal period. Sroufe (1979) believes that these early "mad" expressions are more correctly identified as primitive responses to extreme distress. Anger is more differentiated and readily identified in infants between 4 and 7 months of age. Stenberg and Campos (1990) found that 4-month-old infants displayed angry facial expressions directed toward the source of their frustration (restraint). Expressions of anger become more frequent during the latter half of the first year (Sroufe, 1977; Emde et al., 1976) and gradually increase with age throughout infancy (Lewis & Michalson, 1983). Parents report an increase in the frequency and intensity in their infant's expression of anger after infants begin to creep (Campos, Kermoian, & Zumbahlen, 1992). Obstacles that prevent the infant from obtaining a goal, such as an attractive object, can elicit an angry response.

Young infants usually express anger through crying, angry flushed facial expressions, and increased motor activity. By 1 year of age an infant's angry reactions are likely to include foot stomping, kicking, throwing, or knocking away objects (Sroufe, 1979). Two-year-olds also use defiant verbal expressions ("No!") and aggressive acts such as pushing, biting, and hitting. Their responses are more directly targeted toward the source of anger. The intensity of anger in reaction to frustration or other stimuli at this age is referred to as "rage" (Sroufe, 1996).

Babies react with anger to a variety of situations. The earliest sources of anger are physical restraints that inhibit an infant's movements. Barriers that prevent a baby from reaching a goal, such as a toy, also cause anger. The developing sense of self-awareness and the need for independence result in new sources of anger as the infant's goals come into conflict with parental demands and expectations. For example, infants often react angrily when caregivers put them to bed (Stenberg & Campos, 1990). The "terrible two's" are characterized by increased resistance to adult demands as temper tantrums reach a peak.

Anxiety-Fear

Infants typically begin to show signs of anxiety and fear between 7 and 9 months of age (Izard, 1977). Sroufe (1996) thinks of fear as emerging throughout the infancy period from a more general state of wariness or apprehension rather than an emotion that appears at a specific age. Infants react negatively or warily to strangers, heights (visual cliffs), approaching (looming) objects, separation from their attachment figures, and stimuli associated with pain (doctors' offices). Fear responses in infants include crying, clinging to the caregiver, and a fearful facial expression. The stimuli that elicit fear in infants generally increase in number over the first eighteen months of life (Lewis &

Michalson, 1983) and are connected with the changes in the object concept and other aspects of cognitive development (Sroufe, 1996). During the third year of life, the sources of fear change and begin to include imaginary stimuli such as wild animals. The development of two types of fear—stranger anxiety and separation anxiety—parallel the development of attachment.

Stranger Anxiety. A 9-month-old infant is sitting on the living room floor playing with a ball. A new neighbor who is visiting walks over, kneels down close to the infant, and says, "She is a beautiful baby!" The baby takes one look at the stranger and begins to cry. Fear of strangers emerges during the last half of the first year of life and reaches a peak frequency around 12 months. Girls tend to display negative reactions to strangers a little earlier than boys (Lewis & Michalson, 1983). The incidence declines slightly at the beginning of the second year and rises once again between 18 and 24 months (Scarr & Salapatek, 1970; Lewis & Michalson, 1983). After that time, stranger fear gradually declines.

Infants are less likely to show a fear of strangers if they are being held by a primary caregiver (Mussen, Conger, & Kagan, 1974), and if the strangers are children, especially of the same sex (Brooks & Lewis, 1976). Infants react more negatively to strangers who intrude in familiar, predictable settings (Brookhart & Hock, 1976). Babies who are free to move away are less likely to cry in response to a strange person than babies who are restrained (Bronson, 1972). They also are more likely to be afraid of male than female strangers (Lewis & Brooks, 1974). The extent to which a stranger's behavior is predictable or contingent upon the infant's own responses (e.g., a smile for a smile) is likely to affect the amount of anxiety exhibited (Bronson, 1972).

The infant's responsiveness to strangers is affected by the security of attachment to the mother and experiences within the family. Infants who are securely attached to the mother are much more sociable with strangers than less securely attached infants (Thompson & Lamb, 1984). The quality of the baby's attachment to other family members is also an important influence in stranger sociability. No consistent relationship has been found between the infant's previous experiences with other people outside the family and stranger anxiety (Thompson & Lamb, 1984). However, cross-cultural studies suggest that stranger anxiety is more intense and lasts longer in societies in which infants have more limited contact with strangers than they typically do in America (Super & Harkness, 1982).

Separation Anxiety. An 11-month-old boy is playing in the living room of a neighbor. He looks up and sees his mother disappear into the kitchen with the neighbor. He begins to follow as quickly as possible, crying loudly. This is an example of separation anxiety that is typically seen in infants around 8 or 9 months of age. It reaches a peak around 12 months and begins to disappear toward the end of the second year (Lewis & Michalson, 1983). However, displays of separation anxiety continue longer in some cultures than in others. Separation distress remains longer in infants who are cared for exclusively by the mother than in infants who are also cared for by siblings and other persons (Super & Harkness, 1982).

Both separation and stranger anxiety are emotions that typically are not learned through unpleasant experiences, although that is possible. Some theorists believe that these are among a group of innate emotions that have survival value by keeping the infant close to the parent. The emergence of stranger fear and separation anxiety have also been attributed to cognitive growth, including changes in recall memory, and the object concept (Bronson, 1972). With growing cognitive maturity, infants learn more about the environment and develop a set of expectations. Unfamiliar persons are perceived by infants as discrepant or contradictory stimuli that do not match familiar mental images. The infant thus responds with expressions of anxiety.

Empathy-Sympathy

The experience of participating in the emotional state of another person is referred to as **empathy** (Bischof-Kohler, 1991). Empathy means "feeling as," or sharing the same emotion that another person is experiencing at a given time. **Sympathy** is an emotional response that involves feelings of sorrow and compassion for another person who is in pain and distress. Empathy usually results in expressions of sympathy, such as hugs or other comforting behaviors. On a behavioral level it is

A case of separation anxiety and protest. This infant is reluctant to leave the mother.

difficult to determine when a person is experiencing empathy or sympathy or both. Both empathy and sympathy require the cognitive ability to identify the emotions of others. The term **empathic concern** is sometimes used to describe feelings and behaviors that are a combination of sympathy and empathy (Zahn-Waxler & Radke-Yarrow, 1990).

The capacity to respond to the emotions of others appears so early in life that it is considered to be innate (Bischof-Kohler, 1991). When newborns hear the cries of other babies, they tend to join in with cries of their own. Very young infants also imitate, or match, the facial expressions of adults (e.g., a frown or a smile) that convey emotional states. However, these emotional "mimicry" responses may be attributed to the process of emotional contagion. As such, an infant can share an emotion with others without awareness that the emotion also belongs to someone else. Episodes of emotional contagion are viewed as forerunners, or the raw material, from which empathy develops (Bischof-Kohler, 1991).

Research studies suggest that by 2 years of age, children have the cognitive, emotional, and behavioral capacities to display empathic concern for others in distress (Zahn-Waxler & Radke-Yarrow, 1990). The emergence of empathy may correspond with the achievement of self-recognition. Bischof-Kohler (1991) found that infants, between ages 16 and 24 months of age, who could recognize themselves in a mirror, expressed empathy in an experimental play situation. Infants who did not pass the self-recognition test did not react with empathy-related behaviors. Zahn-Waxler and Radke-Yarrow (1990) observed expressions of empathic concern in 21-month-old infants. They responded to their mother's simulated sadness by looking into her face and making verbal inquires about what is wrong. These expressions were accompanied by looks of concern, hugs, consoling sounds, and statements of sympathy. During the second and third years, children acquire an emotional language through which they can interpret and articulate the distress of others (Hay et al., 1994).

The family environment provides the context for the development of empathic concern. Infants whose parents display affectionate and sensitive interactions are likely to express empathic concern for others. Infants and young children whose parents display extended depression may develop too much empathy that results in exaggerated feelings of responsibility. Later in life, these experiences can lead to preoccupation and overinvolvement with the problems of others, or avoidance of others in distress as a defense mechanism (Zahn-Waxler & Radke-Yarrow, 1990).

INFANTS' UNDERSTANDING OF EMOTIONS

The development of empathy and sympathy or other emotions is related to the infant's understanding of their own emotions and those of others. There is no general agreement about when infants recognize their own emotions (Yarrow, 1979). Due to the neurological immaturity of the newborn and very young infant, it seems likely that external indicators (e.g., crying, facial expressions) of emotional expressions are not reliable indicators of the underlying emotional experience (Campos et al., 1983). For example, when a baby first smiles, it is not necessarily an expression of joy, as it is in an adult. After the first few weeks of life, the baby's emotional expressions more closely match the underlying emotional experiences.

When do infants begin to recognize the feelings of caregivers and other people? This question is important because it involves the infant's capacity to receive emotional signals. There are indications that infants show awareness of different facial expressions of emotions at approximately 2 months of age. Between 4 and 8 months of age, the baby begins to understand and interpret the emotional significance of various facial expressions. (Bornstein & Lamb, 1992; Michalson & Lewis, 1985). At this point, they begin to respond positively or negatively on the basis of emotions exhibited by other people (Campos et al., 1983). For example, infants smile while looking at happy faces, frown at angry faces, or cry in response to angry voices. They also discriminate joy from anger and neutral expressions, as well as surprise from happiness and sadness (Bertenthal & Campos, 1990).

The ability to interpret the emotions of others improves with age. Around 9 months of age, infants begin to look for emotional indicators in the faces, voices, and gestures of their caregivers to decide what to do in uncertain situations. The term **social referencing** is used to describe this tendency (Campos & Stenberg, 1981). For example, infants are more willing to explore a strange toy when the mother smiles than when her facial expressions show fear (Zarbatany & Lamb, 1985).

At about 18 months to 2 years of age, babies begin to comprehend verbal labels that adults use to describe emotional expressions. Michalson and Lewis (1985) found that most 2-year-olds they studied (80 percent) could point to pictures of happy and sad faces. Some of the infants (40 percent) correctly selected surprised and angry faces. The ability to produce these verbal labels ("What kind of face is this?") began to develop at 3 years. The first words infants use to correctly label corresponding facial expressions are "happy," and "sad," and "angry" (Michalson & Lewis, 1985). The following incident illustrates the infant's growing recognition of emotions:

> Today, my husband Jack came home ... in a really good mood. He came in, dancing around, and he kept picking me up and hugging me. Our daughter Jennie (18 months) came running out of the bedroom to see her daddy. When she saw us, she stopped dead in her tracks and started giggling and laughing and started saying, "Kiss, kiss." Then Jack put me down and she came up to us and said, "Me, me, kiss, kiss, love, love," and we gave her a hug (Zahn-Waxler et al., 1984, p. 45).

Two- and three-year-old children also begin to associate emotional expressions with the situations that produced them (Michalson & Lewis, 1985). Bretherton and her colleagues (1980) found that the 28-month-old infants they studied made such cause-effect statements as "I cry [so] lady pick me up and hold me," and "Grandma angry [because] I write on wall." At this stage, infants have begun to understand that others have the same feelings as they do (Zahn-Waxler et al., 1984).

ATTACHMENT

Attachment is not typically listed as a basic, discrete emotion because it is viewed as a "special," emotional relationship between the infant and caregiver (Sroufe, 1996). **Attachment** is defined as "a relatively enduring emotional tie to a specific other person" (Maccoby, 1980, p. 53). Infants display attachment by behaviors such as maintaining close physical contact with the other person, crying when that person leaves, and expressing joy when the person returns (Ainsworth, 1967). The quality of parent-infant attachment has a lasting influence on socioemotional development. The formation of attachment is a two-way process in which the parent becomes attached to the child (bonding) and the child becomes attached to the parent.

Early theories and research on attachment were largely devoted to mother-infant attachment. In recent years however, the importance of concurrent attachments between infants and other caregivers, including fathers, grandparents or other family members, as well as child-care providers has been recognized. Bowlby believed that, at first, infants do not have the capacity to form more than one attachment bond. We now know that infants have the capacity to form multiple attachments (Levitt, 1991). Information is lacking about the relative strength and influence of various attachment relationships. It appears reasonable to expect that infants typically form a hierarchy of attachments, with some relationships being more important, at certain times, than others. In most families, the mother appears to be the most important attachment figure.

Infant-to-Mother Attachment

The most widely used method of assessing infant-mother attachment is the Ainsworth Strange Situation (Ainsworth et al., 1978). This procedure is used in the study of infants 12 to 18+ months of age. An infant is observed during a series of eight episodes in an unfamiliar room with the mother and a stranger. The mother is present part of the time and absent part of the time. The episodes provide an opportunity for researchers to observe the infant's reunion with the mother after being under the stress that results from being alone with a strange person in a strange situation.

Using this procedure, Ainsworth and her associates (1978) initially identified three basic patterns of attachment in 12-month-old infants. The largest number of infants (66 percent) was classified as **securely attached**. These babies were able to use the mother as a secure base to explore the environment. They were interested in the objects in the room, did not cling to the mother, and interacted positively with the stranger. Although they were distressed when the mother left the room, they were easily comforted when the mother returned and soon resumed their play.

A second group of infants was rated as insecurely attached. Two patterns of this type of attachment were observed. A few of the infants (12 percent) were labeled as **avoidant**. They did not protest when separated from their mothers. When the mothers returned, they were avoided or completely ignored. Another group (22 percent) of the infants displayed an ambivalently attached or resistant pattern of attachment (**ambivalent**). These infants were very upset when their mothers left the room. Although they ran to their mothers when they were reunited, they demonstrated insecurity by a mixture of clinging and resistant (kicking and pushing away) behavior.

The attachment behaviors of some infants, however, do not fit well within any of the categories identified above. More recently, an additional type of insecure attachment has been identified. Some infants display behaviors that are labeled as **disorganized-disoriented** attachment. Behaviors observed in these infants during the "strange situation" include freezing all movement, approaching the parent with head averted, stereotypies such as rocking on hands and knees, screaming for the parent upon separation but moving silently away when the parent returns, or turning to greet the parent, and then falling on the floor (Main & Hesse, 1990). These infants' behaviors are viewed as indicating extreme internal conflict. Their mothers often have a history of early psychological trauma and loss in their own lives (Main, Kaplan, & Cassidy, 1985).

Much of the research on infant-mother attachment has been based on the theory of John Bowlby (1969), who identified four stages in the formation of attachment:

1. *Preattachment: Undiscriminating social responsiveness* (birth to 8-12 weeks). During this phase, infants do not typically differentiate one person from another and can be comforted by anyone.
2. *Beginnings of attachment: Discriminating social responsiveness* (3 to 6-8 months). The infant begins to recognize the primary caregiver and a few other familiar people. These preferred adults are usually able to soothe the baby and elicit social responses more quickly than strangers.
3. *Clear-cut attachment: Maintaining proximity* (6-8 months to about 3 years). Around the middle of the first year, infants are typically attached to one specific person. This person is usually the mother, although some infants prefer the father or other caregivers.
4. *Formation of a goal-corrected partnership* (3 to 4 years and on). This phase begins when children recognize that other people have needs and desires of their own and that the mother has to give priority to other activities at times.

Infant-to-Father Attachment

Research studies have shown that most babies become attached to both mother and father at about the same time—7 months (Lamb & Bornstein, 1987). Although infants spend less time interacting with their fathers than their mothers, they seek physical contact and comfort from both parents in about equal proportions (Lamb, 1982c). Infants react to separations from their fathers in much the same way as they do their mothers in laboratory experiments and naturally occurring separations (Parke, 1996). However, infants apparently go through a period, between 12 and 18 months, when they turn to their mothers more than their fathers in stressful situations. The preference for the mother when under stress disappears around 24 months of age (Lamb, 1982c).

Mother-to-Infant Attachment

The process by which a parent becomes attached to an infant is sometimes called **bonding** (Klaus

& Kennell, 1982). In some cases, however, bonding is used more specifically to refer to the establishment of an enduring affectionate attachment of a mother to her infant as the result of skin-to-skin contact during the first few hours after birth (Campos et al., 1983).

The belief that the first few hours after birth represent a "sensitive period" for maternal-infant attachment originated in the study of animals. In some species, such as sheep and goats, the mother will reject her offspring if they are separated from her for a short period of time as soon as they are born. In recent years, researchers have attempted to determine whether or not the sensitive period hypothesis applies to human infants.

A number of studies have reported increased frequencies of affectionate behaviors by mothers who were given extended early contact with their infants (Klaus & Kennell, 1976; Svejda, Pannabecker, & Emde, 1982). These studies, however, have been criticized for serious methodological problems as well as their failure to find any long-term effects (Lamb, 1982a). More carefully controlled studies (e.g., Svejda, Campos, & Emde, 1980) have failed to find evidence that early contact experiences are necessary for bonding to occur. Furthermore, in 80 percent of the world's cultures, mother and infant do not have immediate skin-to-skin contact, and nursing is not started until three days after birth (Super, 1981). Consequently, the belief that mothers will not love their infants adequately if extended skin-to-skin contact does not occur soon after birth seems to be unfounded.

Father-to-Infant Attachment

The importance of father-infant attachment, or bonding, has been recognized in recent years. Researchers have not been successful in identifying a critical or sensitive period for establishing father-infant attachment (Jones, 1985). In one study (Svejda et al., 1982), fathers were given extra contact with their infants during the first two days after delivery. When the interactions of these fathers with their infants were compared with those of another group of fathers who were not given extra contact, no differences were found.

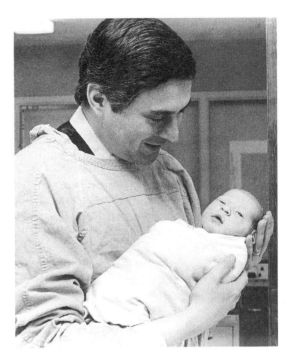

A father becomes as attached to an infant as a mother does.

In any case, though, fathers apparently become just as attached to infants as mothers. Studies (Parke & O'Leary, 1976; Parke & Sawin, 1977) have found fathers to be just as interested as mothers in their infants during the newborn period. Fathers tend to be just as nurturing and stimulating with their infants as mothers. Like mothers, fathers touch, talk to, look at, and kiss their newborns. They are competent caregivers and are responsive to infant distress such as spitting up (Belsky & Volling, 1987).

Importance of Infant-Caregiver Attachment

The formation of attachments is considered to be one of the most important processes of infant development. Bowlby (1969) used a metaphor called an **internal working model** to describe the influence of attachment on human behavior. The concept of an "internal working model" refers to understandings and expectations about oneself and other people in the world that serve as a "script" or a guide for interpersonal relationships. The infant's internal working model develops out of patterns of interactions and attachment relationships with primary caregivers (Bretherton, 1996). Over time, an individual forms and revises the internal working model in response to cognitive changes and new experiences in caregiving. These models determine how infants interpret and anticipate the interpersonal responses from others, what cues they select, and how they respond. Theoretically, infants who have formed secure attachments perceive and respond to people and events very differently from infants whose attachments are insecure.

The importance of attachments is also described in terms of the availability of a **secure base** (Ainsworth et al., 1978). With the mother, or other attachment figure, available as a "secure base," an infant moves away to explore the environment. When frightening or disturbing stimuli are encountered, the infant returns to the mother as a safe haven. Securely attached infants are more likely to use this strategy to learn from the environment. On the other hand, insecurely attached infants are more reluctant to venture from their base of support into strange places. Therefore, these infants have fewer opportunities for learning and establishing feelings of mastery and control over the environment. Even securely attached infants return to their attachment figures from time to time for emotional "refueling."

The security of early attachment establishes the foundation for future behavior. Easterbrooks and Goldberg (1990) found that infants who were securely attached to their mothers as toddlers were likely to become kindergartners who demonstrated emotional stability and expression in situationally appropriate ways; insecurely attached toddlers were more likely to overcontrol impulses and emotions as kindergarteners. Researchers have also found that infants who were securely attached to their mothers and fathers tend to exhibit higher levels of social competency and more positive peer relations as they grow up than insecurely attached infants (Ladd & Le Sieur, 1995).

Influences on Attachment

Caregiver-Infant Interactions. The characteristics of the infant's interactions with the primary caregiver (usually the mother) are probably the most important factor in the attachment process. Caregiver behaviors associated with secure attachment include acceptance, warmth and affection, accessibility, responsiveness, and cooperation with the infant (Maccoby, 1980). Mothers of securely attached infants have been found to be more accepting, sensitive, emotionally expressive, and responsive to needs than mothers of insecurely attached infants (Main et al., 1979; Rosen & Rothbaum, 1993). On the other hand, mothers of insecure attachments are associated with inconsistent care, parental insensitivity, and negligence. Isabella and Beslky (1991) found that securely attached infant-mother relationships were characterized by a predominance of synchronous interactions. As expected, insecure infant-mother relationships were associated with a disproportionate number of behaviors that were miscoordinated or asynchronous. Interactional synchrony will be discussed further below.

Parental Depression. Infants of depressed parents are likely to experience interactions that lead to insecure attachments. A higher proportion of insecure attachments are found in children of parents who suffer major depression than among other groups of children (Cummings & Cicchetti, 1990). Psychological unavailability of parents has been linked with insecure attachments in infants. Depression contributes to attachment problems by interfering with parental responsiveness, availability, and disrupting interactional synchrony. Tronick (1989) found that depressed mothers tend to look away from their infants more, display more anger, are more intrusive, and display less warmth and affection than other mothers.

Contact Comfort. Harlow's studies of infant monkeys reared in isolation from their mothers may offer some clues about the formation of attachment bonds (Harlow & Zimmerman, 1959). The monkeys were reared in a cage with two artificial mothers. One of the mothers was made of wire mesh, and the other consisted of wire mesh covered with terry cloth. The monkeys invariably became attached only to the terry cloth mother, even when the plain mother held the nursing bottle.

Harlow concluded that contact comfort is an important variable in the formation of attachment.

Temperament. The temperament of the infant may be an important source of influence on the way attachment develops. Theoretically, the infant's temperament affects the quality of the parent-infant interaction, which subsequently determines the quality of attachment. For example, infants who are "ambivalently attached" tend to have characteristics of temperament (e.g., irritability, crying) that fit the "difficult child" classification. (Miyake, Chen, & Campos, 1985). After reviewing numerous research studies, Goldsmith and Alansky (1987) concluded that both the caregiver's sensitivity and the infant's temperament play important roles in the attachment process. However, researchers have not been able to confirm a strong relationship among all aspects of temperament and attachment behavior (Bretherton & Waters, 1985).

Multiple Caregiving. In many societies, infants are exposed to a variety of caregivers. Does an infant suffer emotional harm as the result of having to develop emotional ties with several different people? Evidence from infants reared in the Israeli kibbutzim is relevant to this question. A kibbutz is an agricultural settlement where infants are, to a large extent, reared outside the home. Their time is spent largely in "infant houses" under the care of professional caregivers called metaplot (singular: metapelet). The parents, however, are accessible and frequently spend time with their infants. Researchers have found that kibbutz infants demonstrate normal patterns of attachment and emotional development (Super, 1981). In comparison to American infants cared for at home, kibbutz infants demonstrate no significant differences in attachment to their mothers (Maccoby & Feldman, 1972). American parents worry about the disruption of attachment when placing an infant in a child day-care center. The effects of child day-care on attachment will be discussed in Chapter 14.

The Efe (Pygmies) people of the Northeastern Zaire represent another society in which infants are exposed to multiple caregiving (Morelli & Tronick, 1991). The Efe are a seminomadic people who hunt and forage for food and physical needs.

Although the basic social unit is the nuclear family, caregiving by individuals other than the mother is a cultural practice. Immediately after birth the infant is passed around among the other women present so that a mother's first contact does not occur until several hours after birth. Infants are sometimes nursed by another lactating woman. The mother may leave the baby in the camp with other individuals when she leaves to gather food. Infants are also often attended by other people even when the mother is in camp. Morelli and Tronick (1991) observed that the number of different people caring for an infant during the first eighteen weeks of life average approximately fourteen. Observations of infant behaviors around one-year of age indicate they have no problem developing primary attachments to their mothers in the context of multiple caregiving practices.

EMOTION REGULATION

The ability of an infant to regulate emotions is increasingly being viewed as a critical process in healthy emotional development. **Emotion regulation** involves the capacity of individuals to monitor and modify their emotional states and emotional reactions in order to accomplish their goals (Thompson, 1994). Self-regulation of emotions is a key to maintaining self-control, self-reliance, and self-esteem. Currently researchers are studying how physiological processes, such maturation of forebrain inhibitory centers, changes in the production cortisol and other body chemicals, and vagal (heart rate control) processes affect the expression and control of emotions during the infancy period. However, major emphasis is placed on how emotional communication between infants and their caregivers play a critical role in the infant's self-regulatory abilities (Tronick, 1989).

During the first year of life, infants have limited abilities to control emotional states so they are largely dependent upon adults to regulate their environment and emotional stimulation. (Cole, Michel, & Teti, 1994). Gaze aversion, head turning, pushing away, and crying are some of the ways infants attempt to control overstimulating and unpleasant sensations. Around 6 months of age infants put their hands in their mouths or stare at what their hands are doing (e.g., exploring their clothing) as self-calming mechanisms (Toda & Fogel, 1993). Rocking, kicking, and other stereotypical body movements are additional self-calming mechanisms used by infants as they gain control over their body movements. Smiling behavior, vocalizations, leaning toward the caregiver are some mechanisms infants used for eliciting stimulation and maintaining positive emotional states.

Young infants depend upon caregivers to respond to their signals for help in reducing negative emotional states or maintaining desirable emotions. The infant's crying or other emotional signals elicit emotions from the caregiver and influences (regulates) caregiver responses which in turn influence the baby's emotions. This process is sometimes referred to as **mutual regulation** (Robinson & Glaves, 1996). For example, crying usually signals the need for help in regulating distress, while cooing sounds signal a pleasant emotional state the infant wishes to maintain. If the caregiver is emotionally available and responsive, the crying baby receives soothing touch and rocking; or providing time away from stimulation helps the infant reduce stress and restore emotional stability. The cooing baby receives reciprocal "coos" or other caregiver sounds needed to continue the desired feeling (Cole et al., 1994).

These early synchronous interactions are critical in helping the infant establish feelings of adequacy and control. As infants mature, they become increasingly capable of establishing self-regulation of emotions, and external regulation by the caregiver becomes less necessary. (Campos, Campos & Barrett, 1989). However, infants with Down syndrome, maltreated infants, and infants of mothers with mood disorders are at risk for developing emotion regulation difficulties (Cicchetti, Ganiban, & Barnett, 1991).

INTERACTIONAL SYNCHRONY

In order for caregiver-infant relationships to function in ways that promote optimum attachment and emotional development of infants, the interactions must represent a "goodness-of-fit" between the behavior of the infant and the behavior of the caregiver. Successful relationships are characterized by a predominance of **interactional synchrony**. This term is used to refer to behavioral exchanges between caregiver and infant that are reciprocal, harmonious, and mutually rewarding (Isabella & Belsky, 1991). Both baby and caregiver contribute to the interactions and are responsive to each other. Synchronous relationships are also characterized by contingency and entrainment (Brazelton & Cramer, 1990). **Contingency** means the behavior of one partner in the relationship is dependent upon the behavior of the other partner. For example, if the baby smiles in response to a caregiver "peek-a-boo," the game will continue. If the baby's expression does not change, the caregiver will turn away or try something else. The term **entrainment** is used to describe the momentum of the interactional sequences. Once a synchronous "turn-taking" interaction is established, it moves and flows with each partner adding to the momentum until a peak of intensity is reached. The process is sometimes described as a "dance" between the caregiver and the infant.

The first step in establishing a synchronous relationship requires caregivers to adapt their behavior to fit the rhythms of the baby. Initially babies are also dependent upon adults to assume a leadership role in initiating interactions. As they get older, infants assume more initiative and become more active participants in the interactions. An example of a synchronous interaction is seen in the following sequence: The mother smiles and the baby smiles back. After two or three interchanges of smiles that increase in expressiveness, the mother or the baby may add cooing sounds to the interchange. The partner responds with a matching vocalization. After a few such interchanges, the baby looks away to end the sequence (Brazelton & Cramer, 1990).

Infant-caregiver behaviors can quickly become **asynchronous**. This term refers to interactions, or co-occurrences of behaviors that are not reciprocal and mutual (Isabella & Belsky, 1991). Asynchronous interactions occur when behavior becomes one-sided, unresponsive, or overly intrusive. For example, the infant becomes sleepy and closes its eyes. The caregiver jiggles and talks to the baby to keep it awake. The infant becomes agitated and starts fussing or crying. The caregiver then tries to feed the baby who rejects the nipple. The caregiver then puts the baby, who is now wide awake, to bed.

ASSESSING INTERACTIONAL SYNCHRONY: THE BARNARD MODEL

Kathryn Barnard (1979) has developed a model for assessing the adequacy of early caregiver-infant relationships and for helping caregivers understand the interactional processes involved. In this model, both the parent/caregiver and the baby have certain responsibilities for keeping the interaction going. The interactional process is illustrated in Figure 13–1. The breaks in the arrows between caregiver and infant represent an interruption in an interactional sequence. A disruption in the process can originate in the caregiver, the infant, or from an environmental distraction. The responsibilities of infants and caregivers for maintaining the interactional flow are described below.

Clarity of Cues

The responsibility of infants in engaging in synchronous relationships is to send unambiguous cues or signals to the caregiver about their needs. For example, pushing away from the caregiver with

arms and legs is a clear signal that the infant wants to disengage and reduce stimulation. An example of an ambiguous cue is the infant who opens both eyes during sleep. This could easily be interpreted to mean that the infant is awake and ready to engage. An infant's failure to send a clear signal can result in inappropriate caregiving responses and a breakdown of interactional synchrony.

Responsiveness to Caregivers

Another task of the infant is to respond to the caregivers efforts to meet the baby's needs. This means the baby has to "read" the caregiver's signals. If the infant is unresponsive and passive, the caregiver may get discouraged and give up, or engage in intrusive and overstimulating activities in attempts to get a response. An infant's ability to send clear signals and respond to the caregiver can be compromised by a number of factors, including prematurity, low-birthweight, sensory deficits, or numerous congenital disabilities.

Caregiver Sensitivity to the Infant's Cues

An important responsibility of the caregiver is to accurately interpret the signals sent by the infant. Caregivers usually improve with experience and trial and error learning in understanding what the infant wants. However, this process can be improved if parents are given information about specific cues infants typically send and how they should be interpreted. The following is an exam-

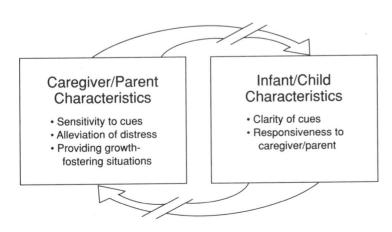

Figure 13–1 Barnard Model of Parent Child Interaction
Sources: Kathryn E. Barnard. (1979). *Nursing child assessment satellite teaching manual (NCAST)*. Seattle: University of Washington. Used by permission.

Caregiver/Parent Characteristics

- Sensitivity to cues
- Alleviation of distress
- Providing growth-fostering situations

Infant/Child Characteristics

- Clarity of cues
- Responsiveness to caregiver/parent

ple of a parent's accurate interpretation of an unambiguous engagement cue sent by an infant: *When I go to change Selma, she sticks this ole flat foot in my face and I kiss it. Then she sticks up the other foot and I kiss it. . . .* (Kubicek, 1996, p. 29).

Caregiver Ability to Alleviate the Infant's Distress

The effectiveness of the caregiver in reducing the distress of an infant is contingent upon the caregiver's ability to recognize the source of the problem and resourcefulness in making an appropriate response. The availability of the parent or other caregiver to respond quickly to a distress signal is important.

Caregiver Growth-Fostering Activities

In addition to interpreting and responding appropriately to the infant's distress signals, parents must also initiate activities that alleviate boredom and lethargy and facilitate development in each of the various growth areas, such as social, emotional, language, and cognitive. This process works best when the caregiver is aware of the infant's developmental level and knows how to provide activities to "match" the infant's needs without being intrusive and overstimulating.

Because infants have limited capacity to control parental behaviors, parents have the major responsibility for making any adaptations necessary for maintaining the flow of interactions. Factors that interfere with the ability of parents and other caregivers to fulfil the three tasks described above include financial worries, emotional problems, marital conflict, substance abuse, and inadequate knowledge.

MENTAL HEALTH AND EMOTIONAL DISORDERS

We don't usually think of babies as having mental health problems. Until recent years relatively few emotional disorders of infants were specified in the professional literature. During the past 20 years,

however, knowledge about infant mental health has mushroomed. The Zero to Three/National Center for Clinical Infant Programs (1994) has published a **Diagnostic Classification: 0-3 Manual** for use by clinicians and other professionals in identifying mental health and developmental disorders in the early years of life. The manual identifies approximately 29 general diagnostic categories under which a variety of specific disorders are described. As an example, the category designated as **disorders of relating and communication** will be described here. Another category that deals with parent-infant relationship disorders will be discussed in Chapter 14.

Disorders of relating and communicating include a group of severe difficulties in relating to and communicating with other people, combined with difficulties in regulating physiological, sensory, attentional, motor, cognitive, and emotional functions (Zero to Three, 1994). Disorders within this category become evident during infancy and early childhood. Problems are diagnosed on a continuum ranging from infants who display a complete lack of interpersonal relationship and communication capacity to infants who have significant impairment in communication, but who reveal some ability or potential for intimacy and closeness in relating to others. One of the most extreme problems is a pervasive developmental disorder referred to as autism or autistic disorder.

Autistic Disorder

A small percentage of these infants (about 2 to 4 per 10,000) are affected by a syndrome known as **infantile autism** or **autistic disorder** (Rutter & Garmezy, 1983). In some infants, the symptoms of this disorder become evident during the first few weeks of life. In other cases, infants display typical development for the first year or two of life before any signs of autism appear (Freeman & Ritvo, 1984). A major characteristic of infants with autistic disorder is their lack of responsiveness to other people. These infants usually do not make eye-to-eye contact or hold out their arms to be picked up and held. They are typically "noncuddlers," although at times they may cling to a caregiver.

Autistic infants apparently do not give or receive pleasure in their relationships with others. Caregivers find them unaffectionate and difficult to engage in games such as peek-a-boo. They tend to be easily upset by changes in their environment and caregiving routines (Freeman & Ritvo, 1984; Rutter & Garmezy, 1983).

Autistic infants also have problems in acquiring speech and nonverbal communication skills. Many do not speak at all, whereas others only echo what another person says. Another group of symptoms involves unusual and uneven patterns of sensorimotor development. Autistic infants tend to either underrespond or overrespond to stimuli. They may engage in repetitive activities and motor movements such as rocking, hand flapping, or staring (Ritvo & Freeman, 1977). Some autistic infants may bang their heads, bite themselves, and engage in other self-destructive behaviors.

Autism occurs at about the same rate all over the world. It affects all races, social classes, and types of families in equal proportions. However, boys are more frequently affected by autism than girls by a ratio of about three or four to one (Freeman & Ritvo, 1983; Rutter & Garmezy, 1983). The problems associated with autism are frequently combined with other syndromes, diseases, and developmental disabilities such as mental retardation and epilepsy (Freeman & Ritvo, 1984).

A few years ago, it was widely believed that this disorder was caused by disturbances in normal mothering and family functioning. However, there is no scientific evidence to support the assumption that autism results from bad parenting. At present, scientists believe that autism is the result of some type of defect in the central nervous system caused by genetic or environmental problems (Ritvo & Freeman, 1984; Wicks-Nelson & Israel, 1991).

Autistic infants have a normal life expectancy, but the outlook for their life's quality is not good. Currently there is no cure for autism. Approximately 75 percent of all autistic infants remain mentally retarded throughout life. Even infants with the mildest form and fewest symptoms continue to have problems in personality, emotional, social, and mental functions. Current methods of treating autism include structured education programs based on behavior-modification technology, along with medications to control some of the symptoms (Ritvo & Freeman, 1984).

Attachment Disorders

Psychologists and psychiatrists are increasingly attributing a variety of problems displayed by older children and adults to **disorders of attachment**. These problems include aggressive, disruptive behaviors, or the inability to form and maintain close relationships later in life (Chinitz, 1995; Smith, 1996). However, this is a very controversial issue and there is no general agreement on how to diagnose or define "attachment disorders" in children or adults. Zeanah, Mammen, and Liberman (1993) have proposed five major types of attachment disorders for infants—nonattached, indiscriminate, inhibited, aggressive, and role-reversed. Researchers have yet to validate such classifications, or to verify any connection between attachment problems and extreme behavioral problems later in life.

FACILITATING EMOTIONAL DEVELOPMENT

Parents cannot control all the factors that influence an infant's emotional development. However, there are numerous practices and activities that parents as well as other caregivers can use to promote healthy emotional development. In general, the most important thing to give the infant is a feeling of being cared for and loved. The same caregivers should be consistently available to play and interact with the baby. The following are some recommended principles and practices.

1. "Woo" the baby. Fall in love with the baby and allow it to fall in love with you. Set aside time for loving and pleasant interchanges, including rocking, hugging, cuddling, smiling, touching, eye contact, talking, and singing.
2. Carefully observe and interpret the baby's cues and signals for attention and distress. Provide prompt, tuned-in responsiveness to the baby's need for play, comfort, or "time-out" (Honig, 1993; Greenspan & Greenspan, 1985).

3. Reassure distressed infants with caresses, calming voice tones and facial expressions. Massage or gently rock tense, crabby babies to induce body relaxation and reduce tension (Honig, 1993).

4. Accept an infant's feelings as real and valid even if the behavior is not acceptable. For example, say, "I can't allow you to hit me, but I understand that you are angry with me right now" (Gonzalez-Mena & Eyer, 1980).

5. Express your own emotions honestly but appropriately. Infants benefit from being exposed to a wide range of emotions (Greenspan & Greenspan, 1985).

6. Help infants identify and label their feelings through reflective listening. ("You feel sad because Mommy has gone to work." "Look at your brother smile. He looks happy!")

7. Help babies find appropriate and alternative ways to express emotional intentions, such as "Show me what you want without crying" (Greenspan & Greenspan, 1985).

8. Some infants need to have a stuffed animal, blanket, and other "security" object to help make the transition from parental dependency to personal independence easier. This is normal as long as it does not represent a deficit in parental attention.

9. Insofar as possible and appropriate, control the stimuli that evoke negative feelings such as anger and fear (e.g., a night light can be provided for the infant who is afraid of the dark). However, infants should not be overprotected.

10. Never use fear and guilt to control an infant's behavior. Avoid statements such as "There is a ghost in that closet that will come out and get you if you don't stop crying!"

11. Provide everyday experiences that are predictable and reassuring (e.g., bathing and naptime) so that the baby gets a secure sense of what to expect and in what sequence (Honig, 1993).

12. Child care facilities should arrange for each caregiver to have responsibility for the same infants each day and move with them when they change age groups or rooms.

Additional suggestions may be found in sources such as Bromwich (1980); Gonzalez-Mena & Eyer, 1997; Grasselli and Hegner, 1980; Greenspan & Greespan, 1985; Honig, 1993; Karnes, 1982; Sparling and Lewis, 1979; Weiser, 1982; and White, 1985. Robert Emde and a multidisciplinary group of researchers and parenting educators at the University of Colorado have developed a program for fostering social-emotional development in the earliest years of life (Fenichel, 1996). This program, called **Partners in Parenting Education (PIPE)**, consists of a set of materials containing concepts, exercises, and activities that can be used in programs for adolescent parents, home-visiting programs, and other early-intervention programs (see Butterfield, 1996; Emde, 1996).

SUMMARY

1. Emotions are generally viewed as complex, subjective experiences that are influenced by a combination of biological and social forces.

2. The various theories of emotional development include biological, socialization, interactionist positions, and systems perspectives.

3. The infant's physiology, temperament, culture, and cognitive sophistication are included among the factors that affect emotional responses.

4. Even though the emotional life of the newborn infant is limited, infants begin to exhibit many of the basic emotions within the first six to nine months of life (e.g., disgust, sadness, surprise, joy, anger, fear). Most emotions have emerged by 3 years of age.

5. Infants begin to use social referencing around 9 months of age as they look for emotional expressions of other people to guide their own behavior. The ability to interpret, label, and comprehend emotions improves with age.

6. Basic patterns of infant-mother attachment include securely attached, anxiously attached, ambivalently attached, and disorganized-disoriented. Bowlby identified four stages in the formation of infant-parent attachment. Infants become equally attached to both fathers and mothers when given appropriate opportunities. In stressful situations, however, 12- to 18-month-old infants prefer their mothers.

7. Research studies have not supported the theory that the first few hours after birth is a critical period for bonding, or parent-infant attachment.

8. Stranger anxiety and separation anxiety are closely related emotions that appear during the second six months of life, after infants have become

attached to their parents. After reaching a peak around 12 months of age, the strength of these emotions declines.

9. The formation of attachment is one of the most important processes of infant development because it affects the formation of one's "internal working model" or view of the world and relationships with people.

10. The formation of attachment and emotional health is facilitated by "interactional synchrony" in caregiver-infant relationships. Other factors that influence attachment relationships are parental depression, parent-infant contact (touch), temperament, and multiple caregiving.

11. The Barnard Model for assessing the adequacy of early caregiver-infant relationships consists of observing the clarity of the babies cues and their responsiveness to caregivers. Parent behaviors that are observed include their sensitivity to infants' cues, ability to relieve distress, and provision of growth-fostering activities.

12. A recently published manual for use by clinicians and other professionals in identifying mental-health problems identifies approximately 29 general diagnostic categories under which a variety of specific disorders of infants are described.

13. Autism is a major disorder of communicating and relating that affects a small percentage of infants. The symptoms of autism, which begin before 30 months of age, include lack of responsiveness to other people, failure to acquire normal speech, repetitive motor activities, and self-destructive behaviors. Boys are more likely to be affected by this disorder than girls. Autism is apparently caused by a defect in the central nervous system.

14. Psychologists and psychiatrists are increasingly attributing a variety of problems displayed by older children and adults, including aggressive and disruptive behaviors, to disorders of attachment. However, there is disagreement among mental-health specialists about the use of attachment disorder as a diagnostic category.

15. To facilitate healthy emotional development, caregivers need to consistently engage in practices that give infants the feeling that they are cared for and loved.

14

Infant Caregiving and Education

Your children are not your children
They are the son's and daughters of Life's
longing for itself.
They come through you but not from you,
And though they are with you yet they belong not
to you . . .
You are the bows from which your children as
living arrows are sent forth . . .
Let your bending in the archer's hand be for
gladness.

—Kahil Gibran

Most infants experience the world and the people in it within the setting of a family. Society assigns primary responsibility for the care of the young to the family. The infant must receive a certain amount of personal care and nurturing for healthy growth and development to occur. The crucial nature of those family experiences for every aspect of infant development cannot be overstated. But the influence is mutual. Infants interact with their caregivers from the beginning. In those interactions, infants influence parents and others just as they are influenced. Infants give as they receive.

In this chapter we consider some of the changes occurring in the American family that have implications for infant development, such as single parenting and maternal employment. A major portion of the chapter is devoted to the experiences infants have in nonparental care outside the home. We also look at various types of early-intervention programs designed to enhance the development of infants from impoverished families. In addition, we consider the characteristics of a favorable home environment, including the processes of parent-infant interaction, discipline, and the provision of appropriate toys and play materials.

FAMILY SYSTEMS PERSPECTIVES

We have long recognized that "the parent-child relationship is unique among human ties" (Maccoby & Martin, 1983, p. 1). More recently, we have begun to appreciate and try to understand the complexity of that relationship within a family systems model. According to this perspective all family members and their behaviors are interconnected. Everything that happens to one family member potentially has an impact on everyone else in the family (Olson & DeFrain, 1994). Family relationships are described in terms of subsystems (husband-wife, parent-child, sibling child, family cohesion (togetherness), and flexibility (ability to change). While much of the earlier research focused on how parents influence infants, we now recognize that parents are influenced by infants, and that parent-child relationships are influenced by mother-father and other relationships within the family. Parents and infants are also influenced by their relations with people in the larger sociocultural network.

CURRENT TRENDS IN THE AMERICAN FAMILY

The form and structure of the American family have changed dramatically in recent decades. A diversity of family forms is emerging to replace the traditional family form made up of the breadwinner father and the homemaker mother. Current variations include dual-worker families, single-parent families, and blended or step families. Increasing divorce rates, the movement of women into the labor force, increased rates of teen-age pregnancy, decreasing family size, and numerous other social changes through the years have contributed to the transformation. Changes that have significant implications for infant development are the increases in the number of single-parent families and the number of working mothers.

Single-Parent Families

The increase in the number of single-parent families during the past two decades has been dramatic. The proportion of single-parent families in the United States increased from 13 percent of all family groups with children less than 18 in 1970 to 31 percent in 1994 (U.S. Bureau of the Census, 1995). This represents more than a 50 percent increase in the one-parent population between 1970 and 1994. The percentage of children raised by a single par-

The number of infants who are reared in two-parent families has declined.

ent varies by race. In 1994, the rate was 25 percent for whites, 65 percent for blacks, and 36 percent for Latinos. There were approximately six times as many one-parent families maintained by mothers as one-parent households maintained by fathers in 1994. There was a small increase (averaging 3 percent) in the number of one-parent households maintained by white, black, and Hispanic fathers between 1970 and 1994. However, single-parent fathers are more likely to have custody of older children than infants. The rise in the number of single-parent households can be attributed mainly to increases in rates of divorce and separation (U.S. Bureau of the Census, 1995). Also, the likelihood of a remarriage after divorce has declined along with an increase in the number of years between divorce and remarriage (Taeuber, 1996).

Impact of Single-Parent Families. Does it make any difference whether an infant grows up in a single-parent family or a two-parent family? It is not easy to answer that question because single-parent families vary widely. For example, a family headed by a 16-year-old mother of an unplanned infant represents a different family unit than that of a 30-year-old single mother of an adopted infant. To some extent, a single-parent family may represent a transition from one family form

to another. While a large number of families may be classified as single-parent households at some point, this designation may be of short duration because of marriage or remarriage (Roberts, 1994). However, many single-parent families share similar problems, including financial instability, inadequate alternative child care, and a high level of stress. The extent to which these and other adverse conditions exist is likely to determine the degree to which infant development is negatively affected by being reared by a single parent. In many instances, single parents have a support network of family member, neighbors and friends that supplement the caregiving process.

Eidusun and colleagues (1982) compared infants who were reared from birth in single-mother families with infants reared in traditional two-parent families and alternative families (communal and unmarried social-contract families). A variety of psychological variables, including attachment, cognitive functioning, and social adjustment, were assessed repeatedly during the infant's first three years. No significant differences between the single-mother infants and infants reared in the other families were discovered. There is little additional research that directly addresses the impact of the single-parent family on infants. Consequently, studies dealing with the effects of divorce, stress, and father absence on children must be examined for additional information on this issue.

Effects of Divorce. Because of their cognitive immaturity, very young infants are expected to be less affected by some of the trauma caused by divorce. However, their immaturity and greater dependency needs may actually make them developmentally more vulnerable to the effects of divorce in some ways. Few studies have isolated the effects of divorce that takes place when the children are infants. Santrock (1970, 1972) assessed the effects of divorce on children who were under age 2 when the divorce occurred. These children displayed less basic trust, more guilt and shame, less industry, and more feelings of inferiority as they grew older. When divorce occurs during infancy, there may also be negative effects upon intellectual development and achievements later in life. Studies on preschool-age children show that boys may be slightly more vulnerable to the effects of divorce on social adjustment than girls (Amato & Keith, 1991). Some studies indicate that younger children are considerably less burdened by divorce than older children (Guttmann, 1993). The extent to which divorce has negative consequences for the development of infants and young children is likely to be determined by the level of parental conflict and stress, the support system, and adequacy of parenting prior to and following the divorce.

Effects of Stress. Single parents experience far greater levels of tension, stress, and conflict in coping with the practical problems of living than parents in intact families. This is particularly true when infants are involved. Some of the most prevalent stresses include economic problems, finding adequate child care, and simply having time and energy to devote to children (Hetherington, 1979).

Wallerstein and Kelly (1980) found that the stress and conflict that accompany divorce result in a "diminished parenting" effect whereby the parents' ability to maintain interaction and communication with their children is lessened. These findings are consistent with the results of other studies. In a laboratory setting, parents were more critical and irritable with their toddlers when they were mildly stressed while performing a task than when the parents were not preoccupied (Zussman, 1980). Hetherington, Cox, and Cox (1982) found that during the first year after divorce, mothers tend to decrease their responsiveness and affection to their children.

The most important factor in the ability of single parent families to cope with stress appears to be the support system available in the extended family network and in society. When adequate economic resources, assistance with child care, housing, and the emotional support of a kinship and social network are available, the potential stresses and problems faced by single-parent families are dramatically reduced (Hetherington, 1979).

Effects of Father Absence. A father may be absent from the home because of death, divorce, desertion, working arrangements, or lack of interest (Parke, 1995). The quality and the degree of the father's involvement, even in the first year of life, are important factors in the child's sex role, personality, and mental development (Biller, 1981). Studies show that male infants whose fathers are absent tend to score lower on tests of cognitive performance than male infants whose fathers are consistently available. The effects of fathers' absence on the intellectual development of daughters apparently do not occur until later in childhood (Parke, 1995).

Apparently father absence does more damage when it occurs during infancy than at later ages (Lamb, 1976). Wachs and Gruen (1982) concluded that boys raised without fathers may have problems establishing appropriate sex-role behavior, such as a tendency to be less masculine or to display an exaggerated masculinity. The effects are particularly noticeable if the separation occurred before 5 years of age. Sex-role development of girls is also negatively affected by father absence, but the effects are not usually observed until adolescence.

Santrock (1970) found that fifth-grade boys who experienced father absence before the age of 2 had more personality problems than boys who lost their fathers at a later age. The boys who experienced father absence during infancy were less trusting, less industrious, and exhibited more feelings of inferiority than boys who were without fathers between 3 and 5 years of age. A study conducted on the Caribbean island of Barbados revealed that school-age males had same-sex identification problems if their father had been absent during the first two years of life (Burton, 1972). Other studies have found early father absence to be associated with increased susceptibility to a variety of behavioral and psychological problems (Biller, 1981).

Maternal Employment

Each year more and more women enter the labor force. The majority of these women are mothers. The number of employed women with children under 3 years of age increased from 33 percent in 1975 to 66 percent in 1994. Out of that group, 68 percent of black mothers were employed as compared with 49 percent of white mothers in 1994. Information was not available for other racial groups. Approximately 59 percent of all women with an infant 1 year of age and under were employed in 1994 (U.S. Bureau of the Census, 1995).

Effects of Maternal Employment

The dramatic increase in maternal employment has generated questions and concerns about how it will affect the development of infants and young children. Many research studies that have been conducted on this issue with conflicting results. Some studies report negative effects of maternal employment on infants' cognitive development (Schacter, 1981), on language development of boys (Chase-Lansdale, Michael, & Desai, 1991), and on child-maternal attachment (Barglow, Vaughn, & Molitor, 1987; Benn, 1986; Lamb, 1982b). Other studies report no effects on cognitive development, social competence, behavioral adjustment (Gottfried, 1991; Hock, 1980; Zimmerman & Bernstein, 1983), nor on child-maternal attachment (Easterbrooks & Goldberg, 1985; Stifter, Coulehan, & Fish, 1993; Weinraub, Jaeger, & Hoffman, 1990). Researchers have also reported that maternal employment does not adversely affect the mental and motor development of relatively healthy preterm infants' at 18

months of age (Youngblut, Loveland-Cherry, & Horan, 1994). Positive effects of maternal employment during the child's first three years have been associated with second-grade reading achievement of children from low-income families (Vandell & Ramanan, 1992).

The contradictory results of research studies on the effects of maternal employment on infant development are not surprising in view of the complexities involved in studying this issue. When comparisons are made between the developmental characteristics of infants being reared by employed mothers versus infants of unemployed mothers, there are numerous environmental and attitudinal factors that can make a difference in the outcomes. Maternal employment status affects infant development only to the extent that it alters family interrelationships and the home environment (Gottfried, 1991; Hoffman, 1989). For example, job related unhappiness and stress may have a "spill over" effect whereby the mother is less nurturing with an infant.

Maternal-employment status is less likely to have a negative impact on infant development if the mother has a choice about working (Youngblut et al., 1994), is satisfied with her job and work role, has a satisfactory child-care arrangement, and does not experience separation anxiety when leaving her infant in alternative child care (Weinraub et al., 1990; Lamb, 1982b; Zaslow, Rabinovich, & Sualsky, 1991). Of these variables, researchers have devoted most of their attention to how nonparental child care affects infant development.

Child-Care Arrangements

Working parents are presented with a variety of options when shopping for a child-care arrangement. The primary choices are usually categorized according to three basic arrangements: care in the infant's own home by a family member or "sitter"; care in another home by a relative, or professional caregiver; and care in a child day-care facility. Approximately 39 percent of children under age 3 are cared for by a relative or a nonrelative in the parent's home; 37 percent are cared for in a relative's or another caregiver's home; 15 percent are

Group day-care is a common experience for infants from many contemporary families.

cared for in organized child-care facilities. Approximately 8 percent of employed mothers care for their infants at work. Fathers are the primary caregivers for about 50 percent of infants who are cared for in their own home (U.S. Bureau of the Census, 1995). Although only a small proportion of infants are enrolled in day-care centers, this is the fastest-growing type of day care offered to the general public.

Effects of Infant Day-Care

Questions and concerns about possible negative effects of nonmaternal care on infants have generated numerous research studies during the past three decades. The earliest studies, conducted in the late 1960s and early 1970s, were limited mostly to high-quality day-care centers designed specifically for research purposes. Since that time additional studies that are more representative of the quality of care available to the general public have emerged. In spite of some of the problems and limitations of the studies, there are a number of consistent findings on how day care affects various aspects of infant development.

Physical Development. In general, day care has not been perceived as a threat to normal physical growth, so very little research has been done in this area. The limited research available indicates that infants from poor families who participate in good-quality day-care experience positive gains

in height, weight, and motor performance. The physical growth of infants from middle-class families apparently is not affected by day care (Clarke-Stewart & Fein, 1983).

Health. Infants who attend any type of day care with more than three other infants can be expected to be sick more frequently than infants who do not participate in day care. They have more incidents of colds, flu, and other respiratory illnesses than infants who stay at home (Strangert, 1976; Kendall, 1983). In addition, type B influenzae, hepatitis A, and diarrhea are some of the most common and persistent health problems that are associated with day care. Young infants are more susceptible to more frequent and severe infections due to immune system immaturity, incomplete immunization, and increased exposure (Link, Kernested, & Ford-Jones, 1993). The transmission of diarrhea and hepatitis is usually the result of the breakdown of proper sanitation practices, such as hand washing after diaper changes (Trump & Karasic, 1983; Snow, 1983).

Safety. Studies on the magnitude of accidental injuries to infants and children who participate in out-of-home care are limited mainly to day-care centers. Child-care injury rates for infants are usually not distinguished from rates for older children. Although rates of injuries requiring medical treatment vary widely from study to study, injury rates of children in day care compare favorably with rates of children injured at home or elsewhere. On the basis of existing studies it has been estimated that 33 to 48 percent fewer serious injuries take place in day-care centers than at home or in other places (Snow et al., 1992).

Social Development. The results of studies that have assessed the effects of day care on social development have produced a mixed picture. While some studies have found no differences between home-reared and day-care subjects, others suggest that day care can have both positive and negative effects on social behavior. Children who begin day care as infants have a tendency to display more aggression and other negative interactions with peers and are less obedient than children who were not enrolled in day care (Belsky, 1988). On the positive side, day-care children have been found to exhibit more social competence in interacting with peers and adults (Snow, 1983).

Emotional Development. Research on the effects of day care on emotional development has been limited mostly to studies on the infant's attachment to the mother. The possibility that nonmaternal infant child care adversely affects the infant's attachment to the mother has been the subject of intense concern by scientists as well as parents. Numerous research studies on this issue have produced contradictory conclusions. There are studies indicating that infant day care does not negatively affect attachment behavior (e.g., Field et al., 1988; Kagan et al., 1978). However, other researchers have concluded that infants under 1 year of age who are enrolled in day care for more than 20 hours per week are at-risk for forming emotionally insecure attachments with their mothers (e.g., Belsky & Rovine, 1988; Lamb, Sternberg, & Prodromidis, 1992).

In 1988, the National Institute of Health and Human Services (NICHD) initiated a large-scale long-term study to resolve the controversy over whether there is an association between nonmaternal infant care and infant-mother attachment, and if so, how it might be explained. The ongoing NICHD Early Child Care Research Network (1996) study includes leading child care researchers from

14 universities throughout the United States. In 1991, infants from approximately 1,300 families were enrolled when they were 1 month old or less, and they are being followed until they are 7 years of age. The infants and families are diverse in terms of race, maternal education, maternal employment status, family income, family structure, and there is diversity in the type, quality, and amount of child care.

The results of the first phase of the study clearly indicate that nonmaternal child care does not, in and of itself, threaten the security of infant-mother attachment. When assessed at 15 months of age, infants who were enrolled in various forms of out-of-home care did not differ in security of attachment from infants who were cared for at home by a parent. However, certain child-care conditions, in combination with certain home environments, apparently increase the likelihood that day care will adversely affect the attachment relationship. There was consistent evidence that infants who were enrolled in poor quality care, unstable child care for more than 10 hours per week were more likely to be insecurely attached **if** their mothers were low in sensitivity and unresponsive to their needs. Overall, the results of the study provide reassurance to working parents that day care does not ordinarily interfere with parent-infant attachment.

Intellectual Development. Through the years research findings have consistently demonstrated that stimulation provided in a high-quality day-care program has positive effects on the cognitive development of infants from economically disadvantaged families. Studies that have focused on infants and children from middle-class families have been less clear-cut, but have tended to conclude that good quality day-care has no obvious harmful or beneficial effects on the intellectual development of these subjects. However, the latest report of the ongoing large-scale study conducted by the NICHD Study of Early Child Care Research Network (1997) shows that various types of good quality day-care contributed to significant gains in cognitive and language development for children from all economic backgrounds during the first 3 years of life. Higher child-care quality was consistently related to better developmental outcomes.

Day-Care Quality

One of the most critical factors in considering the effects of day care on infants is the quality of the care that is used. Under certain conditions, infants and toddlers who attend higher-quality day-care centers have been identified as more likely to be securely attached to their caregivers and more socially oriented than infants in poor or minimally adequate care (Howes, Philips, & Whitebook, 1992; NICHD Early Child Care Research Network, 1996). In addition, the quality of center day care has been associated with cognitive and language development during infancy (Burchinal et al., 1996; NICHD Early Child Care Research Network, 1997).

The quality of child care varies widely among facilities. Child-care quality was rated as ranging from poor to mediocre in a study of 50 nonprofit and 50 for-profit randomly chosen centers in California, Colorado, Connecticut, and North Carolina (Cost, Quality, & Outcomes Team, 1995). The investigators concluded that quality of infant/toddler care at most U.S. child-care centers does not meet the needs for health, safety, warm relationships, and learning. Generally, nonprofit facilities (e.g., municipal agencies, universities, public schools, and employer-sponsored) were rated as superior in quality to other facilities. Unfortunately, the availability of these facilities is very limited.

Much less is known about the quality of family day care in which care is provided in a home other than the child's residence. These facilities are more difficult to identify and study because they are less visible and accessible to researchers. A government-sponsored national day-care home study (Fosberg, 1981) found that the quality of family day care varies considerably among facilities. Generally, homes that were sponsored by a government or nonprofit agency provided better care than homes that were simply registered or licensed or not regulated at all.

Components of Day-Care Quality

Researchers and caregivers have identified many of the factors that are associated with day-care quality. There is general agreement on the major components of day-care quality that can be regulated through government agencies. These features include staff-child ratio, group size, caregiver training, and basic health and safety requirements, and adequate indoor and outdoor space. Staff wages, staff turnover, and parent involvement are also important indicators of day-care quality, but are not typically included in day-care regulations. Additional components of day-care quality include caregiver sensitivity and responsiveness to infant needs and a developmentally appropriate curriculum.

Ratios and Group Size. The maximum number of infants that can be adequately cared for by one caregiver is generally considered to be three or four for infants and five for toddlers (NAEYC, 1991; Ruopp et al., 1979). The maximum recommended group sizes are: six for precrawling infants; nine infants who are mobile (up to 18 months); and twelve for 18 months to 3 years of age (Lally et al., 1995). Unfortunately, licensing laws in most states do not require day-care facilities to meet recommended standards of quality. Although child-care center licensing regulations for staff/child ratios and group size have improved in recent years, in 1995 only 16 states met both staff/child ratio and group size standards recommended by the National Association for the Education of Young Children (NAEYC) in their child-care centers licensing regulations (Snow, Teleki, & Reguero de-Atiles, 1996). In some states, one adult may be allowed to care for as many as eight babies. The caregiver-infant ratio is the major factor affecting the cost of care. Staff salaries are the most expensive part of day care, so when more personnel are employed, the cost of care increases. Thus, most day care facilities do not maintain higher standards than those required by law.

Caregiver Qualifications. Another important factor in assessing the quality of infant day care is the qualifications of the provider. Researchers have found that day-care staff with education and training related to understanding and meeting the needs of infants provide better care with superior results than caregivers without appropriate training (Fosberg, 1981; Ruopp et al., 1979; Honig, 1995). Effective interpersonal skills along with commitment and concern for infants and their families are also important caregiver qualifications (Clarke-Stewart, 1982). Only a few states require day-care providers to have any specialized training or preparation in the care of infants, although most states include in-service training requirements in their child-care licensing regulations (Snow et al., 1996).

Parent Involvement. High-quality day-care programs also include parent involvement and participation as a major component. The more parents are involved in the day-care program, the more children benefit (Zigler & Turner, 1982). Parents can become involved in an infant-toddler day care program in numerous ways, including serving on an advisory board, as a program observer, or helping with special projects. Regular communication between parent and caregiver is viewed as an essential feature of good day care. Unfortunately, parents average only about seven minutes per day in their child's day-care center (Zigler & Turner, 1982). Most of the parent-caregiver contacts occur at "transition points" when children arrive and depart (Powell, 1978).

Staff Turnover. Continuity and stability of caregivers and caregiving arrangements appear to be very important considerations for infants, especially when they are in the peak period for stranger anxiety. Although not all of the research studies have found negative consequences associated with frequent changes in caregivers (e.g., Schiller, 1980), conventional wisdom and much of the research support this conclusion (e.g., Cummings, 1980; Lally et al., 1995; NICHD, 1996). The child's family situation is an important variable that affects the outcome of care in any event. Continuity of care is apparently more important for infants who receive inadequate attention at home (NICHD, 1995).

Infants experience discontinuity of care when they are moved from one child care arrangement to another, when a caregiver leaves a program, or when an infant is changed from one caregiver to another within a facility. Shifting infants from one caregiver to another as often as every six to nine months is a common practice in child-care centers (Lally et al., 1995). Day-care facilities typically have staff-turnover problems because of low wages and lack of fringe benefits. Staff-turnover rates are highest in facilities that pay the lowest wages. Teaching staff earning the lowest wages are twice as likely to leave their jobs as those earning the highest wage (Whitebook, Howes, & Philips, 1989). Among the unregulatable components of day-care quality, staff wages is the most important predictor of the quality of care infants and children receive (Scarr, Eisenberg & Deater-Deckard, 1994).

Assessment of Day-Care Quality

Day-care quality is usually assessed by comparing the regulatable components to the ideal standards as discussed above. Researchers have found that a variety of factors should be used in assessing day-care quality (Scarr et al., 1994). The **Infant-Toddler Day Care Environment Rating Scale (ITERS)** (Harms, Cryer, & Clifford, 1990) is an instrument that can be used to provide an environmental assessment of center-based day care for children under 30 months of age. The ITERS includes 35 items on such "process" factors as personal-care routines, furnishings, learning activities, and caregiver-infant interactions. An overall score and scores on seven subscales can be obtained.

EARLY-INTERVENTION PROGRAMS

As a part of the War on Poverty initiated by the federal government in the 1960s, a variety of early-intervention programs were developed for infants and their parents. These programs were designed primarily to prevent the decline in intelligence scores that often results from environmental deprivation. Many of these efforts were designed as experimental programs to test the effectiveness of intervention in general as well as specific educational models (Beller, 1979). Some of the programs were designed to teach parents how to teach their infants. Other programs focused directly on providing stimulation for the infants. The programs also varied on whether the activities were conducted on an individual basis in the home or in groups at a center. A few model programs were developed in the form of centers designed to work both with parents and their infants.

The first intervention programs were directed primarily at infants considered to be developmentally "at-risk" because of the effects of poverty. More recent programs have been developed to include infants affected by prematurity, genetic disorders, hearing loss, visual impairment or other conditions that threaten growth and development (Trohanis, Cox, & Meyer, 1982).

Lasting Effects of Early Intervention

The results of early-intervention programs are consistent in demonstrating positive short-range effects on the development of economically disadvantaged infants (Beller, 1979). To determine whether or not these benefits last, investigators from twelve early-intervention programs pooled their information and conducted a joint follow-up study. Their participants were aged 9 to 19 at the time. The findings clearly show that the early-intervention programs had long-lasting beneficial effects (Lazar & Darlington, 1979; Lazar & Darlington, 1982). The children who participated in the early-intervention programs were more likely than the control children to perform better in their schools in the following ways:

1. The number of children assigned to special-education classes was reduced by approximately 50 percent.
2. The number of children failing a grade in school was reduced.
3. The program participants achieved superior scores on fourth-grade math tests. There was also a trend toward increased scores on fourth-grade reading tests.
4. The children who received the intervention surpassed their controls on IQ tests for up to three years after

the programs ended. The participants of the three programs, which involved infants and toddlers, maintained superior IQ scores approximately ten to fifteen years after the programs ended.

In addition, mothers' attitudes toward school performance and their vocational hopes for their children were affected in positive ways.

More recently, follow-up results of the Carolina Abercederian Project have provided additional support for the long-term effectiveness of early intervention. This project was a well-designed experiment to determine the extent to which the detrimental effects of poverty could be prevented through an intensive educational program beginning in infancy (Campbell & Ramey, 1994). The researchers found that at age 12, the children who were enrolled in the intervention project maintained an intellectual advantage over the control subjects who did not receive the early educational program. The study supports the theory that, for children from impoverished environments, the earlier in the life span intervention is begun, the greater its benefits are likely to be. A long-term follow-up study of another early intervention program found that its benefits were still evident when the graduates were 27 years old. In comparison to subjects in a control group, the program participants had significantly higher levels of schooling, higher wages, higher percentages of home ownership, with lower percentages receiving social services, or being arrested (Schweinhart, Barnes, & Weikart, 1993).

Current Programs

Early-intervention programs for infants and toddlers who are at-risk for developmental problems have become widespread throughout the United States, encompassing rural, urban, and suburban areas (Hanson, 1996b). The program delivery models vary from home-based, center-based, to a combination of home-based and center-based services. Services are provided by a variety of professionals and agencies with heavy emphasis placed upon family involvement, transdisciplinary programming, and interagency coordination.

THE HOME ENVIRONMENT

The quality of the environment within the home is a critical factor affecting the infant's development. The home environment is directly related to the developmental status of the infant (Gottfried, 1985). What are the characteristics of a favorable home environment for infant development? Betty Caldwell, a nationally recognized expert in infant development and child care, has developed a list of the six environmental characteristics of homes that are most likely to foster early development (Caldwell & Bradley, 1979):

1. Emotional and verbal responsivity of the mother.
2. Avoidance of restriction and punishment.
3. Organization of the physical and temporal (day-to-day) environment.
4. Provisions of appropriate play materials.
5. Maternal (parental) involvement with the child.
6. Opportunities for variety in daily stimulation.

These characteristics have been incorporated into the **HOME Inventory** (Caldwell & Bradley, 1979) that has been used widely in infant research and developmental-screening programs to measure the quality of home environments. The two most important home-environment characteristics that are related to intellectual and language development during infancy are the quantity and quality of parent-infant relations and the availability of play materials (Bradley, 1994; Bradley et al., 1989; Gottfried, 1985). Homes that rate highly on those qualities tend to produce infants who score highest on measures of cognitive performance and language development.

Characteristics of Parent-Infant Relations

In spite of the changes that have occurred in the American family structure, the mother continues to serve as the primary caregiver. Even when the mother is employed, the father spends less time caring for the baby than the mother (Belsky & Volling, 1987; Darling-Fisher & Tiejde, 1990). Mothers average spending 65 to 80 percent more time than fathers in one-to-one interactions with their babies (Parke, 1995). Fathers and mothers differ not only in the amount of time which they spend

with their infants, but in their styles of interaction. A greater proportion of father-infant interactions are spent in play and social interactions, whereas mothers are more involved in routine caregiving activities (Bailey, 1994; Hossain & Roopnarine, 1994). However, this does not mean that fathers are less competent caregivers than mothers. Studies have shown that fathers are as successful as mothers in interpreting a baby's signals and in responding to its needs (Parke & Tinsley, 1987).

In some ways fathers and mothers treat daughters differently from sons. Some studies report that boys are handled more roughly and receive more physical punishment from both parents than girls (Huston, 1983). Other studies report that both parents more often reject, criticize, challenge, control, and reprimand their daughters than their sons (Cowan, Cowan, & Kerig, 1993). Grant (1994) reviewed nine studies that found differences in the mother-infant interaction on the basis of the gender. The overall conclusions were that mothers tended to stimulate or arouse (e.g., burping, handling) their male infant, while mothers of female infants tended to gently caress and stroke their female infants.

Fathers tend to play with infants in different ways than mothers. They are more likely to engage in physical play by bouncing their infants, moving the infant's limbs, and engaging in rough-and-tumble games. In contrast, mothers are more likely to engage in quieter, more conventional playful interactions with toys and games, such as peek-a-boo (Parke & Tinsley, 1987). Some studies report that fathers are more directly involved in the rearing of sons than they are daughters (Lamb, 1981b). Other researchers report that fathers provide less physical contact, overall, for their male infants than for their female infants (Shields & Sparling, 1993).

The reason why fathers sometimes differ from mothers in the treatment of sons and daughters may be related to divergent parenting styles and marital conflict. Cowan and his co-researchers (1993) found that the more husbands and wives differ in parenting styles, the more likely their parenting is affected by whether the baby is a boy or a girl. Fathers were found to be more authoritarian with their daughters than their sons if the mother displayed a different style of parenting. In families where there was marital conflict, the difference

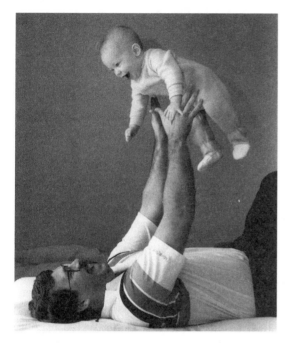

Fathers tend to engage in "rough and tumble" play with their infants.

between the way fathers treated their sons and daughters was intensified.

How Infants Influence Parental Responses. Infants initiate many of the parent-child interactions and are highly effective in gaining parental attention (Maccoby & Martin, 1983). The young infant's sighs, cries, smiles, gaze, state of alertness, helplessness, and "baby face" are some of the characteristics to which parents respond. Yet not all of their responses are positive. Parents typically do not respond as positively to infants with physical impairments, to preterm infants, to noncuddlers, or to "difficult infants" as they do to infants perceived as displaying more postive characteristcs (Maccoby & Martin, 1983; Osofsky & Connors, 1979). Infants are very adaptive, however, and tend to alter many of their responses to match parental behaviors.

How Infants Influence Marital Relations. With the birth of children, the husband-wife relationship changes. The family system changes with the birth of each child (Stafford & Dainton, 1995).

For many couples, the birth of the first child constitutes a crisis that disrupts the marital relationship. For others the "blessed event" requires only minor adjustments (Dyer, 1963; Hobbs, 1968). In most marriages, though, the quality of the husband-wife relationship is apparently affected for better or worse. Approximately 12 percent of a group of 250 married couples experienced a severe decline in marital satisfaction following the birth of the first baby (Belsky & Kelly, 1994). Thirty-eight percent of the couples reported a moderate decline of marital quality. There was no change in marital satisfaction for 30 percent of the couples, while 19 percent felt that their marriage improved.

A number of factors determine the extent to which infants affect the marriage relationship. Couples who are older and who have been married for longer periods of time tend to have fewer problems adjusting to parenthood (Belsky, 1981). The quality of the marriage before the baby is born is another major factor. Couples who report the highest levels of marital satisfaction before pregnancy tend to remain the happiest after the baby is born (Schneck, 1986). The number of children and the years between their birthdays also make a difference. Finally, the individual characteristics of an infant are probably the most important factor in determining how the marriage is affected. Parents of babies who cry more frequently and who are more active tend to be more stressed than parents of less demanding, quieter babies (Russell, 1974).

Marital Relationships and Parenting. The quality of the marriage has important implications for the quality of parenting the infant receives. Belsky found that "in marriages where marital quality declines the most, the bond between mother and child is weakest" (cited in Schneck, 1986, p. 12). Harmonious marriage relationships have been found to be associated with secure toddler-parent attachments and marital discord with insecure attachments (Easterbrooks & Goldberg, 1990). Studies have also shown that marital tension and conflict have a negative impact on the mother's ability to enjoy her baby, to regard it with affection, to be competent as a parent, and to achieve a high quality of infant-mother attachment (Belsky, 1981; Parke & Tinsley, 1987). For example, higher rates of negative behaviors between the father and mother have been found to be associated with a larger number of negative behaviors directed by the mother to the baby (Pederson, Anderson, & Cain, 1980).

The father's involvement in caregiving, playfulness, satisfaction with fatherhood, and competence in caregiving are also linked to the quality of the marriage (Belsky, 1979; Dickie & Matheson, 1984; Feldman, Nash, & Aschenbrenner, 1983). A happy and supportive marital relationship is apparently even more important for the father-infant relationship than it is for the mother-infant relationship. The father may depend more on the mother's support because of uncertainties about how to care for an infant and reluctance to intrude into what is traditionally perceived as the mother's territory (Parke & Tinsley, 1987). Initial differences in parenting styles may be intensified by marital conflict (Cowan et al., 1993), or marital conflict may be intensified by differences in parenting styles.

When fathers spend more time in parenting, both parents benefit. Willoughby and Glidden (1995) found higher participation of fathers in the care of children with disabilities to be associated with greater marital satisfaction for mothers as well as fathers. Those findings are consistent with other studies linking higher levels of father involvement with typically developing children to enhanced marital satisfaction. However, researchers have trouble deciding whether greater marital satisfaction results from more father participation, or whether higher levels of marital satisfaction contribute to increased father participation. The cause-effect relationship may be circular. Fathers who have a higher level of marital satisfaction may tend to become more involved in meeting the needs of their children and enhance marriage satisfaction in the process.

Cultural and Ethnic Diversity in Parenting

On a worldwide scale, parents in all cultures share a common set of goals in their concern for the physical health and survival of their infants and efforts to maximize their future social adjustment and future economic welfare (Levine, 1980). However, the specific childrearing attitudes and strategies parents use in implementing these goals vary widely around the world. In many parts of the world, such as Kenya and South America, infants are held and carried most of the time. Parenting styles are relaxed and casual. Attention is devoted to meeting the baby's physical needs, but efforts are not made to stimulate precocious social or intellectual development (Levine, 1980). In contrast, many American parents are less involved physically with their infants but are more concerned about social and intellectual stimulation. Child-rearing practices vary widely within, as well as between, ethnic and cultural groups. Parents from around the world vary in their perceptions of mechanisms responsible for infant behavior, beliefs about how infants should be treated, educational practices, and patterns of interaction.

In the United States, most of the research on father-infant and mother-infant interactions has been conducted among middle-class Caucasian families. However, experts predict that by the middle of the next century the United States will no longer have any one dominant ethnic group (Chang & Pulido, 1994). Fortunately, information is slowly beginning to accumulate on intracultural and intercultural variations in parenting values and practices among various racial and ethnic groups (see Garcia Coll, Meyer, & Brillon, 1995). Professionals who work with infants and parents in various settings need to understand and be sensitive to different cultural childrearing practices and values in order to improve communication and establish appropriate child-care, early-intervention, or other programs.

African-American Parents. Studies of infant caregiving and interaction among African-American families are finding patterns that differ, but not dramatically, from those observed in other racial groups. African-American mothers, like mothers from other racial classifications in the United Sates, are typically the primary caregiver. However, the rate of involvement in child care by African-American fathers varies from rates identified for Caucasian-American fathers. In one study of intact, middle-class African-American families, fathers reported spending 42 percent as much time as mothers in primary caregiving routines. Whether the mother was employed part-time or full-time did not make any difference (Hossain & Roopnarine, 1994). By comparison, other studies report middle-class Caucasian fathers spend about 33 percent as much time as mothers in caregiving activities when both parents are employed (Lamb, 1987). African-American fathers, compared with African-American mothers, rate themselves as less involved in certain caregiving interactions such as bedtime routines, feeding, comforting a crying infant, or singing to an infant (Hossain & Roopnarine, 1994).

African-American parents tend to emphasize the importance of family ties. Studies reviewed by Garcia Coll and others (1995) indicate that African-American families place a high value on socializing children to respect, obey, and learn from elders in the family and community. Grandparents, other family members, and members from the community tend to support parents in the provision of child care, protection, guidance, and discipline.

Other Minority Parents. Native-American and Hispanic-American (or Latino) families tend to adopt a nurturant, relaxed, and permissive style in rearing infants (Garcia Coll et al., 1995). Responsibilities for child care are typically shared among parents, extended-family members, siblings, and members of the community in both groups. Native-American infants are encouraged to master self-care skills early. Mutual dependence, responsibility, respect for others, courage, optimism, respect for nature, and a spiritual orientation are values that are commonly emphasized in the socialization of infants and children (Olson & DeFrain, 1994). Hispanic-Americans also socialize their infants to be interdependent with family members rather than independent and individualistic. Asian-American parents tend to be lenient, nurturant, and permissive with infants and young children. However, as children get older, their parents impose stricter standards of discipline, encourage self-control, obedience, and emotional maturity (Garcia Coll et al., 1995). Research studies on parenting in lesbian and gay families are very limited, especially in relation to parenting infants (West & Turner, 1995). The results of existing studies have found no evidence to indicate that the gay and lesbian parenting practices and childrearing results differ in noticeable ways from those of heterosexual parents (Patterson, 1995).

Importance of Grandparents

In most families throughout the world grandparents play an important role in infant development. Grandparents, especially grandmothers, influence the development of infants indirectly through the emotional, economic, and other forms of support they provide parents. Grandparents also directly influence the development of infants through contact and interaction (Crockenberg, Lyons-Ruth, & Dickstein, 1993). Although parents across cultures often complain about grandparents being overindulgent and interfering in discipline (Broude, 1995), parents typically value and appreciate the role of grandparents. For many single, adolescent mothers, grandparents are the most important source of support, and often function as the infant's primary caregiver. Research indicates that support from grandparents is associated with more nurturant, sensitive, and responsive caregiving by the infant's mother (Crockenberg et al., 1993). In many families, infants appear to be attached to parents and grandparents alike. Studies also show that the involvement of grandmothers in the care of infants is typically associated with positive developmental outcomes, but is most apparent in cases where parent resources and other sources of support are limited (Crockenberg et al., 1993).

Parenting Infants with Special Needs

Infants who are born with a developmentally challenging condition (e.g., prematurity, Down syndrome, cerebral palsy) display behavioral and physical characteristics that affect interactional patterns with their caregivers. Infants with disabilities tend to be less responsive, less active, and provide less distinct behavioral cues than typically developing infants. For example, infants with Down syndrome engage in less eye contact and less vocal turn-taking with their caregivers than other infants (Widerstrom et al., 1991). Parents may misinterpret their signals and provide excessive stimulation during feeding and other care-giving activities in an effort to elicit responses. On the other hand, because these infants physically appear to be more fragile and less cuddly, parents may provide less stroking, holding, or other nurturing interactions.

Hansen (1996a) reviewed research studies on parent interactions with infants affected by cognitive impairments, physical disabilities, or other developmental challenges. Interaction patterns between mothers and cognitively impaired infants tended to use more structure or directive language than mothers of typically developing infants do in their interactions. Mothers of infants with hearing deficits were found to exhibit less flexibility, less approval, more intrusiveness, and more overprotection in their interactions than mothers of infants without hearing loss. Mothers of infants with vision problems or physical disabilities tend to exhibit similar behaviors (Meadow-Orlans, 1995). Fathers of boys with autism or other communication disorders have been reported to participate less in child-care activities than fathers of boys without disabilities (Bristol, Gallagher, & Schopler, 1988). Shields and Sparling (1995) found that fathers of sick and low-birthweight infants provided less physical contact and affectional touch than fathers of healthy infants. Other studies (see Darke and Goldberg, 1994), however, suggest that fathers of preterm infants and other infants with special needs are more involved in the care of their infants than fathers whose babies are healthy. In all cases, though, mothers of infants with special needs tend to bear a larger share of the work and psychological stress involved in parenting than fathers (Darke & Goldberg, 1994).

In spite of the increased demands involved in parenting infants with disabilities, both mothers and fathers adjust remarkably well. Caregiver-infant interactions are best when caregivers understand and adjust to the characteristics and special needs of infants with developmental problems. Hanson (1996) recommends that intervention programs assist parents in interpreting the infant's unique signaling system, reading and understanding their infant's cues, and providing appropriate interactional responses.

MANAGING INFANT BEHAVIOR: DISCIPLINE

Discipline is an essential part of childrearing. In its broadest meaning, discipline refers to the process of teaching and learning that fosters human growth and development (Dodson, 1970; DuBois, 1952). Discipline gives young children a sense of security by letting them know what they can and cannot do. Children gain approval from others by learning to behave according to socially accepted standards. Discipline thus facilitates the development of self-esteem. Appropriate discipline also fosters achievement motivation and the development of a conscience. The ultimate goal of discipline, though, is the development of self-discipline. Infants begin life with little ability to control their own behavior. They depend upon their caregivers to guide them through the process of establishing impulse control and self-regulation.

Discipline and behavior control are usually not a major concern of parents during the early months of life. Excessive crying and fussing are the behaviors that present the most problems for caregivers before infants begin to move around. As they learn to creep and walk, infants begin to explore the environment and begin to "get out of bounds." As discussed previously, biting, hitting, temper tantrums, failure to comply with requests, clinging, and other types of negative behavior are problem behaviors that develop during the toddler stage. Parents and other caregivers are then faced with decisions about how much freedom to allow, what limits to set, and what methods of discipline and guidance to use.

Setting Limits

Parental expectations of infant behavior and limits must be reasonable to be most effective. Arbitrary and unnecessary limits contribute to negativism, noncompliance, and parent-child conflict. Generally, limits should be designed to (1) ensure the child's health and safety, (2) protect the health, safety, and rights of others, (3) prevent the destruction of property, and (4) teach the moral and social values of the family and society.

Realistic behavioral expectations can be established only if adults keep in mind the age-level characteristics, needs, and limited abilities of infants and toddlers. Cognitive immaturity and limited language ability prevent infants from understanding and complying with adults' wishes, as well as from communicating their own desires. Their struggle to establish autonomy frequently results in negative responses to adult requests. Toddlers need physical activity and freedom of movement. Thus, they have difficulty sitting still and keeping quiet. Infants and toddlers are very egocentric, which means that they view things only from their own point of view. For example, to the parent bath water is used for bathing, but to an infant bath water is something used for playing.

Children need to be informed of the limits that are set and the expectations their caregivers hold. They react to ambiguity with confusion and should not be expected to conform to unclear limits. Toward the end of the first year, infants can begin to understand simple restrictions, such as the meaning of "no." As language development proceeds, verbal explanations can become a little more complex. For young children, it is more important to explain *what* they should do rather than *why* (Greenfield & Tronick, 1980). When possible, directions should be stated in a positive form that tells an infant what to do instead of what not to do ("Keep the sand in the sandbox!").

Strategies for Guiding Behavior

Once limits have been clearly established, they need to be consistently enforced. However, this should be done in positive ways that "preserve the self-respect of the parent as well as the child" (Ginott, 1965, p. 96). The restrictions are applied firmly and kindly without excessive anger or force and without attacking the personality of the child. Children need to be given the right to have feelings, just as adults. Their feelings can be accepted even though the behavior is objectionable. Name-calling and personality attacks, such as "you stupid brat," should never be used. Chamberlain and Patterson (1995) have identified four types of discipline that have been consistently linked with negative childrearing outcomes: (1) inconsistent discipline, (2) irritable, explosive discipline, (3) low supervison and involvement, and (4) inflexible, rigid discipline.

Adults have numerous options for enforcing limits and guiding the behavior of their children. The following are included among the strategies usually recommended for positive guidance of infants and toddlers. Keep in mind, however, that no single technique is equally effective with all children. A child's compliance will vary with the person making the request, the situation, and other factors such as how tired the child is at the time. The temperament of the infant is also an important factor in how resourceful an adult has to be.

Distraction and Redirection. Infants who are crying or engaged in unacceptable activities can be distracted or diverted to another activity. For example, young infants can sometimes be distracted by being held in front of a mirror or a window. They can be moved to a new, more appropriate location. Alternative activities and toys can be provided as substitutes for those that are prohibited. When Tanya was 18 months old, she was found playing in the toilet bowl. Her mother's response was "You need to play somewhere else." She then took Tanya to her room and found some toys for her to play with. Whenever possible, children should be given choices. "Do you want to play here or go outside?" However, a choice should not be given if it is not really available or acceptable.

Environmental Control. Many problem behaviors can be avoided if the environment is properly structured. An infant needs a place to play that is "child-proof." Breakable objects and other valuables should be placed where infants cannot reach them. Safety hazards should be eliminated. An adequate supply of age-appropriate toys and interesting activities should be provided to keep the child busy. Nine-month-old Jamal opened a kitchen cabinet and pulled out the pots and pans from the bottom shelves. Jamal's mother put fasteners on the cabinet doors to keep him away from her cooking utensils. She also put some old pots and pans in a cabinet which she left open for Jamal to play with.

Modeling. It is important for adults to model

the behaviors they want to teach. For example, the best way to teach children to use good manners is for the adult to practice them in caregiving interactions. When adults say "Please" and "Thank you" when making requests, the child will eventually reciprocate. Young children are more likely to imitate a model that is warm and nurturing than one that is cold and aloof.

Positive Reinforcement. Children tend to repeat behaviors that are reinforced with a social reinforcer such as praise, a hug, or a smile. Parents and caregivers are generally encouraged to praise desirable behavior and ignore, as much as possible, behaviors they don't want to encourage. However, praise or other social reinforcers should be sincere and nonmanipulative. Reinforcement should be perceived as a means of fostering the infant's self-esteem rather than simply as a means to achieve behavior control (Seefeldt, 1987).

To be most effective, praise must be given immediately after the behavior. Praise is also most effective when it is a recognition of the child's specific behavior (Ginott, 1965) ("Thank you for sharing your toy! That was a nice thing to do!"). General praise that addresses the child's personality is less helpful ("You're the best child!").

Time-out. The use of time-out to discipline toddlers is another option available to parents and caregivers. In this procedure, a child who is being disruptive is removed from the situation and given a chance to calm down. In some cases, the child is taken to another room and isolated for a while. After a brief interval, the child may return to the situation or resume another activity. This gives the child who is out of control a chance to regain equilibrium and self-control. It is unrealistic, however, to expect an infant or a toddler to sit in a specified place for more than a few seconds. Time-out should be viewed as a teaching act and an opportunity for the infant to establish self-control rather than as a punishment.

Punishment. The use of punishment in controlling the behavior of infants and toddlers is controversial. Scolding, spanking, withdrawal of love, isolation, and other negative responses to a child's behavior are types of punishment commonly used. Punishment is the least desirable means of behavior control. Holden (1983) observed the strategies mothers used in controlling the behavior of 2-year-old infants. Some of the mothers used scolding or reprimands when the infant misbehaved. Other mothers used "preventive" measures such as engaging the child in conversation to control behavior. The mothers who used preventive measures had fewer problems and less conflict with their infants.

Most parents feel that there are times when punishment is necessary, but it should be brief and clearly linked to what the child has done (Laishley, 1983). Punishment is effective in suppressing some behavior, but that does not mean that the behavior is eliminated. Punishment may produce undesirable side effects, such as associating the punishment with the parent. Punishment does not foster the development of internal control and can lead to excessive reliance on external authority for behavioral inhibition (Maccoby, 1980). Punishment is most effective when it immediately follows the problem behavior and when it is consistent. It is also more effective when administered by someone who has a warm and caring relationship with the child (Hetherington & Parke, 1979).

Spanking is the most controversial type of punishment. Most childrearing experts (e.g., Brazelton, 1992; Ginott, 1965) recommend that parents avoid the use of spanking. For example, Ginott (1965) argues that spanking is ineffective and should be avoided: "If spanking is so effective, why do we have such uneasy feelings about it. . . . What is wrong with spanking is the lessons it demonstrates. It teaches children undesirable methods of dealing with frustration. It dramatically tells them: when you are angry—hit!" (p. 107). Ginott's argument is illustrated by the cartoon that shows a father vigorously spanking his son. The caption reads: "That will teach you to hit your younger sister!" The father is right. It will. In actual practice, the majority of parents use spanking as a method of discipline out of a sense of frustration if for no other reason. However, if parents are resourceful, they can find more positive means of behavior control.

Love Withdrawal. One of the most common methods used by parents to control a child's behavior is withdrawal of love. The parent expresses anger and disappointment when the child misbehaves: "I don't like you when you cry like that!" The parent follows up by isolating the child emotionally. The child's efforts to communicate are ignored as the parent turns away from the child, refusing to speak or listen. The parent may even threaten to leave (Maccoby, 1980). Love withdrawal is punitive and implicitly says to the child, "If you don't please me, I won't love you!" The results of love withdrawal are mostly negative. It produces a high level of arousal and anxiety in children and does not lead to the establishment of internal control (Hoffman, 1970). Discipline begins with the loving care that a baby receives (Keister, 1973), so the very foundation of discipline is threatened by the use of love withdrawal.

Parental Attitudes

The effectiveness of any disciplinary technique depends largely upon the nature of the parent-child relationship. Discipline is administered in the context of parental attitudes. The message and meaning of the disciplinary action, especially punishment, are determined to a large extent by the attitude of the disciplinarian. Parental attitudes can be placed on a continuum ranging from love and acceptance to hostility and rejection. The most competent children are reared by parents who use positive methods to control behavior within the context of a warm and loving attitude (Hoffman, 1981). This combination of authority and positive attitudes tends to result in children who are self-reliant, self-confident, curious, and happy (Becker, 1964).

Parent-Infant Relationship Disorders

Understanding the quality of the parent-infant relationship is an important part of diagnosing and treating emotional, behavioral, and other disorders of infants and children. When infants have mental-health problems, relationships with primary caregivers may be part of the problem. Significant relationship difficulties are characterized by negative attitudes, perceptions, emotions, and behaviors of either the parent, the child, or both that lead to disturbed parent-child interactions (Zero to Three, 1994). A **Parent-Infant Relationship Global Assessment Scale (PIR-GAS)** (Zero to Three, 1994) is available for use by clinicians and researchers in assessing the strengths of relationships, as well as the severity of a relationship disorder. Parent-infant (or other caregiver) relationship problems range from less than optimal interaction patterns (**perturbed**) that last for a short period of time, to **grossly impaired** interactions that are so dangerously disorganized and so disturbed that the infant is in danger of physical harm.

The behavioral quality of the interaction, the affective tone, and the level of psychological involvement are used in deciding whether or not there is a relationship disorder. Along with the PIR-GAS, a classification manual is available for use in diagnosing and classifying a variety of relationships disorders. For example, relationships characterized by physical and/or psychological intrusiveness, interference with infant goals, overcontrol, and developmentally inappropriate demands by the caregiver are classified as **overinvolved**. At the other extreme, relationships in which caregivers are unresponsive and insensitive to infant cues and provide low quality of care are classified as **underinvolved.** Other relationship disorders include those classified as **anxious/tense, angry/hostile,** and **abusive**.

SELECTING TOYS AND MATERIALS

Choosing a baby's toys and play materials is as important as choosing the baby's clothing. However, the task is not easy because of the almost endless variety of toys available. Some general criteria should be considered by parents and caregivers in selecting toys and materials for infants and toddlers:

1. Toys and materials should be appropriate for the child's age and developmental level. Fortunately, infants are adaptable and play with toys in their own

way. Information about recommended toys for infants according to age is readily available in numerous publications (e.g., Aston, 1984; Greenfield & Tronick, 1980; White, 1985). Many toy manufacturers label their toys according to a general age range.

2. Toys and materials should provide a challenge to the child without being impossible to master. Adults cannot always predict which toys will present an optimum challenge. However, given a reasonable variety of toys, an infant will select the ones that are most appealing.

3. All toys and play materials should be free from safety hazards (see Chapter 7).

4. The infant's toy collection should be balanced and comprehensive. There should be a variety of toys to cover each area of development, including small and large muscle, sensorimotor, eye-hand coordination, social, emotional, language, and cognitive as well as imagination and creativity.

5. The infant's toy collection should be built around the "basics." It should include play things that can be used in a variety of ways and which are universal and timeless favorites, such as balls, blocks, puzzles, books, records, dolls, and stuffed animals.

6. Toys should be cost effective. A toy should be durable, sturdy, and worth the investment. In some cases this may mean paying more for a better-quality toy and perhaps buying fewer toys. For example, although a wooden puzzle costs more than a cardboard puzzle, the wooden puzzle is a better buy because it lasts longer and "works" better. Parents do not need to purchase a lot of expensive educational toys and materials. Old pots and pans, spools, cans, and other common household items make excellent play materials.

7. Toys should match the available storage and be easily accessible to the infant. Shelves are better than a toy box for organizing and storing toys. Toys should be rotated from time to time. When an infant has grown tired of a toy, it should be stored away and reintroduced at a later time.

SUMMARY

1. Many scholars believe it is important to view the complexity of parent-infant relationships from a family systems model. According to this perspective, emphasis is placed upon the reciprocal or circular nature of relationships in which infants, parents, and other family members influence each other's behavior.

2. Dramatic increases in the number of single-parent families and the number of employed mothers represent changes in the structure of the American family that have affected the ways infants are reared.

3. High rates of divorce and illegitimacy are the main causes of the increased number of single-parent families. Most single-parent families with infants are headed by divorced mothers.

4. Single-parent families share similar problems, including financial instability, inadequate alternative child care, and a high level of stress. The effects of single-parenting are likely to depend upon the extent to which these or other adverse conditions exist.

5. Infants are especially vulnerable to the effects of divorce.

6. The extra stress and conflict experienced by single-parent families are frequently accompanied by a "diminished-parenting" effect.

7. Father absence during infancy has been associated with difficulty in sex role development, intellectual development, and various psychological problems. Males appear to be more adversely affected by father absence than females.

8. Grandparents play an important role in infant development through the emotional, economic, and other forms of support they provide parents as well their direct contact and interactions with infants.

9. Apparently maternal employment does not ordinarily have negative effects on infant development, provided the mother has a choice about working, likes her work, has a satisfactory child-care arrangement, and does not experience separation anxiety when leaving her infant in alternative child care.

10. Good-quality day care for infants has no harmful effects on most aspects of infant development. It has been found to be beneficial to the physical and cognitive development of infants from economically deprived families. However, infants who participate in group day care are sick more frequently than infants who stay at home. Infants are no more likely to be injured at a day-care setting than they are at home. Day care may increase

aggressiveness as an infant gets older. Nonmaternal child care does not threaten the security of infant-mother attachment, unless infants are exposed to poor quality, unstable child care and their mothers are typically unresponsive to their needs.

11. The components of good-quality day care include (a) an adequate caregiver-infant ratio and limited group size, (b) well-qualified caregivers, (c) parental involvement, and (d) continuity of care-givers.

12. The **Infant-Toddler Day Care Environment Rating Scale** is an instrument that can be used, in combination with other standards, to assess the quality of center-based day care for infants.

13. Various types of early-intervention programs were established in the 1960s to facilitate the development of infants from low-income families. The long-term results of those programs show that infant intervention can be effective in alleviating the effects of an impoverished environment. Early-intervention programs for infants and toddlers have become widespread throughout the United States.

14. Two important characteristics of the home environment that are related to infant cognitive and language development are parent-infant interactions and the provision of adequate play materials.

15. In most American families, the mother continues to be the primary caregiver. However, fathers can be just as capable as mothers in taking care of an infant. Fathers and mothers use different styles in playing and interacting with their infants.

16. The quality of a marital relationship tends to decline slightly and level off after the birth of a baby. Couples who have been married longer, couples who were older when they married, and couples who have a relatively high level of marital satisfaction before pregnancy have the least trouble adjusting to parenthood.

17. The decline in the quality of marital relationships is accompanied by a decline in the quality of parenting.

18. Adults who work with infants and parents in various settings need to understand how childrearing values and practices vary within, as well as between, racial, ethnic, and cultural groups.

19. Infants who have special needs display behavioral and physical characteristics that affect interactional patterns with their caregivers. Mothers and fathers tend to adjust remarkably well to the increased demands.

20. Positive discipline is an essential part of effective parent-infant relationships. Useful strategies for guiding the behavior of infants include distraction and redirection, controlling the environment, modeling, positive reinforcement, and the use of time-out. The use of spanking and love withdrawal as means of behavior control should be avoided.

21. Parent-infant relationship problems range from mildly perturbed to grossly impaired interactions. The behavioral quality of the interaction, the affective tone, and the level of psychological involvement are used in deciding whether or not there is a relationship disorder. Relationship disorders include those classified as overinvolved, underinvolved, anxious/tense, angry/hostile, and abusive.

22. Toys and play materials for infants should be (a) appropriate to the child's age and development, (b) challenging but not too difficult, (c) free from safety hazards, (d) available in sufficient types and quantity to cover each area of development, (e) cost effective, and (f) easily stored and accessible.

Glossary

Accommodation. The process of changing existing patterns of thought or behavior to conform to new information or experiences.

Acquired Immune Deficiency Syndrome (AIDS). A disease that attacks the immune system caused by infection with a human immunodeficiency virus (HIV).

Adaptation. The processes by which an individual adjusts and changes to get along in the environment; includes assimilation and accommodation.

Adaptive Behaviors. Self-care activities such as feeding, dressing, and toileting.

Affect. The subjective feeling and expressive components of emotions.

Amniocentesis. The procedure in which a sample of amniotic fluid is withdrawn from the amniotic sac through a hollow needle for laboratory analysis.

Amnion; Amniotic Sac. The inner fluid-filled membrane, resembling a plastic bag, that encloses the developing embryo or fetus; the "bag of waters."

Analgesic. A type of medicine used to reduce or eliminate pain.

Anesthesia. Any type of medicine used to relieve pain by inducing unconsciousness or blocking the transmission of pain signals to the brain.

Anoxia. A condition in which the tissues of the body are not receiving an adequate supply of oxygen.

Apgar Scale. A test administered 1 minute and again 5 minutes after birth to check the physiological condition of the infant.

Apnea. A pause in breathing for 20 seconds or longer.

Artificial Insemination. An attempt to achieve pregnancy through a process whereby a donor's sperm is deposited by a syringe into the vagina.

Assessment of Preterm Infant Behavior Scale (APIB). One of the most widely used instruments for evaluating the developmental status of preterm infants.

Assimilation. The process of incorporating new information into existing patterns of thought or action.

Asynchronous Growth. Development of different parts of the body at different rates.

Attachment. A relatively enduring emotional tie to another person.

At-risk. A condition whereby infants have been exposed, or who may have been exposed, to hazards that are likely to result in developmental delay or atypical development.

Autistic Disorder or **Infantile Autism**. An extreme psychological disorder characterized by a lack of responsiveness to other people, failure to communicate, and other social or emotional disabilities.

Babbling. Sound play consisting of the repetition of consonants and vowels in alternating sequences; thought to be the forerunner of the first meaningful utterances.

Baby diary. A daily record of an infant's behavior recorded by an adult observer, usually a parent-scientist.

The Bayley Scales of Infant Development–II. A widely used norm-referenced instrument for the assessment of cognitive and motor performance of infants from 1 month to 42 months of age.

Beikost. Semisolid, strained baby food.

Blastocyst. A fertilized ovum about the time it enters the uterus and a central cavity is formed inside.

Bottle-mouth Syndrome. A pattern of severe tooth decay teeth that is caused by the pooling of milk or other sugary liquids around the teeth; commonly found among children who are habitually given a bottle to nurse while going to sleep.

Bonding. The process by which a parent forms an emotional attachment to an infant.

Boundary of Viability. The earliest age at which infants can be born and survive.

Braxton Hicks Contractions. Mild contractions of the uterus that occur before true labor begins; sometimes referred to as false labor.

Brazelton Neonatal Behavior Assessment Scale. An instrument used to assess the basic functioning of the newborn infant's nervous system and behavioral response capacities.

Breech Birth. The birth of an infant with the buttocks, feet, or knees as the part that emerges first.

Bronchopulmonary Dysplasia (BPD). A chronic lung disease that affects preterm infants.

Caesarean Section. Childbirth by means of a surgical incision through the abdomen and uterus.

Capacitation. A 7-hour period of conditioning in which sperm become capable of fertilizing an ovum.

Caregiver. A person who provides care for an infant, such as a parent, nurse, or day-care worker.

Cartilage. A rubbery, gristlelike tissue found in the human body and from which the skeleton is formed.

Catchup Growth. The ability of the individual to achieve normal growth potential after a period of malnutrition, intrauterine crowding, illness, or other adversity.

Cephalocaudal Principle. The principle which holds that growth and development proceeds from the upper part of the body to the lower extremities.

Cerebral Palsy. A developmental disorder caused by brain damage; the effects vary from mild motor problems involving one side of the body to severe impairment involving the trunk and all four extremities.

Cervical Pregnancy. A pregnancy in which the fertilized ovum is implanted in or close to the cervix.

Cervix. The mouth, or opening, of the uterus (womb).

Chorion. The outer prenatal membrane that encloses the developing baby. One side of the chorion becomes attached to the uterus as the placenta.

Chorionic Villus Sampling. The procedure whereby a sample of tissue from the chorion is removed and tested for genetic defects.

Circular Reaction. The term Piaget used to describe a continuous response that stimulates its own repetition.

Classical Conditioning. A procedure in which a neutral stimulus and a stimulus that automatically evokes a response are presented at approximately the same time. Eventually, the presentation of the neutral stimulus alone evokes the response.

Cognition. All the mental processes such as thinking, remembering, perceiving, learning, and concept formation.

Colic. A condition that causes an infant to cry with distinctive sounds inconsolably for long periods of time, day in and day out, as if in pain.

Conductive Hearing Loss. A hearing deficit that results from abnormalities in the ear structure or fluid in the middle ear.

Cooing. Vowel-like, rhythmic sounds made by infants during the early part of the prespeech stage.

Competence Motivation. The tendency to seek out and master the most challenging aspects of the environment; a human characteristic considered by some theorists to be innate.

Congenital Malformation. A defect present at birth.

Cordocentesis; also Percutaneous Umbilical Cord Sampling (PUBS). A procedure by which a long needle is inserted through the mother's abdomen into a vein in the umbilical cord to obtain a sample of fetal blood to test for disorders of development.

Cosleeping or **bed sharing**. The practice of allowing an infant to sleep in the same bed with the mother, or father, or both.

Crawling. Locomotion with the head and chest raised while the stomach maintains contact with the surface of the floor.

Creeping. Locomotion on hands and knees or hands and feet.

Crib Speech. Monologues toddlers use to talk to themselves, usually just before going to sleep.

Criterion-referenced Tests. An instrument used to assess the infant's ability to achieve specific, previously determined skills without comparing one infant with a group of other same-age infants.

Critical Period. The span of time when a developing organism is most likely to be permanently influenced by environmental factors.

Cross-modal Transfer. The transfer of information from one sensory system to other sensory systems.

Couvade. A term used to refer to the behavior that is typical of expectant or new fathers, usually related to magical or religious beliefs that are meant to protect the mother and baby.

Crowning. The point during childbirth when the top of the baby's head becomes visible at the vaginal opening.

Cri du Chat Syndrome. A disorder caused by a missing section of chromosome No. 5. characterized by a cry that resembles the meowing of a cat.

Deciduous Teeth. The first set of 20 teeth developed by an infant, which are replaced by 32 permanent teeth; also called temporary, primary, or milk teeth.

Dental Caries. Tooth decay; cavities.

Denver II. One of the most widely used norm-referenced screening tests for infants and children up to 6 years of age.

Dilation. The process by which the cervix opens to its widest capacity to allow a baby to be born.

Discipline. Procedures used by parents and other adults to guide, correct, punish, and control the behavior of children.

Dishabituation. The renewal of interest in a stimulus arising from a noticeable change in the stimulus characteristics.

Disorders of Relating and Communicating. A group of severe difficulties in relating to and communicating with other people, combined with difficulties in regulating physiological, sensory, attentional, motor, cognitive, and emotional functions.

Disorders of Attachment. A controversial term used to classify problems resulting from the failure to form adequate attachments during infancy. Attachment disorders include aggressive, disruptive behaviors, or the inability to form and maintain close relationships later in life.

Dominant Gene. A gene carrying a trait that is always expressed.

Down Syndrome. A developmental disorder caused by the presence of an extra chromosome No. 21, or an extra amount of No. 21 chromosomal material.

Double Substitution Play. The most advanced form of pretend play whereby the infant uses two imaginary objects or materials in a play sequence.

Echolalia. The tendency of an infant to repeat the same sounds over and over.

Ectopic Pregnancy. A pregnancy in which the fertilized ovum becomes implanted outside the uterus.

Ectoderm. The external embryonic layer of cells that forms the nervous system, backbone, the skin, hair, nails, and parts of the eyes and ears.

Effacement. The process during labor through which the cervix becomes thinner and shorter.

Ego. The term used by Freud to label the rational, or thinking, component of personality.

Egocentrism. The inability to see things from another person's point of view.

Embryo. The developing infant from the seventh or eighth day after conception until the end of the eighth week of pregnancy.

Emotion. Feelings; complex internal states consisting of perceptions, thoughts, body responses, and impulses.

Emotion Regulation. The capacity of individuals to monitor and control their emotional states and emotional reactions in order to accomplish their goals.

Empathy. Feeling as, or sharing the same emotion that another person is experiencing at a given time.

Empathic Concern. Feelings and behaviors that are a combination of sympathy and empathy.

Endoderm. The external embryonic layer of cells that will develop into the digestive tract, respiratory system, liver, and various glands.

Endogenous Smile. Spontaneous smile, usually observed when an infant is sleeping, that is triggered by internal body processes.

Epiphyses. Ossification centers which form near the end of the long bones.

Episiotomy. A surgical incision made in the tissue between the vagina and the rectum to facilitate childbirth and prevent tearing of the tissue.

Equilibrium. The term Piaget used to describe a state of balance between assimilation and accommodation.

Established Risk. A category used to classify infants who have been diagnosed with a condition known to result in developmental delay or atypical development.

Exogenous Smile. Smiling behavior elicited by stimuli outside the infant's body.

Expressive Speech. The meaningful vocal utterances and sounds composed and expressed by an individual in communication with others.

Factitious Disorder by Proxy. A disorder involving emotional abuse and other forms of maltreatment whereby the parent fakes or creates symptoms of illness in an infant or child.

Fetal Alcohol Effects (FAE). The term used in cases where prenatal alcohol exposure has been more limited and the observable effects are not as severe as full-blown fetal alcohol syndrome.

Fetal Alcohol Syndrome (FAS). Congenital disabilities, such as overall growth retardation, facial malformations, inadequate brain growth, heart defects, motor problems, skeletal defects, hyperactivity, and other difficulties, resulting from excessive maternal alcohol consumption during pregnancy.

Fetoscope. A surgical instrument used in combination with other special equipment to view the inside of the uterus and to obtain samples of tissue and amniotic fluid for testing.

Fetus. An unborn infant from the eighth prenatal week to birth.

Fontanels. The soft spots in the young infant's skull that harden and disappear as the separate pieces of the skull grow together.

Forceps. An instrument, shaped like tongs, sometimes used in difficult deliveries to help the baby emerge from the birth canal.

Frank Breech. The position of a fetus in which the feet and legs are extended straight up beside the ears and the buttocks are the first part to enter the birth canal.

Full (Complete) Breech. The position of a fetus in which the knees are pulled tightly against the stomach with the feet extended downward and the buttocks are the first part to enter the birth canal.

Functional-relational Play. The second stage of sensorimotor play; the stage is characterized by the infant's ability to use play with two or more objects at the same time in ways that are increasingly appropriate to the relationships of the objects.

Gastrulation. The process through which the three germ layers of the developing embryo are formed.

Gestational Age. The age of the infant calculated from the estimated date of fertilization of the ovum until birth.

Glial Cells. See neuroglial cells.

Goodness-of-fit. The extent to which the caregiving style of the parents appropriately matches the temperament of the infant.

Guided Participation. The process by which children develop through involvement in the cultural practices of their community.

Habituation. The weakening or decline of responsiveness to a stimulus over a period of time.

Haptic Perception. The perceptual process by which infants acquire information about the properties of objects through touch and handling sensations.

Hitching. Locomotion in a sitting position.

Holophrase. A single word considered to be equivalent to a whole phrase or a complete sentence.

HOME Inventory. An instrument that is designed to measure the quality of home environments, including 6 characteristics.

Human Growth Hormone (HGH). A substance produced by the thyroid gland that is necessary for normal body growth.

Hyaline Membrane Disease. See respiratory distress syndrome.

Hypertension. A blood pressure level that is abnormally high.

Hypertonia. Muscle tone that is too stiff and rigid.

Hypotonia. Muscle tone that is too limp and floppy.

Id. The term Freud used to represent the personality component consisting of the basic instincts and physiological urges, such as hunger, thirst, and sex.

Infanticide. Murder of unwanted infants.

Infant State. The baby's level of alertness and availability for contact with the outside world.

Infant-Toddler Day Care Environment Rating Scale (ITERS). An instrument used to provide an environmental assessment of center-based day care "classrooms" for children under 30 months of age.

Intelligence. The ability to think, learn, remember, and solve problems.

Intelligence Quotient (IQ). The score derived from an intelligence test that is typically calculated as: Mental age (Test Score) divided by Chronological Age X 100.

Interactional Synchrony. Behavioral exchanges between a caregiver and an infant that are reciprocal, harmonious, and mutually rewarding.

Interactionist. A theorist who believes that growth and development are the result of the interaction between hereditary and environmental forces.

Internal Working Model. The mental and emotional understandings and expectations about oneself and other people in the world that serve as a "script" or a guide for interpersonal relationships.

Interpersonal Play. The type of play that involves face to face interactions, social games, or routines during which infants have opportunities to enjoy and practice socially appropriate ways of interaction and communication.

Intersensory Perception or **Intermodal Perception.** The ability to combine information from different senses.

Intrauterine. Inside the uterus.

In Vitro Fertilization (IVF). An attempt to achieve a pregnancy by fertilizing an ovum in a "test tube" and transferring the embryo into the uterus.

Iron-deficiency Anemia. A low supply of red blood cell mass caused by an inadequate amount of iron in the diet.

Jargon. Long strings of sophisticated babbling sounds frequently made with gestures and eye contact, also called **conversational babble.**

Jaundice. A yellowish appearance of the skin caused by excessive bilirubin, a pigment formed when the red blood cells are destroyed by disease or by the aging of the blood cells.

Joint Attention. Communication episodes during which infant and caregiver focus on the same object, sounds, or events.

Klinefelter Syndrome. A developmental disorder that occurs when a male child is born with two X chromosomes and one Y chromosome.

Labor Contraction. The tightening and shortening of the muscles in the uterus during the process of childbirth.

Language. Vocal utterances, nonverbal behavior, written expressions, and other behaviors used in the process of communication.

Lanugo. The fine hair that covers the fetus from approximately the twentieth week until the seventh month of pregnancy.

Lateralization. The process by which the different hemispheres of the brain take on special functions.

Learning. The process of acquiring knowledge or skills through experience.

Lightening. The point prior to the onset of labor when the baby's head "drops," or moves into the mother's pelvic opening, thereby reducing pressure on the mother's diaphragm.

Locomotion. The ability to move from place to place.

Long-term Memory. Information that is stored in the mind indefinitely.

Low-birthweight Infant. A baby who weighs less than 5½ pounds at birth.

Maturationist. A theorist who believes growth and development result from the aging process that is largely controlled by a genetic timetable.

Maximally Discriminative Facial Movements Code (MAX). A coding system for rating and analyzing facial expressions of infants as indicators of specific emotions.

Meconium. The greenish black material eliminated in the baby's first bowel movement.

Meiosis. The process through which the body forms reproductive cells (sperm and ovum) by reducing the number of chromosomes from forty-six to twenty-three.

Mesoderm. The middle layer of embryonic cells that form the circulatory, excretory, and reproductive systems, skeleton, muscles, and connecting tissues.

Mitosis. The formation of body cells containing forty-six chromosomes for tissue growth and replacement.

Morpheme. The smallest unit of meaning in a language.

Morula. The fertilized ovum, or zygote, after a mulberry-shaped cluster of sixteen cells has formed at approximately the third day after fertilization.

Motherese. The vocal expressions characteristically used by mothers in talking to their infants, also referred to as **baby talk.**

Motor Biases. The tendency of infants to practice the newest body movements they have learned.

Muscle Strength. The amount of force that the muscles in a particular body part can exert while pushing or pulling against resistance.

Muscle Tone. The amount of tension in the muscles when the body is in a state of rest.

Mutual Regulation. The process whereby infant and caregiver responses control and influence each other's feelings and behavior.

Myelination. The formation of a fatty tissue covering, called myelin, over the nerve cells.

Nativist. A theorist who believes infants are genetically endowed with some basic ideas, feelings, personality, and other characteristics that provide the foundation for future growth and development.

Necrotizing Enterocolitis. A disease that threatens the life of preterm infants caused by an inadequate blood flow to the intestines or infectious bacteria.

Neonate. The newborn baby from birth through the first two weeks of life.

Neuroglial Cells (Glial). Central nervous systems cells that serve as connecting links between the neurons and the blood supply.

Neurons. Basic nerve cells that transmit impulses and control central nervous system functions.

Neurotransmitters. Brain chemicals that facilitate the transmission of signals within the central nervous system.

Neurulation. The process through which the central nervous system begins to develop during the prenatal period.

Niche-picking. A term used to describe the tendency of children to seek out experiences which fit their genetic predispositions.

Nonorganic Failure to Thrive (NOFTT). Growth failure due to physical and emotional neglect.

Norm-referenced Tests. Assessment instruments that provide specific scores or ratings that can be used to compare an infant with the performance of other infants of the same age.

Nutrition. The process by which the body takes in and uses food and other digestible substances.

Object Permanence. The concept of an object as being present somewhere even if it cannot always be seen, touched, or heard.

Object Play. The type of play that involves toys and play materials, characterized by little, if any, interaction with others.

Operant Conditioning. The process by which behavior is repeated or changed as the result of a reward or punishment given as a consequence for a particular response.

Optimal Period. A term that is sometimes used instead of the term **critical period**. It stresses the importance of infancy as a developmental phase, but with less emphasis on the irreversibility of environmental events experienced during the period.

Oral RehydrationTherapy. An effective means of treating dehydration with a special solution containing water, salt, glucose, and other ingredients to replace fluid losses.

Ossification. The process by which cartilage hardens into bone.

Otitis Media. Inflammation of the middle ear.

Otoacoustic Emissions Test. A computerized device used for checking the hearing of newborn infants.

Ovum. The reproductive cell produced by the female.

Parentese. The characteristic vocal expressions used by parents, including fathers, in talking to their infants. (See also *motherese*).

Parent-Infant Relationship Disorders. Significant relationship difficulties characterized by negative attitudes, perceptions, emotions, and behaviors of either the parent, the child, or both that lead to disturbed parent-child interactions.

Peers. Individuals of about the same age or developmental level who interact with each other in some way; equals.

Perceived Personal Effectance. The extent to which infants perceive that they control what happens in their environment.

Perception. The process through which information gathered by the senses is interpreted by the brain.

Personality. The relatively enduring patterns of behavior and personal qualities that establish one's individuality.

Phenylketonuria (PKU). A major recessive genetic disorder which prevents an infant from producing an enzyme necessary for the digestion of an amino acid (phenylalanine) found in milk and many other foods.

Phonemes. The basic units of sounds in a language that are combined to form words.

Pica. The eating of nonfood substances that have no nutritional value.

Placenta. The organ or membrane attached to the unborn baby's umbilical cord on one side and the mother's uterine lining on the other. The baby receives nutrients and oxygen and gets rid of waste products through the placenta.

Placental Previa. A condition in which the placenta is attached too close to the cervix, resulting in a risk of early placental separation and maternal bleeding.

Polygenic Inheritance. Inherited characteristics that result from the combined effects of multiple genes.

Postterm; Postmature. An infant born after 42 weeks of gestational age.

Posture. The adjustment and maintenance of the body position in relation to the forces of gravity.

Potential Risk. A category used to classify infants who have been exposed to adverse biological and/or environmental conditions that have the potential for causing developmental problems.

Pragmatics. The practical aspects of language including the affective and social components; how language is used to relate to others and to get one's needs met.

Pre-embryonic Period. The period of time that begins with the fertilization of the ovum and lasts until the end of the second week, when the embryo begins to form.

Prehension. The ability to grasp with the fingers and thumb.

Prereaching. The first stage of reaching during which infants reflexively reach for or swat at objects with little or no motor coordination or control.

Preterm; Premature. An infant born before 37 weeks of gestational age.

Private Speech. In Vygotsky's theory, this type of speech is defined as inner speech or "self-talk" used for self-communication in solving problems and regulating one's own behavior.

Prostaglandins. A variety of chemical substances found in most tissues of the human body which influence blood pressure, muscle contractions, and numerous other body functions.

Protein Energy Malnutrition (PEM). Malnutrition due to an inadequate supply of protein that can result in growth retardation or failure and possibly mental disabilities.

Proximodistal Principle. The principle which holds that growth and development proceed from the internal parts of the body to the outer extremities.

Psychosocial or **Deprivation Dwarfism**. Growth failure due to emotional stress.

Quickening. The first movements of the fetus that are felt by the mother.

Recall Memory. The ability to retrieve information from the memory in the absence of direct sensory perceptions of the stimulus in question.

Receptive-Emergent Language Test-2. A checklist that is used to screen infants from 1 to 36 months of age for potential delays in receptive and expressive language skills.

Receptive Speech. The meanings and understandings that are attached to the vocal expressions of others.

Recessive Gene. A gene which carries traits that are expressed only if the gene is paired with the identical recessive gene.

Reciprocal Interactions. The process whereby infants and caregivers influence one another's responses.

Recognition Memory. The ability to determine whether a stimulus has been previously encountered; the ability to recognize the correct stimulus (answer) when given a choice.

Reflex. An automatic, involuntary response to a stimulus.

Respiratory Distress Syndrome. A disease of preterm infants caused by a deficiency of surfactant, a substance necessary for efficient breathing.

Retinopathy of Prematurity (ROP) or **Retrolental Fibroplasia**. A disease of preterm and low-birth-weight infants caused by exposure to excess oxygen or other adverse conditions, causing scarring of the eye tissue and possibly blindness.

Rhythmical Stereotypies. Repetitive, rhythmical movements sometimes used by infants to prepare for more advanced and better-coordinated motor activities.

Rooming-in. The practice of allowing the newborn baby to stay in the mother's room rather than in the hospital nursery.

Scaffolding. The term used to describe how adults use special structures of language, social encouragement, and tutoring to promote children's learning.

Scheme. The term Piaget used to label a pattern or unit of thought or action.

Sedative. Medication that has a calming effect and, when taken in sufficient doses, induces drowsiness and sleep.

Self-actualization. A term used by Maslow and Rogers to refer to the need or motivation of humans to achieve their full potential.

Self-awareness. The perception or awareness of oneself as a distinct individual with an existence and identity separate from other people and objects.

Self-concept. The sum total, or composite picture, of how you perceive yourself as an individual.

Self-definition. The ability to define oneself in terms of age, size, gender, personal pronouns, and other verbal labels.

Self-esteem. The evaluation you make of your self-concept, including positive and negative thoughts and feelings.

Self-recognition. The ability of infants to recognize their own images in mirrors, pictures, videotapes, and other forms.

Sensorial Hearing Loss. A type of hearing deficit that results from abnormality of the inner ear, or failure of the nerves to carry sound signals from the inner ear to the brain.

Sensory Memory. Information from immediate sensory impressions that is stored in the mind for an instant.

Separation Anxiety. Emotional distress resulting from an infant's separation from a parent or other attachment figure.

Separation-individuation. The process by which an infant achieves a sense of separateness from the mother.

Sequenced Inventory of Communicative Development-Revised (SICD-R). A diagnostic instrument for measuring the communication skills of infants and children between the ages of 4 months and 4 years.

Sex-linked Disorders. A variety of hereditary disorders that are caused by defective genes carried on the sex chromosomes.

Shaken-Impact Syndrome. Violent shaking of an infant leading to an impact or movement of the brain inside the skull that causes damage to the brain, eyes, or other parts of the head and neck.

Short-term Memory. The ability to recall information that is stored for a brief period of time, usually about a minute.

Social Competence. The ability to use environmental and personal resources to get one's needs met and to achieve a satisfactory developmental outcome.

Socialization. The process through which a person acquires the attitudes, behaviors, and skills needed to get along in a given society.

Socialization of Emotions. The process by which the infants' emotions are influenced, over time, by the responses of parents and other caregivers.

Social Referencing. The use of behavioral cues or indicators displayed by others in deciding how to respond in a situation in which the decision is not clear.

Somites. The budlike segments in the developing embryo from which the skeleton is formed.

Speech. The vocal or spoken component of language.

Sperm. The reproductive cell produced by the male.

Stranger Anxiety. A negative emotional response to a stranger characterized by withdrawal, avoidance, crying, or other signs of distress.

Strawberry Nevi. Large red patches of skin that are sometimes present at birth on Caucasian infants; these marks disappear with age.

Subitization. A perceptual process that people apply in looking at 3 or 4 objects and knowing how many there are without going through the process of enumeration.

Sudden Infant Death Syndrome (SIDS). The sudden, unexpected death of an infant for which no adequate medical explanation can be found.

Superego. The term Freud used to label the personality component which consists of the moral principles and social standards; includes the conscience and the ideal self.

Surfactant. A chemical manufactured by the lungs to facilitate breathing.

Sutures. The narrow seams of cartilage that connect the separate sections of the newborn infant's skull.

Synaptogenesis. The formation of synapses, or connections, between the neurons via their dendrites and axons.

Symbolic Play. The use of pretend games and/or objects to represent something else.

Syntax. Rules that govern the ways words can be combined to form sentences or meaningful phrases.

Sympathy. Feelings of sorrow and compassion for another person who is in pain and distress.

Telegraphic Speech. Linguistic utterances or sentences of limited length that use word order to convey meaning; conjunctions and other nonessential parts of speech are omitted as in a telegram.

Temperament. The stable behavioral and emotional reactions that appear early and are influenced in part by heredity.

Teratogen. Any substance that can produce a developmental abnormality in an embryo or a fetus.

Thermography. A technique using infrared photographic equipment to detect changes in facial skin surface temperature associated with a change in an infant's emotional state.

Theory of Mind. The ability to consider the psychological states of other people.

Thyroxine. A hormone produced by the thyroid gland that is necessary for normal physical growth.

Toddler. An infant who is in the early stage of walking; covers the period of time from approximately 1 year to 3 years of age.

Tranquilizer. A type of drug used to reduce tension and anxiety and to heighten the effects of other medications.

Transactional Perspective. The theory in which developmental outcomes are viewed as the result of reciprocal influences between the child and the environment.

Transdisciplinary Play-Based Assessment (TPBA). A method of assessing the development of infants and young children by a team of professionals and a parent who observe the child in a play session structured in various ways.

Tryphoblasts. The outer layer of cells on the fertilized ovum that bury into the lining of the uterus by secreting enzymes.

Turner Syndrome. A developmental disorder that occurs when a female infant is born with only one sex (X) chromosome.

Ultrasound. A commonly used technique for prenatal assessment whereby high-frequency sound waves are bounced off the fetus to form a live video image called a sonogram.

Umbilical Cord. The ropelike cord containing two arteries and one vein, connecting the unborn infant to the placenta.

Uzgiris-Hunt Ordinal Scales of Psychological Development. An assessment instrument consisting of six subscales based on Piaget's description of cognitive development during infancy; the test items are arranged, or ordered, according to their level of difficulty.

Vacuum Extractor. A device consisting of a metal or a plastic cup that is attached to the top of the baby's head to assist in the birth process.

Vagal Tone. A particular measure of heart rate variability controlled by the vagus nerve of the brain that is considered to be an indicator of changes in emotional states and other psychological functions.

Vernix Caseosa. The whitish, oily substance that covers the fetus to protect the skin from the amniotic fluid.

Visual Preference Technique. An innovative method developed by Robert Fantz to study visual perception by means of a special apparatus equipped with a peephole and a "looking chamber."

Zygote. A fertilized ovum.

Zone of Proximal Development (ZPD). In Vygotsky's theory, the range of tasks and concepts that a child cannot accomplish alone but is capable of mastering with the help of an adult or a more advanced peer.

References

Abbott, S. (1992). Holding on and pushing away: Comparative perspectives on an eastern Kentucky child-rearing practice. *Ethos, 20,* 33–65.

Abel, E. (1983). *Marihuana, tobacco, alcohol, and reproduction.* Boca Raton, FL: CRC.

Abravanel, E. & DeYong, N. (1991). Does object modeling elicit imitative-like gestures from young infants? *Journal of Experimental Child Psychology, 52,* 22–40.

Adams, M. (1985). The descriptive epidemiology of sudden infant deaths among natives and whites in Alaska. *American Journal of Epidemiology, 122,* 637–643.

Adams, R., Maurer, D., & Davis, M. (1986). Newborns' discrimination of chromatic from achromatic stimuli. *Journal of Experimental Child Psychology,41,* 167–281.

Adams, R. & Maurer, D. (1983, April). *A demonstration of color perception in the newborn.* Paper presented at the Society for Research in Child Development, Detroit, MI.

Adams, R. & Maurer, D. (1984, April). *The use of habituation to study newborns' color vision.* Paper presented at the 4th International Conference on Infant Studies, New York, NY.

Adamson, L. (1995). *Communication development in infancy.* Madison, WI: Brown & Benchmark.

Adelson, E. & Fraiberg, S. (1974). Gross motor development in infants blind from birth. *Child Development, 45,* 114–126.

Afriat, C. & Coustan, D. (1995). Birth. In D. Coustan, R. Haning, & D. Singer (Eds.), *Human reproduction: Growth and development* (pp. 307–326). Boston: Little, Brown.

Ainsworth, M. (1967). *Infancy in Uganda: Infant care and the growth of attachment.* Baltimore: Johns Hopkins Press.

Ainsworth, M., Blehar, M., Waters, E., & Wall, S. (1978). *Patterns of Attachment.* Hillsdale, NJ: Erlbaum.

Akerman, B. & Thomassen, P. (1991). Four-year follow-up of locomotor and language development in 34 twin pairs. *Acta Geneticae Medicae et Gemellologiaem, 40,* 21–27.

Alan Guttmacher Institute. (1981). *Teenage pregnancy: The problem that hasn't gone away.* New York: Author.

Alexy, B. & Martin, A. (1994). Breastfeeding: perceived barriers and benefits/enhancers in a rural and urban setting. *Public Health Nursing, 11,* 214–218.

Allen, M. (1993). An overview of long-term outcome. In F. Witter & L. Keith (Eds.), *Textbook of prematurity* (pp. 371–383). Boston: Little, Brown.

Allergy Foundation of America. (1971). *Why are allergies a national health problem?* (Fact Sheet). New York: Author.

Als, H. (1982). Manual for the assessment of preterm infants' behavior (APIB). In H. Fitzgerald, B. Lester, & M. Yogman (Eds.), *Theory and research in behavioral pediatrics* (Vol. 1, pp. 65–132). New York: Plenum.

Amato, P. & Keith, B. (1991). Parental divorce and well-being of children: A meta-analysis. *Psychological Bulletin, 110,* 26–46.

American Academy of Pediatrics. (1978). Breast-feeding. *Pediatrics, 62,* 591–601.

American Academy of Pediatrics. (1982). Task force report: The promotion of breast-feeding. *Pediatrics, 69,* 654–661.

American Academy of Pediatrics. (1985). Prolonged infantile apnea. *Pediatrics, 76,* 129–130.

American Academy of Pediatrics. (1987). Neonatal anesthesia. *Pediatrics, 80,* 446.

American Academy of Pediatrics. (1993). *Toilet training: Guidelines for parents.* (Brochure). Elk Grove, IL: Author.

American Medical Association. (1985). Report of the council on scientific affairs: AMA diagnostic and treatment guidelines concerning child abuse and neglect. *Journal of the American Medical Association, 254,* 796–800.

Andersen, R., Bale, J., Blackman, J., & Murph, J. (1994). *Infections in children: A sourcebook for child-care providers* (2nd ed.). Gaithersburg, MD: Aspen.

Anderson, D. (1993). Nutrition for premature infants. In P. McQueen & C. Lang (Eds.), *Handbook of pediatric nutrition* (pp. 83–106). Gaithersburg, MD: Aspen.

Anderson, S., Chinn, H., & Fisher, K. (1982). History and current status of infant formulas. *American Journal of Clinical Nutrition, 35,* 381–397.

Angleitner, A. & Ostendorf, F. (1994). Temperament and the big five factors of personality. In C. Halverson, G. Kohnstamm, & R. Martin (Eds.), *The developing structure of temperament and personality from infancy to adulthood* (pp. 69–90). Hillsdale, NJ: Erlbaum.

Anisfeld, M. (1996). Only tongue protrusion modeling is matched by neonates. *Developmental Review, 16,* 149–161.

Annis, L. (1978). *The child before birth.* Ithaca, NY: Cornell University Press.

Appleton, T., Clifton, R., & Goldberg, S. (1975). The development of behavioral competence in infancy. In F. Horowitz, (Ed.), *Review of child development research* (Vol. 4, pp. 101–186). Chicago: University of Chicago Press.

Arena, J. (1985, July 27). Duke professor says open commodes danger to kids (Dear Ann Landers). *The News and Observer* (Raleigh, NC), p. C2.

Arnold, J. (1996). Otitis media and its complications. In W. Nelson, R. Behrman, R. Kliegman, & A. Arving (Eds.), *Nelson's textbook of pediatrics* (15th ed., pp. 1814–1819). Philadelphia: Saunders.

Arterberry, M., Craton, L., Yonas, A. (1993). Infants' sensitivity to motion-carried information for depth and object properties. In C. Granrud (Ed.), *Visual perception and cognition in infancy* (pp. 225–234). Hillsdale, NJ: Erlbaum.

Asher, S., Erdley, C., & Gabriel, S. (1994). Peer relations. In M. Rutter & D. Hay, *Development through the lifespan: A handbook for clinicians* (pp. 456–488). Oxford, England: Blackwell.

Ashmead, D. & Perlmutter, M. (1980). Infant memory in everyday life. In M. Perlmutter (Ed.), *New directions for child development: Children's memory* (Vol. 10, pp. 1–16). San Francisco: Josey-Bass.

Aslin, R. (1993). Perception of visual direction in human infants. In C. Granrud (Ed.), *Visual perception and cognition in infancy* (pp. 91–119). Hillsdale, NJ: Erlbaum.

Aslin, R., Pisoni, D., & Jusczyk, P. (1983). Auditory development and speech perception in infancy. In P. H. Mussen (Ed.), *Handbook of child psychology: Vol. 2. Infancy and developmental psychobiology* (4th ed., pp. 573–688). New York: Wiley.

Associated Press. (1996, June 21). Panel says changes needed in way polio vaccine administered. *The Daily Reflector*. Greenville, NC, p. A8.

Associated Press. (1997, June 8). Better floss: Bad gums tied to heart attacks and premature births. *The Daily Reflector* (Greenville, NC), p. A4.

Aston, A. (1984). *Toys that teach your child*. Charlotte, NC: East Woods Press.

Atkinson, J. (1995). Through the eyes of an infant. In R. Gregory, J. Harris, P. Heard, & D. Rose (Eds.). *The artful eye* (pp.141–156). New York: Oxford.

Avery, M. (1995). Editorial: Out of the vortex: Neonatologists' treatment decisions for newborns at risk for HIV. *American Journal of Public Health, 85*, 1484–1485.

Avery, M. & First, L. (1994). *Pediatric medicine* (2nd ed.). Baltimore: Williams & Wilkins.

Bachman, J. (1983). Prenatal care and the normal pregnant woman. *Primary care, 10* (2), 145–160.

Bahrick, L. & Pickens, J. (1994). Amodal relations: The basis for intermodal perception and learning in infancy. In D. Lewkowicz & R. Lickliter (Eds.), *The development of intersensory perception: Comparative perspectives* (pp. 205–233). Hillsdale, NJ: Erlbaum.

Bailey, W. (1994). A longitudinal study of fathers: Involvement with young children: Infancy to age 5 years. *Journal of Genetic Psychology, 155*, 331–339.

Baillargeon, R. (1993). The object concept revisited: New directions in the investigation of infants' physical knowledge. In C. Granrud (Ed.), *Visual perception and cognition in infancy* (pp. 265–315). Hillsdale, NJ: Erlbaum.

Bakker, P. (1987). Autonomous language of twins. *Acta Geneticae Medicae et Gemellologiaem,36*, 233–238.

Baldwin, A. (1967). *Theories of child development*. New York: Wiley.

Bale, J. (1990). The neurologic complications of AIDS in infants and young children. *Infants and Young Children, 3*, 15–23.

Ballachanda, B. (1995). *The human ear canal*. San Diego: Singular.

Ballard, J., Novak, L., & Driver, M. (1979). A simplified score for assessment of fetal maturation of newly born infants. *Journal of Pediatrics, 95*, 769–774.

Bandura, A. (1977). *Social learning theory*. Englewood Cliffs, NJ: Prentice Hall.

Bangs, T. (1982). *Language and learning disorders of the preacademic child* (2nd ed.). Englewood Cliffs, NJ: Prentice Hall.

Banks, M. (1980). The development of visual accommodation during early infancy. *Child Development, 51*, 646–666.

Banks, M., Aslin, R., & Letson, R. (1975). Sensitive period for the development of binocular vision. *Science, 190*, 675–677.

Banks, M. & Bennett, P. (1991). Anatomical and physiological constraints on neonatal visual sensitivity and determinants of fixation behavior. In M. Weiss & P. Zalazo (Eds.), *Newborn attention: Biological constraints on the influence of experience* (pp. 177–217). Norwood, NJ: Ablex.

Banks, M. & Salapatek, P. (1983). Infant visual perception. In P. Mussen (Ed.), *Handbook of child psychology: Vol. 2. Infancy and developmental psychobiology* (4th ed., pp. 435–571). New York: Wiley.

Banks, M. & Shannon, E. (1993). Spatial and chromatic visual efficiency in human neonates. In C. Granrud (Ed.), *Visual perception and cognition in infancy* (pp.1–46). Hillsdale, NJ: Erlbaum.

Barglow, P., Vaughn, B., & Moliter, N. (1987). Effects of maternal absence due to employment on the quality of infant-mother attachment in a low-risk sample. *Child Development, 58*, 945–954.

Barnard, K. (1979). *Nursing child assessment satellite teaching manual (NCAST)*. Seattle: University of Washington.

Barnes, G., Lethin, A., Jackson, E., & Shea, N. (1953). Management of breast-feeding. *Journal of the American Medical Association, 151*, 192–199.

Barness, L. (1990). Bases of weaning recommendations. *Journal of Pediatrics. 117*, 84–85.

Barness, L. & Curran, J. (1996). Nutrition. In W. Nelson, R. Behrman, R. Kliegman, & A. Arving (Eds.).

Nelson textbook of pediatrics (15th ed, pp. 141–172). Philadelphia: Saunders.

Baron-Cohen, S. (1994). Development of a theory of mind: Where would we be without the intentional stance? In M. Rutter & D. Hay (Eds.), *Development through life* (pp. 303–318). Oxford, England: Blackwell.

Barr, H., Streissguth, A., Martin, D., & Herman, C. (1984). Infant size at 8 months of age: Relationship to maternal use of alcohol, nicotine, and caffeine during pregnancy. *Pediatrics, 74,* 336–341.

Barret, D. (1987). Undernutrition and child behavior. In J. Dobbing (Ed.), *Early nutrition and later achievement* (pp. 95–127). London: Academic.

Baruffi, G., Dellinger, W., Stobino, D., Rudolph, A., Timmons, R., & Ross, A. (1984). A study of pregnancy outcomes in a maternity center and a tertiary care hospital. *American Journal of Public Health, 74,* 973–978.

Bates, E., Benigni, L., Bretherton, I., Camaioni, L., & Volterra, V. (1977). From gesture to the first word: On cognitive and social prerequisites. In M. Lewis & L. Rosenblum (Eds.), *Interaction, conversation and the development of language* (pp. 247–317). New York: Wiley.

Bates, E., O'Connell, B., & Shore, C. (1987). Language and communication in infancy. In J. Osofsky (Ed.), *Handbook of infant development* (2nd ed., pp. 149–203). New York: Wiley.

Bates, J. (1980). The concept of difficult temperament. *Merrill-Palmer Quarterly, 25,* 299–319.

Bates, J. (1987). Temperament in infancy. In J. Osofsky (Ed.), *Handbook of infant development* (2nd ed., pp. 1101–1149). New York: Wiley.

Bates, J. (1994). Introduction. In J. Bates & T. Wachs (Eds.), *Temperament: Individual differences at the interface of biology and behavior* (pp. 1–14). Washington, DC: American Psychological Association.

Bates, J. & Bayles, K. (1984). Objective and subjective components in mothers' perceptions of their children from age 6 months to 3 years. *Merrill-Palmer Quarterly, 30,* 111–129.

Bates, J., Wachs, T., & Emde, R. (1994). Toward practical uses for biological concepts of temperament. In J. Bates & T. Wachs (Eds.), *Temperament: Individual differences at the interface of biology and behavior* (pp. 275–306). Washington, DC: American Psychological Association.

Batshaw, M. & Perret, Y. (1992). *Children with handicaps: A medical primer* (3rd. ed.). Baltimore: Brooks.

Bauer, P. (1996). What do infants recall of their lives? Memory for specific events by one-to two-year-olds. *American Psychologist, 51,* 29–41.

Bauer, P. & Hertsgaard, L. (1993). Increasing steps in recall of events: Factors facilitating immediate and long-term memory in 13.5-and 16.5-month-old children. *Child Development, 64,* 1204–1223.

Bauer, P. & Wewerka, S. (1995). One-to two-year-olds' recall of events: The more expressed, the more impressed. *Journal of Developmental Psychology, 59,* 475–496.

Baumrind, D. (1973). The development of instrumental competence through socialization. In A. Picke (Ed.), *Minnesota symposia on child psychology* (Vol. 7, pp. 3–46). Minneapolis: University of Minnesota Press.

Bax, M., Hart, H., & Jenkins, S. (1990). *Child development and health.* Oxford, London: Blackwell.

Baxter, A. (1985). *Techniques for dealing with child abuse.* Springfield, IL: Thomas.

Bayley, N. (1935). The development of motor abilities during the first three years. *Monographs of the Society of Research in Child Development, 1* (Serial No. 1).

Bayley, N. (1965). Comparisons of mental and motor tests scores for ages 1–15 months by sex, birth order, race, geographical location, and education of parents. *Child Development, 36,* 379–411.

Bayley, N. (1993). *Bayley Scales of infant development–II* (2nd ed.). San Antonio: Psychological Corp.

Bayley, N. & Schaefer, E. (1964). Correlations of maternal and child behaviors with the development of mental abilities: Data from the Berkeley Growth Study. *Monographs of the Society for Research in Child Development, 29* (6, Serial No. 97).

Beal, V. (1980). *Nutrition in the life span.* New York: Wiley.

Beauchamp, G. & Cowart, B. (1986, March). When tots taste salt. *Science, 86,* 10.

Beauchamp, G. & Moran, M. (1984). Acceptance of sweet and salty tastes in 2 year old children. *Appetite, 5,* 291–305.

Beck, S. (1979). *Baby talk: How your child learns to speak.* New York: New American Library.

Becker, W. (1964). Consequences of different kinds of parental discipline. In M. Hoffman & L. Hoffman (Eds.), *Review of child development research* (Vol. 1, pp. 169–208). New York: Russell Sage Foundation.

Bedi, K. (1987). Lasting neuroanatomical changes following undernutrition during early life. In J. Dobbing (Ed.), *Early nutrition and later achievement* (pp. 1–49). London: Academic.

Bee, W., Barnard, K., Eyeres, S., Gray, C., Hammond, M., Spietz, A., Snyder, C., & Clark, B. (1982). Prediction of IQ and language skill from perinatal status, child performance, family circumstances and mother-infant interaction. *Child Development, 53,* 1134–1156.

Beedle, G. (1984). Teeth. In C. Kempe, H. Silver, & D. O'Brien (Eds.), *Current pediatric diagnosis and treatment.* (8th ed., pp. 290–293). Los Altos, CA: Lange.

Begley, S. (1996, February 19). Your child's brain. *Newsweek, 127,* 55–61.

Begley, S. (1997, Spring/Summer). How to build a baby's brain. *Newsweek, Special Edition,* 28–32.

Behrman, R. & Vaughan, V. (1983). *Nelson textbook of pediatrics* (12th ed). Philadelphia: Saunders.

Bell, S. & Ainsworth, D. (1972). Infant crying and maternal responsiveness. *Child Development, 43,* 1171–1190.

Beller, E. (1979). Early intervention programs. In J. Osofsky (Ed.), *Handbook of infant development.* (pp. 852–894). New York: Wiley.

Belsky, J. (1979). The interrelation of parental and spousal behavior during infancy in transitional nuclear families: An exploratory analysis. *Journal of Marriage and the Family, 41,* 62–68.

Belsky, J. (1981). Early human experience: A family perspective. *Developmental Psychology, 17,* 3–23.

Belsky, J. (1988). The "effects" of infant day care reconsidered. *Early Childhood Research Quarterly. 3,* 235–272.

Belsky, J. & Kelly, J. (1994). *The transition to parenthood.* New York: Delacorte.

Belsky, J. & Most, R. (1981). From exploration to play: A cross-sectional study of infant free play behavior. *Developmental Psychology, 17,* 630–639.

Belsky, J. & Rovine, M. (1988). Nonmaternal care in the first year of life and the security of infant-parent attachment security. *Child Development, 59,* 157–167.

Belsky, J. & Steinberg, L. (1978). The effects of day care: A critical review. *Child Development, 49,* 929–949.

Belsky, J. & Volling, B. (1987). Mothering, fathering, and marital interaction in the family triad: Exploring family systems processes. In P. Berman & F. Pedersen (Eds.), *Men's transition to parenthood: Longitudinal studies of early family experience* (pp. 37–63). Hillsdale, NJ: Erlbaum.

Bench, J., Collyer, Y., Langford, C., & Toms, R. (1972). A comparison between the neonatal sound-evoked startle response and the head-drop (Moro) reflex. *Developmental Medicine and Child Neurology, 14,* 308–314.

Benenson, J. (1996). Gender differences in the development of relationships. In G. Noam & K. Fischer (Eds.), *Development and vulnerability in close relationships* (pp. 263–286). Mahwah, NJ: Erlbaum.

Benirschke, K. (1995). The biology of the twinning process: How placentation influences outcome. *Seminars in Perinatology, 19,* 342–350.

Benn, R. (1986). Factors promoting secure attachment relationships between employed mothers and their sons. *Child Development, 57,* 1224–1231.

Bennett, F. (1987). The effectiveness of early intervention for infants at increased biologic risk. In M. Guralnick & F. Bennett (Eds.), *The effectiveness of early intervention for at-risk and handicapped children* (pp. 79–112). New York: Academic.

Benson, R. & Pernoll, M. (1994). *Handbook of obstetrics and gynecology* (9th ed.). New York: McGraw-Hill.

Berg, W., Adkinson, C., & Strock, B. (1973). Duration and frequency of periods of alertness in neonates. *Developmental Psychology, 15,* 760–769.

Berk, L. (1996). *Infants, children, and adolescents* (2nd ed.). Boston: Allyn & Bacon.

Berk, L. & Winsler, A. (1995). *Scaffolding children's learning. Vygotsky and early childhood education.* Washington, DC: NAEYC.

Bernhardt, J. (1987). Sensory capabilities of the fetus. *Maternal Child Nursing Journal, 12,* 44–46.

Berry, K. (1975). Developmental study of recognition of antecedents of infant vocalizations. *Perceptual and Motor Skills, 41,* 400–402.

Bertenthal, B. & Campos, J. (1987). New directions in the study of experience. *Child Development, 58,* 560–567.

Bertenthal, B. & Campos, J. (1990). A systems approach to the organizing effects of self-produced locomotion during infancy. In C. Rovee-Collier & L. Lipsitt (Eds.), *Advances in infancy research* (Vol. 6, pp. 1–60). Norwood, NJ: Ablex.

Berthenthal, B., Campos, J., & Bennett, K. (1984). Self-produced locomotion: An organizer of emotional, cognitive, and social development in infancy. In R. Emde & R. Harmon (Eds.), *Continuities and discontinuities of development* (pp. 195–207). New York: Plenum.

Bertenthal, B. & Fischer, K. (1978). Development of self-recognition in the infant. *Developmental Psychology, 14,* 44–50.

Bettleheim, B. (1970). *Food to nurture the mind.* Washington, DC: The Children's Foundation.

Billeaud, F. (1993). *Communication disorders in infants and toddlers.* Boston: Andover.

Biller, H. (1981). Father absence, divorce and personality development. In M. Lamb (Ed.), *The role of the father in child development* (2nd ed., pp. 489–552). New York: Wiley.

Birch, L. & Marlin, D. (1982). I don't like it; I never tried it: Effects of exposure on two-year-old children's food preferences. *Appetite, 3,* 353–360.

Birnholz, J. & Benacerraf, B. (1983). The development of fetal hearing. *Science, 222,* 516–518.

Bischof-Kohler, D. (1991). The development of empathy in infants. In M. Lamb & H. Keller (Eds.), *Infant development: Perspectives from German-speaking countries* (pp. 245–274). Hillsdale, NJ: Erlbaum.

Biswas, M. & Craigo, S. (1994). The course and conduct of normal labor and delivery. In A. DeCherney & M. Pernoll (Eds.), *Current obstetrics and gynecologic diagnosis and treatment* (8th ed, pp.202–227). Norwalk, CT: Appleton & Lange.

Blair, P., Fleming, P., Bensley, D., Smith, I., Bacon, C., Taylor, E., Berry, J., Golding, J., & Tripp, J. (1996). Smoking and the sudden infant death syndrome: Results from 1993–5 case-control study for confidential inquiry into stillbirths and deaths in infancy. *British Medical Journal. 313*, 195–198.

Blanche, S., Mayaux, M., Rouzioux, C., Teglas, J., Firtion, G., Monpoux, F., Ciraru-Virgneron, N., Meier, F., Triciore, J., & Courpotin, C. (1994). Relation of the course of HIV infection in children to the severity of the disease in their mothers at the time of delivery. *New England Journal of Medicine, 330*, 308–312.

Blass, E. & Ciaramitaro, V. (1994). A new look at some old mechanisms in human newborns. *Monographs of the Society for Research in Child Development, 59* (1, Serial No. 239).

Blass, E., Ganchrow, J., & Steiner, J. (1984). Classical conditioning in newborn humans 2-48 hours of age. *Infant Behavior and Development, 7*, 223–235.

Bloom, B. (1964). *Stability and change in human characteristics*. New York: Wiley.

Bloom, L. (1973). *One word at a time: The use of single word utterances before syntax*. The Hague: Mouton.

Bloom, L. (1975). Language development. In F. Horowitz (Ed.), *Review of child development research* (Vol. 4, pp. 245–303). Chicago: University of Chicago Press.

Bloom, L. (1993). *The transition from infancy to language*. New York: Cambridge.

Bock, S. (1987). Prospective appraisal of complaints of adverse food reactions to foods in children during the first 3 years of life. *Pediatrics, 79*, 683–688.

Bock, S. & Sampson, H. (1994). Food allergy in infancy. *Pediatric Clinics of North America, 41*, 1047–1067.

Bohannon, J. (1993). Theoretical approaches to language acquisition. In J. Berko Gleason (Ed.), *The development of langauge* (3rd. ed, pp. 239–297). New York: Macmillan.

Boklage, C. (1980). The sinisitral blastocyst: An embryonic perspective on the development of brain-function asymetries. In J. Herron (Ed.), *Neuropsychology of left-handedness* (pp. 115–137). New York: Academic Press.

Boland, M. & Oleske, J. (1995). The health care needs of infants and children: An epidemiological perspective. In N. Boyd-Franklin, G. Steiner, & M. Boland (Eds.), *Children and families with HIV/AIDS: Psychosocial and therapeutic issues* (pp. 19–51). New York: Guilford.

Boring, E. (1923, June). Intelligence as the tests test it. *New Republic, 35*, 35–37.

Bornstein, M. (1981). Psychological studies of color perception in human infants. Habituation, discrimination and categorization, recognition, and conceptualization. In L. Lipsitt (Ed.), *Advances in infancy research* (Vol. 1, pp. 2–40). Norwood, NJ: Ablex.

Bornstein, M. (1985). Human infant color vision and color perception. *Infant Behavior and Development, 8*, 109–113.

Bornstein, M. & Lamb, M. (1992). *Development in infancy* (3rd ed.). New York: McGraw-Hill.

Borovsky, D. & Rovee-Collier, C. (1990). Contextual constraints on memory retrieval at six-months. *Child Development, 61*, 1569–1583.

Bossey, J. (1980). Development of olfactory and related structures in staged human embroyos. *Anatomy of Embryology, 161*, 225–236.

Bowen, S. & Miller, B. (1980). Paternal attachment behavior as related to presence or absence at delivery and parenthood classes: A pilot study. *Nursing Research, 29*, 307–311.

Bower, T. (1977). *A primer of infant development*. San Francisco: Freeman.

Bower, T.(1977). Blind babies see with their ears. *New Scientist, 73*, 255–257.

Bower, T. (1982). *Development in infancy* (2nd ed). San Francisco: Freeman.

Bower, T., Broughton, J., & Moore, M. (1970). Demonstration of intention in the reaching behavior of neonate humans. *Nature, 228*, 679–681.

Bowerman, M. (1978). The acquisition of word meaning: An investigation into some current conflicts. In N. Waterson & C.E. Snow, (Eds.), *The development of communication* (pp. 263–287). New York: Wiley.

Bowlby, J. (1969). *Attachment and loss. Vol. 1: Attachment*. New York: Basic.

Boyson-Bardies, B. (1994). Speech development: Contributions from cross-linguistic studies. In A. Vyt, H. Bloch, & M. Bornstein (Eds.), *Early child development in the French tradition: Contributions from current research* (pp. 191–206). Hillsdale, NJ: Erlbaum.

Brackbill, Y. (1979). Obstetrical medication and infant behavior. In J. Osofosky, (Ed.), *Handbook of infant development* (pp. 76–125). New York: Wiley.

Bradley, R. (1972). Development of the taste bud and gustatory papilae in human fetuses. In J. Bosma (Ed.), *The third symposium of oral sensation and perception: The mouth of the infant* (pp. 137–162). Springfield, IL: Thomas.

Bradley, R. (1974). *Husband coached childbirth*. New York: Harper & Row.

Bradley, R. (1994). The HOME Inventory: Review and reflections. In H. Reese (Ed.), *Advances in child development and behavior* (Vol. 25, pp. 241–288). San Diego: Academic.

Bradley, R., Rock, S., Barnard, K., Gray, C., Hammon, M., Mitchel, S., Siegel, L., Ramey, C., Gottfried, A., & Johnson, D. (1989). Home environment and cognitive development in the first 3 years of life: A collaborative study involving six sites and three ethnic groups in North America. *Developmental Psychology, 25*, 217–235.

Brambati, B. & Oldrini, A. (1986). Methods of chorionic villus sampling. In B. Brambati, G. Simoni, & S. Fabro (Eds.), *Chorionic villus sampling* (pp. 73–97). New York: Dekker.

Braungart, J., Plomin, R., Defries, J., & Fulker, D. (1992). Genetic influence on tester-rated infant temperament as assessed by Bayley's Infant Behavior Record: Nonadoptive and adoptive siblings and twins. *Developmental Psychology, 28,* 40–47.

Brazelton, T. (1973). Neonatal behavioral assessment scale. *Clinics in Developmental Medicine*, No. 50. Philadelphia: Lippincott.

Brazelton, T. (1992). *Touchpoints.* Reading, MA: Addison-Wesley.

Brazelton, T. & Cramer, B. (1990). *The earliest relationship.* Reading, MA: Addison-Wesley.

Bredberg, G. (1985). The anatomy of the developing ear. In S. Trehub & B. Schmeiter (Eds.), *Auditory development in infancy* (pp. 3–20). New York: Plenum Press.

Bremner, J. (1988). *Infancy.* New York: Basil Blackwell.

Brengman, S. & Burns, M. (1983). Vaginal delivery after C-section. *American Journal of Nursing, 83,* 1544–1547.

Brennan, W., Ames, E., & Moore, R. (1966). Age differences in infants' attention patterns to different complexities. *Science, 151,* 354–356.

Bretherton, I. (1996). Internal working models of attachment relationships as related to resilient coping. In G. Noam & K. Fischer (Eds.), *Development and vulnerability in close relationships* (pp. 3–27). Mahwah, NJ: Erlbaum.

Bretherton, I., Beeghly-Smith, M., Williamson, C., & McNew, S. (1980, April). *"I hurt your feelings cause I was mean to you." Toddlers' person knowledge as expressed in their language.* Paper presented at the meeting of the International Conference on Infant Studies. New Haven, CT.

Bretherton, I. & Waters, E. (Eds.). (1985). Growing points of attachment theory and research. *Monographs of the Society of Research in Child Development, 50* (1–2, Serial No. 209).

Briggs, J. (1970). *Never in anger: Portrait of an Eskimo family.* Cambridge, MA: Harvard University.

Bristol, M., Gallagher, J., & Schopler, E. (1988). Mothers and fathers of young developmentally disabled and nondisabled boys: Adaptation and spousal support. *Developmental Psychology, 24,* 441–451.

Brody, S. (1951). *Patterns of mothering.* New York: International University Press.

Bromwich, R. (1980). *Working with parents and infants: An interactional approach.* Baltimore: University Park Press.

Bronfenbrenner, U. (1979). *The ecology of human development.*Cambridge, MA: Harvard University.

Bronson, G. (1972). Infants' reactions to unfamiliar persons and novel objects. *Monographs of the Society of Research in Child Development, 37* (3, Serial No. 148).

Brookhart, J. & Hock, E. (1976). The effects of experimental context and experimental background on infants' behavior toward their mothers and strangers. *Child Development, 47,* 333–340.

Brooks, J. & Lewis, M. (1976). Infants' response to strangers: Midget, adult and child. *Child Development, 47,* 323–332.

Brooks, J. & Lewis, M. (1976, July). *Visual self-recognition in infancy: Contingency and the self-other distinction.* Paper presented at the Southeastern Conference 21st International Congress, Paris.

Brooks-Gunn, J. & Lewis, M. (1979). The effects of age and sex on infants' playroom behavior. *Journal of Genetic Psychology, 134,* 99–105.

Brooks-Gunn, J. & Lewis, M. (1982). The development of self-knowledge. In C. Kropp & J. Krakow (Eds.), *The child: Development in a social context* (pp. 333–387). Reading, MA: Addison-Wesley.

Brooten, D. & Jordan, C. (1983). Caffeine and pregnancy: A research review and recommendations for clinical practice. *JOGN Nursing, 12*(2), 190–195.

Broude, G. (1995). *Growing up: A cross-cultural encylopedia.* Santa Barbara, CA: ABC-CLIO.

Brown, R. (1973). *A first language: The early stages.* Cambridge, MA: Harvard University Press.

Brown, R. (1977). Introduction. In C. E. Snow & C. Ferguson (Eds.), *Talking to children* (pp. 1–27). London: Cambridge University Press.

Brown, R. & Fraser, C. (1963). The acquisition of syntax. In C. Cofer & B. Musgrave (Eds.), *Verbal behavior and learning: Problems and processes* (pp. 158–197). New York: McGraw-Hill.

Browne, S. & Miller, B. (1980). Paternal attachment behavior as related to presence during delivery and preparenthood classes. *Nursing Research, 29,* 307–311.

Brownell, C. & Brown, E. (1992). Peers and play in infants and toddlers. In V. Van Hasselt & M. Hersen (Eds.), *Handbook of social development: A lifespan perspective* (pp.183–200). New York: Plenum.

Brownell, C. & Kopp, C. (1991). Common threads, diverse solutions: Concluding commentary. *Developmental Review, 11,* 288–303.

Bruck, K. (1961). Temperature regulation in the newborn infant. *Biologic Neonatorum, 3,* 65–119.

Brunelle, J. & Carlos, J. (1990). Recent trends in dental caries in U.S. Children and the effects of water fluoridation. *Journal of Dental Research, 69,* 723–727.

Bruner, J. (1978). Learning the mother tongue. *Human Nature, 1,* 42–49.

Bruner, J. (1982). The formats of language acquisition. *American Journal of Semiotics, 1,* 1–16.

Bruner, J. (1983). *Child's talk.* New York: Norton.

Bryden, M. & Steenhuis, R. (1991). The assessment of handedness in children. In J. Obrzut & G. Hynd (Eds.), *A handbook of issues, methods, and practice* (pp. 411–436). San Diego: Academic.

Bryen, D. (1982). *Inquiries into child language.* Boston: Allyn & Bacon.

Buchsbaum, H. & Emde, R. (1990). Play narratives in thirty-six-month-old children: Early moral development and family relationships. *The Psychoanalytic Study of the Child, 40,* 129–155.

Buer, G., Ewald, L., & Dubanoski, R. (1991). Breastfeeding and cognitive development of three-year-old children. *Psychological Reports, 68,* 1218–1222.

Burchinal, M., Roberts, J., Nabors, L., & Bryant, D. (1996). Quality of center child care and infant cognitive and language development. *Child Development, 67,* 606–620.

Burnett, C. & Johnson, E. (1971). Development of gait in childhood: Part 2. *Developmental Medicine and Child Neurology, 13,* 207.

Burroughs, A. (1986). *Bleier's maternity nursing* (5th ed.). Philadelphia: Saunders.

Burton, B., Schulz, C., Angle, B., & Burd, L. (1995), An increased incidence of haemangiomas in infants born following chorionic villus sampling (CVS). *Prenatal Diagnosis. 15,* 209–214.

Burton, R. (1972). Cross-sex identity in Barbados. *Developmental Psychology, 6,* 365–374.

Bushnell, E. & Boudreau, J. (1991). The development of haptic perception during infancy. In M. Heller & W. Schiff (Eds.), *The psychology of touch* (pp.139–161). Hillsdale, NJ: Erlbaum.

Bushnell, E. (1985). The decline of visually guided reaching during infancy. *Infant Behavior and Development, 8,* 139–155.

Bushnell, E. & Bourdeau, J. (1993). Motor development and the mind: The potential role of motor abilities as a determinant of aspects of perceptual development. *Child Development, 64,* 1005–1021.

Bushnell, I. & Sai, F. (1987). *Neonatal recognition of mother's face.* University of Glasglow Report 87/1.

Buss, A. (1989). Temperaments as personality traits. In G. Kohnstamn, J. Bates, & M. Rothbart (Eds.), *Temperament in childhood* (pp. 49–58). New York: Wiley.

Buss, A. & Plomin, R. (1975). *A temperament theory of personality.* New York: Wiley.

Butler, N. & Goldstein, H. (1973). Smoking in pregnancy and subsequent child development. *British Medical Journal, 4,* 573.

Butterfield, E. & Sipperstein, G. (1974). Influence of contingent auditory stimulation upon nonnutritional suckle. In J. Bosma (Ed.), *Third symposium on oral sensation and perception: The mouth of the infant* (pp. 313–334). Springfield, IL: Thomas.

Butterfield, P. (1996). The partners in parenting education program: A new option in parent education. *Zero to Three, 17*(1), 3–10.

Butterworth, G. & Hopkins, B. (1993). Origins of handedness. *Developmental Medicine and Child Neurology, 35,* 177–184.

Byard, R. (1994). Is co-sleeping in infancy a desirable or dangerous practice. *Journal of Paediatrics and Child Health, 30,* 198–199.

Byers, T., Graham, S., Rzepka, T., & Marshall, J. (1985).

Lactation and breast cancer. *American Journal of Epidemiology, 121,* 644–674.

Bzoch, K. & League, R. (1991) *The Receptive-Emergent Language Test-2.* Los Angeles: Western Psychological Services.

Caldwell, B. (1964). The effects of infant care. In M. Hoffman & L. Hoffman (Eds.), *Review of child development research* (Vol. 1, pp. 9–87). New York: Russell Sage Foundation.

Caldwell, B. & Bradley, R. (1979). *Home observation for measurement of the environment.* Little Rock, AR: University of Arkansas.

Callen, P. & Filley, R. (1990). Amniotic fluid evaluation. In M. Harrison, M. Golbus, & R. Filly (Eds.), *The unborn patient: Prenatal diagnosis and treatment* (2nd ed., pp. 139–149). Philadelphia: Saunders.

Campbell, F. & Ramey, C. (1994). Effects of early intervention on intellectual and academic achievement: A follow-up study of children from low-income families. *Child Development, 65,* 684–698.

Campos, J., Barrett, K., Lamb, M., Goldsmith, H., & Stenberg, C. (1983). Socioemotional development. In P. Mussen (Ed.), *Handbook of child psychology: Vol. 2. Infancy and developmental psychobiology* (4th ed., pp. 784–915). New York: Wiley.

Campos, J., Bertenthal, B., & Kermoian, R. (1992). Early experience and emotional development: The emergence of wariness of heights. *Psychological Science, 3,* 61–64.

Campos, J., Campos, R., & Barrett, K. (1989). Emergent themes in the study of emotional development and emotion regulation. *Developmental Psychology, 25,* 394–402.

Campos, J., Kermoian, R., & Zumbahlen, M. (1992). Socioemotional transformations in the family system following infant crawling onset. *New Directions for Child Development, 55* (Spring), 25–56.

Campos, J. & Stenberg, C. (1981). Perception, appraisal, and emotion: The onset of social referencing. In M. Lamb & L. Sherrod (Eds.), *Infant social cognition: Empirical and theoretical considerations* (pp. 273–314). Hillsdale, NJ: Erlbaum.

Canadian Paediatric Society Nutrition Committee. (1979). Infant feeding. *Canadian Journal of Public Health, 70,* 376–385.

Capaldi, E. & VandenBos, G. (1991). Taste, food exposure and eating behavior. *Hospital and Community Psychiatry, 42,* 787–789.

Capute, A., Shapiro, B., Palmer, F., Ross, A., & Wachtel, R. (1985). Normal gross motor development: The influence of race, sex, and socioeconomic status. *Developmental Medicine and Child Neurology, 27,* 635–643.

Carey, S. (1996). Perceptual classification and expertise. In R. Gelman & T. Au (Eds.), *Perceptual and cognitive development* (pp. 49–69). San Diego: Academic.

Carey, W. & McDevitt, S. (1978). Revision of the Infant Temperament Questionnaire. *Pediatrics, 61,* 735–739.

Carlson, V., Cicchetti, D., Barnett, D., & Braunwald, K. (1989). Disorganized/ disoriented attachment relationships in maltreated children. *Developmental Psychology, 25,* 525–531.

Carr, D. (1971). Chromosome studies on selected spontaneous abortions: Polyploidy in man. *Journal of Medical Genetics, 8,* 164.

Casaer, P (1992). Development of motor functions: A developmental-neurological approach. In A. Kalverboer, B. Hopkins, & R. Geuze (Eds.), *Motor development in early and later childhood: Longitudinal approaches* (pp.125–136). Cambridge, England: Cambridge University.

Cataldo, C. (1983). *Infants and toddler programs: A guide to very early education programs.* Reading, MA: Addison-Wesley.

Cattell, P. (1940). *The measurement of intelligence of infants and young children.* New York: Psychological Corp.

Caudill, W. & Schooler, C. (1973). Child behavior and child rearing in Japan and the United States: An interim report. *Journal of Nervous and Mental Disease, 157,* 323–338.

Centers for Disease Control. (1995). Recommended childhood immunization schedule. *Morbidity and Mortality Weekly Report, 44*(RR-5), 1–8.

Centers for Disease Control. (1996). Sudden infant death syndrome—United States, 1983–1994. *Morbidity and Mortality Report, 45,* 859–861.

Centers for Disease Control. (1997). Recommended childhood immunization schedule United States, January-December 1997. *Morbidity and Mortality Weekly Report, 46,* 35–37.

Chamberlain, P. & Patterson, G. (1995). Discipline and child compliance in parenting. In M. Bornstein (Ed.), *Handbook of parenting* (Vol. 4, pp. 205–225). Mahwah, NJ: Eralbaum.

Chandler, L., Andrews, M., & Swanson, M. (1980). *Movement assessment of infants: A manual.* Rolling Bay, WA: Infant Movement Research.

Chang, H. & Pulido, D. (1994). The critical importance of cultural and linguistic continuity for infants and toddlers. *Zero to Three, 15*(2), 9–11.

Charney, R. (1980). Speech roles and the development of personal pronouns. *Journal of Child Language, 7,* 509–528.

Chase-Lansdale, P., Michael, R., & Desai, S. (1991). Maternal employment during infancy. In J. Lerner & N. Galambos (Eds.), *Employed mothers and their children: An analysis of "Children of the national longitudinal survey of youth"* (pp. 37–62). New York: Garland.

Chase-Lansdale, P. & Owen, M. (1987). Maternal employment in a family context: Effects of infant-mother and infant-father attachment. *Child Development, 58,* 1505–1512.

Chess, S., Thomas, A., & Birch, H. (1965). *Your child is a person.* New York: Viking.

Child, I. (1968). Personality in culture. In E. Borgatta & W. Lambert (Eds.), *Handbook of personality theory and research* (pp. 82–145). Chicago: Rand McNally.

Chinitz, S. (1995). Intervention with children with developmental disabilities and attachment disorders. *Developmental and Behavioral Pediatrics, 16*(3), S17–S20.

Chisholm, J. (1981). Prenatal influences on aboriginal-white Australian differences in neonatal irritability. *Ethology and Sociobiology, 2,* 67–73.

Chomsky, N. (1968). *Language and mind.* New York: Harcourt, Brace, Jovanovich.

Chomsky, N. (1975). *Reflections on language.* New York: Pantheon.

Chugani, H. (1993). Poistron emission tomography scanning: Applications in newborns. *Clinics in Perinatology, 20,* 395–409.

Cicchetti, D. (1991). Fractures in the crystal: Developmental psychopathology and the emergence of self. *Developmental Review, 11,* 271–287.

Cicchetti, D., Ganiban, J., & Barnett, D. (1991). Contributions from the study of high-risk populations to understanding the development of emotion regulation. In J. Garber & K. Dodge (Eds.), *The development of emotion regulation and dysregulation* (pp.15–48). New York: Cambridge University.

Clark, E. (1973). What's in a word: On the child's acquisition of semantics in his first language. In T. Moore (Ed.), *Cognitive development and the acquisition of language* (pp. 65–110). New York: Academic Press.

Clark, E. (1995). Language acquisition: The lexicon and syntax. In J. Miller & P. Eimas (Eds.), *Speech, language , and communication* (pp. 303–337). San Diego: Academic.

Clark, H. & Clark, E. (1977). *Psychology and language.* New York: Harcourt, Brace, Jovanovich.

Clarke-Stewart, A. (1982). *Daycare.* Cambridge, MA: Harvard University Press.

Clarke-Stewart, A. & Fein, G. (1983). Early childhood programs. In P. Mussen (Ed.), *Handbook of child psychology: Vol. 2. Infancy and developmental psychobiology* (4th ed., pp. 917–999). New York: Wiley.

Clarke, S. & Taffel, S. (1995). Changes in cesarean delivery in the United States, 1988 and 1993. *Birth, 22,* 63–67.

Clements, D. (1992). Haemophilus influenzae type b. In S. Krugman, S. Katz, A. Gershon, & C. Wilfert, (Eds.), *Infectious diseases of children* (9th ed., pp. 127–142), St. Louis: Mosby.

Clifton, R., Perris, E., & Bullinger, A. (1991). Infants' perception of auditory space. *Developmental Psychology, 27,* 187–197.

Cloud, H. (1993). Developmental disabilities. In P.

McQueen & C. Lang (Eds.), *Handbook of pediatric nutrition* (pp. 400–421). Gaithersburg, MD: Aspen.

Cockburn, F. (1984). The newborn. In J. Forfar & G. Arneil (Eds.), *Textbook of pediatrics* (3rd ed.), (Vol. 1, pp. 117–258). New York: Churchill Livingstone.

Cogan, R. (1980). Effects of childbirth preparation. *Clinical Obstetrics and Gynecology, 23*, 1–14.

Cohen, F. (1984). *Clinical genetics in nursing practice.* Philadelphia: Lippincott.

Cohen, S. (1978). Maternal employment and mother-child interaction. *Merrill-Palmer Quarterly, 24*, 189–197.

Colburn, D. (1986, June 19). *Children still perish for lack of vaccine.* Greenville Daily Reflector, p. 22.

Cole, P., Michel, M., & Teti, L. (1994). The development of emotion regulation and dysregulation: A clinical perspective. In N. Fox (Ed.), *Monographs of the Society for Research in Child Development, 59*, 73–100 (Serial No.240).

Collin, M., Halsey, C., & Anderson, C. (1991). Emerging developmental sequelae in the 'normal' extremely low birth weight infant. *Pediatrics, 88*, 115–120.

Collins, E. & Turner, G. (1975). Maternal effects of regular salicylate in gestation in pregnancy. *Lancet, 2*, 335–337.

Columbo, J.(1993). *Infant cognition: Predicting later intellectual functioning.* Newbury Park, CA: Sage.

Comer, J. & Poussaint, A. (1976). *Black child care.* New York: Pocket Books.

Committee on Injury and Poison Prevention. American Academy of Pediatrics. (1995). Injuries associated with infant walkers. *Pediatrics, 95*, 778–779.

Committee on Nutrition. American Academy of Pediatrics. (1974). Salt intake and eating patterns of infants and children in relation to blood pressure. *Pediatrics, 53*, 115–121.

Committee on Nutrition. American Academy of Pediatrics. (1976a). Commentary on breast-feeding and infant formulas, including proposed standards for formulas. *Pediatrics, 57*, 287–285.

Committee on Nutrition. American Academy of Pediatrics. (1976b). Iron supplementation for infants. *Pediatrics, 58*, 765–768.

Committee on Nutrition. American Academy of Pediatrics. (1979). Fluoride supplementation: Revised dosage schedule. *Pediatrics, 63*, 150–152.

Committee on Nutrition. American Academy of Pediatrics. (1980). On the feeding of supplemental foods to infants. *Pediatrics, 65*, 1178–1181.

Committee on Nutrition. American Academy of Pediatrics. (1985). *Pediatric nutrition handbook* (2nd ed.). Elk Grove Village, IL: American Academy of Pediatrics.

Committee on Nutrition. American Academy of Pediatrics. (1993). *Pediatric nutrition handbook* (3rd. ed.). Elk Grove Village, IL: American Academy of Pediatrics.

Committee to Study the Prevention of Low Birth Weight. (1985). *Preventing Low Birth Weight.* Washington, DC: National Academy Press.

Condon, W. & Sander, L. (1974). Synchrony demonstrated between movements of the neonate and adult speech. *Child Development, 45*, 456–462.

Condry, J. & Condry, S. (1976). Sex differences: A study of the eye of the beholder. *Child Development, 47*, 812–819.

Connolly, K. & Stratton, P. (1969). An exploration of some parameters affecting classical conditioning in the neonate. *Child Development, 40*, 431–441.

Connor, F., Williamson, G., & Siepp, J. (Eds.). (1978). *Program guide for infants and toddlers with neuromotor and other developmental disabilities.* New York: Teachers College Press.

Consumer Reports. (1995). Child safety seats: Are they always safe? *Consumer Reports, 60*, 580–585.

Conway, D., Prediville, W., Morris, A., & Stirrat, C. (1984). Management of spontaneous rupture of the membranes in the absence of labor in primigravid women at term. *American Journal of Obstetrics and Gynecology, 150*, 947–951.

Cooksey, N. (1995). Pica and olfactory cravings of pregnancy: How deep are the secrets. *Birth, 22*, 129–136.

Coopersmith, S. (1967). *The antecedents of self-esteem.* San Francisco: Freeman.

Coplan, J. (1995). Normal speech and language development. *Pediatrics in Review, 16*, 91–100.

Corkum, V. & Moore, C. (1995). Development of joint visual attention in infants. In C. Moore & J. Dunham (Eds.), *Joint attention: Its origins and role in development* (pp. 61–83). Hillsdale, NJ: Erlbaum.

Cornelius, M., Taylor, P., Geva, D., & Day, N. (1995). Prenatal tobacco exposure and marijuana use among adolescents: Effects on offspring gestational age, growth, and morphology. *Pediatrics, 95*, 738–743.

Corsaro, W. & Eder, D. (1990). Children's peer cultures. *Annual Review of Sociology, 16*, 197–220.

Cost, Quality, & Outcomes Team. (1995). *Cost, quality, and child outcomes in child care centers: Executive summary* (2nd ed.). Denver, CO: University of Denver.

Courage, M. & Adams, R. (1990). Visual acuity assessment from birth to three years old using the acuity card procedures: Cross-sectional and longitudinal samples. *Optometry and Vision Science, 67*, 713–718.

Coustan, D. (1995a). Obstetric analgesia and anesthesia. In D. Coustan, R. Haning, & D. Singer (Eds.), *Human reproduction: Growth and development* (pp. 327–340). Boston: Little, Brown.

Coustan, D. (1995b). Obstetric complications. In D. Coustan, R. Haning, & D. Singer (Eds.), *Human reproduction: Growth and development,* (pp. 431–455). Boston: Little, Brown.

Cowan, P., Cowan, C., & Kerig, P. (1993). Mothers, fathers, sons, and daughters: Gender differences in family formation and parenting style. In P. Cowan, D. Field, D. Hansen, A. Skolnick, & G. Swanson (Eds.), *Family, self, and society* (pp. 165–195). Hillsdale, NJ: Erlbaum.

Cox, J. & Gallagher-Allred, C. (1980). *Normal diet: Age of dependency.* Columbus, OH: Ohio State

Craig, K., Whitfield, M., & Grunau, R., Linton, J., & Hadjistavropoulos, H. (1993). Pain in the preterm neonate: Behavioral and physiological indices. *Pain, 52,* 287–299.

Crais, E. & Roberts, J. (1996). Assessing communication skills. In M. McLean, D. Bailey, & M. Wolery (Eds.), *Assessing infants and toddlers with special needs* (pp. 334–397). Columbus, OH: Merrill.

Cratty, B. (1979). *Perceptual and motor development in infants and young children* (2nd ed.). Englewood Cliffs, NJ: Prentice Hall.

Cravioto, J. & Robles, B. (1965). Evolution of adaptive and motor behavior during rehabilitation from kwashiorkor. *American Journal of Orthopsychiatry, 35,* 449–464.

Crittenden, P. (1985). Maltreated infants: Vulnerability and resilience. *Journal for Child Psychology and Psychiatry, 26,* 85–96.

Crockenberg, S. (1987). Predictors and correlates of anger toward and punitive control of toddlers by adolescent mothers. *Child Development, 58,* 964–975.

Crockenberg, S., Lyons-Ruth, K., & Dickstein, S. (1993). The family context of infant mental health: II. Infant development in multiple family relationships. In C. Zeanah (Ed.), *Handbook of infant mental health* (pp. 38–55). New York: Guilford.

Crook, C. (1977). Taste and the temporal organization of neonatal sucking. In J. Weiffenbach (Ed.), *Taste and development: The genesis of sweet preference* (pp. 146–158). Bethesda, MD: National Institutes of Health. (DHEW Pub No. NIH 771068).

Crook, W. (1975). *Your allergic child.* Jackson, TN: Professional Books.

Cruttenden, A. (1970). A phonetic study of babbling. *British Journal of Disorders in Communication, 5,* 110–118.

Cryer, D., Harms, T., & Bourland, B. (1987). *Addison-Wesley active learning series: Active learning for infants.* Menlo Park, CA: Addison-Wesley

Cummings, E. (1980). Caregiver stability and day care. *Developmental Psychology, 16,* 31–37.

Cummings, M. & Cicchetti, D. (1990). Toward a transactional model of relations between attachment and depression. In M. Greenberg, D. Cicchetti, & E. Cummings, *Attachment in the preschool years: Theory, research and intervention* (pp. 339–372). Chicago: University of Chicago.

Curtis, D. (1990). Infant nutrient supplementation. *Journal of Pediatrics, 117,* S110–118.

Daehler, M. & Greco, C. (1985). Memory in very young children. In M. Pressley & C. Brainerd (Eds.), *Cognitive learning and memory in children* (pp. 49–79). New York: Springer-Verlag.

Dahl, L. (1972). Salt and hypertension. *American Journal of Clinical Nutrition, 25,* 231.

Dahl, R., Scher, M., Williamson, T., Robles, N., & Day, N. (1995). A longitudinal study of prenatal marijuana use. Effects on sleep and arousal at age 3 years. *Archives of Pediatric and Adolescent Medicine, 149,* 145–150.

Dale, P. (1976). *Language and development* (2nd ed.). New York: Holt, Rinehart & Winston.

D'Alton, M. (1994). Prenatal diagnostic procedures. *Seminars in Perinatology, 18,* 140–162.

Damon, W. & Hart, D. (1982). The development of self-understanding from infancy through adolescence. *Child Development, 53,* 841–864.

Daniels, D. & Plomin, R. (1985). Differential experience of siblings in the same family. *Developmental Psychology, 21,* 747–760.

Daniels, D., Plomin, R., & Greenhalgh, J. (1984). Correlates of difficult temperament in infancy. *Child Development, 55,* 1184–1194.

Dannemiller, J. & Stephens, B. (1988). A critical test of infant pattern preference models. *Child Development.* 59, 210–216.

Darke, P. & Goldberg, S. (1994). Father-infant interaction and parent stress with healthy and medically compromised infants. *Infant Behavior and Development, 17,* 3–14.

Darley, F. & Winitz, H. (1961). Age of the first word: Review of research. *Journal of Speech and Hearing Disorders, 26,* 272–290.

Darling-Fisher, C. & Tiedje, L. (1990). The impact of maternal employment characteristics on fathers' participation in child care. *Family Relations, 39,* 20–26.

Dart, R. & Rumack, B. (1994). Poisoning. In W. Hay, J. Groothuis, A. Hayward, & M. Levin. *Current pediatric diagnosis & treatment* (12th ed., pp. 316–343). Norwalk, CT: Appleton & Lange.

Darwin, C. (1877). A biographical sketch of an infant. *Mind, 2,* 285–294.

Davis, H., Gartner, J., Galvis, A., Michaels, R., & Mestad, P. (1981). Acute upper airway obstruction: Croup and epiglottis. *Pediatric Clinics of North America, 28,* 859–880.

Davis, J. & Rovee-Collier, C. (1983). Alleviated forgetting of a learned contingency in 8-week-old infants. *Developmental Psychology, 19,* 353–365.

Day, N. & Richardson, G. (1991). Prenatal alcohol exposure: A continuum of effects. *Seminars in Perinatology, 15,* 271–279.

Day, R. (1967). Factors influencing offspring. *American Journal of Diseases of Children, 142,* 6.

Decarie, G. & Ricard, G. (1996). Revisiting Piaget revisited. In G. Noam & K. Fischer (Eds.), *Development and vulnerability in close relationships* (pp. 113–132). Mahwah, NJ: Erlbaum.

Decarie, T. (1969). A study of the mental and emotional development of the thalidomide child. In B. Foss (Ed.), *Determinants of infant behavior* (Vol. 4, pp. 110–114) London: Methuen.

DeCasper, A. & Fifer, W. (1980). Of human bonding: Newborns prefer their mothers' voices. *Science, 208,* 1174–1176.

DeCasper, A. & Prescott, P. (1984). Human newborns' perception of male voices: Preference, discrimination and reinforcing value. *Developmental Psychobiology, 17,* 481–491.

DeCasper, A. & Spence, M. (1986). Prenatal maternal speech influences newborns' perception of speech sounds. *Infant Behavior and Development, 9,* 133–150.

DeKaban, A. (1970). *Neurology of early childhood.* Baltimore: Williams & Wilkins.

de Mause, L. (1974). The evolution of childhood. In L. de Mause (Ed.), *The history of childhood* (pp. 1–73). New York: Psychohistory Press.

Dennis, W. (1941). Infant development under conditions of restricted practice and of minimal social stimulation. *Genetic Psychology Monographs, 23,* 143–191.

Dennison, B., Rockwell, H., & Baker, S. (1997). Excess fruit juice consumption by preschool-aged children is associated with short stature and obesity. *Pediatrics, 99,* 15–22.

Derryberry, D. & Rothbart, M. (1984). Emotions, attention and temperament. In C. Izard, J. Kagan, & R. Zajonc (Eds.), *Emotions, cognition, and behavior* (pp. 132–166). London: Cambridge University Press.

Desmond, M., Wilson, G., Alt, E., & Fisher, E. (1980). The very low birth weight infant after discharge from intensive care: Anticipatory health care and developmental course. *Current Problems in Pediatrics, 10,* 1–59.

Desor, J., Maller, O., & Andrews, K. (1975). Ingestive responses of human newborns to salty, sour and bitter stimuli. *Journal of Comparative and Physiological Psychology, 89,* 966–970.

Desor, J., Maller, O., & Greene, L. (1977). Preference for sweet in humans: Infant children and adults. In J. Wiffenbach (Ed.), *Taste and development: The genesis of sweet preference* (pp. 161–172). Bethesda, MD: National Institutes of Health. (DHEW Pub. No. NIH 77–1068).

Desrochers, S., Morissette, P., & Ricard, M. (1995). Two perspectives on pointing in infancy. In C. Moore & J. Dunham (Eds.), *Joint attention: Its origins and role in development* (pp 85–101). Hillsdale, NJ: Erlbaum.

de Villiers, J. & de Villiers, P. (1978). *Language acquisition.* Cambridge, MA: Harvard University Press.

de Villiers, J. & de Villiers, P. (1979). *Early language.* Cambridge, MA: Harvard University Press.

Dewey, K., Heinig, J., & Nommsen-Rivers, L. (1995). Differences in morbidity between breast-fed and formula-fed infants. *Journal of Pediatrics, 126,* 696–702.

Dick-Read, Grantley. (1972). *The practice of natural childbirth.* New York: Harper & Row.

Dickie, J. & Matheson, P. (1984, August). *Mother-father-infant: Who needs support.* Paper presented at the meeting of the American Psychological Association, Toronto, Ontario.

Dobbing, J. (1976). Vulnerable periods in brain growth and somatic growth. In D. Roberts & A. Thomson (Eds.), *The biology of human fetal growth* (pp. 137–147). New York: Halsted Press.

Dobbing, J. (1993). Nutrition, the developing brain and intelligence. *Professional Care of Mother and Child, 3,* 64–69.

Dobbing, J. & Smart, J. (1974). Vulnerability of developing brain and behavior. *British Medical Bulletin, 30,* 164.

Dodson, F. (1970). *How to parent.* New York: Signet.

Doman, G. (1982). *Teach your baby math.* New York: Pocket Books.

Doman, G. (1984). *How to multiply your baby's intelligence.* New York: Doubleday.

Draper, P. & Cashdan, E. (1988). Technological change and child behavior among the Young. *Ethnology, 27,* 339–365.

Dreikurs, R. (1958). *The challenge of parenthood* (Rev. ed.). New York: Hawthorn.

Drillien, C. (1964). *The growth and development of the prematurely born infant.* Edinburgh: Livingstone.

Dryden, R. (1978). *Before birth.* London: Heinemann.

DuBois, F. (1952). The security of discipline. *Mental Hygiene, 36,* 353–372.

Dubowitz, L., Dubowitz, V., & Goldberg, C. (1970). Clinical assessment of gestational age in the newborn infant. *Journal of Pediatrics, 77,* 1–10.

Dubowitz, V. (1980). *The floppy infant* (2nd ed.). Philadelphia: Lippincott.

Dunham, P., Dunham, F., & Curwin, A. (1993). Joint-attentional states and lexical acquisition at 18 months. *Developmental Psychology, 29,* 827–831.

Dunham, P. & Dunham, R. (1992). Lexical development during middle infancy: A mutually driven infant-caregiver process. *Developmental Psychology, 28,* 414–420.

Dunn, J. (1986). Pretend play in a family. In A. Gottfried & C. Brown (Eds.), *Play interactions* (pp. 149–162). Lexington, MA: Heath.

Dunn, J. (1987). The beginnings of moral understanding: Development in the second year. In J. Kagan & S. Lamb (Eds.), *The emergence of morality in young children* (pp. 91–112). Chicago: University of Chicago.

Dunn, J. (1988). *The beginnings of social understanding.* Oxford: Basil Blackwell.

Dunnihoo, D. (1992). *Fundamentals of gynecology and obstetrics* (2nd ed.). Philadelphia: Lippincott.

Dunst, C. (1980). *A clinical and educational manual for*

use with the Uzgiris and Hunt Scales of infant psychological development. Austin, TX: Pro-Ed.

Durand, A. (1992). The safety of home birth: The farm study. *American Journal of Public Health, 82,* 450–452.

Dwyer, T. & Ponsonby, A. (1995). SIDS epidemiology and incidence. *Pediatric Annals, 24,* 350–356.

Dyer, E. (1963). Parenthood as crisis: A restudy. *Marriage and Family Living, 25,* 488–496.

Eagan, B., Whelan-Williams, S., and Brooks, W. (1985). The abuse of infants by manual shaking: Medical, social and legal issues. *Florida Medical Association Journal, 72,* 503–507.

Easterbrooks, M. & Goldberg, W. (1985). Effects of early maternal employment on toddlers, mothers, and fathers. *Developmental Psychology, 21,* 774–783.

Easterbrooks, M. & Goldberg, W. (1990). Security of toddler-parent attachment: Relation to sociopersonality functioning during kindergarten. In M. Greenberg, D. Cicchetti, & E. Cummings, *Attachment in the preschool years: Theory, research and intervention* (pp. 221–244). Chicago: University of Chicago.

Eastham, E. & Walker, W. (1977). Effect of cow's milk on the gastrointestinal tract: A persistant dilemma for the pediatrician. *Pediatrics, 60,* 477.

Eckerman, K. & Whatley, J. (1977). Toys and social interaction between infant peers. *Child Development, 48,* 1146–1156.

Eddy, T. (1973). *Past and present malnutrition and its effect on health today. Childhood and society.* New York: Norton.

Edwards, C. (1995). Parenting toddlers. In M. Bornstein (Ed.), *Handbook of parenting* (Vol. 1, pp. 41–64). Mahwah, NJ: Erlbaum.

Eichorn, D. (1979). Physical development: current foci of research. In J. Osofsky (Ed.), *Handbook of infant development* (pp. 253–282). New York: Wiley.

Eiduson, B., Kornfein, M., Zimmerman, I., & Weisner, T. (1982). Comparative socialization practices in traditional and alternative families. In M. Lamb (Ed.), *Nontraditional families: Parenting and child development* (pp. 315–346). Hillsdale, NJ: Erlbaum.

Eilers, R. & Minifie, F. (1975). Fricative discrimination in early infancy. *Journal of Speech and Hearing Research, 18,* 158–167.

Eimas, P. (1975). Speech perception in early infancy. In L. Cohen & P. Salapatek (Eds.), *Infant perception: From sensation to cognition* (Vol. 2, pp. 193–231). New York: Academic Press.

Eimas, P., Siqueland, E., Juzcyk, P., & Vigorito, J. (1971). Speech perception in early infancy. *Science, 171,* 303–306.

Eisenberg, R. (1976). *Auditory competence in early life.* Baltimore: University Park Press.

Eliason, M. & Williams, J. (1990). Fetal alcohol syndrome and the neonate. *Journal of Perinatal and Neonatal Nursing, 3,* 64–72.

Elkind, D. (1981). *The hurried child: Growing up too fast too soon.* Reading, MA: Addison-Wesley.

Emde, R. (1980). Levels of meaning for infant emotions: A biosocial view. In W. Collins (Ed.), *Minnesota symposia of child psychology: Vol. 13. Development of cognition, affect and social relations* (pp. 1–38). Hillsdale, NJ: Erlbaum.

Emde, R. (1996). Thinking about intervention and improving early socioemotional development: Recent trends in policy and knowledge. *Zero to Three, 17*(1), 11–16.

Emde, R., Biringen, Z., Clyman, R., & Oppenheim, D. (1991). The moral self of infancy: Affective core and procedural knowledge. *Developmental Review, 11,* 251–270.

Emde, R., Gaensbauer, T., & Harmon, R. (1976). *Emotional expression in infancy: A bio-behavioral study. Psychological Issues* (Vol. 10, No. 1) (Monograph 37) New York: International Universities Press.

Emde, R., Johnson, W., & Easterbrooks, M. (1987). The do's and don'ts of early moral development: Psychoanalytic tradition and current research. In J. Kagan & S. Lamb (Eds.), *The emergence of morality in young children* (pp. 245–277). Chicago: University of Chicago.

Ensher, G. & Clark, D. (1994). *Newborns at risk: Medical care and psychoeducational intervention* (2nd ed.). Gaithersberg, MD: Aspen.

Entwisle, D. & Doering, S. (1981). *The first birth.* Baltimore: Johns Hopkins University.

Eppler, M., Adolph, K., & Weiner, T. (1996). The developmental relationship between infants' exploration and action on slanted surfaces. *Infant Behavior and Development, 19,* 259–264.

Epstein, H. (1978). Growth spurts during brain development: Implications for educational policy and posture. In J. Chall & A. Mirsky (Eds.), *Education and the brain: The seventy-seventh yearbook of the National Society for the Study of Education* (pp. 343–370). Chicago: University of Chicago Press.

Erikson, E. (1963). *Childhood and society* (2nd ed.) New York: Wiley.

Ervin-Tripp, S. (1966). Language development. In L. Hoffman & M. Hoffman (Eds.), *Review of child development research* (Vol. 2, pp. 55–105). New York: Russell Sage Foundation.

Espenschade, A. & Eckert, H. (1967). *Motor development.* Columbus, OH: Merrill.

Etaugh, C., Grinnel, K. & Etaugh, A. (1989). Development of gender labeling: Effect of age pictured children. *Sex Roles, 21,* 769–773.

Evans, G. & Hall, J. (1976). The older sperm. *Ms., 4* (7), 48–50.

Ewy, D. & Ewy, R. (1982). *Preparation for childbirth: A Lamaze guide.* Boulder, CO: Pruett.

Fabry, P. & Tepperman, J. (1970). Meal frequency: A

possible factor in human pathology. *American Journal of Clinical Nutrition, 23,* 1059.

Fagan, J. (1971). Infants' recognition memory for a series of visual stimuli. *Journal of Experimental Child Psychology, 11,* 244–250.

Fagard, J. (1990). The development of bimanual coordination. In C. Bard, M. Fleury, & L. Hay (Eds.). *Development of eye-hand coordination across the life span* (pp. 262–282). Columbia, SC: University of South Carolina.

Fagot, B. (1995). Parenting boys and girls. In M. Bornstein (Ed.), *Handbook of parenting* (Vol. 1, pp.163–183). Mahwah, NJ: Erlbaum.

Fagot, B. & Hagan, R. (1991). Observations of parent reactions to sex-stereotyped behaviors: Age and sex effects. *Child Development, 62,* 617–628.

Fagot, B. & Leinbach, M. (1989). The young child's gender schema: Environmental input, internal organization. *Child Development, 60,* 663–672.

Fagot, B. & Leinbach, M. (1993). Gender-role development in young children: From discrimination to labeling. *Developmental Review, 13,* 205–224.

Family Life Council of Greater Greensboro. (1973). *North Carolina's battered children.* (Leaflet.)

Fantz, R. (1958). Pattern vision in young infants. *Psychological Review, 8,* 43–49.

Fantz, R. & Nevis, S. (1967). Pattern preferences and perceptual-cognitive development in early infancy. *Merrill-Palmer Quarterly, 13,* 77–108.

Feldman, S. (1978). *Choices in childbirth.* New York: Grosset and Dunlop.

Feldman, S., Nash, S., & Aschenbrenner, B. (1983). Antecedents of fathering. *Child Development, 54,* 1628–1636.

Fenichel, E. (1996). Editor's note. *Zero to Three, 17*(1), 2.

Fenson, L., Dale, P., Reznick, J., Bates, E., Thal, D., & Pethick, S. (1994). Variability in early communicative development. *Monographs of the Society for Research in Child Development, 59* (5, Serial No. 242).

Fenson, L., Kagan, J., Kearsley, R., & Zelazo, P. (1976). The developmental progression of manipulative play in the first two years. *Child Development, 47,* 232–236.

Fergusson, D., Horwood, L., & Shannon, F. (1987). Breast-feeding and subsequent social adjustment in six-to eight-year-old children. *Journal of Child Psychology, 28,* 378–386.

Fernald, A. (1984). The perceptual and affective salience of mothers' speech to infants. In L. Feagans, C. Garvey, & R. Golinkoff (Eds.), *The origins and growth of communication* (pp. 5–29). Norwood, NJ: Ablex.

Fernald, A. (1989). Intonation and communicative intent in mother's speech to infants: Is the melody the message? *Child Development, 60,* 1497–1510.

Fernald, A., Taeschner, T., Dunn, J., Papousek, M.,

Boyson-Bardies, B., & Fukui, I. (1989). A cross-language study of prosodic modifications in mothers' and fathers' speech to preverbal infants. *Journal of Child Language, 16,* 477–501.

Fetters, L. (1996). Motor development. In M. Hanson (Ed.), *Atypical infant development* (2nd. ed, pp. 403–450). Austin, TX: Pro-Ed.

Field, T. (1990). *Infancy.* Cambridge, MA: Harvard University.

Field, T. (1995). Massage therapy for infants and children. *Developmental and Behavioral Pediatrics, 16,* 105–111.

Field, T., Cohen, D., Garcia, R. & Greenberg, R. (1984). Mother-stranger face discrimination by the newborn. *Infant Behavior and Development, 7,* 19–25.

Field, T., Masi, W., Goldstein, S., Perry, S., & Parl, S. (1988). Infant day care facilitates preschool social behavior. *Early Childhood Research Quarterly, 3,* 341–359.

Filer, L. (1990). Iron needs during rapid growth and mental development. *Journal of Pediatrics. 117,* S143–146.

Filer, L. (1995). Iron deficiency. In F. Lifshitz (Ed.), *Childhood nutrition* (pp. 53–59). Boca Raton: CRC.

Finberg, L. (1990). Modified fat diets: Do they apply to infancy? *Journal of Pediatrics, 117,* 132–133, 168.

Finberg, L., Kiley, J., & Luttrell, C. (1963). Mass accidental salt poisoning in infancy. *Journal of the American Medical Association, 184,* 121–124.

Finkelstein, N., Dent, C., Gallagher, J., & Ramey, C. (1978). Social behavior of infants and toddlers in a daycare environment. *Developmental Psychology, 14,* 257–262.

Fiscus, S., Adimora, A., Schoenbach, V., Lim. W., Mckinney, R., Rupar, D., Kenny, J., Woods, C., & Wilfert, C. (1996). Perinatal HIV infection and the effect of Zidovudine therapy on transmission in rural and urban counties. *Journal of the American Medical Association, 275,* 1483–1488.

Fleischer, K. (1955). Unterschugen zur entuicklung der inneohrfunktion (intrauterine kindsbewegungen nach schallreizen). *Laryngologie, Rhinologie, Otologie, 34,* 733–740.

Fleming, P., Blair, P., Bacon, C., Bensley, D., Smith I., Taylor, E., Berry, J., Golding, J., & Tripp, J. (1996). Environments of infants during sleep and risk of the sudden infant death syndrome: Results of 1993–5 case-control study for confidential inquiry into still-births and deaths in infancy. *British Medical Journal, 313,* 191–195.

Fogel, A. (1997). *Infancy: Infant, family, and society* (3rd ed.). Mineapolis/St. Paul: West.

Foman, S. (1993). *Nutrition of normal infants.* St. Louis: Mosby.

Foman, S., Lloyd, J., Thomas, A., & Ziegler, E. (1979). Recommendations for feeding normal infants. *Pediatrics, 63,* 52–58.

Foman, S., Thomas, L., & Filer, L. (1970). Acceptance of unsalted strained foods by normal infants. *Journal of Pediatrics, 76,* 242.

Ford, C. (1945). *A comparative study of human reproduction.* Yale University Publications in Anthropology No. 32. New Haven, CT: Yale University Press, 84–85.

Fosberg, S. (1981). *Family day care in the United States: Summary of findings* (Vol. 1). Final report of the national day care home study. Cambridge, MA: ABT Associates.

Foundation for the Study of Infant Death and the British Paediatric Respiratory Group. (1985). Apnoea monitors and sudden infant death. *Archives of Disease of Children, 60,* 76–80.

Fowler, W. (1980). *Infant and child care: A guide to education in group settings.* Boston: Allyn & Bacon.

Fox, N. (1985). The organization of cerebral lateralization during infancy. *Infant Mental Health Journal, 6,* 175–184.

Fox, M. & Porges, S. (1985). The relation between neonatal heart period patterns and developmental outcome. *Child Development, 56,* 28–37.

Fraiberg, S. (1971). Interaction in infancy: A program for blind infants. *Journal of the American Academy of Child Psychiatry, 10,* 381–405.

Fraiberg, S. (1974). Blind infants and their mothers: An examination of the sign system. In M. Lewis & L. Rosenblum (Eds.), *The effect of the infant on its caregivers* (pp. 215–232). New York: Wiley.

Fraiberg, S., Smith, M., & Adelson, E. (1969). An educational program for blind infants. *Journal of Special Education, 3,* 121–139.

Frank, D., Bauchner, H., Parker, S., Huber, A., Kyei-Aboagyke, K., Cabral, H., & Zuckerman, B. (1990). Neonatal body proportionality and body composition after in utero exposure to cocaine and marijuana. *Journal of Pediatrics. 117,* 622–626.

Frank, L. (1968). Play is valid. *Childhood Education, 44,* 433–440.

Frankel, K. & Bates, J. (1990). Mother-toddler problem solving: Antecedents in attachment, home behavior, and temperament. *Child Development, 61,* 810–819.

Frankenburg, W., Dodds, J., Archer, P., Bresnick, B., Mashka, P., Edelman, N., Shapiro, H. (1992). *Denver II* (2nd ed.). Denver, CO: Denver Developmental Materials, Inc.

Frankenburg, W., Dodds, J., & Fandal, A. (1973). *Denver Developmental Screening Test.* Denver, CO: Denver Developmental Materials, Inc.

Freed, E. Steinschneider, A., Glassman, M., & Winn, K. (1994). Sudden infant death syndrome prevention and an understanding of selected clinical issues. *Pediatric Clinics of North America, 41,* 967–989.

Freedman, E., Sachtleben, M., Dahrouge, D., & Neff, R. (1984). Long term effects of labor and delivery on offspring: A matched pair analysis. *American Journal of Obstetrics and Gynecology, 150,* 941–945.

Freeman, B. & Ritvo, E. (1984). The syndrome of autism: Establishing the diagnosis and principles of management. *Pediatric Annals, 13,* 284–296.

Freud, S. (1917). *Psychopathology of everyday life.* New York: Macmillan.

Freud, S. (1940). *An outline of psychoanalysis.* New York: Norton.

Fried, P. & Makin., J. (1987). Neonatal behavioral correlates of prenatal exposure to marijuana, cigarettes, and alcohol in a low risk population. *Neurobehavioral Toxicology ad Teratology.* 79–85.

Fried, P., Watkinson, B., & Willan, A. (1984). Marijuana use during pregnancy and decreased length of gestation. *American Journal of Obstetrics and Gynecology, 150,* 23–27.

Friedman, D. (1981). Ethnic differences in babies. In E. Hetherington & R. Parke (Eds.), *Contemporary readings in child psychology* (pp. 6–12). New York: McGraw-Hill.

Friedman, J. & Polifka, J. (1994). *Teratogenic effects of drugs: A resource for clinicians.* Baltimore: Johns Hopkins.

Frietas, B. (1984). The development of taste acceptance in human infants. *Dissertation Abstracts International, 44*(7–5), 2272. (University Microfilms No. DA83226288).

Fuhrmann, W., & Vogel, F. (1983). *Genetic counseling* (3rd ed.). New York: Springer-Verlag.

Furuno, S., O'Reilly, K., Hosaka, C., Inatsuka, T., Zeisloft-Falbey, B., & Allman, T. (1988). *Hawaii early learning profile (Help).* Palo Alto, CA: Vort.

Gallahue, D. (1982). *Understanding motor development in children.* New York: Wiley.

Galler, J. & Ross, R. (1993). Malnutrition and mental development. In R. Suskind & L. Lewinter-Suskind (Eds.), *Textbook of pediatric nutrition* (2nd ed., pp. 173–179). New York: Raven.

Gamble, T. & Zigler, E. (1986). Effects of infant day care: Another look at the evidence. *American Journal of Orthopsychiatry, 56,* 26–41.

Garcia Coll, C. & Meyer, E. (1993). The sociocultural context of infant development. In C. Zeanah (Ed.), *Handbook of infant mental health* (pp.56–69). New York: Guilford.

Garcia Coll, C., Meyer, E., & Brillon, L. (1995). Ethnic and minority parenting. In M. Bornstein (Ed.), *Handbook of parenting* (Vol. 2, pp. 189–210). Mahwah, NJ: Erlbaum.

Garmel, S. & D'Alton, M. (1994). Diagnostic ultrasound in pregnancy: An overview. *Seminars in Perinatology, 18,* 117–132.

Garn, S. (1966). Body size and its implication. In L. Hoffman & M. Hoffman (Eds.), *Review of child development research* (Vol. 2, pp. 529–566). New York: Russell Sage Foundation.

Gasser, R. (1975). *Atlas of human embryos.* New York: Harper & Row.

Gellis, S. & Kagan, B. (1986). *Current pediatric therapy.* Philadelphia: Saunders.

Gerber, M. (1981). What is appropriate curriculum for infants and toddlers? In B. Weissbound & J. Musick (Eds.), *Infants: Their social environments* (pp. 77–85). Washington, DC: National Association for the Education of Young Children.

Gerrard, J., Mackenzie, J., Goluboff, N., Garson, J., & Maningas, C. (1973). Cow's milk allergy: Prevalence and manifestations in an unselected series of newborns. *Acta Paediatrica Scandinavica,* (Suppl. 234), 1–21.

Gershon, A. & LaRussa, P. (1992). Varicella-zoster virus infections. In S. Krugman, S. Katz, A. Gershon, & C. Wilfert (Eds.), *Infectious diseases of children* (9th ed., pp. 587–614). St. Louis: Mosby.

Gesell, A. (1925). *The mental growth of the preschool child.* New York: MacMillan.

Gesell, A. (1940). *The first five years of life: A guide to the study of preschool child.* New York: Harper & Brothers.

Gesell, A. (1945). *The embryology of behavior.* New York: Harper.

Gesell, A. (1954). The ontogenesis of infant behavior. In L. Carmichael (Ed.), *Manual of child psychology* (2nd ed., pp. 335–373). New York: Wiley.

Gesell, A. & Ames, L. (1947). The development of handedness. *Journal of Genetic Psychology, 70,* 155–175.

Gesell, A. & Ilg, F. (1937). *Feeding behavior of infants.* Philadelphia: Lippincott.

Gesell, A. & Thompson, H. (1934). *Infant behavior: Its genesis and growth.* New York: McGraw-Hill.

Ghent, W., DaSylva, N., & Farren, M. (1985). Family violence: Guidelines for recognition and management. *Canadian Medical Association Journal, 132,* 541–549.

Giattino, J. & Hogan, J. (1975). Analysis of father's speech to his language learning child. *Journal of Speech and Hearing Disorders, 40,* 524–537.

Gibson, D., Sheps, S., Schechter, M., & McCormick, A. (1990). Retinopathy of prematurity-induced blindness: birthweight-specific survival and the new epidemic. *Pediatrics, 86,* 405–412.

Gibson, E. (1969). *Principles of perceptual learning and development.* New York: Appleton.

Gibson, E. (1992). How to think about perceptual learning: Twenty-five years later. In H. Pick, P. Van Den Broek, & D. Knill (Eds.), *Cognition: Conceptual and methodological issues* (pp. 215–237). Washington, DC: American Psychological Association.

Gibson, E. & Walk, R. (1960). The "visual cliff." *Scientific American, 202,* 64–71.

Gibson, J. (1969). *The senses considered as perceptual systems.* Boston: Houghton Mifflin.

Gielen, A., Faden, R., O'Campo, P., & Paige, D. (1992). Determinants of breast-feeding in a rural WIC population. *Journal of Human Lactation, 8* (1), 11–15.

Ginott, H. (1965). *Between parent and child.* New York: Macmillan.

Glassman, M. (1994). All things being equal: The two roads of Piaget and Vygotsky. *Developmental Review, 14,* 186–214.

Gleason, C. & Durand, D. (1993). Respiratory complications. In F. Witter & L. Keith (Eds.), *Textbook of prematurity* (pp. 279–303). Boston: Little, Brown.

Gleason, J. (1975). *Fathers and other strangers: Men's speech to young children.* Georgetown University 26th Round Table on Language and Linguistics. Washington, DC: Georgetown University.

Gleason, J. (1993). Studying language development. In J. Gleason (Ed.), *The development of language* (3rd. ed., pp. 1–37). New York: Macmillan.

Gold, E. (1996). Almost extinct diseases: Measles, mumps, rubella, and pertussis. *Pediatrics in Review, 17,* 120–127.

Golden, M. & Birns, B. (1976). Social class and infant intelligence. In M. Lewis (Ed.), *Origins of intelligence: Infancy and early childhood* (pp. 299–352). New York: Plenum.

Goldfield, B. (1987). The contributions of child and caregiver to referential and expressive language. *Applied Psycholinguistics, 8,* 267–280.

Golding, J., Limerick, S., & Macfarlane, A. (1985). *Sudden infant death syndrome: Patterns, puzzles and problems.* Seattle: University of Washington Press.

Goldman, A. (1984). Drugs and the mechanism of the drug induced teratogenesis. In L. Stern (Ed.), *Drug use in pregnancy* (pp. 68–98). Balgowlah, Australia: ADIS Health Science.

Goldsmith, H. (1983). *Emotionality in infant twins: Longitudinal results.* Abstracts of the Fourth International Congress on Twin Studies. London.

Goldsmith, H. & Alansky, J. (1987). Maternal and infant temperamental predictors of attachment: A metaanalytic review. *Journal of Consulting and Clinical Psychology, 55,* 805–816.

Goldsmith, H., Buss, A., Plomin, R., Rothbart, M., Thomas, A., Chess, S., Hinde, R., & McCall, R. (1987). Roundtable: What is temperament? Four approaches. *Child Development, 58,* 505–529.

Goldsmith, H. & Rothbart, M. (1991). Contemporary instruments for assessing temperament by questionnaire and in the laboratory. In J. Streulau & A. Anglettner (Eds.), *Explorations in temperament* (pp. 249–272). New York: Plenum.

Goldstein, G. & Heiner, D. (1970). Clinical and immunological perspectives in food sensitivity. *Journal of Allergy, 46,* 270–291.

Gonzalez-Mena, J. & Eyer, D. (1980). *Infancy and caregiving.* Palo Alto, CA: Mayfield.

Gonzalez-Mena, J. & Eyer, D. (1997). *Infants, toddlers,*

and caregivers (4th ed.). Mountain View, CA: Mayfield.

Gordon, I., Guinagh, B., & Tester, R. (1977). The Florida parent education infant and toddler programs. In M. Day & R. Parker (Eds.), *The preschool in action* (2nd ed., pp. 95–127). Boston: Allyn & Bacon.

Gordon, J. & Haire, D. (1981). Alternatives in childbirth. In P. Ahmed (Ed.), *Pregnancy, childbirth, and parenthood* (pp. 287–313). New York: Elsevier.

Gormican, A., Valentine, J., & Sutter, E. (1980). Relationships of maternal weight gain and infant birthweight. *Journal of the American Dietetic Association, 77,* 662–668.

Gotlin, R., Kappy, M., Eisenbarth, G., & Chase, P. (1995). Endocrine disorders. In W. Hay, J. Groothuis, A. Hayward, & M. Levin (Eds.), *Current pediatric diagnosis and treatment* (12th ed., pp. 881–883). Norwalk, CT: Appleton.

Gottfried, A. (1984). Touch as an organizer of human development. In C. Brown (Ed.), *The many facets of touch* (pp. 114–120). Skillman, NJ: Johnson & Johnson.

Gottfried, A. (1985). The relationship of play materials and parental involvement to young children's development. In C. Brown & A. Gottfried (Eds.), *Play interactions: The role of toys and parental involvement in children's development* (pp. 181–185). Somerville, NJ: Johnson & Johnson.

Gottfried, A. (1991). Maternal employment in the family setting: Developmental and environmental issues. In J. Lerner & N. Galambos (Eds.), *Employed mothers and their children: An analysis of "Children of the national longitudinal survey of youth"* (pp. 63–84). New York: Garland.

Gottwald, S. & Thurman, K. (1995). Parent-infant interaction in neonatal intensive care units; Implications for research and delivery of service. In J. Blackman (Ed.). *Infant development and mental health in early intervention* (pp. 26–27). Gaithersberg, MD: Aspen.

Graeber, J. & Schwartz, T. (1993). In F. Witter & L. Keith (Eds.), *Textbook of prematurity* (pp. 321–332), Boston: Little, Brown.

Graham, G. & Adrianzen, T. (1972). Late "catch-up growth" after severe infantile malnutrition. *Johns Hopkins Medical Journal, 131,* 204.

Granrud, C. & Yonas, A. (1984). Infants perception of pictorial specified interposition. *Journal of Experimental Child Psychology, 37,* 500–511.

Granrud, C., Yonas, A., & Opland, E. (1985). Infants' sensitivity to depth cue of shading. *Perception and Psychophysics, 37,* 415–419.

Granrud, C., Yonas, A., Smith, I., Arterberry, M., Gliksman, M., & Sorknes, A. (1984). Infants' sensitivity to accretion and deletion of texture and information for depth at an edge. *Child Development, 55,* 1630–1636.

Grant, V. (1994). Sex of infant differences in mother-infant interaction: A Reinterpretation of past findings. *Developmental Review, 14,* 1–26.

Grantham-McGregor, S. & Schofield, W., & Powell, C. (1987). Development of severely malnourished children who received psychosocial stimulation: Six-year follow-up. *Pediatrics, 79,* 247–254.

Grasselli, R. & Hegner, P. (1980). *Playful parenting.* New York: Putman.

Gravett, M. (1984). Causes of preterm delivery. *Seminars in Perinatology, 8,* 246–257.

Greco, C., Rovee-Collier, C., Hayne, H., Greisler, P., & Earley, L. (1986). Ontogeny of early event memory: I. Forgetting and retrieval by 2-and 3-month-olds. *Infant Behavior and Development, 9,* 441–461.

Greenfield, P. & Tronick, E. (1980). *Infant curriculum: The Bromley-Heath Guide to the care of infants in groups* (rev. ed.). Santa Monica, CA: Goodyear.

Greenough, W., Black, J., & Wallace, C. (1987). Experience and brain development. *Child Development, 58,* 539–559.

Greenspan, S. & Greenspan, N. (1985). *First feelings: Milestones in the emotional development of your baby and child.* New York: Viking.

Greenspan, S. & Meisels, S. (1996). Toward a new vision for the developmental assessment of infants and young children. In S. Meisels and E. Fenichel (Eds.), *New visions for the developmental assessment of infants and young children* (pp. 11–26). Washington, DC: Zero to Three.

Groome, L. Swiber, M., Bentz, L., Holland, S., & Atterbury, J. (1995). Maternal anxiety during pregnancy: Effect on fetal behavior at 38 to 40 weeks of gestation. *Developmental and Behavioral Pediatrics, 16,* 391–396.

Guerrero, V. & Rojas, O. (1975). Spontaneous abortion and aging of human ova and spermatozoa. *New England Journal of Medicine, 293,* 573–575.

Guillory, A., Self, P., & Paden, L. (1980, April). *Odor sensitivity in one month infants.* Paper presented at the International Conference on Infant Studies, New Haven, CT.

Gunnar, M. (1978). Changing a frightening toy into a pleasant toy by allowing the infant to control its actions. *Developmental Psychology, 14,* 157–162.

Gunnar, M. (1980). Control, warning signals and distress in infancy. *Developmental Psychology, 16,* 281–289.

Gunnar, M. (1994). Psychoendocrine studies of temperament and stress in early childhood: Expanding current models. In J. Bates & T. Wachs (Eds.). *Temperament: Individual differences at the interface of biology and behavior* (pp. 175–198). Washington, DC: American Psychological Association.

Gunnar, M., Brodersen, L., Krueger, K., & Rigatuso, R. (1996). Dampening of behavioral and adrenocortical reactivity during early infancy: Normative changes and individual differences. *Child Development, 67,* 877–889.

Guntheroth, W. (1995). *Crib death: The sudden infant death syndrome* (3rd. ed.). Armonk, NY: Futura.

Gurney, J. (1979). The young child: Protein-energy malnutrition. In D. Jelliffe & E. Jelliffe (Eds.), *Nutrition and growth* (pp. 185–216). New York: Plenum.

Guttmann, J. (1993). *Divorce in psychosocial perspective: Theory and research.* Hillsdale, NJ: Erlbaum.

Hagekull, B. (1994). Infant temperament and early childhood functioning: Possible relations to the five-factor model. In C. Halverson, G. Kohnstamm, & R. Martin (Eds.), *The developing structure of temperament and personality from infancy to adulthood* (pp. 227–240). Hillsdale, NJ: Erlbaum.

Hainline, L. & Lemerise, E. (1982). Infants' scanning of geometric forms varying in size. *Journal of Experimental Child Psychology, 33,* 235–256.

Haith, M. (1979). Visual competence in early infancy. In R. Held, H. Leibowitz, & H. Teuber (Eds.), *Handbook of sensory physiology: Vol. 8. Perception* (pp. 311–356). Berlin: Springer-Verlag.

Haith, M., Bergman, T. & Moore, M. (1977). Eye contact and face scanning in early infancy. *Science, 198,* 853–855.

Hall, C. & Lindzey, G. (1978). *Theories of personality* (3rd ed.). New York: Wiley.

Hall, D. (1985). The outlook for low birth weight babies. *The Practitioner, 229,* 779–783.

Hall, E. (1969). *The hidden dimension.* New York: Doubleday.

Hall, G. (1891). *Notes on the study of infants.* The Pedagogical Seminary, 1, 127–138.

Halliday, M. (1975). *Learning how to speak: Explorations in the development of language.* New York: Elsevier.

Halpern, R. (1993). Poverty and infant development. In C. Zeanah (Ed.). *Handbook of infant mental health* (pp. 73–86), New York: Guilford.

Halverson, H. (1931). An experimental study of the prehension in infants by means of systematic cinema records. *Genetic Psychology Monographs, 10,* 107–286.

Hamill, P., Johnston, F., & Lemeshaw, S. (1972). *Height and weight of children: Socio-economic status: United States.* Rockville, MD: U.S. Department of Health, Education and Welfare. Pub. No. HRA 73–1601.

Hamilton, M. (1984). *Basic maternity nursing* (5th ed.). St. Louis: Mosby.

Hanawalt, B. (1977). Childrearing among the lower classes of late medieval England. *Journal of Interdisciplinary History, 8,* 1–22.

Hanna, E. & Meltzhoff, A. (1993). Peer imitation by toddlers in laboratory, home, and day-care contexts: Implications for social learning and memory. *Developmental Psychology, 29,* 701–710.

Hanson, M. (1996a). Early interactions: The family context. In M. Hanson (Ed.), *Atypical infant development* (2nd ed., pp. 235–272). Austin, TX: Pro-Ed.

Hanson, M. (1996b). Early intervention: Models and practices. In M. Hanson (Ed.), *Atypical infant development* (2nd ed., pp. 451–476). Austin, TX: Pro-Ed.

Harkins, D. & Uzgiris, I. (1991). Hand use matching between mothers and infants during the first year. *Infant Behavior and Development, 14,* 289–298.

Harlow, H. & Zimmerman, R. (1959). Affectional responses in the infant monkey. *Science, 130,* 431–432.

Harms, T., Cryer, D. & Clifford, R. (1990). *The infant and toddler environmental rating scale.* New York: Teachers College.

Harrigan-Hamamoto, K. (1983). *Pain in infants.* Unpublished master's thesis, California State University, Long Beach.

Harris, P. (1989). *Children and emotion: The development of psychological understanding.* New York: Basil Blackwell.

Hart, B. & Risley, T. (1995). *Meaningful differences in the everyday experience of young American children.* Baltimore: Brookes.

Hartshorn, K. & Rovee-Collier, C. (1997). Infant learning and long-term memory at 6 months: A confirming analysis. *Developmental Psychobiology, 30,* 71–85.

Hartup, W. (1983). Peer relations. In P. Mussen (Ed.), *Handbook of child psychology: Vol. 4. Socialization, personality and development* (4th ed., pp. 103–196). New York: Wiley.

Harvey, E., Boife, J., Honeyman, M., & Flannery, J. (1985). Prenatal x-ray exposure and childhood cancer in twins. *New England Journal of Medicine, 312,* 541–545.

Hassid, P. (1984). *Textbook for childbirth educators* (2nd ed.). Philadelphia: Lippincott.

Hauth, J., Goldeberg, R., Andrews, W., DuBard, M., & Cooper, R. (1995). Reduced incidence of preterm delivery with metronidazole and erythromycin in women with bacterial vaginosis. *New England Journal of Medicine. 333,* 1732–1735.

Hawkins, J. & Higgins, L. (1981). *Maternal and gynecological nursing.* Philadelphia: Lippincott.

Hay, D. (1994). Prosocial development. *Journal of Child Psychology and Psychiatry, 35,* 29–71.

Hay, D., Caplan., M., Castle, J., & Stimson, C. (1991). Does sharing become increasingly rational in the second year of life? *Developmental Psychology, 27,* 987–993.

Hay, D., Castle., & Jewett, J. (1994). Character development. In M. Rutter & D. Hay (1994), *Development through the lifespan: A handbook for clinicians* (pp. 319–349). Oxford, England: Blackwell.

Hay, D., Castle, J., Stimson, C., & Davies, L. (1995). The social contruction of character in toddlerhood. In M. Killen & D. Hart (Eds.), *Morality in everyday life* (pp. 23–51). New York: Cambridge University.

Haywood, K. (1993). *Life span motor development* (2nd ed.). Champaign, IL: Human Kinetics.

Health Watch. (1997). *NBC Nightly News*, January 7.

Hecaen, H. & Ajuriagurra, J. (1964). *Left-handedness: Manual superiority and cerebral dominance*. New York: Grune & Stratton.

Hedrick, D., Prather, E., & Tobin, A. (1984). *Sequenced Inventory of Communicative Development-Revised*. Los Angeles: Western Psychological Services.

Heidelise, A., Tronick, E., Lester, B., & Brazelton, T. (1979). Specific neonatal measures: The Brazelton Neonatal Behavioral Assessment Scale. In J. Osofsky (Ed.), *Handbook of infant development* (pp. 185–215). New York: Wiley.

Heins, M. (1984). The battered child revisited. *Journal of the American Medical Association, 251*, 3295–3300.

Held, R. (1993). What can rates of development tell us about underlying mechanisms. In C. Granrud (Ed.), *Visual perception and cognition in infancy* (pp. 75–89). Hillsdale, NJ: Erlbaum.

Held, R. & Hein, A. (1963). A movement-produced stimulation in the development of visually guided behavior. *Journal of Comparative Physiological Psychology, 56*, 872–876.

Helms, D. & Turner, J. (1976). *Exploring child behavior: Basic principles*. Philadelphia: Saunders.

Henig, R. & Fletcher, A. (1983). *Your premature baby*. New York: Rawson Associates.

Hermes, P. (1981, February 10). WD Medical update: Crib death. *Woman's Day, 43*, 14, 16–17.

Hershenson, M. (1964). Visual discrimination in the human newborn. *Journal of Comparative and Physiological Psychology, 58*, 270–276.

Hershenson, M., Munsinger, H., & Kessen, W. (1965). Preferences for shapes of intermediate variability in the human newborn. *Science, 147*, 630–631.

Hetherington, E. (1979). Divorce: A child's perspective. *American Psychologist, 34*, 851–858.

Hetherington, E. & Parke, R. (1979). *Child psychology: A contemporary viewpoint* (2nd ed.). New York: McGraw-Hill.

Hetherington, E., Cox, M., & Cox, R. (1982). Effects of divorce on parents and children. In M. Lamb (Ed.), *Nontraditional families* (pp. 233–288). Hillsdale, NJ: Erlbaum.

Hill, L. & Breckle, R. (1983). Current uses of ultrasound in obstetrics. *Primary Care, 10*(2), 205–223.

Hill, L. & Kleinberg, F. (1984a). Effects of drugs and chemicals on the fetus and newborn (First of two parts). *Mayo Clinic Proceedings, 59*, 707–716.

Hill, L. & Kleinberg, F. (1984b). Effects of drugs and chemicals on the fetus and newborn (Second of two parts). *Mayo Clinic Proceedings, 59*, 755–765.

Hillier, S., Nugent, R., Eschenbach, D., Krohn, M., Gibbs, R., Martin, D., Cotch, M., Edelman, R., Pastorek, J., Rao, V., Mcnellis, D., Regan, J., Carey, J., & Klebanoff, M. (1995). Association between bacterial vaginosis and preterm delivery of a low-birthweight infant. *New England Journal of Medicine, 333*, 1737–1742.

Himmelberger, D., Brown, B., & Cohen, E. (1978). Cigarette smoking during pregnancy and the occurrence of spontaneous abortion and congenital abnormality. *Journal of Epidemiology, 108*, 470.

Hinton, S. & Kerwin, D. (1981). *Maternal, infant and child nutrition*. Chapel Hill, NC: Health Services Consortium.

Hirst, J., Teixeira, F., Zakar, T. & Olson, D. (1995). Prostaglandin endoperoxide-H synthase-1 and -2 messenger ribonucleic acid levels in human amnion with spontaneous labor onset. *Journal of Clinical Endocrinology and Metabolism, 80*, 517–523.

Hjelle, L. & Ziegler, D. (1976). *Personality theories: Basic assumptions and research applications*. New York: McGraw-Hill.

Hobbs, D. (1968). Transition to parenthood: A replication and extension. *Journal of Marriage and the Family, 30*, 413–417.

Hock, E. (1980). Working and nonworking mothers and their infants: A comparative study of maternal caregiving characteristics and infant social behavior. *Merrill-Palmer Quarterly, 26*, 79–101.

Hodapp, R. & Mueller, E. (1982). Early social development. In B. Wolman (Ed.), *Handbook of developmental psychology* (pp. 284–300). Englewood Cliffs, NJ: Prentice Hall.

Hoffman, L. (1974). Effects of maternal employment on the child: A review of the research. *Developmental Psychology, 10*, 204–228.

Hoffman, L. (1979). Maternal employment: 1979. *American Psychologist, 34*, 859–865.

Hoffman, L. (1989). Effects of maternal employment in the two-parent family. *American Psychologist, 44*, 283–292.

Hoffman, M. (1970). Moral development. In P. Mussen (Ed.), *Carmichael's handbook of child psychology* (Vol. 2, pp. 261–359). New York: Wiley.

Hoffman, M. (1981). Development of moral thought, feeling and behavior. In E. Hetherington & R. Parke (Eds.), *Contemporary readings in child psychology* (2nd ed., pp. 366–373). New York: McGraw-Hill.

Hogge, W. (1990). Teratology. In I. Merkatz & J. Thompson (Eds.), *New perspectives on prenatal care* (pp.117–121). New York: Elsevier.

Hogue, C. & Hargraves, M. (1995). Preterm birth in the African-American community. *Seminars in Perinatology, 19*(4), 255–262.

Holden, G. (1983). Avoiding conflict: Mothers as tacticians in the supermarket. *Child Development, 50*, 1020–1035.

Holmes, D., Reich, J., & Pasternak, J. (1984). *The development of infants born at risk*. Hillsdale, NJ: Erlbaum.

Holmes, S., Reef, S., Hadler, S., Williams, W., & Wharton. M. (1996). Recommendations of the Advisory Committee on Immunization Practices. *Morbidity and Mortality Weekly Report, 45*(RR-11), 1–23.

Homan, W. (1973). Mother's milk or other milk? In *Annual editions: Readings in human development '73–'74* (pp. 72–76). Guilford, CT: Dushkin.

Honig. A. (1993). Mental health for babies: What do theory and research teach us? *Young Children, 48*(3),69–76.

Honig, A. (1995). Choosing child care for young children. In M. Bornstein (Ed.), *Handbook of parenting* (Vol. 4, pp. 411–435). Mahwah, NJ: Erlbaum.

Hook, E. & Lindsjo, A. (1978). Down's syndrome in live births by single year maternal age interval in a Swedish study: Comparison with results from a New York study. *American Journal of Human Genetics, 30,* 19–27.

Hooker, D. (1952). *The prenatal origin of behavior.* Lawrence, KS: The University of Kansas Press.

Hopkins, B. & Westra, T. (1988). Maternal handling and motor development: An intracultural study. *Genetic, Social, and General Psychology Monographs, 114,* 377–420.

Hopper, H. & Naremore, R. (1978). *Children's speech: A practical introduction to communication development* (2nd ed.). New York: Harper & Row.

Horowitz, F. (1982). Methods of assessment for high-risk and handicapped infants. In C. Ramey & P. Trohanis (Eds.), *Finding and educating high-risk and handicapped infants* (pp. 101–118). Baltimore: University Park Press.

Hossain, Z. & Roopnarine, J. (1994). African-American fathers' involvement with infants: Relationship to their functional style, support, education, and income. *Infant Behavior and Development, 17,* 175–184.

Hottinger, W. (1977). Motor development: Conception to age five. In C. Corbin (Ed.), *A textbook of motor development* (pp. 1–28). Dubuque, IA: Brown.

Hoving, K., Spencer, T., Robb, K., & Schulte, D. (1978). Developmental changes in visual information processing. In P. Ornstein (Ed.), *Memory development in children* (pp. 21–67). Hillsdale, NJ: Erlbaum.

Howes, C. (1987). Peer interaction of young children. *Monographs of the Society of Research in Child Development, 53*(1, Serial No. 217).

Howes, C. & Olenick, M. (1986). Family and child care influences on toddler's compliance. *Child Development, 57,* 202–216.

Howes, C., Philips, D., & Whitebook, M. (1992). Thresholds of quality: Implications for the social development of children in center-based child care. *Child Development, 63,* 449–460.

Hronsky, S. & Emory, E. (1987). Neurobehavioral effects of caffeine on the neonate. *Infant Behavior and Development, 10,* 61–80.

Hubel, D. & Wiesel, T. (1970). The period of susceptibility to the physiological effects of unilateral eye closure in kittens. *Journal of Physiology, 206,* 419–436.

Hunziker, U. & Barr, R. (1986). Increased carrying reduces infant crying: A randomized control trial. *Pediatrics, 43,* 641–648.

Huston, A. (1983). Sex-typing. In P. Mussen (Ed.), *Handbook of child psychology: Vol. 4. Socialization, personality and development* (4th ed., pp. 387–367). New York: Wiley.

Huttenlocher, J., Haight, W., Bryk, A., Seltzer, M., & Lyons, T. (1991). Early vocabulary growth: Relation to language input and gender. *Developmental Psychology, 27,* 236–248.

Huttenlocher, P. (1994). Synaptogenesis in human cerebral cortex. In G. Dawson & K. Fischer (Eds.), *Human behavior and the developing brain* (pp. 137–152). New York: Guilford.

Illingworth, R. (1991). *Normal child: Some problems of the early years and their treatment* (10th ed.). London: Churchill Livingstone.

Irwin, O. C. (1948). Infant speech: Development of vowel sounds. *Journal of Speech and Hearing Disorders, 13,* 31–34.

Isabella, R. & Belsky, J. (1991). Interactional synchrony and the origins of infant-mother attachment: A replication study. *Child Development, 62,* 373–384.

Izard, C. (1977). *Human emotions.* New York: Plenum.

Izard, C. (1978). On the ontogenesis of emotions: Cognition relationships in infancy. In M. Lewis & L. Rosenblum (Eds.), *The development of affect* (pp. 389–413). New York: Plenum.

Izard, C. (1979). *The maximally discriminative facial movement coding system (Max).* Newark, DE: University of Delaware, Instructional Resources Center.

Izard, C. (1993). Organizational and motivational functions of discrete emotions. In M. Lewis & J. Haviland (Eds.), *Handbook of emotions* (pp. 631–641). New York:Guilford.

Izard, C. & Malatesta, C. (1987). Perspectives on emotional development: Differential emotions theory of early emotional development. In J. Osofsky (Ed.), *Handbook of infant development* (2nd ed, pp. 494–554). New York: Wiley.

Jacklin, C. & Maccoby, E. (1983). Issues of gender differentiation in normal development. In M. Levine, W. Carey, A. Crocker, & R. Gross (Eds.), *Developmental-behavioral pediatrics* (pp. 175–184). Philaelphia: Saunders.

Jacobson, J., Tianen, R., Wille, D., & Aytck, D. (1986). Infant-mother attachments and early peer relations: The assessment of behavior in an interactive context. In E. Mueller & C. Cooper (Eds.), *Process and outcome in peer relations* (pp. 57–78). New York: Academic Press.

Jakobsson, I. & Lindberg, T. (1978). Cow's milk as a cause of infantile colic in breast-fed infants. *Lancet, 2,* 237–239.

James, T. (1985). Editorial comment: Crib death. *Journal of the American College of Cardiology, 5,* 1185–1187.

James, W. (1890). *The principles of psychology.* New York: Henry Holt.

Jelliffe, D. & Jelliffe, E. (1977). Breast fed is best: Modern meanings. *New England Journal of Medicine, 297,* 912–915.

Jenista, J., Powell, K., and Menegus, M. (1984). Epidemiology of neonatal enterovirus infection. *Journal of Pediatrics, 104,* 685–694.

Jensen, A. (1969). How much can we boost IQ and scholastic achievement? *Harvard Educational Review, 39,* 1–123.

Jirasek, J. (1983). *Atlas of human prenatal morphogenesis.* Boston: Martinus Nijhoff.

Johnson, C. (1996). Nonorganic failure to thrive. In W. Nelson, R. Behrman, R. Kliegman, & A. Arving (Eds.), *Nelson's textbook of pediatrics* (15th ed., pp. 119–120). Philadelphia: Saunders.

Johnson, G., Purvis, G., & Wallace, R. (1981). What nutrients do our infants really get? *Nutrition Today, 16*(4), 4–10.

Johnson, J. & Ershler, J. (1982). Curricular effects on the play of preschoolers. In D. Pepler & K. Rubin (Eds.), *Contributions to human development: Vol. 5. The play of children: Current theory and research* (pp. 130–143). Basel, Switzerland: S. Karger.

Johnson, M., Dziurawiee, S., Ellis, H., & Morton, J. (1991). Newborns' preferential tracking of face-like stimuli and its subsequent decline. *Cognition, 40,* 1–19.

Jones, L. (1985). Father-infant relations in the first year of life. In M. Hanson & F. Bozett (Eds.), *Dimensions of fatherhood* (pp. 93–114). Beverly Hills, CA: Sage.

Juscyck, P. (1995). Language acquisition: Speech sounds and the beginning of phonology. In J. Miller & P. Eimas (Eds.). *Speech, language, and communication* (pp. 263–301). San Diego: Academic.

Kagan, J. (1979). Overview: Perspectives on human infancy. In J. Osofsky (Ed.), *Handbook of infant development* (pp. 1–25). New York: Wiley.

Kagan, J. (1981a). *The second year: The emergence of self awareness.* Cambridge, MA: Harvard University Press.

Kagan, J. (1981b). Universals in human development. In R. H. Munroe, R. L. Munroe, & B. Whiting (Eds.), *Handbook of cross-cultural human development* (pp. 53–62). New York: Garland.

Kagan, J. (1991). The theoretical utility of constructs of self. *Developmental Review, 11,* 244–250.

Kagan, J. (1994). *Galen's prophecy: Temperament and human nature.* New York: Basic Books.

Kagan, J. & Klein, R. (1973). Cross-cultural perspectives on early development. *American Psychologist, 28,* 947–961.

Kagan, J., Kearsley, R., & Zelazo, P. (1978). *Infancy: Its place in human development.* Cambridge, MA: Harvard University Press.

Kagan, J. & Lewis, M. (1965). Studies in the attention of the human infant. *Merrill-Palmer Quarterly, 11,* 95–127.

Kallings, L. (1993). HIV infection in the nineties. *Vaccine, 11,* 525–528.

Kaminer, R. & Jedrysek, E. (1983). Age of walking and mental retardation. *American Journal of Public Health, 73,* 1094–1096.

Kane, D. (1985). *Environmental hazards to young children.* Phoenix: Onyx Press.

Kaplan-Sanoff, M., Parker, S. & Zuckerman, B. (1991). Poverty and early childhood development: What do we know and what should we do? *Infants and Young Children, 4,* 68–76.

Karnes, M. (1982). *You and your small wonder: Book II.* Circle Pines, MN: American Guidance Service.

Kaufman, J. & Zigler, E. (1987). Do abused children become abusive parents? *American Journal of Orthopsychiatry, 57,* 186–192.

Kaufmann-Hayoz, R. (1991). Perceptual development. In M. Lamb & H. Keller, (Eds.), *Infant development: Perspectives from German-speaking countries* (pp. 219–243).

Kaye, K. (1980). Why we don't talk `baby talk' to babies. *Journal of Child Language, 7,* 489–507.

Keister, M. (1973). *Discipline: The secret heart of child care.* Greensboro, NC: The University of North Carolina at Greensboro.

Kellman, P. & Spelke, E. (1983). Perception of partly occluded objects in infancy. *Cognitive Psychology, 15,* 483–454.

Kellman, P. (1996). The origin of object perception. In R. Gelman & T. Au (Eds.), *Perceptual and cognitive development* (pp. 3–8). San Diego: Academic.

Kelly, D. & Shannon, D. (1982). Sudden infant death syndrome and near sudden infant death syndrome: A review of the literature, 1964–1982. *Pediatric Clinics of North America, 29,* 1241–1261.

Kempe, C. & Helfer, R. (1972). *Helping the battered child and his family.* Philadelphia: Lippincott.

Kendall, E. (1983). Child care and disease: What's the risk. *Young Children, 38*(5), 68–77.

Kendrick, A., Kaufman, R., & Messenger K. (Eds.). (1988). *Healthy young children: A manual for programs.* Washington, DC: National Association for the Education of Young Children.

Kent, R. (1980). Articulatory and acoustic perspectives on speech development. In A. Reilly (Ed.), *The communication game: Perspectives on the development of speech, language and nonverbal communication skills* (pp. 38–48). Skillman, NJ: Johnson & Johnson.

Kilkenny M. & Lumley, J. (1994). Ethnic differences in the incidence of the sudden infant death syndrome in Victoria, Australia 1985–1989. *Paediatric and Perinatal Epidemiology, 8,* 27–40.

King, J. & Ashworth, A. (1991). Contemporary feeding practices in infancy and early childhood in developing countries. In F. Falkner (Ed.), *Infant and child nutrition worldwide: Issues and perspectives.* Boca Raton: CRC.

King, W. & Seegmiller, B. (1973). Performance of 14-to 22-month-old black firstborn male infants on two tests of cognitive development. *Developmental Psychology, 8,* 317–326.

Kinsbourne, M. (1978). *Asymmetrical function of the brain.* London: Cambridge University.

Klaus, M. & Kennell, J. (1976). *Maternal-infant bonding.* St. Louis: Mosby.

Klaus, M. & Kennell, J. (1982). *Parent-infant bonding* (2nd ed.). St. Louis: Mosby.

Klein, J. (1992). Otitis media. In S. Krugman, S. Katz, A. Gershon, & C. Wilfert, (Eds.), *Infectious diseases of children* (9th ed.; pp. 285–293). St. Louis: Mosby.

Knight-Ridder News Service. (1991). 13-ounce baby holding his own in Florida hospital. *News and Observer.* May 24, p. 4.

Knittle, J. (1972). Obesity in childhood: A problem in adipose tissue cellular development. *Journal of Pediatrics, 81,* 1048–1059.

Knobloch, H., Stevens, F., & Malone, A. (1980). *Manual of developmental diagnosis.* New York: Harper & Row.

Kolb, B. (1989). Brain development, plasticity, and behavior. *American Psychologist, 44,* 1203–1212.

Kold, B. & Whishaw, I. (1990). *Fundamentals of human neuropsychology* (3rd. ed). New York: Freeman.

Kopp, C. (1992). Emotional distress and control in young children. *New Directions for Child Development, 55*(Spring), 41–56.

Kopp, C. & Brownell, C. (1991). The development of self: The first 3 years. *Developmental Review, 11,* 195–196.

Kopp, C. & Krakow, J. (1982). *The child: Development in a social context.* Reading, MA: Addison-Wesley.

Kopp, C. & Parmelee, A. (1979). Prenatal and perinatal influences on infant development. In J. Osofsky (Ed.), *Handbook of infant development* (pp. 29–75). New York: Wiley.

Korner, A. (1984). The many facets of touch. In C. Brown (Ed.), *The many facets of touch* (pp. 107–113). Skillman, NJ: Johnson & Johnson.

Krashen, S. (1973). Lateralization, language learning, and the critical period: Some new evidence. *Language Learning, 23*(1), 63–74.

Krugman, R. (1984). Child abuse and neglect. *Primary Care, 11,* 527–534.

Krugman, S, Katz, S., Gershon, A., & Wilfert, C. (1992). (Eds.), *Infectious diseases of children* (9th ed). St. Louis: Mosby.

Kubicek, L. (1996). Helping young children to become competent communicators: The role of relationships. *Zero to Three, 17*(1), pp. 25–30.

Kuhl, P. (1981). Auditory category formation and developmental speech perception. In R. Stark (Ed.), *Language behavior in infancy and early childhood* (pp. 165–183). New York: Elsevier.

Kuhl, P. & Meltzoff, A. (1982). The bimodal perception of speech in infancy. *Science, 218,* 1138–1141.

Kulka, A., Walter, R., & Fry, C. (1966). Mother-infant interaction as measured by simultaneous recording of physiological processes. *Journal of American Academy of Child Psychiatry, 5,* 496.

Kullander, S. & Kaellen, B. (1971). A prospective study of smoking and pregnancy. *Acta Obstetrics and Gynecology of Scandanavia, 50,* 83.

Ladd, G. & Le Sieur, K. (1995). Parents and peer relationships. In M. Bornstein (Ed.), *Handbook of parenting* (Vol. 4, pp. 377–409). Mahwah, NJ: Erlbaum.

Lagercrantz, H. & Slotkin, T. (1986). The stress of being born. *Scientific American, 254,* 100–108.

Lagerspetz, K., Nygard, M., & Strandwick, C. (1971). The effects of training in crawling on the motor and mental development of infants. *Scandinavian Journal of Psychology, 12,* 192–197.

Laishley, J. (1983). *Working with young children.* London: Edward Arnold.

Lally, J., Griffin, A., Fenichel, E., Segal, M., Szanton, E., Weissbourd, B. (1995). *Caring for infants and toddlers in groups.* Arlington, VA: Zero to Three/ NationalCenter.

Lamaze, F. (1970). *Painless childbirth: The Lamaze method.* Chicago: Henry Regency.

Lamb, M. (1976). *The role of the father in child development.* New York: Wiley.

Lamb, M. (1981a). Developing trust and perceived effectance in infancy. In L. Lipsitt (Ed.), *Advances in infancy research* (Vol. 1, pp. 101–127). Norwood, NJ: Ablex.

Lamb, M. (1981b). Fathers and child development: An integrative review. In M. Lamb (Ed.), *The role of the father in child development* (2nd ed., pp. 1–73). New York: Wiley.

Lamb, M. (1982a). Early context and maternal-infant bonding: One decade later. *Pediatrics, 70,* 763–768.

Lamb, M. (1982b). Maternal employment and child development: A review. In M. Lamb (Ed.), *Nontraditional families: Parenting and child development* (pp. 45–69). Hillsdale, NJ: Erlbaum.

Lamb, M. (1982c). Parent-infant interaction, attachment and socioemotional development in infancy. In R. Emde & R. Harmon (Eds.), *The development of attachment and affiliative systems* (pp. 195–214). New York: Plenum.

Lamb, M. (Ed.). (1987). *The father's role: Cross-cultural perspectives.* Hillsdale, NJ: Erlbaum.

Lamb, M. & Bornstein, M. (1987). *Development in*

infancy: An introduction (2nd ed.). New York: Random House.

Lamb, M. & Campos, J. (1982). *Development in infancy.* New York: Random House.

Lamb, M., Sternberg, K. & Prodromidis, M. (1992). Non-maternal care and the security of infant-mother attachment: A reanalysis of the data. *Infant Behavior and Development, 15,* 71–83.

Langer, W. (1975). Infanticide: A historical survey. In L. deMause (Ed.), *The new psychohistory* (pp. 55–67). New York: Psychohistory Press.

Langlois, J., Roggman, L., Casey, R., Ritter, J., Reiser-Dammer, L., & Jenkins, V. (1987). Infant preferences for attractive faces: Rudiments of a stereotype? *Developmental Psychology, 23,* 363–369.

Lazar, I. & Darlington, R. (1979). *Lasting effects after preschool: Summary report.* (DHEW Publication No. OHDS 79-30179). Washington, DC: U.S. Department of Health, Education and Welfare.

Lazar, I. & Darlington, R. (1982). Lasting effects of an early education. *Monographs of the Society for Research in Child Development, 47* (2–3, Serial No. 195).

Lazarus, R. & Monat, A. (1979). *Personality* (3rd ed.). Englewood Cliffs, NJ: Prentice Hall.

Leach, C., Greenspan, J., Rubenstein, S., Shaffer, T., Wolfson, M., Jackson, J., Delmos, R., Fuhrman, B., et al. (1996). Partial liquid ventilation with perflubron in premature infants with severe respiratory distress syndrome. *New England Journal of Medicine, 335,* 761–767.

Leach, P. (1976). *Babyhood.* New York: Knopf.

Leach, P. (1984). *The child care encyclopedia.* New York: Knopf.

Leavitt, L. (1980). The development of speech comprehension and speech production. In A. Reilly (Ed.), *The communication game: Perspectives on the development of speech, language and non-verbal communication skills* (pp. 21–30). Skillman, NJ: Johnson & Johnson.

Leavitt, R. & Eheart, B. (1985). *Toddler day care: A guide to responsive caregiving.* Lexington, MA: Heath.

Leboyer, F. (1975). *Birth without violence.* New York: Knopf.

Lechat, M., Borlee, I., Bouckaert, A., & Mission, C. (1980). Caffeine study (letter to the editor). *Science, 207,* 1296–1297.

Ledoux, J. (1993). Emotional networks in the brain. In M. Lewis & J. Haviland (Eds.), *Handbook of emotions* (pp. 109–118). New York: Guilford.

Lee-Parritz, A. & Heffner, L. (1995). Gestational diabetes. In F. Brown & J. Hare (Eds.), *Diabetes complicating pregnancy* (pp. 15–40). New York : Wiley.

Legerstee, M.(1991). The role of person and object in eliciting early imitation. *Journal of Experimental Child Psychology, 51,* 423–433.

Lehane, S. (1976). *Help your baby learn.* Englewood Cliffs, NJ: Prentice Hall.

Leibel, R. (1991). Obesity. In O. Brunser, F. Carrazza, M. Gracey, B. Nichols, & J. Senterre (Eds.), *Clinical nutrition of the young child* (pp.155–166). New York: Raven.

Lempers, J., Flavell, E., & Flavell, J. (1977). The development in very young children of tacit knowledge concerning visual perception. *Genetic Psychology Monographs, 95,* 3–53.

Lenneberg, E. (1967). *Biological foundations of language.* New York: Wiley.

Lenneberg, E., Rebelsky, G., & Nichols, I. (1965). The vocalizations of infants born to deaf and hearing parents. *Human Development, 8,* 23–27.

Lester, B. (1985). There's more to crying than meets the ear. In B. Lester & C. Boukydis (Eds.), *Infant crying: Theoretical and research perspectives* (pp. 1–27). New York: Plenum.

Lester, B., Boukydis, C., Garcia Coll, C., Hole, W., & Peucker, M. (1992). Infantile colic: Acoustic cry characteristics, maternal perception of cry, and temperament. *Infant Behavior and development, 15,* 15–26.

Lester, B. & Dreher, M. (1989). Effects of marijuana use during pregnancy on newborn cry. *Child Development, 60,* 765–771.

Leventhal, A. & Lipsitt, L. (1964). Adaptation, pitch discrimination, and sound localization in the neonate. *Child Development, 35,* 759–767.

Leventhal, J. (1996). Child maltreatment: Neglect to abuse. In A. Rudolph, J. Hoffman, & C. Rudolph (Eds.), *Rudolph's pediatrics* (20th ed., pp. 145–152). Stamford, CT: Appleton & Lange.

Leventhal, J., Edgerter, S., & Murphy, J. (1984). Reassessment of the relationship of perinatal factors and child abuse. *American Journal of Diseases of Children, 138,* 1034–1039.

Levin, G. (1983). *Child Psychology.* Monterey, CA: Brooks/Cole.

Levine, R. (1980). A cross-cultural perspective on parenting. In M. Fantini & R. Cardenas (Eds.), *Parenting in a multicultural society* (pp. 17–40). New York: Longman.

Levitt, M. (1991). Attachment and close relationships: A life-span perspective. In J. Gewirtz & W. Kurtines (Eds), *Intersections with attachment* (pp. 183–205). Hillsdale, NJ: Erlbaum.

Levy, J. (1973). *The baby exercise book.* New York: Random House.

Levy, M. & Koren, G. (1992). Clinical toxicology of the neonate. *Seminars in Perinatology, 16*(1), 63–75.

Lewis, C. (1979). *The infant nutrition trip.* Chapel Hill, NC: University of North Carolina School of Nursing, (Filmstrip).

Lewis, M. (1986). Origins of self-knowledge and individual differences in early self-recognition. In J. Suls & A. Greenwood (Eds.), *Psychological perspectives on the self* (Vol. 3, pp. 55–78). Hillsdale, NJ: Erlbaum.

Lewis, M. (1987). Social development in infancy and early childhood. In J. Osofsky (Ed.), *Handbook of infant development* (2nd ed., pp. 419–494). New York: Wiley.

Lewis, M. (1991). Ways of knowing: Objective self-awareness or consciousness. *Developmental Review, 11*, 231–244.

Lewis, M. (1993). The emergence of human emotions. In M. Lewis & J. Haviland (Eds.), *Handbook of Emotions* (pp. 223–246). New York: Guilford.

Lewis, M. & Brooks, J. (1974). Self, others and fear: Infants reactions to people. In M. Lewis & L. Rosenblum (Eds.), *The origins of fear* (pp. 195–227). New York: Wiley.

Lewis, M. & Brooks, J. (1978). Self-knowledge in emotional development. In M. Lewis & L. Rosenblum (Eds.), *The development of affect* (pp. 205–226). New York: Plenum.

Lewis, M. & Brooks-Gunn, J. (1979). *Social cognition and the acquisition of self.* New York: Plenum.

Lewis, M. & Freedle, R. (1973). Mother-infant dyad: The cradle of meaning. In P. Pliner, L. Krames, & T. Alloway (Eds.), *Communication and affect: Language and thought* (pp. 127–155). New York: Academic Press.

Lewis, M. & Michalson, L. (1983). *Children's emotions and moods: Developmental theory and measurement.* New York: Plenum.

Lewis, M. & Saarni, C. (1985). Culture and emotions. In M. Lewis & C. Saarni (Eds.), *The socialization of emotions* (pp. 1–17). New York: Plenum.

Lewis, M., Stanger, C., & Sullivan, M. (1989). Deception in 3-year-olds. *Developmental Psychology, 25*, 439–443.

Lickona, T. (1983). *Raising good children.* New York: Bantam.

Linder, T. (1993). *Transdisciplinary play-based assessment* (Rev. ed.). Baltimore: Brookes.

Lindfors, J. (1980). *Children's language and learning.* Englewood Cliffs, NJ: Prentice Hall.

Link, A., Kernested, D., & Ford-Jones, E. (1993). Young infants. In L. Donowitz (Ed.), *Infection control in the childcare center and preschool* (pp. 23–29). Baltimore: Williams & Wilkins.

Linn, P., Horowitz, F., & Fox, H. (1985). Stimulation in the NICU: Is more necessarily better? *Clinics in Perinatology, 12*, 407–422.

Linn, S., Schoenbaum, S., Monson, R., Rosner, B., Subblefield, P., & Ryan, K. (1982). No association between coffee consumption and adverse outcomes of pregnancy. *New England Journal of Medicine, 306*, 141–145.

Linn, S., Schoenbaum, S., Monson, R., Rosner, B., Stubblefield, P., & Ryan, K. (1983). The association of marijuana use with outcome of pregnancy. *American Journal of Public Health, 73*, 1161–1164.

Lipsitt, L. (1977). Taste in human neonates: Its effect on sucking and heart rate. In J. Weiffenbach (Ed.), *Taste and development: the genesis of sweet preference* (pp. 125–141). Bethesda: MD: National Institutes of Health. (DHEW Pub. No. NIH 77–1068).

Lipsitt, L., Engen, T., & Kaye, H. (1963). Developmental changes in the olfactory threshold of the neonate. *Child Development, 34*, 371–376.

Lipsitt, L. & Levy, N. (1959). Electrotactual threshold in the neonate. *Child Development, 30*, 547–554.

Litovsky, R. & Clifton, R. (1992). Use of sound-pressure level in auditory distance discrimination by 6-month-old infants. *Journal of the Acoustical Society of America, 92*, 794–802.

Little, A., Lipsitt, L., & Rovee-Collier, C. (1984). Classical conditioning and retention of the infant's eyelid response: Effects of age and interstimulus interval. *Journal of Experimental Child Psychology, 37*, 512–524.

Littman, H., Medendorp, S., & Goldfarb, J. (1994). The decision to breast-feed. *Clinical Pediatrics, 33*, 214–219.

Locke, J. (1961). *An essay concerning human understanding.* London: Dent. (Originally published in 1690).

Lorenz, K. (1965). *Evolution and modification of behavior.* Chicago: University of Chicago Press.

Lourenco, O. & Machado, A. (1996). In defense of Piaget's theory: A reply to 10 common criticisms. *Psychological Review, 103*, 143–164.

Lowrey, C. (1978). *Growth and development of children* (7th ed.). Chicago: Medical Yearbook.

Lowrey, C. (1986). *Growth and development of children* (8th ed.). Chicago: Medical Yearbook.

Lozoff, B., Wolff, A. & Davis, N. (1984). Cosleeping in urban families with young children in the United States. *Pediatrics, 74*, 171–182.

Lubchenco, L., Hansman, C., Dressler, M., & Boyd, E. (1963). Intrauterine growth as estimated from liveborn birth-weight data at 24 to 42 weeks of gestation. *Pediatrics, 32*, 793–796.

Lucas, A., Morley, R., Cole, T., Lister, G., Lesson-Payne, C. (1992). Breastmilk and subsequent intelligence quotient in children born preterm. *Lancet, 339*, 261–264.

Lumley, J. & Astbury, J. (1980). *Birth rites, birth rights.* Melbourne, Australia: Sphere Books.

Lunt, R. & Law, D. (1974). A review of the chronology of eruption of deciduous teeth. *Journal of the American Dental Association, 89*, 872–879.

Maccoby, E. (Ed.). (1966). *Development of sex differences.* Stanford, CA: Stanford University Press.

Maccoby, E. (1980). *Social development: Psychological growth and the parent-child relationship.* New York: Harcourt, Brace, Jovanovich.

Maccoby, E. (1990). Gender and relationships: A developmental acount. *American Psychologist, 45,* 513–520.

Maccoby, E. & Feldman, S. (1972). Mother-attachment and stranger-reaction patterns in the third year of life. *Monographs of the Society for Research in Child Development, 37*(1, Serial No. 146).

Maccoby, E. & Martin, J. (1983). Socialization in the context of the family. In P. Mussen (Ed.), *Handbook of child psychology: Vol. 4. Socialization, personality and social development* (4th ed., pp. 1–101). New York: Wiley.

MacFarlane, J. (1975). Olfaction in the development of social preferences in the human neonate. In *Parent-infant interaction: Ciba Foundation Symposium 33* (new series; pp. 103–117). Amsterdam: Elsevier.

Machado, J. & Meyer-Botnarescue, H. (1997). *Student teaching guide: Early childhood practicum guide* (3rd ed.). Albany, NY: Delmar.

Mackey, M. (1995). Women's evaluation of their childbirth performance. *Maternal-Child Nursing Journal, 23,* 57–72.

MacMahon, B., Lin, T., Lowe, C., Mirra, A., Roynihor, B., Salber, E., Trichopoulos, D., & Valaloras, V. (1970). Lactation and cancer of the breast: Summary of an international study. *Bulletin WHO, 42,* 185.

MacMillan, H., MacMillan, J. & Oxford, D. (1993). Periodic health examinations, 1993 update: 1. Primary prevention of child maltreatment. *Canadian Medical Association Journal, 148,* 151–163.

Mahler, M. (1968). *On human symbiosis and the vicissitudes of individuation.* New York: International Universities Press.

Mahler, M., Pine, F., & Bergman, A. (1975). *The psychological birth of the human infant.* New York: Basic Books.

Main, M. & George, C. (1985). Responses of abused and disadvantaged toddlers to distress in agemates: A study in a day care setting. *Developmental Psychology, 21,* 407–412.

Main, M. & Hesse, E. (1990). Parents' unresolved traumatic experiences are related to infant disorganized attachment status. In M. Greenberg, D. Cicchetti, & E. Cummings (Eds.), *Attachment in the preschool years: Theory, research and intervention* (pp. 161–220). Chicago: University of Chicago.

Main, M., Kaplan, N., & Cassidy, J. (1985). Security in infancy, childhood, and adulthood: A move to the level of representation. In. I. Bretherton & E. Waters (Eds.), Growing points of attachment theory and research (pp. 66–104). *Monographs of the Society of Research in Child Development, 50*(1–2, Serial No. 209).

Main, M., Tomasini, L., & Tolan, W. (1979). Differences among mothers of infants judged to differ in security. *Developmental Psychology, 15,* 72–73.

Malatesta, C. & Haviland, J. (1982). Learning display rules: The socialization of emotion expression in infancy. *Child Development, 53,* 991–1003.

Malatesta, C. & Haviland, J. (1985). Signals, symbols and socialization: The modification of emotional expression in human development. In M. Lewis & C. Saarni (Eds.), *The socialization of emotions* (pp. 89–116). New York: Plenum.

Malina, R. (1973a). Environmental factors in motor development. In C. Corbin (Ed.), *A textbook of motor development* (pp. 46–58). Dubuque, IA: Brown.

Malina, R. (1973b). Physical development factors in motor performance. In C. Corbin (Ed.), *A textbook of motor development* (pp. 36–46). Dubuque, IA: Brown.

Malina, R. & Bouchard, C. (1991). *Growth, maturation, and physical activity.* Champaign, IL: Human Kinetics.

Mandler, J. (1984). Representation and recall in infancy. In M. Moscovitch (Ed.), *Advances in the study of communication and affect: Vol. 9. Infant memory* (pp. 75–101). New York: Plenum.

Mandler, J. (1990). A new perspective on cognitive development in infancy. *American Scientist, 78,* 236–243.

Manion, J. (1977). A study of fathers and infant caretaking. *Birth and the Family Journal, 4,* 174–178.

Mans, L., Cicchetti, D., & Sroufe, L. (1978). Mirror reactions of Down's syndrome infants and toddlers: Cognitive underpinnings of self-recognition. *Child Development, 49,* 1247–1250.

Marks, M. (1985). *Pediatric infectious diseases for the practitioner.* New York: Springer-Verlag.

Martin, A. (1996). Now that's a lot of babies: Multiple births take off. *The News and Observer*, February 9, p. 6D. Raleigh, NC.

Martin, B. (1975). Parent-child relations. In F. Hetherington (Ed.), *Review of research in child development* (Vol. 4, pp. 463–540). Chicago: University of Chicago Press.

Martin, E. & Beal, V. (1978). *Robert's nutrition work with children* (4th ed.). Chicago: University of Chicago Press.

Martin, H. P. (1973). Nutrition: Its relation to physical, mental and emotional development. *American Journal of Clinical Nutrition, 26,* 766–775.

Martinez, G. & Dodd, D. (1983). 1981 milk feeding patterns in the United States during the first 12 months of life. *Pediatrics, 71,* 166–170.

Marzollo, J. (1977). *Super tot: Creative activities for children from one to three.* New York: Harper & Row.

Maslansky, E., Cowell, C., Carol, R., Berman, S., & Grossi, M. (1974). Survey of infant feeding practices. *American Journal of Public Health, 64,* 780–785.

Maslow, A. (1970). *Motivation and personality* (2nd ed.). New York: Harper & Row.

Matsungaga, E., Tonomura, A., Oishi, H., & Kikuchi, Y. (1978). Re-examination of paternal age effect in Down syndrome. *Human Genetics, 40,* 259–268.

Maurer, D. & Barrera, M. (1981). Infants perception of natural and distorted arrangements of a schematic face. *Child Development, 52,* 196–202.

Mawhinney, S. & Pagano, M. (1994). Distribution of the latency period for perinatally acquired AIDS. *Statistics in Medicine, 13,* 2031–2042.

May, J. (1988). Microbial contaminants and antimicrobial properties of human milk. *Microbiology Science, 5,* 42.

Mayer, J. (1965). Genetic factors in human obesity. *Annals of the New York Academy of Science, 131,* 412–421.

Mayhall, P. & Norgard, K. (1983). *Child abuse and neglect.* New York: Wiley.

Maziade, M., Boudreault, M., Cote, R. & Thivierge, J. (1986). Influence of gentle birth delivery procedures and other perinatal circumstances on infant temperament: Developmental and social implications. *The Journal of Pediatrics, 108,* 134–136.

McCall, R. (1974). Exploratory manipulation and play in the human infant. *Monographs of the Society of Research in Child Development, 39* (2, Serial No. 155).

McCall, R. & Melson, W. (1970). Complexity, contour, and area as determinants of attention in infants. *Developmental Psychology, 3,* 343–349.

McCandless, B. (1967). *Children: Behavior and development* (2nd ed.). New York: Holt, Rinehart, & Winston.

McCarthy, D. (1954). Language development in children. In L. Carmichael (Ed.), *Manual of child psychology* (pp. 492–630). New York: Wiley.

McCarthy, P. (1979). Controversies in pediatrics: What tests are indicated for the child under 2 with fever? *Pediatric Review, 1,* 51–56.

McClenaghan, B. & Gallahue, D. (1978). *Fundamental movement: A developmental and remedial approach.* Philadelphia: Saunders.

McCormick, C. & Maurer, D. (1988). Unimanual hand preferences in 6-month-olds: Consistency and relation to familial-handedness. *Infant Behavior and Development, 11,* 21–29.

McCormick, K. (1996). Assessing cognitive development. In M. McLean, D. Bailey, & M. Wolery (Eds.). *Assessing infants and children with special needs* (2nd ed., pp. 268–304). Columbus, OH: Merrill.

McDonald, K. (1980). Enhancing a child's positive self concept. In T. Yawkey (Ed.), *The self-concept of the young child* (pp. 51–61). Provo, UT: Brigham Young University Press.

McDonald, R. & Avery, D. (1983). *Dentistry for the child and adolescent* (4th ed.). St. Louis: Mosby.

McGraw, M. (1966). *The neuromuscular maturation of the human infant.* New York: Hafner.

McKenna, J. & Mosko, S. (1993). Evolution and infant sleep: An experimental study of infant-parent cosleeping and its implication for SIDS. *Acta Paediatrics, Supplement 389,* 31–36.

McKenna, J., Mosko, S., Richard, C., Drummond, S., Hunt, L., Cetel, M., & Arpaia, J. (1994). Experimental studies of infant-parent cosleeping: Mutual physiological and behavioral influences and their relevance to SIDS. *Early Human Development, 38,* 187–201.

Mckusick, V. (1981). The genetics of birth defects: A map of chromosomes in relation to diagnosis and management. In A. Bloom & L. James (Eds.), *Birth Defects: Original Article Series, 17* (1), 229–248.

McLaren, D. & Burman, D. (1982). *Textbook of paediatric nutrition* (2nd ed.). London: Churchill Livingstone.

McNeil, D. (1970). The development of language. In P. Mussen (Ed.), *Carmichael's manual of child psychology* (Vol. 1, pp. 1061–1161). New York: Wiley.

Meadow-Orlans, K. (1995). Parenting with a sensory or physical disability. In M. Bornstein (Ed.), *Handbook of parenting* (Vol. 4, pp. 57–84). Mahwah, NJ: Erlbaum.

Mehl, M. & Peterson, G. (1981). Home birth versus hospital birth: Comparisons of outcomes of matched populations. In P. Ahmed (Ed.), *Pregnancy, childbirth, and parenthood* (pp. 315–334). New York: Elsevier.

Meier, J. & Malone, P. (1979). *Facilitating children's development* (Vol. 1). Baltimore: University Park Press.

Meisels, S. (1996). Charting the continuum of assessment and intervention. In S. Meisels & E. Fenichel (Eds.), *New visions for the developmental assessment of infants and young children* (pp. 27–52). Washington, DC: Zero to Three.

Meltzoff, A. (1988a). Infant imitation and memory: Nine-months-olds in immediate and deferred tests. *Child Development, 59,* 217–225.

Meltzoff, A. (1988b). Infant imitation after a 1-week delay: Long-term memory for novel acts and multiple stimuli. *Developmental Psychology, 24,* 470–476.

Meltzoff, A. & Borton, R. (1979). Intermodal matching by human neonates. *Nature, 282,* 403–404.

Meltzoff, A., Kuhl, P., & Moore, M. (1991). Perception, respresentation, and the control of action in newborns and young infants: Toward a new synthesis. In M. Weiss & P. Zelazo (Eds.), *Newborn attention: Biological constraints and the influence of experience* (pp. 377–412). Norwood, NJ: Ablex.

Meltzoff, A. & Moore, M. (1977). Imitation of facial and normal gestures of human neonates. *Science, 198,* 75–78.

Meltzoff, A. & Moore, M. (1983). Newborns imitate adult facial gestures. *Child Development, 54,* 702–709.

Meltzoff, A. & Moore, M. (1989). Imitation in newborns: Exploring the range of gestures imitated and the underlying mechanisms. *Developmental Psychology, 25,* 954–962.

Meltzoff, A. & Moore, M. (1992). Early imitation within a functional framework: The importance of person identity, movement, and development. *Infant Behavior and Development, 15,* 479–505.

Meltzoff, A. & Moore, M. (1994). Imitation, memory, and representation of persons. *Infant Behavior and Development, 17,* 83–99.

Melzack, R. (1984). The myth of painless childbirth. *Pain, 19,* 321–337.

Melzack, R., Kinch, R., Dobkin, P., LeBrun, M., & Taenzer, P. (1984). Severity of labour pain: Influence of physical as well as psychologic variables. *Canadian Medical Association Journal, 130,* 579–584.

Mendelson, M. & Haith, M. (1976). The relation between audition and vision in the human newborn. *Monographs of the Society of Research in Child Development, 41* (Whole No. 167).

Menn, L. & Stoel-Gammon, C. (1993). Phonological development: Learning sound patterns. In J. Gleason (Ed.), *The development of langauge* (3rd. ed., pp. 65–113). New York: Macmillan.

Mennella, J. & Beauchamp, G. (1991). Maternal diet alters the sensory qualities of human milk and the nursling's behavior. *Pediatrics, 88,* 737–744.

Mennella, J. & Beauchamp, G. (1993). Early flavor experiences: When do they start? *Zero To Three. 14*(2), 1–7.

Menyuk, P. (1982). Language development. In C. Kopp & J. Krakow (Eds*.), The child: Development in a social context* (pp. 282–331). Reading, MA: Addison-Wesley.

Meryash, D. (1995). Genetics. In D. Coustan, R. Haning, & D. Singer (Eds.), *Human reproduction: Growth and development* (pp. 99–120). Boston: Little, Brown.

Metropolitan Life Insurance Co. (1985). The risky first year of life. *Statistical Bulletin, 66*(1), 2–8.

Meyer, M. (1982). Smoking and pregnancy. In J. Niebyl (Ed.), *Drug use in pregnancy* (pp. 133–153). Philadelphia: Lea & Febiger.

Michalson, L. & Lewis, M. (1985). What do children know about emotions and when do they know it? In M. Lewis & C. Saarni (Eds.), *The socialization of emotions* (pp. 117–139). New York: Plenum.

Miles, R., Rutherford, G., & Coonley, R. (1983). *Structural entrapment hazards to infants and children.* Washington, DC: U.S. Consumer Product Safety Commission.

Milgrom, J., Westley, D., & McCloud, P. (1995). Do infants of depressed mothers cry more that other infants? *Journal of Paediatrics and Child Health, 31,* 218–221.

Miller, H., Hassanein, K., & Hensleigh, P. (1976). Fetal and growth retardation in relation to maternal smoking and weight gain in pregnancy. *American Journal of Obstetrics Gynecology, 125,* 55–61.

Miller, J. & Eimas, P. (1983). Studies on the categorization of speech by infants. *Cognition, 13,* 135–165.

Miller, P. (1993). *Theories of developmental psychology* (3rd ed.). New York: Freeman.

Miller, S. (1987). *Developmental research methods.* Englewood Cliffs, NJ: Prentice Hall.

Milner, A. (1985). Apnoea monitors and sudden infant death. *Archives of Disease in Childhood, 60,* 76–80.

Mistretta, C. & Bradley, R. (1977). Taste in utero: Theoretical considerations. In J. Weiffenbach (Ed.), *Taste and development: The genesis of sweet preference* (pp. 51–64). Bethesda: MD: National Institutes of Health, (DHEW Pub. No. NIH 77-1068).

Miyake, K., Campos, J., Kagan, J, & Bradshaw, D. (1986). Issues in socioemotional development in Japan. In H. Azuma, I. Hakuta, & H. Stevenson (Eds.), *Kodomo: Child development and education in Japan* (pp. 239–261). San Francisco: Freeman.

Miyake, K., Chen, S., & Campos, J. (1985). Infant temperament, mothers mode of interaction, and attachment in Japan: An interim report. In I. Bretherton & E. Waters (Eds.), *Growing points of attachment theory and research* (pp. 276–297). Monographs of the Society for Research in Child Development, 50, (1–2, Serial No. 209).

Mizukami, K., Kobayashi, N., Ishii, T., Iwati, H. (1990). First selective attachment begins in early infancy: A study using telethermography. *Behavior and Development, 13,* 257–271.

Moffitt, A. (1971). Consonant cue perception by 20-24 week old infants. *Child Development, 42,* 717–731.

Monckeberg, F. (1991). Protein energy malnutrition: Marasmus. In O. Brunser, F. Carrazza, M. Gracey, B. Nichols, & J. Senterre. (Eds.), *Clinical nutrition of the young child* (pp.121–132). New York: Raven.

Montagu, A. (1964). *Life before birth.* New York: American Library.

Montagu, A. (1971). *Touching: The human significance of skin.* New York: Columbia University Press.

Moore, K. (1983). *Before we are born* (2nd ed.). Philadelphia: Saunders.

Moore, K. & Persaud, T. (1993). *The developing human: Clinically oriented embryology* (5th ed.). Philadelphia, Saunders.

Moore, M. (1978). *Realities in childbearing.* Philadelphia: Saunders.

Moreli, G., Oppenheim, D., Rogoff, B., & Goldsmith, D. (1992). Cultural variations in infants' sleeping arrangements: Questions of independence. *Developmental Psychology, 28,* 604–613.

Morelli, G., Rogoff, B., Oppenheim, D., & Goldsmith, D. (1992). Cultural variations in infants' sleeping arrangements: Questions of independence. *Developmental Psychology, 28,* 604–613.

Morelli, G. & Tronick, E. (1991). Efe multiple caretaking and attachment. In J. Gewirtz & W. Kurtines

(Eds.), *Intersections with attachment* (pp.41–51). Hillsdale, NJ: Erlbaum.

Morisset, C., Barnard, K., & Booth, C. (1995). Toddlers' language development: Sex differences within social risk. *Developmental Psychology, 31,* 851–865.

Morley, R., Cole, T., Powell, R., & Lucas, P. (1988). Mother's choice to provide breast milk and developmental outcome. *Archives of Disease in Childhood, 63,* 1382–1385.

Morse, P. (1972). The discrimination of speech and non-speech stimuli in early infancy. *Journal of Child Language, 6,* 199–204.

Morton, J. & Johnson, M. (1991). CONSPEC and CONLERN: A two-process theory of infant face recognition. *Psychological Review, 98,* 164–181.

Moss-Salentijn, L. & Hendricks-Klyvert, M. (1990). *Dental and oral tissues: An introduction* (3rd ed.). Philadelphia: Lea & Febiger.

Mrazek, P. (1993). Maltreatment and infant development. In C. Zeanah (Ed.), *Handbook of infant mental health* (pp.159–172). New York: Guilford.

Mueller, C. (1996). Multidisciplinary research of multimodal stimulation of premature infants: An integrative review of the literature. *Maternal-Child Nursing Journal, 24,* 18–31.

Mueller, E. & Vandell, D. (1979). Infant-infant interaction. In J. Osofsky (Ed.). *Handbook of infant development* (pp. 591–622). New York: Wiley.

Muir, D. (1985). The development of infants' auditory spatial sensitivity. In S. Trehub & B. Schneider (Eds.), *Auditory development in infancy* (pp. 51–84). New York: Plenum.

Muir, D. & Field, J. (1979). Newborn infants orient to sound. *Child Development, 50,* 431–436.

Murphy, K. & Smyth, C. (1962). Response of fetus to auditory stimulation. *Lancet, 1,* 972–973.

Murphy, L. (1983). Issues in the development of emotion in infancy. In R. Plutchik & H. Kellerman (Eds.), *Emotion: theory, research and experience: (Vol. 2). Emotions in early development* (pp. 1–34). New York: Academic Press.

Mussen, P., Conger, J., & Kagan, J. (1974). *Child development and personality* (4th ed.). New York: Harper & Row.

Naeye, R. (1979). Weight gain and the outcome of pregnancy. *American Journal of Obstetrics and Gynecology, 135,* 3–9.

Naeye, R. (1983). Maternal age, obstetric complications and the outcome of pregnancy. *Obstetrics and Gynecology, 61,* 210–216.

Nash, M. (1997, February 3). Fertile minds. *Time, 149,* 48–56.

Nathanson, L. (1994). *The portable pediatrican for parents.* New York: Harper/Collins.

National Association for the Education of Young Children (NAEYC). (1991). *Accreditation criteria and*

procedures of the National Academy of Early Childhood Programs* (Rev. ed.). Washington, DC: Author.

National Center for Health Statistics. (1976, June). NCHS Growth Charts, 1976. *Monthly Vital Statistics Report,* (Vol. 25, No. 3, Supplement, HRA 76-1120). Rockville, MD: U.S. Department of Health, Education and Welfare.

National Center for Health Statistics. (1984). Midwife and out-of-hospital deliveries: United States. *Vital and Health Statistics.* Series 21, No. 40 DHS Publication No. (PHS) 84–1918. Washington, DC: U.S. Government Printing Office.

National Center for Health Statistics (1994). *Vital and health Statistics: Cesarean delivery in the United States, 1990.* Hyattsville, MD: U.S. Department of Health and Human Services.

National Center for Health Statistics. (1995). *Healthy people 2000 review, 1994* (DHSS Hyattsville Publication No. PHS 95-1256-1). Hyattsville, MD: U.S. Government Printing Office.

National Research Council. (1989). *Recommended dietary allowances* (10th ed.). Washington, DC: National Academy Press.

National Safety Council. (1987). *Accident facts.* Chicago: Author.

National Safety Council. (1996). *Accident facts.* Chicago: Author.

Needham, R. (1996). Assessment of growth. In R. Behrman, R. Kleigman, & A. Arvin (Eds.), *Nelson's textbook of pediatrics* (15th ed., pp. 63–67). Philadelphia: Saunders.

Needleman, R. (1996). Fetal growth and development. In W. Nelson, R. Behrman, R. Kliegman, & A. Arving (Eds.), *Nelson's textbook of pediatrics* (15th ed., pp. 33–36). Philadelphia: Saunders.

Neisser, U. (1991). Two perceptually given aspects of the self and their development. *Developmental Review, 11,* 197–209.

Nelms, B. & Mullins, R. (1982). *Growth and development: A primary care approach.* Englewood Cliffs, NJ: Prentice Hall.

Nelson, K. (1973). Structure and strategy in learning to talk. *Monographs of the Society for Research in Child Development, 38* (Whole No. 149).

Nelson, K. (Ed.). (1989). *Narratives from the crib.* Cambridge, MA: Harvard.

Nelson, L. (1996). Disorders of the eye. In R. Behrman, R. Kleigman, & A. Arvin (Eds.), *Nelson's textbook of pediatrics* (15th ed., pp. 1746–1747). Philadelphia: Saunders.

Nelson, N., Enkin, M., Saigel, S., Bennet, K., Milner, R., & Sackett, D. (1980). A randomized clinical trial of the Leboyer approach to childbirth. *New England Journal of Medicine, 202,* 655–660.

Newberger, J. (1997). New brain development research: A wonderful opportunity to build public support for early childhood education. *Young Children, 52,*(4), 4–9.

Newborg, J., Stock, J., Wnek., L., Guiduabaldi., J., & Sviniski., J. (1988). *Battelle developmental inventory screening test.* Chicago: Riverside.

Newell, K. (1984). Physical constraints to motor development. In J. Thomas (Ed.), *Motor development during childhood and adolescence* (pp. 105–122). Minneapolis: Burgess.

Newport, E., Gleitman, H., & Gleitman, L. (1977). Mother I'd rather do it myself: Some effects and noneffects of maternal speech style. In C.E. Snow & C. Ferguson (Eds.), *Talking to children* (pp. 109–149). London: Cambridge University Press.

News and Observer, Raleigh, NC, *Burlington wife has miracle baby.* (1979, July 17, p. 6).

NICHD Early Child Care Research Network. (1996, April). *Infant child care and attachment security: Results of the NICHD study of early child care.* Symposium, International Conference on Infant Studies, Providence, RI.

NICHD Early Child Care Research Network (1997, April). *Mother-child interaction and cognitive outcomes associated with early child care: Results of the NICHD study.* Poster symposium, Society for Research in Child Development, Washington, DC.

Nicoll, A., Newell, M., Van Praag, V., Van de Perre, P., & Peckham, C. (1994). Infant feeding policy and practice in the presence of HIV-1 infection. *Current Science, 9,* 107–119.

Niebyl, J. (1982). *Drug use in pregnancy.* Philadelphia: Lea & Febiger.

Nilsson, L. & Hamberger, L. (1990). *A child is born.* New York: Delacorte.

Novak, J. & Broom, B. (1995). *Ingall's and Salerno's maternal and child health nursing* (8th ed.). St. Louis: Mosby.

Nowakowski, R. (1987) Basic concepts of CNS development. *Child Development, 58,* 568–595.

O'Brien, M. (1992). Gender identity and sex roles. In V. Van Hasselt & M. Hersen (Eds.), *Handbook of social development* (pp. 325–345). New York: Plenum.

O'Connor, B. (1993). The home birth movement in the United States. *The Journal of Medicine and Philosophy, 18,* 147–174.

Oates, R. (1996). *The spectrum of child abuse: Assessment, treatment, and prevention.* New York: Bruner/Mazel.

Obler, K. (1985). Language through the life-span. In J. Gleason (Ed.), *The development of language* (pp. 277–305). Columbus, OH: Merrill.

Odom, S. & Munson, L. (1996). Assessing social performance. In M. McLean, D. Bailey, & M. Wolery (Eds), *Assessing infants and preschoolers with special needs* (2nd ed., pp. 398–434). Columbus, OH: Merrill.

Oleske, J. (1994). The many needs of the HIV-infected child. *Hospital Practice, 29,* 81–87.

Oller, D. & Eilers, R. (1982). Similarity in Spanish and English learning babies. *Journal of Child Language, 9,* 565–577.

Oller, D., Willmar, L., Doyle, W., & Ross, C. (1976). Infant babbling and speech. *Journal of Child Language, 3,* 1–12.

Olney, R. & Scholnick, E. (1976). Adult judgements of age and linguistic differences in infant vocalizations. *Journal of Child Language, 3,* 145–156.

Olsen, J., Pereira, A., & Olsen, S. (1991). Does maternal smoking modify the effect of alcohol on fetal growth? *American Journal of Public Health, 81,* 69–73.

Olson, D. & DeFrain, J. (1994). *Marriage and the family: Diversity and strengths.* Mountain View, CA: Mayfield.

Olson, G. & Strauss, M. (1984). The development of infant memory. In M. Moscovitch (Ed.), *Advances in the study of communication and affect: Vol. 9. Infant memory* (pp. 29–48). New York: Plenum.

Olson, H. (1994). The effects of prenatal alcohol exposure on child development. *Infants and Young Children, 6,* 10–25.

Osofsky, J. & Connors, K. (1979). Mother-infant interaction: An integrative review. In J. Osofsky (Ed.), *Handbook of infant development* (pp. 519–548). New York: Wiley.

Osofsky, J. & Jackson, B. (1994). Parenting in violent environments. *Zero to Three, 14* (3), 8–12.

Otake, M. & Schull, W. (1984). In utero exposure to A-bomb radiation and mental retardation: A reassessment. *British Journal of Radiology, 57,* 409–414.

Overby, K. (1996). Pediatric health supervision. In A. Rudolph, J. Hoffman, & C. Rudolph (Eds.), *Rudolph's pediatrics* (20th ed., pp. 26–30). Stamford, CT: Appleton & Lange.

Oxorn, H. (1980). *Oxorn-Foote human labor and birth* (4th ed.). New York: Appleton-Century-Crofts.

Padilla, A. & Lindholm, K. (1976). Acquisition of bilingualism: A descriptive analysis of the linguistic structures of Spanish/English speaking children. In H. Keller (Ed.), *Bilingualism in the bicentennial and beyond* (pp. 97–142). New York: Bilingual Review Press.

Painter, G. (1971). *Teach your baby.* New York: Simon & Schuster.

Painti, D. (1982). Mid-cavity forceps delivery. *British Journal of Obstetrics and Gynecology, 89,* 495–500.

Palmer, F., Capute, A., & Shapiro, B. (1988). Mandated interventions and clinical trials: A time of proof. *Developmental and Behavioral Pediatrics, 9,* 79–81.

Panneton, R. & DeCasper, A. (1982, March). *Newborns are sensitive to temporal and behavioral contingencies.* Paper presented at the meeting of the International Conference on Infant Studies, Austin, TX.

Panskepp, J. (1993). Neurochemical control of moods

and emotions: Amino acids and neuropeptides. In M. Lewis & J. Haviland (Eds.), *Handbook of emotions* (pp. 87–107). New York: Guilford.

Pansky, B. (1982). *Review of medical embryology*. New York: Macmillan.

Papousek, M. & Papousek, H. (1991). Early verbalizations as precursors of language development. In M. Lamb & H. Keller (Eds.), *Infant development: Perspectives from German speaking countries* (pp. 299–328). Hillsdale, NJ: Erlbaum.

Papousek, M., Papousek, H. & Harris, B. (1987). The emergence of play in parent-infant interactions. In D. Gorlitz & J. Wohlwill (Eds.), *Curiosity, imagination, and play* (pp. 215–246). Hillsdale, NJ: Erlbaum.

Parfitt, R. (1977). *The birth primer*. Philadelphia: Running Press.

Parke, R. (1978). The father's role in infancy: A re-evaluation. *Birth and the Family Journal, 5*, 211–213.

Parke, R. (1989). Social development in infancy: A 25-year perspective. In H. Reese (Ed.), *Advances in child development and behavior* (Vol. 21, pp. 1–35). New York: Academic.

Parke, R. (1995). Fathers and families. In M. Bornstein (Ed.), *Handbook of parenting* (Vol. 3, pp. 27–63). Mahwah, NJ: Erlbaum.

Parke, R. (1996). *Fatherhood*. Cambridge, MA: Harvard University.

Parke, R. & O'Leary, S. (1976). Family interaction in the newborn period. In K. Riegal & J. Meacham (Eds.), *The developing individual in a changing world. Vol. 2: Social and environmental issues* (pp. 49–62). The Hague: Mouton.

Parke, R. & Sawin, D. (1977, March). *The family in early infancy: Social interactional and attitudinal analysis*. Paper presented at the Society for Research in Child Development, New Orleans.

Parke, R. & Tinsley, B. (1987). Family interaction in infancy. In J. Osofsky (Ed.), *Handbook of infant development* (2nd ed., pp. 579–641). New York: Wiley.

Parks, W. (1996). Human immunodeficiency virus. In W. Nelson, R. Behrman, R. Kliegman, & A. Arving (Eds.), *Nelson's textbook of pediatrics* (15th ed., pp. 916–919). Philadelphia: Saunders.

Parmelee, A., Wenner, W., & Schulz, H. (1964). Infant sleep patterns from birth to 16 weeks of age. *Journal of Pediatrics, 65*, 576–582.

Patterson, C. (1995). Lesbian and gay parenthood. In M. Bornstein (Ed.), *Handbook of parenting* (Vol. 3, pp. 255–274). Mahwah, NJ: Erlbaum.

Paul, R. & Miller, D. (1995). Cesarean birth: How to reduce the rate. *American Journal of Obestrics and Gynecology, 172*, 1903–1911.

Pedersen, F., Rubenstein, J., & Yarrow, L. (1979). Infant development in father-absent families. *The Journal of Genetic Psychology, 135*, 51–61.

Pederson, F., Anderson, B., & Cain, R. (1980). Parent-infant and husband-wife interactions observed at age five months. In F. Pederson (Ed.), *The father-infant relationship* (pp. 71–86). New York: Praeger.

Peeples, D. & Teller, D. (1975). Color vision in two month old human infants. *Science, 189*, 1102–1103.

Perkin, J. (1990). Maternal influences on the development of food allergies in the infant. *Topics in Clinical Nutrition, 5*, 6.

Perris, E. & Clifton, R. (1988). Reaching in the dark toward sound as a measure of auditory localization in infants. *Infant Behavior and Development, 11*, 473–491.

Peterson, C. (1974). *A child grows up*. New York: Alfred.

Peterson, G., Mehl, L., & Leiderman, P. (1979). The role of some birth-related variables in father attachment. *American Journal of Orthopsychiatry, 49*, 330–338.

Phillips, J. (1975). *The origins of intellect: Piaget's theory*. San Francisco: Freeman.

Piaget, J. (1929). *The child's conception of the world*. New York: Harcourt & Brace.

Piaget, J. (1951). *Play, dreams and imitation in childhood*. New York: Norton.

Piaget, J. (1952). *The origins of intelligence in children* (M. Cook, Translator). New York: International Universities Press.

Piaget, J. (1954). *The construction of reality in the child*. New York: Basic Books.

Piaget, J. (1962). *Play, dreams and imitation in childhood*. New York: Norton.

Piaget, J. (1971). *Biology and knowledge*. Chicago: University of Chicago Press.

Pickens, J. (1994). Perception of auditory-visual distance relations by 5-month-old infants. *Developmental Psychology, 30*, 537–544.

Pikler, E. (1968). Some contributions to the study of gross motor development of children. *Journal of Genetic Psychology, 113*, 27–39.

Piper, M. & Darrah, J. (1993). *Motor assessment in the developing infant*. Philadelphia: W. B. Saunders.

Pipes, P. (1982). Nutrition in infancy and childhood. *Primary Care, 9*, 497–516.

Pipes, P. & Trahms, C. (1993). *Nutrition in infancy and childhood* (5th ed.). St Louis: Mosby.

Pipp-Siegel, S. & Pressman, L. (1996). Developing a sense of self and others. *Zero to Three, 17*(1), 17–24)

Plomin, R. & DeFries, J. (1980). Genetics and intelligence: Recent data. *Intelligence, 4*, 15–24.

Plomin, R. & DeFries, J. (1985). *Origins of individual differences in infancy: The Colorado Adoption Project*. New York: Academic Press.

Plomin, R., Chipuer, H., & Loehlin, J. (1990). Behavior genetics and personality. In L. Pervin (Ed.), *Handbook of personality theory and research* (pp. 222–243). New York: Guilford.

Plomin, R., DeFries, J., & McClearn, G. (1990). *Behavioral genetics: A primer*. New York: Freeman.

Plomin, R. & Saudino, K. (1994). Quantitative genetics

and molecular genetics. In J. Bates & T. Wachs (Eds.), *Temperament: Individual differences at the interface of biology and behavior* (pp. 143–171). Washington, DC: American Psychological Association.

Pollock, L. (1983). *Forgotten children: Parent-child relations from 1500 to 1900*. Cambridge, London: Cambridge University Press.

Powell, D. (1978). Correlates of parent-teacher communication frequency and diversity. *Journal of Educational Research, 71*, 331–341.

Press, B. & Greenspan, S. (1985a). Ned and Dan: The development of a toddler friendship. *Children Today, 14*, 24–29.

Press, B. & Greenspan, S. (1985b). The toddler group: A setting for adaptive social-emotional development of disadvantaged one-and two-year-olds in a peer group. *Zero to Three, 5*(4), 6–11.

Preyer, W. (1888). *The mind of the child: Part 1. The senses and the will*. New York: Appleton-Century-Crofts.

Price, J. (1984). Allergy in infancy and childhood. In M. Lessof (Ed.), *Allergy: Immunological and clinical aspects* (pp. 127–173). New York: Wiley.

Pritchard, J., MacDonald, P., & Gant, N. (1985). *Williams obstetrics* (17th ed.). Norwalk, CT: Appleton-Century-Crofts.

Provence, S. (1967). *Guide for the care of infants in groups*. New York: Child Welfare League of America.

Prudden, B. (1964). *How to keep your child fit from birth to six*. New York: Harper & Row.

Prudden, S. & Sussman, J. (1972). *Suzy Prudden's creative fitness for baby and child*. New York: Morrow.

Public Health Service. (1986). Premature mortality due to sudden infant death syndrome. *Mortality and Morbidity Weekly Report, 35*, 169–170.

Public Health Service. U.S. Department of Health and Human Services. (1980). *Immunizations against disease: 1980*. Atlanta, GA: Author.

Pulaski, M. (1978). *Your baby's mind and how it grows*. New York: Harper & Row.

Quigley, M., Sheehan, K., Wilkes, M., & Yen, S. (1979). Effects of maternal smoking on circulating catecholamine levels and fetal heart rates. *American Journal of Obstetrics and Gynecology, 133*, 685–690.

Ranly, D. (1980). *A synopsis of craniofacial growth*. New York: Appleton-Century-Crofts.

Rappoport, D. (1976). Pour une naissance sans violence: Resultats d'une premiere enquete. (For a birth without violence: Results of a first inquiry.) *Bulletin Psychologie, 29*, 552–560.

Rebelsky, F. & Hanks, C. (1971). Fathers' verbal interactions with infants in the first three months of life. *Child Development, 42*, 63–69.

Redshaw, M., Rivers, R., & Rosenblatt, B. (1985). *Born too early: Special care for your preterm infant*. Oxford, NY: Oxford University Press.

Reimish, J. (1981). Prenatal exposure to synthetic progestins increases potential for aggression in humans. *Science, 211*, 1171–1173.

Reinisch, E. & Minear, R. (1978). *Health of the preschool child*. New York: Wiley.

Reissland, N. (1988). Neonatal imitation in the first hour of life: Observations in rural Napal. *Developmental Psychology, 24*, 464–469.

Remington, J. & Klein, J. (Eds.). (1983). *Infections of the fetus and newborn infant* (2nd ed.). Philadelphia: Saunders.

Ridenour, M. (1978). Programs to optimize infant motor development. In M. Ridenour (Ed.), *Motor development: Issues and implications* (pp. 39–61). Princeton, NJ: Princeton Book Co.

Rimell, F., Thome, A., Stool, S., Reilly, J., Rider, G., Wilson, C. (1995). Characteristics of objects that cause choking in children. *JAMA, 274*, 1763–1766.

Ritvo, E. & Freeman, B. (1977). National Society for Autistic Children. Definition of the syndrome of autism. *Journal of Pediatric Psychology, 4*, 146–148.

Ritvo, E. & Freeman, B. (1984). A medical model of autism: Etiology, pathology and treatment. *Pediatric Annals, 13* (4), 298–305.

Rivara, F. & Brownstein, D. (1996). In W. Nelson, R. Behrman, R. Kliegman, & A. Arving (Eds.), *Nelson's textbook of pediatrics* (15th ed., pp. 226–232). Philadelphia: Saunders.

Roberts, T. (1994). *A systems perspective on parenting*. Pacific Grove, CA: Brooks/Cole.

Robinson, J. & Glaves, L. (1996). Supporting emotion regulation and emotional availability through home visitation. *Zero to Three, 17*(1), pp. 31–35.

Rogan, W. & Gladen, B. (1993). Breast-feeding and cognitive development. *Early Human Development, 31*, 181–193.

Rogers, C. (1961). *On becoming a person*. Boston: Houghton Mifflin.

Rogoff, B. (1990). *Apprenticeship in thinking: Cognitive development in social context*. New York: Oxford University Press.

Rogoff, B., Mistry, J., Goncu, A., & Mosier, C. (1993). Guided participation in cultural activity by toddlers and caregivers. *Monographs of the Society for Research in Child Development, 58*(8, Serial No. 236).

Rogoff, B. & Morelli, G. (1989). Perspectives on children's development from cultural psychology. *American Psychologist, 44*, 343–348.

Roopnarine, J. & Field, T. (1983). Peer-directed behaviors of infants and toddlers during nursery school play. *Infant Behavior and Development, 6*, 133–138.

Roquer, J., Figueras, J., & Jimenez, R. (1995). Influence on fetal growth of exposure to tobacco smoke during pregnancy. *Acta Paediatrics, 84*, 118–121.

Rose, N. & Mennuti, M. (1995). Periconceptual folic

acid supplementation as a social intervention. *Seminars in Perinatology, 19*, 243–254.

Rose, S. (1984). Preterm responses to passive, active, and social touch. In C. Brown (Ed.), *The many facets of touch* (pp. 91–106). Skillman, NJ: Johnson & Johnson.

Rose, S. (1994). From hand to eye: Findings and issues in infant cross-modal transfer. In D. Lewkowicz & R. Lickliter (Eds.), *The development of intersensory perception: Comparative perspectives* (pp. 265–284). Hillsdale, NJ: Erlbaum.

Rose, S. & Ruff, H. (1987). Cross modal abilities in human infants. In J. Osofsky (Ed.), *Handbook of infant development* (2nd ed., pp. 318–362). New York: Wiley.

Rosen, K. & Rothbaum, F. (1993). Quality of parental caregiving and security of attachment. *Developmental Psychology, 29*, 358–357.

Rosenblith, J. & Sims-Knight, J. (1985). *In the beginning: Development in the first two years of life.* Monterey, CA: Brooks/Cole.

Rosenzweig, M., Bennett, E., & Diamond, M. (1972). Brain changes in response to experience. *Scientific American, 226*, 22–29.

Ross Mothers Survey. (1996). *Updated breast-feeding trend: 1987–1995* (Rev). Columbus, OH: Ross Laboratories.

Ross, H. (1974). Forms of exploratory behavior in young children. In B. Foss (Ed.), *New perspectives in child development* (pp. 138–163). Harmondsworth, England: Penguin.

Ross, H. & Lollis, S. (1987). Communication with infant social games. *Developmental Psychology, 23*, 241–248.

Rothbart, M. (1973). Laughter in young children. *Psychological Bulletin, 80*, 247–256.

Rothbart, M. (1981). Measurement of temperament in infancy. *Child Development, 52*, 569–578.

Rothbart, M. (1982). The concept of difficult temperament. *Merrill-Palmer Quarterly, 28*, 35–39.

Rothbart, M. & Derryberry, D. (1981). Development of individual differences in temperament. In M. Lamb & A. Brown (Eds.), *Advances in developmental psychology* (Vol. 1, pp. 37–86). Hillsdale, N J: Erlbaum.

Rothman, K., Moore, P., Singer, M., Nguyen, U, Mannino, S., & Milunsky, A. (1995). Teratogenicity of high Vitamin A intake. *New England Journal of Medicine, 333*, 1372–1373.

Rovee-Collier, C. & Shyi, C. (1992). A functional and cognitive analysis of infant long-term retention. In C. Howe, C. Brainerd, & V. Reyna (Eds.), *Development of long-term retention* (pp. 3–55). New York: Springer-Verlag.

Rowland, C. & Hargroves, M. (1995). Preterm birth in the African-American community. *Seminars in Perinatology, 19*, 255–262.

Rugh, R. and Shettles, L. (1971). *From Conception to Birth.* New York: Harper & Row.

Ruopp, R., Travers, J., Glantz, F. & Coelen, C. (1979). *Children at the center: Final report of the national day care study* (Vol. 1). Cambridge, MA: ABT Associates.

Russell, C. (1974). Transition to parenthood: Problems and gratifications. *Journal of Marriage and the Family, 36*, 294–301.

Russell, M. (1976). Human olfactory communication. *Nature, 260*, 520–522.

Rust, O. & Morrison, J. (1993). Surveillance for onset of preterm labor and prophylactic therapy. In F. Witter & L. Keith (Eds.), *Textbook of prematurity* (pp. 47–64), Boston: Little, Brown.

Rutherford, G. & Kelly, S. (1981). *Accidental strangulations (ligature) of children less than 5 years of age.* Washington, DC: U.S. Consumer Product Safety Commission.

Rutkowska, J. (1993). *The computational infant.* New York: Harvester/Wheatsheaf.

Rutter, M. (1985). Family and school influences on cognitive development. *Journal of Child Psychology and Psychiatry, 26*, 683–704.

Rutter, M. (1987). Continuities and discontinuities from infancy. In J. Osofsky (Ed.), *Handbook of infant development* (2nd ed., pp. 1256–1296). New York: Wiley.

Rutter, M. & Garmezy, N. (1983). Developmental psychopathology. In P. Musen (Ed.), *Handbook of child psychology: Vol. 4. Socialization, personality and social development* (4th ed., pp. 775–911). New York: Wiley.

Sachs, J. (1993). The emergence of intentional communication. In J. Gleason (Ed.), *The development of language* (3rd. ed., pp. 39–64). New York: Macmillan.

Sachs, J. & Devlin, J. (1976). Young children's use of age appropriate speech styles in social interaction and role playing. *Journal of Child Language, 3*, 81–98.

Sadler, T. (1990). *Langman's medical embryology* (6th ed.). Baltimore: Williams & Wilkins.

Sagi, A. (1981). Mothers' and non-mothers' identification of infant cries. *Infant Behavior and Development, 4*, 37–40.

Sagor, S., Feinbloom, R., Spindel, P., & Brodsky, A. (1983). *Home birth: A practitioner's guide to birth outside the hospital.* Rockville, MD: Aspen.

Salisbury, G. & Hart, R. (1970). Gamete aging and its consequences. *Biology of Reproduction, 2* (Supplement), 1.

Sameroff, A. (1968). The components of sucking in the human newborn. *Journal of Experimental Psychology, 6*, 607–623.

Sameroff, A. (1993). Models of development and developmental risk. In C. Zeanah (Ed.), *Handbook of infant mental health* (pp. 3–13). New York: Guilford.

Sameroff, A. & Cavanagh, P. (1979). Learning in infancy: A developmental perspective. In J Osofsky (Ed.) *Handbook of infant development* (pp. 344–392). New York: Wiley.

Sammons, W. & Lewis, J. (1985). *Premature babies: A different beginning.* St. Louis: Mosby.

Sanson, A., Oberklaid, F., Pedlow., R., & Prior, M. (1991). Risk indicators: Assessment of infancy predictors of preschool behavioral maladjustment. *Journal of Child Psychology and Psychiatry, 32,* 609–626.

Santos, J. I., Arrendo, J. L., & Vitale, J. J. (1983). Nutrition, infection and immunity. *Pediatric Annals, 12*(3), 182–194.

Santrock, J. (1970). Influence of onset and type of parental absence on the first Ericksonian crisis. *Developmental Psychology, 3,* 272–274.

Santrock, J. (1972). Relation of type and onset of father absence to cognitive development. *Child Development, 42,* 1721–1734.

Satter, E. (1983). *Child of mine: Feeding with love and good sense.* Palo Alto, CA: Bull.

Satter, E. (1990). The feeding relationship: Problems and interventions. *Journal of Pediatrics, 117,* S181–189.

Saudino, K. & Eaton, W. (1991). Infant temperament and genetics: An objective twin study of motor activity level. *Child Development, 62,* 1167–1174.

Scarr, S., Eisenberg, M., & Deater-Deckerd, K. (1994). Measurement of quality in child care centers. *Early Childhood Research Quarterly, 9,* 131–151.

Scarr, S. & McCartney, K. (1983). How people make their own environments: A theory of genotype AE environment effects. *Child Development, 54,* 424–435.

Scarr, S. & Salapatek, P. (1970). Patterns of fear development during infancy. *Merrill-Palmer Quarterly, 16,* 53–90.

Scarr, S. & Weinberg, R. (1978, April). Attitudes, interests and IQ. *Human Nature, 1,* 29–36.

Scarr-Salapatek, S. (1983). An evolutionary perspective on infant intelligence: Species patterns and individual variation. In M. Lewis (Ed.), *Origins of intelligence* (2nd ed., pp. 191–223). New York: Plenum.

Schaffer, H. (1979). Acquiring the concept of dialogue. In M. Bornstein & W. Kessen (Eds.), *Psychological development from infancy* (pp. 279–306). Hillsdale, NJ: Erlbaum.

Schanler, R. & Hurst, N. (1994). Human milk for the hospitalized preterm infant. *Seminars in Perinatology, 18,* 476–484.

Scherz, R. (1981). Fatal motor vehicle accidents of child passengers from birth to four years of age in Washington state. *Pediatrics, 68,* 572–575.

Schiff, W., Benasich, A., & Bornstein, M. (1989). Infant sensitivity to audiovisually coherent events. *Psychological Research, 51,* 102–106.

Schiller, J. (1980). *Child care alternatives and emotional well being.* New York: Pregena.

Schmitt, B. & Berman, S. (1984). Ear, nose and throat. In H. Kempe, H. Silver, and D. O'Brien (Eds.), *Current Pediatric Diagnosis and Treatment* (8th ed., pp. 297–328). Los Altos, CA: Lange.

Schmitt, B. & Krugman, R. (1992). Abuse and neglect of children. In R. Behrman (Ed.), *Nelson's textbook of pediatrics* (14th ed., pp. 78–83). Philadelphia: Saunders.

Schmitt, B. & Roxann, H. (1994). Ambulatory pediatrics. In W. Hay., J. Groothuis, A. Hayward, & M. Levin. *Current pediatric diagnosis & treatment* (12th ed., pp. 283–315). Norwalk, CT: Appleton & Lange.

Schneck, M. (1986, April). And baby makes three. *Human Development Research at Penn State, 3,* 10–12.

Schneider-Rosen, K. & Wenz-Goss, M. (1990). Patterns of compliance from eighteen to thirty months of age. *Child Development, 61,* 104–112.

Schoendorf, K., Hogue, C., Kleinman, J., & Rowley, D. (1992). Mortality among infants of black as compared with white college-educated parents. *The New England Journal of Medicine, 326,* 1522–1526.

Schweinhart, L. Barnes, H., & Weikart, D. (1993). *Significant benefits: The High/Scope Perry preschool study through age 27. Monographs of the High/Scope Educational Research Foundation Number 10.* Ypsilanti, MI: High/Scope.

Scott, E., Jan, J., & Freeman, R. (1977). *Can't your child see?* Baltimore: University Park Press.

Scrutton, D. (1969). Footprint sequences of normal children under five years old. *Developmental Medicine and Child Neurology, 115,* 44–51.

Seefeldt, C. (1987). Praise—good or bad? *Dimensions, 15* (4), 18–20.

Senter, S. (1983). *Infant communication: Learning to understand your baby.* Irvine, CA: National Pediatric Support Services.

Shelov, S. (1994). *The American Academy of Pediatrics: Caring for your baby and young child.* New York: Bantam.

Shepherd, T. (1991). *Catalog of teratogenic agents* (7th ed.). Baltimore: Johns Hopkins.

Shepherd-Look, D. (1982). Sex differentiation and the development of sex roles. In B. Wolman (Ed.), *Handbook of developmental psychology* (pp. 403–433). Englewood Cliffs, N J: Prentice Hall.

Sherrod, K., Vietze, P., & Friedman, C. (1978). *Infancy.* Monterey, CA: Brooks/Cole.

Shields, M. & Sparling, J. (1993). Fathers' play and touch behaviors with their three-month-old infants. *Physical & Occupational Therapy in Pediatrics, 13,* 39–59.

Shirley, M. (1931). *The first two years: A study of twenty-five babies: Vol. 1. Postural and locomotor development.* Minneapolis: University of Minnesota Press.

Shoemaker, W. & Tower, W. (1970). Out of the oven and into the winner's circle. *Sports Illustrated, 32,* 20–25.

Siegler, R. (1991). *Children's thinking* (2nd ed.). Englewood Cliffs, NJ: Prentice-Hall.

Siegler, R. (1993). Commentary: Cheers and lamentations. In C. Granrud (Ed.), *Visual perception and cognition in infancy* (pp.333–344). Hillsdale, NJ: Erlbaum.

Silberg, J. (1993). *Games to play with babies* (Rev ed.). Beltsville, MD: Gryphon.

Silva, P., Buckfield, P., and Spears, G. (1978). Some maternal and child development characteristic associated with breast-feeding. *Australian Pediatrics. 14*, 265–268.

Silver, H. (1984). Growth and development. In C. Kempe, H. Silver, & D. O'Brien (Eds.). *Current pediatric diagnosis and treatment.* (8th ed., pp. 9–25). Los Altos, CA: Lange.

Sinclair, D. (1978). *Human growth after birth* (3rd ed.). New York: Oxford University Press.

Sinclair, H. (1994). Early cognitive development and the contribution of peer integration: A Piagetian view. In S. Friedman & H. Haywood (Eds.), *Developmental follow-up* (pp. 129–138). San Diego: Academic.

Singer, D. (1995). Human embryogenesis. In D. Coustan, R. Haning, & D. Singer (Eds.), *Human reproduction: Growth and development* (pp.27–98). Boston: Little, Brown.

Singh, G. & Stella, M. (1995). Infant mortality in the United States: Trends, differentials, and projections, 1950 through 2010. *American Journal of Public Health, 85,* 957–964.

Singh, G. & Yu, S. (1995). Infant mortality in the United States: Trends, differences, and projections, 1950 through 2010. *American Journal of Public Health, 85,* 957–964.

Siqueland, E. (1968). Reinforcement and extinction in human newborns, *Journal of Experimental Child Psychology, 6,* 431–442.

Skinner, B. (1957). *Verbal behavior.* New York: Appleton-Century-Crofts.

Skinner, B. (1961). *Cumulative record.* New York: Appleton-Century.

Skinner, B. (1972). *The shaping of a behaviorist.* New York: Knopf.

Slater, W. (1983, April 20). A short and tragic life for Michael M. *Greenville Daily Reflector*, p. 26.

Sleigh, G. & Ounsted, M. (1975). Present-day practice in infant feeding. *Lancet, 1,* 7909.

Slocum, D. & James, S. (1968). Biomechanics of running. *Journal of the American Medical Association, 97,* 205.

Smedler, A., Faxelius, G., Bremme, K., & Lagerstrom, M. (1992). Psychological development in children born with very low birth weight after severe intrauterine growth retardation: A 10-year follow-up study. *Acta Paediatrics, 81,* 197–203.

Smelser, N. & Smelser, W. (1963). *Personality and social systems.* New York: Wiley.

Smith, L. (1996, July 26). 'Attachment disorder' hot diagnosis of troubled kids. *The News and Observer,* Raleigh, NC, p. 4D.

Smith, M. & Lifshitz, F. (1994). Excess fruit juice consumption as a contributing factor in nonorganic failure to thrive. *Pediatrics, 93,* 438–443.

Smith, M. (1926). An investigation of the development of vocabulary in young children. *University of Iowa Studies in Child Welfare, 3,* No. 5.

Smith, N. (1973). *The acquisition of phonology: A case study.* Cambridge, England: Cambridge University Press.

Smith, P. (1989). Assessing motor skills. In D. Bailey & M. Wolery (Eds.), *Assessing infants and preschoolers with handicaps* (pp.301–338). Colmbus, OH: Merrill.

Smoll, F. (1982). Developmental kinesiology. In J. Kelso & J. Clark (Eds.), *The development of movement control and co-ordination.* New York: Wiley.

Snow, C. E. (1977). The development of conversation between mothers and babies. *Journal of Child Language, 4,* 1–22.

Snow, C. W. (1983, November). *As the twig is bent: A review of research on the consequences of day care with implications for caregiving.* Paper presented at the annual meeting of the National Association for the Education of Young Children, Atlanta, GA. (Eric Document Reproduction Service No. Ed 238–590).

Snow, C.W., Teleki, J., Cline, D., & Dunn, K. (1992). Is day care safe? A review of research on accidental injuries. *Day Care and Early Education, 19*(3), 28–31.

Snow, C.W., Teleki, J., & Reguero de-Atiles, J. (1996). Child care licensing standards in the United States: 1981 to 1995. *Young Children, 51(6),* 36–41.

Snyder, L., Bates, E., & Bretherton, I. (1981). Content and context in early lexical development. *Journal of Child Language, 8,* 565–582.

Soken, N. & Pick, A. (1992). Intermodal perception of happy and angry expressive behaviors by seven-month-old infants. *Child Development, 63,* 787–795.

Solomons, G. (1984). Child abuse and neglect. In J. Blackman (Ed.), *Medical aspects of developmental disabilities* (pp. 39–41). Rockville, MD: Aspen.

Soutullo, D., Hernandez, M. & Bahrick, L. (1992, May). *Infants bimodal perception of adult and child faces and voices.* Presented at the International Conference on Infant Studies, Miami Beach, FL.

Sparling, J. & Lewis, I. (1979). *Learning games for the first three years.* New York: Berkley Books.

Sparrow, S., Balla, D., & Cicchetti, D. (1984). *Interview edition, expanded form manual, Vineland adaptive behavior scales.* Circle Pines, MN: American Guidance Service.

Speer, F. (1973). Management of food allergy. In F. Speer & R. Dockhorn (Eds.), *Allergy and immunology in children.* Springfield, IL: Thomas.

Spelke, E. (1979). Perceiving bimodally specified events in infancy. *Developmental Psychology, 15,* 626–636.

Spelke, E. & Hermer, L. (1996). Early cognitive development: Objects and space. In R. Gelman & T. Au (Eds.), *Perceptual and cognitive development* (pp. 71–114). San Diego: Academic.

Spelt, D. (1948). The conditioning of the human fetus in utero. *Journal of Experimental Psychology, 38,* 375–376.

Spencer, J. (1995). The management of term labor. *Archives of Diseases in Childhood, 72,* F55–F61.

Sperry, L. & Sperry, D. (1995). Young Children's presentations of self in conversational narration. *New Directions for Child Development, 69*(Fall), 47–60.

Spitz, R. (1945). Hospitalism. *Psychoanalytic Study of the Child, 1,* 45–74.

Spitz, R., Emde, R., & Metcalf, D. (1970). Further prototypes of ego formation: A working paper from a research project on early development. *The Psychoanalytic Study of the Child, 25,* 417–441.

Spock, B. & Rothenberg, M. (1992). *Dr. Spock's baby and child care* (6th ed.). New York: Pocket.

Spreen, O., Risser, A., & Edgell, D. (1995). *Developmental neurology.* New York: Oxford.

Sroufe, L. (1977). *Knowing and enjoying your baby.* Englewood Cliffs, NJ: Prentice Hall.

Sroufe, L. (1979). Socioemotional development. In J. Osofsky (Ed.), *Handbook of infant development* (pp. 462–516). New York: Wiley.

Sroufe, L. (1996). *Emotional development.* New York: Cambridge University.

Sroufe, L. & Waters, E. (1976). The ontogenesis of smiling and laughing: A perspective on the organization of development in infancy. *Psychological Review, 83,* 173–189.

Sroufe, L. & Wunsch, J. (1972). The development of laughter in the first year of life. *Child Development, 43,* 1326–1344.

Stafford, L. & Dainton, M. (1995). Parent-child communication within the family system. In T. Socha & G. Stamp (Eds.), *Parents, children, and communication* (pp. 3–21). Mahwah, NJ: Erlbaum.

Stangler, S., Huber, C., & Routh, D. (1980). *Screening growth and development of preschool children.* New York: McGraw-Hill.

Stansbury, K. & Gunar, M. (1994). Adrenocortical activity and emotion regulation. In N. Fox (Ed.), The development of emotion regulation: Biological and behavioral considerations. *Monographs of the Society for Research in Child Development* (pp. 108–134), *59*(Serial No.240).

Stark, R. (1978). Features of infant sounds: The emergence of cooing. *Journal of Child Language, 5,* 379–390.

Stark, R. (1979). Prespeech segmental feature development. In P. Fletcher & M. Garman (Eds.), *Language acquisition* (pp. 15–32). Cambridge, England: Cambridge University Press.

Starr, R. (1979). Child abuse. *American Psychologist, 34,* 872–878.

Stechler, G. & Halton, A. (1982). Prenatal influences on human development. In B. Wolman (Ed.), *Handbook of developmental psychology* (pp. 175–189). Englewood Cliffs, N J: Prentice Hall.

Stein, Z. & Kline, J. (1983). Smoking, alcohol and reproduction. *American Journal of Public Health, 73,* 1154–1156.

Stein, Z., Susser, M., Saenger, G., & Morolla, F. (1974). *Famine and human development: The Dutch hunger winter of 1944–1945.* New York: Oxford University Press.

Steiner, J. (1977). Facial expressions of the neonate indicating the hedonics of food related chemical stimuli. In J. Wiffenbach, (Ed.), *Taste and development: The genesis of sweet preference* (pp. 173–204). Bethesda, MD: National Institute of Health. (DHEW Pub. No. NIH 77-1068).

Steinmetz, J. (1994). Brain substrates of motion and temperament. In J. Bates & T. Wachs (Eds.), *Temperament: Individual differences at the interface of biology and behavior* (pp. 17–45). Washington, DC: American Psychological Association.

Stenberg, C. & Campos, J. (1990). The development of anger expressions in infancy. In N. Stein, B. Leventhal, & T. Trabasco (Eds.), *Psychological and biological approaches to emotion* (pp. 247–282). Hillsdale, NJ: Erlbaum.

Stene, J., Fischer, G., Stene, E., Mikkelesen, M., & Petersen, E. (1977). Paternal age effect in Down's syndrome. *American Human Genetics, 40,* 299–306.

Stern, D. (1985). *The interpersonal world of the infant.* New York: Basic Books.

Steuer, F. (1994). *The psychological development of children.* Pacific Grove, CA: Brooks/Cole.

Stewart, J., Manchester, D., & Sujansky, E. (1995). Genetics and dysmorphology. In W. Hay, J. Groothuis, A. Hayward, M. Levin (Eds.), *Current pediatric diagnosis and treatment* (12th ed., pp. 947–987). Norwalk, CT: Lange.

Stifter, C., Coulehan, C., & Fish, M. (1993). Linking employment to attachment: The mediating effects of maternal separation anxiety and interactive behavior. *Child Development, 64,* 1451–1460.

Stipek, D., Gralinski, J., Kopp, C. (1990). Self-concept development in the toddler years. *Developmental Psychology, 26,* 972–977.

Strangert, K. (1976). Respiratory illness in preschool children with different forms of day care. *Pediatrics, 57,* 219–229.

Straus, M., Celles, R., & Steinmetz, S. (1979*). Behind closed doors: Violence in the American family.* Garden City, NY: Doubleday/Anchor.

Strelau, J. (1994). The concepts of arousal and arousability as used in temperament studies. In J. Bates & T. Wachs (Eds.), *Temperament: Individual differences at the interface of biology and behavior* (pp. 117–141). Washington, DC: American Psychological Association.

Streri, A. & Spelke, E. (1988). Haptic perception of objects in infancy. *Cognitive Psychology, 20*, 1–23.

Streri, A. & Spelke, E. (1989). Effects of motion and figural goodness on haptic object perception in infancy. *Child Development, 60*, 1111–1125.

Stunkard, A., Foch, T., & Krubec, Z. (1986). A twin study of human obesity. *JAMA, 256*, 51–54.

Suomi, S. (1982). Biological foundations and developmental psychobiology. In C. Kopp & J. Krakow (Eds.), *The child: Development in a social context* (pp. 42–91). Reading, MA: Addison.

Super, C. (1981). Behavioral development in infancy. In R. H. Munroe, R. L. Munroe, & B. Whiting (Eds.), *Handbook of cross-cultural human development* (pp. 181–270). New York: Garland.

Super, C. & Harkness, S. (1982). The development of affect in infancy and early childhood. In D. Wagner & H. Stevenson (Eds.), *Cultural perspectives in child development* (pp. 1–19). San Francisco: Freeman.

Svejda, M., Campos, J., & Emde, R. (1980). Mother-infant "bonding": Failure to generalize. *Child Development, 51*, 775–779.

Svejda, M., Pannabecker, B., & Emde, R. (1982). Parent-to-infant attachment: A critique of the early "bonding model." In R. Emde & R. Harmon (Eds.), *The development of attachment and affiliative systems* (pp. 83–93). New York: Plenum.

Swain, I., Zelazo, P., & Clifton, R. (1993). Newborn infants' memory for speech sounds retained over 24 hours. *Developmental Psychology, 29*, 312–323.

Taber-Flusberg, H. (1994). Language development. In M. Rutter and D. Hay (Eds.), *Development through life: A handbook for clinicians* (pp. 212–238). London: Blackwell.

Taeuber, C. (1996). *Statistical handbook on women in America* (2nd ed.). Phoenix, AZ: Oryx.

Tanner, J. (1990). *Fetus into man.* Cambridge, MA: Harvard University.

Tarmin, O., Newman, T., Lifshitz, F. (1995). Cholesterol screening and dietary intervention in childhood for prevention of adult onset cardiovascular disease. In F. Lifshitz (Ed.), *Childhood nutrition* (pp. 13–20). Boca Raton: CRC.

Tatzer, E., Schubert, M., Timisch, W., & Simbruner, G. (1985). Discrimination of taste preference for sweet in premature babies. *Early Human Development, 12*, 23–30.

Taubman, B. (1984). Clinical trial of the treatment of colic by modification of parent-infant interaction. *Pediatrics, 74*, 998–1003.

Taylor, B. (1977). Breast versus bottle feeding. *New Zealand Journal of Medicine, 85*, 235–238.

Teller, D. & Lindsey, D. (1993). Motion nulling techniques and infant color vision. In C. Granrud (Ed.), *Visual perception and cognition in infancy* (pp.47–73). Hillsdale, NJ: Erlbaum.

Teplin, S. (1995). Visual impairment in infants and young children. *Infants and Young Children, 8*, 18–51.

Tesh, J. & Glover, T. (1969). Aging of rabbit spermatozoa in the male and its effect on fertility. *Journal of Reproductive Fertility, 20*, 573.

Thacker, S. & Banta, H. (1983). Benefits and risks of episiotomy: An interpretative review of the English language literature 1860–1980. *Obstetrical and Gynecological Survey, 38*, 232–250.

Thelen, E. (1981). Rythmical behavior in infancy: An ethological perspective. *Developmental Psychology, 17*, 237–257.

Thelen, E., Fisher, D., & Ridley-Johnson, R. (1984). The relationship between physical growth and a newborn reflex. *Infant Behavior and Development, 7*, 479–493.

Thelen, E. & Fogel, A. (1989). Toward an action-based theory of infant development. In J. Lockman & N. Hazen (Eds.), *Action in social context: Perspectives on early development* (pp. 23–64). New York: Plenum.

Thelen, E., Ulrich, B., & Jensen, J.(1989). The developmental origins of locomotion. In M. Woollacott & A. Shumway-Cook (Eds.), *The development of posture and gait across the lifespan* (pp. 25–47). Columbia, SC: University of South Carolina Press.

Thoman, E. (1993). Obligation and option in the premature nursery. *Developmental Review, 13*, 1–30.

Thomas, A. & Chess, S. (1977). *Temperament and development.* New York: Brunner/Mazel.

Thomas, A. & Chess, S. (1985). The behavioral study of temperament. In J. Strelau, F. Farley, & A. Gale (Eds.), *The biological bases of personality and behavior: Vol. 1. Theories, measurement, techniques and development* (pp. 213–225). Washington, DC: Hemisphere.

Thomas, R. (1996). *Comparing theories of child development* (4th ed.). Pacific Grove, CA: Brooks/Cole.

Thomasello, M. (1995). Joint attention as social cognition. In C. Moore & P. Dunham (Eds.), *Joint Attention: Its origins and role in development* (pp. 103–130). Hillsdale, NJ: Erlbaum.

Thompson, M., McInnes, R., & Willard, H. (1991). *Thompson & Thompson: Genetics in Medicine* (5th ed.). Philadelphia: Saunders.

Thompson, R. (1994). Emotion regulation: A theme in search of definition. In N. Fox (Ed.), The development of emotion regulation: Biological and behavioral considerations. *Monographs of the Society for Research in Child Development* (pp. 25–52), *59*(Serial No.240).

Thompson, R. & Lamb, M. (1984). Infants, mothers, families and strangers. In M. Lewis (Ed.), *Beyond the dyad* (pp. 195–221). New York: Plenum.

Tiedemann, D. (1787/1972). Observations on the mental development of a child. In W. Dennis (Ed.), *Historical readings in developmental psychology* (pp. 11–31). New York: Appleton-Century-Crofts.

Tizard, I. (1995). *Immunology: An introduction* (4th ed.). Philadelphia: Saunders.

Toda, S. & Fogel, A. (1993). Infant response to the still-face situation at 3 and 6 months. *Developmental Psychology, 29,* 532–538.

Townsend, T. (1993). Hepatitis A; Hepatitis B. In L. Donowitz (Ed.), *Infection control in the child care center and preschool* (2nd ed., pp. 151–156). Baltimore: Williams & Wilkins.

Traub, A., Morrow, R., Ritchie, J., & Dornan, K. (1984). A continuing use of Kielland's forceps? *British Journal of Obstetrics and Gynecology, 91,* 894–898.

Treem, W. (1994). Infant colic: A pediatric gasterenterologist's perspective. *Pediatric Clinics of North America, 41,* 1121–1138.

Trehub, S., Trainor, L., & Unyk, A. (1993). Music and speech processing in the first year of life. In H. Reese (Ed.), *Advances in child development and behavior* (Vol. 24; pp. 1–35). San Diego: Academic.

Trevarthen, C. (1978). The psychobiology of speech development. *Neurosciences Research Program Bulletin, 12* (4), 570–585.

Trohanis, P., Cox, J., & Meyer, R. (1982). A report on selected demonstration programs for infant intervention. In C. Ramey & P. Trohanis (Eds.), *Finding and educating high-risk and handicapped infants* (pp. 137–191). Baltimore: University Park Press.

Tronick, E. (1989). Emotions and emotional communication. *American Psychologist, 44,* 112–118.

Trotter, R. (1987). You've come a long way, baby. *Psychology Today, 21*(5), 34–45.

Troyer, L. & Parisi, V. (1993). In T. Moore, R. Reiter, R. Rebar, & V. Baker (Eds.), *Gynecology and obstetrics: A longitudinal approach* (pp. 575–590). New York: Churchill Livingstone.

Trump, C. & Karasic, R. (1983). Management of communicable diseases in day care centers. *Pediatric Annals, 12,* 219–229.

Turner, G. & Collins, E. (1975). Fetal effects of regular salicylate ingestion in pregnancy. *Lancet, 2,* 338–339.

Tweedie, J. (1987). *Children's hearing problems: Their significance, detection, and management.* Bristol, England: Wright.

U.S. Bureau of the Census. (1995). *Statistical Abstract of the United States* (115th ed.). Washington, DC: U. S. Government Printing Office.

U.S. Bureau of the Census. (1996). *Statistical Abstract of the United States* (116th ed.). Washington, DC: U. S. Government Printing Office.

Ungerer, J., Brody, L., & Zelazo, P. (1978). Long-term memory for speech in 2-4-week-old infants. *Infant Behavior and Development, 1,* 177–186.

United Nations Children's Fund (1996). *The progress of nations 1996.* New York: UNICEF.

USDHEW. (1972). *Tips for tots.* DHEW Publication No. (FDA) 73–7012. Washington, DC: U.S. Government Printing Office.

Uzgiris, I. (1967). Ordinality in the development of schemes for relating to objects. In J. Hellmuth (Ed.), *Exceptional infant: Vol. 1. The normal infant* (pp. 315–334). New York: Bruner/Mazel.

Uzgiris, I. & Hunt, I. (1975). *Assessment in infancy.* Urbana, IL: University of Illinois Press.

Uzgiris, I. & Raeff, C. (1995). Play in parent-child interactions. In M. Bornstein (Ed.), *Handbook of parenting* (Vol. 4, pp. 353–376). Mahwah, NJ: Erlbaum.

Valadian, I. & Porter, D. (1977). *Physical growth and development from conception to maturity.* Boston: Little, Brown.

Vandell, D. & Mueller, E. (1980). Peer play and friendships during the first two years. In H. Foot, A. Chapman, & J. Smith (Eds.), *Friendship and social relations in children* (pp. 181–208). New York: Wiley.

Vandell, D. & Ramanan, J. (1992). Effects of early and recent maternal employment on children from low-income families. *Child Development, 63,* 938–949.

Vandell, D. & Wilson, K. (1987). Infants' interactions with mother, sibling, and peer contacts: Contrasts and relations between interaction systems. *Child Development, 58,* 176–186.

Vandell, D., Wilson, K., & Buchanan, N. (1980). Peer interaction in the first year of life: An examination of its structure, content and sensitivity to toys. *Child Development, 51,* 481–488.

Vander Vliet, W. & Hafez, E. (1974). Surviving and aging of spermatozoa: A review. *American Journal of Obstetrics and Gynecology, 118,* 1006.

Vedam, S. & Kolodji, Y. (1995). Guidelines for client selection in the home birth midwifery practice. *Journal of Nurse-Midwifery, 40,* 508–521.

Verba, M. (1994). The beginnings of collaboration in peer interaction. *Human Development, 37,* 125–139.

Von Hofsten, C. (1982). Eye-hand coordination in the newborn. *Developmental Psychology, 18,* 450–461.

Von Hofsten, C. (1984). Developmental changes in the organization of prereaching movements. *Developmental Psychology, 20,* 378–388.

Von Hofsten, C. (1992). Studying the development of goal-directed behavior. In A. Kalverboer, B. Hopkins, & R. Geuze (Eds.), *Motor development in early and later childhood: Longitudinal approaches* (pp. 89–108). Cambridge, England: Cambridge University.

Vorhees, C. & Mollnow, E. (1987). Behavioral teratogenesis: Long term influences on behavior from early exposure to environmental agents. In J. Osofosky (Ed.), *Handbook of infant development* (pp. 913–971). New York: Wiley.

Vulliamy, D. (1982). *The newborn child* (5th ed.). London: Churchill Livingstone.

Vygotsky, L. (1962). *Thought and language*. Cambridge, Mass: MIT Press.

Vygotsky, L. (1978). *Mind in society: The development of higher mental processes*. Cambridge, MA: Harvard University.

Wachs, T. (1982). *Relation of home noise-confusion to infant cognitive development*. Paper presented at the meeting of the American Psychological Association, Washington, DC.

Wachs, T. & Gruen, G. (1982). *Early experiences and human development*. New York: Plenum.

Walco, G., Cassidy, R., Schechter, N. (1994). Pain, hurt, and harm: The ethics of pain control in infants and children. *New England Journal of Medicine, 331*, 541–544.

Walden, T. & Garber, J. (1994). Emotional development. In M. Rutter & D. Hay (Eds.), *Development through the lifespan: A handbook for clinicians* (pp. 403–455). Oxford, England: Blackwell.

Waldenstrom, U. & Nilsson, C. (1994). Experience of childbirth in birth center care: A randomized control study. *Acta Obstetricia et Gynecologica Scandinavica, 73*, 547–554.

Waletzky, L. (1979). Breast-feeding and weaning: Some psychological considerations. *Primary Care, 6*(2), 341–364.

Walk, R. & Gibson, E. (1961). A comparative and analytical study of visual depth perception. *Psychological Monographs, 75* (Whole No. 519).

Walker, A. (1982). Intermodal perception of expressive behaviors by human infants. *Journal of Experimental Child Psychology, 33*, 514–535.

Walker-Andrews, A. (1986). Intermodal perception of expressive behaviors: Relation of eye and voice? *Developmental Psychology, 22*, 373–377.

Walker-Andrews, A. (1994). Taxonomy for intermodal relations. In D. Lewkowicz & R. Lickliter (Eds.), *The development of intersensory perception: Comparative perspectives* (pp. 39–56). Hillsdale, NJ: Erlbaum.

Wallerstein, J. & Kelly, J. (1980). *Surviving the breakup: How children and parents cope with divorce*. New York: Basic Books.

Walter, E. & Shurin, P. (1992). Acute respiratory infections. In S. Krugman, S. Katz, A. Gershon, & C. Wilfert, (Eds.), *Infectious diseases of children* (9th ed., pp. 329–376). St. Louis: Mosby.

Wasserman, G. & Stern, D. (1978). An early manifestation of differential behavior toward children of the same and opposite sex. *Journal of Genetic Psychology, 133*, 129–137.

Wasz-Hocket, O., Lind, J., Vucrenkoski, V., Partenen, T., & Valanne, E. (1968). The infant cry: A spectrographic and auditory analysis. *Clinics in Developmental Medicine, 29*. London: Heinemann.

Waters, E. & Sroufe, L. (1983). Social competence as a developmental construct. *Developmental Review, 3*, 79–97.

Wechsler, D. (1944). *The measurement of adult intelligence* (3rd. ed). Baltimore: Williams & Wilkins.

Weiffenbach, J., Daniel, P., & Cowart, B. (1979). Saltiness in developmental perspective. In M. Kare, M. Fregly, & R. Bernard (Eds.), *Biological and behavioral aspects of salt intake* (pp. 13–30). New York: Academic Press.

Weiner, I. & Elkind, D. (1972). *Child development: A core approach*. New York: Wiley.

Weinraub, M. Clements, L., Sockloff, A., Ethridge, T., Gracely, E., & Meyers, B. (1984). The development of sex role stereotypes in the third year: Relationships to gender identity, sex typed toy preferences. *Child Development, 55*, 1493–1503.

Weinraub, M., Jaeger, E., & Hoffman, L. (1990). Predicting infant outcome in families of employed and nonemployed mothers. In N. Fox & G. Fein (Eds.), *Infant day care: The current debate* (pp. 127–144). Norwood, NJ: Ablex.

Weir, R. (1966). Some questions on the child's learning of phonology. In F. Smith & G. Miller (Eds.), *The genesis of language* (pp. 153–169). Cambridge, MA: MIT.

Weir, R. (1970). *Language in the crib*. The Hague: Mouton.

Weiser, M. (1982). *Group care and education of infants and toddlers*. St. Louis: Mosby.

Weissbluth, M. & Green, O. (1984). Plasma progesterone concentrations and infant temperament. *Developmental and Behavioral Pediatrics, 5*, 251–253.

Wekselman, K., Spiering, K., Hetteberg, C., Kenner, C., & Flandermeyer, A. (1995). Fetal alcohol syndrome from infancy through childhood: A review of the literature. *Journal of Pediatric Nursing, 10*, 296–303.

Wellman, B. (1937). Motor achievements of preschool children. *Childhood Education, 13*, 311–316.

Wellman, H. (1994). Early understanding of mind: The normal case. In S. Baron-Cohen, H. Tager-Flusberg, & D. Cohen (Eds.), *Understanding other minds* (pp. 10–39). New York: Oxford University.

Werner, E. (1979). *Cross-cultural child development*. Monterey, CA: Brooks/Cole.

Werner, L. & VandenBos, G. (1993). Developmental psychoacoustics: What infants and children hear. *Hospital and Community Psychiatry. 44*, 624–626

West, R. & Turner, L. (1995). Communication in lesbian and gay families: Building a descriptive base. In T. Socha & G. Stamp (Eds.), *Parents, children, and communication* (pp. 147–169). Mahwah, NJ: Erlbaum.

Weston, W., Lane, A., & Weston, J. (1980). Diaper dermatitis: Current concepts. *Pediatrics, 66*, 532–536.

Whaley, K. (1990). The emergence of social play in infancy: A proposed developmental sequence of infant-adult play. *Early Childhood Research Quarterly, 5*, 347–358.

Whaley, K. & Rubenstein, T. (1994). How toddlers "do"

friendship: A descriptive analysis of naturally occuring friendships in a group child care setting. *Journal of Social and Personal Relationships, 11,* 383–400.

Wheeler, C. (1995). Labour: Normal and dysfunctional. In D. Coustan, R. Haning, & D. Singer (Eds.), *Human reproduction: Growth and development* (pp. 291–305). Boston: Little, Brown.

Whetnall, E. & Fry, D. (1964). *The deaf child.* London: Heinemann.

White, B. (1975). *The first three years of life.* Englewood Cliffs, NJ: Prentice Hall.

White, B. (1985). *The first three years of life* (Rev. ed.). Englewood Cliffs, NJ: Prentice Hall.

White, B. & Watts, J. (1973). *Experience and environment* (Vol. 1). Englewood Cliffs, NJ: Prentice Hall.

White, R. (1959). Motivation reconsidered: The concept of competence. *Psychological Review, 66,* 297–333.

Whitebook, M., Howes, C., & Philips, D. (1989). *Who cares? Child care teachers and the quality of care in America. Executive summary of the national child care staffing study.* Oakland, CA: Child Care Employee Project.

Whitehurst, G. (1982). Language development. In B. Wolman (Ed.), *Handbook of developmental psychology* (pp. 367–386). Englewood Cliffs, NJ: Prentice Hall.

Whitten, C. & Stewart, R. (1980). The effect of dietary sodium in infancy on blood pressure and related factors. *ACTA Paediatrica Scandinavica,* (Suppl. 279), 1–17.

WHO/UNICEF. (1981). *Infant and young child feeding: Current issues.* Geneva: World Health Organization.

Whorf, B. (1956). *Language, thought and reality.* Cambridge, MA: MIT Press.

Wicks-Nelson, R. & Israel, A. (1991). *Behavior disorders of childhood* (2nd ed.). Englewood Cliffs, NJ: Prentice-Hall.

Wickstrom, R. (1983). *Fundamental motor patterns* (3rd ed.). Philadelphia: Lee & Febiger.

Widerstrom, A., Mowder, B., & Sandall, S. (1991). *At-risk and handicapped newborns and infants: Development, assessment, and intervention.* Englewood Cliffs, NJ: Prentice-Hall.

Wiese, D. & Daro, D. (1995). *Current trends in child abuse reporting and fatalities: The results of the 1994 annual fifty state survey.* Chicago, IL.: NCPCA.

Wiesenfeld, A., Malatesta, C., & Deloache, L. (1981). Differential parental response to familiar and unfamiliar infant distress signals. *Infant Behavior and Development, 4,* 281–295.

Williams, H. (1983). *Perceptual and motor development.* Englewood Cliffs, NJ: Prentice Hall.

Williams, R. (1996, October). Breast feeding best for babies. *FDA Consumer Magazine* [On line]. Available: http://www.fda.gov/fdac/features/895_brstfeed.html.

Willinger, M. (1995). SIDS prevention. *Pediatric Annals, 24,* 358–364.

Willinger, M., James, L., & Catz, C. (1991). Defining suddent infant death syndrome (SIDS). *Developmental Pediatric Pathology, 11,* 677–684.

Willoughby, J. & Glidden, L. (1995). Fathers helping out: Shared child care and marital satisfaction of parents of children with disabilities. *American Journal on Mental Retardation, 95,* 399–406.

Winick, M. (1976). *Malnutrition and brain development.* New York: Oxford University Press.

Winick, M. (1979). Nutrition and brain development. In F. Balli (Ed.), *Nutritional problems in childhood.* Padova, Italy: Piccin Medical Books.

Winick, M., Meyer, K., & Harris, R. (1975). Malnutrition and environmental enrichment by early adoption. *Science, 190,* 1173–1175.

Woelfel, J. (1984). *Dental Anatomy* (3rd ed.). Philadelphia: Lea & Febiger.

Wolff, P. (1963). Observations on the early development of smiling. In B. Foss (Ed.), *Determinants of infant behavior* (Vol. 2, pp. 113–138). London: Methuen.

Wolff, P. (1966). The causes, controls, and organization of behavior in the neonate. *Psychological Issues, 5* (1, Whole No. 17), 7–11.

Wolff, P. (1969). The natural history of crying and other vocalizations in early infancy. In B. Foss (Ed.), *Determinants of infant behavior* (Vol. 4, pp. 81–109). London: Methuen.

Wolk, S., Zeanah, C., Garcia Coll, C., & Carr, S. (1992). Factors affecting parents' perception of temperament in early infancy. *American Journal of Orthopsychiatry, 62,* 71–82.

Wollman, L. (1981). A case of galoctapoiesis in a male. *Journal of the American Society of Psychosomatic Dentistry and Medicine, 28,* 2.

Wood, B. (1976). *Children and communication: Verbal and nonverbal language development.* Englewood Cliffs, NJ: Prentice Hall.

Wood, B. & Walker-Smith, J. (1981). *Mackeith's infant feeding and feeding difficulties* (6th ed.). London: Churchill Livingstone.

Woodruff, C. (1978). The science of infant nutrition and the art of infant feeding. *JAMA, 240,* 657–661.

Woollacott, M. (1992). Early postnatal development of posture control: Normal and abnormal aspects. In A. Kalverboer, B. Hopkins, & R. Geuze (Eds.), *Motor development in early and later childhood: Longitudinal approaches* (pp.89–108). Cambridge, England: Cambridge University.

World Health Organization. (1985). *Treatment and prevention of acute diarrhoea.* Geneva: Author.

Worthington-Roberts, B. & Williams, S. (1996). *Nutrition throughout the life cycle* (3rd. ed.). St. Louis, MO: Mosby.

Wortman, C., Loftus, E., Marshall, M. (1992). *Psychology* (4th ed.). New York: McGraw-Hill.

Wray, J. (1991). Breast-feeding : An international and historical review. In F. Falkner (Ed.), *Infants and child nutrition worldwide: Issues and perspectives* (pp. 62–113). Boca Raton: CRC.

Wyly, M. (1995). *Premature infants and their families: Developmental interventions.* San Diego: Singular.

Wynbrandt, J. & Ludman, M. (1991). *The encyclopedia of genetic disorders and birth defects.* New York: Facts on File.

Wynn, K. (1992). Addition and subtraction by human infants. *Nature, 357,* pp. 52–53.

Yarrow, L. (1979). Emotional development. *American Psychologist, 34,* 951–957.

Ymada, H. (1983). *Pediatric cranial computed tomography.* New York: Medical Publishers.

Youngblut, J., Loveland-Cherry, C., & Horan, M. (1994). Maternal employment effects on families and preterm infants at 18 months. *Nursing Research, 43,* 331–337.

Zahn-Waxler, C., Cummings, E., & Cooperman, G. (1984). Emotional development in childhood. In G. Whitehurst (Ed.), *Annuals of child development* (Vol. 1, pp. 45–106). Greenwich, CT: JAI Press.

Zahn-Waxler, C. & Radke-Yarrow, M. (1990). The origins of empathic concern. *Motivation and Emotion, 14,* 107–130.

Zarbatany, L. & Lamb, M. (1985). Social referencing as a function of information source: Mothers versus strangers. *Infant Behavior and Development, 8,* 25–33.

Zaslow, M. Rabinovich, B., & Sualsky, J. (1991). From maternal employment to child outcomes: Preexisting group difference and moderating variables. In J. Lerner & N. Galambos (Eds.), *Employed mothers and their children: An analysis of "Children of the national longitudinal survey of youth"* (pp. 237–290). New York: Garland.

Zeanah, C. (1994). The assessment and treatment of infants and toddlers exposed to violence. *Zero to Three, 14*(3), 29–37.

Zeanah, C., Mammen, O. & Liberman, A. (1993). Disorders of attachment. In C. Zeanah (Ed.), *Handbook of infant mental health* (pp. 332–349). New York: Guilford.

Zelazo, P., Zelazo, N., & Kolb, S. (1972). Walking in the newborn. *Science, 176,* 314–315.

Zero to Three/National Center for Clinical Infant Programs. (1994). *Diagnostic classification: 0-3: Diagnostic classification of mental health and developmental disorders of infancy and early childhood.* Arlington, VA: Author.

Zeskind, P. (1983). Cross-cultural differences in maternal perceptions of cries of low- and high-risk infants. *Child Development, 54,* 1119–1128.

Zeskind, P., Sale, J., Maio, M., Huntington, M., & Wiseman, J. (1984, April). *Adult perceptions of pain and hunger cries: A synchrony arousal.* Paper presented at the International Conference on Infant Studies, New York, NY.

Zigler, E. & Turner, P. (1982). Parents and day care workers: A failed partnership? In E. Zigler & A. Gordon (Eds.), *Day care: Scientific and social policy issues* (pp. 174–182). Boston: Auburn House.

Zimmerman, I. & Bernstein, M. (1983). Parental work patterns in alternative families: Influence on child development. *American Journal of Orthopsychiatry, 53,* 418–425.

Zlatnik, F. (1995). Normal labor and delivery. In J. Scott, P. DiSaia, C. Hammond, & W. Spellacy (Eds.), *Danforth's obstetrics and gynecology* (7th ed., pp. 105–128), Philadelphia: Lippincott.

Zuckerman, B., Bauchner, H., & Parker, S. (1990). Maternal depressive symptoms during pregnancy and newborn irritability. *Journal of Developmental and Behavioral Pediatrics, 11,* 190–194.

Zuckerman, B., Frank, D., Hingson, R., Amaro, H., Levenson, S., Kayne, H., Parker, S., Vinci, R., Aboagye, K., Fried, L., Cabral, H., Tiemperi, R., & Bauchner, H. (1989). Effects of maternal marijuana and cocaine use on fetal growth. *New England Journal of Medicine, 320,* 762–768.

Zussman, J. (1980). Situational determinants of parental behavior; Effects of competing cognitive activity. *Child Development, 51,* 792–800.

GIRLS: BIRTH TO 36 MONTHS
PHYSICAL GROWTH
NCHS PERCENTILES*

Appendix 1   Growth Curves for Girls: Birth to 36 Months
             Length by Age and Weight by Age

Source: National Center for Health Statistics, *NCHS Growth Charts*, (1976). Adapted by Ross
Laboratories. Reprinted by permission.

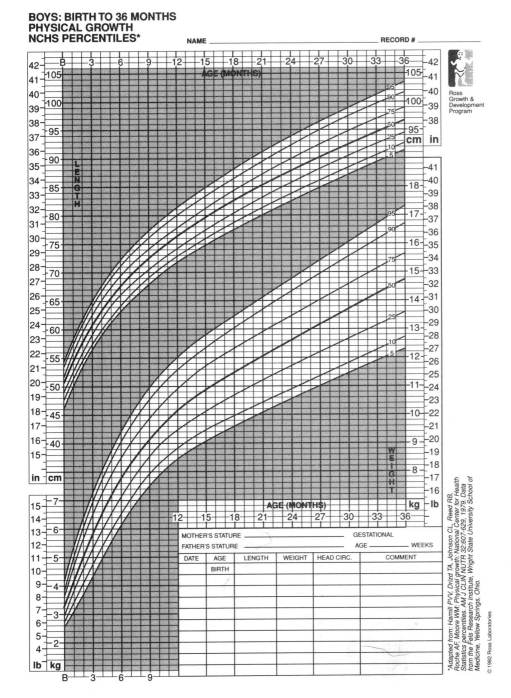

**BOYS: BIRTH TO 36 MONTHS
PHYSICAL GROWTH
NCHS PERCENTILES***

Appendix 2   Growth Curves for Boys: Birth to 36 Months
Length by Age and Weight by Age

Source: National Center for Health Statistics, *NCHS Growth Charts,* (1976). Adapted by Ross
Laboratories. Reprinted by permission.

GIRLS: BIRTH TO 36 MONTHS
PHYSICAL GROWTH
NCHS PERCENTILES*

NAME _____ RECORD # _____

DATE	AGE	LENGTH	WEIGHT	HEAD CIRC.	COMMENT

in vivo performance ...
SIMLAC® Infant Formulas
in vivo performance ...
closet to mother's milk
ISOMIL® Soy Protein Formulas
When the baby can't take milk.
ADVANCE® Nutritional Beverage
Instead of 2% milk.

ROSS LABORATORIES
COLUMBUS, OHIO 43216
DIVISION OF ABBOTT LABORATORIES, USA

G105(0.05)/DECEMBER 1985   LITHO IN USA

Adapted from: Hamill PVV, Drizd TA, Johnson CL, Reed RB, Roche AF, Moore WM: Physical growth: National Center for Health Statistics percentiles. AM J CLIN NUTR 32:607-629, 1979. Data from the Fels Research Institute, Wright State University School of Medicine, Yellow Springs, Ohio.

© 1982 Ross Laboratories

Appendix 3   Growth Curves for Girls: Birth to 36 Months
Head Circumference and Length by Weight
Source: National Center for Health Statistics, *NCHS Growth Charts,* (1976). Adapted by Ross Laboratories. Reprinted by permission.

**BOYS: BIRTH TO 36 MONTHS
PHYSICAL GROWTH
NCHS PERCENTILES***

NAME _____   RECORD # _____

DATE	AGE	LENGTH	WEIGHT	HEAD CIRC.	COMMENT

Appendix 4   Growth Curves for Boys: Birth to 36 Months
Head Circumference and Length by Weight
Source: National Center for Health Statistics, *NCHS Growth Charts,* (1976). Adapted by Ross
Laboratories. Reprinted by permission.

Credits

Subject Index

329

Name Index